BONG HiTS 4 JESUS

BONG HiTS 4 JESUS

A Perfect Constitutional Storm in Alaska's Capital

• • •

James C. Foster

University of Alaska Press
Fairbanks

University of Alaska Press
P.O. Box 756240
Fairbanks, AK 99775-6240

second printing 2011

ISBN 978-1-60223-089-7

Library of Congress Cataloging-in-Publication Data

Foster, James C. (James Carl)
BONG HiTS 4 JESUS : a perfect constitutional storm in Alaska's capital /
by James C. Foster.
p. cm.
Includes bibliographical references and index.
ISBN 978-1-60223-089-7 (pbk. : alk. paper)
1. Morse, Deborah, school principal—Trials, litigation, etc. 2. Frederick, Joseph—Trials,
litigation, etc. 3. City and Borough of Juneau School District—Trials, litigation, etc.
4. Freedom of speech—United States. 5. Students—Legal status, laws, etc.—Alaska.
6. Students—Legal status, laws, etc.—United States. I. Title.
KF229.M67F67 2010
342.7308'53—dc22
2010006347

This publication was printed on acid-free paper that meets the minimum
requirements for ANSI / NISO Z39.48-1992 (R2002) (Permanence of Paper
for Printed Library Materials).

Cover design by Dennis Roberts
Clay Good's front cover photo of students hoisting the BONG HiTS 4 JESUS banner
used by permission of ZUMA Press, Inc.
Brian Wallace's back cover photo of Joseph Frederick used by permission of
Polaris Images Corporation.
Art Lien's back cover drawing of Doug Mertz arguing before the U.S. Supreme Court
used with kind permission of the artist, © Art Lien.
Evan Vucci's back cover photo of Deborah Morse standing in front of the U.S. Supreme
Court, accompanied by former drug policy czar Barry McCaffrey and her lawyer Kenneth
Starr used by permission of AP/Wide World Photos.
Charles Barsotti's cartoon used by permission of the Cartoon Bank, Condé Nast
Publications, © Charles Barsotti/Condé Nast Publications/www.cartoonbank.com.

Contents

● ● ●

Purity is on the edge of evil, they say.
—Ursula K. Le Guin, *Always Coming Home*

We are seeking, in the widened sense of the term in which it encompasses very much more than talk, to converse with [natives], a matter a great deal more difficult, and not only with strangers, than is commonly recognized.
—Clifford Geertz, *The Interpretation of Cultures*

The limits of my language mean the limits of my world.
—Ludwig Wittgenstein, *Tractatus Logico-Philosophicus*

Acknowledgments

● ● ●

WHEN I EMBARKED on this journey, little did I know where the trip would take me or how long I would travel. What began in the fall of 2007 as a run-of-the-mill conference discussion about a quirky Supreme Court decision evolved into a two-and-a-half-year odyssey. The deeper I investigated the backstory of *Morse v. Frederick*, 551 U.S. 393 (2007), the more antecedent circumstances and events came to the fore. Beyond context simply becoming crucial to understanding that particular case, eventually the Supreme Court case became my vehicle for exploring the context itself. My journey immersed me in the roots of Juneau's ongoing schism over student rights and school authority. Ultimately, my journey yielded lessons about the importance of keeping civil civic conversation going—and about the perils of not doing so.

Along my journey lots of folks have enabled me to keep this particular conversation going. I am delighted to thank them at the outset.

The book you are reading was made possible by the willingness of Elisabeth Dabney, University of Alaska (UA) Press managing editor for acquisitions, and her colleagues serving on the UA Press editorial board to embrace my project in its fairly early stages. This book almost died abornin'. Having been curtly informed, in no uncertain terms, by series editors at another university press that prominently publishes Supreme Court case studies, that a book about *Morse v. Frederick* "had no place on their list," I was chagrined but undaunted. I persisted, writing the first couple of chapters and submitting them to UA Press. What better place, I reasoned, for a book about a Supreme Court case originating in Juneau, Alaska, than that state's university press? Elisabeth agreed, and served as enthusiastic "matchmaker." You're holding the result. Thank you, Elisabeth.

Twenty-four extensive interviews, which I conducted over the course of about a year, figure centrally in my telling the story of a "perfect constitutional storm in Alaska's capital." When I began thinking about who I wanted to talk with, I drew up an ambitious list. My list included jurists involved in the prolonged litigation, from U.S. District Court Judge John W.

Sedwick on up to U.S. Supreme Court Justice John Paul Stevens—with lots of their judicial colleagues in between. An exchange of e-mails with colleague Steve Wasby served to disabuse me of my naive aspirations. Stalwart student of appellate courts, and disabuser par excellence, Steve administered a pointed, abbreviated course in judicial ethics and interview protocols, bringing me up short and causing me to rethink who I would interview—and why. Thank you, Steve.

All work with human subjects in a university setting must be submitted to, and approved by, the Institutional Review Board (IRB) of the institution with which the principal investigator is affiliated. Those IRB procedures, which are salutary and necessary, also can be a labyrinthine distraction. Oregon State University IRB Program Representative Donna Stevenson shepherded me through submitting my original proposal, and then renewing its approval. Thank you, Donna.

Then there are my twenty-seven interviewees themselves. They are listed at the back of the book. Each of these people unstintingly shared their time and their stories with me. Without their forthright expression of their take on events leading up to, surrounding, and following the January 24, 2002, incident on Glacier Avenue, I could not have fashioned my account. Hearty thanks to each one of you.

I want to single out four of my interviewees for especial appreciation: Joe Frederick and Deborah Morse—of course—and their respective attorneys, Doug Mertz and David Crosby. Without these four collaborators this book would have been a nonstarter. It is to them in particular that I address my commitment, articulated (in the context of *The Laramie Project*) in my introduction: "Father Schmit [Catholic priest in Laramie] believes that Matthew Shepard served Laramie well. He trusts that the authors of a play about the events surrounding Matthew's service will do him, and his town, justice. I have endeavored to do no less for the people who trusted me and rendered invaluable assistance in telling this story" (p. 4).

A sabbatical from Oregon State University–Cascades, fall term 2008, together with being appointed faculty leader of the 2008 fall semester Washington, D.C., program by Lewis & Clark College, enabled me to live and work in our nation's capital for fifteen weeks. During that time I was able to share early chapters with a few East Coast colleagues and, crucially, conduct interviews with six attorneys who were involved in writing and submitting amicus briefs in *Morse v. Frederick*. I appreciate this institutional support from my undergraduate alma mater (Lewis & Clark), and my primary employer (Oregon State). Fellow Lewis & Clark alum William Cummings, long an attorney in Juneau, twice provided my partner, Mindy, and me with hospitable lodging during our stays in Alaska's capital. Bill is smart, witty, and one of our favorite people. In Fairbanks, Mindy and I enjoyed the warm welcome extended to us by Michelle Bartlett, director of summer sessions and lifelong learning at the University of Alaska Fairbanks. Thanks to you both.

Speaking of sharing work with colleagues, my work and I have benefited enormously from a rich diversity of associates and coworkers who have read materials and offered comments along my journey. Early on Don Crowley, Susan Leeson, and Carolyn N. Long read and commented on draft proposals and a chapter or two. While I was in Washington, D.C., Lou Fisher, David Hudson, and Philippa Strum read and commented on early chapters. Back in Oregon, as I continued writing, I enjoyed the advantage of having two librarians, a coordinator of international programs, and professors of English and speech communication—all affiliated with Oregon State University–Cascades—give my drafts close readings. By name, these folks are Michele DeSilva and Lynne Hart, Cynthia Engel, Neil Browne and Natalie Dollar. To Michele and Neil in particular: your rigorous scrutiny coupled with your supportive attentiveness significantly improved the style and substance of my final work product (not to mention kept me heartened to carry on). To Natalie: chapter 9 would not be what it is without your work and your edits. Lief Carter chipped in his thoughts on chapter 8. To this variegated list of astute and encouraging readers, I'd add a social worker, Mindy Soules. I'd also add Sarah Foster, Brittney Rickman, and Jeremy Guericke for their loving support. Thank you, all.

When my manuscript was complete, Elisabeth Dabney handed it off to her UA Press colleague, production editor Sue Mitchell. Sue oversaw a professional team that took my typescript and produced this book. Melanie Gold did the copyediting. Rachel Fudge did the interior design, layout, and proofreading. Dennis Roberts did the cover. My thanks to each of you.

And to Mindy: As in all aspects of our lives, we've been partners in this endeavor. "*Cherish* is the word I use to describe. . . ."

Introduction

● ● ●

ONE FEATURE of the annual fall meeting of the Pacific Northwest Political Science Association (PNWPSA) is the Supreme Court Roundtable. For academics from around the region, and beyond, who specialize in law, courts, and judicial politics, the event is something of a gathering of The Clan. While there are facilitators who divvy up and dissect highlights of the Supreme Court's previous October Term, their role is primarily as conversation starters. Much like oral argument before the Court itself, lively give-and-take usually supplants set-piece presentations. At the fall 2007 PNWPSA meeting, I exercised my prerogative as Roundtable organizer and assigned myself a fascinating and curious Supreme Court case originating in Alaska's capital: *Deborah Morse and the Juneau School Board, et al. v. Joseph Frederick*, 551 U.S. 393 (2007).

Initially, I found *Morse v. Frederick* interesting for several reasons. First, the case seemed particularly suited to my pedagogical and scholarly style. I approach studying and teaching American constitutional law by situating the U.S. Supreme Court's (SCOTUS) doctrinal work within surrounding historical context, shorn of which doctrine is reduced to arid legal rules lacking meaning and significance. Concurrently, as a political scientist teaching about law, I employ SCOTUS work products as windows into political dynamics and governmental policies. First Amendment doctrines lend themselves very well to exploring the interfaces between law, politics, and society. The Free Speech clause—those "ten little words," as I refer to them with my students—is especially steeped in American history. As a speech case, then, *Morse* attracted me. Second, *Morse v. Frederick* is a student speech case, and *Morse* is the only such First Amendment dispute the SCOTUS has agreed to hear in nineteen years, since it decided *Hazelwood School District v. Kuhlmeier*, 484 U.S. 260 (1988). Not only relatively uncommon as a case before the highest court, *Morse* also could be potentially consequential as its lineage traced to the iconic late Warren Court student rights decision, *Tinker v. Des Moines Independent Community School District*, 393 U.S. 504 (1969). Not only unique and important, *Morse* is intrinsically appealing to my Oregon State University students, who are themselves only recently graduated from the high school setting within which *Morse* arose. Then, too, there is

Morse v. Frederick's locale of origin. Juneau, Alaska, is distant enough to be exotic, and not so far removed as to be foreign.

Yet another intriguing aspect of *Morse v. Frederick* is that an infrequent student speech rights case was going to be heard by a new Court. "Every time a new justice comes to the Supreme Court, 'it's a different court,' Justice Byron R. White liked to say—and he was in a position to know, having witnessed the arrival of thirteen new justices during his own thirty-one-year tenure."[1] The final Rehnquist "natural court," that is, the period during which no personnel changes took place, lasted over eleven years, from August 3, 1994, when Justice Stephen Breyer took his seat, until September 29, 2005, when Chief Justice John G. Roberts Jr. was seated to replace his deceased predecessor. The first natural court under Roberts lasted a mere ninety-three days, from September 29, 2005, until January 1, 2006, when Samuel A. Alito Jr. succeeded the retiring Justice Sandra Day O'Connor. This new court was notable for Justice Alito, who was anticipated to align with the Court's three most conservative members (Roberts, Scalia, and Thomas) having replaced Justice O'Connor, who was variously described as pragmatic, centrist, and a swing vote. It was this new "Roberts 2" tribunal, altering the "mix of ideology, personality, principle and politics,"[2] that granted Deborah Morse's petition for a writ of certiorari on December 1, 2006. By this date, the BONG HiTS 4 JESUS banner incident on Glacier Avenue, January 24, 2002, that had precipitated the controversy between student Joseph Frederick and Principal Deborah Morse was almost five years old.

My initial interest in *Morse v. Frederick*—the decision—led me to present it to the PNWPSA Roundtable. For that event, my focus was narrow and technical. One might say, lawyerly. The discussion with my colleagues assayed the meaning of "disruptive" speech, identified a "drug speech" exception to *Tinker*, traced converging First and Fourth Amendment precedents underlying that exception, and evaluated the *Morse* majority's deferring to school authority to trump student speech rights. Even in the process of parsing the decision, I wanted to know more about the case and the stories animating it. As I delved more deeply, a SCOTUS work product took on human faces, becoming a tale of community discord. *Morse v. Frederick* was growing curiouser and curiouser. My PNWPSA presentation was evolving into a book project.

In the process, my academic mantra—context, context, context—was reasserting itself. What I refer to as my milieu principle started driving my inquiry. That principle was generating questions about how, and what, and why circumstances and personalities clashed on Glacier Avenue, across from Juneau-Douglas High School, that January Thursday, followed by almost seven years of increasingly acrimonious disputing. Then, in spring 2008, just as I was growing increasingly intrigued, a fortuitous coincidence occurred. I had tried to contact Joseph Frederick's and Deborah Morse's lawyers. I thought that talking with Doug Mertz and David Crosby, respectively, would provide informative points of departure, and might provide me access to their clients. But Mertz and Crosby live in Juneau, Alaska, while I live in Bend, Oregon. Connecting with them in person was going to be time-consuming, not to mention costly. It just so happened that Doug Mertz's son Edward was graduating from Willamette University in Salem, Oregon, a couple of hours' drive from Bend. My partner, Mindy Soules, and I met Doug and his wife, Margo Waring, in Salem for lunch and conversation about the dispute that had occupied Doug since early 2002. I left our discussion with one overriding impression: Doug Mertz deeply felt and personally experienced Joe Frederick's case. I heard negligible professional distancing. On the contrary, for Mertz the legal work that preceded and culminated in *Morse v. Frederick*, then continued after the SCOTUS decision, was not a job. It was a First Amendment crusade. (When I eventually met and conversed with David Crosby in September 2008, I was left with an identical impression—from the opposing perspective, of course.)

My impression piqued my already budding curiosity to understand the antagonisms firing such passion. My inquiry broadened and deepened. When I set out, I thought of my project as a tidy case study, a narrow-gauged investigation. What had begun as an account of a weighty novelty—adolescent BONG HiTS 4 JESUS banner leads to First Amendment drug exception—became a study in how human relationships can go off the rails. The Bering Sea and the Gulf of Alaska, in the North Pacific, are known as weather makers, giving birth to ferocious storms. Playing the role of jurisprudential meteorologist, metaphorically speaking, I set about endeavoring to understand and explain the atmospheric genesis of that perfect constitutional storm in Alaska's capital known as *Morse v. Frederick*.

As my focus expanded, my analytical inquiry changed. Or rather, my analysis diversified. The chapters that follow draw upon a rich variety of legal, political science, anthropological, and literary materials. I take the reader on a journey from storytelling, through analysis of history and doctrine and judicial process, back again to storytelling. In adopting role models, I have aimed high. The book you are reading has been inspired by my admiration for, and use in my teaching of, works by Alan F. Westin,[3] Frank B. Freidel,[4] John A. Garraty,[5] Michael C. Dorf,[6] Fred W. Friendly,[7] Anthony Lewis,[8] Peter H. Irons,[9] and Richard Polenberg.[10] If these scholars provide role models, Clifford Geertz is my muse. I first encountered Professor Geertz's "interpretive anthropology"[11] as a young professor over thirty years ago.[12] Since then, both as a Socratic teacher who seeks to meet students where they are in order to educate them (from Latin: *educere*, "to lead forth") and a scholar who sees writing as a political activity, a basic point of departure for me is "the native's point of view"[13] meaning that "[t]he trick is not to get [myself] into some inner correspondence of spirit with [my] informants. . . . The trick is to figure out what the devil they think they are up to."[14]

Now, I am not doing interpretive anthropology here. What I am doing is trying to make sense of the origins and consequences of the perfect constitutional storm that engulfed Joseph Frederick, Deborah Morse, and the other "natives" whose stories shape this book. In the end, I venture to offer some thoughts about how educators might avoid other such perfect storms—which are Acts of neither God nor Nature. Such perfect storms result from the conjunction of particular circumstances at a specific place. As Geertz wrote of "local knowledge,"

> Like sailing, gardening, politics, and poetry, law and ethnography are crafts of place: they work by the light of local knowledge. The instant case, *Palsgraff* or the *Charles River Bridge*, provides for law not only the ground from which reflection departs but also the object toward which it tends; and for ethnography, the settled practice, potlatch or couvades, does the same. Whatever else anthropology and jurisprudence may have in common—vagrant erudition and a fantastical air—they are alike absorbed with the artisan task of seeing broad principles in parochial facts. "Wisdom," as an African proverb has it, "comes out of an ant heap."[15]

If I manage to mine a modicum of wisdom from the *Morse v. Frederick* "ant heap," then Clifford Geertz's hand, sadly posthumously, is at work.

One other preliminary thought: I have done my best to get this story right, as I honestly understand it. To the people who have shared their stories with me, I owe being conscientiously devoted to truth-telling. Their generosity, candor, and trust demand no less. I do not expect everyone to agree with my interpretation. The disparate people between these covers are not going to circle up and sing "Kumbaya." I do expect them to hold me to the standard articulated by Father Roger Schmit, the Roman Catholic priest in the play about Matthew Shepard and the townspeople of the Wyoming city where he was murdered, *The Laramie Project*. When two participants in the Tectonic Theater Project came to interview him, Father Schmit said, "I will speak with you. I will trust that if you write a play of this, that you say it right. You need to do your best to say it correct."[16]

Father Schmit believes that Matthew Shepard served Laramie well. He trusts that the authors of a play about the events surrounding Matthew's service will do him, and his town, justice. I have endeavored to do no less for the people who trusted me and rendered invaluable assistance in telling this story.

Given the duration and complexity of Joseph Frederick's and Deborah Morse's dispute, readers might find the following time line useful.[17]

Charting the Perfect Constitutional Storm in Juneau

January 24, 2002
- Joe Frederick and thirteen others hoist a banner reading BONG HiTS 4 JESUS as Winter Olympic torch relay passes Juneau-Douglas High School on Glacier Avenue.
- Deborah Morse, Juneau-Douglas High School principal, suspends Frederick for ten days, adding a criminal trespass order for duration of suspension.

February 25, 2002
- Gary Bader, Juneau school district superintendent, upholds Morse's suspension of Frederick, reducing suspension to eight days served.

March 19, 2002
- Juneau School Board unanimously upholds Morse's suspension of Frederick.

Spring 2002
- Avrum M. Gross, former head of the American Civil Liberties Union of Alaska and attorney general for the state of Alaska, 1974–1980, unsuccessfully attempts to mediate the dispute between Frederick and Morse and the school district.

April 25, 2002
- Douglas Mertz, Frederick's attorney, files suit against Morse and the Juneau School District in the U.S. District Court, District of Alaska.

May 27, 2003

- Judge John W. Sedwick, U.S. District Court, District of Alaska, rules in favor of Morse and the Juneau School District, granting defendant's summary judgment, *Frederick v. Morse, and the Juneau School Board* (No. J 02-008 CV [JWS]).

July 8, 2004

- Douglas Mertz appeals Judge Sedwick's decision to the Ninth U.S. Circuit Court of Appeals.

March 10, 2006

- Three-judge panel of the Ninth U.S. Circuit Court of Appeals reverses the U.S. District Court's decision, finding Morse personally liable for violating Frederick's First Amendment rights, 439 F.3d 1114 (9th Cir. 2006).

August 28, 2006

- Kenneth Starr and his law firm, Kirkland & Ellis, representing Morse and the Juneau School District pro bono, file a petition for a writ of certiorari with the U.S. Supreme Court on behalf of their clients.

December 1, 2006

- U.S. Supreme Court grants Morse and the Juneau School District cert, agreeing to hear their appeal, 127 S. Ct. 722 (2006).

March 19, 2007

- U.S. Supreme Court hears oral arguments in *Morse v. Frederick*, 06-278.

June 25, 2007

- U.S. Supreme Court, 5–4, finds for petitioners in *Morse v. Frederick*, 551 U.S. 393 (2007).

July 2007

- Per *Morse v. Frederick*, 551 U.S. 393 (2007), Ninth Circuit reverses its ruling in *Frederick v. Morse*, 439 F. 3d 1114 (2006).

August 2, 2007

- David Crosby, Deborah Morse's and Juneau School District's attorney, files with the U.S. District Court for the District of Alaska a suggestion of mootness and motion to dismiss.

August 7, 2007

- Ninth Circuit Court of Appeals returns *Morse v. Frederick* to the U.S. District Court for the District of Alaska for further proceedings.

September 10, 2007

- Ninth Circuit Court of Appeals enters an order referring the ongoing litigation to Judge Sedwick.

October 10, 2007
- Judge Sedwick issues final judgment in *Frederick v. Morse*, No. J02-008 CV (JWS), holding that Frederick's remaining claims for declaratory and injunctive relief under Alaska law are moot.

November 2007
- Juneau School District rejects Douglas Mertz's settlement offer.
- Douglas Mertz appeals Judge Sedwick's judgment to Ninth Circuit Court of Appeals.

January 2008
- Juneau School District attorney David Crosby files motion with the U.S. District Court for the District of Alaska to compel Frederick to pay $5,000 in costs the school district incurred litigating at the U.S. Supreme Court, and the second U.S. District Court action.

Late Winter and Spring 2008
- Ninth Circuit's chief mediator, Claudia L. Bernard, unsuccessfully seeks to mediate the dispute between Frederick and Morse under auspices of Court's Mediation and Settlement Program.

September 9, 2008
- Same three-judge panel of the Ninth Circuit Court of Appeals that heard and decided *Frederick v. Morse*, 439 F.3d 1114 (9th Cir. 2006), hears oral arguments for a second time.

Fall 2008
- Ninth Circuit reopens negotiations between parties.

November 3, 2008
- Joseph Frederick and Juneau School District agree to terms specified in Settlement Agreement and Mutual Release.

Prologue

A Tale of Three Wars and Zero Tolerance

*A*NNUS HORRIBILIS means "terrible year." *Merriam-Webster's* Online Dictionary and the *Oxford English Dictionary*, respectively, trace the term's origins to 1983 and 1985. It was in 1992, however, that Queen Elizabeth II launched *annus horribilis* into common parlance by famously invoking the words during her November 24 Guildhall speech. Her Majesty's speech was scheduled to commemorate a joyful occasion, the fortieth anniversary of her accession to the throne. Whatever happiness attended that event, in the royal household and throughout Britain, was tarnished by a year-long series of family scandals and a major mishap. The indignities were stock Windsor family foibles, marital separations and dissolutions and a tell-all book, which materialized seemingly monthly throughout the year, compounded by rapacious coverage in the tabloid press. The misfortune was a calamitous fire at Windsor Castle that broke out four days prior to the Queen's Guildhall speech. Starting in Elizabeth II's private chapel, the fire burned for fifteen hours, severely damaging one-fifth of the castle's total floor space.

Rising to acknowledge the hospitality of the Lord and Lady Mayor of the City of London, who hosted her anniversary event at the City of London Corporation's eight-hundred-year-old home, Elizabeth II told the notables assembled in the Guildhall, "1992 is not a year on which I shall look back with undiluted pleasure. In the words of one of my more sympathetic correspondents, it has turned out to be an 'annus horribilis.'" These two sentences are about all that is remembered of the Queen's brief remarks, which culminated in a toast. Significantly, Her Majesty went on to wax thoughtful about the year she had just experienced. "I sometimes wonder," the Queen reflected, "how future generations will judge the events of this tumultuous year." She continued:

> I dare say that history will take a slightly more moderate view than that of some contemporary commentators. Distance is well-known to lend enchantment, even to the less attractive views. After all, it has the inestimable advantage of hindsight.

But it can also lend an extra dimension to judgement, giving it a leavening of moderation and compassion—even of wisdom—that is sometimes lacking in the reactions of those
whose task it is in life to offer instant opinions on all things great and small.[1]

The Queen's implicit plea for compassion is completely understandable, coming from a person who no doubt felt as though she had spent 1992 besieged, absorbing hostile incoming fire while coping with personal losses. My concern in this prologue is with the other dimension of judgment—moderation—twice referenced by Her Majesty. As a preamble to my concerns in the book you are holding, I want to reflect on the salient aspect of the first decade of the twenty-first century, our own *anni horribili* eschewing "instant opinions" in lieu of bringing to bear judgment leavened by moderation.

Moderation was in scarce supply during *anni horribili* 2000–2009. Extremism is the decade's defining characteristic. Drawing lines in the sand was the prevailing modus operandus. Over the past ten years, the decade during which the "perfect constitutional storm in Alaska's capital" that I explore in the following chapters was played out, varieties of dogmatism shaped sweeping aspects of American domestic politics and foreign policy, not to mention macro- and micro-relations among and between state and nonstate actors throughout the world. As we will see, excess also infected community relations in Juneau, Alaska. This book could just as well be subtitled *Self-Righteousness in Alaska's Capital City.* The story I tell could just as well have taken place in any number of other cities in the United States.

The two protagonists of this book, Joseph Frederick and Deborah Morse, each in their own way demonstrated an exaggerated awareness of his own rights and her own virtuousness: Frederick, the Hero of student expression; Morse, the Protector of student safety. Both were piously certain of their own morality, personifying the immoderate ethos of our time. An essential aspect of that ethos, it seems to me, is our proclivity to go to war—literally and figuratively, in both foreign and domestic policy realms. War pervades American life. Since World War II, Americans have lived in a garrison state, based on a permanent war economy, suffused with martial imagery. This country has engaged in a seemingly endless series of regional hostilities, incursions, brushfire conflicts, and sundry other euphemistically named military operations. Since September 11, 2001, we have pursued a War on Terror. At home, over the past half century, we declared War on Poverty, then a War on Drugs. War figures appreciably in this book. First, a Supreme Court decision during a particularly divisive conflict serves as the point of departure for my legal analysis. Second, the D.A.R.E. campaign serves as my backdrop. Third, a central theme is the tendency to resort to combat, in the form of litigation. The "Tale of Three Wars" in the prologue title refers to the Vietnam War, the War on Drugs, and the state of war in which two Juneau citizens found themselves embroiled. In its many modes, warring breeds zero tolerance. Zero tolerance is a conversation stopper. And when conversation stops, people are inclined to fight, thereby creating a vicious cycle of resorting to extreme measures. Paraphrasing the late Barry M. Goldwater, my vantage point on war and intolerance, as species of hubris, is that extremism in the defense of one's presumptions is no virtue.

Zero tolerance can assume many forms. The December 1965 policy adopted by principals in the Des Moines Independent Community School District, which banned wearing black armbands to school, did not brook exceptions. The principals just said, "No!" They backed up their prohibition with the threat of suspension. The Tinker children's opposition to the war in Vietnam motivated them to wear the banned armbands to school. Their subsequent suspension motivated them to oppose being silenced. Their landmark case, *Tinker v. Des Moines Independent Community School District*, 393 U.S. 503 (1969), established the rule that remains the baseline for conversations about students' constitutional rights. As we will see, that conversation has evolved in ways that minimally modify, and arguably erode, the extent of students' protections under the First and Fourth Amendments. Nevertheless, the Vietnam War gave rise to an initial judicial rejection of school policies having the effect of not tolerating student speech.

Like the school principals in Des Moines, those prosecuting the War on Drugs just say, "No!" A primary object of their zero tolerance is use of illegal drugs by adolescents. But this absolute stricture entails auxiliary unconditional measures. Specifically, in the service of implementing a zero tolerance drug policy, high school students' expectation of privacy on campus approached zero. Beginning in 1985, three U.S. Supreme Court opinions severely curtailed students' Fourth Amendment rights by, among other things, replacing individualized suspicion and probable cause with dragnet drug testing. *New Jersey v. T.L.O.*, 469 U.S. 325 (1985), *Vernonia School District, 47J v. Acton*, 515 U.S. 646 (1995), and *Board of Education of Independent School District of Pottawatomie County v. Earls*, 536 U.S. 822 (2002) set the doctrinal table, so to speak, for the incident on Glacier Avenue, January 24, 2002, across from Juneau-Douglas High School (JDHS).

When JDHS Principal Deborah Morse observed Joe Frederick and his buddys hoist their banner emblazoned with BONG HiTS 4 JESUS just as the Winter Olympics torch relay runner approached, she just said, "No." The moment Morse crossed Glacier Avenue and ordered the assembled students to take down their banner, the stage was set for Juneau, Alaska, to go to war over the First Amendment. Hostilities lasted for six years and eleven months. Dangerous drug speech or sophomoric student stunt? Interpreting the chapters that follow, readers will have ample opportunity to judge. Readers also will have lots to mull over. The facts are messy, not only because circumstances are fundamentally disputed but especially because circumstances are deeply embedded in the major players' identities. In point of fact, the differing perceived realities are at war.

The period between their January 24, 2002, encounter and their eventual settlement on November 3, 2008, was Joseph Frederick's and Deborah Morse's very own *anni* horribili. Their zero tolerance for each other led them to make lasting war. What began as a test of wills in the context of mutual estrangement was escalated, in characteristic early twenty-first-century fashion, into a full-blown, knock-down-drag-out battle. Invoking the metaphor I employ in my title, their interpersonal excesses blew up Frederick's and Morse's squall into the perfect constitutional storm. Unable to hear, much less credit, their adversary's story, they resorted to that (usual) American version of taking up arms: litigating. Each sought to impose their dogma on the other. Their instructive plight reminds me of Justice Robert H. Jackson's observation in another public school case:

Probably no deeper division of our people could proceed from any provocation than from finding it necessary to choose what doctrine and whose program public educational officials shall compel youth to unite in embracing. Ultimate futility of such attempts to compel coherence is the lesson of every such effort from the Roman drive to stamp out Christianity as a disturber of its pagan unity, the Inquisition as a means to religious and dynastic unity, the Siberian exiles as a means to Russian unity, down to the fast failing efforts of our present totalitarian enemies. Those who begin coercive elimination of dissent soon find themselves exterminating dissenters. Compulsory unification of opinion achieves only the unanimity of the graveyard. (*West Virginia State Board of Education v. Barnette*, 319 U.S. 624, 641 [1943])

Of course, Justice Jackson was speaking here of state actors imposing doctrinal and programmatic unity upon public school pupils via a compulsory flag salute. Yet understood more abstractly, as a general insight into the folly and the danger attending any attempt by one person arbitrarily to compel another to agree with their view of things, Jackson's opinion is highly pertinent to the story I tell in the following pages. Understood, at its base, as a caution about the short distance between refusing to take notice and putting out of existence, Justice Jackson's wisdom animates Linda Loman's reproach, when she demands of her grown sons in *Death of a Salesman*, "attention must be paid. . . . Attention, attention must finally be paid to such a person."

1

Harmonic Convergence in Juneau

(In)famous for Fifteen Minutes

EVERY SUPREME COURT case begins as a story. At the heart of each story is a quarrel—a fight. Fundamentally, these fights can be over the nature of the story itself. The very narrative becomes contested terrain. When "truth" itself is at issue, more than mere facts are up for grabs. The devil may reside in the details, but Supreme Court cases can turn on the manner in which a majority of the justices connects the discrete dots. *Morse v. Frederick* can be described as originating from an incident that occurred midmorning, Thursday, January 24, 2002, as the Olympic torch relay passed Juneau-Douglas High School (JDHS) on Glacier Avenue. But this description begs crucial questions. Worse, it reduces a complex and contradictory social reality to a stark series of isolated facts—time, date, place, and event—that only Joe Friday could love.[1] Joe Frederick's and Deborah Morse's stories are a lot messier than "just the facts." Their stories also are more interesting, and revealing. The roots of their dispute run deep. Unbeknownst to the people who were generating it, a perfect constitutional storm was brewing in Juneau, Alaska.

Pride Goeth before a Fall

A renowned Japanese film director provides a useful way of making sense of this storm. Akira Kurosawa's 1950 film *Rashomon* explores how stories we tell are suffused with self. For Kurosawa, when we recount an event, we are revealing who we are. *Rashomon* revolves around two events: a rape and a killing.[2] Nevertheless, Kurosawa is not interested in either of these two stubborn facts per se—any more than the raw fact that Joe Frederick and his buddies unfurled a fourteen-foot banner reading BONG HiTS 4 JESUS as the 2002 Olympic torch relay passed Juneau-Douglas High School on January 24, 2002, concerns me here. Both *Rashomon* and *Morse v. Frederick* are *about* humans as storytellers. "[I]n telling and in the retelling, the people reveal not the action but themselves."[3] In other words, both *Rashomon* and *Morse v. Frederick* engage the complementary questions: What do we make of our life experiences? How do we define ourselves in the process of defining our reality?

Donald Richie is a student of Japanese cinema. He has written extensively on Kurosawa's work. He reads *Rashomon* broadly in terms of Kurosawa's most basic artistic purpose: "Here then, more than in any other single film, is found Kurosawa's central theme: the world is illusion, you yourself make reality, but this reality undoes you if you submit to being limited by what you have made."[4] Richie's rendering of Kurosawa contains two elements. First, we are the authors of the reality we occupy. Second, we need to take care not to be trapped by our own certainties.[5] While transcribing my interview with Sally Smith, Juneau's mayor from 2000 to 2003, I was struck by how pertinent Richie's insights are to my project of elucidating the "iceberg" of which *Morse v. Frederick* is merely the tip. Mayor Smith talked about reacting with "total disappointment" that the torch relay had become a "national brouhaha":[6]

> As the mayor of the community, so excited about having the torch in Alaska, for the first time, and the only place it was coming in Alaska, and to have this get blown up into something—I just shook my head, and went "Whose egos are having a problem here?"[7]

Dueling egos and competing stories: this is how constitutional brouhahas like *Morse v. Frederick* are spawned. Kurosawa's cinematic insights into human beings go beyond discerning the paradox that we are agents prone to trapping ourselves within our own creations. According to Richie, Kurosawa suggests that the reason we tend to ensnare ourselves is pride. We tend to identify with the tangled web we have woven, investing our creations not only with credibility but with self-esteem. As Richie observes:

> All the [*Rashomon*] stories have in common one single element—pride. . . . *Rashomon* is like a vast distorting mirror or, better, a collection of prisms that reflect and refract reality. By showing us its various interpretations . . . [Kurosawa] has shown first, that human beings are incapable of judging reality, much less truth, and, second, that they must continually deceive themselves if they are to remain true to the ideas of themselves that they have.[8]

Acting out scripts we ourselves author, we become the characters we create, locked into roles of our own design. "Very often it is the wide discrepancy between the situation as it seems to others and the situation as it seems to the individual that brings about the overt behavior difficulty. . . . If men define situations as real, they are real in their consequences."[9] It is as though we are walking reifications, agents who have forgotten our own agency.[10]

In light of Richie's take on Kurosawa, one might conclude that Joe Frederick and Deborah Morse were destined to clash. That certainly is one possible reading of their story. Paraphrasing art critic Parker Tyler, Richie articulates this determinist view in compelling terms, terms with which Mayor Smith appears to agree. Here is Richie:

> Each [*Rashomon* character] is proud of what he did because, as he might tell you: "it is just the sort of thing that I would do." Each thinks of his character as being fully formed, of being a *thing*, like the rape or the dagger is a thing, and of his therefore (during an emergency such as this) being capable of only a certain number of (consistent) reactions. They are *in character* because they have defined their own character for themselves and will admit none of the sur-

prising opportunities which must occur when one does not. They "had no choice"; circumstances "forced" their various actions; what each did "could not be helped." It is no wonder that the reported actions refuse to agree with each other.[11]

Here is Sally Smith's take on how "destiny" played out in Juneau: "[It's] just a harmonic convergence of all the wrong things . . . There, again, what a perfect storm: you know, a wrong time to be wrong, and the wrong person to be wrong with."[12]

Perceived in Richie's and Smith's terms, Joe Frederick's and Deb Morse's collective story takes on the proportions of a Greek tragedy—with a twist. The twist being that, unlike characters in Greek drama, who are driven by fatal flaws beyond their ken and control, the failings of Frederick's and Morse's characters, like those of Kurosawa's characters, are of their own manufacture. While grappling with Frederick's and Morse's stories for some time, I have grown increasingly convinced that their interactions are not a simple matter of "he said/she said." So, at first glance, a determinist account is somewhat attractive. Richie's and Smith's view breaks out of a dichotomous mental straitjacket that confines one rigidly to right/wrong, truth/lies, good/bad dyads, and joins Frederick and Morse in a confrontational dance in which neither partner led (or both did, blindly). In circumstances in which each side claims a monopoly of What Really Happened, finding a way to bridge the apparently unbridgeable is welcome. *Morse v. Frederick* as an act of nature: Fate—even when personally contrived—has its attractions. It is comfortable to escape blame; to abdicate control and release responsibility for one's actions.

I am troubled, nevertheless, that while enabling escape from the puerile blame game, this quasi-fateful explanation also diminishes human volition and, with it, human responsibility. I use *diminishes* because Richie (and, I suspect, Mayor Smith[13]) never rejects outright humans' capacity to rewrite our respective scripts. In the middle of his statement of the determinist view quoted above, note that Richie uses the word "will": "They are in character because they have defined their own character for themselves and *will* admit none of the surprising opportunities which must occur when one does not" (emphasis added). I believe that we choose not to choose, most of the time. I also believe that recognizing how people routinely abdicate choice is not the same as asserting that humans are incapable of choosing.[14] The trick, or perhaps more accurately the challenge, is to step outside of one's role—which also is one's self. Doing so is no easy matter. Doing so clearly entails being a "traitor" to one's self, divorcing who you are from a range of potentials as yet only dimly perceived—and perhaps having to do so amid exigent circumstances. The reward of doing so is, as Richie observes, "surprising opportunities."

Just because redefining our character is daunting does not relieve us of the human duty of undertaking the task. Richie names failure to undertake rewriting our script as "bad faith." And, he adds, "[w]e know what Kurosawa thinks about this. From Sugata Sanshiro on, his villains have been in bad faith; that is, they see themselves as a kind of person to whom only certain actions, certain alternatives are open. In the effort to create themselves they only codify."[15] In the process of behaving in character, Frederick and Morse not only fixed on a collision course, they foreclosed other possible interactions. Unfortunately—perhaps even tragically—by acting in bad faith they lost sight of the "important corollary" to Kurosawa's central theme, namely: "you are not . . . truly subject to this reality, you can break free from it."[16] On occasion, I have thought of this whole episode in terms of an irresistible force (Frederick) meeting an immovable object (Morse). But that view is entirely too mechanistic. Although their conflict often took on a patina of inevitability, in the final analysis almost everything about Joseph's and Deborah's interactions was avoidable.[17] Rashomon's central ambiguities are set in a bamboo grove. Frederick's and Morse's drama of ambiguity initially unfolded in a rain forest.

"Juneau"

Juneau is a state of mind. That sentence is not a travel agency slogan. Rather, it is designed to shift our frame to facilitate understanding Juneau in psychological and interpersonal terms, as well as a physical place. To be sure, Juneau is a particularly stunning location. How many venues can offer the amenities of a small university town (University of Alaska Southeast) contained within a national forest (Tongass)? Originally a gold-mining town, "[t]hese days, in summer, cruise ship passengers have replaced miners, funneling down the gangplanks of huge floating cities like the *Regal Princess* and *Noordam*, to fill the attenuated downtown, wedged between the [Gastineau] channel and the 3,500-foot summits of Mount Juneau and Mount Roberts."[18]

Juneau remains Alaska's capital—for the time being. The perennial potboiler over moving the capital continues to simmer. In 1994, former two-term Alaska governor Jay Hammond offered his typical candidly irreverent take on the mix of logic, expediency, and self-interest fueling then recent versions of an ongoing debate:

> [C]apital move proponents argued since half of Alaska's population lived in Anchorage, the capital should be relocated in the area of greatest population density and easiest access. Juneau, they argued, unconnected by road to any other Alaskan community, was inconvenient and too expensive to reach by air for citizens who wished to berate the legislature and governor. This faction maintained that government would improve by removing the legislature from its sequester in remote, often-fog-bound Juneau and hauling it north, where, "if we could just get our hands on those rascals' throats, they might shape up."
>
> Actually, the motives of many "pro-move" advocates were less noble. Land speculators, businessmen, contractors, and labor unions salivated over prospects of building a "Brasilia of the North." No matter its costs, the prospect of snatching the economic plum that Juneau had snatched from Sitka years before led many to invest heavily in hopes of tapping state oil revenues to finance their aspirations. Juneauites not only opposed the move; they knew as long as there remained a threat of moving the capital, potential local development prospects were grounded in Juneau, while they soared elsewhere.[19]

Threats to relocate the capital continue. Before she resigned as governor, Sarah Palin made no secret of her interest in shifting state government north, to Anchorage or, preferably, to the Matanuska-Susitna (Mat-Su) Borough where the city of Wasilla is located. During the 2008 legislative session, Republican Representative Mark Neuman, from Wasilla, introduced House Bill 54 that purported to establish a competition that would allow communities from around the state to bid on the opportunity to build a new legislative hall building. Many saw the proposal as a transparent attempt to quit Juneau. Neuman's bill died at session end without coming to a floor vote. Nevertheless, incrementally, state government officials continued to leave town.[20]

While working steadily to marginalize Juneau in state politics, Governor Palin did not hesitate to use Juneau as a picturesque backdrop for her 2007 bid for a national political role. Learning that two cruise shiploads of conservative Republican luminaries, organized respectively by Rupert Murdoch's *Weekly Standard* and the late William F. Buckley Jr.'s *National Review*, were scheduled to visit Juneau that summer,[21] Palin launched a charm offensive housed in the very governor's mansion where she refused to live on a regular basis, symbolically rejecting remote Juneau in lieu of the "real" Alaska. The situation was a convergence of opportunity and ambition. John McCain's presidential campaign was desperately seeking a woman with conservative credentials and star power to join him on the ticket. Sarah Palin was looking for a larger stage than the largest state in the Union.[22]

In a couple of revealing twists of circumstance that rival fiction, two aspects of the "Palin's Love Boats"[23] episode illustrate Juneau as a state of mind. In both, Juneau conveniently assumed the proportions of a symbol. First, after lunch, the governor took her initial group of guests on a "flightseeing" trip to the Kensington Gold Mine in Berners Bay, north of town. Her field trip itself was a partisan gold mine. At the time, the Kensington Gold Mine was at the center of litigation pitting the Southeast Alaska Conservation Council, Lynn Canal Conservation, and the Juneau Group of the Sierra Club against the mine's owner, Coeur Alaska, Inc., and the state itself. Narrowly, the issue was whether, under federal law, mining by-products that Coeur Alaska, Inc. proposed to dump into the adjacent Lower Slate Lake were prohibited "discharge" or acceptable "tailings." Among Alaska conservatives, the dispute had assumed the proportions of "obstructionist environmentalists" versus "jobs for Southeast Alaskans." Ironically, the procedural contours of this dispute bore a striking resemblance to *Morse v. Frederick* in that the mining company had won at the U.S. District Court level, but had lost on appeal at the Ninth Circuit. In both disputes, Alaskan conservatives were counting on the Roberts Court to reverse an out-of-step "liberal Ninth Circuit."[24] Playing on this parallel, in a second coup, Sarah Palin invited Deborah Morse to join her and her conservative guests for lunch—one week before the Supreme Court announced its BONG HiTS decision. In the space of a single afternoon, Governor Palin adroitly aligned herself with two of contemporary Juneau's conservative icons. Her efforts to woo influential Republican queen makers proved decisive:

> By the end of February 2008, the chorus of conservative pundits for Palin was loud enough
> for the mainstream media to take note. . . . By the spring, the McCain Campaign had report-
> edly sent scouts to Alaska to start vetting Palin as a possible running mate. A week or so
> before McCain named her, however, sources close to the campaign say, McCain was intent
> on naming his fellow-senator Joe Lieberman. . . . David Keene, the chairman of the Amer-
> ican Conservative Union . . . believed that "McCain was scared off" in the final days, after
> warnings from his advisers that choosing Lieberman would ignite a contentious floor fight at

the Convention, as social conservatives revolted against Lieberman for being, among other things, pro-choice.

"They took it away from him," a longtime friend of McCain . . . said of the advisers. "He was furious. He was pissed. It wasn't what he wanted." Another friend disputed this, characterizing McCain's mood as one of "understanding resignation."[25]

Whatever John McCain's view of the events leading up to selecting Sarah Palin as his running mate, two things are clear. First, Sarah Palin stage-managed the process in a masterful way. Second, Juneau was a pawn in her game. A "besieged gold mine" and a "beleaguered high school principal" became means for her to establish her conservative bona fides.[26]

Leaving the realm of presidential electoral theatrics, one continues to encounter Juneau as a state of mind. Repeatedly, during my conversations with both Juneau residents and other Alaskans, people would refer to Juneau in ways both notably distinguishing and mildly disparaging. Juneau comes off as a unique place—a place both apart from, and out of step with, the rest of Alaska. For instance, in terms of voting patterns, Juneau is described as "a blue island in a sea of red." "One thing about Juneau," remarked *Juneau Empire* reporter Eric Morrison, "I often tell people that we're a blue city in a red state. Juneau is very different than the rest of Alaska. We almost vote, traditionally, exactly the opposite the way that the state votes. So, like for governor and for president [in 2008], Juneau voted overwhelmingly for Obama—for all the Democratic candidates pretty much. And it goes that way pretty much every election. . . . That's one thing to take into context, here. . . . There's pockets of conservatives in town. . . . But, like I said, there's a majority of liberal-type people in Juneau."[27]

Not only do Juneau's Democratic voting trends set it apart from "Sourdough Alaska,"[28] you can't get to Juneau from anywhere else in the state—or anywhere else, period. Strictly speaking, of course, it is incorrect to say that one cannot get to Juneau. One cannot get to Juneau by motor vehicle, because Juneau resides on a road that goes nowhere.[29] Depending on one's point of view, the absence of road access is either a badge of honor and civic pride or a source of frustration and embarrassment. In Juneau, the "road to nowhere" is more controversial than the infamous "bridge to nowhere."[30] Mayor Sally Smith talked about how the 2002 Olympic torch relay visit to Juneau illustrated misconceptions about what some (mostly in the travel industry) call the "Little San Francisco,"[31] while creating an opportunity briefly to bridge local divisions. "This is pretty incredible," Smith enthused:

> To bring something like this to Juneau, Alaska, where there is no road, and one of the political issues that's been a hot topic for some time is whether or not to have a road. So, to some extent, the excitement of the torch coming here was, in our minds, linked with this issue of we're supposed to be so inaccessible and isolated. . . . What was interesting to us about [meeting with Salt Lake Olympics organizing officials] . . . is the fact that they really didn't have any concept of where it was they were bringing the torch. They really didn't. You know, they thought they were gonna drive in. They counted on the weather being snowy. They had stereotypical thoughts of this place that didn't meet what we know it to be. So, after a couple of meetings . . . we forged a couple of special agreements that were very unusual for the torch relay. One of which was merchandising. They thought they

were gonna bring their vans up here. I mean, that's how they make their money, and that was their big plan is that they would have these merchandising vans. They couldn't get them here—[they would have to] come by barge. And so they allowed us to design our own T-shirts and to have our own logo. . . . They thought that it would be really great to have a dog team mushing. And we said, "We can't promise you snow, and a dog team is not indigenous to this part of the country." . . . The flame has to come! And so they were— they have their own private jet. And we went, "No guarantees!" [*laughs*]. . . . You've got to have special equipment, and GPS wasn't all the rage then that it is now, and if you weren't GPS-equipped, you weren't coming in. At least the likelihood was very strong. But Alaska Airlines had the special equipment, so we actually convinced [the Salt Lake officials] to bring up a sister plane on Alaska Airlines. . . . That was a biggie. And Alaska Airlines and their little jet got in. But, about half an hour after their little jet got in, it wouldn't have—it was that close. The weather turned to snow; it turned to winter.[32]

The Olympic torch relay was a big deal, in part because it served as a release valve, siphoning off part of the stresses endemic to Juneau, that relatively inaccessible small-town capital city pressure cooker. To have the incident on Glacier Avenue distract from this unifying event was distressing. "Juneau is a very polarized community," Mayor Smith said.

It's the state capital. It's a small town. Those are the only explanations I can come up with. Juneau is both liberal and ultra-conservative. And each side just hates the other, regardless— even if they just agree with each other, they'll find a reason not to agree. . . .

We were dismayed that [BONG HiTS] became a national news sort of focus. When you had Ethel Lund [member of Tlingit dance group Yun Shu Ka]—you know the other parallel piece out there—you had this remarkable woman canoeing [*laughs*] [the torch] on January 24th across Gastineau Channel. . . . We had Norman Vaughan out there—he was in his nineties at the time—and he was upset because he didn't get to run [the torch] in front of the capital. Norman Vaughan was an antarctic explorer [and 1932 Olympic dogsled racer] and has a mountain named for him. He's dead now, and that was probably the last public appearance that he made; and he made a big splash. . . . This wonderful piece of the true tradition of the torch goes out on national media. Then that made me feel really good. . . . I think most people locally just kinda rolled their eyes [at the BONG HiTS episode]. . . . And they just sort of dismissed it. This place was really high on having the torch. And [BONG HiTS] was just the nasty little nuisance over there![33]

Fueling Juneau's civic leaders' dismay was their embarrassment—and their annoyance. Having the "dustup" on Glacier Avenue eventually eclipse their long-anticipated, much-celebrated torch relay amounted to rain falling on their parade—big time. Understandably proud of their coup to the point of being proprietary about the torch run, Juneau's municipal elites were mightily displeased that an initially intrusive "nasty little nuisance" threatened to swallow it and supersede the main event. More was at risk than Juneau's image as an Olympic torch relay host city, however. The reputations of Juneau's governing officials were on the line.

Of course, reputation is notoriously ephemeral and essentially a matter of perception. It is, in other words, yet another state of mind. As the competing narratives of Frederick and Morse unfolded, their reputations became arenas of struggle, contested terrain. Their disparate stories themselves became the story.

Joseph Frederick[34]

Joe is a civil rights hero, and a bad actor. He is highly intelligent, and not always smart. In short, he's human. Clay Good,[35] retired biology teacher at JDHS and former president of the Juneau Education Association (the teachers' union), spoke about Joe in clear-eyed terms:

> I heard of Joe, he came on my radar as a teacher, 'cause teachers get together in the lounge or the copy room, or wherever, and they'll talk about whatever's going on in a day, and his name would come up often enough as a student of concern to teachers, even if you didn't have him in your class. Most teachers had an idea of who he was, and the mischief he was up to. . . . He was not beyond being a prankster. And he wasn't one to enjoy authority, and I think he flaunted his independence a bit. . . . Joe delighted in provoking. And, so, it's not like he is a victim of random circumstances. . . . You know, it's like a kid in my own class, who's the troublemaker, will then complain to me because I'm always on him, 'cause I'm always watching him. And I say, "Well, whadda guess, buddy?! Gonna cause trouble? Yeah, I'm gonna keep an eye on ya." That's what we do as teachers. . . . I think my peers would agree. Not that any of us were "Get rid of Joe" mentality. But we care a lot about all the students, including the ones who are struggling, or who are provocateurs. They're a valuable part of the community, and shaping their energy or values is, I think, what most teachers attempt to do; and did so with Joe. At the same time, teachers have a strong sense of—I don't know, it's almost a strong sense of paternalistic or maternalistic protecting others. And Joe didn't have a great deal of empathy for other people, and stepped on toes and didn't always look out for other people. . . . And so part of . . . teachers' concern [was] is this guy stepping on other people? Is he hurtin' other people? Does he have enough regard for the safety and concerns of others? He's just spinnin' a little bit faster than most other students, so naturally he gets looked at more closely.[36]

Joe Frederick is a prankster: a contemporary Till Eulenspiegel.[37] Perhaps a historical figure who lived in the fourteenth century, Till Eulenspiegel became legendary in sixteenth-century German *Schwank-literatur* or "fool's literature." "He is a unique, complex and mysterious character. . . . He is a mischief maker. . . . While he does trick the dishonest, harsh, cruel, stupid, conceited, obnoxious, boring and pretentious—in short, the deserving—he also preys on the naive, the gullible, and the innocent."[38] At the end of Richard Strauss' tone poem (1894–1895), "Till Eulenspiegle's Merry Pranks," Strauss' romanticized antihero receives his comeuppance on the gallows, only to have the last laugh via a reprise at the end. Who knows, had Joe Frederick lived five centuries ago, he might have been hanged. Instead, he was suspended from high school.

Joe Frederick arrived in Juneau in the summer of 2000. Joe's father, Frank Frederick, had preceded him to Juneau, in late 1999, accepting employment with Alaska Public Entity

Insurance (APEI). Frank had left a job in Seattle, where he and his son had moved following Frank's contentious divorce from his wife in northeast Texas, which had left Frank deeply bitter.[39] According to Frank, he opted to relocate to Juneau, even though his Seattle employer offered to match the APEI salary offer, because Joe did not like Thomas Jefferson High School (TJHS), the Federal Way, Washington, school Joe attended his sophomore year. Joe told his dad that his unhappiness resulted from antipathy directed toward him by TJHS boys, who were jealous because Joe's lingering Southern accent made him attractive to TJHS girls, and because Joe had run-ins with what Joe called "Asian gangbangers."[40]

In retrospect, Frank believes that Joe paid a price for their somewhat nomadic existence. He contrasted Joe's experience while they still lived in Texas with Joe's subsequent difficulties. "Joe always got along with everybody and was well liked in Texas," Frank observed.

> So I guess moving around does cause some adjustments. . . . You go to a new school, and you didn't grow up with the kids, they don't know you. You gotta make new friends. Joe has— don't get me wrong, Joe has a lot of friends in Juneau. Joe makes a lot of friends. But he'd never told me he'd gotten in any fights at school. But I heard about 'em—it was after he graduated. But he never came home and told me he'd gotten into a fight. . . . I found out later— you know, Joe didn't tell me a lot of things. . . . [H]e had a Camaro, and . . . he was new to the school, and he played soccer, and so I had a few of his friends tell me later—this is after he even graduated—how Joe had to get into a couple of fisticuffs with football players that would start pickin' on him, but he wouldn't back down.[41]

Joe's version of his troubled transition resembles Frank's. Listening to both accounts, Joe became an "outsider." Joe was doubly an outsider. First, he was a newcomer, a stranger who moved into town, enrolling at JDHS as a junior—at his third school in three years. Social relations in the stratified, hyper-status-conscious environment that is high school had long since been sorted and solidified by the time Joe showed up.[42] The JDHS pecking order had been fixed. Second, responding to being marginalized, Joe assertively turned his disadvantage into an asset, proudly assuming the mantle of Outsider as his defining identity. Arriving amid already-established social groups, Joe cast himself in antisocial terms. Joe's outsider script and rebellious character were colored by his reading of Albert Camus, but his behavior often resembled Tom Petty's Eddie: a rebel without a clue.[43]

Joe traces his difficulties with JDHS administrators to his survival strategy. Shunned by model students, Joe chose to associate with students who shunned being model:

> Part of the reason, probably, . . . why [JDHS] administration . . . liked to pick on me; when high school students transfer to new schools, it's usually the counterculture-oriented students that are more open to making friends, rather than the students who are old-time from that city that are more like—I'm trying to think how to describe it—it's hard to describe. Like, for instance, kids who are quite healthy and have always lived in that town and played on sports teams, they already have their groups of friends, and stuff. So, it's more kids that are into counterculture. Also, you could say, experimentation with drugs and stuff like that— those type of kids in high school are much more friendly and open to making new friends.

So, therefore I did make friends with a lot of kids in Juneau who would not be your choice, straight-A students that follow all the rules. . . . So, many of the people I associated with were troublemakers, or got into trouble more often than other people did that already sort of have their "in" crowds.[44]

I asked Joe when his concerns about being singled out by JDHS administrators, due to his being part of the counterculture group, started to get focused on student speech issues and First Amendment issues. Joe's answer further sheds light on his pride in the outsider "trickster" role in which he cast himself.[45]

Well, I've always been, my method of thinking has always been different than many people. I've always liked to think hypothetically: "Let's see, oh actually, then I could do this." Or whatever. My parents would always say something—"Yeah, but you shouldn't." . . . Well, for instance, before this [banner thing] all happened, actually . . . One day, it was probably my third time to be in court for either possession of tobacco or minor consuming alcohol, or something.[46] And I thought about it . . . how often students come to the court, and I know you have a right to a trial, no matter what. So, one day I decided to drop a bombshell on the Juneau Courthouse. When they called me to come up, and they asked me to enter my plea, I said "Not guilty." [laughs] . . .

But what had happened was I was guilty. I had been drinking with friends at the skate park. . . . I was getting into my car, and I was standing there, I had my keys in my car door by the skate park, and I was holding a six-pack of beer, and I heard someone say, "Freeze." And then I looked, and I saw in the reflection of my car door, I could see the outline of police officers and the badge. . . . So, instead of go into the car where I would get a driving charge which would be serious, I pulled my keys back, turned around, took off running, and smashed the bottles on the concrete. And one of the cops managed to run me down. . . .

Anyways, I pled not guilty. And I couldn't get a jury trial because there was no jail time at risk. . . . The penalty's only a fine, so I only get a trial in front of one judge, whose—I'd been in his Minor Consuming Court before: [Peter B.] Froehlich. And I did my research. I invoked the rule making—forcing—officers to leave the room, 'cause there were two officers and I made them leave the room during each other's testimony. . . . I requested, made a—what do you call it . . . I made a motion of discovery . . . and I listed everything: audio, video surveillance they had, any testimony the officers would give, anything. . . . The police department didn't respond. The court dates comes. I think if I had an attorney and I wasn't representing myself, it would have been thrown out over this, because the prosecution starts and I object and say, "Hey, I filed a motion of discovery two weeks ago. I haven't been provided any of this." And, instead of throwing away the case, and dismissing it, which I think would have happened if I was an actual attorney, the judge says, "Oh"—he sort of got on the prosecution—he said, "You guys have to honor his request, and I'm going to give you two more weeks. Come back in two weeks." Two weeks later, they gave me their stuff.

But I'd made a diagram of the skate park, the entire place. I'd drawn it up on AutoCAD, had all the parameters. And I even had lots of evidence of pictures, because they didn't have any bottles to bring in, of course, because I knew I'd smashed 'em—right? And if I smashed 'em, there was no alcohol in 'em, and how could they prove there was alcohol in 'em before they were smashed or not? I got the officers to contradict on almost every possible point they possibly could. They couldn't even agree on whether or not it was raining that night. . . . I had pictures of the skate park, which is always littered with beer cans, and empty beer bottles, and broken bottles, anyways. Any given day you can go up there and pick up a hundred empty beer cans. So, the fact that [the police officers] found empty bottles, or broken bottles there doesn't really prove anything. So the officer says, "Well, I knew that [the bottles had] just been broken because the ground was wet." I said, "Because the ground was wet." And then I think I made a comment about the percentage of time it's precipitating in Juneau, at any given time. . . . But [the officers] contradicted on every point. I even asked them to point out where I was, and where they were, when I threw the bottles. And something about the testimony showed that, like, they couldn't have possibly seen me throw the bottles, because they said I was off—here—and they were off—here—but there's a building in the way. But they contradicted on lots of stuff.

And then, at the end of it, Judge Froehlich says, "You know, Mr. Frederick, you could make a hell of an attorney one day. You basically proved that you had nothing to drink that night. But, I feel like you're guilty—$300." . . . Basically, the Judge at the end told me I'd make a great attorney. I'd proved I wasn't drinking—but he knew I was, and found me guilty anyways. . . . [This episode] was maybe a few months before [the torch run].[47]

Joe's accounts of his counterculture friends at JDHS, and the episode in Judge Froehlich's court, display key elements of the role he played out during his junior and senior years. Basically, he portrays himself as resourceful outsider. Joe likely would neither employ those particular words nor endorse them as self-descriptions. Still, Joe saw the world oppositionally, and thought of himself as a clever survivor. He divided the world into "them," i.e., authority figures and those who collaborate with them, versus "us," i.e., those who reject established authority and pay a price for rebelling. He took pride in his skill at tweaking The Establishment, and was convinced that the Juneau police and JDHS officials persecuted him precisely for his being adept at being annoying. "It's sort of like trying to fight against them," Joe observed. "And, you know, try to learn to play by the rules, and still beat them. Like, play it like a game of chess."[48]

Joe's chess reference is not entirely apt. Although he delighted in outmaneuvering his opponents skillfully, he saw no need to play by rules that he believed were unfairly skewed and arbitrarily enforced. For him, the "chess game" was rigged by people to whom he was unattached.[49] As far as Joe was concerned, this circumstance gave him license to mischievously pick and choose among rules as he went along.[50] "I'm trying to think why I pushed the envelope more than other people around here," Joe mused just before recounting his version of the incident on Glacier Avenue. "Maybe [it's] because I'm new in the community. . . . Whereas, if I'd grown up here . . . I'd be less likely to do it because, if I'd grown up in this community, probably many of the people who work at the high school [would] also [be] associated with my family. . . . For me, it's like I have no association with these people, and I don't view them the same as like somebody who'd grown up here. For instance, it's like: 'Oh, Mrs. Morse—your mother's friend.' So, I have a lot more freedom in this respect."[51] Instead of being his mother's friend, Deborah Morse became Joe's adversary.

Deborah Morse[52]

Deborah Morse has been bruised by the incident on Glacier Avenue and, especially, by the ensuing contentiousness. She sees herself as misunderstood by many colleagues and community members, mistreated by the media, and outright misrepresented by some parties to the controversy spawned on January 24, 2002.[53] Ironically, Deborah is every bit as firmly convinced as Joe that she did the right thing that Thursday morning—and just as righteously indignant at being perceived otherwise. On several occasions, her lawyer, David Crosby, told me that his client is "snakebit" over the entire six-year-plus episode. Although her counsel would persuade the U.S. Supreme Court to hear Morse's case, and she would win before that tribunal, Deborah Morse did not emerge unscathed.

Kenneth Starr argued Deb Morse's case before the Supreme Court. She was in Washington, D.C., to hear the oral arguments on Monday, March 19, 2007. The previous day, she had attended the preparatory moot courts conducted at the Kirkland & Ellis office in Washington, D.C. "I remember this one point," Deb recalled, "where Ken turned around, looked at me, and he goes: 'You just weren't what I expected!' You know, I thought—I guess they were expecting this old battle ax [*laughter all around*] administrator. And he goes: 'You just seem too nice.'"[54]

Deb Morse is nice. Saying that is not damning her with faint praise. Genuinely pleasant and polite, Deborah Morse decidedly is no old battle ax administrator. Neither is she a babe in the woods. Ken Starr said she just seems "too nice." Too nice, in what context? Too nice to be a high school principal? Too nice to mete out discipline? Too nice to be sued by a high school student? Too nice to be the villain portrayed in some media reports, blog posts, and letters to the editor? It is unlikely we will ever know what Starr had in mind. No matter. In the context of how our self-defined roles can confine us, Deborah Morse is too nice for her own good. Her defining conception of herself as kind, likable, and agreeable precludes entertaining the possibility that she might have acted otherwise.

Deb evinces a sense of hurt bewilderment that anyone could see her in another, less positive light. On three occasions during our one-hundred-minute-plus interview, Deborah Morse was overcome with emotion. Each time, she obviously was struggling with how her interactions with Joe had played out in her office, following their encounter on Glacier Avenue. She clearly regretted what became a second altercation. Still, Morse's regrets did not enable her to break out of her "too nice" role. She was very upset that her conscientious efforts to disarm a dicey situation—to resolve this bit of unpleasantness agreeably—were for naught. Joe had sabotaged her.

> My intention had been to [*tears up*]—I'm sorry—would have been to bring [Joe] into my office and talk about it, and that would have been it.... It would have been just trying to talk to him.... And—I'm so sorry—he was just belligerent.... Definitely ... I felt like he was being very belligerent and not cooperative.... So, I was filling out the [disciplinary] paperwork ... and just because he kept jumping up and got agitated, and almost threatening

towards me . . . I could just tell he wasn't getting it. . . . I'm sorry that I'm getting upset. . . . I'm feeling he's not getting it. . . . Just the whole situation.[55]

Toward the end of our interview, I asked, "So, Deb, looking back on it, how do you feel about the whole situation?" She began her reply facetiously—sort of: "I wish that we had never participated [*smiles*], and I never had to experience all this. But it wouldn't have changed what happened." She continued:

> I think I did the right thing at the time. And I really just wanted to talk to the student. If he had just come to my office [when I'd asked him to], we probably would have had a—I would think a different outcome. I don't know if that would have been within his character to have had it turn out any other way.[56]

According to Deborah Morse, the drama on Glacier Avenue, and subsequently in her JDHS office, features a caring administrator—and an antagonistic scoundrel. If only Joe Frederick had the strength of character to capitulate, to comply, and to cooperate, the two of them could have talked things out. Because Joe behaved roguishly, Principal Morse regrettably had no choice but to abandon her original intention in lieu of disciplining him. That outcome was not nice, and it was not her responsibility.[57]

Another way of understanding the role Morse played is in terms of cognitive dissonance. It seems to me that a key aspect of Deb "being too nice for her own good" is that she clearly experienced difficulty reconciling her image of who she is as a person with the circumstances broadly surrounding her conflict with Joe Frederick. "I have a hard time imagining," remarked reporter Eric Morrison, of the *Juneau Empire*, "that [Morse] would have done what she did, if she would have known where it would have taken her. . . . I don't think she had a very pleasant time dealing with this whole situation, especially as it grew and grew, and became—had so much national interest there at the end."[58]

Above, while discussing Ken Starr's expression of pleasant surprise at Morse being "too nice," I speculated about possible meanings of his comment. When drafting that passage I originally wrote, then deleted, a fifth question: What's a nice person like you doing, having to defend your actions before the U.S. Supreme Court? I suppose that Deb puzzled along similar lines: How did this happen to a nice person like me?[59] The "this" in that sentence likely refers to several related dimensions of her life after January 24, 2002, the most salient being the persistent litigation leading up to, culminating in, and continuing after *Morse v. Frederick*, and her attendant exposure to public scrutiny. There are a couple of collateral dimensions, which I will pose as questions, implicit in Morse's rueful lament. First, how did a nice person like Deborah Morse end up being a controversial principal? Second, how did a nice person like Deborah Morse end up with "egg on her face"?[60]

Morse's four-year tenure as JDHS principal (2000–2004) became increasingly problematic.[61] *Problematic* pertains to a basic sense that those four years grew increasingly troubling for her, because being nice did not comport easily with some of her experiences as principal. First, Morse was conflicted over her concern with maintaining order and the exigencies of doing so. She wanted to run a tight ship while avoiding the conflicts that unavoidably attend doing so. Second, Morse presided over almost two thousand staff, faculty, and students when she seemed more comfortable with brick-and-mortar projects than with people. Presiding over the $27 million JDHS renovation project may have been the highlight of her time as principal.[62] Third, as principal, Deb Morse had considerable authority but the very process of exercising her authority made her a target—no more so than on January 24, 2002. A well-known Gary Larson cartoon illustrates this last point. Two deer are standing in the woods. One deer has a prominent red bull's-eye on its chest. The other deer says: "Bummer of a birthmark, Hal." Deb Morse was not marked from birth. Being targeted for doing her job was no less of a bummer.

I asked former JDHS teacher Clay Good what he and his colleagues' informal conversations were about Morse's administration. His answer—as clear-eyed as his views about Joe—summarizes what was problematic about Morse as JDHS principal.

> Oh, you know, Deb I found to be a highly competent manager, but a very reclusive one. . . . If you're gonna have somebody be authoritarian and just make decisions, you want somebody who makes good decisions and makes them well informed, and sort of saves you a lot of trouble. And that was my regard for her. We had to go toe-to-toe ourselves a couple of times. My role in the high school, besides being the lucky knucklehead with the camera at the right moment [laughs], was also that I was a union president and powerful in those circles, and had to work with Deb at pretty high power levels from time to time. Authority's important to her. And what I enjoyed about Deb was that she was competent taking care of the nuts-and-bolts stuff. But she wasn't out and about hobnobbing with the students or the teachers. [She] didn't have a great relationship with most folks—I mean, not a bad relationship, but sort of a nonrelationship. . . . Deb—if you had power, or if you were male, or if she could avoid conflict—she would. And so she and I didn't have that many problems. And, generally I was treated well and always got what I wanted. And so I presumed, or would project, that that was true of others. And the voice you hear from the other side is that: "Yeah, she took care of you, Clay, because she's protecting her own thing." But, if she sensed a vulnerability, or a different status, or was threatened by other women, she would use her authority in ways that [some JDHS female faculty members][63] felt weren't positive or benevolent. . . . Like I said, our dance was one of a power balance, and we found a comfortable place to be. But I'm not sure many other people enjoyed the power I did.[64]

Political scientists who seek to gauge the influence that the chief justice wields over decisions made by justices on the U.S. Supreme Court differentiate between the chief's roles as "task leader" and "social leader."[65] A task leader is more or less effective at facilitating the work of the institution she heads. Competent task leaders get the job done. A social leader is more or less successful at knitting together the people working in the institution over which she presides. Competent social leaders get people pulling together. My sense from my interviews (including my interview with Deb herself) is that Morse was more comfortable with the task leader aspects of her role as JDHS principal, especially when the task involved bricks and mortar, than with being a social leader. The problem lies in the fact that a central task of a high school principal entails being a social leader.[66] An essential part of the job to be done is creating a collegial, inclusive, and safe learning space. Creating such an environment entails talking, among other social skills. "[W]hat needs to happen," observed Superintendent Carol Comeau in the context of describing the Anchorage School District's efforts to confront hateful, bullying school atmospheres targeting LGBTQ (lesbian, gay, bisexual, transgender, and questioning) students—"what needs to happen, [is] we need to not be afraid to have these difficult conversations, and empower kids to be part of that, rather than come down with the heavy club."[67] Since Deb Morse may have found the social dimensions of her leadership task uncongenial, leaving the JDHS principal's job to become Juneau School District's coordinator of facilities planning may have been a relief.

Regrettably, while she probably found managing physical plants nicer than negotiating various faculty and student minefields, Morse remained tarred by the BONG HiTS unpleasantness. Deb's job change may have diminished her being discomforted by any question along the lines of: How did a nice person like me end up being a controversial principal? Nevertheless, switching occupational hats did not alleviate the persistent question: How did a nice person like me end up with egg on her face?

The phrase *egg on her face* is *Juneau Empire* reporter, Eric Morrison's. The phrase was mentioned three times during our interview in conjunction with how the BONG HiTS episode played out in Deborah Morse's life. "As I was told," Eric explained:

> [Morse] didn't get fired from being the [JDHS] principal, but it was kind of a forced move within the district. It was kind of seen as a promotion in a way.... And so it was kind of a move up into a new administration. She was still gonna be well employed within the district, but it's because of—what I always understood and, I mean, I could be wrong—she could have willingly wanted to be out of the principal's position because of all this.... I can't tell her thoughts, but I think she feels like she's got a little bit of egg on her face in the community.... I think she has a little bit of egg on her face just 'cause she has to live here in this community, still. And she's become notorious for that action on that one day. And so I think there's a lot of people in town—she probably has to interact with them on quite an almost daily basis I imagine—and people in the district, even. Probably—I'm sure she had relationships that probably changed because of it, just daily interactions with people....[68]
>
> Then we had this new school kind of debacle.... Our population, by all—apparently by what people are telling us, is that the community is shrinking. The new school [Thunder Mountain High School], it went: [Juneau] voted to have the school, and there was a revote to not have the school, then there was a revote to have the school. And so this school took years and years. And so, while this BONG HiTS 4 JESUS issue was going on, they were also building this school, and there was tons of money being poured into it. It kept increasing in cost—cost overruns.... So it just became this huge issue. And now our population has shrunk. There was an overcrowding issue, but now we have too much school for not enough kids....[69]

Assessments of Morse's response to the incident on Glacier Avenue are more nuanced than being a simple matter of Morse having reasons to be embarrassed. For instance, civic officials and school administrators I talked with unanimously believe that high school principals, like Deb Morse, have authority to make judgments about student behavior.

Furthermore, these folks—Morse's professional colleagues and peers—all were aghast at the attempt to hold Morse personally liable for damages as a result of her particular judgment call regarding Joe Frederick's behavior on January 24, 2002. They all unequivocally opposed this aspect of Frederick's lawsuit. Carol Comeau, Anchorage School superintendent, articulated the collective view:

> [The school board and I] had some real mixed feelings about this case. The one part—we absolutely disagreed with Joe [in] that we did not believe the principal should have been sued personally. . . . Absolutely—that part; if that had been the only issue, I can guarantee you we would have joined in [with Morse], because we believed she was absolutely operating within her job description, following Board policy, procedures—all of that. That part of the lawsuit—I was furious when I saw it. Why would anyone want to be a principal or an educator, if [it] ends up that they are personally liable for doing their job? So, we felt really strongly about that.[70]

By the same token, while standing shoulder-to-shoulder with Deborah Morse regarding the extent of her authority, and her legal immunity while exercising it, some interviewees voiced concerns they and others had about her specific decision around the Glacier Avenue incident. For instance, former Juneau Mayor Sally Smith observed:

> I think most people locally just kinda rolled their eyes [at the banner incident]. And, of course, I didn't know the kid. But those who knew the kid said: "You gotta consider the kid! And he's a low-life troublemaker. It's all about him." And they just sorta dismissed it. You know, they were—this place was really high on having the torch, and that was just the nasty little nuisance over there. [The] more I heard—as much as I love Deb Morse—was that Deb handled it wrong. That seemed to be the water-cooler-coffee-pot discussion, was that Deb overreacted. . . . Overreacted . . . [S]he probably shoulda just said [to Joe]: "Not a good idea! You need to learn how to make better choices." Talk to the parents, agree on some detention or something. But it probably didn't merit suspension. The real incident occurred when she suspended him. . . . Most people thought the kid was a jerk. Most people thought Deb overreacted. Probably she'd had many altercations with this kid, and [the banner] was the straw that broke the camel's back—unfortunately. . . . And she just finally lost it. And she's a human being. But that seemed to be the general consensus around the community, was what a shame it had to be over this, and what a shame it had to turn into a court case.[71]

Having lived with Deborah Morse and Joseph Frederick vicariously for several years, then having met and talked with each of them in person, when I think of our storytellers, two pairs of adjectives consistently come to mind to describe them: wounded/wary (Deb Morse); brazen/brash (Joe Frederick).[72] Yet, in the very act of writing those descriptors— as I engrave black letters on a white page—I realize that I am engaging in precisely the sort of reductionism and, worse, reification that I seek to combat with this project. I face a dilemma: wanting to convey fully my sense of those who are telling these tales, I risk being implicated in foreclosing to our players the "surprising opportunities which must occur" when one is not locked within one's self-created role. So, resisting the temptation to add more layers of interpretation, I will avoid the risk of further rubricizing[73] Morse and Frederick by stopping to let Joe and Deb recount their stories in their own words.

Rashomon in Juneau

Joe Begins His Story[74]

The banner itself—it was not that well planned. . . . I think it was all within twenty-four hours of [the torch relay] that we decided we wanted to do something[,] . . . because there were TV cameras. . . . But we also wanted to piss people off, like they couldn't do anything about it.[75]

We wanted something that—we just wanted to hold up a banner for the TV cameras, and we wanted it to be something pushy. So we threw in Jesus as a religious thing, to where something that could be controversial or funny or whatever you wanted it to be, or nothing if you don't—I mean, I don't see it as deep, deep thought or philosophy or anything, you know. It's just anything . . .

Q.[76] Now, you said you wanted to be pushy. What do you mean by being "pushy"?

A. Well, not pushy, just somewhat to where you are testing something. If we held up a banner that said "Hi," or "Hello," you know . . . that's not really testing free speech at all.

Q. So you wanted it to be something controversial?

A. Yes.

Q. And how did you see this phrase as being controversial?

A. Well, it is all in preferences, once again. One way it could be controversial is if you take "bong" as in the definition that you [Crosby] found on the Internet many times, and put it "for Jesus." Christian people . . . I believe that they are anti-drugs, so if you put that together, it's somewhat ironic. Some people might just look at it as a joke or whatever. . . .[77]

We made the banner. . . . We got some paper and duct tape and drove up to the parking garage above the [Juneau Public] Library downtown, and laid out the paper. And, then at that point, we still weren't sure what to write on it. I mean, it was, I don't know—maybe we just decided, somebody might have suggested—and we're like, "Yeah, let's do 'Bong Hits for Jesus.'"[78]

The phrase I used doesn't matter. I could have used another phrase and still [have] been going for the same message. It's just to say what you want. I mean, the Constitution doesn't just protect, like, deep speech or legal speech. . . . I wasn't trying to spread any idea. I was just trying to assert my right.

Q. Were you trying to prompt a debate about the message "Bong hits for Jesus"?

A. No, not really. Just to be able to say something. . . . The content of the banner was not anywhere nearly as important as everybody seems to think it was. . . . All that we wanted was to hold up a sign, be able to do it because the Bill of Rights says we can. . . . We weren't trying to put out a deep message to anybody. We weren't trying to put out a message at all; just to show people that, "Look, you have the right to free speech." . . . I don't see how it's advocating anything.[79]

[A] lot of people might think [the banner] was stupid; like the student body and stuff. Which, actually, the student body—we didn't get a reaction out of them. I don't think anybody cared. Most of them were sitting there, like: "This [torch relay] is so lame!" Like there's nothing. There's a guy running down with a torch, and there's a couple of cars or something. "It's too cold to be out here for this." They're all sitting there like this: "Let's go back inside!" And then, when Ms. Morse came across and started tearing [the banner] down, that's when it was like a big deal. If she hadn't torn it down, nobody would have even thought twice about the banner, or even remembered it.[80]

Q. And at what point did you unfurl the banner?

A. Right as the camera was passing us. The camera was in the truck in front of the runner, so right as it passed we were being shot, and we held it up.

Q. Why didn't you unfurl it earlier?

A. Because we were waiting for the camera.

Q. So the sole point was to have this shown on the camera?

A. Yes. . . .

Q. All right. W[hen] you held the banner up, what happened then?[81]

A. She [Morse] crossed the street, and started saying, "No, no, no!" and started tearing the sign down. And all the kids holding the sign—which wasn't me, actually—I wasn't holding the sign until she started to tear it down. That's when I grabbed the sign. 'Cause the whole time, if you look at the pictures, I'm not holding the sign. I'm like standing there yelling, and telling the people, like directing them: "You guys hold it up higher, higher" and organizing. And most of the people . . . when they[82] tore it down, they took off running.[83]

A lot of people were just dropping [the banner] when she came over because—I don't know. They didn't have faith in their rights of free speech, I guess, and they were scared because they didn't trust the Constitution to protect them, I guess. But I had faith in it, so I held it.[84]

As she took it down, I said, "What happened, I thought we were in America, don't we have free speech?" And I made these comments to her. And she didn't care. She might even have said something along the lines of "Not in high school."[85]

She said, "Not here." I said, "Why not? It's free speech. We're not on school grounds." And she said that—she repeated to take it down. I said, "No. What happened to the Bill of Rights? This is our right to do this. It's a free speech exercise." And she said, "Not here it's not." . . . And she asked me to come to her office. I said I'd be there.[86]

Deb Begins Her Story[87]

Here's what happened. We were at an admin. meeting . . . and the school board president came in—Mary Becker—and she was on the committee for the Olympic torch coming through Juneau. And she came and asked that the district be part of that, and that we find ways to involve students and, also, to make sure that as many students in the district could actually see the torch. . . . And I actually remember thinking right then, at that moment, that bringing the entire student body out in front of the high school, it was a huge school assembly and that it was going to take effort to make sure that everything was supervised, and making sure all the times fell right. . . . The plan was that we wouldn't be out there [on Glacier Avenue] more than thirty minutes. And we went out, there was lots of snow, it was really cold. . . .

And then what happened was the Coke truck came by and they were handing out banners, little banners—I Saw the Torch!—or something like that, and then they were also handing out plastic bottles of pop, twenty-ounce bottles of pop to kids. . . . And then, there had been a couple of incidences right after that. . . . I was walking back and forth, and a snowball had gone by me, and I knew the area, and the group of students. And they were kinda grouped together.[88]

I had had several interactions with that group of students [where Joe was standing], that had been an ongoing issue; the snowball, then the snowball, the [pop] that was thrown at the vehicle, and also the snowball that came—that hit the driver's side window of the police officer's car, as well as students in that group throwing [pop] at each other. So we had—I'd had numerous interactions with that group at that point. . . .

Q.[89] What I'm trying to get at is whether or not you know that any of the students holding the banner were before that throwing things or fighting.

A. I wouldn't have known that because we're standing there watching car—a car goes by and then the next thing you see is the pop bottle hitting the back of the vehicle and then you see where it's coming from but not exactly who threw it. . . .

Q. If you didn't know that the students holding the banner had engaged in throwing things or fighting, what's the connection? What's the logic there that made you think that the banner itself would contribute to an unruly situation?

A. It was a sequence of events that happened that were sparked by incidents coming out of that group of students.

Q. Even if some of the students holding the banner had in fact thrown things, why did you think that the banner would contribute to an unruly situation?

A. Well, it definitely was part of it and so it . . . was one contributing factor to the ongoing interactions that I have had with that group of students at that time. . . . The snowball coming from there was part of it . . . the pop hitting the vehicle was part of it, the sequence of events and the events that happened. The students throwing things at each other was part of it, as well as the banner was part of it. The interactions I'd had with that group of students.[90]

And then we saw a truck come by, and then directly behind it was the torch bearer. And just as they're going by, I see across the street this banner come up. And, at that point, I'm watching that. I didn't even really see the torch . . . 'cause I'm like going [*shrugs shoulders, vocalizes quizzically*] lookin' at [the banner]. . . . And I just walked over, and I remember saying, "Put the banner down." And I remember Joe saying something about, "What about my First Amendment rights?" And then I'm saying, "This isn't the right place; this isn't the appropriate place to do this." "Well, I'm on public property." And I'm sayin' to him, "Well, you're in the middle—this is a school activity, a school event. It's not the right place." . . . And I said, "Come to my office—we'll talk about it." My feet were freezing [*laughs*] and I really just wanted to get into the building.[91]

Joe Continues His Story

I did go to her office fairly shortly. I didn't, like, hold her hand and go to the office with her. That's one of her big things, is that I didn't immediately report to her office. . . . But, I mean, it was, like, within ten minutes, or something.[92]

I said I'd be there. "I'm going to go grab my books out of my car on the way." She didn't say anything. Then she walked off, and I went to my car, got my books, and I walked back into the school.

On the way to the office I stuck my head in the door of my next class, which was physics, I believe. I said, "I've got to go to the office. I'll be back," so he wouldn't count me absent.

And then as I was walking out the door, I saw Ms. Morse and Mr. Staley [assistant principal], and they told me to come to the office. I said I was already on my way.

I got to their office, and they told me I was going to be suspended for disruptive behavior. I said, "What disruptive behavior?" And then they said I was defiant as well. I asked them how I was defiant. They said that I didn't put the banner down at first, and that I was questioning why they were suspending me. And then I said, "How can you all be mad about the banner? It was pure speech, and don't we have the Bill of Rights still?" Mr. Staley said not in school because it doesn't apply. Then I quoted Thomas Jefferson to them in the office, saying that "Free speech can't be limited without being lost." They told me to stop arguing because I just got another five days [suspension] right after I quoted Jefferson. . . .

Q. Who was it that informed you that the suspension had been increased from five days to ten days?

A. Ms. Morse.

Q. And she made that remark immediately after you quoted Thomas Jefferson?[93]

A. Yes.

Q. Did you remain seated during your period of time in the office with Ms. Morse?

A. Yes.

Q. Did you ever, at any time, stand up and lean over her desk?

A. To get a pen.

Q. Beg pardon?

A. To get a pen to write something down.

Q. Did you ever stand up and lean over and demand to see what was on her computer screen?

A. I don't believe so. . . .

Q. Did Ms. Morse ask you what "Bong HiTS for Jesus" meant?

A. Yes.

Q. What did you tell her?

A. It could mean anything. She said, "Doesn't it mean drug paraphernalia?" And I said that it could mean anything. "How do you know it's not an acronym?" . . .

When she said that she thought it was a reference to drugs, I said, "How do you know it's not something else, like not an acronym?" She said, "What else could it mean?" I said, "How do you know it doesn't mean 'Better Olympic National Games Head Into Town for Jesus'?" [Emphasis added.]

Q. Is that what you meant?

A. I didn't mean anything. I have already said that. I'm just saying that it could be anything. You can't directly link anything.

Q. Did you make that up on the spur of the moment?

A. Yes.[94] . . .

After the banner incident, life started getting really difficult for me in Juneau. . . . They [Ms. Morse] had given me a schematic, while I was suspended, of the school and their rules. And their rules said while I'm on suspension I cannot enter Juneau-Douglas property, and there was no listing of "within 300 feet," or anything like that. And I went in to pick up my girlfriend from school, and I parked at the Augustus Brown city swimming pool—the city swimming pool.[95] You can go down there and there are big signs all over the parking lot: "This is not school property." "Student parking not allowed." "Parking for pool patrons only." 'Cause they have a big problem that people can't park at the city pool because the high school students take up the lot. So they'd made a big distinction, and posted signs all over the place saying, "Students not allowed. This is city property." There are signs everywhere.

Anyways, the school called and told the police to bust me because I was violating my trespass order, from being suspended. And, meanwhile, somehow, because the school had also told them I was a drug dealer, I guess a local judge had told them [the Juneau police] that they didn't have evidence to go and arrest me for being a drug dealer on hearsay, but if they had another reason to arrest me, he would issue them a search warrant to search for drugs. So a team of—I don't know—four or five squad cars and about eight officers like swarmed in, yanked our doors open, drug us out of the car, and I believe some of them may have even pulled guns—or at least had their hand on their gun, like ready to pull. And they impounded my car. They refused to let another driver of legal age, of eighteen years of age, drive it. They refused to allow me to call my father, the owner of the car. They impounded it. And my boss, who was my ex-girlfriend's father, who I work construction for, usually in the afternoons, 'cause I was only usually going to school in the morning; I work construction in the afternoon with him. He sees it. And he's an old-time Alaskan. His parents came here in the '30s or '40s. So he knows many, many people around the city, including the tow truck driver who's driving this car to police impound. So he waves him down and says, "What's the deal with this car?" And the tow truck driver says, "Oh, I just picked this up from the high school. Police say this guy's going down for a long time. Big-time drug dealer. They're expecting to get lots of drugs and money out of the car." And he says, "Really?!"

Anyway, that also added to the [false arrest] suit against the police, defamation and libel, because there were no drugs in the car. I had fifteen cents in my pocket when they arrested me. . . . The police did claim they found stuff. They claim they did find drug paraphernalia in the car. It was a full-sized straw that was still in the Taco Bell cup. But, technically, a plastic straw is drug paraphernalia. Oh, and they also seized bags with a brown, crumbly brown powder, which turned out to be leftover sugar cookies my girlfriend's mother had given us, that they were hoping was hashish or some type of strange drug. They had found that when they were initially digging through the car, and they were excited. And, after further looking into this, they realized they were wrong. They had to release me. It was within twenty-four hours. The district attorney got very angry with the police. He was like, "You idiots. First of all, he wasn't trespassing. Second of all, he has nothing in his car. And, third, you did this in front of the entire city." Because they did it—I was picking up my girlfriend from school, so it was right when school gets out. And you've got the entire staff, all the student body walking by and watching this. And, whatever happens later, people still have this image of me, on the pavement . . . they cuffed me, put me in the squad car.[96]

Deb Continues Her Story

I went into my office to find out where Joe's class would have been, 'cause I didn't know if he'd gone into a class, or what he had done. . . . I knew that I didn't know what direction he went. . . . So, I went in my office and I pulled up his class schedule, and it said that he was in shop first and his next period, that we were currently in, was a science class. And so, I asked the two assistant principals that have offices right with me to go down with me. We just went right down the staircase. Myself and Mr. Staley waited, and we had Katherine Milliron, which would have been, actually, Joe's administrator, go in; and then they came right out. . . .

He came into my office, and I remember consciously leaving my door open 'cause my admin. assistant's [Pam Tippets'] desk is right there and she can see in. . . . I started looking up his parent information . . . and I was getting ready to call his dad, and he immediately informed me that he didn't want me to call his dad, and he would sue me if I did. He said, "I'm eighteen and you can't call my dad. I don't live at home." He immediately . . . he wrote a note that said, "I'm eighteen and I don't give you permission to contact my dad." . . . He hadn't gone to [his first-period] class, and I said something about, "Well then you were skipping." And then he said, "Well, I was stuck in the snow." And he stood up and started writing on my notepad a pass about excusing himself, because he was eighteen, because he was late. . . . It was like this. When I said about skipping, he jumped up and was very agitated, and was coming across the desk towards me. Or he would come back behind [my desk] and want to see my computer screen. And he would go: "Are you gonna suspend everybody? Are you gonna suspend everybody who's skipping? . . . And I said, "Well, it depends on what the circumstances are." "Show me! I want you—show me that you suspend everybody!" . . . And he goes, "What about your son (who was a senior in the high school at the time)? Do you suspend him every time he skips?" And I remember saying, "Well, he never skips. He knows not to." . . .

[David Crosby[97]:] Now, how about the business of quoting Jefferson? Did he quote it? Where did he quote it? What did it have to do with the decision that you made?

[Morse:] I just remember him saying, "What about my First Amendment rights?" out on the sidewalk. And never did I say, "You're suspended for a week, and now it's two weeks," or anything like that.

The procedure is you go over the infractions, what the consequences are. I remember looking at his prior incidences in his file, because a lot of time they'll hold days in abeyance. It might be a ten-day suspension, but you only are out for five days, or two days, as long as you never do that type of infraction again; where those days in abeyance can come back into play. And I remember looking at that, didn't feel that, necessarily, that that would automatically jump back some of those additional days. But, definitely, because of the multiple—I felt like he was being very belligerent and not cooperative. That he definitely didn't follow my directive when I asked him to come with me, directly to my office. And the inappropriate materials that he had displayed. And the skipping—that jumped it up to the next level, a Category I. And, looking at that, I felt that a ten-day suspension was appropriate.[98]

[A]s I'm filling out all the paperwork, I did decide to . . . fill out a criminal trespass form because in my opinion Joseph clearly wasn't getting that this was inappropriate. . . .

I . . . felt that possibly he wouldn't get the directive that during the suspension of ten days that he was to remain off campus, and so I did fill out a criminal trespass and explained that to him. . . .

Q. Okay. And then what?

A. Then I directed Joseph to—that he was to then leave campus. I walked out of the office with him and I asked him to leave the school by way of the front door.

Q. As you were going out of the office you told him to go out by the front door?

A. Right. I said, "This is a criminal trespass," because he was very agitated, he was very argumentative, and I could tell—I suspected that he would be resistant and so I asked him to please exit the building out the front doors.

Q. And what did he respond?

A. He continued walking down the hall right outside my office. I followed him out, was a couple of steps behind him and repeated several times, "Joseph, I've asked you to exit the front doors of the high school." And he . . . would waive [*sic*] the papers and ignored—did respond to that.

Q. And then what?

A. We kept walking. . . . I continued to speak because the bell had just rung. It was right at the lunch hour. Students were streaming into the halls and I continued to ask him to, "Joseph I've directed you to go out the front door of the building." . . . A student approached him. [Joe] was still—had the papers going. I continued to ask him to—"I've . . . directed you to leave campus." And as the student[s] come up, they said, "What's going on?" "I've been suspended for skipping." And then he yelled, "Do you suspend everyone who skips?" and kept going. And I kept repeating, "Joseph, I've asked you to leave campus." And then he went off into the parking lot . . . and left campus.[99]

Joe Frederick appealed Principal Morse's ten-day suspension to Gary Bader, then Juneau School District superintendent.[100] Upon bringing the appeal, the remainder of Frederick's suspension, which already had run eight days, was held in abeyance. Gary Bader recalled that he "had no knowledge of Joseph until . . . this issue developed with his suspension." He continued: "Whatever happened between the principal and Joseph—I mean there are disciplinary actions at the high school all the time that don't rise to the attention of the superintendent. . . . This one was unusual in the sense that Joseph was given a criminal trespass order—you're not to come on the campus—when he was suspended by the principal."[101] The former superintendent described the appeals hearing he conducted as an informal process, not a judicial process. "It was kind of a back-and-forth."[102] Participating were Joe; his father, Frank; Doug Mertz; and Deborah Morse. Following the hearing, Bader went to work drafting his decision.

I went home, and I spent the better part of a weekend writing this opinion. And I got copies of the court cases . . . and set out to do the best job I could do of making a determination about the incident which sparked the whole disrespectful behavior, and all the other things attendant to it. That, to me, was the threshold, so I did address that, I think, at length in my opinion. . . . First of all, I didn't accept that his speech was protected speech. . . . I guess that I believe that the *Tinker* case did not limit itself to only political speech, but that political speech was at the heart of the *Tinker* case. And this clearly wasn't political speech, in my mind.

I don't think you'll find many, if any, superintendent appeals while I was superintendent that went to the length of the letter that I wrote. . . . I guess I just had a sense that this thing was gonna be—this record needs to be tight. I did the best I could. I'm not an attorney or anything like that. But I remember, when we concluded the hearing, that I didn't know how I was gonna find. I mean, there had already been seven days of suspension. Joseph said [in response to the question I had asked him, earlier, at the courthouse (see fn. 101)]: "I just want it to go away." . . . I want to point out that, in one sense, it did just go away. . . . I mean, you cannot unring a bell, but as best as a superintendent can do.[103]

Gary Bader handed down his decision on February 25, 2002, a month and a day after the interactions that eventually spawned litigation. The superintendent upheld Principal Morse's judgment regarding the five infractions, devoting half of his findings (four-plus pages, out of eight) to violation 2:12, Display of Offensive Material. Bader specified that the "offensive material" was Joe's banner that appeared to advocate using illegal drugs, a message the superintendent found both potentially disruptive and inconsistent with the school's educational mission.[104] In the end, Bader limited Joe's suspension to time spent out of school (eight days), and ordered that suspension days previously held in abeyance be removed from Frederick's discipline. Per school district policy, Bader's decision specified that Joe had five days from receipt of the document to appeal to the Juneau-Douglas School Board.

Accordingly, Joe appealed Superintendent Bader's decision to the full board. The Juneau School Board conducted a hearing in Frederick's case, lasting over four hours, on March 13, 2002.[105] In addition to the seven board members,[106] attending the hearing were Joe and Frank Frederick, Gary Bader, Deborah Morse, and attorneys Doug Mertz and Ann Gifford. The hearing was a precursor of things to come. First, it was contentious. Testy exchanges between the two lawyers pepper the proceedings. Second, like the subsequent litigation, the hearing was something of a marathon (the transcript runs 205 pages). In the end, however, it took the board almost no time at all to vote unanimously to uphold Joe Frederick's suspension. On March 19, 2002, Mary Becker called the board to order at 6 p.m. Immediately, the board went into executive session "to discuss a matter which may tend to prejudice the reputation or character of a person or persons. The matter to be discussed is student suspension #02-01." Ten minutes later, at 6:10 p.m., the board reconvened in regular session, and immediately affirmed "the suspension of Student #02-01 for the reasons given in the Superintendent's decision."[107] Mary Becker remembers that "it was not any easy hearing."

It was the most difficult I've ever held. . . . And I knew at that point that we were not—this was not necessarily going to go away. Because you get lawyers in there, and it's an ACLU, First Amendment rights issue. And you get a little suspicious that, maybe, there's gonna be more than there is to it. . . . It was a unanimous decision by the board to support the decision of the superintendent. And we did not write up our own opinion. And it was my recommendation not to, but just to come out and say, "the school district"—I don't know the exact words—but "supports the decision of the superintendent." Because, had we written up all of our justifications, and all of our—we put, "for the reasons given." I think that was the way we put it. . . . Because, if we had tried to write up a resolution, a brief on why, we would have needed to get a lawyer. You know [*laughs*], and Ann [Gifford] was already the lawyer. . . . So, we were very careful.[108]

The school board was well advised to proceed cautiously. On both sides of the disagreement, positions were hardening and tempers rising.

Sometime after the school board's decision, toward the end of May, early June, Avrum M. Gross became involved in attempting to mediate the dispute between Frederick and Morse and the school district. Before he retired, Av Gross, as he is known, was a highly visible public figure in Alaska. He remains widely respected for being a savvy, skilled, and fair-minded lawyer. A Democrat, and former head of the American Civil Liberties Union of Alaska, Gross was appointed by Republican governor Jay Hammond to be attorney general for the State of Alaska, a post Gross occupied from 1974 to 1980.[109] An overture to negotiate a settlement was made to Gross at the initiative of Alaska Public Entities Insurance, the Juneau School District's underwriter.[110] The particular details of Av Gross' efforts are private, shielded under the Alaska Rules of Evidence as a species of settlement negotiation. As one of Av Gross' legal colleagues explained the situation to me: "Being in mediation is like Las Vegas. What happens there stays there. In other words it's a confidential proceeding . . ."[111]

Instructively, like the underlying dispute between Joseph Frederick and Deborah Morse itself, accounts of Av Gross' efforts—and why they failed—diverge significantly. Each side accuses the other of bad faith. Both parties evade responsibility. Even two Juneau School District colleagues, Superintendent Gary Bader and Board President Mary Becker, recount different versions of Av Gross' task. Bader remembers:

I believe that his brokering, if you will—I mean he didn't try give-and-take, he just said, "Guys, this is silly. Why don't you guys just agree that you stepped on his rights or something like that" [*laughs*]. Because we would have wanted to do that. I don't think anybody had any interest in this—spending the money, and, particularly, the time. Time is so precious to a school administrator, a central office administrator. And then, of course, it took the school board's time. And then, the community, some people polarized.[112]

According to Bader, Av Gross focused on persuading the school district to compromise. By contrast, Becker recalls that Gross sought to persuade student Frederick and lawyer Mertz to come to their senses:

[Av Gross was involved] . . . [b]ecause we wanted there to be—the board asked for it, too. We wanted Av Gross. Av Gross had been successful in doing things, and he's a very respected and a very good man. A real good lawyer and a good judge—not judge, but a good person at these kinds of things. We thought, maybe, he could talk sense into both of them [Frederick and Mertz] and have this dropped.[113]

"Talking sense" here is elastic. It could have meant that Av Gross sought to prevail on the school district to acknowledge encroaching on Joe, or it could have meant that Gross wanted to prevail on Joe and his counsel to terminate their unrelenting appeals. Then again, "talking sense" could have meant both—or something else altogether. In any event, Av Gross' efforts clearly function as a sort of "Rorschach test," revealing as much about the observer as about the circumstances observed.

The disparity characterizing Bader's and Becker's explanations grows deeper (not to mention antagonistic) when it comes to how each party explains why negotiations failed. The extent of the gulf separating the two explanations illustrates how easily the line between elucidating and justifying can be blurred. The gap also is symptomatic of how positions were hardening. Ironically, at the very time Gross was attempting to defuse the dispute, battle lines were being drawn. Here is Ann Gifford's version of the reasons why no settlement was achieved:

> [Av] did try really hard. . . . One of the things . . . that was very galling to me is that . . . at various times [Frederick and Mertz] have said, "This whole thing would have been over if the district had just agreed to have a forum[.] . . . It wasn't exactly the way that they wanted it to be. . . . Av went back and forth, back and forth, and they did all these different iterations of their offers, and what they were willing to do. And the last one the district was willing to do included a forum, with recognized authorities. And it would be like an in-service, but students could participate. . . . At that point the focus was more on educating staff, but students could participate. . . . But, in any event, they put all this stuff together, and that was one of the things they were willing to do. And they were gonna expunge his record. The only thing [laughs] they weren't willing to do is say, "Oh yeah, that was wrong, and we can never discipline a student in these circumstances." But they didn't want to deal with a lawsuit. It wasn't worth it. And they didn't have a vendetta against Joseph Frederick. They didn't want to chase him into his adult life with stuff. They just wanted to maintain their authority to discipline kids, when the kids did this—you know, promoted drugs at school. . . .
>
> Av's reports back to us were that he understood that Doug [Mertz] thought that was all a good idea, and that Doug thought it was a reasonable settlement and was gonna try and persuade his client to do it. And then, in the end, Joseph Frederick rejected it. ["And what's your sense of why Joe rejected it?"—JCF] I don't know. ["David (Crosby) said something about part of the sticking point, as he understood it, was Joe and Doug insisting that ACLU was involved in the forum."—JCF] I don't know if that was the sticking point about why Joseph rejected it at the end. That's definitely how they wanted it to be. That was the thing that was different, as far as the school board's offer was constructed. [The school board] didn't want to just say, "Okay—you pick whoever it is; you control." And so they didn't want to do that. But I don't know if that was the sticking point, or what. I don't know why Joseph didn't want that settlement in the end.[14]

Here is Doug Mertz's version of the reasons why no settlement was achieved:

At one point in [Av Gross'] mediations we made the offer to have a student assembly, with a person from the ACLU and a person of their choosing talk to students about their student rights. And the thing would be wiped off Joe's record. And the lawsuit would be withdrawn. That was it. And they turned it down. . . . There was never any counter offer that involved a forum on the same terms, where, basically one of us got to talk about it. And, at some point—not then, but later—[David] Crosby talked to me about why they wouldn't accept a forum, namely that, students being students—they would listen to the ACLU perspective and not the school's perspective. So they were very conscious of the possibility and what, to them, would be the result, and they didn't want it. Therefore, they turned it down. In fact, I was just floored when, at the forum [held at Juneau-Douglas High School, March 20, 2009, as part of the eventual settlement], Ann claimed the opposite. . . . And there's no doubt, they could have made it go away by accepting those two points—period.[115]

Ann Gifford found Doug Mertz's explanation "galling." Doug Mertz was "floored" by Ann Gifford's explanation. Fundamentally, Av Gross' mediation efforts foundered on the parties' (and their lawyers') mutual distrust.[116] School district officials did not trust Joe's motives in insisting on a student assembly where ACLU speakers would participate. Joe didn't trust the district's motives in rejecting his forum proposal. Within just over three months of the incident on Glacier Avenue, bridges were being burned.

Joe Frederick's and Deborah Morse's fight had taken a decisive turn—becoming a federal case—when, on April 25, 2002, Frederick sued Morse and the Juneau School District in the U.S. District Court for the District of Alaska. Technically, Doug Mertz filed suit under 42 U.S.C. § 1983, "Civil action for deprivation of rights."[117] A series of motions and cross-motions for summary judgment were filed around two issues: declaratory and injunctive relief, as well as damages and punitive damages. Basically, Frederick asked Judge Sedwick to find that Morse had violated his First Amendment rights and that, consequently, Morse and the Juneau School Board, of which she was an agent, were liable for damages. Morse and the school district, represented by David Crosby at this point, replied that they opposed the motions for relief, and that they had qualified immunity from any damage claims.

Judge John W. Sedwick heard *Frederick v. Morse, and the Juneau School Board* (No. J 02-008 CV (JWS).[118] Originally, oral arguments had been scheduled in the case for June 10, 2003, but both parties withdrew the request. By the time Frederick's suit came before him, Judge Sedwick had been serving on the federal bench for over nine years. Educated at Dartmouth College (B.A., 1968) and Harvard Law School (J.D., 1972), Sedwick had been in private practice, and served for one year as director of the Division of Land and Water Management, Department of Natural Resources, State of Alaska, prior to becoming a federal judge. He was appointed to the U.S. District Court by President George H. W. Bush on July 2, 1992, receiving his commission on October 9, 2002.[119] In an opinion and order, dated May 27, 2003, and an order dated May 29, 2003, Judge Sedwick sided with the defendants on all issues.[120] In particular, he denied Frederick's motion for summary judgment on Frederick's claims for declaratory and injunctive relief, while granting Morse's and the school district's summary judgment motions on qualified immunity.

The supreme irony of Judge Sedwick's rulings is that he granted summary judgments. In a dispute where, as I wrote above, Frederick's and Morse's "disparate stories themselves became the story," Judge Sedwick adjudged one version of the story (Morse's) more "factual" than the other (Frederick's). The leitmotif of Judge Sedwick's opinion is captured in his phrase "[c]ontrary to Frederick's claim, there is no issue of fact."[121] Now, in the interest of judicial economy, summary judgment is a powerful tool. "The purpose of summary judgment is to avoid unnecessary trials. It may also simplify a trial, as when partial summary judgment dispenses with certain issues or claims."[122] According to Rule 56 of the Federal Rules of Civil Procedure, summary judgment hinges on the absence of disputed facts.[123] As Judge Sedwick summarized the standard of review, "Rule 56 of the Federal Rules of Civil Procedure provides that summary judgment should be granted if there is no genuine dispute as to material facts and if the moving party is entitled to judgment as a matter of law."[124] Judge Sedwick found no authentic factual disagreement between the plaintiff and the defendant because he regarded the latter's account as more valid than the former's. Judge Sedwick's decision in *Frederick v. Morse* can be understood as judicial discounting trumping judicial fact finding. "Although [Frederick's] evidence is admissible," Sedwick wrote, "these facts are beside the point."[125] By disposing of *Frederick v. Morse* in this manner, Judge Sedwick perpetuated the fundamental dispute separating the parties: What happened on January 24, 2002? Judge Sedwick's ruling also guaranteed that questions of fact would run throughout the subsequent litigation like Ariadne's thread.

The district court outcome returns us to the beginning of this chapter—and to my concern to do justice to a complicated and conflicted situation. I am reminded of the starkly different stories surrounding Matthew Shepard's death. As tragic as Matthew being assaulted on October 7, 1998, and consequently dying five days later were, the circumstances surrounding the January 24, 2002, incident on Glacier Avenue are as controversial. Many frame Shepard's death as a hate crime.[126] Others see it as drug-related.[127] This excerpt from a National Public Radio (NPR) report captures the contested ambiguity—and the tendency to think dichotomously—characterizing these different yet similar situations:

[NPR REPORTER, ELIZABETH] BLAIR: [T]here is yet a third way to look at the Matthew Shepard story.

MS. JOANN WYPIJEWSKI (Journalist): Of course it had to do with homophobia. Of course it had to do with drugs. Of course it had to do with violence in the culture.

BLAIR: JoAnn Wypijewski is a journalist who also wrote a story on Matthew Shepard for *Harper's* magazine. She has problems with "The Laramie Project" and the "20/20" report. She says both have too narrow an explanation for why Shepard was killed.

MS. WYPIJEWSKI: If you say it's just about hate or just about drugs, you so simplify the story.

BLAIR: Wypijewski believes it's not either-or and that many factors were involved that night, including hate and drugs. Wypijewski believes that oversimplifications started as soon as Matthew Shepard was held up as an emblem for hate crimes.

MS. WYPIJEWSKI: Emblematic stories need emblematic victims. And so Matthew needed to be an emblematic victim. And as soon as you have to do that, you start creating a kind of myth.

BLAIR: ["The Laramie Project"] [p]laywright Moisés Kaufman knows very well that which story you tell and which story you choose to believe depend a lot on your own agenda.

MR. MOISÉS KAUFMAN: Stories are malleable and that history is malleable and that we have to be doubly vigilant when we listen to history and we listen to stories.[128]

No sooner than Joe Fredrick became emblematic of either a "bad actor" or a "civil liberties hero" and Deborah Morse was rubricized as either an "authoritarian principal" or a "stalwart principled administrator" did the oversimplifying and myth making began. Truth—such as it is—resides in a more artful understanding. The late Robert Altman understood that truth resembles a kaleidoscope. He spoke about Kurosawa's genius in *Rashomon*:

> The main thing here is that, when one sees a film, you see the characters on screen. It's not like reading where you imagine certain things. You see very specific things. You see a tree. You see a sword. So, you take that—one takes that as Truth. But in this film, you take it as Truth, and then you find out that it is not necessarily true. And you see these various versions of the episode that has taken place that these people are talking about. And you're never told which is true and which isn't true, which leads you to the proper conclusion that it is all true—and none of it's true. So it becomes a poem. And it cracks this visual thing that we have in our minds that, if we see it, it must be a fact. . . . The trial or the testimony scenes, that we keep going back to . . . we never see the interrogator. So this person is speaking to the audience but—as if the audience is the interrogator. It's as if I, the audience, were saying: "What happened?! I saw—this other guy told me something else." And you get a different version. There's one fact that takes place in all of 'em, and that's the death of this one man. The rest of it is—it's a poem. And it's dramatic, and it works. . . . And everybody that you would talk to about it—if you'd sit down and make a person see the film, and ask him questions, you would not get the same answers from anybody. Which is the art of art. It's what art is.[129]

Questions remain as the *Rashomon* credits roll. Questions remained, as well, after Judge Sedwick ruled in *Frederick v. Morse*. Joseph Frederick would pursue his queries before the Ninth Circuit Court of Appeals. Still, it was not for lack of conscientious effort on Sedwick's part that his answers rang untrue to some. Unlike film directors of Kurosawa's ilk who make art films, judges endeavor to fashion certain answers out of ambiguity. Somewhat like alchemists, the judge's vocation entails telling us what is true.[130] In order to accomplish such transformations, judges have to shape, to winnow, and to freeze kaleidoscopic social reality—and there is a cost. Legal truth may have the assuring ring of authority about it. Legal truth also has the aura of contrivance about it. Eventually, three judges on the Ninth Circuit would have their chance at truth telling. Before discussing that episode in Joe's and Deb's stories, I want to set the stage by analyzing the doctrinal context within which *Morse v. Frederick* unfolded, specifically *Tinker v. Des Moines Independent Community School District*, 393 U.S. 503 (1969), as well as how changes in U.S. Supreme Court membership reshaped that context.

The Tentative *Tinker* Rule

W HEN THREE YOUNG Iowans were suspended from their respective secondary schools for wearing black armbands in December 1965 to protest the war in Vietnam, they probably did not "define the troubles they endure[d] in terms of historical change and institutional contradiction."[1] "[T]he intricate connection between the patterns of their own lives and the course of world history"[2] likely was not at the front of John and Mary Beth Tinker and Christopher Eckhardt's minds. Yet, by taking their stand to mourn those whose lives had been lost and to oppose continuing the carnage, John, Mary Beth, and Christopher's personal troubles intersected with public issues in ways that continue to influence both the lives of particular high school students and the contours of American constitutional law.

"*Tinker* is the starting point for virtually every judicial discussion of the first amendment rights of children."[3] Yet, despite being treated as a First Amendment icon,[4] there is both less—and more—to *Tinker v. Des Moines School Dist.*, 393 U.S. 503 (1969) than meets the eye. Tinker is usually taken to be synonymous with Justice Abe Fortas' dictum, announced with "Holmesian flourish,"[5] "[i]t can hardly be argued that either students or teachers shed their constitutional rights to freedom of speech or expression at the schoolhouse gate." But Justice Fortas' pronouncement begs the question at issue in *Tinker*, namely, the status of students' First Amendment rights within a school setting. Fortas' ringing proclamation diverts attention from the actual *Tinker* ruling, which struck a cautious balance between two competing values: student expression and school order. Reducing *Tinker* to a resonant sound bite obscures several circumstances that render *Tinker* as much an instructive historical artifact as a resounding protection of student speech. In this case, symbolism eclipses substance.

We need to demystify *Tinker*. We can do so by, first, situating the case within its doctrinal context and then by recounting the social circumstances out of which it arose. After locating *Tinker*, we can examine the majority ruling as well as the two concurring and two dissenting opinions handed down on February 24, 1969. Finally, we can assay *Tinker*'s ambiguous legacy.

The Supreme Court did not address the Free Speech Clause of the First Amendment until the second decade of the twentieth century.[6] The Court did not address rights in an educational context until about the same time, and the two cases where it did dealt primarily with rights of parents, teachers, and educational institutions.[7] Student speech rights, specifically, first came to the fore in *West Virginia State Board of Education v. Barnette*, 319 U.S. 624 (1944). This case was brought by parents and children, practicing Jehovah's Witnesses, who challenged the mandatory recitation of the Pledge of Allegiance. On January 9, 1942, the West Virginia State Board of Education had adopted a resolution "ordering that the salute to the flag become 'a regular part of the program of activities in the public schools,' that all teachers and pupils 'shall be required to participate in the salute honoring the Nation represented by the Flag; provided, however, that refusal to salute the Flag be regarded as an Act of insubordination, and shall be dealt with accordingly.' . . . Failure to conform [was] . . . dealt with by expulsion. Readmission [was] denied by statute until compliance."[8] Writing for himself and five colleagues, Justice Robert H. Jackson overturned the resolution. The Court held that "local authorities in compelling the flag salute and pledge transcends constitutional limitations on their power and invades the sphere of intellect and spirit which it is the purpose of the First Amendment to our Constitution to reserve from all official control."[9]

In light of the majority's reasoning twenty-five years later in *Tinker v. Des Moines*, it is useful to highlight three points Justice Jackson made. First, although *Barnette* had been brought by Jehovah's Witnesses, the Court conceived of the central issue not in terms of the students' religious freedom, but more broadly in terms of students' freedom of (silent) dissent. Jackson wrote:

> [T]he issue as we see it [does not] turn on one's possession of particular religious views or the sincerity with which they are held. While religion supplies appellees' motive for enduring the discomforts of making the issue in this case, many citizens who do not share these religious views hold such a compulsory rite to infringe constitutional liberty of the individual.[10]

Second, Justice Jackson made a point of noting that the schoolchildren's refusal to participate in the pledge ritual created no "clear and present danger"[11] to the school environment. In other words, the students' protest did not threaten the school's educational mission:

> It is now a commonplace that censorship or suppression of expression of opinion is tolerated by our Constitution only when the expression presents a clear and present danger of action of a kind the State is empowered to prevent and punish. It would seem that involuntary affirmation could be commanded only on even more immediate and urgent grounds than silence. But here the power of compulsion is invoked without any allegation that remaining passive during a flag salute ritual creates a clear and present danger that would justify an effort even to muffle expression.[12]

Third, the Court took judicial notice of the fact that the Jehovah's Witnesses' actions were not disruptive and conflicted with no other rights:

> The freedom asserted by these appellees does not bring them into collision with rights asserted by any other individual. It is such conflicts which most frequently require intervention of the State to determine where the rights of one end and those of another begin. But the refusal of these persons to participate in the ceremony does not interfere with or deny rights of others to do so. Nor is there any question in this case that their behavior is peaceable and orderly. The sole conflict is between authority and rights of the individual.[13]

The First Amendment interpretive linkages between *Barnette* and *Tinker* are compelling. Both ambivalently embrace students' rights. On the one hand, "[b]oth . . . provide strong support to the proposition that student speech activity is entitled to robust First Amendment Protection."[14] Robust protection, perhaps, yet, on the other hand, "*Barnette*'s actual holding is fairly limited: students cannot be compelled 'to declare a belief'";[15] and "contained within *Tinker* are two dramatically different models about students' rights."[16]

Janus is the Roman god of thresholds. Usually depicted as having two faces looking in opposite directions, Janus protected portals into and out of buildings as well as beginnings and endings, temporally and in a person's life. The first month of the Julian and Gregorian calendars is named after Janus. *Tinker v. Des Moines* is Janus-like in that Justice Fortas' majority opinion and Justice Hugo Black's dissent interpret the First Amendment rights of secondary school students in diametrically different ways. Although Black's dissent may be viewed as somewhat surprising in light of conventional takes on his "absolutist trope,"[17] vis-à-vis the First Amendment ("no law means no law"), disagreements over what the First Amendment requires are hardly unique. Given the inherent ambiguity of language, even in a case like *Tinker* where the language of the particular constitutional language at issue—"Congress shall make no law . . . abridging the freedom of speech"—is seemingly explicit, justices unavoidably read the text through the lenses of their biographies, their assumptions, and their values.[18] Justices Fortas and Black came to opposing conclusions in *Tinker* because they saw the issues posed by *Tinker* in opposite ways. Their opinions are Janus epitomized.

If one focuses strictly on Justice Fortas' rhetoric in dicta, *Tinker* is about "fundamental rights," "akin to pure speech," that "school officials banned and sought to punish." He notes that the district court that dismissed the Tinkers' and Eckhardt's complaint recognized that wearing armbands to express certain views falls under the protection of the First Amendment. He then asserts, in the most often quoted portion of his opinion, that "[i]t can hardly be argued that either students or teachers shed their constitutional rights to freedom of speech at the schoolhouse gate."[19] Adding that "[t]his has been the unmistakable holding of this court for almost 50 years,"[20] Justice Fortas cites *Meyer v. Nebraska*, 262 U.S. 390 (1923), *Bartels v. Iowa*, 262 U.S. 404 (1923), and nine additional cases (including *Barnette*) to support his contention. Thus "[o]ur problem lies in the area where students in the exercise of First Amendment rights collide with the rules of the school authorities."[21] But Fortas does not begin with this definition of the problem. Rather, he begins by first quoting from an opinion from the Fifth Circuit Court of Appeals, *Burnside v. Byars*, 363 F.2d 744 (5th Cir. 1966). The *Burnside* court formulated the constitutional problem as "the wearing of symbols like the armbands cannot be prohibited unless it 'materially and substantially interfere[s] with the requirements of appropriate discipline in the operation of the school.'"[22] This formulation differs significantly from Justice Fortas' more unqualified language.

Burnside v. Byars was handed down simultaneously with *Blackwell v. Issaquena County Board of Education*, 363 F.2d 749 (5th Cir. 1966). The similarities—and ultimately the difference—between these two companion cases are instructive. Both cases resulted from struggles to register blacks to vote, and "Freedom Schools," during 1964's "Mississippi (later Freedom) Summer." Both cases arose in all-black segregated Mississippi high schools. Both cases arose when students wore "freedom buttons" to school in protest of segregated education. (Freedom buttons, half black/half white, bore the slogan "ONE MAN ONE VOTE" around the letters "SNCC" for Student Non-Violent Coordinating Committee.) Both schools' administrators banned students from wearing the buttons.

At this point the circumstances in each case diverge. For over a week, first 30, then 150, and eventually over 300 Henry Weathers High School students, in Issaquena County, wore freedom buttons to school. During this period the school routine and discipline were disrupted by noisy conversations in hallways, by some students pinning buttons on classmates who had not requested one, as well as by some students showing a general lack of courtesy and hostility toward administrators. Upward of three hundred students were suspended. When some of the suspended students petitioned the U.S. District Court for an injunction to prevent Issaquena County school officials from enforcing the ban on wearing buttons, they were denied. On appeal, based on the record in the case, the Fifth Circuit Court of Appeals, through Judge Walter Gewin, upheld the lower court. Judge Gewin wrote in *Blackwell*: "It is always within the province of school authorities to provide by regulation the prohibition and punishment of acts calculated to undermine the school routine. This is not only proper in our opinion but is necessary."[23] In *Burnside* the record showed no disruption[24] at Booker T. Washington High School where around forty students wore freedom buttons on campus. Based on the absence of disruption, the Court of Appeals came to a different conclusion when Booker T. Washington students who had been suspended for a week challenged the school's prohibition. It ruled the regulation "an infringement upon students' right of free expression." Still, Judge Gewin also noted that the First Amendment does not guarantee "an absolute right to speak," and that "the law recognizes that there can be an abuse of such freedom."

Although he quotes from Judge Gewin's *Burnside* opinion four times in the space of eight pages, Justice Fortas' excerpts do not convey the contingent nature of the right *Burnside* protects. Gewin starts from the premise that school officials must have authority to maintain order and discipline in the face of student misconduct. Only then, and within this context, does he recognize students' right to free expression. If students behave, (only) then may they engage in speech:

> But *with all of this in mind* we must also emphasize that school officials cannot ignore expressions of feelings with which they do not wish to contend. They cannot infringe on their students' right to free and unrestricted expression as guaranteed to them under the First Amendment to the Constitution, where the exercise of such rights in the school buildings and schoolrooms do not materially and substantially interfere with the requirements of appropriate discipline in the operation of the school [*emphasis added*].[25]

It is tempting to say that *Tinker* was an "afterthought" to *Burnside*, in the sense that Justice Fortas applied the Fifth Circuit's balancing formulation to the particulars of the armband case.[26] Even though tempting, it is not helpful. Portraying Justice Fortas' opinion in *Tinker* as the mere shadow of the *Burnside* opinion is not only inaccurate, such a portrayal does not further the task of demystifying *Tinker*. Key to understanding why *Tinker* is seen as an icon of student expression is grasping the vital difference in emphasis between Justice Fortas' opinion and Judge Gewin's. One way we might think of this difference is between rights and responsibilities. When it comes to siding with students because they behaved, the *Tinker* holding is virtually identical to that in *Burnside*.[27] "But it is not for this balancing approach to rights that *Tinker* is cited. Rather it is for Justice Fortas' sweeping dicta regarding the Constitutional rights of students."[28] Fortas places students' rights squarely in the foreground.[29] Students' responsibilities fade into the backdrop. Decisively, Fortas' dicta is full of references to "fundamental rights," "pure speech," and "hazardous freedom." "In our system," Fortas declares, "state-operated schools may not be enclaves of totalitarianism." One might be forgiven for being seduced by Fortas' soaring rhetoric.[30] As constitutional poetry, there is more to *Tinker* than meets the eye. As constitutional law, there is less.

Two very short concurring opinions amplify *Tinker*'s tentativeness. Perhaps discerning the potential for expansive interpretation inherent in Justice Fortas' rhetorical flourishes, Justice Potter Stewart and Justice Byron White each sought to trim their colleague's sails by highlighting distinctions they thought important. Justice Stewart wrote that he "cannot share the Court's uncritical assumption that, school discipline aside, the First Amendment rights of children are co-extensive with those of adults."[31] The decisive criterion for Stewart was developmental: because they possess different capacities for individual choice, adults and children had different First Amendment rights.[32] Justice White stated his view "that the Court continues to recognize a *distinction* between communicating by words and communicating by acts or conduct which sufficiently impinges on some state interest" (emphasis added). In the same sentence, White also said that he did not "subscribe to everything the Court of Appeals said about free speech in *Burnside v. Byars*."[33] Although, from his cryptic remark, one cannot know for certain which specific part(s) of the Fifth Circuit's *Burnside* opinion Justice White rejected, given the way he links an act or conduct (as distinct from words) with impinging on state interest, it is reasonable to surmise that he was troubled by what he saw as the Appeals Court's conflation of symbolic speech with "pure speech," especially in a school setting. It appears, then, that White saw *Burnside*, "a case relied on by the Court in the matter now before us," as doubly dubious. First, for him, the Court of Appeals uncritically assumed that wearing black armbands rose to the same level as verbal expression for purposes of the First Amendment.[34] Second, it protected such symbolic expression in a forum where the state has significant interests in maintaining discipline so as to pursue its educational mission.

Justice Black shared none of his brethren Stewart's and White's ambivalence. He knew *Tinker* had been wrongly decided. Responding to Justice Fortas' opinion, which conveyed the *Burnside* analysis in language portraying expansively students' First Amendment rights, Black launched a solo frontal attack on the assumptions, reasoning, and conclusions of the majority. He worded his attack in terms both strident and foreboding. Lest anyone mistake his reading of the case, in the very first paragraph of his five-page opinion (matching in length Justice Fortas') Justice Black referred to all four Tinker children and Christopher Eckhardt as "defying pupil[s]."[35] What follows might be described as a "controlled rant" in which Black doubts the finding that the Des Moines students' protest was not disruptive, rejects the majority's analysis of symbolic speech in schools as a "myth,"[36] and defends a model of education in which students are to be seen but decidedly not heard.[37] Ultimately, as a second bookend to complement his derisive reference to "defying pupil[s]," Justice Black "wholly disclaim[s] any purpose on my part to hold that the Federal Constitution compels teachers, parents, and elected school officials to surrender control of the American public school system to public school students."[38]

Along the way, Justice Black offers his colleagues two cautionary tales. First, he chides the majority for adopting what he calls "the McReynolds reasonableness doctrine."[39] The "McReynolds" in question is, of course, Justice James McReynolds. He wrote the two lead opinions (*Meyer* and *Bartels*) of the eleven opinions that Justice Fortas cites as precedents supporting the "unmistakable" proposition that neither "students [n]or teachers shed their constitutional rights to freedom of speech or expression at the schoolhouse gate." One can almost hear Justice Black retort: "Poppycock!" For Black, the majority's "unmistakable" proposition derives from employing the much-disparaged substantive due process test of *Lochner*[40]—the "constitutional boogeymen"[41] "that brought on President Franklin Roosevelt's well-known Court fight." Restating his familiar assessment, Black wrote that the *Lochner* test maintained "that judges have the power to hold laws unconstitutional upon the belief of judges that they 'shock the conscience' or that they are 'unreasonable,' 'irrational,' 'contrary to fundamental 'decency,' or some other such flexible term without precise boundaries."[42] Although President Roosevelt's "Court-Packing" scheme failed, "the fight left the 'reasonableness' constitutional test dead on the battlefield."[43] For Black, there "the McReynolds reasonableness doctrine" should lie, not to be "resurrected" to usher in a "new revolutionary era of permissiveness . . . fostered by the judiciary."[44]

Black's fear that the majority's opinion would lead to school chaos fueled his second warning. His point of departure was that "[u]ncontrolled and uncontrollable liberty is an enemy to domestic peace." He continues:

> One does not need to be a prophet or the son of a prophet to know that after the Court's holding today some students in Iowa schools and indeed in all schools will be ready, able, and willing to defy their teachers on practically all orders. This is the more unfortunate for the schools since groups of students all over the land are already running loose, conducting break-ins, sit-ins, lie-ins, and smash-ins. . . . Turned loose with lawsuits for damages and injunctions against their teachers as they are here, it is nothing but wishful thinking to imagine that young, immature students will not soon believe it is their right to control the schools[.] . . . This case, therefore, wholly without constitutional reasons in my judgment, subjects all the public schools in the country to the whims and caprices of their loudest-mouthed, but maybe not their brightest students.[45]

Even if Justice Black's jeremiad was not prescient in the sense that his dire prediction of an educational apocalypse came to pass, his views on student behavior and school authority were influential. Disciplining student speech would take precedence over protecting student expression in subsequent Supreme Court rulings. (See Chapter 3.) Why? One part of the answer can be framed in terms of the *Tinker* Paradox. This paradox is rooted in the tension between the *Tinker* rhetoric and the *Tinker* rule. On the one hand, *Tinker* asserts that students do not "shed their constitutional rights to freedom of speech or expression at the schoolhouse gate." On the other hand, *Tinker* holds that student expression must not "'materially and substantially interfere with the requirements of appropriate discipline in the operation of the school'" (Fortas quoting *Burnside v. Byars*). Justice Fortas' dictum (which attracted a bare majority) notwithstanding, the *Tinker* rule is hardly an unequivocal sanctioning of student speech in the school setting. Justice Stewart's and White's concurring opinions deepen *Tinker*'s ambiguity. Justice Black's and Harlan's dissents reject even the modest *Tinker* ruling. In summary fashion, the *Tinker* vote might be described as $(5+1+1)/(-1-1)$, protecting safe student speech.[46] The rub, of course, is that "safe" is open to widely diverging interpretations.[47]

But this is not the whole story. To round out the picture of how *Tinker* set the stage for subsequent retreats from protecting students' First Amendment rights, we need to discuss three additional problematic aspects of *Tinker* which render its protection of student speech uncertain. We also need to appreciate the unique political climate within which *Tinker* was decided.

A significant characteristic of *Tinker* is that its legal analysis is fact-driven. Relying as it does on a dispositive difference between the *Blackwell* and *Burnside* records (the lack of disruption in *Burnside*) and the resultant different outcomes, the *Tinker* rule does not turn on students' First Amendment right to free expression, but rather on how they exercise that right. Only nondisruptive behavior absolves the right. "The key point is that the focus of the First Amendment analysis is on the result or effect of student expression."[48] "*Tinker* was an easy case," observes law professor Thomas C. Fischer, "there simply was no 'disorder.'" Or was there? Justice Black found disruption in the *Tinker* record where the majority found none. Facts are notoriously fungible. Fischer continues: "It is not always so simple to discern the prospect of extent of potential disruption. . . . Should school authorities be held to a high standard of proof of disruption, or can on campus expression be entirely prohibited if the reviewer is able to demonstrate some ground to believe that the exercise of expression would be potentially harmful to some students?"[49]

The picture that emerges is that not only is the *Tinker* rule tentative, its application is "treacherous." Mark G. Yudof, who employs that term, explains:

> *Tinker* employs a mixed fact-law rule [i.e., students have a constitutional right to free expression which, if exercised disruptively, might be suppressed by school officials]. I have always thought this rule rendered *Tinker*'s application treacherous, difficult, and hard to predict. When I was a law professor, I used to ask my students the following questions: What counts as a disruption? How much disruption will outweigh the assertion of the right? How are these interests balanced? Is this rule, with its emphasis on identifying disruption in schools, a rule at all, or is it just an invitation to judges to assert their personal ideologies and persuasions?[50]

As we will see in Chapter 3, subsequent to *Tinker*, "other justices ascended to the high bench; Justices Powell, Rehnquist, and O'Connor, and Chief Justice Burger appeared less eager than Justices Fortas, Brennan, Douglas, and Marshall, and Chief Justice Warren, to recognize and extend civil liberties, and would even support curtailing student rights."[51]

A second characteristic of *Tinker* rendering it tentative is that the case dealt with expression that was unalloyed political speech—"pure speech," as Justice Fortas put it.[52] Like the apparent absence of disruption in the *Tinker* record distracts from the difficulty of judging what amounts to disruption, the clearly political character of the plaintiffs' black armband protest obscures the definitional challenge in specifying protected symbolic speech. Again, *Tinker* presents the easy case. Professor Joseph Russomanno waxes lyrical about the "heart" of *Tinker* being "the freedom to express dissent":

> *Tinker* . . . serves as a case study not only in expressing dissenting opinions, but the inherent value of a system that protects such expression. Such a system epitomizes the Miltonian model, allowing ideas into the marketplace where they can compete with one another. Only with that juxtaposition can the "best" ideas be seen as "good." Only in that way can ideas lacking in quality be properly rejected.[53]

These are lovely and important sentiments. But not all forms of symbolic student speech are as explicitly political as were the protests in Des Moines. Indeed, the term *symbolic political speech* itself might be said to resemble what philosopher W. B. Gallie called an "essentially contestable" concept. For Gallie, the use of essentially contested concepts "inevitably involves endless disputes about their proper use on the part of their users."[54] Paradoxically, an essentially contested concept is "a concept whose correct use is for its correct use to be contestable."[55] As Samantha Beeson writes:

> The "essentiality" of its contestability does not mean that the disagreements that surround its meaning are objectively irresolvable, but that, on the one hand, disputes about the meaning of the concept go to the heart of the matter and can generate rival paradigms and criteria of application and that, on the other, it is part of the very meaning and essence of the concept to be contested and to raise questions as to its nature.[56]

Essentially contestable concepts are problematic concepts because they inherently give rise to basic disagreements.

The Court's own struggles over the extent to which the First Amendment protects symbolic political expression illustrate Gallie's and Beeson's point: at the core of "symbolic speech" are debates over what amounts to symbolic speech.[57] It was not until 1931, in *Stromberg v. People of State of California*, 283 U.S. 359, that the Supreme Court recognized that nonverbal elements of communication were protected by the First Amendment[58]—and then it did so indirectly. Nineteen-year-old Yetta Stromberg was a teacher at the Pioneer Summer Camp, a place in the San Bernardino Mountains run by members of the Young Communist League for working-class children, aged ten to fifteen. The camp was targeted by an anti-communist organization, the Better America Foundation, which persuaded the San Bernardino County sheriff to search the venue for subversive materials. The search turned up "a camp-made reproduction of the flag of Soviet Russia, which was also the flag of the

Communist Party in the United States."[59] The flag was raised daily, accompanied by the children reciting a pledge of allegiance. Stromberg was charged with and convicted of violating a California statute adopted in 1919. Section 403a of that law made it a felony to display "a red flag, banner, or badge or any flag, badge, banner, or device of any color or form whatever in any public place or in any meeting place or public assembly, or from or on any house, building, or window as a sign, symbol, or emblem of opposition to organized government or as an invitation or stimulus to anarchistic action or as an aid to propaganda that is of a seditious character."[60] Writing for himself and six colleagues, Chief Justice Charles Evan Hughes overturned Stromberg's conviction. His ruling keyed on the California District Court of Appeal's recognition of "indefiniteness and ambiguity" in §403a.[61] Thus the law was held void for vagueness. By distinguishing between §403a's unconstitutional ban on displaying a flag "as a sign, symbol, or emblem of opposition to organized government," on the one hand, and the constitutional "punishment of those who indulge in utterances which incite to violence and crime and threaten the overthrow of organized government by unlawful means[;] conduct abhorrent to our institutions,"[62] on the other hand, the Supreme Court implicitly extended the First Amendment to symbolic speech.

Justice Jackson was explicit—one might say ringing—in discussing the symbolic aspects of protected political speech in his 1943 *Barnette* opinion. Upholding the right of Jehovah's Witnesses' children to refrain from reciting the Pledge of Allegiance, an act of pure speech, Jackson linked their protected silence to the communicative content of symbols:

> Symbolism is a primitive but effective way of communicating ideas. The use of an emblem or flag to symbolize some system, idea, institution, or personality, is a short cut from mind to mind. Causes and nations, political parties, lodges, and ecclesiastical groups seek to knit the loyalty of their followings to a flag or banner, a color or design. The State announces rank, function, and authority through crowns and maces, uniforms and black robes; the church speaks through the Cross, the Crucifix, the altar and shrine, and clerical reiment. Symbols of State often convey political ideas just as religious symbols come to convey theological ones. Associated with many of these symbols are appropriate gestures of acceptance or respect: a salute, a bowed or bared head, a bended knee. A person gets from a symbol the meaning he puts into it, and what is one man's comfort and inspiration is another's jest and scorn.[63]

Immediately following these observations, Justice Jackson cites *Stromberg*.

To the underlying question, whether the flag salute ceremony "may be imposed upon the individual by official authority under powers committed to any political organization under our Constitution,"[64] the *Barnette* Court answered "No." But it did not do so unanimously. Justices Stanley Reed and Owen Roberts dissented without opinion. Justice Felix Frankfurter wrote a forceful dissent, the key to which is his hallmark insistence on judicial restraint: "Judges should be very diffident in setting their judgment against that of a state in determining what is and what is not a major concern, what means are appropriate to proper ends, and what is the total social cost in striking the balance of imponderables."[65] In this vein, apparently in direct reply to Justice Jackson, Frankfurter wrote:

We are told that symbolism is a dramatic but primitive way of communicating ideas. Symbolism is inescapable. Even the most sophisticated live by symbols. But it is not for this Court to make psychological judgments as to the effectiveness of a particular symbol in inculcating concededly indispensable feelings, particularly if the state happens to see fit to utilize the symbol that represents our heritage and our hopes. And surely only flippancy could be responsible for the suggestion that constitutional validity of a requirement to salute our flag implies equal validity of a requirement to salute a dictator. The significance of a symbol lies in what it represents. To reject the swastika does not imply rejection of the Cross. And so it bears repetition to say that it mocks reason and denies our whole history to find in the allowance of a requirement to salute our flag on fitting occasions the seeds of sanction for obeisance to a leader. To deny the power to employ educational symbols is to say that the state's educational system may not stimulate the imagination because this may lead to unwise stimulation.[66]

The Jackson-Frankfurter exchange further illustrates the fact that symbols are essentially contestable. Justice Jackson contends that a symbol's meaning is in the eye of the beholder: one person's object of patriotic devotion—the American flag—is another's graven image. In Justice Frankfurter's opinion, a symbol's meaning inheres in the object: the American flag represents "our heritage and our hopes"; saluting our flag pays respect to what it stands for, nothing else.

The next, and in many respects most instructive, symbolic speech case prior to *Tinker* is *United States v. O'Brien*, 391 U.S. 367 (1968). The story of how the justices struggled among themselves over the concept of symbolic speech, and whether the First Amendment protects such expression, is a salient chapter in the story of how "symbolic political speech" engenders "endless disputes about [its] proper use."[67] If *Tinker* was a relatively easy case, when it comes to protected symbolic speech, *O'Brien* was hard. *O'Brien* originated at a time when American involvement in Vietnam was being escalated,[68] and "The War at Home"[69] in opposition to American policies was in its early stages. On March 31, 1966, David Paul O'Brien and three others burned their draft cards on the steps of the South Boston Courthouse. Immediately, it became all but impossible to untangle their conduct from their message—what they did from what they "said." FBI agents present had to rescue O'Brien and his fellow protesters from a large crowd so outraged by the gesture that its members had bodily attacked the four. Burning one's Selective Service registration card not only generated intense anger in some American quarters, doing so was illegal. After a *Life* magazine story covering a July 29, 1965, demonstration by some four hundred antiwar protesters at a New York City induction center featured a photograph of a young man burning his draft card, South Carolina Congressman Mendel Rivers and South Carolina Senator Strom Thurmond introduced a bill to criminalize willful destruction or mutilation of a draft card. The latter described draft card burning as "treason."[70] The Rivers-Thurmond bill was adopted by a voice vote in the Senate. The House passed it by a vote of 393–1. "The *New York Daily News* published a cartoon depicting draft card burners as rats and demanded that the government immediately prosecute such 'Communist-incited beatniks, pacifists, and damned idiots.'"[71]

David O'Brien was convicted of violating the 1965 Amendment to the Universal Military Service and Training Act, and "sentenced . . . to the custody of the Attorney General for a maximum period of six years for supervision and treatment."[72] On appeal, the First Circuit overturned O'Brien's conviction under the 1965 Amendment, ruling that the "1965 Amendment ran afoul of the First Amendment by singling out persons engaged in protests for special treatment."[73] Nevertheless, the Court of Appeals upheld O'Brien's conviction on the lesser charge of non-possession of a draft card. When the U.S. government appealed the First Circuit's ruling on the 1965 Amendment, the stage was set for a revealing internal debate among the justices of the U.S. Supreme Court.

Right at the outset of considerations, Justice Douglas voted not to grant the government's petition for certiorari. Professor Michael Belknap speculates that, "apparently realizing what his colleagues would do if they reviewed"[74] the First Circuit's decision on the 1965 Amendment, staunch civil libertarian Douglas sought to head off that result. He was outvoted 8–1. The Court was not inclined to affirm the First Circuit's ruling. In the first place, there was considerable skepticism among the justices that burning a draft card was symbolic speech. After the case had been argued and taken under advisement, at conference Chief Justice Warren shared his rejection of O'Brien's lawyer's argument that the 1965 Amendment "is unconstitutional as applied to the facts of this case because the conduct it seeks to punish is a peaceful act of symbolic speech."[75] At this point, Warren's assessment appeared to be shared by seven of his brethren. He took on writing the opinion himself, and assigned the actual drafting to one of his clerks, Larry G. Simon. In his draft, which he undertook shortly after the Tet offensive,[76] Simon attempted to dance around the fact that the Court's own precedents embraced the concept of symbolic speech. Nevertheless, Simon's draft stated: "We hold that O'Brien's conduct of burning his certificate was not speech within the meaning of the First Amendment."[77] This stance lost Justices Brennan, Fortas, and Harlan. Not surprisingly, given his subsequent Tinker dissent, only Black signed on this initial draft.

Responding critically to Warren's "symbolic speech" analysis, Justice Harlan wrote and circulated a draft concurring opinion that eventually became the basis of the O'Brien majority. Harlan's approach, rejected by Warren, balanced O'Brien's First Amendment right to symbolic expression against the compelling governmental interest to prevent destruction of draft cards. Professor Belknap quotes from Harlan's draft:

> "I am unable," Harlan wrote, "to endorse a doctrine which dictates that all . . . nonverbal modes of expression are entirely without the ambit of the First Amendment when regulated in aid of any state interest, no matter how trivial, which is not connected with their communicative impact." . . . "I would . . . hold that governmental interference with the performance of any act undertaken to aid in the communication of an idea, and reasonably capable of performing that function, may raise questions under the 'speech' clause of the First Amendment." . . . "I am of the opinion that the Government's interest in preventing O'Brien from destroying his draft card outweighed the communicative values of that action."[78]

Harlan did get all that he wanted in Warren's revised opinion for the Court. The basic difference between Harlan's draft opinion, on which Warren relied but did not embrace, is the extent to which Harlan was willing to be open to varieties of symbolic expression, and to entertain affording such communicative acts First Amendment protection. Here is the key passage in Warren's opinion for the Court:

We cannot accept the view that an apparently limitless variety of conduct can be labeled "speech" whenever the person engaging in the conduct intends thereby to express an idea. However, even on the assumption that the alleged communicative element in O'Brien's conduct is sufficient to bring into play the First Amendment, it does not necessarily follow that the destruction of a registration certificate is constitutionally protected activity. This Court has held that when "speech" and "nonspeech" elements are combined in the same course of conduct, a sufficiently important governmental interest in regulating the nonspeech element can justify incidental limitations on First Amendment freedoms. . . . [W]e think it clear that a government regulation is sufficiently justified if it is within the constitutional power of the Government; if it furthers an important or substantial governmental interest; if the governmental interest is unrelated to the suppression of free expression; and if the incidental restriction on alleged First Amendment freedoms is no greater than is essential to the furtherance of that interest.[79]

Harlan replied to Warren in a concurring opinion:

I wish to make explicit my understanding that [the Court's balancing test] does not foreclose consideration of First Amendment claims in those rare instances when an "incidental" restriction upon expression, imposed by a regulation which furthers an "important or substantial" governmental interest and satisfies the Court's other criteria, in practice has the effect of entirely preventing a "speaker" from reaching a significant audience with whom he could not otherwise lawfully communicate. This is not such a case, since O'Brien manifestly could have conveyed his message in many ways other than by burning his draft card.[80]

In the end, five members of the Court—Black, Brennan, Fortas, Stewart, and White— joined the Chief Justice's limited (some would say cramped)[81] symbolic speech analysis.[82] With the chips down, and growing numbers of Americans seeking avenues to express peacefully their opposition to the Vietnam War, the Supreme Court had responded by narrowing the options.

A third characteristic of the Tinker rule that renders it tentative is that the holding rests on a conception of adolescent students and a model of secondary education both of which are controversial. Justice Fortas wrote: "First Amendment rights, applied in light of the special characteristics of the school environment, are available to teachers and students."[83] Just what are these "special characteristics"? Fortas began by answering the question in the negative. "In our system," he wrote, "state-operated schools may not be enclaves of totalitarianism. School officials do not possess absolute authority over their students."[84] Fortas then articulated three attributes of students and their school environment that he saw as definitive. First, students participate actively in learning. "In our system, students may not be regarded as closed-circuit recipients of only that which the State chooses to communicate. They may not be confined to the expression of those sentiments that are officially approved." Second, students are individuals. Here Justice Fortas cited the contrast that Justice McReynolds drew in *Meyer v. Nebraska* between Spartan education, designed "to submerge the individual," and "this Nation's repudiation of the principle that a state might so conduct its schools as to 'foster a homogeneous people.'"[85] Third, schools are forums for the discussion of ideas. Justice Fortas cites Justice Brennan's opinion in *Keyishian v. Board of Regents*, 385 U.S. 589 (1967):

> "The vigilant protection of constitutional freedoms is nowhere more vital than in the community of American schools." The classroom is peculiarly the "marketplace of ideas." The Nation's future depends upon leaders trained through wide exposure to that robust exchange of ideas which discovers truth "out of a multitude of tongues, [rather] than through any kind of authoritative selection."[86]

In sum, embracing a conception of student "agency," Justice Fortas adopts what might be called a "communicative model" of secondary education:

> The principal use to which schools are dedicated is to accommodate students during prescribed hours for the purposes of certain types of activities. Among those activities is personal intercommunication among the students. This is not only an inevitable part of the process of attending school; it is also an important part of the educational process.[87]

Read through the eyes of, say, John Dewey and other proponents of "progressive" education, Justice Fortas' view may appear unexceptionable. But not everyone shares this "educational ideology."[88] In particular, the Supreme Court has not subscribed to any unambiguous, much less unanimous, view of how to resolve the often conflicting "two requirements of public education—the need to integrate children into society and the need to allow them to develop as individuals."[89] In an insightful Note, William B. Senhauser derives three streams of educational ideology from the work of Lawrence Kohlberg and Rochelle Mayer[90]—cultural transmission, romanticism, and progressivism—and analyzes them as they play out in Supreme Court decisions. "Supreme Court opinions," Senhauser contends, "over the past half century represent each of the[se] . . . ideologies, and a pattern of development emerges upon closer inspection."[91] That pattern, as Senhauser discerns it, shows the Court growing increasingly skeptical in the early twentieth century of the cultural transmission[92] model, and tending to favor progressivism.[93] Senhauser specifies *Meyer v. Nebraska* and *West Virginia State Board of Education v. Barnette*, both cited in the *Tinker* majority opinion, as exemplifying this trend. These two cases (along with Justice McReynolds' opinion in another early case, *Pierce v. Society of Sisters*, 268 U.S. 510 [1925]), inaugurated the pattern that the *Tinker* Court adopted. For Senhauser, Justice Fortas took his cues directly from John Dewey:

> In implicitly applying Dewey's progressive ideology to primary and secondary public education, the Court discounted both the inculcative interest of the state and the alleged immaturity of students at the secondary educational level—factors that support a disparate treatment between higher and lower public education. The *Tinker* Court described the relationship between the student and the state as reciprocal rather than inculcative, and as a relationship characterized by a robust exchange of ideas extending to all aspects of the school environment and serving both individual students' interests and broader societal interests. By imposing no age or maturity limitations on the exercise of student expression, the majority assumed that all

students may benefit from and contribute to this exchange of ideas without also assuming that children have a full capacity for individual choice. Furthermore, by imposing the non-interference principle and accepting the value of maximum student discourse, the majority implicitly rejected discipline in and of itself as one of the goals of education.[94]

We know that Fortas' implicit rejection of discipline per se as an educational goal particularly exercised Justice Black. He was not alone. Several commentators have rejected the underlying educational ideology informing Fortas' opinion. In a particularly pointed critique of the trend toward liberating youth from "centuries of seen-but-not-heard childhood," education policy scholar Kay S. Hymowitz pointed to *Tinker* as "a signal moment in our evolution into this new arrangement."[95] Siding with Justice Black, Hymowitz raised concerns about the "anti-cultural" and anarchic potential in the model of the "democratic child" inherent in the *Tinker* opinion. Although "not all, or even most, high schools in the United States have degenerated into . . . [a] kind of 'Lord of the Flies' chaos[,]" she wrote, "a fear of new adolescent power drove administrators and teachers to keep classes amiable and nonthreatening or, in other words, unchallenging."[96] Citing Horace Mann, Hymowitz endorses the *Tinker* classroom that promotes "independent and vigorous minds." In the end, however, she views *Tinker* as subversive of democratic debate:

In practice, it is not so easy to distinguish—as the Supreme Court tried to do—speech "that intrudes upon the work of schools" and speech which merely expresses an "unpopular" or "controversial" point of view. Thus, although *Tinker* probably did discourage some authoritarian educators from censoring some political ideas, it also weakened the kinds of benign authority that go into shaping an ideal classroom. Required to allow speech to flow freely and to remain neutral about its content, educators are rendered impotent in any attempt to instruct students in the discipline and responsibilities of rational, democratic debate. Instead of advancing political maturity and free thought, *Tinker* ends up reinforcing the more natural obsessions of the teen imagination, which is already getting plenty of sustenance from the media and the peer group. *Tinker* has indeed encouraged free expression on the issues that really concern the Darwinian teen: sex and violence.[97]

Writing in a less polemical, more theoretical vein, law professor (and former public school teacher) Anne Proffitt Dupre also raises doubts about the conception of the public school that informs Tinker. Professor Dupre posits a continuum bounded by "two models of school power: social reproduction and social reconstruction."[98] Under the first model, society confers power upon public schools to advance the mission of inducting children into society. The social reproduction model thus resembles the "cultural transmission ideology" William Senhauser analyzed, in that both focus on inculcation of existing social values. By contrast, under Dupre's second model, social reconstruction, cultural change supplants cultural transmission as the primary educational goal. Social reconstruction resembles Senhauser's "progressive ideology."[99] One might say that social reproduction is societally focused; social reconstruction is child focused. Echoing the substance, if not the tone, of Justice Black's dissent, Professor Dupre criticizes *Tinker*'s "reconstruction motif"—the "shade of *Tinker*": "Black espoused the 'original idea of schools' that was the essence of the reproduction model: 'that children had not yet reached the point of experience and wisdom which enabled them to teach all of their elders.'"[100] In order to come "out of the shade of *Tinker*," Dupre proposes "a new school power paradigm."[101] Her proposal seeks to refine the "bluntly . . . tutelary, custodial and guardian-like"[102] paradigm that Justice Scalia articulated in his opinion for the Court in *Vernonia School Dist. 47J v. Acton*, 515 U.S. 646 (1995). She calls her refinement "an attorneyship model." Derived from the rebuttable presumption underlying Justice Harlan's *Tinker* dissent—that school officials act in students' best interest—Dupre's paradigm sees public school officials

> entrusted with the delegated responsibility to act in the best pedagogical interest of pres-
> ent and future students while fulfilling an obligation of continued communication with both
> student and parent. In short, parents would delegate to school officials—teachers and princi-
> pals—the power to make independent judgments regarding "legitimate school concerns."[103]

Dupre raises concerns that, while stated in terms seemingly related to those Professor Mark Tushnet discusses in his analysis of free expression and the young adult,[104] the effect is very different. For Dupre, the desired outcome is orderly learning. For Tushnet, by contrast, the desired outcome is vindicating *Tinker*'s "deep insight . . . that children [are] persons protected by the first amendment."[105] Tushnet's point of departure is that "[k]nowledge of what life is like for young adults in schools is the sine qua non to establishing workable, coherent constitutional law for young adults in schools."[106] His basic argument is that two "standards" are required to establish such a constitutional law. These standards are grounded in students' rights of self-expression and to receive information. Starting with the second right, Tushnet contends that because schoolchildren cannot yet participate in the electoral process, they must depend on "surrogates"—parents and school professionals[107]—to provide them access to materials so they can learn what potential voters need to know in order to cast an intelligent vote.

To some extent, Tushnet's surrogates concept resembles Dupre's attorneyship model. Both key on school officials acting on behalf of students' "best" interest. Nevertheless, there are two essential differences. First, the best interest Tushnet has in mind requires conveying "political truth" to students because "the broadest range of information and opinion is necessary for the pubic intelligently to exercise its democratic power to design and pursue society policies."[108] For Dupre, it is in the best interest of students for "public educators to implement necessary disciplinary measures so that serious learning can and will take place."[109] Second, if surrogates "do not choose to provide the information, the young adult has only a limited technique for review—protest. This conclusion leads to consideration of the second major category of first amendment rights, those relating to self-expression."[110] Tushnet's considerations lead him to conclude that the *Tinker* approach to students' self-expression is "correct,"[111] even if he is not sanguine that judges will implement that analysis. More probable, he suggests, "the doctrines presented are susceptible to manipulation to conform with a judge's likely misperceptions of today's schools."[112]

Did *Tinker* mark the advent of developing students' free speech rights—or the high water mark? An answer to that question, implicit in the title of this chapter and the discussion here, is explored more explicitly in Chapter 3. As a bridge to the following chapter, it is useful to take note of the context within which *Tinker* was decided. *Tinker* exists on the cusp. The decision is a product of its time and, to coin a phrase, those times were a-changin'. Historian John Morton Blum nicely situates *Tinker* and specifies central characteristic of its era with the title of his 1991 book, *Years of Discord: American Politics and Society, 1961–1974*.[113] The leitmotif of Professor Blum's book is the trials and tribulations of what he calls the "liberal spirit."[114] Between the covers of his book, Blum traces the antecedents of the liberal spirit in the Franklin D. Roosevelt administration, its tortured path through subsequent three Democratic presidencies, and its eventual exhaustion in 1974. If John F. Kennedy's narrow electoral victory in 1960 signaled the beginning of this period, Richard M. Nixon's resignation on August 9, 1974, marked its close. Smack dab in the middle of this divisive time stood the Warren Court. The Court that decided *Tinker* epitomized the liberal spirit. Chief Justice Earl Warren personified it; he was a salient lightning rod for the country's discord. The Warren Court, writes Blum, also was "flawed":

> As the Great Society was flawed, so was the Warren Court. Qualities of haste in drafting legislation and of sloppiness in administration damaged the functioning of the Great Society. Similar qualities characterized the majority opinions of the Warren Court. Those opinions lacked the judicial craftsmanship to protect them from future modification, as the dissents from them suggested. That vulnerability played into the hands of conservatives determined to see the decisions over-turned. And that political threat endangered the democratic results of the Warren Court's rulings.[115]

Consider two other aspects of *Tinker*'s time. First, the United States was at war. Historically, during war, when Americans' civil liberties are often most at risk, the Supreme Court is least likely to come to their defense. "Throughout our history periods of war tension have been marked by serious infringements on freedom of expression."[116] What this means is that, for all the bold language in the *Tinker* ruling in defense of student speech, the ruling is not an unequivocal bulwark. It has its limits—limits marked by the narrow convergence of views in the majority opinion. As Michael Belknap wrote in explaining the "barren record [of liberal legalism] in Vietnam Cases," "it was, after all, simply the use of law to implement a liberal political agenda. Where there was no liberal consensus, it could accomplish very little. Indeed, in such a context legal liberalism could not function. It was a casualty of the Vietnam War."[117] Another casualty of the Vietnam War was the liberal spirit itself. The second aspect of *Tinker*'s time is that the decision virtually closed the door on the Warren Court. "*Tinker* was decided in 1969," writes Erwin Chemerinsky:

> the last year of the Warren Court. Chief Justice Earl Warren had already announced his resignation and was soon to be replaced by the much more conservative Warren Burger. The author of the majority opinion in *Tinker*, Justice Abe Fortas, already had been denied confirmation as Chief Justice when *Tinker* was released, and Justice Fortas would shortly resign from the Court amidst a scandal. Justice Fortas' successor, Justice Harry Blackmun, would be a strong conservative voice and a consistent conservative vote in his first years on the Court.[118]

3

From Black Armbands to Colliding Tubas

IN THE FINAL sentence of the last chapter of his book *Years of Discord*, historian John Morton Blum observes that, by Richard M. Nixon's resignation from the presidency on August 9, 1974, "the liberal spirit was spent."[1] For Blum, the liberal spirit refers to a political stance that seeks to employ the federal government to advance social justice and social welfare. The title of Blum's book evokes two characteristics of this era: dissention fueled by war abroad coupled with domestic social struggles and deep division over the merits of the liberal spirit itself. *Tinker v. Des Moines School Dist.* is a microcosm of the liberal and discordant times of which it is a part. *Tinker* held great, albeit ambiguous, promise—which it clearly fell short of realizing. Blum's epilogue, "Retreat and Revival," nicely captures *Tinker's* ambivalent time:

> It was primarily in domestic social and economic policies that the programs of the Federal government had been most salubrious during the Kennedy and Johnson period. . . . But the New Frontier and the Great Society failed to address the endemic nature of American poverty. . . . Further, the Vietnam War absorbed federal energies and funds necessary for continued social reform. The expectations of the dispossessed remained unfulfilled. The consequent riots in the streets and violence at the universities might have occurred solely because of the growing tensions over race and class. As it happened, they were provoked by the war itself. . . . The resulting discord, no longer wholly peaceful, molded the politics of 1968. Its reverberations persisted for at least twenty years.[2]

This chapter discusses the ways in which the reverberations to which Blum refers played out in key aspects of constitutional jurisprudence affecting secondary school students between 1985 and 2002. One might say that this chapter traces the constitutional consequences of the exhaustion of the liberal spirit. Specifically, it tells the story of a recalibration of student speech rights, a recalibration that some conclude is a retreat. Yet that story cannot be told by focusing solely on the First Amendment. The reverberations of the years of discord encompassed more than student expression.

Chief Justice Earl Warren retired on June 23, 1969. At the time of his departure from the Court, Warren was both much revered and much reviled. As noted in Chapter 2, Chief Justice Warren personified the liberal spirit. As it played out during the almost sixteen-year tenure of the "Warren Court,"[3] that tendency not only harbored an internal contradiction. The tendency also generated vitriolic opposition. Liberal legalism[4] was born of intellectual debates among lawyers, legal scholars, and judges that took place during the tumultuous years of the late nineteenth century and into the contentious first three decades of the twentieth.[5] It incorporates a basic progressive impulse, born of sociological jurisprudence and legal realism, that views law and courts as instruments of social change. On the other hand, liberal legalism contains a residual aversion to judges second-guessing legislative policies, an aversion traceable to debates over judicial nullification of economic regulatory statutes deemed class legislation (*"Lochner*izing").[6] These elements generated the fault lines characteristic of the early Warren Court dividing, say, Justice William Brennan from Justice Felix Frankfurter. Professor Tushnet traces this particular Warren Court divide to differences among justices on the Warren Court's immediate precursor, Franklin Roosevelt's New Deal Court:

> As the New Deal Justices justices considered their predecessors, they divided over what had gone wrong. For some the pre-New Deal Court was wrong because it was conservative and obstructed the adoption of progressive social programs. For those holding this view, there would be nothing wrong with a liberal Court that advanced progressive programs, even beyond what Congress and state legislatures wanted. For others the pre-New Deal Court was wrong because it invalidated legislation on grounds that had no support in the Constitution itself. These justices needed a theory to explain when and how the Court could properly find statutes unconstitutional. The early years of the New Deal Court were dominated by a search for theoretical bases to rest judicial review on; but by 1962, when the late Warren Court came into being, those disputes had played themselves out.[7]

What is conventionally thought of as the Warren Court, then, did not coalesce until those New Deal justices who had an aversion to employing law to advance policy goals left the Supreme Bench.

While these specific intramurals among the Warren Court justices may have largely played out by 1962 (with Justice Charles Whittaker's and Justice Frankfurter's respective departures), external opposition to the Warren Court's liberal jurisprudence was unabated.[8] Richard M. Nixon targeted the Warren Court during his 1968 presidential campaign. Against the backdrop of Southern outrage at the Warren Court's liberal decisions in areas affecting race relations, Nixon singled out the Warren Court's path-breaking decisions extending various due process protections to criminal defendants (a segment of American society where people of color are overrepresented). As "Impeach Earl Warren" billboards littered the country,[9] Nixon accused the Court under Warren's leadership of "going too far in weakening the peace forces against the criminal forces." Nixon pledged to appoint Justices he termed "strict-constructionist" who would "interpret, not try to make laws."[10] Upon his election President Nixon sought to make good on his pledge, first by nominating Warren E. Burger to replace the outgoing presiding justice. Then, after two unsuccessful attempts to get his nominees confirmed, in June 1970 Nixon placed Harry Blackmun on the Court to replace Abe Fortas, who had resigned amid partisan rancor and a scandal occasioned by Fortas' accepting a retainer from Louis Wolfson, a Wall Street financier who was eventually convicted in two separate federal securities prosecutions.

Between Chief Justice Warren's retirement in June 1969 and August 1993, when President Bill Clinton named Ruth Bader Ginsburg to the Court, every justice appointed—eleven in all (including William Rehnquist's original appointment, then elevation to chief justice)—was nominated by a Republican president. This is not the place to assess the decisional trends resulting from those appointments.[11] Rather, two points bear on this discussion. First, Richard Nixon's, Ronald Reagan's, and George H. W. Bush's views on constitutional jurisprudence were antithetical to the liberal legalism of the Warren Court. Whether they were successful in "remaking" the Supreme Court—or not[12]—these three presidents avowedly sought to change its direction via their appointments. Second, for purposes of assessing the extent to which the Supreme Court has "retreated" from its *Tinker v. Des Moines* decision, it is useful background information to know that, in the period covered by this chapter—1985 to 2002—all but two justices had been appointed by presidents who were explicitly committed to rebalancing what these chief executives saw as a tilt toward civil liberties during the Warren Court era, a tilt that undermined the legitimate state interest in maintaining order.

Consider the concerns President Reagan expressed in his first radio broadcast of 1984. His topic was school violence and discipline. Here, in essence, is what the president said:

Today I want to talk about a subject which . . . deals with violence and is on our minds as the holidays end and our children go back to school—the problem of classroom discipline. The sad truth is, many classrooms across the country are not temples of learning, teaching the lessons of good will, civility, and wisdom important to the whole fabric of American life; many schools are filled with rude, unruly behavior, and even violence. . . .

Today American children need good education more than ever. But we can't get learning back into our schools until we get the crime and violence out. It's not a question of anyone asking for a police state. . . .

Today I'm asking Americans to renew our commitment to school discipline.

The Department of Education will study ways to prevent school violence, publicize examples of effective school discipline, continue its joint project with the National Institute of Justice to find better ways for localities to use their resources to prevent school crime.

The Department of Justice will establish a National School Safety Center. This center will publish handbooks informing teachers and other officials of their legal rights in dealing with disruptive students and put together a computerized national clearinghouse for school safety resources. I've also directed the Justice Department to file court briefs to help school administrators enforce discipline.

But despite the importance of these efforts, we can't make progress without help from superintendents and principals, teachers, parents, and students themselves.[13]

President Reagan's speech extolling school discipline should be read in conjunction with Reagan's oft-stated goal: a federal judiciary "made up of judges who believe in law and order and a strict interpretation of the Constitution."[14]

This chapter looks closely at five U.S. Supreme Court decisions[15] bearing on secondary school students' rights. Its main purpose is to understand the extent to which the Court has retreated from how it employed the First Amendment to protect student expression in *Tinker*. As noted above, however, undertaking this task requires broadening the scope of the inquiry. These five cases are the important decisions addressing student rights prior to *Morse v. Frederick*, 551 U.S. 393 (2007). They provide insight into where the Court stands with regard to balancing student rights against school authority and school discipline. Three of the cases—*T.L.O.*, *Vernonia*, and *Earls*—raise Fourth Amendment issues. The remaining two cases—*Fraser* and *Kuhlmeier*—are First Amendment cases. One cannot understand the ways *Morse v. Frederick* "morphs First and Fourth Amendment analysis in a very troubling way"[16] without considering the doctrinal background staked out in these five decisions. Separately, each is a snapshot of ongoing struggles to balance civil rights with educators' authority in school contexts. Together, these cases comprise a line of analysis that resolves the tentative *Tinker* rule into a picture of deference to authority.

Key to understanding all five cases is the fact that these conflicts between rights and authority all took place within a school context. Noting this context is not merely stating the obvious. Rather, focusing on the salient characteristics of the common venue from whence all five of these cases originated provides a "unifying thread"[17] which explains how the Court read the First and Fourth Amendments. Professor James E. Ryan notes that public schools are charged with carrying out two basic missions, one academic and the other social.[18] Ryan's basic argument is that, on occasions when the constitutional protection of free speech or the constitutional proscription of unreasonable searches and seizures come into conflict with school's academic mission, the Court predictably will side with school authorities against students:

> It appears that the more a particular policy has to do with the academic function of schools, the more likely it is that the Court will uphold the policy, even if it means truncating a constitutional right. Thus, the core principle that has survived in the free speech cases is that schools are free to limit speech that would disrupt the learning process. Similarly, the Fourth Amendment cases can be understood as representing a belief, reasonable if contestable, that warrantless and even suspicionless searches are permissible in order to preserve an atmosphere that is safe and conducive to learning. . . . In short, one way to understand why the Court treats the government as "educator" in some cases but not others is to recognize that school officials and teachers perform different roles within the school setting. Of these various roles, the Court has privileged the academic.[19]

An important theme running through the analysis of the five Supreme Court decisions that follows is that, even if students' constitutional rights do not stop at the schoolhouse gate, within school they take on subsidiary status. Academic pursuits, as defined by school officials, trump student expression and student privacy.

Aspects of how the Court's privileging schools' academic function overrides students' rights are on display in *New Jersey v. T.L.O.* 469 U.S. 325 (1985)—the first of the five cases analyzed in this chapter. It is tempting to characterize the Court's 6–3 ruling as resulting in a "Fourth Amendment—Lite." While the *T.L.O.* majority neither removes Fourth Amendment protection from students nor denies that students have a reasonable expectation of privacy while at school, it fashions a standard vitiating both. Early in his opinion for the Court, Justice White cited *Tinker* to bulwark the Court's view that school administrators and teachers do not act in loco parentis and, hence, are subject to the Fourth Amendment. "In carrying out searches and other disciplinary functions pursuant to such policies," White wrote, "school officials act as representatives of the State, not merely as surrogates for the parents, and they cannot claim the parents' immunity from the strictures of the Fourth Amendment."[20] Nevertheless, he continued, to hold this "is only to begin the inquiry into the standards governing . . . [school] searches."[21]

The circumstances which set the Supreme Court's inquiry in motion unfolded at Piscataway High School, located in Middlesex County, New Jersey. On a March day in 1980 a teacher came upon two girls smoking in a lavatory. Smoking violated school policy. When the teacher took the two girls to Assistant Vice Principal Theodore Choplick's office, one of the two confessed to smoking. The other girl, fourteen-year-old freshman T.L.O., denied that she had been smoking. She claimed that she did not smoke at all. In response, Principal Choplick demanded to see T.L.O.'s purse. Choplick opened T.L.O.'s purse and found a cigarette package. He also saw cigarette rolling papers, which prompted him to examine thoroughly the entire contents of the purse. His search yielded a small amount of marijuana, a pipe, a number of plastic bags, a large number of one-dollar bills, and what appeared to be a list of students who owed T.L.O. money, as well as a couple of letters implicating T.L.O. in dealing marijuana.

T.L.O. was charged with delinquency in the Juvenile and Domestic Relations Court of Middlesex County. She challenged the admissibility of the evidence obtained from her purse under the Fourth Amendment. The Juvenile Court denied T.L.O.'s motion to suppress. It held:

> [A] school official may properly conduct a search of a student's person if the official has a *reasonable* suspicion that a crime has been or is in the process of being committed, or *reasonable* cause to believe that the search is necessary to maintain school discipline or enforce school policies.[22]

The concept of "reasonableness" turned out to be the hub on which *New Jersey v. T.L.O.* turned. When T.L.O. appealed to the New Jersey Supreme Court, that body agreed with the lower court's view of the appropriate standard, namely, "that a warrantless search by a school official does not violate the Fourth Amendment so long as the official 'has reasonable grounds to believe that a student possesses evidence of illegal activity or activity that would interfere with school discipline and order.'"[23] Nevertheless, the New Jersey tribunal held, 5–2, that Principal Choplick's search was not reasonable and ordered suppression.[24]

In language squarely related to Professor Ryan's analytical framework, Justice White framed the question before the U.S. Supreme Court thusly: "How, then, should we strike the balance between the schoolchild's legitimate expectations of privacy and the school's equally legitimate need to maintain an environment in which learning can take place?"[25] Paraphrasing the Court's answer to this question, the appropriate balance is a "reasonable" balance that must be struck in situ, that is, in the place—the school—where an equilibrium is required. "[W]hat is reasonable depends on the context within which a search takes place."[26] In the school context, considerations of discipline and order dictate both that the Fourth Amendment warrant requirement be waived, and that the central Fourth Amendment concept of "reasonableness" be redefined. "It is evident that the school setting requires some easing of the restrictions to which searches by public authorities are ordinarily subject."[27] Such "easing" is "best served by a Fourth Amendment standard of reasonableness that stops short of probable cause."[28] Under the *T.L.O.* majority's standard, a reasonable search "will be permissible in its scope when the measures adopted are reasonably related to the objectives of the search and not excessively intrusive in light of the age and sex of the student and the nature of the infraction."[29]

In all, the justices wrote five opinions in *T.L.O.* Justices Powell and Blackmun both concurred. (Justice O'Connor joined the former.) Justices Brennan and Stevens both dissented. (Justice Marshall joined them.) Of these, Powell's concurrence and Brennan's dissent are most pertinent to our concern here. Justice Powell elaborated on a concern that Justice Stewart had briefly articulated in his *Tinker* concurrence. Recall that Stewart sought to temper the *Tinker* majority's ringing assertion of students' First Amendment rights. Stewart wrote: "I cannot share the Court's uncritical assumption that, school discipline aside, the First Amendment rights of children are coextensive with those of adults."[30] Powell's *T.L.O.* concurrence extends Stewart's view to the Fourth Amendment. "I agree with the Court's decision," Justice Powell wrote, "and generally with its opinion." He continued:

> I would place greater emphasis, however, on the special characteristics of elementary and secondary schools that make it unnecessary to afford students the same constitutional protections granted adults and juveniles in a nonschool setting.[31]

Here is Powell's analysis:

> However one may characterize their privacy expectations, students properly are afforded some constitutional protections. In an often quoted statement, the Court said that students do not "shed their constitutional rights . . . at the schoolhouse gate." *Tinker* . . . The Court also has "emphasized the need for affirming the comprehensive authority of the states and of school officials to prescribe and control conduct in the schools." Id. . . . The Court has balanced the interests of the student against the school officials' need to maintain discipline by recognizing qualitative differences between the constitutional remedies to which students and adults are entitled.[32]

Note that Powell makes passing reference to *Tinker* on his way to emphasizing his (and Justice O'Connor's) primary concern—school discipline—thereby striking a balance that the *Tinker* Court did not.

Justice Brennan would have none of the balance struck by the *T.L.O.* majority. In his opinion, that balance "defaced"[33] Fourth Amendment protections. Following a review of "this Court's Fourth Amendment jurisprudence,"[34] culminating in his asserting the centrality of the concept of probable cause to protecting the individual's "zone of privacy,"[35] and ultimately "the right to be let alone—the most comprehensive of rights and the right most valued by civilized men,"[36] Brennan writes:

> I thus do not accept the majority's premise that "[t]o hold that the Fourth Amendment applies to searches conducted by school authorities is only to begin the inquiry into the standards governing such searches." For me, the finding that the Fourth Amendment applies, coupled with the observation that what is at issue is a full-scale search, is the end of the inquiry.[37]

Toward the end of his dissent, Justice Brennan speculates on "the real force underlying"[38] the Court's *T.L.O.* decision. Pointing to the three different opinions, suggesting "a majority that cannot agree on a genuine rationale,"[39] Brennan intimates that such "doctrinally destructive nihilism,"[40] merely patched over by balancing tests, is, in fact, an "unanalyzed exercise of judicial will."[41] What is the object of this exercise? Justice Brennan's answer brings us back to James Ryan's analysis. "[I]t may be that the real force underlying today's decision is the belief that the Court purports to reject—the belief that the unique role served by the schools justifies an exception to the Fourth Amendment on their behalf."[42]

The very next term, on July 7, 1986 (*T.L.O.* was decided January 15, 1985), Justice Brennan concurred in a 7-2 judgment that again deferred to school officials' authority. This time the context was the First Amendment. *Bethel School Dist. No. 403 v. Fraser*, 478 U.S. 675 (1986) arose when Matthew N. Fraser delivered a short speech to six hundred students attending a Bethel High School assembly in Spanaway, Pierce County, Washington. Fraser's speech supported the nomination of Jeff Kuhlman, a fellow student, for student body vice president. A clever and, no doubt, somewhat mischievous fellow, Fraser wrote a deliberately provocative speech. His address was an extended double entendre.[43] Bethel High officials were not amused. They found Fraser in violation of this Bethel High School rule: "Conduct which materially and substantially interferes with the educational process is prohibited, including the use of obscene, profane language or gestures."[44] Fraser was suspended for three days (he actually returned to school after two days). School officials also struck Fraser's name from the list of candidates eligible for election as commencement speaker. (Despite his removal, Bethel High School students wrote in Fraser's name, electing him to be a graduation speaker, a role he was allowed to carry out only after the district court enjoined school officials from banning him.) "The school officials martyred me," Fraser later observed.[45]

Matthew Fraser may have been a hero to his fellow Bethel High students but, to six justices of the U.S. Supreme Court, he was merely a "confused boy" who "indulged" in "lewd, indecent, . . . offensive speech and conduct."[46] Chief Justice Warren Burger wrote for himself and five others (Justice Brennan joined the judgment only). Burger's opinion can be read as gloss on *Tinker* by someone who was "shocked, shocked" by Fraser's suggestive imagery.[47] The chief justice's opinion, pro forma, begins and ends with *Tinker*.

Seemingly by rote, Burger begins by invoking *Tinker*: "students do not 'shed their constitutional rights to freedom of speech or expression at the schoolhouse gate.'"[48] Nevertheless, he devotes most of his brief opinion to distinguishing Fraser's nominating speech from the Tinkers' silent symbolic protest—that and to reiterating the now familiar view that the special character of schools' educational mission limits students' rights. The Ninth Circuit held that Fraser's "speech was indistinguishable from the protest armband in *Tinker*."[49] This ruling was in error, the chief justice argued, because lewd speech is not the same as passive political speech:

> The marked distinction between the political "message" of the armbands in *Tinker* and the sexual content of respondent's speech in this case seems to have been given little weight by the Court of Appeals. In upholding the students' right to engage in nondisruptive, passive expression of a political viewpoint in *Tinker*, this Court was careful to note that the case did "not concern speech or action that intrudes upon the work of the schools or the rights of other students."[50]

Not only is lewd speech constitutionally unprotected political speech, it is uncivil speech, and the mission of public school to inculcate norms of civility. For Burger, Fraser not only strayed way off the constitutional reservation, so to speak, his speech ran afoul of "[t]he role and purpose of the American public school system."[51] Schools' inculcative[52] rationale requires that school officials be given significant latitude to maintain discipline and order. In practice, this requires curtailing students' rights. Citing the previous term's Fourth Amendment case, Burger reiterates the Court's view of the First Amendment:

> The First Amendment guarantees wide freedom in matters of adult public discourse. . . . It does not follow, however, that simply because the use of an offensive form of expression may not be prohibited to adults making what the speaker considers a political point, the same latitude must be permitted to children in a public school. In *New Jersey v. T.L.O.* . . . we reaffirmed that the constitutional rights of students in public school are not automatically coextensive with the rights of adults in other settings.[53]

Note how Burger connects his First Amendment analysis with the Court's Fourth Amendment analysis in *T.L.O.* Despite different fact patterns implicating different constitutional provisions, the warrantless search of a student's purse, upheld in *T.L.O.*, and the censoring of a student's suggestive speech, upheld in *Fraser*, share two doctrinal underpinnings—one explicit, another implicit. First, Burger expressly asserts that students' constitutional rights are not coextensive with adults' constitutional rights. Second, implicit in such a differentiation is the twofold assumption that students enjoy diminished constitutional protection because they are children and because they go to school. Inside the schoolhouse gate, the First and Fourth Amendments exist on the same circumscribed plane.

I noted above that, in his *T.L.O.* dissent, Justice Brennan speculated about "the real force underlying" the decision. One might ponder a similar question with regard to the *Fraser* outcome. Regarding *Fraser*, the answer is not too hard to discern. In the penultimate paragraph of his opinion, Chief Justice Burger returns to *Tinker*. But it is on Justice Black's dissent that he relies, not Justice Fortas' majority opinion. Restating his points that Fraser's nominating speech was "unrelated" to the Tinkers' protest, and that the First Amendment does not prevent school officials from banning "a vulgar and lewd speech," Burger cites Black's repudiation of permissiveness. In the end, for the *Fraser* Court, balancing student rights against official authority amounts to a struggle for control:

> I wish therefore, . . . to disclaim any purpose . . . to hold that the Federal Constitution compels the teachers, parents, and elected school officials to surrender control of the American public school system to public school students.[54]

Justice Brennan concurred in the Court's judgment. In his concurring opinion, he attempted to square his conclusion that Bethel High School officials were acting within their authority to punish Matthew Fraser for his talk with his conviction that those officials' actions mark the outer limits of what the First Amendment allows. Although his effort might be seen as resembling a contortionist's acrobatics,[55] clearly Justice Brennan chose to join the majority judgment in order to limit its scope.[56] He argued that *Fraser* was fact-driven, and that the case could be decided comfortably under the *Tinker* rule:

> Respondent's speech may well have been protected had he given it in school but under different circumstances, where the school's legitimate interests in teaching and maintaining civil public discourse were less weighty. In the present case, school officials sought only to ensure that a high school assembly proceed in an orderly manner. . . . Thus, the Court's holding concerns only the authority that school officials have to restrict a high school student's use of disruptive language in a speech given to a high school assembly.[57]

Brennan's reading of the case avoids—implicitly rejecting—the majority's distinguishing Matthew Fraser's speech from the Tinkers', the majority's overriding emphasis on inculcating norms of civility (purging "lewd" student speech), and, ultimately, the majority's choosing sides in any "struggle to control" public school education.

By contrast, Justice Marshall in his short dissent,[58] while agreeing with Brennan's analysis, explicitly denies that the school district satisfied the *Tinker* rule's requirement of demonstrating disruption. "[W]e may not unquestioningly accept," he wrote, "a teacher's or administrator's assertion that certain pure speech interfered with education."[59] Whether Justice Brennan's or Justice Marshall's approach more effectively protects *Tinker* is debatable.[60]

Fraser was one of two final cases decided by the Court under Chief Justice Warren Burger.[61] By the time the justices convened to hear *Hazelwood School District v. Kuhlmeier*,[62] on October 13, 1987, the country had a new chief justice and a new associate justice. Warren Burger had resigned as of September 26, 1986. President Reagan elevated William Rehnquist to chief. Then he appointed Antonin Scalia to fill Rehnquist's open seat. Still, the Court remained short-handed. On the day *Hazelwood* was argued the country was embroiled in acrimonious hearings before the Senate Judiciary Committee on Reagan's nomination of Judge Robert H. Bork to replace Lewis F. Powell Jr., who had resigned on June 26, 1987. Ten days after the Hazelwood oral arguments, the full Senate rejected Bork's nomination, 42-58, on October 23, 1987. It was not until the following February that Anthony Kennedy was sworn in as Justice Powell's successor.

With two key changes in membership, one might have anticipated that the jurisprudence of student rights might change accordingly. In two respects, it did not. First, *Tinker* continued to provide the backdrop against which student rights were debated. It is notable that Justice White, who wrote the majority opinion in *Hazelwood*, began by invoking *Tinker*:

> Students in the public schools do not "shed their constitutional rights to freedom of speech or expression at the schoolhouse gate." *Tinker* . . . They cannot be punished merely for express- ing their personal views on the school premises—whether "in the cafeteria, or on the play- ing field, or on the campus during authorized hours—*unless* school authorities have reason to believe that such expression will "substantially interfere with the work of the school or impinge upon the rights of other students" [emphasis added].[63]

Second, although *Tinker* set the stage, it continued to be peripheral to the focal point of the action. The "special circumstances" of public schools and the "special needs" of public edu- cation shaped the script. In short, the singular characteristics of the educational environ- ment took the lead. "When reviewing policies that are related to the academic function of school, the Court has characterized schools as unique and has downplayed the possibility that constitutional standards applied in schools could easily be applied elsewhere"[64]—and, one might add, vice versa.

Cathy Kuhlmeier was layout editor of the *Spectrum*, a newspaper published by Hazel- wood East High School in St. Louis County, Missouri. Like most American high school newspapers, students produced the *Spectrum* in conjunction with a class, in this case Jour- nalism II. Their teacher for most of the 1982–1983 school year was Robert Stergos. He oversaw production of the *Spectrum* issue scheduled to appear on May 13, 1983. Published roughly every three weeks, the *Spectrum* had a circulation of 4,500, distributed to stu- dents, school personnel, and community members. For the May 13 issue, Kuhlmeier and her fellow student journalists produced, among other items, two stories dealing, respec- tively, with students' experiences with pregnancy and the impact of divorce on Hazelwood East students. Toward the completion of the production process, and before publication, teacher Stergos resigned to take a job in the private sector. He was replaced as Journalism II teacher/*Spectrum* advisor by Howard Emerson.

Standard operating procedure at Hazelwood East required Emerson to submit *Spectrum* page proofs to the school's principal, Robert Eugene Reynolds. Principal Reynolds had sev- eral concerns about the two articles in question. He objected to the first article's reference to sexual activity and birth control as inappropriate reading for younger students. He wor- ried that, despite the use of pseudonyms, the specific pregnant students to which the article referred might be identified. Regarding the divorce article, Reynolds believed that, given the pointed criticisms leveled in print by the student who was the article's focus, her parents should have been afforded the chance to respond. Emerson had delivered the *Spectrum* page proofs to Reynolds on May 10—three days in advance of publication. In light of his reservations, and not having much time, Reynolds ordered Emerson to publish the May 13 edition of the *Spectrum* without the two offending articles. In response, Cathy Kuhlmeier and two fellow *Spectrum* staffers, Leslie Smart and Leann Tippett, sued Reynolds, Emerson, and other Hazelwood East officials in federal court. They sought to enjoin Reynolds' deletion order, based on a declaration that their First Amendment rights had been violated.

The trial court and the Eighth Circuit Court of Appeals divided on the controversy. Kuhlmeier's request for injunctive relief was denied by the U.S. District Court for the Eastern District of Missouri following a bench trial.[65] School officials, the district court concluded, "may impose restraints on students' speech in activities that are 'an integral part of the school's educational function' . . . so long as their decision has 'a substantial and reasonable basis.'"[66] On the record, the district court found Principal Reynolds' deletion order reasonable. The Appeals Court disagreed, and reversed. In his majority opinion, Judge Gerald Heaney viewed the *Spectrum* as a public forum as well as part of the Hazelwood East curriculum. As a public forum school officials were precluded "from censoring its contents except when 'necessary to avoid material and substantial interference with school work or discipline . . . or the rights of others' . . . *Tinker*."[67]

Recall that I referred to Justice White's *T.L.O.* opinion as fashioning a "Fourth Amendment—Lite."[68] In *Hazelwood* he creates the corollary: "First Amendment—Lite." Initially, White says *Tinker* is not relevant to the *Spectrum*. Rejecting the Eight Circuit's public forum analysis, Justice White argued that "[s]chool officials did not evince either 'by policy or by practice' . . . any intent to open the pages of Spectrum to 'indiscriminate use,' . . . by its student reporters and editors, or by the student body generally. Instead, they 'reserve[d] the forum for its intended purpos[e],' . . . as a supervised learning experience for journalism students. Accordingly, school officials were entitled to regulate the contents of Spectrum in any reasonable manner." "It is this standard," White holds, "rather than our decision in Tinker, that governs this case."[69] Next, White distinguishes *Tinker*. "The question whether the First Amendment requires a school to tolerate particular student speech—the question that we addressed in *Tinker*—is different from the question whether the First Amendment requires a school affirmatively to promote particular student speech."[70] Finally, White concludes that "we cannot reject as unreasonable Principal Reynolds' conclusion that neither the pregnancy article nor the divorce article was suitable for publication in *Spectrum*."[71]

Equally instructive as Justice White's analysis leading to the *Hazelwood* result is the doctrinal foundation he lays out to underpin that analysis. His analysis walks the reader away from *Tinker*, toward endorsing a reasonableness test grounded in school officials' need "to set high standards . . . standards that may be higher than those demanded . . . in the 'real' world."[72] In a single paragraph at the beginning of his opinion, immediately after reaffirming *Tinker*, Justice White offers the following summary of the Court's constitutional path to *Hazelwood*:

> We have nonetheless recognized that the First Amendment rights of students in the public schools "are not automatically coextensive with the rights of adults in other settings," *Bethel School District No. 403 v. Fraser* . . . , and must be "applied in light of the special characteristics of the school environment." *Tinker*, cf. *New Jersey v. T.L.O.* . . . . A school need not tolerate

student speech that is inconsistent with its "basic educational mission," *Fraser*, even though the government could not censor similar speech outside the school. Accordingly, we held in *Fraser* that a student could be disciplined for having delivered a speech that was "sexually explicit" but not legally obscene at an official school assembly, because the school was entitled to "dissociate itself" from the speech in a manner that would demonstrate to others that such vulgarity is "wholly inconsistent with the 'fundamental values' of public school education." [*Fraser*]. We thus recognized that "[t]he determination of what manner of speech in the classroom or in school assembly is inappropriate properly rests with the school board, id, rather than with federal courts. It is in this context that respondents' [Kuhlmeier, Smart, and Tippett] First Amendment claims must be considered.[73]

Clearly, the path to *Hazelwood* leads from *Tinker*. But to what effect? Justice Brennan's *Hazelwood* dissent facilitates addressing that question. His dissent reads like a mini-disquisition into *Tinker*: once and future reigning doctrine. Brennan canvases *Tinker's* status. The gist of his findings is that *Tinker* not only remains good law (in the sense of remaining valid)—*Tinker* is pertinent law (in the sense of intrinsically controlling). For Brennan, *Tinker* is neither wrong nor inapposite. It's the *Hazelwood* majority that errs by "abandoning"[74] the ruling.

Justice Brennan's inquiry can be read as a "civics lesson."[75] He begins and ends his dissent by noting the ironic lesson that the Hazelwood school officials' original act of censorship and the Supreme Court's legitimization of that act taught students. Little did the novice journalists who produced the *Spectrum* anticipate that their work would be suppressed, much less that the nation's highest court would find that the First Amendment is impotent to stop such silencing. "This case arose," Brennan writes, "when the Hazelwood East administration breached its own promise, dashing students' expectations. . . . In my view the principal broke more than just a promise. He violated the First Amendment's prohibitions against censorship of any student expression that neither disrupts classwork nor invades the rights of others."[76] According to Justice Brennan, but for the majority's mistaken abandonment of *Tinker*, not only would *Hazelwood* have had a very different outcome—not endorsing "brutal censorship"[77]—the Court would not have adopted "vaporous nonstandard[s]"[78] such as "potential topic sensitivity"[79] which is of a kind with "'public welfare, peace, safety, health, decency, good order, morals or convenience' . . . [all of which invite] manipulation to achieve ends that cannot permissibly be achieved through blatant viewpoint discrimination and chills student speech to which school officials might not object."[80] For Justice Brennan, then, *Hazelwood* "aptly illustrates how readily school officials (and courts) can camouflage viewpoint discrimination as the 'mere' protection of students from sensitive topics."[81]

In the fall of 1989, a year and a half after *Hazelwood* was decided, Vernonia School District 47J in Oregon, implemented a mandatory Student Athlete Drug Policy. Vernonia is a small town, population under 2,500. It is located on the Nehalem River in Columbia County in northwestern Oregon. The Vernonia School Board adopted its Student Athlete Drug Policy "to prevent student athletes from using drugs, to protect their health and safety, and to provide drug users with assistance programs."[82] Vernonia school administrators adopted their policy, entailing both blanket and random suspicionless drug testing of student athletes, because they had come to their "wits end"[83] due to increasing disciplinary problems, disruptive behavior, and a student culture idealizing and using drugs. Vernonia school officials were convinced that student athletes were at the core of the district's drug problem. Two years into the administration of Vernonia's Student Athlete Drug Policy, Washington Grade School seventh grader James Acton signed up to play football. He was told he could not participate because he and his parents refused to sign the mandatory drug testing permission form. Joined by his parents, Judy and Wayne, James Acton sued District 47J. Among other things,[84] they argued that the Student Athlete Drug Policy violated the Fourth Amendment. Their claim was denied and their action dismissed by the U.S. District Court for the District of Oregon. The Ninth Circuit Court of Appeals reversed.

By the time the Actons' suit was argued before the Supreme Court on March 28, 1995, the Court's membership, since *Hazelwood*, had changed again. David H. Souter had replaced William J. Brennan Jr. on October 19, 1990. Clarence Thomas succeeded Thurgood Marshall on October 19, 1991. Ruth Bader Ginsburg followed Byron R. White on August 10, 1993. Steven G. Breyer filled Harry A. Blackmun's seat on August 3, 1994. No matter. A 5–3 vote in favor of the Hazelwood School District was complemented by a 6–3 decision favoring Vernonia School District 47J.[85] The Supreme Court's "abandonment"[86] of *Tinker* continued unabated.

Justice Scalia wrote the majority opinion in *Vernonia*.[87] Despite arising in a Fourth Amendment context, Scalia's analysis essentially resembles Justice White's First Amendment calculus in *Hazelwood*. Recall that, after invoking *Tinker*, Justice White argued "nonetheless[,]"[88] "the First Amendment rights of students in the public schools are not automatically coextensive with the rights of adults in other settings."[89] Likewise, Justice Scalia also qualifies *Tinker*— this time using a conjunction: "while children assuredly do not shed their constitutional rights[90] . . . Fourth Amendment rights, no less than First and Fourteenth Amendment rights, are different in public schools than elsewhere."[91] Why do students' constitutional rights differ in the school context? Again, Justice White's and Justice Scalia's analyses are substantially similar. They both embrace a conception of education, and a view of adolescents, that is grounded in the principle that any action "a reasonable guardian and tutor might undertake"[92] is, ipso facto, a constitutional action. *Guardian and tutor*—if those words have a paternalistic ring it is because the Court's current view of schools and students centers on regulating conduct.

Regulating conduct, if not its fundamental predicate, is apparent in White's *Hazelwood* opinion. A key paragraph in his opinion begins: "Educators are entitled to exercise greater control over [student speech that is part of the school curriculum]."[93] Why?

> [T]o assure that participants learn whatever lessons the activity is designed to teach, that readers or listeners are not exposed to material that may be inappropriate to their level of maturity, and that the views of the individual speaker are not erroneously attributed to the school. . . . Otherwise, the schools would be unduly constrained from fulfilling the role as a principle instrument in awakening the child to cultural values, in preparing him for later professional training, and in helping him to adjust normally to his environment.[94]

Characteristically, Justice Scalia cuts to the chase: school officials must be given wide latitude to enforce reasonable controls over student behavior because their charges are mere kids.

"Central, in our view, to the present case," Scalia writes, "is the fact that the subjects of the [Vernonia] Policy are (1) children, who (2) have been committed to the temporary custody of the State as schoolmaster."[95] His fundamental premise is that—in effect, if not in law—public schools stand in the place of parents. Although Justice Scalia acknowledges that the Court rejected this predicate in *New Jersey v. T.L.O.*, he contends that "*T.L.O.* did not deny, but indeed emphasized, that the nature of [the State's power over schoolchildren] is custodial and tutelary, permitting a degree of supervision and control that could not be exercised over free adults." In loco parentis thus underpins the post-*Tinker* analysis of student rights.

Writing for the dissenters,[96] Justice O'Connor took the majority to task for endorsing Vernonia's suspicionless search procedure. She noted the irony that, since much "of the evidence the [school] District introduced to justify its suspicionless drug-testing program consisted of first- or second-hand stories of particular, identifiable students acting in ways that plainly gave rise to reasonable suspicion of in-school drug use,"[97] the Court could have treated *T.L.O.* as controlling. But it did not. Instead, the majority ignored the circumstances on the ground in *Vernonia*; the Court "dispenses with a requirement of individualized suspicion"[98] and, in so doing, ignores the Fourth Amendment that "dictates that a mass, suspicionless search regime is categorically unreasonable."[99] Having left both the Fourth Amendment requirements of a warrant and of probable cause at the schoolhouse gate in *T.L.O.*, the *Vernonia* Court also jettisons individualized suspicion for school athletes. Justice O'Connor frames the consequences for *Tinker* in terms of a question and an answer:

> The instant case . . . asks whether the Fourth Amendment is . . . so lenient that students may be deprived of the Fourth Amendment's only remaining, and most basic, categorical protection: its strong preference for an individualized suspicion requirement, with its accompanying antipathy toward personally intrusive, blanket searches of mostly innocent people. . . . [I]f we are to mean what we often proclaim—that students do not "shed their constitutional rights . . . at the schoolhouse gate," *Tinker* . . .—the answer must plainly be no.[100]

For O'Connor, then, judged by Justice Fortas' *Tinker* truism, the *Vernonia* majority is incorrect, hypocritical, or both. Random, suspicionless searches of students playing high school athletics belie the Court's extolling of student athletes' constitutional rights. Apparently, students shed their privacy at the gymnasium door.

Almost seven years to the day after the *Vernonia* opinion came down, the other Fourth Amendment shoe dropped. By a 5–4 vote, the Supreme Court sanctioned extending suspicionless blanket drug searches to all middle or high school students who wanted to participate in any extracurricular activity. In *Board of Education of Independent School District No. 92 of Pottawatomie County v. Earls*, 536 U.S. 822 (2002), all the *Vernonia* justices except Ginsburg[101] voted to uphold the Student Activities Drug Testing Policy (SADTP) that the Pottawatomie County Board of Education, in Tecumseh, Oklahoma, implemented in fall 1998. SADTP requires every student who elects to participate in competitive extracurricular activities to submit to drug testing.

Vernonia prepared the way for *Earls*. Another way to put the relationship is that *Earls* is *Vernonia* on steroids. Much of Justice Thomas' *Earls* opinion resembles Justice Scalia's

Vernonia opinion. In fact, Thomas characterizes the *Earls* outcome in terms of "[a]pply-ing the principles of *Vernonia* to the somewhat different facts of this case, . . . [to] conclude that Tecumseh's Policy is also constitutional." But the *Earls* majority ventures considerably beyond the four cases analyzed thus far, "painting the big picture of what the Constitution requires and permits of educators."[102]

The case was brought by Lindsay Earls and Daniel James. Lindsay participated in show choir, marching band, the academic team, and the National Honor Society. James wanted to participate in the academic team, but his grades rendered him ineligible.[103] They and their parents sued the Pottawatomie County School District, arguing that SADTP, both facially and as implemented, violated the Fourth Amendment. Earls and James also argued that the school district did not identify any "special need" that justified testing all students involved in extracurricular activities. The U.S. District Court for the Western District of Oklahoma granted summary judgment for the school district. On appeal, the Tenth Circuit Court of Appeals reversed. In doing so the Tenth Circuit rejected the school district's argument that "students involved in non-athletic activities are at risk for physical harm from drug abuse. For example, the district argued, band members carry heavy instruments, Future Farmers of America members wrestle large animals at times, and since these groups travel they have less supervision than regular students."[104] Key to the Tenth Circuit's ruling was its conclu-sion that "[b]efore imposing a suspicionless drug testing program, . . . a school 'must dem-onstrate that there is some identifiable drug abuse problem among a sufficient number of those subject to the testing, such that testing that group of students will actually redress its drug problem.'"[105] Because the school district failed to make such a showing, SADTP was unconstitutional.

The concept of "special needs," understood largely as "unique environment," lies at *Earls*' core. Justice Thomas' majority opinion, as well as Justice Breyer's concurrence, rely significantly on the good faith determination by conscientious Pottawatomie County "guardians and tutors"[106] that SADTP was justified by their struggle to address the prob-lem of student drug use in their schools. Thus, the lodestar for the Court's understanding of "special needs" is the unique character of secondary schools. For instance, Justice Thomas wrote that "the context of the public school environment serves as the backdrop for the analysis of the privacy interest at stake and the reasonableness of the drug testing policy in general."[107] Employing this context-of-responsible-guardians-and-tutors frame, Thomas proceeds to conclude that Pottawatomie County students participating in extracurricular activities have attenuated privacy expectations, that the intrusiveness of collecting urine samples from Pottawatomie County students for drug testing is minimal, and that epidemic national drug use mitigates the need for any particular school district, like Pottawatomie County, to demonstrate a local crisis. Four sentences from the end of his opinion for the Court, Justice Thomas writes (with no apparent sense of irony): "Within the limits of the Fourth Amendment, local school boards must assess the desirability of drug testing school children."[108] Given the overall trajectory of his *Earls* analysis, one need not add emphasis to Thomas' statement to discern where his priorities in that particular sentence lie: rely-ing on *Vernonia*'s emphasis on "public school's custodial responsibilities,"[109] the *Earls* court deferred to the custodians' judgment.[110]

At the outset of her dissent, in direct rejoinder to the *Earls* majority's sweeping rule, Justice Ginsburg replies pointedly: "Although 'special needs' inhere in the public school context, those needs are not so expansive or malleable as to render reasonable any program of student drug testing a school district elects to install."[111] The remainder of her dissent can be read as an effort to refute the basis of the majority's deference; a yielding to authority she holds undercuts students' Fourth Amendment rights by ignoring the fact that *Earls* "presents circumstances dispositively different from those in *Vernonia*."[112] The majority's deference derives from its broad-gauged misapplication of *Vernonia*. The mistakes are twofold. First, by lumping student athletes with, say, student band members, the *Earls* majority conflates *Vernonia*'s targeted focus on drug use by student athletes with dragnet drug searches of public school students. *Vernonia* does not stand for the proposition that, because drug use poses a generalized threat to all schoolchildren, all schoolchildren are subject to suspicionless search. "[T]hat the children are enrolled in school scarcely allows government to monitor all [dangerous] activities[,]" Ginsburg wryly observes. "Had the *Vernonia* Court agreed that public school attendance, in and of itself, permitted the State to test each student's blood or urine for drugs, the opinion in *Vernonia* could have saved many words."[113] Second, the majority erroneously equates students participating in interscholastic sports with students participating in extracurricular activities: they do both "voluntarily," hence, both are attended by a lowered expectation of privacy. Not so, says Ginsburg. The voluntariness of the two situations is "hardly equivalent."[114] By going out for sports, students accept the circumstances of traveling to unfamiliar places, where they change clothes and shower in public dressing rooms in order to engage in highly demanding physical activities that often involve rough bodily contact. It is not a huge leap (if not necessarily a compelling one) to argue that the inherent exposure characteristic of school sports reduces student athletes' legitimate expectation of privacy. Having put themselves "out there" by suiting up to play, producing a urine specimen for a drug test is a small intrusion—especially since the test is for their own good. Justice Ginsburg buys the argument, thus far. "[S]chools cannot offer a program of competitive athletics without intimately affecting the privacy of students, *Vernonia*."[115]

By contrast, participating in extracurricular activities entails nowhere near the crossing of personal boundaries and risky physical exertion as sports. In treating sports and again, say, band as the same for purposes of suspicionless drug testing, the *Earls* majority commits a sort of category error. It attributes the locker room and playing venue properties of school sports to practicing fingerings and fine-tuning precision drill. "Urging that the safety interest furthered by drug testing is undoubtedly substantial for all children, athletes and nonathletes alike, . . . the Court cuts out an element essential to the *Vernonia* judgment."[116] Seeking to counter the way the majority blurs a key *Vernonia* distinction in order to defer to Tecumseh's SADTP, Justice Ginsburg challenges head on the school district's (as well the United States' as amicus) omnibus view of risk. Her discussion is puckish, slightly surreal, and instructive:

> At the margins, of course, no policy of *random* drug testing is perfectly tailored to the harms it seeks to address. The School district cites the dangers faced by members of the band, who must "perform extremely precise routines with heavy equipment and instruments in close

proximity to other students," and Future Farmers of America, who "are required to individually control and restrain animals as large as 1500 pounds." . . . For its part, the United States acknowledges that "the linebacker faces a greater risk of serious injury if he takes the field under the influence of drugs than the drummer in the half-time band," but parries that "the risk of injury to a student who is under the influence of drugs while playing golf, cross country, or volleyball (sports covered by the policy in *Vernonia*) is scarcely any greater than the risk of injury to a student . . . handling a 1500-pound steer (as [Future Farmers of America] members do) or working with cutlery and other sharp instruments (as [Future Homemakers of America] members do)." . . . One can demur to the Government's view of the risks drug use poses to golfers . . . for golfers were surely as marginal among the linebackers, sprinters, and basketball players targeted to testing in Vernonia, as steer-handlers are among the choristers, musicians, and academic-team members subject to urinalysis in Tecumseh. Notwithstanding nightmarish images of out-of-control flatware, livestock run amok, and colliding tubas disturbing the peace and quiet of Tecumseh, the great majority of students the school district seeks to test in truth are engaged in activities that are not safety sensitive to an unusual degree. There is a difference between imperfect tailoring and no tailoring at all.[117]

Wither goest *Tinker*? Where has this journey, from black armbands in 1969 to colliding tubas in 2002, taken us? What can we say about where the line of cases discussed in this chapter leaves student rights? The first thing to say is that little definitive can be said. While each case adds to the mix in fairly clear ways, it is in the nature of constitutional jurisprudence to remain relatively open-textured. The controversies—and the conversations—continue. Nevertheless, it is in the nature of lawyering (and professing) to assert certainty amid ambiguity. So, there is a large literature made up of interpretations, analyses, theses, and appraisals addressing aspects of the questions posed in this paragraph.[118] One might array assessments of where *Tinker* stands along an imaginary continuum. Doing so, one can find documentation at one end of the continuum that *Tinker* is merely a "euphemism"; "only . . . an obligatory greeting."[119] Conversely, at the continuum's opposite end, others assert that *Tinker* "continues to resonate. Its influence is unmistakable. Its application is widespread and regular."[120] Both views are snapshots—"Prokofiev moments,"[121] if you will. They are freeze frames asserting either that *Tinker* is dead and gone, or that *Tinker* is alive and well. Both opinions, because they are dichotomous, are erroneous. More accurately, as of *Earls*, *Tinker* is in limbo.[122]

Justice William Brennan's assessment of *Tinker*, in his *Hazelwood* dissent, comes close to the mark. Recall that, for Brennan, *Tinker* is neither wrong nor inapposite. It's the *Hazelwood* majority that errs by "abandoning" the ruling.[123] Three times in just over a single page, Brennan employed the word abandon to describe the majority's treatment of *Tinker*. The gist of his critique is that the *Hazelwood* Court deserts *Tinker* without destroying it. Brennan "disentangles"[124] the majority's rationale. First, he argued that the *Hazelwood* majority's "rationale for abandoning Tinker . . . [is] no more than an obscure tangle of three excuses to afford educators 'greater control' over school-sponsored speech than the *Tinker* test would permit ."[125] Second, Brennan explained why *Tinker* addresses educators' legitimate concern to exercise curricular control. While agreeing with the *Hazelwood* majority that, under the

First Amendment, educators must be able to supervise school curriculum, Brennan said "[t]hat [interest] is . . . the essence of the *Tinker* test, not an excuse to abandon it." "Under *Tinker*," Brennan continued, "school officials may censor . . . such student speech as would 'materially disrup[t]' a legitimate curricular function."[126] Third, Brennan distinguished between Principal Reynolds censoring the two *Spectrum* articles and Hazelwood East dissociating itself from particular student expression. *Tinker* forbids silencing student journalists. By contrast:

> [W]e need not abandon *Tinker* to reach [the] conclusion . . . [that] an educator [has] the prerogative not to sponsor the publication of a newspaper article that is "ungrammatical, poorly written, inadequately researched, biased or prejudiced," or that falls short of the "high standards for . . . student speech that is disseminated under [the school's] auspices[.] [W] e need only apply [*Tinker*]. . . . The educator may, under *Tinker*, constitutionally "censor" poor grammar, writing, or research, because to reward such expression would "materially disrup[t]" the newspaper's curricular purpose. The same cannot be said of official censorship designed to shield the *audience* or dissociate the *sponsor* from the expression.[127]

Dissociating entails separating oneself from, say, poor grammar or sloppy research. Part of what faculty do when they evaluate student essays is to dissociate themselves from shoddy work. Such distancing is legitimate. By contrast, censoring entails suppressing. It is unacceptable for faculty to punish a student for expressing a particular opinion. For Justice Brennan, the *Hazelwood* Court abandons *Tinker* because the majority fails to grasp that, under *Tinker*, Principal Reynolds could have dissociated himself from the *Spectrum* articles without censoring them.

In the next to last sentence of his *Hazelwood* dissent, Justice Brennan regrets that the majority "teach[es] youth to discount important principles of our government as mere platitudes."[128] Brennan was referring, of course, to "*Tinker*'s time-tested proposition that public school students 'do not shed their constitutional rights to freedom of speech or expression at the schoolhouse gate.'"[129] For Brennan, the unfortunate "civics lesson" that the *Hazelwood* Court teaches results directly from its abandoning *Tinker*. That abandonment "denudes high school students of much of the First Amendment protection that *Tinker* itself prescribed."[130] Similarly, it is clear that the Court's desertion of *Tinker* in *T.L.O.*, *Fraser*, *Vernonia*, and *Earls* further "denudes" secondary school students of First and Fourth Amendment rights. By abandoning *Tinker*, the Court has deserted its tentative embrace of students' rights in lieu of school administrators' good-faith judgments. The Court thereby has relegated *Tinker* to a place of "restraint or confinement; a place or state of neglect or oblivion."[131] Nevertheless, the practical fact that *Tinker* has gone into eclipse does not mean that *Tinker* no longer exists. The Court also has banished *Tinker* to an "intermediate or transitional place or state; a state of uncertainty."[132] *Tinker* remains only a few votes away from being applied in practice.[133] The Court that abandoned *Tinker* can always potentially embrace it.

4

A New Century, a Different Court

Throughout American history, presidents have attempted to shape the federal judiciary to advance their particular policy agendas. In the aftermath of the Jeffersonian "Revolution of 1800," outgoing Federalist president John Adams appointed the so-called "midnight judges."[1] Faced with the possibility that the Supreme Court might invalidate key aspects of his prosecution of the Union cause during the Civil War, in 1863 Abraham Lincoln lobbied Congress to add a tenth Supreme Court justice to keep that body "safe" and "right."[2] Perhaps most familiar is Franklin D. Roosevelt's 1937 effort to "pack" the U.S. Supreme Court in order to end-run its "horse-and-buggy definition of inter-state commerce."[3] As is also well known, while FDR lost the court-packing battle, he won the doctrinal war. His appointment of nine justices, between 1937 and 1943, established the New Deal constitutional order. That jurisprudential regime, grounded in liberal legalism and possessed of a thoroughgoing liberal spirit, reached its apex in the Warren Court.[4]

A central feature of how the Warren Court interpreted the Constitution is a halting assertion of individual rights over varieties of institutional authority. In this regard, *Tinker v. Des Moines* is the quintessential Warren Court decision. As we have seen, Justice Fortas' opinion speaks boldly of students' First Amendment speech rights in general, then proceeds cautiously when vindicating students' actual practice of those rights. Despite the "tentative" character of the original *Tinker* rule, and although, in five decisions handed down over the thirty-three years since, the scope and reach of *Tinker* has been confined, *Tinker's* endorsement of student rights over school authority remains emblematic of the post-1937 constitutional arrangement that Republicans reject.

This chapter explores the thirty-four-year skirmish (some would say total war) over the New Deal regime, focusing primarily on Republican efforts to remake the U.S. Supreme Court between William H. Rehnquist's swearing in, on January 7, 1972, and Sandra Day O'Connor's departure, on January 31, 2006. More specifically, this chapter tells the story of how Justice O'Connor's resignation and Chief Justice Rehnquist's death—events occurring within two months of each other in 2005—gave President George W. Bush the opportunity to build on previous Republican appointments to create "critical mass" around a policy regime opposed to the Roosevelt Court's economic liberalism and the Warren Court's civil liberties jurisprudence. This story might well be subtitled "A Tale of Two Arizonans."

William Rehnquist arrived at the Supreme Court ten years before Sandra Day O'Connor. The decade he served as an associate justice prior to her arrival is a prologue to the main events discussed in this chapter. Rehnquist's initial experience in the nation's capital had been as a law clerk to Justice Robert H. Jackson during the Court's 1952–1953 term. Following his sixteen-month service, Rehnquist settled in Phoenix, Arizona. There he practiced law, immersed himself in conservative Republican politics, and eventually served as a legal advisor to Senator Barry Goldwater's 1964 presidential campaign. When Richard M. Nixon was elected president in 1968, Rehnquist returned to Washington. From 1969 until 1971, Rehnquist headed the Office of Legal Counsel, serving as an assistant under Attorney General John Mitchell in Nixon's Justice Department. Within three years of his inauguration as president in January 1969, Richard M. Nixon had elevated three associate justices and a chief justice to the Supreme Court. William Rehnquist was among the associate justices.

Despite his impeccable conservative credentials, Rehnquist was something of an improbable candidate for a Nixon appointment. A relaxed, casual person given to sporting long sideburns and garish attire in the manner of the seventies, Rehnquist was the antithesis of the uptight Nixon. After meeting his future nominee, Nixon is reported to have said: "This guy Renchberg looks like a clown with his pink shirt, psychedelic tie, and mutton chops."[5] Nixon already had appointed the "anti-Warren"[6]—Warren Burger—chief justice. Then, following two failed attempts to elevate Southern jurists, who held controversial views (and modest-to-dubious qualifications), to the Supreme Bench, Nixon had been obliged to appoint two relatively moderate justices—Harry Blackmun and Lewis Powell. After the debacles of the G. Harrold Carswell and Clement F. Haynsworth Jr. nominations, resulting from Nixon's "petulance,"[7] Rehnquist joked that he had no chance of being nominated, "because I'm not from the South, I'm not a woman, and I'm not mediocre."[8] Even after he was nominated, Rehnquist's confirmation was not a foregone conclusion. During the controversy over Lyndon Johnson's failed attempt to elevate Justice Fortas to chief justice, the Senate had taken to exercising its role of advice and consent more assertively.[9] Rehnquist's conservatism rankled Democrats. Interest groups, like civil rights activists, also were playing a more active role in the nominating process.[10] A memo that Rehnquist wrote to his boss while clerking for Justice Jackson, titled "A Random Thought on the Segregation Cases," had surfaced. In that memo Rehnquist opined: "I realize that this is an unpopular and unhumanitarian position for which I have been excoriated by 'liberal' colleagues, but I think *Plessy v. Ferguson* was right and should be re-affirmed."[11] *Plessy*, of course, is the 1896 decision upholding a Jim Crow law that the Supreme Court overturned in *Brown v. Board of Education*. Rehnquist survived his contested confirmation hearings, and was approved by a Senate vote of 68–26. Nevertheless, he received the highest number of no votes of any successful Supreme Court nominee since the 52–26 vote on Charles Evans Hughes's nomination to be chief justice in 1930.

Several factors explain the configuration of Rehnquist's confirmation vote. His controversial opinions on civil rights made him a high-profile target. Second, control of the national government when President Nixon nominated Rehnquist was divided between Republicans and Democrats.[12] Republican Nixon was in the White House. At the other end of Pennsylvania Avenue, Democrats controlled both Houses of Congress. Perhaps most important, and certainly most pertinent to this chapter's concerns, Nixon was endeavoring to nominate justices committed to undoing the policy regime created by the New Deal and Warren Courts. In this regard, Nixon's Supreme Court nominations represent "a set of commitments in opposition to a resilient regime."[13] Seeking to practice a "politics of preemption," Nixon was:

> [i]ntruding into an ongoing polity as an alien force[. Such presidents] interrupt a still vital political discourse, and try to preempt its agenda by playing upon the political divisions within the establishment that affiliated presidents instinctively seek to assuage. Their programs are designed to aggravate interest cleavages and factional discontent within the dominant coalition, for therein lies the prospect of broadening their base of support and sharpening their departure from the received formulas.[14]

The "received formula" from which Nixon anticipated his Supreme Court nominees would depart was the jurisprudence of the Warren Court—the "judicial Camelot"[15] of economic liberalism and individual rights. The vehicle for their departure was to be "strict construction."

Rehnquist became "Nixon's strict constructionist."[16] "Although 'strict constructionism' was more of a political slogan than a sharply defined analytical concept, both Nixon and his audience understood that it mainly represented an opposition to the innovative [Warren Court] judicial decisions of the prior decade, especially those relating to social issues and individual rights."[17] "In a practical sense, strict construction judges were those who would give greater scope to the conservative attitudes that Nixon's election represented."[18] On the Burger Court, Rehnquist's strict constructionist stance meant that he was an outlier—the "Lone Ranger" as he came to be called. Rehnquist dissented solo fifty-four times during his fifteen-year tenure as an associate justice.

Rehnquist was an outlier on the Burger Court because Nixon failed in his effort to "preempt" legal liberalism. As the title of perhaps the most well-known analysis of the Supreme Court under Warren Burger (on which Associate Justice Rehnquist served for fourteen years and nine months) has it, the Burger Court was "the counter-revolution that wasn't."[19] Noting that Nixon's judicial appointments fell short of achieving his constitutional goals is not to argue that the changed Court effected no changes to important aspects of constitutional law and policy. Clearly, changes occurred—look at *T.L.O.* and *Fraser* compared to *Tinker* in the realm of students' rights. The point is that the Burger Court was unable to reverse key elements of the New Deal/Warren Court policy regime.

In metaphorical terms, while the Burger Court pruned key legal liberal precedents— trimming here, reducing there—it did not uproot the entire tree. Professor Blasi's contribution to the collection of essays he edited assessing the Court under Burger is aptly titled: "The Rootless Activism of the Burger Court," rootless because of an absence of any particular judicial philosophy around which majorities could consistently coalesce. In his foreword to the Blasi collection, Anthony Lewis also adopts botanical imagery:

> On the Supreme Court, only Justice William Rehnquist really goes back to first premises in his opinions and is willing to rethink doctrines in terms of personal constitutional ideology. . . . Perhaps this is only a transitional period. Perhaps Justice Rehnquist will be joined by others as ready as he is to uproot established doctrine. Then the Burger years might be seen in history as no more than what Justice Holmes called "that period of dry precedent which is so often to be found midway between a creative epoch and a period of solvent philosophical reaction." But as it stands, the Burger Court is doing what comes naturally to judges in the post-Warren era: trimming here and there, notably where egalitarianism looks to have costly consequences, but also building on the cases of the 1950s and 1960s when the spirit moves it. . . . [20]

Undoubtedly the most notable instance where the post-Nixon Court built upon the Warren Court's cases is *Roe v. Wade*, 410 U.S. 113 (1972). That decision, written by Nixon appointee Harry A. Blackmun (and joined by Nixon appointees Burger and Powell), partially relies on reasoning articulated in *Griswold v. Connecticut*, 381 U.S. 479 (1965), which was written by the quintessentially liberal William O. Douglas. Whether examined in terms of constitutional interpretation or socially conservative political values, there is no hint of "strict constructionism" in *Roe v. Wade*.

Warren Burger retired as chief justice on September 26, 1986. By the time of his departure, a firestorm had developed around *Roe v. Wade*. No issue came to define Supreme Court nomination politics more completely in the final two decades of the twentieth century than abortion. Neither debates over the death penalty, nor over religion in schools, nor over the rights of criminal defendants approached the passion and the vitriol of abortion disputes. By the time Chief Justice Burger left the Bench for a more congenial (and suitable) job as chairman of the Commission on the Bicentennial of the U.S. Constitution, reshaping the Court largely had become synonymous with overturning *Roe v. Wade*. By the time Burger had gone, Ronald Reagan had been elected president, and he had made his first appointment to the Supreme Court. She was Sandra Day O'Connor.

Given the political circumstances prevailing in July 1981, O'Connor's nomination was little surprise. Reagan Republicanism had transformed the GOP in ways that created challenges for attracting mainstream women voters. "The 1980 Republican party platform had abandoned the Equal Rights Amendment (ERA) and added a 'family' plank, which was worded such that it could be construed as antithetical to women's autonomy."[21] To compensate for the resulting electoral gender gap, presidential candidate Reagan promised to nominate a woman to the Supreme Court "at one of his earliest opportunities."[22] When Justice Potter Stewart announced his retirement, the pool of Republican female candidates deemed eligible totaled six. O'Connor's name quickly rose to the top of this very abbreviated list. Once nominated, her confirmation was all but a foregone conclusion.

As with William Rehnquist's contested nomination in 1971, several factors explain Sandra Day O'Connor's easy path to confirmation. First, and most salient, the fact that she is a woman made opposing O'Connor both politically unwise and costly. Second, Republicans controlled the Senate at the time of her confirmation hearing. Third, Reagan was what political scientist Kevin J. McMahon, following Stephen Skrowronek,[23] refers to as a "reconstructive president." Thomas Jefferson, Andrew Jackson, Abraham Lincoln, and Franklin Roosevelt all were reconstructive presidents. All were elected under opportune circumstances. The key opportunities were created by the transitional nature of their respective presidencies. "[T]heir political identity is opposed to a preexisting political regime in sharp decline."[24] Although McMahon includes Reagan among the two twentieth-century reconstructive presidents, Reagan should be thought of as a junior member of this club. Why? Because, when it comes to Supreme Court appointments, the defining characteristic of a reconstructive presidency is to prevail. Here, FDR is the pure type. He was nine for nine. By contrast, Reagan was four for five, with one of his nominees, William Rehnquist to be chief justice, being highly contested. McMahon acknowledges Reagan's "lower level of reconstructive authority."[25] He also describes Reagan's motives in appointing O'Connor as less transformative than "to both make history and [as] a political statement that would enhance his image among women voters who were increasingly voting for Democrats."[26] O'Connor was confirmed, 99–0.

Sandra Day O'Connor arrived on the Court on September 25, 1981. She joined her fellow Arizonan William Rehnquist as an associate justice. Although both served on a bench presided over by Chief Justice Burger until Burger retired five years later, it is a misnomer to refer to this period as the Burger Court, for two reasons. First, Warren E. Burger possessed neither the wit, nor the temperament, nor the charm to be an effective chief justice. He ran the Court's conferences in a manner, at once indifferent and meddlesome, that frustrated and annoyed his colleagues. Second, the putative chief justice left little impression on the Court's constitutional jurisprudence between 1969 and 1986. He was given to reducing constitutional doctrine to formulaic "tests," as illustrated by his opinions in *Lemon v. Kurtzman*, 403 U.S. 602 (1971), an Establishment Clause case, and *Miller v. California*, 413 U.S. 115 (1973) attempting to define "obscenity." Burger looked the part of chief justice: "He was a handsome, heavyset man with a dignified carriage; his most striking feature was a mane of flowing white hair. Even his voice—a deep baritone—fit the standard image of his office. In short, if his abilities had matched his appearance, Warren Burger would surely be remembered as one of the greatest of all chief justices."[27] They did not.

> To put it simply, Warren Burger was a hard-working, conservative justice of average to below-average abilities by Supreme Court standards, a product of midwestern Republicanism whose legacy will rest in a number of landmark Supreme Court decisions (which would have been historic almost regardless of who wrote for the majority) and several innovative administrative reforms (which were distinctively Burger's).[28]

The High Tribunal between 1969 and 1986 is more accurately described as the Nixon-Reagan Court because of the efforts of those two Republican presidents to reshape constitutional law and policy through their appointments.

In terms of judicial philosophy, however, describing the Supreme Court as the "Brennan Court" during those seventeen years provides even more insight. Students of the U.S.

Supreme Court refer to "natural courts."[29] The term conventionally pertains to a cohort of Supreme Court justices who have served together continuously without an appointment. The latest natural Court, which existed from August 3, 1994, when Stephen G. Breyer joined the Court until John G. Roberts' arrival on September 29, 2005, is the longest nine-member natural court in American history, lasting eleven years. If one focuses on constitutional jurisprudence instead of continuity of membership, one might say that the "natural court" between October 1956 and June 1986 was the "Brennan Court." As Mark Tushnet has observed:

> [I]t might be a mistake to accept Earl Warren's tenure [or Warren Burger's] as demarcating a distinctive period of constitutional adjudication. A strong contender for an alternative label would be the "Brennan Court." The Brennan Court decided all the central cases of the Warren Court except *Brown v. Board of Education*, which the Brennan Court enthusiastically endorsed and extended. The Brennan Court went on to decide *Roe v. Wade* and the gender discrimination cases as well. Thus an appropriate descriptive theory for the Brennan Court would be a rights-based theory . . .[30]

It is important not to make too much of labels.[31] Tushnet's reference to "a rights-based theory" gets closer to the heart of the matter: however one designates the Court during the period from, say, *Tinker* (1969) to *Fraser* (1986), it did not repudiate legal liberalism, often embracing it. "In the 1970s and 1980s, long after Warren, Douglas, and Black had departed, Brennan still carried the liberal torch."[32]

When Warren Burger announced his resignation toward the end of May 1986, the Reagan administration seized the opportunity to make a "two-for-one" shot. On the same day, during a single press briefing, Reagan nominated conservative William Rehnquist as chief justice then, to fill Rehnquist's seat, he nominated conservative Antonin G. Scalia. This tactical move resulted in a net gain of one (Scalia), for a total of two intellectually deft, philosophically consistent, and dependably conservative justices. The Reagan White House had little trouble settling on Rehnquist to replace Burger. "He was smart, experienced, reliably conservative, and well liked by his colleagues."[33] As for Rehnquist's open seat, initially, two equally attractive possibilities existed, both Reagan-appointed judges sitting on the D.C. Circuit Court of Appeals: Scalia and Robert H. Bork. President Reagan opted for Scalia because appointing him to the Supreme Court would give Reagan another "first"—the first Italian American justice. Scalia was confirmed by a Senate vote of 98–0. (Bork's fate, when subsequently nominated by Reagan to replace Lewis Powell, is well known: the Senate refused to confirm him, 42–58.[34])

The respective confirmation processes of Rehnquist and Scalia are a study in stark contrasts. "No one was going to lay a glove on 'Nino' Scalia."[35] He was a smart, fluent, and convivial nominee. He possessed both sterling academic credentials, having graduated from Georgetown University and Harvard Law and taught at the University of Chicago, and solid judicial experience as a sitting judge on the D.C. Circuit Court of Appeals. Scalia was conservative, but he would be replacing another conservative, William Rehnquist. Then, too, Scalia had a minimal judicial record, with no "skeletons" in his biographical closet. He presented a relatively low profile. By comparison, William Rehnquist was a known quantity and, being well known, was a high-value target. As Republican Sen. Orrin Hatch, one of Rehnquist's supporters complained, Democrats "left no stone unthrown."[36] In addition to the infamous "*Plessy* memo" Rehnquist had written while clerking for Justice Robert H. Jackson in 1952, which had resurfaced, another incendiary memo reappeared. In this communication, clerk Rehnquist suggested that Justice Jackson might dissent in *Terry v. Adams*, 345 U.S. 461 (1953), a case originating in Texas in which the Court banned whites-only primaries, 8–1. "It is about time," Rehnquist opined, "the Court faced the fact that the white people of the South don't like the colored people: the constitution restrains them from effecting this dislike thru state action, but it most assuredly did not appoint the Court as a sociological watchdog to rear up every time private discrimination raises its admittedly ugly head."[37] Justice Jackson did not follow his clerk's advice.

Two other embarrassing episodes dogged Rehnquist through his confirmation process. First, opponents resurrected the charge that during elections in 1962 and 1964, in his capacity as legal advisor to Republican "ballot-security" teams, Rehnquist had challenged the credentials of black voters. Second, opponents disclosed that the deed to Rehnquist's Vermont summer home contained a covenant prohibiting its sale or rental "to any member of the Hebrew race," and that the deed to his Phoenix house barred its sale or rental to "any person not of the white or Caucasian race." Rehnquist and his allies denied the first charge and successfully disarmed the matter of the restrictive covenants by saying Rehnquist knew nothing of them. Still, these controversies resulted in Rehnquist taking "a thrashing,"[38] even though Republicans controlled the Senate. On September 17, 1986, the Senate confirmed Rehnquist as the sixteenth chief justice of the United States. One-third of the Senate, thirty-three senators, voted against him. This is the largest number of nay votes a successful chief justice nominee has ever received.

In addition to the distinctions between the circumstances surrounding each nominee, four tactical factors explain Scalia's and Rehnquist's different confirmation experiences. First, the White House purposely nominated the two at the same time in order to shield Scalia. "In the final analysis, the [Reagan] administration made an educated bet that [Rehnquist] could survive the expected liberal firestorm while at the same time deflecting liberal opposition from the Scalia appointment."[39] Kevin McMahon specifies the other three factors:

> First, when the Senate was simultaneously considering (or about to consider) two candidates for High Court vacancies during the past century, it contested or rejected one of the President's nominees on four of the five occasions. To those senators itching for conflict, such a scenario provides a perfect opportunity to display both their willingness to compromise and their readiness to fight for their principles. Second, the Senate was far more eager to contest or reject nominees for chief justice than nominees for an associate slot. . . . Finally, when a nominee for chief had already served as an associate, the Senate viewed the appointment with a very critical eye.[40]

Despite their very different confirmation experiences, by their swearing in on September 26, 1986, William Rehnquist and Antonin Scalia embodied Ronald Reagan's success in reshaping the Supreme Court's membership. They would be followed, on February 18, 1988, by Reagan's final appointee, Anthony M. Kennedy. Together with Sandra Day O'Connor these four justices would comprise the heart of the Court under the new chief justice. By 1991 the Court's two remaining Warren Court justices—William Brennan and Thurgood Marshall—were gone.[41] The Court had been remade. Whether or not it had been redirected remained the question.

For the next twenty years, until she left the Court on July 1, 2006, Justice O'Connor would provide a key—many would argue the key—to answering that question. Arguably, Sandra Day O'Connor was the center of gravity on the Court presided over by Chief Justice Rehnquist. "No one ever pursued centrism and moderation, those passionless creeds, with greater passion than O'Connor. . . . The way to win a majority in the Rehnquist Court was to earn O'Connor's support . . . [she] was willing to entertain suitors from her queenly perch as the center of the Court."[42]

Justice O'Connor's pivotal influence can be attributed to several factors. First, she served on a Court that was delicately balanced between shifting coalitions of "liberals" and "conservatives." She could play the role of fulcrum because, between 1986 and 2006, no single faction of the Court was consistently able to marshal majorities. Second, the Court's membership during Rehnquist's tenure was remarkably stable. There were only five turnovers in membership during his nineteen years as chief justice and, as we have seen, for the last eleven of those nineteen years a natural court existed. So, although divided, the Court was constant. Third, by temperament and experience, Justice O'Connor was inclined to seek the middle ground. She cut her political teeth working in venues where collaboration counted, doing volunteer work and serving as a legislator in the Arizona Senate where she eventually became Majority Leader (her first "first" as an American woman). After O'Connor joined the Court, centrist Justice Lewis F. Powell was her friend and mentor. Powell has been described as the "balance wheel of the [Burger] Court."[43] Finding the middle ground thus became her modus operandi. Fourth, Justice O'Connor has a down-to-earth frame of mind. One might say that, as a judge, she was less a thinker, in the sense of being given to grand theorizing, than a problem solver. The adjective often used to describe her approach to judging is "pragmatic."[44]

Another term one might apply to how Justice O'Connor decided cases is "split-the-difference jurisprudence."[45] Critically analyzed by Circuit Judge J. Harvie Wilkinson III, this mode of judicial decision making is quintessentially moderate and realistic. In its incrementalism, "split-the-difference jurisprudence" resembles the sort of judging that law professor Cass Sunstein describes as taking "one case at a time."[46] Judge Wilkinson sees three manifestations of "split-the-difference jurisprudence":

> Sometimes, the result of a case, or set of cases, transparently bespeaks of a split-the-difference approach. In other cases, an opinion scrupulously balances statements appealing to one side with statements attractive to the other and adopts an in-between approach to resolve the issue before it. A third manifestation of split-the-difference jurisprudence occurs when a court steers a course that obviously threads the needle between two polar positions in a broader political debate.[47]

Judge Wilkinson notes that "[t]hese three categories will, of course overlap at times, and a given case may appropriately belong in more than one."[48] He also observes that, while the

Rehnquist Court "raised this form of jurisprudence to an art form . . . often, but not always, Justice O'Connor . . . actually split the difference."[49]

Justice O'Connor's split-the-difference approach is most prominently on display in decisions involving two of the most knotty, controversial issues the Court faced during her tenure: abortion and affirmative action. In *Planned Parenthood of Southeastern Pennsylvania v. Casey*, 505 U.S. 833 (1992) Justice O'Connor's opinion, written jointly with Justices Kennedy and Souter, split the difference between reaffirming *Roe v. Wade*, 410 U.S. 113 (1973) on the one hand, while upholding all but the spousal notification requirements of Pennsylvania's amended Abortion Control Act. The linchpin of O'Connor's *Casey* opinion is the concept of "undue burden." "A finding of an undue burden," she wrote,

> is a shorthand for the conclusion that a state regulation has the purpose or effect of placing a substantial obstacle in the path of a woman seeking an abortion of a nonviable fetus. A statute with this purpose is invalid because the means chosen by the State to further the interest in potential life must be calculated to inform the woman's free choice, not hinder it.[50]

Eleven years later, in *Grutter v. Bollinger*, 539 U.S. 306 (2003), Justice O'Connor split the difference between affirming the University of Michigan Law School's race-conscious university admissions policy, on the one hand, while rejecting rigid numerical quotas. Like Justice Powell's opinion in the previous landmark university affirmative action case, *Regents of the University of California v. Bakke*, 438 U.S. 265 (1978), after which she modeled her opinion, the linchpin in *Grutter* is a diverse student body:

> Justice Powell approved the university's use of race to further only one interest: "the attainment of a diverse student body." With the important proviso that "constitutional limitations protecting individual rights may not be disregarded," Justice Powell grounded his analysis in the academic freedom that "long has been viewed as a special concern of the First Amendment." . . . In seeking the "right to select those students who will contribute the most to the 'robust exchange of ideas,'" a university seeks "to achieve a goal that is of paramount importance in the fulfillment of its mission." Both "tradition and experience lend support to the view that the contribution of diversity is substantial."[51]

While Justice O'Connor's *Casey* and *Grutter* opinions are more famous (or infamous, as the case may be), her split-the-difference jurisprudence also can be seen in three of the five students' rights cases decided since *Tinker*. In *T.L.O.*, *Vernonia*, and *Earls*, O'Connor "appeared less concerned with allegiance to any . . . [doctrinal] sacred cows than with fairly deciding the case in front of her, using whatever tools seemed necessary."[52] Characteristically, Justice O'Connor's approach to student rights in the school setting is nondogmatic and practical. She looks for the useful answer.

In *New Jersey v. T.L.O.* O'Connor joined Justice Powell's brief concurring opinion. Recall that Justice White, writing for the 6–3 Court, upheld the search of a student's purse conducted by an assistant vice principal. Along the way to that conclusion, Justice White held that the Fourth Amendment's prohibition of unreasonable searches and seizures applies to searches conducted by school officials—adding that this holding "is only to begin the inquiry into the standards governing such searches."[53] In upholding the search, the Court struck a balance between "the schoolchild's legitimate expectation of privacy and the school's equally legitimate need to maintain an environment in which learning can take place."[54] Joined by Justice O'Connor, Justice Powell's "emphasis [was] somewhat different."[55] Instead of balancing competing social values, Powell differentiated between the constitutional rights of students within a school setting, on the one hand, and the "full panoply of constitutional rights" enjoyed by adults in the context of "enforcement of criminal law."[56] The key is the character of the school environment:

> The special relationship between teacher and student . . . distinguishes the setting within which schoolchildren operate. Law enforcement officials function as adversaries of criminal suspects. These officers have the responsibility to investigate criminal activity, to locate and arrest those who violate our laws, and to facilitate the charging and bringing of such persons to trial. Rarely does this type of adversarial relationship exist between school authorities and pupils. Instead, there is a commonality of interests between teachers and their pupils. The attitude of the typical teacher is one of personal responsibility for the student's welfare as for his education.[57]

Stated differently, although students do not "shed their constitutional rights . . . at the schoolhouse gate" (*Tinker*), there is a "qualitative difference between the constitutional remedies to which students and adults are entitled."[58] Neither embracing students' rights fully, nor rejecting them, Powell—with O'Connor—split the difference.

By the time the Court moved from validating suspicion-based warrantless searches of students' personal possessions in *T.L.O.*, to ratifying random suspicionless drug tests of student athletes ten years later in *Vernonia*, Justice O'Connor had parted company with the majority. For O'Connor, pragmatically setting apart students' constitutional rights in school from adults' constitutional rights generally, due to the unique needs and characteristics of the educational environment, is one thing. It is an entirely different matter to dispense "with a requirement of individualized suspicion" thereby opening all student athletes "to an intrusive bodily search."[59] Splitting the difference, realistically,[60] between students' and adults' rights is not the same as obliterating students' Fourth Amendment rights:

> [A] suspicion-based search regime is not just any less intrusive alternative; the individualized suspicion requirement has a legal pedigree as old as the Fourth Amendment itself, and it may not be easily cast aside in the name of policy concerns. It may only be forsaken, our cases in the personal search context have established, if a suspicion-based regime would be ineffectual. . . . The great irony of this case is that most (though not all) of the evidence the [Vernonia] District introduced to justify its suspicionless drug-testing program consisted of first- or second-hand stories of particular, identifiable students acting in ways that plainly give rise to reasonable suspicion of in-school drug use—and thus that would have justified a drug-related search under our *T.L.O.* decision.[61]

From Justice O'Connor's point of view, when the sensible *T.L.O.* distinction would have sufficed, the *Vernonia* majority abandoned that "measured intrusion on constitutional rights" in lieu of a "suspicionless policy . . . [that] sweeps too broadly."[62] Once again, O'Connor regrets that the majority opts for a wholesale rule in lieu of case- and context-specific deliberation.

Justice O'Connor's take on *Board of Education of Independent School District No. 92 of Pottawatomie County v. Earls*, 536 U.S. 822 (2002) is that two wrongly decided decisions do not remotely amount to a right-headed approach to high school drug use. "I dissented in *Vernonia School District 47J v. Acton*, 515 U.S. 646 (1995)," she wrote, "and continue to believe that case was wrongly decided." O'Connor continued: "Because *Vernonia* is now this Court's precedent, and because I agree that petitioners' program fails under even the balancing approach adopted in that case, I join Justice Ginsburg's dissent."[63] Remember that the *Earls* majority validated the Tecumseh, Oklahoma, school district's Student Activities Drug Testing Policy, which mandated suspicionless drug testing of all middle and high school students wanting to participate in any extracurricular activity, 5–4. Basically, the slim *Earls* majority extended the *Vernonia* ruling to include all student activities, not just athletics. To this extension, Justice Ginsburg, joined by Justice O'Connor (and Justices Souter and Stevens), replied: "[T]his case resembles *Vernonia* only in that the School Districts in both cases conditioned engagement in activities outside the obligatory curriculum on random subjection to urinalysis. The defining characteristics of the two programs, however, are entirely dissimilar." In other words, for the *Earls* dissenters, O'Connor among them, rather than splitting the difference in a practical manner to solve the problem of adolescent drug use, the majority conflated key differences between the Vernonia and Tecumseh programs in ways that compromised students' Fourth Amendment rights.

Justice O'Connor submitted her resignation to President George W. Bush on July 1, 2005. She made her resignation "effective upon the nomination and confirmation of my successor." That process was prolonged beyond her expectations by Chief Justice Rehnquist's death on September 3, 2005, which vaulted replacing Rehnquist over filling O'Connor's seat in the Bush administration's priorities. O'Connor's successor, Samuel A. Alito Jr., was not sworn in until January 31, 2006.

Commentaries on, and assessments of, the Court under Chief Justice Rehnquist began appearing years before the man himself had departed.[64] By the time of this writing, the literature is fairly voluminous and growing. A few themes have emerged, however. Among the most instructive for understanding the Court on which Sandra Day O'Connor served is *New York Times* Supreme Court correspondent Linda Greenhouse's periodization of the Rehnquist era. Greenhouse writes about the last of three "Rehnquist Courts."[65] As her point of departure, Greenhouse uses an influential article by law professor Thomas W. Merrill.[66] Merrill divides the Court during Chief Justice Rehnquist's tenure into the first, lasting from October 1986 until July 1994, and the second, which commenced the first Monday in October 1994 and, according to Merrill, was continuing as of the spring 2003 publication date of his article. Merrill's analysis is sophisticated, and not easily summarized. Basically, he argues that five "phenomena"[67] distinguish the first from the second Rehnquist Court and, drawing on three explanations offered by prominent political science students of the Court plus a fourth of his own coinage,[68] he seeks to explain these distinguishing characteristics. One can read Merrill's article as sort of a cautionary tale urging, for lack of a better term, a catholic (more accurately, perhaps, interdisciplinary) approach to analyzing the Supreme Court. Merrill's conclusions suggest that lawyers and law professors, on the one hand, would benefit from dialogue with political scientists—and vice versa. The former ought to supplement their "normative analysis of legal questions" with "a healthy dose of realism." "Understanding the preferences and the strategies that lie behind the jurisprudence may provide insights into what kinds of arguments are likely to succeed and why, and it may give us some sense of how permanent the jurisprudential preferences of the current Justices are likely to be." The latter ought to supplement their quest for "universal," reductionistic models of judicial behavior with the realization that "[i]t is quite possible . . . that in studying an institution like the Supreme Court, where the behavior of each individual plays such a critical role in the performance of the institution, a more complex or multi-dimensional theory of judicial behavior will have more explanatory power than a single-dimensional theory."[69]

Without taking any position regarding Merrill's recommendations, Greenhouse argues that beginning in 2003 a third "Rehnquist Court" emerged. That year, contends Greenhouse, was "[t]he year Rehnquist may have lost his court."[70] Like Merrill's, Greenhouse's supporting analysis resists being reduced to a few summary lines. Nevertheless, the defining characteristics of her third Rehnquist Court—its "dynamic"[71]—can be briefly stated: it is, first, a Court where Chief Justice Rehnquist regularly dissented in defining cases and, second, it is a Court divided over how far to push precedents established by previous Rehnquist Courts. Greenhouse specifies fourteen cases she deems especially significant where Rehnquist dissented.[72] Inter alia, these decisions addressed affirmative action, the words "under God" in the Pledge of Allegiance, gay rights, the death penalty, and medical marijuana. Seemingly, the only hot-button issue missing was abortion. Rehnquist also was on the losing side in cases pertaining to states' rights and property rights, two of his signature issues. That noted, Greenhouse asserts that merely toting up losses in landmark cases tells neither the entire story of Chief Justice Rehnquist's final years nor the most revealing tale. More interesting is the fact that in two cases, the significance of which she holds would be "difficult to overstate,"[73] Rehnquist wrote for majorities that stopped short of extending a couple of key precedents dear to the Chief's heart, one involving immunizing states from suit, the other involving accommodation of religion.

In *Nevada Dept. of Human Resources v. Hibbs*, 538 U.S. 721 (2003) the Court had the chance to hone further its use of the Eleventh Amendment as a doctrinal vehicle to exempt states from suits authorized by various congressional statutes (such as the 1990 Americans with Disabilities Act). In a line of cases tracing back seven years,[74] the Rehnquist Court had fashioned a jurisprudence making the legitimacy of such suits contingent upon a showing that Congress was addressing a specifically protected right, under Section 5 of the Fourteenth Amendment,[75] in order to abrogate state Eleventh Amendment immunity. The provision challenged in *Hibbs* was a part of the 1993 Family and Medical Leave Act (FMLA). William Hibbs had sued his employer, the Welfare Division of the Nevada Department of Human Resources, for violating the FMLA provision of up to twelve weeks of unpaid annual medical leave, thereby precluding him caring for his ailing wife. Hibbs had sued under the FMLA provision, creating a private right of action. The district court awarded Nevada summary judgment, holding that Hibbs'

FMLA claim was barred by the Eleventh Amendment and that his Fourteenth Amendment rights had not been violated. Surprisingly, declining the invitation to enhance its "newly muscular"[76] Eleventh Amendment state rights jurisprudence, the Court, 6–3, sided with Hibbs. Noting the long history of sex discrimination in the United States, Chief Justice Rehnquist wrote: "the States' record of unconstitutional participation in, and fostering of, gender-based discrimination in the administration of leave benefits is weighty enough to justify the enactment of prophylactic §5 legislation [such as FMLA]."[77]

In *Locke v. Davey*, 540 U.S. 712 (2004) the Court had the opportunity to extend its 2002 ruling that using publicly funded vouchers to support parochial school education was not prohibited by the Establishment Clause.[78] The question *Locke* posed was whether the Free Exercise Clause required Washington State to pay Joshua Davey's tuition at Northwest College, an Assemblies of God school, through the state's Promise Scholarship Program. Chief Justice Rehnquist said no. He observed that the "Establishment Clause and the Free Exercise Clause, are frequently in tension," noting "there is room for play in the joints" between them.[79] Just because employing publicly funded vouchers in parochial schools is not an Establishment of religion under the First Amendment, it did not follow that the Free Exercise Clause of the First Amendment mandates that a public-funded scholarship must be available to students pursuing pastoral studies at religious schools. Chief Justice Rehnquist wrote: "The State's interest in not funding the pursuit of devotional degrees is substantial and the exclusion of such funding places a relatively minor burden on Promise Scholars. If any room exists between the two Religion Clauses, it must be here."[80]

Greenhouse's analysis of *Hibbs* and *Locke* brings us back to Justice O'Connor's split-the-difference jurisprudence. Referring to *Hibbs* and *Locke*, Greenhouse comments, "[y]ou can almost picture the majority peering over the cliff and deciding not to jump."[81] In terms of doctrine, it would have been no stretch either to extend the *Seminole-Garrett* line to *Hibbs* or to expand the *Zellman* precedent to *Locke*. Nonetheless, taking either step would have been politically risky, exposing the Court to a storm of controversy. Under these circumstances, the Court decided to proceed cautiously, one case at a time.[82] "So this is the third Rehnquist Court: a majority that has fractured over how far to go—over 'when to hold 'em and when to fold 'em,' in the words of the Kenny Rogers song, over when to stop at the edge of the cliff and when to jump."[83] Greenhouse's imagery suggests two hallmarks of Justice O'Connor's jurisprudence: political savvy and practical decision making. In terms of Greenhouse's "twin imperatives," O'Connor consistently struck a serviceable balance between "consistency and pragmatism."[84] That balance is evident in the *Hibbs* and *Locke* outcomes.[85] To appropriate Greenhouse's language and imagery again, Justice O'Connor's "comfort level"—her "felt need"[86]—gave her a uniquely down-to-earth take on "the surrounding constitutional culture." When Greenhouse explains what she means by "constitutional culture,"[87] she could just as well be describing Justice O'Connor's modus operandi and her consequent point of view:

By perception of constitutional culture, I mean . . . a . . . personal orientation on the part of individual Justices. Amid the cacophony of commentary, which voices—present or anticipated, formally expressed or simply part of the background music, within our borders or without—are most salient? At which point do various Justices decide that it is necessary in the Court's interest, or the country's, to subordinate "craft to outcome" and engage in the "sacrifice of cogency for wisdom," to borrow from John Jeffries's recent reappraisal of Justice Powell's performance in *Bakke*.[88]

As a master of a pragmatic jurisprudence, it turns out that Justice O'Connor was The Gambler on the Third Rehnquist Court—par excellence.[89] She discerned the wisdom in Falstaff's observation: "The better part of valour is discretion; in the which better part I have saved my life."[90]

On January 31, 2006, Samuel A. Alito Jr. replaced Sandra Day O'Connor. Since then, six years into a new century, the U.S. Supreme Court has been a different Court. It is too early to tell just how different the current Court will be. Informed speculation is rife, and educated guesses abound.[91] Early indications suggest that contemporary controversies over, say, the death penalty, leave the current Court deeply divided,[92] and that Justice Anthony Kennedy's vote often is pivotal.[93] Nevertheless, now is not the time, and this project is not the place, to engage in crystal-ball gazing about where a Supreme Court without Justice O'Connor might be heading. One can say that the present Court is defined by her absence. Gone are her interpersonal skills, her savvy political instincts, and her pragmatic jurisprudential impulse. Assaying the consequences of O'Connor leaving is not furthered by designating her an "icon,"[94] nor consigning her to a subtitle: "Most Influential Justice."[95] The picture is more subtle—and complex. Two assessments, published a decade apart, by a political scientist and a law professor respectively, provide useful insights into what Justice O'Connor brought to her quarter-century on the Court—and what her exit from that stage signifies.

Nancy Maveety authored her 1996 analysis of Justice O'Connor to counter the prevalent tendency to reduce the justice to merely a famous first. Concerned that, fifteen years into O'Connor's tenure, common perceptions of the justice did not go much deeper than seeing her as a novelty (female) justice, or as Ronald Reagan's path-breaking nominee, Maveety sought to offer a more sophisticated analysis grounded in a close reading of O'Connor's work on the Court. At the time, Maveety's characterization of Justice O'Connor as a "quiet leader"[96] on Courts presided over by Warren Burger and William Rehnquist was unusual. Of course, in years subsequent to 1996 it became commonplace to use some variation of the term *leader* in conjunction with Justice O'Connor. Maveety's contribution to our understanding of Justice O'Connor's legacy derives less from Maveety's description of her as a leader than from Maveety's analysis of what made O'Connor influential.

For Maveety, Sandra Day O'Connor was "a key strategist shaping the collective outputs of the Burger and Rehnquist Courts"[97] because she was an "accommodationist judge."[98] O'Connor's strategically significant work as an "accommodationist" jurist had three interrelated tendencies, manifested in two aspects. O'Connor's three accommodationist tendencies are "contextual conservatism," "coalitional propensities," and "pragmatic centrism"[99]:

> These three tendencies are the unifying themes through which O'Connor's work on the Court are critically examined . . . This study demonstrates the definitive impact O'Connor has had on both constitutional doctrine and the conventions of collegiality of the contemporary Supreme Court.[100]

Maveety argues that Justice O'Connor introduced "a new, more choral convention of coop-erative decision-making on the Supreme Court," a convention that Maveety says resembles a "more legislative method of forming opinions—one that relies heavily on a contextual and serial reasoning process." O'Connor's method made her "the Court's accommodation-ist strategist and the epitome of the conservatism of the contemporary Court."[101]

Justice O'Connor's inclinations were evident in her approach to law and to the way in which she operated in a small-scale collegial decision-making body. Maveety terms O'Connor's approach and her modus operandi, respectively, "jurisprudential accommoda-tionist" and "behavioral accommodationist." The former refers to "an approach to doctrinal analysis and precedential rule following that is flexible, contextual, and fact specific." The latter pertains to "a strategic understanding of voting and coalitional behavior that includes swing voting, separate opinion writing, and conditional cooperation with political allies."[102] In short, Justice O'Connor fashioned a uniquely effective style of leadership that one might characterize as keyed on staying open to possibilities.

O'Connor's intellectual and interpersonal openness can be likened to remaining avail-able. Widely appreciated for being a keen and accessible person, Justice O'Connor employed her supple mind and her winning personality in chambers in ways that garnered support among her judicial colleagues. In a 2006 law review article published after Justice O'Connor's resignation, Wilson Ray Huhn presented a complementary analysis to Maveety's. His argu-ment is that O'Connor's judicial philosophy can be understood, at bottom, as a mode of pro-moting growth.[103] As the title of, and epigraph to, his essay, Huhn quotes from O'Connor's short concurring opinion in *Michael H. v. Gerald D.*, 491 U.S. 110 (1989), 132: "I would not foreclose the unanticipated by the prior imposition of a single mode of historical analysis."[104] In a strikingly similar vein, Maveety quotes Justice O'Connor, concurring in *Capitol Square Review and Advisory Board v. Pinnett*: "flexibility is a virtue and not a vice."[105] Do not fore-close the unanticipated. Perceive flexibility as a virtue. Justice O'Connor, it seems, sought to nurture a judicial sense of wonder. Here is Professor Huhn:

> Justice O'Connor has been faithful to precedent and attentive to detail, while at the same time demonstrating a constant willingness to rethink her position on matters of funda-mental importance. Beyond her contribution to our understanding of the Constitution, Sandra Day O'Connor has also enlarged our understanding of human potential. Her most enduring lesson for us all is that throughout all stages of life we are capable of remarkable growth.[106]

It is no surprise that Justice O'Connor drove Justice Scalia to distraction.[107] It would be hard to imagine two more diametrically opposed judges. I am not referring here merely to their respective judicial attitudes. Ironically, reduced to raw ideology, O'Connor and Scalia likely would agree surprisingly often. What distinguishes the two is more fundamental—more holistic, for lack of a better term. (The words *gestalt* and *Weltanschauung* are approxima-tions.) If Justice O'Connor approached judging as a matter of wondering, for Justice Scalia judging entails knowing. For O'Connor the "answer" is contingent. For Scalia, the answer is clear.

What Justice O'Connor's departure signifies, then, is that a receptive voice has been silenced. We will never know how she would have responded to the specific issues raised in *Morse v. Frederick*. More broadly, we will never know how Justice O'Connor thought about disciplining student speech in the context of the "zero-tolerance" atmosphere created by simultaneous wars on terror—domestic and foreign—and on drugs. What we do know is that the Supreme Court to which Deborah Morse brought her appeal was not the same body that saw Justice O'Connor dissent in *Vernonia* and *Earls*.

The Ninth Circuit Weighs In

JOSEPH FREDRICK'S appeal took him to the most innovative and controversial Circuit Court of Appeals in America: the Ninth. The Ninth Circuit Court of Appeals is among twelve regionally organized courts which, along with the Circuit Court of Appeals for the Federal Circuit, comprise the core of the nation's intermediate appellate tribunals. Borrowing Wallace Stegner's description of the West, former Justice O'Connor referred to the Ninth Circuit as "the largest and most diverse federal circuit in the 'big country.'"[1] Nine states, one territory, and one commonwealth fall within the jurisdiction of the Ninth Circuit.[2] Covering much of the western third of the United States, it stretches from the Arctic Circle to the Mexican border, from eastern Montana to the south-central Pacific Ocean. It encompasses fifteen federal judicial districts.[3] Almost one-fifth of all Americans live within its authority. Vast, rather than big, might be a more apt characterization of the Court's geographical breadth. Most fundamentally, the court to which Frederick appealed cannot be understood apart from the federal character of American government, as well as the history of the region within which the Ninth Circuit is embedded.

The structure of the courts in the United States judicial system reflects the federal nature of American government. Divided governing authority is a defining feature of American government. As Justice Kennedy famously observed in a 1995 concurrence:

> Federalism was our Nation's own discovery. The Framers split the atom of sovereignty. It was the genius of their idea that our citizens would have two political capacities, one state and one federal, each protected from incursion by the other. The resulting Constitution created a legal system unprecedented in form and design, establishing two orders of government, each with its own direct relationship, its own privity, its own set of mutual rights and obligations to the people who sustain it and are governed by it.[4]

Following the bifurcating tenets of federalism, from their origins the courts of the United States have been organized around states and combinations of states. U.S. District Courts have existed within states, or within parts of states. Judicial circuits have combined groups of districts.[5] Although circuit courts were first established by the Judiciary Act of 1789, between that statute and the Evarts Act of 1891 circuit courts combined both original and appellate jurisdiction. The specifics of such combined jurisdiction, as well as the configuration of states comprising different circuits, shifted throughout the nineteenth century as Congress grappled haltingly, on an ad hoc basis, with staffing the benches of U.S. Courts.

One challenge to effective court reform was that, while the expanding geographical scope and population of the country, together with the Civil War Amendments, generated mushrooming case loads in U.S. courts, Congress clung to the mythology that U.S. Supreme Court justices—"riding circuit"[6]—largely supplemented by other federal judges filling both trial and appellate roles, could handle the crowded dockets. The mythology was deceiving. "By one estimate, in approximately eight-ninths of all cases brought in a four-year period during the 1880s, the same district judge heard and decided the appeal for rehearing or new trial."[7] Another obstacle to reform was federalism itself. In the aftermath of the extension of national governmental authority attending the Civil War, supporters of states' rights balked at any moves that would expand the reach of Washington, D.C. "[B]ecause an expanded federal court appellate system would entrench power in the national government, certain interests in Congress resisted enacting further reforms. The sectional rivalries and concern for states' rights that had been prevalent in the Civil War era were not completely dead."[8] Thus, lingering regional divisions and embedded federalism concerns stymied responses to overcrowded federal court dockets.

Despite inertia and resistance, the Evarts Bill became law on March 3, 1891. It created nine intermediate circuit courts of appeals.[9] Thus began the history of the unique court to which Joseph Frederick appealed.[10]

Three dimensions define the uniqueness of the Ninth Circuit: its regional history, its procedural innovations, and ongoing controversies over some of its rulings.[11] As a preface to scrutinizing how a three-judge panel of the Ninth disposed of Frederick's appeal, it is useful to discuss briefly each facet. My intention is not to suggest that these three factors explain the outcome in *Frederick v. Morse*[12] in any causal sense. Rather, it is both useful and interesting to contextualize the venue that heard Frederick's appeal.

Courts, as is well known, are not self-starters. Courts' work products—judicial decisions—are shaped by the sorts of cases that litigants bring to them.[13] The substance of the cases brought is produced by a dynamic amalgam of time and space. That is to say that the particular cases and controversies[14] courts hear result from a confluence of circumstances situated within a specific historical period and located in a given place. To say that the Ninth Circuit Courts of Appeals is a Western court tells us something about its work. As the Court's premier historian, David C. Frederick, notes: "Despite the broad diversity of the vast region within the court's jurisdiction, many issues that arose in one section also affected others."[15] But knowing that the Ninth is located in the Western United States is not enough. Westerners not only confront issues unique to their region which create distinctive legal questions, those issues change over time. So, for instance, while railroads played a central part on the Ninth Circuit docket in the 1890s, computer technology was significant in the 1990s—controversies surrounding Leland Stanford's Central Pacific Railroad Company were supplanted by fights over Shawn Fanning's Napster.

Some of the chapter titles in David Frederick's history of the Ninth Circuit convey the flavor of the characteristically Western concerns coming before that court, as those concerns evolved from 1891 until 1941. He discusses "Railroads, Robber Barons, and the Saving of Stanford University" (chapter 2); "Testing Tolerance: Chinese Exclusion and the Ninth Circuit" (chapter 3); "The Judicial Faultline: Battles over Natural Resources" (chapter 5); "War, Liquor, and the Quest for Order" (chapter 7); "Adjudicating the New Deal" (chapter 9). A helpful supplement to these headings are the summary highlights of significant cases Ninth Circuit judges heard between 1905 and 2005.[16] The summary was compiled as part of the centennial commemoration of the Ninth's San Francisco Courthouse (now the James R. Browning United States Courthouse).

Picking one thematic thread from among many illustrating how the Ninth addressed specifically regional disputes throughout the twentieth century, various parties brought cases involving different aspects of racial and ethnic discrimination to the court. *United States v. Ah Sou*[17] involved a Chinese slave girl brought to the West Coast of the United States illegally by her master. Ah Sou escaped and entered into a sham marriage intended to allow her to remain in the country. Washington District Judge Cornelius Hanford stayed her deportation under the Thirteenth Amendment. The Ninth Circuit reversed, holding such an interpretation would effectively nullify the federal 1882 Chinese Exclusion Act.

Thirty-eight years later, it was an American citizen of Japanese descent who brought a case to the Ninth. On May 30, 1942, Fred Toyosaburo Korematsu had been arrested in San Leandro, California, for violating Civilian Exclusion Order No. 34. This order was promulgated to enforce military orders that excluded all Japanese Americans from "Military Area No. 1," made up of the entire Pacific coastline, Southern California, and the Arizona–Mexico border area.[18] Following his conviction, Korematsu appealed to the Ninth Circuit in March 1943. A three-judge panel affirmed his conviction, but not without divergent views.[19] Only one judge, Albert Lee Stephens, wholly deferred to executive branch authority to exclude Japanese Americans during wartime. Writing the majority opinion, Judge Curtis D. Wilbur held that the outcome in Korematsu's appeal was controlled by the U.S. Supreme Court's then newly minted decision in *Hirabayashi v. United States*, 302 U.S. 81 (1943). Despite the fact that Hirabayashi pertained narrowly to a curfew ordered pursuant to Executive Order 9066, not the Civilian Exclusion Order No. 34, the three Ninth Circuit judges reasoned that, by extension, *Hirabayashi*'s validation of the former applied to the latter as well. Judge William Denman reluctantly joined his brethren. Although he excoriated Japanese American "exclusion" policies as euphemistic and racially discriminatory, he nevertheless saw them as evils necessitated by wartime emergencies.[20]

By 1947 circumstances and attitudes regarding race and ethnicity were changing. When a group of Mexican-American parents filed a class-action suit challenging the legally segregated schools in Orange County, California, the outcome differed from those in the Chinese and Japanese-American exclusion cases. *Westminster School District of Orange County v. Mendez*[21] is a landmark Ninth Circuit decision, albeit a curious one. It is a milestone because

Mendez is a crucial step on the road to *Brown v. Board of Education.*[22] Gonzalo Mendez and his fellow class members argued, inter alia, that Orange County's mandatory school segregation deprived their children of equal protection of the laws, in violation of the Fourteenth Amendment. Thurgood Marshall and two colleagues[23] filed an amicus brief for the National Association for the Advancement of Colored People supporting the parents. The trial judge, senior judge of the Southern District of California, Paul J. McCormick, agreed with the constitutional challenge.[24] While affirming Judge McCormick's ruling, the Ninth Circuit did not embrace his reasoning. Avoiding a direct Fourteenth Amendment analysis of school segregation, likely because such analysis would have obliged the circuit court to uphold the Westminster District policy under existing precedents,[25] the seven Ninth Circuit judges overturned the Westminster District policy as illegal under relevant state statutes. Employing the maxim of statutory construction, *expressio unius est exclusio alterius* (the mention of one thing in a statute implies the exclusion of another thing not mentioned), the judges held:

> [T]he state law permits of segregation only as we have stated, that is, it is definitely confined to Indians and certain named Asiatics. That the California law does not include the segregation of school children because of their Mexican blood, is definitely and affirmatively indicated as the trial judge pointed out, by the fact that legislative action has been taken by the State of California to admit to her schools, children citizens of a foreign country, living across the border. Mexico is the only foreign country on any California boundary.
>
> It follows that the acts of respondents were and are entirely without authority of California law, notwithstanding their performance has been and is under color or pretense of California law. Therefore, conceding for the argument that California could legally enact a law authorizing the segregation as practiced, the fact stands out unchallengeable that California has not done so but to the contrary has enacted laws wholly inconsistent with such practice.[26]

The Ninth Circuit Court's unanimous opinion thus upheld the rights of Mexican-American schoolchildren by default. The court did not exactly vindicate their rights. Rather it said that, because California had not exercised its (unquestioned) authority specifically to segregate Mexican American schoolchildren based on their ethnicity, local Orange County school officials could not unilaterally do so. Exactly two months after the *Mendez* decision, California state officials acted affirmatively to protect the equal education rights of "Indians . . . and children of Chinese, Japanese or Mongolian parentage,"[27] as well as other racial and ethnic minorities. On June 14, 1947, Governor Earl Warren signed into law an act repealing all remaining vestiges of segregation in the California Education Code. Just shy of seven years later, Chief Justice Earl Warren would preside over the U.S. Supreme Court's rejection of school segregation on Fourteenth Amendment equal protection grounds.[28]

Not only has the Ninth Circuit Court of Appeals been in the thick of a particularly Western version of ongoing American controversies over race and ethnicity, as the three cases discussed above illustrate, the court also has been on the cutting edge of appellate court reform. Innovation is the second of the three dimensions defining the uniqueness of the Ninth Circuit. In a classic example of the wisdom contained in the cliché that necessity is the mother of invention, the various new policies and procedures adopted by the Ninth Circuit have been driven by exigencies related to caseload, compounded by geographical size. Jonathan Matthew Cohen has characterized the litigation burden on U.S. Courts of Appeals generally as "the caseload albatross hanging from [judges'] necks."[29] Cohen's Coleridge reference raises two knotty questions in the context of appellate court reform: (1) what specific sorts of reform should be undertaken to ameliorate the workload problem? and (2) how can such changes be designed and implemented in ways that enhance, rather than undermine, the distinctiveness of U.S. Courts of Appeals? This chapter is not the place to detail the experiments undertaken, and the debates such reforms have engendered, much less to address the general topic of appellate court reform.[30] Still, continuing to contextualize the Ninth Circuit's decision in *Frederick v. Morse*,[31] a brief look at the Circuit's use of "limited" en banc panels illustrates the Ninth Circuit's innovations—and their controversial nature.

En banc, French for "on the bench," refers to a judicial hearing by the full complement of judges sitting on any given bench, or court. Typically, in practice, en banc entails appellate courts sitting as a whole, compared to dividing into smaller groups—panels—composed of fewer judges than the complete court. Given the weighty claims on appellate judges' time, most cases brought before them are heard by panels. For "multiple reasons,"[32] however, lawyers and (mostly) the court's own sitting judges sometimes call for a rehearing en banc. Confronted with the competing concerns to get its work finished, and to get its work done right,[33] alone among two eligible circuits,[34] in August 1980 the Ninth Circuit authorized an intermediate approach, called limited en banc.[35] To some a "safety valve,"[36] to others an "oxymoron,"[37] the Ninth Circuit's en banc procedure provides that eleven judges may sit, and act, for the court as a whole.[38] Judith A. McKenna, director for the Federal Judicial Center's 2003 Project on Structural and Other Alternatives for the Federal Courts of Appeal, reports these assessments of the Ninth Circuit's novel approach:

> The Federal Courts Study Committee [1990] recommended that all courts of appeal be permitted to perform their *en banc* functions by panels of whatever size the court chooses and prescribes the rule, so long as the panels include nine or more judges in those courts having nine or more authorized judgeships. The Judicial Conference [of the United States] has taken no position on this recommendation. Our survey reveals that appellate judges are divided on the desirability of the limited en banc procedure—about 37% strongly or moderately support it and about 30% strongly or moderately oppose it. Most, of course, have no experience with it, so individual circuit analyses are instructive. Ninth Circuit appellate judges overwhelmingly support increased use of limited *en banc* panels (44% strongly, 30% moderately). The American Bar Association's subcommittee report on circuit size reported observing no problems with the limited *en banc* practice to date and recommended that other circuits consider adopting it as they grow larger.[39]

By contrast, active Ninth Circuit Judge Pamela Ann Rymer dissents from the three-quarters of her colleagues cited in the passage just above. Judge Rymer concludes that her court's "limited" en banc procedure is a "glass half empty": "[W]hile the limited *en banc* concept has the merit of affording another level of review short of calling upon the resources of the full court," Rymer writes, "it nevertheless has built-in shortcomings that curtail the unifying and stabilizing functions of true, full-bench review."[40] The debate over limited en banc captures important distinguishing traits of the Ninth Circuit—innovative, diverse, and controversial. The debate further illustrates how the Ninth Circuit is highly visible—more accurately, conspicuous—because it is in the forefront.

To some extent, controversies swirling around the Ninth Circuit are a subset of more widespread debates over the role of the federal judiciary in American society. Although most attention paid to judicial recruitment focuses on the highly politicized U.S. Supreme Court appointment and confirmation process,[41] the process of staffing the U.S. Courts of Appeals has become just as partisan. Stark partisanship has developed relatively recently. The late Professor Harold W. Chase's pioneering 1972 analysis of how Article III judges are recruited sounds quaint.[42] Under the heading "partisanship," Chase speaks of "political pressures" which, in his telling, bear a striking resemblance to patronage and old-boy networking:

> If [a] candidate wins and then has the responsibility of appointing or helping to appoint to high office, he has a coterie of people well known to him who have demonstrated that they are like-minded in political philosophy and that they are able. What is more natural in such a situation than to seek to place such people in high governmental posts? . . . To the degree that an appointment is made on qualification and ability, it is inaccurate to describe it as a "purely political" appointment. But political considerations exert enormous pressures on the appointment-makers. Here, "political" is used in its grossest sense to describe considerations which enable, or are thought to enable, a party or candidates to win elections.[43]

The "electoral connection"[44] terms in which Chase defines politics have been supplemented, often to the extent of being supplanted, by policy concerns. The contemporary appointment process—an "interaction of a number of people with varying and, to some extent, countervailing powers attempting to influence each other"[45]—is largely driven by relatively narrow-gauge (parochial) goals.[46] In other words, shaping policy outcomes shapes the appellate judge selection process.[47]

As I said above, appointing circuit judges became a partisan affair relatively recently. How recently—and why? The abbreviated answers are since 1969—and because of judicial discretion. But such short answers come up short. The story is more complex.

"Politics has pervaded federal judicial appointments since the United States was founded," remarks law professor Carl Tobias. "Nonetheless," Tobias continues:

> some observers of the selection process contend that politicization has escalated over the last three and a half decades, beginning in the Republican Administration of President Richard Nixon, who secured election with a promise to retain "law and order" by placing on the federal bench conservative jurists who would be "strict constructionists." However, a rather modern strain originated when the Senate rejected District of Columbia Circuit Judge Robert Bork, whom President Ronald Reagan had nominated for the Supreme Court in 1987.[48]

Tobias' view of how federal judges are selected is helpful because, while he notes the fact that "partisan political considerations"[49] always have been important, he also points out that the "blatant uses"[50] of partisanship have escalated to where "infighting and divisiveness"[51] have swallowed the process. Clearly, presidents and senators always have jockeyed to place their cronies, their supporters, and their fellow travelers at all levels on the federal bench. Just as clearly, beginning with the Nixon administration, this "old-fashioned" politics of networking and reward coexisted with a new politics of ideological litmus tests and voting the party line.

Early in the Nixon administration, on March 25, 1969, a White House staffer drafted and sent a seven-page memo up the line. Tom Charles Huston's message to President Nixon was crystal clear: the administration's policy agenda could be advanced by strategic use of the presidential power to appoint District and Circuit Court judges. "Through his judicial appointments," Huston wrote, "a President has the opportunity to influence the course of national affairs for a quarter of a century after he leaves office." Huston continued, italicizing for emphasis: "*In approaching the bench, it is necessary to remember that the decision as to who will make the decisions affects what decisions will be made.*" He concluded that if the president "establishes *his* criteria and establishes *his* machinery for insuring that the criteria are met, the appointments he makes will be *his*, in fact, as in theory."[52] Invoking a Watergate-era image, political scientist Elliot E. Slotnick terms the Huston memo "the 'smoking gun' of the policy implications of judicial selection."[53] Nevertheless, the Nixon administration formalized neither the criteria nor machinery that Huston had recommended.

What Tom Huston proposed, Jimmy Carter started to implement. What Carter implemented, Reagan and George W. Bush perfected.[54] The result of the self-conscious, systematic attention successive presidential administrations paid to linking their respective policy agendas to the process of judicial appointment is that "[w]e now witness a presidentially centered system with highly partisan and divisive senatorial coalitions aligned with or in opposition to the President's judicial selection pursuits."[55] Underlying this system is the awareness shared by Republicans as well as Democrats that, "for presidents who want to influence the direction of the judiciary and the course of public law and policy long after they have left office,"[56] judges are the key actors.

Judges are key policy actors because discretion is inherent in the judicial role. Discretion is inherent in judging because language is ambiguous and law, a linguistic phenomenon, is unavoidably indeterminate.[57] The indeterminacy of law does not mean that any given legal problem has an infinite number of solutions, any more than judicial discretion means that judges can decide any way they see fit. Law is not open-ended. Judges are not unfettered. Rather, law's indeterminate nature means that legal rules do not necessarily dictate inevitable outcomes; not always are there inescapable conclusions. Concomitantly, when judges[58] interpret law they must weigh alternative meanings and choose among them. But that is not all judges consider. They read the meaning of any given legal language within the context of what it was designed to accomplish. Laws are not merely linguistic artifacts. They also are vehicles for managing—for governing—public affairs. Judging is thus an amalgam of semantics and civics.[59] Judges seek to ascertain a law's meaning as well as to discern its purpose. Because neither a law's meaning nor its purpose is always self-evident, judging often entails "filling in the blanks." Sheldon Goldman observes:

The core constituencies of both parties, as well as scholars of law and courts, understand that judging is an art and not a science. It is a process of applying the provisions of statutes or constitutions—which may be vaguely worded—to a specific set of facts. The judge must figure out for herself what the words of the Constitution, the statute, or the precedent mean as applied to the case at hand.[60]

Although politicians characteristically deny and/or decry judicial choice as "legislating from the bench," these same politicians, very many of whom are lawyers, realize full well that judges exercise bounded discretion. Why else would politicians of opposing stripes want *their* judges on the bench? Judicial decision *making* is hardly a well-kept secret; politicians merely posture as though it were. It is a rhetorical tactic to cloak their policy agendas in the mantle of legitimacy and inevitability imparted by the talisman, the rule of law.

Contemporary partisan warfare over appointments to the federal bench is symptomatic of a deep divide over what policy agenda will shape the nation's judiciary. Although, as just noted, conflicts over federal judicial appointments take place behind a feigned veil of ignorance purporting to be innocent of politics, it is precisely because, as Tom Huston reminded President Nixon, "the decision as to who will make the decisions affects what decisions will be made" that these conflicts are so bitterly fought.[61] For reasons analyzed in the foregoing pages, the Ninth Circuit Court of Appeals is a particular focal point of such conflicts. The critical narrative about the Ninth is that it is too activist, too liberal— and too large. Two points made previously[62] bear repeating here: first, the Ninth Circuit is conspicuous because it is in the forefront; second, controversies swirling around the Ninth Circuit are a subset of more widespread debates over the role of the federal judiciary in American society. "The cacophony that surrounds the Ninth Circuit"[63] thus is both symptomatic of broader debates over the federal judiciary and possessed of its own distinctive characteristics. Hanging over all critical scrutiny of the Ninth Circuit's work is an ongoing debate over splitting the Circuit.

Two Ninth Circuit decisions provide both convenient chronological bookends to, and useful glimpses into, the disputes underlying proposals to split the Circuit. In a June 19, 2005 *New York Times* article, "Lawmakers Trying Again to Divide Ninth Circuit," then Ninth Circuit Chief Judge Mary M. Schroeder set the stage:

"The reason that the issue of splitting the circuit comes up repeatedly is because of dissatisfaction in some areas with some of our decisions," said Mary M. Schroeder, chief judge of the Ninth Circuit and a strong opponent of any split. "This has a long historic basis beginning with some fishing rights decisions in the 60's and going forward to the Pledge of Allegiance case and presently some of the immigration decisions."[64]

The contemporary history of efforts to split the Ninth Circuit accompanies heated controversies over Native American fishing rights in the Pacific Northwest. In the 1960s, Native tribes began aggressively to assert treaty-based[65] rights to take fish off as well as on their reservations. They did so in the face of opposition from commercial and game fishers and in violation of state regulations limiting catches as part of overall conservation management policies. Tribal members began to engage in civil disobedience, staging "fish-ins" at places throughout Oregon and Washington. Indian fishing rights became a cause célèbre—and a hotbed of dispute. In one highly publicized incident, on September 9, 1970, over two hundred law enforcement officers stormed, arresting sixty protesters, and dismantled a fishing camp that Natives had set up on the Puyallup River. The increasingly volatile situation led the U.S. Justice Department to file suit against the State of Washington on behalf of thirteen tribes. The suit sought to require Washington agencies charged with regulating the state's fisheries to enforce Native treaty rights to fish off reservation.

On February 12, 1974, U.S. District Court Judge George H. Boldt sided with the United States and the tribes.[66] Judge Boldt not only found Washington State to be in violation of tribal members' treaty rights to fish off reservation. He held that Natives' treaty fishing rights trump other citizens' fishing rights. Furthermore, Boldt decided, "[while] non-treaty fishermen shall have the opportunity to take up to 50% of the harvestable number of fish that may be taken by all fishermen at usual and accustomed grounds and stations . . . treaty right fishermen [also] shall have the opportunity to take up to the same percentage of harvestable fish."[67] Thus, Native treaties entitled tribal fishers to fully half of all harvestable fish that were taken off reservation. Adding insult to injury, from Washington State's and nontreaty fishers' point of view, Judge Boldt required state agencies to enforce restrictions on commercial and sport fishers in order to effectuate the 50/50 rule.[68] The decision kindled a firestorm. *United States v. Washington* morphed into simply the *Boldt* decision. Judge Boldt was hung in effigy. Bumper stickers proclaiming "Can Judge Boldt, Not Salmon" and "Let's Give 50 percent of the Indians to Judge Boldt" appeared on cars in the state.[69] The Ninth Circuit Court of Appeals affirmed Judge Boldt's decision the following year.[70] Washington State's reaction was reminiscent of state acts of nullification during the antebellum nineteenth century. Law professor and former federal fisheries administrator Martin H. Belsky details Washington's defiant response:

> The State of Washington refused to accept the Ninth Circuit's decision and went to its own courts to nullify it. *Boldt* required the Washington State Department of Fisheries to adopt regulations to implement the decision. Immediately after the Department issued the regulations, commercial fishermen, assisted by State of Washington officials, filed suit in Washington state court seeking a writ of mandate "ordering the Director of Fisheries to issue regulations which apply equally and in a nondiscriminatory fashion to both treaty and non-treaty fishermen."
>
> In two decisions, *Puget Sound Gillnetters Ass'n v. Moos* and *Washington Commercial Passenger Fishing Vessel Ass'n. v. Tollefson*, the Washington Supreme Court ultimately held the federal court actions invalid and forbade the Department of Fisheries to comply with the federal injunction. Specifically, in *Puget Sound*, the court held that Washington law allowed regulations of fisheries for conservation purposes only, and that Indians, as citizens of the State of Washington, are subject to the laws of the State of Washington. The court added that no court, including a federal court, had the authority to order a state agency to do any act inconsistent with its statutory authority. The court asserted that it, not the federal district court, had the authority to interpret state statutes as to the power of state agencies and had at least equal authority as federal courts to interpret Indian treaties.[71]

The Washington Supreme Court was not prepared to recognize the *Boldt* decision until the U.S. Supreme Court upheld the opinion.[72] The U.S. Supreme Court upheld Judge Boldt's decision in *Washington v. Washington State Commercial Passenger Fishing Vessel Ass'n*, 443 U.S. 658 (1979).[73] Even so, because its affirmance stood, the Ninth Circuit was tarred with siding with minority Indians against majority white fishers.

Twenty-five years after the U.S. Supreme Court upheld the Ninth Circuit's affirmance of Judge Boldt's divisive 1974 opinion, the U.S. Supreme Court "dodged a bullet" propelled its way by the Ninth Circuit. In an Establishment Clause challenge to the phrase *under God* in the Pledge of Allegiance, Dr. Michael Newdow sought to enjoin the Elk Grove Unified School District in California, where his daughter was enrolled, from its daily practice of reciting the Pledge. Although reciting the Pledge is voluntary at the school Newdow's daughter attended, Dr. Newdow argued that his daughter was injured by being compelled to "watch and listen as her state-employed teacher in her state-run school leads her classmates in a ritual proclaiming that there is a God, and that our's [sic] is 'one nation under God.'"[74] Newdow's original suit was dismissed at the district court level. A three-judge panel of the Ninth Circuit reversed. Writing for himself and Judge Stephen Reinhardt, Judge Alfred T. Goodwin penned an opinion that immediately became notorious to the point of being radioactive.[75] In a manner similar to how Judge Boldt's decision was received, Judge Goodwin's opinion was perceived to add insult to injury. The "injury" consisted of declaring unconstitutional both the 1954 congressional statute adding the words *under God* to the Pledge and the school district's daily recitation of the Pledge, as violating the Establishment Clause. The "insult" resulted from the Ninth Circuit employing the U.S. Supreme Court's own deeply divided and much criticized Establishment Clause jurisprudence as the basis of its holding.[76] In effect, the Ninth Circuit used the Supreme Court's own problematical precedents to fashion a widely resented outcome.

Five of the High Court justices, sitting on a tribunal itself polarized over many Establishment Clause matters, wanted nothing to do with the Ninth Circuit's toxic decision.[77] When the Elk Grove Unified School District appealed, a bare majority of the eight participating justices ducked. More precisely, the majority avoided reaching the merits of Michael Newdow's Establishment Clause claim by holding that Newdow lacked standing to sue. Construing Dr. Newdow's complaint as a domestic dispute between Newdow and his daughter's mother, Sandra Banning, Justice Stevens wrote, "[o]ne of the principal areas in which this Court has customarily declined to intervene is the realm of domestic relations."[78] Noting that California state court had granted Banning legal custody of her daughter, Stevens concluded:

> In our view, it is improper for the federal courts to entertain a claim by a plaintiff whose standing to sue is founded on family law rights that are in dispute when prosecution of the lawsuit may have an adverse effect on the person who is the source of the plaintiff's claimed standing. When hard questions of domestic relations are sure to affect the outcome, the prudent course is for the federal court to stay its hand rather than reach out to resolve a weighty question of federal constitutional law.[79]

Justice Stevens' stance may, or may not, have been "prudent" from the standpoint of exercising what the late constitutional scholar Alexander Bickel recommended as the "passive virtues"[80] of husbanding judicial authority by not deciding constitutional issues unnecessarily. Without a doubt, it was "prudent" of the U.S. Supreme Court to avoid the hornets' nest the Ninth Circuit had created. Although perhaps not "dead on arrival," as one legal analyst[81] declared *Newdow I,*[82] "[p]raise for the panel's decision was muted[,] . . . criticism of the decision was swift and, mostly, harsh."[83] In fact, Justice Scalia recused himself from participating in *Elk Grove* because, on January 12, 2003, less than six months after *Newdow I* came down, Scalia had delivered a speech in which he attacked the Ninth Circuit's holding.[84]

Do decisions like those affirming *Boldt* and overturning the 1954 version of the Pledge of Allegiance demonstrate that the Ninth Circuit is too activist and too liberal? Do such rulings justify calls to break up the Ninth Circuit? These are large questions. Much ink has been spilled, and much rhetoric expended, debating them.[85] Still, in the spirit of the stage-setting purpose of the foregoing pages, perhaps it is useful to observe in passing that contemporary arguments over the Ninth Circuit are reminiscent of the fights occasioned by Franklin D. Roosevelt's Judiciary Reorganization Bill of 1937. Recall that President Roosevelt thought the U.S. Supreme Court too activist and too conservative. Instead of breaking up the Court, he sought to supplement its membership. Asserting that the aging justices were overworked, FDR sought to add one judge for every sitting justice over seventy years of age who did not retire. Had Roosevelt's "Court-packing bill" passed, it would have authorized the president to appoint up to six additional justices. As is well known, the bill failed. It is also well known that Roosevelt's solicitous concern over the Court's workload was a ruse to remake the Court along lines more amenable to the New Deal.[86] Are worries about an overburdened Ninth Circuit Court of Appeals a case of history repeating itself?

The reader may well be asking at this point, why this lengthy discussion about the court that decided *Frederick v. Morse*?[87] What does this analysis of the Ninth Circuit have to do with understanding that case? The answer has three dimensions. As I said above, my intention is not to suggest that the Ninth Circuit's regional history, its procedural innovations, and ongoing controversies over some of its rulings specifically explain the outcome in *Frederick v. Morse* in any causal sense. Rather, for three reasons, it is both useful and interesting to contextualize the venue that heard Joseph Frederick's appeal. First, the foregoing situates *Frederick v. Morse* historically, providing a sense where the case fits within a larger picture. A second aspect of how the preceding discussion contextualizes *Frederick v. Morse* is that it provides a flavor—a feel, if you will—for the sort of court that heard and decided Frederick's appeal as well as how that court is perceived. Knowing that the Ninth is a conspicuous and controversial tribunal, the decisions of which usually are scrutinized closely, underscores the fact that, whatever the outcome in *Frederick v. Morse*, that result would be examined attentively—especially during a time of rancorous partisan division over federal courts. Thus, the foregoing attunes us to the significance of *Frederick v. Morse*. Third, it contextualizes *Frederick v. Morse* by locating the case within ongoing judicial process. By itself, *Frederick v. Morse* is only a way station; an important destination, to be sure, but also part of a more extensive legal journey.

In appellate proceedings like *Frederick v. Morse* before the Ninth Circuit, opposing counsel pursue this journey by means of filing legal briefs. Briefs are pictorial devices. Employing verbal imagery more or less artfully, lawyers paint a picture they want the relevant decision maker to adopt. In appellate cases, the decision maker is a judge, or, in the case of the Ninth Circuit, a panel of judges. In *Frederick v. Morse* the randomly selected panel was composed of Cynthia Holcomb Hall, Andrew J. Kleinfeld, and Kim McLane Wardlaw. At the time *Frederick v. Morse* was argued before them on July 8, 2004, in Anchorage, these three judges had a total of thirty-nine years of service on the Ninth Circuit between them.

Judge Hall was not only the senior Ninth Circuit judge on the *Frederick v. Morse* panel, she had taken senior circuit judge status as of August 31, 1997.[88] Born in 1929 in Los Angeles, California, Hall was educated at Stanford University (A.B., L.L.B) and New York University (L.L.M.). Her legal practice focused on tax law. Her judicial career began in 1972 when the Nixon administration appointed her to the U.S. Tax Court. She and her husband, John Hall, were the first husband-and-wife team simultaneously appointed to posts in Washington, D.C., a move that was criticized at the time because it resulted in a single family drawing two salaries from the federal government. President Ronald Reagan nominated Hall to the U.S. District Court for the Central District of California in October 1981. She served on that body until August 1, 1984, when the Reagan administration elevated her to the Ninth Circuit Court of Appeals. Her resident chambers are in Pasadena, California.

Judge Kleinfeld has served on the Ninth Circuit since 1991 when he was appointed by President George H. W. Bush. Although a native New Yorker, born in 1945, Kleinfeld has spent most of his career in Alaska. After graduating from Wesleyan University (1966) and Harvard Law School (1969), for three years he clerked for Judge J. A. Rabinowitz on the Alaska Supreme Court. Between 1971 and 1986, Kleinfeld was in private practice in Fairbanks, also serving briefly as a part-time U.S. Magistrate (1971–1974), until President Reagan appointed him to the U.S. District Court, District of Alaska in March. In May 1991, George H. W. Bush nominated Kleinfeld to the Ninth Circuit. His resident chambers are in Fairbanks.

The only Democratic appointee on the panel that heard and decided *Frederick v. Morse* was Judge Kim McLane Wardlaw. Born in 1954 in Los Angeles, California, Wardlaw earned both her bachelor's degree and her law degree from the University of California, Los Angeles. Following a clerkship with U.S. District Court Judge William P. Gray, Wardlaw joined the law firm of O'Melveny and Myers as an associate in 1980. She became a partner seven years later. Wardlaw and her husband, Bill, are very active in Democratic Party politics. Wardlaw served as a Clinton delegate at the 1992 Democratic National Convention, and Bill chaired Bill Clinton's 1992 and 1996 presidential campaigns in California. President Bill Clinton appointed Kim Wardlaw to the U.S. District Court for the Central District of California in August 1995, and elevated her to the Ninth Circuit Court of Appeals in January 1998. The daughter of a Scotch Irish father and a Mexican American mother, Judge Wardlaw is the first Hispanic woman confirmed by the Senate to a seat on a federal appeals court. Her resident chambers are in Pasadena, California.

To judges Hall, Kleinfeld, and Wardlaw, attorneys Douglas K. Mertz, for Joseph Frederick, and David C. Crosby, for Deborah Morse, directed their arguments. Like all lawyers worth their salt, Mertz and Crosby sought to tell a convincing story—to paint a compelling picture—and to connect their story to the pertinent law. Each sought to characterize the major players, to represent the events involving those players, and to clothe their players' actions in legal legitimacy. Although many facts were in dispute and relevant legal materials were malleable, both lawyers employed the standard rhetorical strategy: convert uncertainties into absolutes. Each presented his client's point of view as the whole story.

For plaintiff Frederick, lawyer Mertz told a tale about a concerned student who, due to the rash actions of a school administrator, was deprived of his well-established First Amendment right to free expression. Two passages from the "Statement of Facts" section of Mertz's brief capture the gist of his injury narrative:

> On January 24, 2002, the day on which the [Winter Olympics] torch relay was run, Joseph and several friends went to the route of the relay and stood waiting for it on a public sidewalk. The sidewalk was clearly off school property, in front of private homes and across the street from the municipal swimming pool and Juneau-Douglas High School. He parked his car several blocks away, on a city street, and had not entered school grounds that day or even been on the same side of the street as the school before the banner was displayed. . . .
>
> As the relay approached, Joseph and his friends unfurled the banner in a way that he hoped would be visible to television cameras filming the relay. As soon as she saw the banner, the High School principal, Deborah Morse, left the school property and ran across the street and demanded that Joseph put the banner down. When he responded by asking about his free speech rights, she grabbed the banner from his hands, and the other people holding the banner dropped it. She rolled up the banner and took it and instructed Joseph to meet her in her office.[89]

Notably, Mertz relates that Joseph Frederick attended the Olympic torch relay intending to exercise his First Amendment rights and was thwarted in doing so. But for Principal Morse's intemperate intervention, he and his friends would have hoisted their banner and had their innocuous nonsense message immortalized on television. Morse damaged Frederick by making what was just good fun into an incident followed by punishment.

In sharp contrast, for defendant Morse, lawyer Crosby recounted a tale about a conscientious school principal who, during an official school event, observed a group of students raise a fourteen-foot-long banner displaying a message advocating drug use in violation of school district policy, and took decisive action. Two passages from the "Statement of Relevant Facts" section of Crosby's brief illustrate his accountability narrative:

> Believing that the [Olympic torch relay] event had educational value and significance to the community, the Juneau School Board decided to let students participate and observe the relay during school hours. Throughout the school district, supervised release time and transportation was made available for students who were not on the relay route so that they could participate in the event.
>
> High School Principal and appellee/defendant Deborah Morse gave teachers the option of permitting their classes to observe the torchbearers from the sidewalks on either side of

the street in front of the High School. The students were not "released" from school, but rather remained under the supervision of teachers and school administrators for the limited purpose of observing the relay. . . .

Plaintiff insists that he displayed the banner in order to test his First Amendment rights and to get on the TV cameras. He denies that he was trying to communicate any message to anyone. He was aware at the time that he made the banner, however, that a "bong" is a water pipe that may be used for smoking marijuana, that a "hit" is slang for inhaling marijuana, and that the phrase "BONG HITS FOR JESUS" would be construed by many people as a reference to drugs and could offend Christians by associating the name of Jesus with drugs.[90]

Notably, Crosby tells of how Deborah Morse sought to preserve the integrity of an official school district event by stopping Joseph Frederick from converting that event into an occasion to display prominently an offensive, pro-drug message. But for her responsible and timely depriving him of his banner, Joseph Frederick would have gotten away with a disruptive and dangerous act.

Injury versus accountability—the opposing narratives woven by attorneys Doug Mertz and David Crosby set up their divergent legal arguments. For the former, the law dictated that Joseph Frederick was entitled to injunctive relief and damages because his First Amendment rights had been infringed. For the latter, the law required the outcome that, in fact, U.S. District Judge John W. Sedwick had announced, namely, summary judgment for Deborah Morse and the Juneau School District because no constitutional rights had been violated and appellees enjoyed qualified immunity. Mertz and Crosby fought out their legal differences in the arena of case law. Right at the start of the "Summary of Argument" section of his Ninth Circuit brief, Mertz argued that judicial interpretations of students' speech rights under the First Amendment showed that "[a] public school official may restrict student speech only under narrow circumstances. . . . None of those circumstance exists here."[91] In the opening paragraph of the "Summary of Argument" section of his Ninth Circuit brief, Crosby countered that court opinions support the conclusion that "Principal Morse properly construed Frederick's 'BONG HITS FOR JESUS' banner as advocating or promoting illegal drug use. . . . [H]er conduct in disciplining Frederick did not violate the first amendment."[92] The legal terms of the debate thus complement the competing narratives: case law supports redress of Joseph Frederick's injury resulting from being deprived of his First Amendment rights versus case law vindicates Deborah Morse in the discharge of her responsibility to hold accountable an errant student.

Not surprisingly, the basic contest before the Ninth Circuit that July day in 2004 was the status of *Tinker v. Des Moines Ind. Comm. School Dist.*, 393 U.S. 503 (1969). In Chapter 3, I observed that "Tinker is in limbo."[93] That state of uncertainty created the space for the opposing parties in *Frederick v. Morse* to offer conflicting readings of student rights in light of prevailing case law. Thirty-five years, and multiple federal court decisions, later the interpretive ripples resulting from judicial glosses on *Tinker* continued to play out in controversies between students and school administrators.

Framing the debate between opposing counsel in *Frederick v. Morse* was the Ninth Circuit's own reading of students' speech rights and school officials' authority in light of *Tinker* and two of its progeny, *Bethel School District No. 403 v. Fraser,* 478 U.S. 675 (1986) and *Hazelwood School Dist. v. Kuhlmeier,* 484 U.S. 260 (1988). In 1992 the Ninth had handed down a decision in *Chandler v. McMinnville School District.*[94] The circumstances giving rise to this case involve two students wearing buttons to school in support of their respective parents, who were among a group of striking teachers in the district. The buttons displayed a variety of slogans containing the word *scab* on them. When school authorities prohibited the students from wearing the buttons or face sanctions, the students sued, claiming that the ban violated the First Amendment. Citing *Tinker,* the Ninth Circuit sided with the students. Specifically, the Ninth, Chief Judge J. Clifford Wallace writing, "discerned three distinct areas of student speech from the Supreme Court's school precedents":

> (1) vulgar, lewd, obscene, and plainly offensive speech; (2) school-sponsored speech; and (3) speech that falls into neither of these categories. We conclude . . . that the standard for reviewing the suppression of vulgar, lewd, obscene, and plainly offensive speech is governed by *Fraser,* school-sponsored speech by [*Kuhlmeier*], and all other speech by *Tinker.*[95]

Employing this "comprehensive, three-part categorical scheme,"[96] and reasoning that neither the first (*Fraser*-governed) nor the second (*Hazelwood*-governed) category applied to the facts in *Chandler,* the Ninth Circuit decided that *Tinker* controlled:

> The district court held that the "scab" buttons were inherently disruptive, but nothing in the complaint or the analysis of the district court substantiates this conclusion. We conclude that the district court erred in holding, without more, that the "scab" buttons were inherently disruptive.[97]

Chandler operates as an interpretive rule. It can be read as instructing that *Fraser* and *Hazelwood* are exceptions to *Tinker* which, while modifying *Tinker* in important ways, nevertheless do not vitiate *Tinker* as the point of departure regarding student speech rights. If a given fact pattern in a student speech case pertains to neither *Fraser* nor *Hazelwood,* then *Tinker* controls. In other words, under *Chandler, Tinker* is the default rule.

The distance separating the parties' legal arguments in *Frederick v. Morse* can be conveniently summarized in terms of *Chandler.* Doug Mertz contended that his client's case resembled that of Chandler and Depweg, the two McMinnville students who brought suit over the "scab" buttons, hence *Tinker* controlled. David Crosby maintained that his clients' case implicated both the *Fraser* and *Hazelwood* precedents (not to mention *Vernonia School District 47J v. Acton,* 515 U.S. 646 [1995] and *Board of Education v. Earls,* 536 U.S. 822 [2002]), hence *Tinker* was superseded.

Doug Mertz told a *Tinker* story. His account of what happened on Glacier Avenue on January 24, 2002, dovetails with his legal argument, tailored to the *Chandler* rule, that Joe Frederick was engaging in protected speech. Mertz's constitutional argument has five parts—all designed to narrow the focus to *Tinker.* First, "Students Have First Amendment Rights."[98] Quoting the ultimate *Tinker* language about students not shedding their constitutional rights to freedom of speech or expression at the schoolhouse gate, Mertz observes:

"The Ninth Circuit Court of Appeals has cited this language in a number of cases in which it found that school officials had improperly infringed on student's First Amendment rights."[99] Second, "School Officials May Not Restrict Student Rights to Free Expression, with Only a Few Narrow Exceptions Which Do Not Apply Here."[100] In what may be the heart of his brief, Mertz sought to align himself with the Ninth Circuit's *Chandler* ruling, distinguishing his client's case from *Fraser* and *Hazelwood* and asserting the primacy of *Tinker*. Summarizing his argument, Mertz wrote: "[T]he Supreme Court has held that on campus, a school can punish obscene speech or speech which presents a clear and present danger of imminent harm or substantive evil, such as violence of a substantial interference with the educational process, and is likely to produce such conduct. Mere inconvenience, discomfort, or controversy are not sufficient reasons to sustain sanctions against speech."[101] Mertz then immediately quoted the Ninth Circuit's *Chandler* three-part categories, after which he wrote: "Since Joseph Frederick's banner was not vulgar, lewd, plainly offensive, or school sponsored, it falls into the third category and so is governed by *Tinker*."[102]

Third, "Off-Campus, the Ability of a School Official to Punish Free Speech Is Even More Restricted."[103] In the previous section of his argument, Mertz sought to refute the Juneau School District's assertion that, because the Olympic torch relay was a *Hazelwood*-like school-sanctioned activity, Principal Morse could censor Frederick's banner. In the third section, Mertz argued affirmatively that the "BONG HiTS" banner incident took place off-campus and furthermore, under *Tinker*, school officials may not punish nondisruptive speech, wherever it occurs:

> 1) First, Mr. Frederick was not part of any organized school activity when he displayed the banner. He had not even been on campus that day and was not watching the relay with a class that had been released. He joined his friends on a sidewalk, off the campus, and that group included both students and non-students. By the school officials' logic, a school could extend its control over student free speech by the mere act of giving students the option to attend a non-school event held off campus. There are literally no cases which support such a broadening of public school officials' authority to control the independent activities of a student when not on campus.
>
> 2) The *Tinker* standard still applies to this speech . . . and under *Tinker*, a school official may not punish on campus speech unless it creates an imminent and substantial danger to the educational process. The school officials have admitted here there was no disruption of that process. They cannot punish such speech on or off campus.[104]

Fourth, "The School District's Claim That the Banner *Could* Be Interpreted by Some Persons as Advocating Drug Use, Which *May* Someday Cause a Disruption of the Educational Process, Is Too Remote to Justify Punishing an Exercise of Pure Speech." Mertz sought to carry two arguments in this section. Initially, he characterized the school district's contention that the message on Frederick's banner *might* lead to future disruptive drug-related behavior as "tenuous."[105] Next, bringing the reader back to *Tinker*, he reiterated his account of the circumstances leading to Frederick's suspension:

There were no threats. There was no advocacy of violence. There were no racial epithets or demeaning racial language that could lead to violence. There was no obscenity as in *Fraser*. There was no use of school facilities as in the school newspaper cases [*Hazelwood*], so that there was no possibility of confusion between the school's position and that of the persons holding the banner. There was merely a quiet and respectful display of a banner with a message that the plaintiff intended as a humorous, non-harmful satire on a topic of public debate. . . . In short, nothing about the incident invoked *any* of the exceptions to freedom of student speech.[106]

Finally, Mertz took aim at how the district court's reading of *Fraser* unjustifiably expanded the school district's authority: "The District Court's Reliance on Fraser Is Inappropriate under the Controlling Case Law and Leaves Public Officials with Nearly Unlimited Discretion to Define and Punish 'Offensive' Speech."[107] The thrust of Mertz's argument in this section is that the district court interpreted *Fraser* in such a way that it supplants, rather than supplements, *Tinker*. Directing the Ninth Circuit's attention to its own *Chandler* decision, Mertz reminded the court that it had rejected the view that the term "plainly offensive" in *Fraser* is an accordion-like concept that can be expanded to absorb any speech deemed objectionable by school officials:

> The *Fraser* case itself concerned a student who used obscene and sexually suggestive language at a school assembly. In contrast, in *Chandler*, the students were making a serious point on a matter of public debate—use of replacement teachers during a strike. In rejecting the school officials' claim that the use of "scab" and similar words was "plainly offensive" under *Fraser*, the [Ninth Circuit] made clear its concern that the "vulgar and lewd" category not be expanded so far that it would allow suppression of non-lewd speech which is part of a debatable public issue. That is precisely the situation here. The District Court erred when it used the *Fraser* rather than the *Tinker* test.[108]

Mertz's *Tinker* story follows an arc of adding insult to injury. Joe Frederick was injured when Deborah Morse, acting in her official capacity, tore down his banner then suspended him in contravention of his First Amendment rights. When the district court for the District of Alaska granted defendants Morse and the Juneau School District summary judgment—on the theory that Frederick's banner was a patently offensive pro-drug message displayed during a school-sanctioned activity—it added insult to the original constitutional injury. Mertz offered the Ninth Circuit *Tinker* as the remedy to Frederick's injury, and the redress to his being insulted.

David Crosby told a *Fraser* story. Just as Mertz's factual and legal arguments dovetailed, Crosby's legal arguments interlock with his accountability narrative. The final line of Crosby's brief nicely illustrates the connection. He wrote: "As this Court [the Ninth Circuit] has said on several occasions, it is not '. . . unfair to require that one who deliberately goes perilously close to an area of proscribed conduct shall take the risk that he may cross the line.'"[109] Crosby's legal arguments are divided into two sections, with the first having three subsections.

The first section reads: "A. Under *Fraser* and *Chandler*, Frederick could be disciplined for displaying a banner emblazoned 'BONG HITS FOR JESUS' because the banner was 'plainly offensive' and 'inconsistent with the school district's basic educational mission' to teach safe and healthy lifestyles."[110] Under this heading, the first subsection is: "1. The School Board rightly prohibits messages that advertise or advocate use of illegal drugs as inconsistent with the district's educational mission and disruptive to the district's educational program."[111] In this subsection Crosby sought to align Juneau School Board policies with existing case law. He argued that high school drug use is recognized as a nationwide problem, and that the Juneau School District has a mandate to combat the scourge. He quoted, first, from *Board of Education v. Earls*, 536 U.S. 822 (2002), then from *Vernonia School District 47J v. Acton*, 515 U.S. 646 (1995) to make the points that the drug epidemic requires a war against drugs, and that a drug-infested school disrupts the educational process.[112] In this context, Crosby noted:

> Consistent with its policies of educating students in healthy lifestyles and prohibiting use or possession of illegal drugs or alcohol by students, the [Juneau] school board has adopted policies proscribing display of messages that promote or advertise illegal drugs or alcohol. Such messages are properly regarded by the Board as "inconsistent with the district's educational mission and disruptive to the district's educational program," as well as "interfer[ing] with the orderly operation of the educational program."[113]

Crosby's second subsection builds on the first: "2. Principal Morse's determination that 'BONG HITS FOR JESUS' advertises or advocates use of illegal drugs was reasonable and should not be second-guessed by the Court."[114] Citing six federal court decisions, two involving drug-related references and four *Fraser*-related language, Crosby argued that case law held that school administrators were better situated than courts to make judgments about the content of student speech. "Frederick continues to claim that the phrase bong hits is ambiguous and nonsensical. Principal Morse's interpretation was certainly a reasonable one, however, and should not be second-guessed by the Court."[115]

The third subsection heading reads: "3. Under *Fraser*, Principal Morse could seize the 'BONG HITS' banner even if it were not vulgar or school-sponsored and did not disrupt classroom activities."[116] David Crosby's central argument here is that the message on Joseph Frederick's banner is so unambiguously pro-drug that it is inherently "plainly offensive"— vulgar per se[117]—under *Fraser* and, hence, subject to being censored. Seeking to recast the Ninth Circuit's *Chandler* three-part categorical interpretive scheme, Crosby argued that, when dealing with pro-drug speech, the concept "plainly offensive," derived from *Fraser*, trumps both *Hazelwood* and *Tinker*. He wrote:

> . . . Frederick and the amici take a far too restrictive view of *Fraser*.
>
> The *Fraser* Court was not simply being prudish. The Court was concerned that the speech in question "intrude[d] on the work of the schools or the rights of other students," that it "undermined the school's basic educational mission," and was "wholly inconsistent with the 'fundamental values' of public school education." All of these concerns apply with equal force to messages that advocate or promote illegal drugs, such as "BONG HITS FOR JESUS." . . .

Frederick and the *amici* simply ignore the question of whether pro-drug messages ought to be treated differently: whether such messages are so plainly offensive or inconsistent with the basic educational mission of the schools as to warrant their suppression under *Fraser* . . .[118]

Almost as afterthought, Crosby completed the above sentence by writing, "or so inherently disruptive as to warrant suppression under the *Tinker* standard."[119] Clearly, Crosby hung his constitutional hat, so to speak, on the *Fraser* peg. Just as Mertz, in a key passage of his brief, sought to align his arguments with the Ninth Circuit's *Chandler* schema, Crosby mainly sought to bring his clients' case under the umbrella of the U.S. Supreme Court's *Fraser* rule.

That said, as a veteran attorney David Crosby knew a lawyer needs several arrows in his quiver. The second main section of his legal arguments seeks the cover of *Hazelwood*-related claims: "B. Principal Morse had the power to discipline Frederick because he was present with fellow students observing a school sanctioned and supervised event during school hours."[120] In an illustrative footnote where he reiterates that *Fraser* controls, Crosby refers to *Hazelwood*'s jurisdiction-conferring and authorizing force:

Amici misconstrue the district court's opinion as holding that because the banner was unfurled at a "school-sponsored" event, the school could therefore censor any message under *Hazelwood*. The district court was clearly relying on *Fraser*, not *Hazelwood*, and considered the issue of school-sponsorship or supervision only to determine the jurisdictional extent of Principal Morse's disciplinary authority.

Nevertheless, Crosby continued:

Even under *Hazelwood*, Principal Morse was entitled to suppress a pro-drug banner prominently displayed as a school-supervised event in order to prevent any inference that the School approves of such conduct or messages.[121]

Crosby's *Fraser* story follows an arc of irresponsible behavior thwarted by timely and conscientious action under fire. Deborah Morse is his story's hero. Acting decisively amid chaotic circumstances, she removed Frederick's sophomoric banner and, with it, a pro-drug message that was offensive, disruptive, and dangerous and, for these reasons, in violation of Juneau School District policies. When the district court for the District of Alaska granted her summary judgment, that court vindicated her judgment. It also held Joseph Frederick accountable. David Crosby offered the Ninth Circuit *Fraser* as a vehicle to uphold Judge John W. Sedwick's ruling and, in so doing, to reinforce school administrators' authority while forewarning potential student provocateurs.

I have said that Mertz told an injury narrative and Crosby an accountability narrative. I could just as accurately say that Mertz told a free speech narrative and Crosby a drug control narrative. In fact the latter narratives are implicit in the former—and vice versa. Yet another take on each lawyer's competing representation of his respective client's case implicates a basic, abiding tension in American constitutional law, namely that between individual rights and social order. In this regard, Doug Mertz and David Crosby were asking the Ninth Circuit to engage in a line-drawing exercise as venerable as the First Amendment itself.[122] Line drawing is what the Ninth Circuit did in its March 10, 2006, opinion.

Judge Andrew J. Kleinfeld wrote for the three-judge Ninth Circuit panel. The first sentence of his opinion for the unanimous court suggests where it was going to draw the line: "This is a First Amendment student speech case."[123] Of the two narratives explained above, the Ninth Circuit found plaintiff Frederick's more persuasive, siding with student expressive rights over school authority to punish speech it found offensive. Judge Kleinfeld's account of the facts focuses on the absence of any disruption attributable to Frederick's banner. He noted that "[i]n their answers to interrogatories, Appellees never contended that the display of the banner disrupted or was expected to disrupt classroom work."[124] Rather, Kleinfeld continued, "the principal did not rip down the sign at the rally because she anticipated or was concerned about such possible consequences. . . . She told [Frederick] to take the banner down because she 'felt that it violated the policy against displaying offensive material, including material that advertises or promotes use of illegal drug.'"[125]

Turning to legal analysis, Judge Kleinfeld commenced by explicitly rejecting the district court's—and the Juneau School District's—point of departure. Kleinfeld wrote: "The district court reasoned that *Bethel School District No. 403 v. Fraser* as opposed to *Tinker v. Des Moines Independent Community School District* governed Frederick's speech. We disagree."[126] With *Tinker* trumping *Fraser*, the defining inquiry turned on whether or not Frederick's banner resulted in disruption:

> [T]he question comes down to whether a school may, in the absence of concern about disruption of educational activities, punish or censor non-disruptive, off-campus speech by students during school-authorized activities because the speech promotes a social message contrary to the one favored by the school. The answer under controlling, long-existing precedent is plainly "No."[127]

The Ninth Circuit distinguished both *Fraser* and *Hazelwood* as inapposite. *Fraser*, the court held, dealt with sexually offensive speech, not politically offensive speech.[128] *Hazelwood*, the court held, dealt with speech occurring as part of an officially endorsed or sponsored school activity, not off-campus speech during "a Coca-Cola and Olympics activity" that students were released to attend.[129]

Judge Kleinfeld next directed his attention to what, in the court's view, was the heart of the matter: drawing a line around school authority to punish nondisruptive student speech. Because it clearly explains the Ninth Circuit's view of *Frederick v. Morse*, Kleinfeld's reasoning bears quoting in full:

> There has to be some limit on the school's authority to define its mission in order to keep *Fraser* consistent with the bedrock principle of *Tinker* that students do not "shed their constitutional rights to freedom of speech or expression at the schoolhouse gate." Had the school in that case defined its mission as instilling patriotic duty or promoting support for national objectives, it still could not have punished the students for wearing the black arm-bands. All sorts of missions

are undermined by legitimate and protected speech—a school's anti-gun mission would be undermined by a student passing around copies of John R. Lott's book, *More Guns, Less Crime*; a school's anti-alcohol mission would be undermined by a student e-mailing links to a medical study showing less heart disease among moderate drinkers than teetotalers; and a school's traffic safety missions would be undermined by a student circulating copies of articles showing that traffic cameras and automatic ticketing systems for cars that run red lights increase accidents.[130]

For the Ninth Circuit, *Frederick v. Morse* came down to a choice between "vague and nonsensical"[131] speech versus unchecked school authority. The court drew the line at Principal Morse's behavior. Under Judge Kleinfeld's opinion, Morse's basic mistake was acting on her sweeping, on-the-spot judgment that Frederick's banner was "offensive." For the court, Joseph Fredrick's banner was not analogous to Matthew Fraser's offensive campaign speech. "Sexual speech can be expected to stimulate disorder among those new to adult hormones,"[132] opined Judge Kleinfeld. Sanctioning Fraser for delivering a sexually suggestive speech during a school assembly was one thing. Removing Frederick's banner, then suspending him, crossed the line into arbitrariness. As the Ninth Circuit read precedent, in contrast to Fraser's patently lewd allusions, Frederick's cryptic allusions to drug use more resembled political speech because, like gun control, abstemiousness, and using drones to regulate traffic, antidrug policies are controversial.[133] Hence, absent disruption, "BONG HiTS 4 JESUS" was protected speech.

I said above that attorneys Crosby and Mertz asked the Ninth Circuit to engage in constitutional line drawing. In drawing the line in Joseph Frederick's favor, Judges Hall, Kleinfeld, and Wardlaw tilted the balance in favor of students' First Amendment rights over school officials' authority to maintain order. Their particular judgment is debatable. Their authority to render judgment is not. Their authority derives, in part, from a written constitution containing language in need of interpretation and application. This is what I mean when I say that the Ninth Circuit's line-drawing exercise is as venerable as the First Amendment itself. John Stuart Mill conveyed the inherent worth of line drawing as well as its intrinsically debatable character when he wrote in 1859:

> There is a limit to the legitimate interference of collective opinion with individual independence: and to find that limit, and maintain it against encroachment, is as indispensible to a good condition of human affairs, as protection against political despotism.
>
> But though this proposition is not likely to be contested in general terms, the practical question, where to place the limit—how to make the fitting adjustment between individual independence and social control—is a subject on which nearly everything remains to be done.[134]

Line drawing is valuable—and inconclusive. In other words, line drawing is political. In *Frederick v. Morse*, the Ninth Circuit weighed in on the question of where to draw the line between students' speech rights and school administrators' authority to maintain order. Not satisfied with where the three-judge panel surveyed the line, on March 21, 2006, the Juneau School District petitioned for a rehearing en banc. The Ninth Circuit denied that petition on April 18, 2006. Just over four months later, on August 28, 2006, Deborah Morse and the Juneau School District petitioned the U.S. Supreme Court to hear their case.

6

Not-So-Brief Battles,
Not Such Odd Bedfellows

JOSEPH FREDERICK had a lot of friends when he answered Deborah Morse's United States Supreme Court challenge to his victory before the Ninth Circuit Court of Appeals. Of the fifteen amicus curiae briefs filed in *Morse v. Frederick*, twelve supported respondent Frederick. Although the raw numbers of amicus briefs favored Frederick, three heavyweights sided with petitioner Morse. D.A.R.E. America[1] and the National School Boards Association[2] supported Morse. So did then U.S. Solicitor General Paul D. Clement,[3] on behalf of the United States. Whether having the most friends, or having a few influential friends, shapes judicial outcomes—or whether having friends makes any difference at all; these are fascinating, instructive, and debatable questions. There is a rich scholarly literature assaying amicus curiae briefs in American judicial process. Aspects of this literature provide useful context to telling the story about which groups and organizations sided with whom in *Morse v. Frederick*, and why. Discussing this literature sheds light on an important subtext to the "BONG HiTS" story. The amici amplify the social controversies and legal issues underlying what, on the surface, may appear to be merely a case of an uppity high school senior crossing paths with a reactive administrator. More than providing an engaging sidebar, then, the fifteen amicus briefs in *Morse v. Fredrick* are a window into key parts of the backstory.

As the expression is used in the American judicial system, the term *amicus curiae* is something of a misnomer.[4] Literally Latin for "friend of the court,"[5] the term describes a practice more accurately rendered "friend of a party" *(amicus postulator* [plaintiff] */amicus reus* [defendant]). Terminology aside, throughout American history, courts have allowed third parties to intervene in litigation on behalf of on one side or the other. Although important advantages can accrue to appellate courts from receiving amicus briefs, and while such advantages are not simply incidental, amicus briefs are primarily instrumental tools rather than altruistic assistance. They are advocacy vehicles as much as helpful aids. In 1992, Michael K. Lowman, then senior articles editor of the *American University Law Review*, now a partner at Jenner & Block warned: "No longer a mere friend of the court, the amicus has become a lobbyist, an advocate, and, most recently, the vindicator of the politically powerless."[6] Low-man read the history of amicus participation in a way that led him to be concerned that, unbridled,[7] such involvement threatens the integrity of American judicial process. Other students of amicus curiae are more sanguine or, at least, less alarmed.[8]

"oral shepardizer"[9]   "litigating amicus"[10]

Figure 6.1: Range of Amicus Roles

Key to understanding the range of opinion among these analysts is where they situate amicus briefs on an imaginary continuum (see Figure 6.1 above). This continuum displays the range of functions amici might play in judicial process, from neutral advisor to partisan advocate. At the left pole, amici are helpers, pure and simple. Their role is to facilitate a court's work by helping jurists avoid errors of law and of fact. As the term *oral shepardizer* suggests, in this mode amici might assist by validating a legal citation in support of an argument, or by pointing out citation errors, or by finding additional relevant cases for a specific point of law. Moreover, "shepardizing" amici also might provide additional pertinent information of use to a court. Although scholars disagree over whether the American amicus practice traces its roots to a similar Roman device or to English use,[11] the conventional view is that "[t]he role of amicus curiae . . . enjoys a rich pedigree . . . [which] allowed an unbiased or neutral outsider to a legal action to provide information to an appellate court in a case in which the amicus was not named as a party."[12]

This conception of amici as neutral friend of the court is deeply ingrained in American judicial consciousness. A 1979 First Circuit Court of Appeals decision, *New England Patriots Football Club v. University of Colorado*,[13] exemplifies the widespread conventional view. This case originated when several people associated with the University of Colorado sought to importune Charles L. (Chuck) Fairbanks to come coach football for the university while he was still under contract to the New England Patriots. Although Fairbanks was not a party to the resulting lawsuit, the First Circuit granted the University of Colorado counsel's request that Fairbanks be granted leave to file an amicus brief. An offended court rued its decision to allow a "self-serving" "contract-breaker"[14] to file as an amicus. The court's regret was grounded in its view that Fairbanks had abused his amicus role:

> In granting permission we had assumed, wrongly, it proved, that counsel knew what an amicus is, namely, one who, "not as parties, . . . but, just as any stranger might," *Martin v. Tapley*, 1875, 119 Mass. 116, 120, "for the assistance of the court gives information of some mat-ter of law in regard to which the court is doubtful or mistaken," *Bouvier's Law Dictionary* 1 (3d ed., 1914), 188, rather than one who gives a highly partisan ("eloquent," according to defen-dants) account of the facts.[15]

In the First Circuit's complaint we see all the elements common to the "oral shepardizer" conception of being an amicus curiae. First, amici are outsiders. Second, amici are disinterested. Third, amici serve the court. Fourth, amici provide useful information. One might characterize this view as a "good Samaritan" understanding of the amicus role.

At the other end of the continuum is the "litigating amicus." One might characterize this view as a "surreptitious party" understanding of the amicus role in that, while not formally a party to the legal action in question, a "litigating amicus" de facto becomes a "stealth" participant in that lawsuit. If the "oral shepardizer" view tends to idealize amici, the "litigating amicus" view can demonize amici. Put differently, while the "oral shepardizer" view tends to celebrate amici as salutary, indeed necessary, features of the American legal landscape, the "litigating amicus" view criticizes the practice as burdensome and a threat to adversarial norms underlying American jurisprudence. For the former, "the amicus brief is an important part of 'deliberative democracy,' a theory that favors fully informed debate as a condition to democratic society."[16] For the latter, "[t]he amicus curiae device may be likened to democracy . . . but its application to everyday litigation would be impracticable, resulting in confusion and delay."[17]

Located somewhere along the "Range of Amicus Roles" continuum are two bodies of literature that might be described as more empirical and corrective than normative writings tending toward one or the other poles. One might term these works "realistic" in the sense that, accepting amicus briefs as a key institution firmly embedded in American judicial practice, their authors either seek to determine the influence such devices have on judicial decision making, or they seek to reform the tool.

This literature, discussed below, accepts, as its point of departure, the fallacy of what law professor Stuart Banner called "the myth of the neutral amicus."[18] In an important 2003 article published in *Constitutional Commentary*, Banner effectively debunked "this supposed history"[19] with an empirical study of 308 reported cases with amicus participation, between 1790 and 1890.[20] Here is how Banner traces the lineage of the misnomer ("friend of the court") that derives from the neutrality myth:

> The misnomer is conventionally understood to be a vestige of a time when *amici* actually did render disinterested advice, for the purpose of helping the court rather than one of the parties. The original role of the amicus, on this view, was that of a neutral bystander, someone without a stake in the outcome of the case, who offered information to the court gratuitously, just to help the court avoid error. The function of the *amicus* has changed, the story goes, but the name has not. This understanding of the *amicus*'s history traces back to a 1963 *Yale Law Journal* article by the political scientist Samuel Krislov, who located the supposed "shift from neutrality to advocacy" in the nineteenth century. Krislov's conclusion has been repeated many times since.[21]

In light of Banner's data, Krislov's influential conclusion was wrong. Since 1790, there has been no "shift" in the function of amici. Their function always has included advocacy:

> There were more neutral *amici* than partisan *amici* in 1790–1820 (thirteen of twenty cases). In 1821–1830 the numbers of neutral and partisan *amici* were equal. In every decade from 1831–1840 through 1881–1890, however, there were many more partisan *amici* than neutral *amici*. After 1831–1840 the percentage of *amici* who were neutral never rose above 18%.[22]

Banner concludes:

> These percentages suggest that since 1790 there never has been a time in American practice in which the *amicus curiae* was exclusively neutral. The *amicus* was most neutral before the 1830s, but even then it was a device that seems to have been understood to be available regardless of whether the *amicus* was neutral or partisan.[23]

The left-hand pole of the continuum in Figure 6.1 is labeled "*oral* shepardizer." One of Banner's insights is his suggestion that the practice of neutral amicus curiae was an artifact of nineteenth-century legal disputation in which verbal argumentation predominated. It was the oral mode in which lawyers debated, then, that fostered an environment in which neutrality existed. "As more American case reports and treatises began to be published," notes Banner, "there would have been fewer occasions on which a lawyer hanging around the courtroom would have had knowledge of a relevant precedent not known by the court or the lawyers for the parties. As lawyers began to make their legal arguments primarily in written briefs rather than in open court, eavesdroppers to litigation would have become less likely to offer unsolicited suggestions."[24]

In his nationally syndicated newspaper column Will Rogers wrote on October 20, 1929, about the lobbying activities of one Joseph R. Grundy, a Republican who served as president of the Pennsylvania Manufacturers' Association from 1909 to 1930. A leading protectionist, Grundy was lobbying the Senate at the time to pass additional tariff legislation. Rogers' exact words in his column that day were, with Rogers' own spelling and grammar:

> I knew you was going to ask, "What is Grundy doing in Washington?" That is where his offices are.
>
> "What's his offices doing in Washington when he is President of the Manafactures Association of Pennsylvania? Why ain't they in Pennsylvania?"
>
> Say, Grundy has more offices in Washington than Hoover. Hoover only tells the Senate what they should do. Grundy tells 'em what they will do.[25]

A bit over half a century later, two political scientists, Karen O'Connor and Lee Epstein, squarely brought amicus briefs within the purview of lobbying.[26] O'Connor and Epstein demonstrated that what Stuart Banner had shown to be the case in the nineteenth century, also held true for the late twentieth century: amicus briefs were a form of advocacy—of lobbying. In so doing, they initiated a line of inquiry that has generated an influential body of scholarly literature illustrating, if not definitively explaining, the influence of amicus briefs on courts. O'Connor and Epstein's foil was two publications, authored by political scientist Nathan Hakman, in which Hakman "disparaged"[27] the argument that interest groups employ amicus briefs to lobby the U.S. Supreme Court as "Political Science 'folklore.'"[28] Clearly, Hakman did not buy Krislov's 1963 message about the shift "from friendship to advocacy."[29] O'Connor and Epstein chided that Hakman's research was outdated[30] and that, consequently, his conclusions ran counter to the interest-group paradigm of politics supported by more current research on amicus participation. Their updated judgment was that

[a] legion of scholars has described the judicial lobbying efforts of interest groups. . . . Virtually all recent research . . . has found evidence of a significant systematic organizational role in Supreme Court litigation. . . . Whether or not Hakman was correct in disparaging the "folklore" of studies of judicial interest group activity, the same conclusion could not be drawn today.[31]

O'Connor and Epstein reinvigorated scholarly inquiry into judicial lobbying via amicus briefs.[32] Subsequent to their seminal "Research Note," "the literature of amicus briefs has focused on interest group use of the [Supreme] Court,"[33] and other judicial forums. Embarking from the premise that amicus are advocates, recent scholarship has focused (significantly, if not exclusively) on understanding the influence of such lobbying.

At the end of the 1980s, the same decade that O'Connor and Epstein rekindled scholarly interest in amicus advocacy, two other political scientists published an analysis of amicus briefs and "agenda setting" in the U.S. Supreme Court. Gregory A. Caldeira and John R. Wright's important 1988 article, published in the discipline's preeminent journal, the *American Political Science Review*, is a study of how amicus briefs affect Supreme Court justices' decisions regarding petitions for writs of certiorari.[34] Caldeira and Wright hypothesized that the "greater number of *amicus curiae* briefs filed for a given case—either in favor of, or in opposition to, *certiorari*—the greater the likelihood that the case will be granted a *writ of certiorari*."[35] In other words, Caldeira and Wright theorized that participation by amicus advocates at the "gatekeeping"[36] stage of Supreme Court decision-making figures in persuading the justices to open their courthouse gate to a full hearing on the merits. "The presence of *amici* during case selection," Caldeira and Wright observed, "communicates to the Supreme Court information about the constellation of interests involved, and this information . . . is both valued and heeded by the justices and their clerks."[37] Based on their data analysis, Caldeira and Wright concluded that "our statistical results indicate strong support for our primary hypothesis . . . the proposition that justices pay close attention to the demands of outside parties when making *certiorari* decisions."[38] In an article based on the same data set, published two years after their initial analysis, Caldeira and Wright revisited the participation of amici at the "cert" stage of the U.S. Supreme Court review process.[39] They reported that 29 percent of amicus participation took place at the agenda-setting stage. "These numbers attest not only to the perceived importance of the Court's case selection process, but they also reveal that the overall level of amicus activity is considerably higher than that observed in full opinion cases only."[40] Demonstrably, then, amicus advocacy at the "cert" stage is both extensive and effective.

Both of Caldeira's and Wright's studies are based on data derived from the 1982 term of the U.S. Supreme Court. Recently, Adam Chandler posted a study of "private groups and advocacy organizations pushing cert. petitions" in which he drew on a sample of U.S. Supreme Court cases from between May 19, 2004, and August 15, 2007.[41] Chandler's counting shows how thoroughly amicus briefing at the pre-merits stage is dominated by pro-business and anti-regulation groups.[42] More pertinent to the concerns of this chapter, Chandler also shows that these business-oriented "repeat players"[43] are highly successful players in terms of writs of certiorari granted. The overall success rate is 27.13 percent, ranging from 39.13 percent (Washington Legal Foundation) to 0 percent (Reporters Committee for Freedom of the Press, and Society of Professional Journalists).[44] Chandler cautions against exaggerating the significance of his findings, while nevertheless relating them to Caldeira and Wright's research:

> [T]he influence of a cert.-stage amicus brief should not be overestimated from the success percentages of the top sixteen groups. While the overall success rate of the groups in the chart is far higher than the success rate of a cert. petition in general (about 27% compared to a general success rate of less than 5% for a paid petition), it also stands to reason that the petitions they throw their weight behind would alone have a reasonable chance of being granted. Moreover, the 27% overall success rate is inflated by the instances in which multiple groups from the top sixteen filed briefs at the cert. stage in the same granted cases.
>
> Nevertheless, political science professors Greg Caldeira and Jack Wright . . . have shown briefs of cert.-stage *amici*, whether in support of granting the petition or not "substantially increase" the likelihood that the Court will grant.[45]

Taken together, these three modest quantitative studies indicate that amicus advocacy, while not "invincible,"[46] wields influence during the agenda-formation stage of the U.S. Supreme Court's review process.

Suggestive qualitative analysis comes from a recent article by Richard J. Lazarus, "Advocacy Matters Before and Within the Supreme Court: Transforming the Court by Transforming the Bar."[47] Lazarus argues that, beginning in the mid-1980s a revitalized bar of the U.S. Supreme Court has been transformed into a coterie of specialized, expert lawyer elites. Lazarus keys his analysis on prestigious law firms seeking to build in-house Supreme Court proficiency (and success), "replicating"[48] that of the U.S. Solicitor General's office, by hiring former solicitor generals, initially Rex Lee by Sidley Austin in 1985. Another example of a firm hiring a former solicitor general is Kenneth W. Starr, currently of counsel with Kirkland & Ellis. Starr argued Deborah Morse's case before the Supreme Court. Efforts to create a "shadow Solicitor General's Office"[49] kindled kindred efforts by states, corporations, and business groups such as, preeminently, the U.S. Chamber of Commerce to hire personnel with Supreme Court track records. "It is hard . . . ," writes Lazarus, "to sort out to what extent the consequent rise in the Supreme Court Bar was primarily supply- rather than demand-driven. What seems most likely is that a symbiotic relationship arose between the two."[50]

Lazarus finds no difficulty in specifying one salient consequence of the rise in the Supreme Court Bar for shaping the Supreme Court's plenary agenda: a transformed Supreme Court Bar is altering the kind of cases the Court is agreeing to hear. He refers to this process as "sheeting the plenary docket."[51] In spite of a significant decline in the overall number of cases the Court agrees to hear, the sort of cases granted cert. has been profoundly shaped by elite members of the Supreme Court Bars' amicus advocacy on behalf of corporate interests. Lazarus describes an ensemble of factors whereby expert advocacy coalesces with workload, in-house time constraints, division of labor (Supreme Court law clerks reviewing cert. petitions), and, for lack of a better term, "clubiness"[52] to affect case selection. Here is how Lazarus explains effective written advocacy at work:

The expert Supreme Court advocates do not merely discern the existing priorities of the Justices. They deliberately and systematically educate the Justices concerning what the priorities should be. Through repeated filings of cases and *amicus* support from weighty authorities and interest groups, the advocates identify what legal issues are sufficiently important for the Court to resolve. They demonstrate that controversy in the lower court arising from an existing Supreme Court precedent, federal constitutional provision, or federal statute or regulation warrants the Court's attention. They establish the serious practical consequences of the problem. And, even if their presentation is not enough, standing alone, to convince the Court to grant review, the expert advocates at least persuade the Court to ask the Solicitor General to file an *amicus* brief at the jurisdictional stage addressing the question whether *certiorari* is warranted.[53]

Lazarus invokes the spirits of former Solicitor General John W. Davis and former Solicitor General and Supreme Court Justice Thurgood Marshall as representing two powerful complementary lawyering skills—craft and strategy[54]—characteristic of the current generation of elite Supreme Court advocates. He worries that the very efficacy of the new Supreme Court Bar, deployed to advance business interests, creates an "advocacy gap."[55] Lazarus notes, nevertheless, that one partially offsetting trend is the tendency for elite Supreme Court advocates to take on pro bono work on behalf of a greater diversity of clients.

Ken Starr's pro bono representation of Deborah Morse and the Juneau School District before the Supreme Court exemplifies this trend. At the time Morse and her colleagues were considering a U.S. Supreme Court appeal, Rick Richmond[56] was a partner in Kirkland & Ellis, and a colleague of Ken Starr's. Richmond was the principal in-house proponent of Kirkland & Ellis taking on Deborah Morse's and the Juneau School District's case. Richmond and Starr, among others, collaborated on the petitioners' brief in *Morse v. Frederick*. Starr, joined by Deputy Solicitor General Edwin S. Kneedler, argued Deborah Morse's and the Juneau School Board's case before the Supreme Court on March 19, 2007.

On September 9, 2008, I interviewed Rick Richmond about his firm's involvement in *Morse v. Frederick*.[57] He explained that David Crosby, the attorney who represented Deborah Morse, initiated contact with a telephone call. Prior to Crosby's phone call, neither Richmond nor anyone else at Kirkland & Ellis had any relationship with any of the parties to *Morse v. Frederick*. According to Richmond, attorney Crosby told him that his client had lost at the Ninth Circuit Court of Appeals and had no funds to pursue an appeal. Would Ken Starr and Kirkland & Ellis be willing to take on Deborah Morse's case pro bono? Crosby asked. Crosby's request initiated what Richmond described as a process of in-house "winnowing" by Kirkland & Ellis's pro bono committee.[58] Exercising "healthy skepticism,"[59] this group weighed a mix of logistic, tactical, and policy factors, leading it eventually to decide to represent Deborah Morse on appeal. First, the committee asked, are there individuals in the firm who would be interested in taking on Morse's case? Second, does this case merit allocating the firm's available resources? Third, in light of the fact that Alaska has relatively lenient marijuana laws and, given the "Cert. Pool" procedure,[60] which delegates to law clerks at the Court the responsibility for reviewing and summarizing petitions for the justice for whom they work, is there a better than negligible chance we can get cert.? The key is to capture the Court's attention, especially given the fact that "the odds are, and always have been, strongly against a grant of review."[61]

According to Richmond, several circumstances militated in favor of Kirkland & Ellis signing on to Morse's appeal. First, the Ninth Circuit's holding that Morse was personally liable for confronting then suspending Frederick was troubling. This ruling might catch the attention of the justices, Richmond recalled thinking. Second, the Ninth Circuit's reputation for being exceptionally liberal made its decision in *Frederick v. Morse*—from Kirkland & Ellis' point of view—an inviting vehicle to challenge that Court's holding. Third, the fact pattern in the "BONG HiTS" case made it "odd and interesting."[62] It was the sort of case that might catch the attention of Supreme Court law clerks and just might command the votes of four justices required to grant cert. Fourth, Ken Starr is widely respected in appellate lawyers' circles. He is often recruited for Supreme Court work, being asked for his judgment, advice, and editing skills. "His name means a lot at the Supreme Court."[63] Ultimately, the pro bono committee reported to David Crosby that "[Crosby's] getting Ken, and Kirkland & Ellis."[64]

Before Ken Starr would be able to argue Deborah Morse's case before the U.S. Supreme Court, four justices had to vote to grant her petition for a writ of certiorari. A writ of certiorari ("cert.") is an order that a higher court issues to a lower court, to certify the records of a particular decision to the superior court for its review. Currently, cert. is the primary path to full appellate review of a case by the Supreme Court.[65] The "rule of four" is an informal Supreme Court procedure, adopted after Congress expanded the Court's discretionary docket in the Judiciary Act of 1925, through which the Court grants cert. to a petitioner upon the votes of four justices to do so.[66]

Deborah Morse's petition for a writ of certiorari was filed on August 28, 2006. One month later, on September 28, 2006, two prominent organizations—D.A.R.E. America (Drug Abuse Resistance Education) and the National School Boards Association (NSBA)[67]—filed amicus curiae briefs supporting Morse's petition. As noted above, "amicus advocacy . . . wields influence during the agenda-formation stage of the U.S. Supreme Court's review process."[68] Both statistically valid relationships, and an advocacy link, suggest that amicus briefs increase the likelihood that the justices will vote to hear a case. Further evidence, demonstrating how cert. votes relate to votes on the merits, suggests that the justices vote "strategically," that is, with an eye to outcomes. This evidence comes from research reported in a 1999 article, "Sophisticated Voting and Gate-Keeping in the Supreme Court."[69] The researchers, political scientists Gregory A. Caldeira, John R. Wright, and Christopher J. W. Zorn, argue that "justices engage in sophisticated voting, defined as looking forward to the decision on the merits and acting with that potential outcome in mind."[70] They add:

> [Our] findings provide solid support for the proposition that justices employ sophisticated strategies when voting on *cert*. In particular, we show a substantial relationship between not only a justice's own ideological position and his or her vote, but also between the position of the other members of the Court and that vote.[71]

Although at this point in time we are not privy to either the conversations preceding or the cert. vote itself regarding *Morse*, within the Court's "sanctum sanctorum,"[72] given the eventual Supreme Court outcome in *Morse v. Frederick*, and knowing how the justices voted on the merits, it is reasonable to speculate that five members of the Court—Alito, Kennedy, Roberts, Scalia, and Thomas—voted to grant Deborah Morse's cert. petition. Again, in the context of the final vote and the ultimate alignment of these justices, it seems valid to conjecture that the NSBA and D.A.R.E. briefs figured in that vote to grant cert. By articulating specific arguments tactically designed to convince these five justices to vote strategically to grant cert., NSBA and D.A.R.E. helped to boost Deborah Morse's case onto the Court's plenary agenda.

The NSBA and D.A.R.E. amicus briefs supporting Deborah Morse's petition for certiorari can be understood as complementary. Each raised two aspects of the same zero-tolerance argument: high school students should not be able to advocate illegal drug use, and school officials should have the authority to sanction any students who do—a "one-two" rhetorical punch, of sorts.

The NSBA proffered two major "reasons for granting the writ."[73] The NSBA's first reason is: "[The Supreme Court] Should Provide Much Needed Clarification of Student Free Speech Jurisprudence to Guide Schools in Balancing Students' Free Speech Rights with the Schools' Need to Perform Their Educational Mission."[74] This argument asks the Court to grant cert. in order "to afford critical guidance to school administrators regarding student free speech rights."[75] This first "clarification" rationale has six subheadings. These can be read to consist of a major premise follow by five subsidiary requests for judicial explication. The NSBA's major premise sought a ruling that school districts can incorporate combating drugs as part of their educational mission:

> The Ninth Circuit's decision in *Frederick* . . . disregards precedent from this Court and other courts, and circumscribes the manner in which school districts may *define* and *implement* their educational mission. In essence, the Ninth Circuit minimizes a school district's legitimate and good faith efforts to enforce anti-drug messages as part of their educational mission by simply concluding that the Juneau School District was "not entitled to suppress speech that undermines whatever mission the school defines for itself."[76]

The NSBA brief continued:

> By imposing restrictions on the right of school districts *to establish their own* education mission, including anti-drug messages, and to uphold this mission by regulating inconsistent student speech, the Ninth Circuit apparently sought to prevent what it viewed as unbridled school discretion from swallowing the *Fraser* rule. But in fact, what the court effectively did was to eliminate the rule entirely. Accordingly, this Court should grant review to remove the Ninth Circuit's unwarranted restrictions on a school district's right to *define* its educational mission.[77]

The NSBA's linchpin cert. argument was that school administrators required a Supreme Court ruling that would free them from the Ninth Circuit's unjustifiably corseted reading of *Fraser*.[78] In other words, school administrators needed expansive discretion to "define and implement" their respective districts' "education mission" so as to combat illegal drug messages. The breadth of the rule for which the NSBA was asking is illustrated by the sixth of its derivative clarifications: "This Court Should Clarify Whether 'Bong Hits 4 Jesus' Is Speech Worthy of First Amendment Protection."[79] Here the NSBA argued, essentially, that regardless of any message Joseph Frederick was attempting to convey—"nonsense" or pro-drug—school officials should have the authority to regulate student speech. This argument envisioned school administrators as ultimate First Amendment campus watch dogs, able to determine what speech, if any, inside the schoolhouse gate deserved protection, and what speech could be proscribed. "In other words, whether the words are deemed nonsense or a pro-drug message, Principal Morse's action in regulating [Frederick's] speech would be constitutionally acceptable."[80]

The NSBA argued that the second reason the Supreme Court should grant cert. is that "The Ninth Circuit's Departure from Well-Established Qualified Immunity Principles Denies School Administrators Their Longstanding Authority to Ensure a Positive Learning Environment."[81] Although standing on its own bottom, this rationale also can be seen as related to the NSBA's basic concern to enhance school administrators' discretion. The way in which the NSBA frames its qualified immunity argument makes the link. Administrators, noted the NSBA, often must make consequential snap judgments, sometimes under stressful and rapidly shifting circumstances. The Ninth Circuit's rule imposing damages on Deborah Morse directly penalizes her for doing her job. "Administrators must make these decisions at the risk of a legal challenge, and if the Ninth Circuit is correct, personal liability."[82] Adopting a novel twist on a phrase well-known in First Amendment jurisprudence, the NSBA worries that the Ninth Circuit's "refusal to provide Principal Morse with qualified immunity creates an untenable *chilling* effect on the hundreds of thousands of administrators who are charged with maintaining order and discipline in our schools and with ensuring that students, while in our schools' charge, receive messages that promote the district's educational goals."[83] For the NSBA then, the Ninth Circuit added injury to insult by limiting school officials' discretion, and punishing them for exercising it.

D.A.R.E.'s amicus brief complements the NSBA's. D.A.R.E.'s central argument focused on the authority of high school officials to fight adolescent illicit drug use: "The Decision Below Forces Schools to Tolerate Student Advocacy of Illegal Drug Use at School Events."[84] D.A.R.E. argued that the Supreme Court's review

> is warranted to confirm that courts must defer to a school's decision to prohibit pro-drug speech[.] . . . The Ninth Circuit's ignorance of the student drug use problem, or its willingness to tolerate that problem, should not be allowed to hamstring our school authorities and endanger the health and safety of our children.[85]

D.A.R.E. attorneys sandwiched its defense of school officials' authority between a discussion of the "enormous proportions" of "teenage drug abuse" in the United States[86] and its assertion that the Ninth Circuit's ruling is "unworkable" and "unenforceable."[87] In the first instance D.A.R.E. painted a picture of widespread regular drug usage across the country—particularly among Alaska youths. "In Alaska, the drug problem is particularly severe," D.A.R.E. observed, "and especially with marijuana. Sixty percent of Juneau students have used marijuana by the time they graduate from high school. And, in a 2003 survey of Alaska high school students, 6.5% reported using marijuana on school property within the last thirty days, and 13.1% reported that they had used marijuana for the first time *before* they turned 13."[88] Second, D.A.R.E. contended that, given the nationwide drug epidemic, particularly acute in Alaska, the Ninth Circuit's decision is incoherent and threatening. Appropriating the same civil liberties imagery as the NSBA brief, D.A.R.E. argued the Ninth Circuit's "sweeping holding— that pro-drug messages are neither offensive nor inherently disruptive—combined with an unworkable disruption standard, and the threat of personal liability for any misstep, will *chill* enforcement of anti-drug policies far beyond the requirements of the First Amendment."[89]

Perhaps most striking is D.A.R.E's specification of the "educational mission" that school officials ought to be authorized to enforce. We have seen how the NSBA argued on behalf of school administrators' expansive discretion to "define and implement" their respective districts' education mission. D.A.R.E. reduces that mission to zero tolerance. The D.A.R.E. brief cites *Vernonia*[90] and *Earls*[91]—both random drug search cases, neither involving student speech—to illustrate its point that the U.S. Supreme Court, unlike the Ninth Circuit Court of Appeals, recognizes the fact that "the nationwide drug epidemic makes the war against drugs a pressing concern in every school."[92] This national emergency requires a commensurate response, and that response is the very one the Ninth Circuit vitiates:

> [T]he Ninth Circuit failed to recognize the school's interest in enforcing a zero-tolerance policy for pro-drug student messages. . . . In fact, the decision below itself exemplifies the perception that the Juneau School Board policy is designed to combat: that illegal drug use by high school students is no big deal.[93]

D.A.R.E. countered that student illegal drug use, especially in Alaska, is a very big deal. Given this epidemic, student advocacy of drug use also is a big deal. In light of these two circumstances, the Ninth Circuit's ruling frustrating enforcement of zero-tolerance policies toward student drug speech is the biggest deal of all. "If allowed to stand, the decision will send the message that courts, rather than schools, have the exclusive say on what manner of speech is 'plainly offensive' to the educational functions of the public schools."[94]

D.A.R.E. and the NSBA filed their amicus briefs supporting the petition for a writ of certiorari that Deborah Morse and the Juneau School Board had filed on August 28, 2006. Ken Starr is listed on that petition as counsel of record.[95] Rick Richmond reflected on how he and his colleagues perceived key aspects of their clients' case.[96] In constitutional terms, he said the litigation raised questions pertaining to whether a kid can say and do whatever he wants in a school setting. "Kids are not free agents in school," he opined. Educationally, *Morse v. Frederick* is a "pretty serious case. Here's a principal doing her job, acting in a way that seems not to be controversial, and she could get herself and the school district sued." As a social matter, Richmond said that the case involved the serious problem of drugs and youth. Kirkland & Ellis' petition addressed all of these concerns; concerns that were reinforced by arguments made by D.A.R.E. and the NSBA in their respective amicus briefs.

The first sentence of Kirkland & Ellis' petition nicely summarizes its two key arguments, as well as their importance: "In a case that has drawn the attention—and deep concern—

of school boards and administrators nationwide, the Ninth Circuit has profoundly upset settled understandings of First Amendment and qualified immunity principles."[97] Most of the petition, eleven of sixteen pages devoted to articulating reasons for granting the writ, focuses on asking the Supreme Court to clarify "whether the First Amendment requires public schools to tolerate mixed messages about illegal drugs."[98]

The Kirkland & Ellis attorneys divided their First Amendment analysis into five sections. The collective message is that the Ninth Circuit's March 10, 2006, ruling in *Frederick v. Morse*[99] is out of step, out of touch, and disruptive. First, the petition directs the Supreme Court's attention to "the so-called *Tinker-Fraser-Hazelwood* trilogy,"[100] as the basic framework within which lower courts have interpreted student speech rights under the First Amendment. Second, despite the fact that "not all student speech falls neatly into"[101] the *Tinker-Fraser-Hazelwood* trilogy categories,[102] the petitioners make a case that lower courts other than the Ninth Circuit, and commentators, and school boards together with Juneau's—all these entities agree that "schools enjoy authority to proscribe student expression promoting illegal substances without any heightened evidentiary requirement (of showing disruption to school operations)."[103] "The Ninth Circuit has dramatically altered the legal landscape."[104] Third, the petitioners hold that the Ninth Circuit's "inflexible"[105] approach "is at war with"[106] the Supreme Court's view that school boards and school administrators should "enjoy considerable deference in carrying out their demanding and sensitive responsibilities"—especially in the context of adolescent illegal drug use.[107] Fourth, in comparison with the Ninth Circuit's "muddled message as to what constitutes permissible school speech,"[108] petitioners urge that school districts require "definitive guidance"[109] that will afford them "significant latitude in discouraging substance abuse."[110] Fifth, because teenage drug use is so dangerous, petitioners conclude that pro-drug messages targeting adolescents need to be treated differently under the First Amendment, a conclusion petitioners say is supported by Supreme Court precedents relating to speech promoting other hazardous substances. "By refusing to differentiate the pro-drug message on Frederick's banner from the armbands in *Tinker*, the Ninth Circuit trivializes the drug crisis in our nation's schools."[111]

Kirkland & Ellis' First Amendment analysis is of a piece with its two amici's arguments. The trajectory of all three arguments supporting a grant of cert. is that the Ninth Circuit's decision in *Frederick v. Morse*, by limiting and punishing Deborah Morse's exercise of discretion that January 24, 2002, on Glacier Avenue, cast a chill over her ability to enforce legitimate school district policy and, in so doing, undercut the war on drugs. Although there are differences between the petition and its two amici, these are matters of emphasis. Kirkland & Ellis' petition is relatively more legalistic. It focused on clashes between the Ninth Circuit's *Frederick* opinion and other lower courts' and law writers'. It also highlighted the distance separating the Ninth Circuit's restrictive view of school authority from the Supreme Court's more deferential approach. The two amici briefs are relatively more policy oriented. Unsurprisingly, the D.A.R.E. amicus brief sets its sights on how the Ninth Circuit's *Frederick* opinion jeopardized efforts to combat teenagers using illegal drugs. Also unsurprising is the NSBA's concern with how *Frederick* straitjacketed school administrators, not only in their exercise of authority but also in their ability to define the educational mission underpinning that authority. In fine, all three documents sought to persuade the Supreme Court to review the Ninth Circuit Court of Appeals' *Frederick* ruling because that lower court made grave errors of law and policy needing remedy.

Responding on Joseph Frederick's behalf, attorney Douglas Mertz argued there are four reasons why the petition for a writ of certiorari should be denied.[112] Before specifying these reasons, Mertz laid out a four-and-a-half page "counter-statement of the case." Mertz's counterstatement was central to his view of the case that the Juneau School District's (together with Principal Morse) action as largely premised on the petitioners having "misstated facts and ignored other facts."[113] "The actual facts of this case," Mertz began, "are hard to recognize from Petitioner's statement."[114] Mertz was not concerned about minor errant facts and trivial details. But for these errors, he held, the petitioners would have no case. J. D. Tuccille nicely captured Mertz's position when Tuccille posted to his blog, Disloyal Opposition: "Does the authority of school officials reach beyond the classroom—even off school grounds? . . . What's important to remember is that, even if Frederick had pulled his stunt on school grounds, the case wouldn't be a slam-dunk for school officials. . . . But Frederick was, in fact, on a public street."[115]

Mertz's counterstatement dovetails with his first reason why cert. should not be granted: "The facts of this case simply do not present the issues on which the petitioners seek certiorari." In Chapter 5, I distinguish the "injury narrative" Mertz presented from the "accountability narrative" recounted by David Crosby, the school district's and Deborah Morse's attorney. The former recounts a story about Frederick being deprived of his First Amendment rights. The latter tells a story about Morse enforcing school antidrug policies. "Injury versus accountability—the opposing narratives woven by attorneys Doug Mertz and David Crosby set up their divergent legal arguments."[116] Not only this. These two opposing narratives also rested on widely different versions of what had happened on January 24, 2002. Ultimately, the outcome each party sought was traceable to Morse's and Frederick's antithetical accounts. Mertz keys his opposition brief to contesting Morse's and the Juneau School District's version of the facts:

> The petition seeks a writ of *certiorari* based on a factual scenario that is not presented in this case[.] . . . Respondent's speech did not occur on campus, did not occur at a school-sponsored event, and did not cause any disruption of the educational process. Based on those actual facts, the holding below is a narrow one, and fully consistent with this Court's controlling precedents. It is the petitioners who seek to change the law based on an idiosyncratic set of facts and without any clearly demonstrated need. This Court should decline that invitation.[117]

Second, Mertz sought to show that "there is no conflict among the circuits." His basic argument is that circuit court opinions agree that on-campus student displays (which Frederick's banner was not) of what school officials might interpret as "pro-drug" messages are protected speech—absent a showing of disruption. Third, Mertz debunks the petitioners' portrayal of the Ninth Circuit's ruling as causing a "crisis among schools throughout this nation by disturbing a settled expectation about pre-existing law . . . [N]othing could be farther from the truth."[118] "This case," claims Mertz:

arises in a unique factual setting that is not likely to recur: a student who had not been to school that day joined with non-students to display a banner, off school grounds, with a political message utilizing parody, during an event that was not sponsored by the school but which students were allowed to leave school and watch. Such idiosyncratic facts simply do not provide an appropriate vehicle for this Court's review of First Amendment rules that have been well-settled for nearly two decades.[119]

Fourth, Mertz addressed the qualified immunity dispute. Answering the petitioners' arguments, Mertz characterizes their objections as "result-oriented and not based in fact."[120] In point of fact, he says, the Ninth Circuit quoted the *Saucier* test correctly and applied it accurately to the case at hand, holding "that a reasonable principal in Morse's shoes would have understood that Frederick's suspension was unlawful under *Tinker*. None of those holdings is surprising or exceptional."[121]

The not-so-brief battle over the Juneau School Board's and Deborah Morse's petition for a writ of certiorari concluded with a reply memorandum written and filed by their Kirkland & Ellis attorneys on October 9, 2006. Short in length, running ten pages, the Kirkland & Ellis reply is long on pointed characterizations. Respondent's opposition brief, assert Starr and his colleagues, amounts to "caviling." It "obfuscates the record and paints a misleading portrait of governing law." It "weaves a web of semantic quibbles, misleading factual characterizations, and record-barren assertions." All this in the first paragraph. At the end of the first page, the respondent's brief is dismissed as a "mosaic of wishful thinking."[122]

In the remaining nine pages, the Kirkland & Ellis lawyers revisit their three main arguments for granting cert. First, "This Case Raises Vital Issues of Practical Importance under the First Amendment in the Recurring Context of Student Speech."[123] Here petitioners' lawyers sought to rebut Mertz's "baseless"[124] argument that the School Board's and Morse's case is "idiosyncratic."[125] Rather, *Morse v. Frederick* "presents an attractive vehicle for shaping the cacophonous body of First Amendment law in the context of school officials seeking to enforce policies against promoting illegal substances."[126] Once again, the clash between Frederick's injury narrative and Morse's accountability narrative is joined. Second, "The Instability and Confusion Infecting the Law of Student Speech Have Been Exacerbated in Recent Weeks."[127] Here respondent's argument that no conflict exists between circuit courts is labeled "wrong" and a "law office pretense." Reading several lower court decisions pertinent to varieties of student speech, the memorandum seeks to show that the respondent's opposition brief is "an exercise in willful blindness," erroneous assertion, and distorted holdings[128] Third, "The Ninth Circuit's Qualified Immunity Analysis Departs from This Court's Jurisprudence in a Profoundly Unsettling Manner."[129] Here the petitioner's accountability narrative was associated with concern to shield school administrators as they carry out their essential duties. "If qualified immunity can be so recklessly tossed aside, as it was in *Frederick*, then the tens of thousands of public school officials who support this petition will find themselves preoccupied with litigation risks when called upon to fulfill their vital role in maintaining school discipline and decorum."[130]

With all the parties' documents, and those of the two amici, pertaining to the question of certiorari in hand by early October 2006, the U.S. Supreme Court conferred about *Morse v. Fred-*

erick for slightly less than two months. The Court granted cert. on December 1, 2006. Merits briefs, and any replies, were to be filed by February 16, 2007. This deadline was later extended to February 20, 2007, for the respondent, and to March 12, 2007, for the petitioners' reply brief.

Having jousted over the issue of granting certiorari for six months—the first phase of the two-stage Supreme Court review process—the parties rejoined the fight, this time over the merits. As during the first phase, the amici curiae allied with each party. Supporting Deborah Morse and the Juneau School Board were D.A.R.E. America, the National School Boards Association, and the Solicitor General of the United States. These entities, "heavyweights" as I characterized them at the beginning of this chapter, were outnumbered by the twelve groups supporting Joseph Frederick.[131] As with the cert. phase, there is a valuable literature analyzing the ways in which amicus curiae briefs influence Supreme Court decision making on the merits. This literature can be summarized as scrutinizing a "group model," an "informational model," or a "litigator model" explanation of Supreme Court participation and outcomes. These are not air-tight categories. For instance, it has been argued that when interest groups engage in direct discord with opponent amici they "alter the information environment at the Court by drawing the justices' attention to points of law and fact in their opponent's briefs."[132] Or, as another example: "Members of the U.S. Supreme Court need reliable information. Experienced lawyers know how to provide it."[133] Briefly summarizing the landscape of recent, salient empirical research provides a useful backdrop to the ultimate round of (also not so) brief battles before the Supreme Court in *Morse*.

Although different researchers explore the question of amici curiae influence and the choices Supreme Court justices make on the merits, from differing angles, employing different methodologies, and arriving at different conclusions, as above regarding amici and cert. grants,[134] it is possible to synthesize a prevailing view. That view has three elements: (1) amicus briefs filed by various groups matter, (2) especially when filed by experienced counsel (conspicuously, the solicitor general), and (3) what makes amicus briefs matter is the information they provide. Thus all three explanations—the "group model," "informational model," and "litigator model"—come into play. Jenner & Block partner and frequent Supreme Court advocate Bruce J. Ennis accurately summarized the gist of the prevailing view in a 1984 article, "Effective Amicus Briefs." "Let's begin," Ennis started his article, "by dispelling . . . common misconceptions about amicus briefs." He continued:

> The first is that amicus briefs are not very important; that they are at best only icing on the cake. In reality, they are often the cake itself. Amicus briefs have shaped judicial decisions in many more cases than is commonly realized. Occasionally, a case will be decided on a ground suggested only by an amicus, not by the parties. Frequently, judicial rulings, and thus their precedential value, will be narrower or broader than the parties had urged, because of a persuasive amicus brief. Courts often rely on factual information, cases or analytical approaches provided only by an amicus. A good idea is a good idea, whether it is contained in an amicus brief or a brief of a party.[135]

Ennis' analysis provides tantalizing insight into how Joseph Frederick's amici moderated the Supreme Court's majority opinion in *Morse v. Frederick*.[136] This particular aspect of the broader story about student speech rights and school administrators' discretion can be understood to entail Joseph Frederick's amici successfully engaging in "damage control" by influencing Justice Alito's concurring opinion that narrows the majority's endorsement of school officials' authority to censor "drug-related" student speech. There is more on this aspect below, and in Chapter 8.

For now, as context to detailing briefing battles on the merits, it is important to understand that amici participation is widespread, and influential. Two in-depth studies of amici participation during two separate Supreme Court terms, 1982 and 1995 document the contours of interest group participation in litigation before the Court. I have already referred to Caldeira and Wright's studies, based on a data set derived from the 1982 term,[137] which found extensive amicus participation at the agenda-setting stage of the Supreme Court process. Using one of Caldeira and Wright's studies as their point of departure,[138] political scientists Paul M. Collins Jr. and Lisa A. Solowiej find further evidence of widespread and diverse amicus involvement in the 1995 term.[139] Significantly, Collins and Solowiej, like Bruce Ennis, link amicus influence to providing information:

> If . . . the justices are hearing from a multitude of voices in the Court, this increases the chances that each organized group offers the Court novel argumentation that might otherwise be unavailable to it. Simply put, groups of the same organizational typology are likely to rely on similar presentation styles and authorities in their advocacy efforts. As such, a heterogeneous choir of interest group voices in the Court suggests that the justices receive a wide range of information that might aid them in creating efficacious law.[140]

Several instructive studies explore this nexus between amicus participation, providing information to the justices, and influencing their decisions. Three such studies in particular stand out.

First, in 2000 law professors Joseph D. Kearney and Thomas W. Merrill published an article pertinently titled "The Influence of Amicus Curiae Briefs on the Supreme Court."[141] Their ambitious study employs a data base including 6,141 cases from forty-nine Supreme Court terms (1946–1995) to test three hypotheses derived from three competing models of Supreme Court decision making. Simply stated, the "attitudinal model" insists that justices make decisions based upon their political beliefs; the "interest group model" holds that justices resolve cases according to interests articulated by groups participating in the controversy; and the "legal model" maintains that justices employ rules, rights, and policy arguments to fashion lawful outcomes.[142] Restating these three explanations in terms of hypothesized explanations of Supreme Court outcomes, we have: ideology trumps; group influence counts; and legality matters. In a nuanced interpretation of their findings, Kearney and Merrill argue that, although their data "provide some support"[143] for all three models, legal doctrine appears to provide the most compelling explanation.

> In arguing that the legal model is best supported by our findings, we do not suggest that the legal model provides the sole explanation for Supreme Court decisions, or that our data do not also provide some support for the rival models. We do believe, however, that our study provides evidence that amicus briefs that speak to the requirements of the law exert some

influence on the outcomes reached by the Court. In other words, law matters, and because law matters, amicus briefs that speak to the requirements of the law matter.[144]

Law matters. Because law matters, amicus briefs communicating information in compelling ways about the legal issues raised by the case at bar are effective at persuading justices that the arguments of the party with whom the amicus is allied are meritorious. Because legally sophisticated amicus briefs matter, the quality of legal advocacy is essential to amici's effectiveness. A clear implication of Kearney and Merrill's study is that the experience of one's legal representative can be decisive.[145]

Four years after Kearney and Merrill's study, political scientist Paul M. Collins Jr. revisited variants of the "interest group" and "legal" models. Collins began by noting that "virtually none of [the previous] research has explicitly examined why amicus briefs influence litigation success. . . . The numerous other studies . . . are generally either focused on a few groups . . . or specific issue areas or do not control for established influences on litigation success."[146] As Collins formulated them, he sought to test an "affected groups hypothesis" and an "information hypothesis." The first posits that the number of groups filing amicus briefs influences Supreme Court decision making; the second posits that the information amici provide influences Supreme Court decision making. "[T]he affected groups hypothesis, holds that amicus briefs are efficacious because they signal to the Court that a wide variety of outsiders to the suit will be affected by the Court's decision. . . . [T]he information hypothesis asserts that amicus briefs are effective, not because they signal how many affected groups will be impacted by the decision, but because they provide litigants with additional social scientific, legal, or political information supporting their arguments."[147] As with Kearney and Merrill's study, in Collins' research neither "groups" nor "information" are air-tight categories. Both are important to explaining Supreme Court decision making. Still, while amici are key players, the information their briefs convey is the crucial explanatory factor. Or, to put it another way, amici are the media—information is the message. Collins' model "shows strong support that it is amicus brief support that increases the probability of litigation success, and not amicus participant support. Consequently, it appears the Court values the information found within amicus briefs and not the information found on the covers of these briefs."[148]

Third, political scientist Paul Chen authored a textual study of how the amicus briefs "may have influenced"[149] the Supreme Court's decision, and the justices' four opinions, in a medical marijuana case, *Gonzales v. Raich*, 545 U.S. 1 (2005). Chen's approach differs from methodologies characteristic of most political science research into how amici influence U.S. Supreme Court decision making. Not satisfied with conventional large-scale statistical data analyses,[150] Chen adopts a different approach, offering a case study of how justices employ information contained in amicus briefs. Putting *Raich* under a microscope, as it were, Chen finds evidence of pervasive amicus influence in Justice John Paul Stevens' opinion for the Court, as well as Justice Antonin Scalia's concurrence and the dissents by Justices Sandra Day O'Connor and Clarence Thomas. "The arguments and information presented in the AC briefs had an impact on the Court's substantive decision-making[,] the issues the justices considered in deciding the case, the concerns they addressed in their opinions, and the arguments and information they marshaled to justify their positions."[151]

Chen's findings are instructive, albeit less surprising than corroborating by how they "annotate" amici influence on Supreme Court decision making evidenced in the other, more quantitative studies I have discussed. More pertinent to my concerns in this chapter are Chen's reflections on the light his results shed on amicus participation and information processing. Because Chen's concluding observations are so pertinent, and lucid, they are worth quoting at length.

> The information provided in the AC briefs is important, not for the purpose of reflecting the political interests or public opinion surrounding an issue, but for legally-relevant arguments and information pertaining to the case. The informational theory of AC impact hypothesizes that justices seek alternative arguments, in addition to the ones offered by the parties, to find support for their positions, especially when the parties' arguments are weak. The findings discussed here lend support to the view that "the addition of outside counsel, in the form of amicus briefs, may aid a party in better realizing its litigation objectives" [quoting Paul M. Collins Jr.]. Although the submission of twice as many AC briefs in support of Respondents [in *Raich*] did not help them win, nevertheless the influence of AC's arguments and information is discernable in all of the justice's opinions.
>
> But more than just winning the case, what each side really wants is the Court to adopt its argument so that it becomes legal precedent. Winning by itself matters little in political litigation, unless the outcome is also based on the arguments that will be favorable to that side's cause in future litigation. As [Susan] Behuniak-Long explains, "while the main purpose of an amicus brief is to persuade the Court to rule on behalf of a particular litigant, the impact of amici is not limited to this result alone. Interest groups may also claim success if the Court adopts the language or perspective of the brief, or if the litigant's argument is strengthened by the endorsement of the amicus." Ultimately, this research provides further insight into and support for the legal approach to Supreme Court decision making, in which legal arguments are viewed as exerting influence on the Court's substantive decisions.
>
> Finally, this examination of AC brief impact in *Raich* lends support to [James F.] Spriggs and [Paul J.] Wahlbeck's finding that AC briefs that have the most influence on the Court are not those which offer completely novel arguments or information in addition to those offered in the parties' briefs, but those briefs that, while reiterating the parties' arguments, thus signaling for the Court the salience of the legal issues, also offer additional information or a different perspective from the AC's particular standpoint. Briefs that provided unique information or arguments, without framing that material within a salient legal argument raised by the parties, seemed more likely to be ignored by the Court.[152]

Chen's reflections prepare the ground for my analysis, just below. As we will see, the amici competing in *Morse v. Frederick* not only sought to persuade the Court to their side, they sought primarily to carry the day rhetorically—that is to say, to win the argument. In terms of how I have characterized the debate, the opposing amici sought to influence the Court to couch its ruling in language incorporating either the accountability narrative (Morse) or the injury narrative (Frederick)—or at least nuances of both. The amici pursued this goal by dovetailing their arguments with those of the party whom they supported. To the extent amici went off on a tangent, they were less effective.

The Supreme Court granted cert. on two questions: what are the speech rights of high school students under the First Amendment, and do high school principals enjoy qualified immunity from damages? Of course, in their respective briefs, each party posed these questions in terms designed to highlight their answers. Kirkland & Ellis' answer, for Deborah Morse and the Juneau School Board, can be summed up in six words: "The Ninth Circuit was doubly wrong."[153] Building their case around what I am calling an "accountability narrative," Ken Starr and his colleagues argued that the Ninth Circuit should be reversed because its "uncompromising libertarian vision"[154] erroneously hampers school administrators' efforts to hold students accountable for their behavior—and more unacceptably, punishes such officials for acting responsibly by levying damages.[155] The leitmotif of the petitioner's brief is combating advocacy of illegal drug use. Deborah Morse was carrying out her "bedrock duty"[156] when she crossed Glacier Avenue and ordered Joseph Frederick to take down his banner proclaiming BONG HiTS 4 JESUS; she ought not to be penalized for doing so. As a matter of law, "The *Tinker-Fraser-Kuhlmeier* trilogy permitted Juneau school official to discipline Frederick for promoting illegal substances":

> Frederick's "bong hits" banner did not involve the passive expression of a political viewpoint. Rather, his slang marijuana reference was part of an antisocial publicity stunt designed to draw attention away from an important (and historic) school activity. . . . The message was therefore strictly contrary to the school's basic educational mission of promoting a healthy, drug-free lifestyle. . . . The trilogy—when distilled to its essential principles—stands for the proposition that students have limited free speech rights balanced against the School District's right to carry out its educational mission and to maintain discipline.[157]

Given the "flinty reality"[158] of teenage drug abuse in America, Deborah Morse should be commended, not condemned. Frederick's "message was trebly wrong. It was the wrong message, at the wrong time, and in the wrong place."[159] Principal Morse "represents the paradigmatic conscientious public servant for whom [the] bedrock qualified immunity principles were designed to protect."[160]

Two of the three amici supporting the petitioners, D.A.R.E. and the National School Boards Association (NSBA), respectively amplified upon the twin themes of Kirkland & Ellis' brief: accountability and immunity. Counting two former "Drug Czars"[161] among the six parties on its brief, D.A.R.E. claimed unique authority to address the dangerous tendencies[162] of Joseph Frederick's banner. D.A.R.E.'s submission is interspersed with references to "the fight against illegal drug use by our nation's teens"[163] as "of particular concern to amicus curiae," "[a]s these amici can attest," and "[a]s these amici know from first-hand experience.[164] What D.A.R.E. argues it singularly understands is that "had Principal Morse failed to react to Frederick's inappropriate display, she would have foregone an opportunity to teach her students—including Frederick—that they should be law-abiding. And she would have failed to protect her students from further exposure to a harmful message."[165] For D.A.R.E., then, accountability is paramount.

For the NSBA,[166] immunity in the exercise of administrative discretion is paramount. NSBA's major concern is to protect public school officials who carry out their educational mission by combating illegal drug use. The most revealing passage in its brief appears half-way through under this heading: "Local School Boards Need Reasonable Latitude to Define Their Educational Mission, and School Officials Should Be Afforded Reasonable Professional Discretion to Determine When Speech Is Inconsistent with That Mission or Interferes with Maintaining a Safe and Effective Learning Environment."[167] The gist of the NSBA's argument is that courts should defer to—not penalize—local educational officials' determination of what sorts of student speech run afoul of any given school's educational mission as understood by the relevant school administrator. "[T]he education of the Nation's youth," the NSBA insists, is primarily the responsibility of parents, teachers, and state and local school officials, and not federal judges. . . . [S]chool boards and school administrators are in the best position to determine whether student speech interferes with the particular school's educational mission."[168] Because school administrators are best situated to make judgment calls, they are on the front lines of the war on drugs. Without immunity from damages resulting from their essential work, these warriors will be disadvantaged and, hence, discouraged from pursuing careers in school administration. "Refusing to grant immunity to school administrators despite the lack of clarity over student free speech rights will have a deleterious impact on the more than 15,000 school districts and 225,000 school administrators across this nation."[169]

I interviewed Naomi Gittins, an NSBA staff attorney for twenty-five years. She talked about the process leading up to, and shaping, her organization's two amicus briefs (supporting certiorari and on the merits). Gittins said she believed that the Juneau School District contacted NSBA and asked it to consider supporting their position.[170] Gittins also confirmed that immunizing school officials from liability figured centrally in the NSBA's decision to support Deborah Morse and the Juneau School Board. NSBA looked at the case—looked at the pros and cons, "which is what we always do. We like to take more of a policy approach to our briefs rather than a strict legal approach."[171]

> [O]ne of the main things we try to do in a lot of our briefs . . . is to try and give the Court an idea of what day-to-day school life is like on the particular issue for a school administrator, or a teacher . . . [*Morse v. Frederick*] was one where—is an area of law that—lacks a lot of clarity and that schools are always struggling with to come up with the right approach of balancing students' rights with their need to maintain safety and order in the classroom. And, for school officials, I think one of the scary things about this particular case was that the principal was denied qualified immunity, so that she could be personally liable. And I guess our approach to that was that school administrators—most of them, of course not all of them—are making a good faith effort to do that sort of balancing and, when the law's not clear one way or the other, we felt like, well they really don't need to be on the hook from a personal liability standpoint. So we felt it was important to support the case for that reason.[172]

I asked Gittins whether it would be fair to characterize the issue of qualified immunity as a "red flag" that caught the NSBA's attention. "It definitely is something that we pay attention to," she replied. "School administrators . . . have a lot of issues that they need to work with on a daily basis. They need to be able to make judgment calls. . . . School districts want to be able to recruit people . . . [who] don't have to worry about: 'If I do something wrong, or if I make a judgment about what's best for my particular school on a particular issue, that my personal assets are gonna be at risk.'"[173]

Joining the NSBA and D.A.R.E. as amici supporting Deborah Morse and the Juneau School District was the United States, with Solicitor General Paul D. Clement as counsel of record. In Supreme Court litigation, the solicitor general is widely viewed as the amicus of all of amici, to the extent of being perceived as the "tenth justice."[174] Among scholars who have analyzed the solicitor general's amicus participation, a consensus exists that the solicitor general (SG), and hence the party with which that office is allied, enjoys significant success before the Supreme Court.[175] "[W]ith friends like this, you can't lose."[176] Agreement breaks down when it comes to explaining why. Paul M. Collins Jr. recently observed that "While the findings with respect to the SG's influence is in accord with the separation of powers model, it should be recognized that there is some ambiguity in the extant literature whether this is entirely supportive of a separation of powers model or is more generally reflective of the SG's almost unparalleled advocacy experience as compared to other members of the Supreme Court bar."[177] Irrespective of lingering uncertainty surrounding the reasons explaining the SG's influence, having that influence in one's camp is much coveted.

Solicitor General Clement aligned the United States squarely with the petitioners' view of the case. Right at the outset, in the first two sentences of its brief, the United States articulates its interests in terms of the petitioners' accountability narrative: "This case concerns the authority of public schools to prohibit student speech that promotes illegal drug use, and the qualified immunity of school officials who punish students for engaging in such speech. The United States has a substantial interest in those questions."[178] In summary terms, the SG argued that the case at bar was not a Tinker-related matter but, instead, a *Fraser/Kuhlmeier* matter. The crux is proscribing drug-related speech. When Joseph Frederick hoisted his BONG HiTS 4 JESUS banner he "violated the [school] policy against displaying offensive material, including material that advertises or promotes use of illegal drugs."[179] Because it ran afoul of school policies designed to facilitate the educational mission of the Juneau School District, Frederick's display was unprotected by the First Amendment. On the contrary, Deborah Morse had ample legal authority to banish his banner. The SG identified three reasons why student speech deemed "advocacy of illegal drug use at a school event"[180] is unprotected speech. First, illegal drugs pose a severe threat to America's schoolchildren. Second, illegal drugs undermine the entire school curriculum and the whole educational process. Third, promoting any sort of illegal behavior threatens the ability of school to inculcate respect for law.[181] On these grounds, "[t]his case is governed not by *Tinker*, which applies when a school merely seeks to avoid controversy and prevent disturbance, but instead by *Fraser* and *Kuhlmeier*, which confirm that a school can prohibit speech inconsistent with its basic educational mission."[182] By making these arguments, the SG representing United States made the petitioners' position its own.

Doug Mertz, attorney for Joseph Frederick, arrayed his Respondent's arguments along a by now well-established skirmish line in the *Morse v. Frederick* briefing battle. Mertz's brief reads somewhat like a mirror image of the SG's. Whereas the SG reasoned that *Tinker* did not pertain to the case being argued, Mertz foregrounded *Tinker* as controlling. "This case is not about drugs[,]" began Mertz. "This case is about speech."[183] He continued: "Petitioners ask this Court to return to a pre-*Tinker* world. The rule they propose would open the door to an enforced orthodoxy that this Court has consistently condemned, and would effectively immunize all but irrational school censorship from constitutional scrutiny."[184]

Mertz characterized the rule that the petitioners sought as a "per se" rule. He maintained that such a general holding would sweep unconstitutionally broadly, restricting student speech by relieving school administrators of the responsibility of having to assess the specific circumstances of each occurrence. He wrote:

> Since *Tinker*, this Court's approach to student speech has been balanced and contextual. Petitioners cannot prevail under that approach. Accordingly, they propose a blanket rule that would prohibit any student speech that advocates illegal conduct or, alternatively, any student speech that promotes drug or alcohol use, or that is contrary to what the school defines as its "mission." . . .
>
> The cure they propose, however, is worse than the disease. Under our constitutional system, respect for law cannot be compelled through censorship.
>
> A *per se* rule prohibiting students from engaging in speech that "promotes" unlawful conduct undermines the values it is designed to protect.[185]

Mertz argued that neither petitioners' references to *Fraser* and *Kuhlmeier*[186] nor attempted analogies to *Vernonia* and *Earls*[187] displace *Tinker*. Frederick's speech was not offensively lewd, vulgar, or obscene. His banner was not school-sponsored. Student drug testing under the Fourth Amendment does not correspond to disciplining student speech under the First Amendment. Inside the Juneau-Douglas High School gate, *Tinker* protects Frederick's speech.[188]

Twelve amicus briefs supporting Joseph Frederick were submitted by a collective total of eighteen parties.[189] As I said in opening this chapter, Joseph Frederick had a lot of friends when he answered Deborah Morse's U.S. Supreme Court challenge to his victory before the Ninth Circuit Court of Appeals. With this many voices seeking to be heard, amici faced the challenge of adding dimensions to Doug Mertz's arguments while remaining pertinent to the petitioner's injury narrative. Former assistant to the SG, then deputy SG, Stephen M. Shapiro offers this instructive list of reasons why amicus briefs fail:

> The Court is flooded each term with short amicus briefs that say little more than "me too"— the amicus agrees with one side in the controversy. Other amicus briefs repeat the analysis of one of the parties with slightly varied phraseology. Still other amicus groups file documents so one-sided that they fail to meet the countervailing arguments, and thus they fail to assist the Court in comparing and evaluating competing claims. In addition, some amicus briefs insist on discussing issues that are far removed from the issues before the Court, and thus they contribute nothing to the analysis of the case. Finally, some amicus groups plague the Court with filings that are little more than political or economic editorials, and thus they fail to acknowledge and analyze the relevant statutory or constitutional principles, or even the decisions of the Supreme Court itself.[190]

Shapiro's cautions recall Paul Chen's findings, discussed above,[191] that effective amici reinforce the arguments of the party they are supporting and also enhance their ally's case. Their task is to be original without becoming irrelevant. In short, Joseph Frederick's friends had to walk a fine line between cloning and straying off the reservation.

Frederick's friends had to walk this line while playing defense. Allying with the Respondent obliged amici supporting Frederick to assume the posture of articulating arguments crafted to dissuade a majority of the justices from disturbing the status quo—namely the Ninth Circuit's ruling in *Frederick v. Morse*. Frederick's amici were advocating inaction. Unlike D.A.R.E, the NSBA, and the United States, all of which urged the Court to reverse the Ninth Circuit's ruling as a remedy, Frederick's amici sought to shield the lower court. The former asked the justices to reject the Ninth Circuit's decision in order to vindicate Deborah Morse's authority to hold Joseph Frederick accountable for advocating illegal drug use. The latter urged the justices not to disturb the Ninth Circuit outcome in order to protect Joseph Frederick from the injury caused by Deborah Morse's abuse of discretion.

Frederick's friends came to his cause from three different points of departure. The organizations filing amicus briefs can be divided broadly—and roughly—into three types: free expression advocates, religious speech advocates, and drug policy reform advocates.[192] Much was made at the time (March 2007) of what "strange bedfellows" these divergent groups were.[193] Journalists, bloggers, and pundits remarked on the apparent curiosity of Joe Frederick's impromptu display bringing together, for instance, Liberty Counsel ("Restoring the Culture One Case at a Time by Advancing Religious Freedom, the Sanctity of Human Life and the Traditional Family") with Lambda Legal Defense and Education Fund ("[T]he oldest national organization pursuing high-impact litigation, public education and advocacy on behalf of equality and civil rights for lesbians, gay men, bisexuals, transgender people and people with HIV."); associating Students for Sensible Drug Policy ("[A]n international grassroots network of students who are concerned about the impact drug abuse has on our communities, but who also know that the War on Drugs is failing our generation and our society") with Alliance Defense Fund ("[A] legal alliance defending the right to hear and speak the Truth through strategy, training, funding, and litigation"). Actually, Frederick's amici were not such odd bedfellows at all. They were united by their shared preventive task. Pursuing that project, they adopted various complementary approaches.[194]

One sensible way to sort these approaches is to categorize Respondent's amicus briefs by what they "specifically add to the dialogue."[195] That phrase is Dan Schweitzer's, Supreme Court counsel to the National Association of Attorneys General. In his 2003 "Fundamentals of Preparing a United States Supreme Court Amicus Brief," Schweitzer suggested nine "ideas" about how an amicus might "add to the dialogue." I have sorted the twelve amicus briefs supporting Frederick into five of these nine categories: "The 'Different Legal Argument' Brief"; "The 'Damage Control' Brief"; "The 'Amplify One Issue' Brief"; "The 'Answer the Other Side's Amici' Brief"; and "The 'Surprising Source' Brief."[196] Because these are not airtight silos, and because some of Frederick's amici sought to add more than one dimension to his case, I have placed some of the twelve amici under more than one heading.

Schweitzer describes the "The 'Different Legal Argument' Brief" as follows:

A party sometimes entirely excludes an argument that you believe should be brought to the Court's attention. Whatever the reason for this—be it institutional or based on differing legal analysis—an amicus brief can aid the Court by alerting it to another legal argument in support of the party's claim.[197]

Five amici offered arguments that differed, more or less, from those Doug Mertz made on Frederick's behalf. First, alleging "factual sogginess," counsel of record for the American Center for Law and Justice (ACLJ) Jay Alan Sekulow argued that the Court should dismiss the writ of certiorari as improvidently granted. "This is a poor test case for student free speech," ACLJ maintained.

The case at bar is a far cry from a crisp, sharply delineated presentation of competing claims. . . . It would be regrettable if the Court were to resolve the important questions of constitutional law at issue here in the context of a jokester's prank, rather than a student's bearing of a serious message (as in *Tinker*). It would likewise be regrettable if the Court decided these important questions on a factual record based in significant respects upon an inference (e.g., as to whether the school policies applied and whether respondent Frederick meant to advocate drugs at all).[198]

Second, amicus Lambda Legal Defense and Education Fund (LLDEF) took a different tack by reminding the Court about the distinction between protected student speech and harassing speech, cautioning the justices not to shield the latter as it reaffirmed the former. LLDEF first answered one of Kenneth Starr's arguments (another of Schweitzer's nine suggestions), urging the Court to defend Frederick's First Amendment right to hoist his banner: "Unable to demonstrate a risk of substantial disruption, Petitioners resort to the claim here that Frederick's banner 'was the wrong message, at the wrong time, and in the wrong place.' This argument is eerily similar to the claim rejected in *Tinker* that 'the schools are no place for demonstrations.'"[199] Having invoked *Tinker* to support Frederick's speech rights, LLDEF then warned that *Tinker* does not immunize disruptive harassing school speech: "Many courts have recognized that student speech that torments other students based on their personal characteristics implicates *Tinker*'s concern that student expression might in some instances collide with other students' rights."[200] Clearly, LLDEF sought to bring Frederick's speech within *Tinker*'s mantle while excluding speech targeting lesbians, gays, bisexuals, and transgendered individuals.

Third, in another argument that falls under a couple of Schweitzer's categories (answering the other side and different legal argument), the National Coalition against Censorship (NCAC) took head on the argument that Frederick's alleged advocacy of illegal drug use disqualified him from First Amendment protection. NCAC rejected the petitioners' reliance on *Fraser* "as a catch-all standard" because doing so "would create a classic slippery slope on which no student speech would be safe from the risk of administrative censorship."[201] NCAC then characterized the "conflict" between Frederick and the school as "a purely ideological one."[202] The petitioners "belabor"[203] the Safe and Drug Free Schools and Communities Act (SDFSCA) as justification for censoring Frederick's banner, asserted NCAC. NCAC replies that "[n]owhere does SDFSCA require that schools prohibit or otherwise limit student speech having to do with drugs, and in fact, to the extent the statute implicates speech at all, its emphasis rests squarely on the promotion of speech and other forms of disseminating information on the subject."[204] It turns out, says NCAC, "that the best [First Amendment] antidote to objectionable speech is more speech."[205]

Fourth, offering an argument distinct from yet complementary to NCAC's, Students for Sensible Drug Policy (SSDP) contended that the legal standard sought by the petitioners would "stifle legitimate student speech about drug policy."[206] Not only is censoring drug-related speech indefensible under SDFSCA and the First Amendment, SSDP argued, doing so would silence students regarding a matter of immediate concern to them. SSDP specified four reasons why "students have a constitutional right to discuss issues relating to drug policies":

> Drug Policies Affect Students From Elementary School Through College.
> Students Are Often A Focal Point Of The National Drug Policy Debate.
> Because Students Often Are At The Center Of Government Efforts To Prevent Drug Abuse, Their Constitutionally Protected Right of Speech Is Of Particular Importance On Issues Relating To Drug Policy.
> Student Speech Relating To Drug Policy Should Be Protected Because Students Offer An Invaluable Perspective Regarding How To Curb Drug Abuse.[207]

I interviewed attorney Alex D. Kreit, who was on the SSDP brief. Kreit was a member of one of the five original founding chapters of SSDP while an undergraduate at Hampshire College, and was a SSDP board member throughout its formative years. After the Supreme Court granted cert. in *Morse v. Frederick* Kreit e-mailed back and forth with SSDP colleagues about filing an amicus brief. Kreit suggested that "SSDP would have a unique perspective to bring in to the case. . . . So we started e-mailing about that."[208] The actual drafting process "started out with a conference call with [SSDP Executive Director] Kris Krane, myself, and [counsel of record] Brooks [M. Beard] talking about what—getting from Kris—what perspective does SSDP want to bring. What does SSDP want to say in this brief? What are the values of what SSDP wants to say? . . . Where do they want to come at it from?"

Kreit continued:

> The unusual thing in an amicus brief situation—I think usually your client's objective is to win the case; to get the best result. . . . Usually the strategy is mostly, it's mostly just the legal strategy of how do we end up winning this case or minimizing the damage . . . But for an amicus brief I think there's a difference in that, there, the objective is—obviously you want to write a brief that's going to help the side your client's on succeed—but it's also a little bit more policy focused. It's saying what does this group want to contribute to this dialogue? . . . Here I think it's also . . . what do they want to contribute to the discussion; what's their unique perspective as a group? Because, in doing an amicus brief that's the main thing: getting it so that the group has something unique to contribute because, otherwise [why bother]?"

During our conversation, Kreit reinforced the nexus SSDP advanced in its amicus filing between uncensored student speech and students' ability to shape drug policies. He said:

We knew the chief—the main brief was going to be obviously talking about the ultimate constitutional issues, and generally what constitutional rules there should be for student speech. . . . Especially with SSDP, [its] organizational interest is obviously, they've got these student chapters. They have some high school student chapters, and they've had high school student chapters that have had problems with administrators not letting them talk about issues on campus. So we wanted to make it clear . . . that, although this case involved a pretty ridiculous phrase, there's a lot of student discussion about drug policy that is just like the discussion of any other policy. And especially because students bring a unique perspective to drug policy issues, . . . that they are often in the cross-hairs of drug policy . . . centered around the idea of protecting students from drugs. And I think students, better than anyone, know how well that works. . . . We wanted to argue the point that, if there's a broad rule here that chills and inhibits student speech over drug policy issues, that's not going to be helpful to anybody. The only way that we can hope to get a better drug policy—to get a drug policy that's actually more effective at reducing drug use and abuse among young people—is if young people are able to freely discuss drug policy issues on their campus.

The next sort of amicus briefs supporting Joe Frederick fall under Schweitzer's category "The 'Damage Control' Brief." He describes this type of submission as "a variant of the 'more restrained than the party' brief." "Sometimes," Schweitzer writes, "you are afraid the Court will use a case to set forth a broad rule that you do not desire. Your amicus brief can explain to the Court why, based on the particular facts or procedural posture, it should issue a narrow opinion and reserve the broader issue for a later date."[209] To a significant extent, given that they were playing defense in *Morse v. Frederick*, most of the respondent's amici were engaging in damage control. To a considerable degree, they were advancing variants on an argument to the effect: "If the Court grants petitioners' desired rule it would damage student speech rights; but if the justices must do so, they ought to craft as limited a standard as possible." The SSDP brief analyzed just above, illustrates this sort of damage control. As Alex Kreit said:

> [I]f [Frederick's] speech is interpreted as [direct advocacy of illegal behavior], then that's a pretty broad ruling. It could chill a lot of speech. But we also were realistic in thinking about how might this come out. . . . So a lot of what we want to do is get into the brief—hammer home the idea that if they're going to rule for the school district, hammer home that it's important to note that this is a limited holding. . . . Our worry was we don't want an opinion that sort of just makes it sound like, "Hey, if [students] start talking about drugs, then they can be punished."[210]

Another already cited amicus brief in which a variation of damage control plays a major role is the LLDEF filing which cautioned the Court not to rule so broadly, if it announced the LLDEF's desired outcome by vindicating Joseph Frederick's speech rights, that the Court's holding could be understood as protecting hate speech.

Two other amici illustrate alternative approaches to damage control in *Morse v. Frederick*. First, Michael E. Rosman, counsel of record for the Center for Individual Rights (CIR), filed an amicus brief supporting Frederick "to point out the dangers of adopting" a standard that "is far too expansive and vague."[211] CIR's central concern was that, were the Court to adopt the standard proposed by the petitioners and their amici, school administrators' discretion would be unbounded and, consequently, students' speech rights would be destroyed. Rosman wrote: "Under the school's version of its 'basic educational mission,' the term can be defined in any way it likes." He continued, "if a school can define its 'basic educational mission'—or, as the School and its amici put it when discussing *Tinker*, the 'work of the school'—as broadly as it wishes and punish speech inconsistent with that 'mission' or 'work,' it is hard to envision what a school cannot regulate." Ultimately, Rosman urged in no uncertain terms that "lines must be drawn if students' entire lives are not to be given over to schools' speech-suppressing agenda."[212]

I interviewed Michael Rosman about CIR's involvement in *Morse v. Frederick*.[213] Early in our conversation, he pointedly identified why CIR came on board: "We decided that the theories that the petitioners had of the scope of schools' ability to regulate speech were very . . . dangerous, and that it was important, then, to try and cabin those theories to the extent that we could." He added that "[a]t the beginning we were just concerned that this was an example of the War on Drugs trumping everything, including the Bill of Rights."[214] I asked Rosman if the language I quoted in the previous paragraph from CIR's brief about "lines must be drawn" is CIR's core argument. "Yeah," he replied,

> one of the things we try [to do] is sort of appeal to anyone on the Court who happened to be a lawyer (which is sort of a joke) [*laughs*], and who would actually think, "Oh well, there's conflicting evidence, there's lines to be drawn; maybe we should give this more thought. Maybe we shouldn't have taken this case to begin with." 'Cause chances are, when the Court takes a case, they're doing it because they don't particularly like the result of the court below. Chances are, when the Court takes a case from the Ninth Circuit [*laughs*], they're really doing it to reverse the judgment of the court below. . . . And so, we were just trying to say: "Listen, this is going way overboard." . . . So, this is the reductio ad absurdum, where-is-the-line-drawing, slippery-slope kind of argument that you see in [the language you quoted to me].

Second, the Liberty Legal Institute's amicus brief also exemplifies damage control. If anything, the Liberty Legal Institute (LLI) was even more forthright than CIR in stating its concern. On page one the authors wrote: "The cryptic message at issue in this case is not cause for diminishing *Tinker* and derailing almost forty years of jurisprudence protecting the political and religious speech of students."[215] LLI describes itself on its Web site as "Protecting Religious Freedoms and First Amendment Rights: A network of over 120 dedicated attorneys successfully battling in the courts for religious freedoms, students' rights, parental rights, the definition of the family, and other freedoms."[216] Given LLI's mission, Morse's request for a Supreme Court rule endorsing broad administrative discretion to sanction student speech raised red flags. "What amicus fears most," LLI stated, "is that a loosely worded opinion, holding that students have no First Amendment right to promote drug use, will fatally undermine protection for core religious and political speech in public schools. The vague and deferential standard proposed by petitioner and her amici invites this consequence." Even more explicitly, LLI worried that "[i]f the Court adopts petitioner's proposed subjective test, religious speech would be censored by public schools seeking to establish 'neutrality,' especially given religious speech is always contrary to the 'basic educational mission' because no school may adopt the advancement of religion as its mission."[217] Seeking to minimize any such damage that might result from a majority of the justices aligning with Deborah Morse's and the Juneau School Board's position, the LLI attorneys offered this suggestion: "If the Court wishes to reverse in this case, it could carve out an explicit exception for advocacy of the use of illegal drugs and add that explicit exception to the sexually explicit speech identified in *Bethel Sch. Dist. v. Fraser*, 478 U.S. 675 (1986). But it must be very clear about the basis for that exception."[218]

Dan Schweitzer described "The 'Amplify One Issue' Brief" in these terms: "A party often sets forth numerous independent reasons why it should prevail. As a consequence, the party may only briefly address an argument that you believe merits greater consideration. An amicus brief can fill that gap, spending (for example) twenty to twenty-five pages on an argument on which the party spends only five pages."[219] In his merits brief, Doug Mertz devoted three pages to arguing that the record did not support any "nexus between the speech and the school"[220]—a nexus required as a threshold to make *Tinker* applicable. In its amicus brief supporting Joseph Frederick, the Rutherford Institute devoted seventeen of twenty-eight pages to amplifying Mertz's argument that Morse is not a school speech case.

By arguing that Morse is not a school speech case, the Rutherford Institute put itself squarely at odds with the Ninth Circuit panel which had said, in the first sentence of its opinion in *Frederick v. Morse*, "This is a First Amendment student speech case."[221] Conspicuously rejecting this point of departure, the Rutherford Institute opened its amicus brief with a uniquely extensive Statement of Facts. Rutherford's attorneys divided its six-page appraisal into "Undisputed Facts" and "Disputed Facts."[222] The three authors[223] of the brief argued that "only undisputed facts in the record . . . should be relied upon for decision."[224] Despite this correct procedural posture, they contend:

> Petitioners' Brief mistakenly blends conflicting versions of disputed and undisputed facts to reach the desired legal end. . . . Numerous . . . significant "disputed facts" that are identified in the following text above should be recognized as such and not relied upon as the basis for the Court's decision in this case. Otherwise, the case should be remanded for trial on these disputed issues.[225]

A key disputed fact, Rutherford attorneys contend, is "Petitioner Morse's assertion that the Olympic torch relay was a 'school-sponsored/sanctioned' function or activity."[226] Building on this alleged ambiguity, the Rutherford attorneys devoted the remainder of their amicus brief to reasoning that *Tinker* is inapplicable. "*Tinker* and its progeny dealt with student speech that either occurred within the metes and bounds of the school, at school assemblies, or in school curriculums."[227] By contrast

> Frederick's speech clearly occurred outside the metes and bounds of the school in a quintessentially public forum—a public sidewalk during a publicly-viewed parade promoted by a commercial sponsor, commemorating an international public event, surrounded by people who themselves were engaged in various types of expression. There was admittedly no disruption of school. It was in this context that Frederick unfurled his banner with a message expressing disdain for the event, in effect mocking it with a silly message. This does not disqualify it as

protected speech under the First Amendment, nor does it permit the school system to censor it because of embarrassment or because it otherwise disagrees with its message."[228]

In advancing this argument, the Rutherford attorneys amplified on Doug Mertz's "passing" contention that Joseph Frederick was not subject to Juneau School officials' authority. Their amicus brief thereby added to the colloquy about students' speech rights vis-à-vis school administrators' discretion.

I interviewed Rutherford Institute founder John W. Whitehead about his organization's amicus brief.[229] Whitehead began by saying, "We decided to do our own brief. . . . I thought we could add something a little different." He elaborated on his view of the case:

> The basic, bottom line, issue as I saw it; you had a kid across the street—I think [the event] was sponsored by Coca-Cola—I didn't see how it could be a school-sanctioned event. I don't think there was anything in the record to that. . . . I don't see how it fit in the *Tinker* mode— they couldn't prove disruption, it didn't happen at school. It didn't fit in the *Fraser* mode because it wasn't in the school. Beyond the constitutional issues, my main concern was, since the mid-1990s, we've been doing a lot of zero-tolerance cases. . . . I'm avidly opposed to most zero-tolerance policies. A sort of draconian atmosphere has enveloped the schools, very anti-free speech, anti-civil libertarian. I think this case epitomizes it. What bothers me is, can a school reach out beyond the limits—even if it's just peripheral in its relationship to the school—and bring in that behavior within the school confines and control.

Dan Schweitzer suggests that amici might write what he terms "The 'Answer the Other Side's' Brief. "You can often help the respondent by focusing your energies on arguments made primarily by petitioner's amici. This allows the respondent to save its firepower for the arguments the petitioner itself has made."[230] Footnote eleven of the Rutherford Institute's amicus brief illustrates what Schweitzer proposes. Appended to the passage from the Rutherford brief I quoted on the previous page, footnote eleven takes the solicitor general to task: "The Solicitor General attempts to transform this case into a referendum on society's effort to eliminate the scourge of illegal drugs and, in effect, to impose the school system's anti-drug orthodoxy on students throughout the community." The Rutherford attorneys continue:

> He argues, in essence, that censorship of dissident student speech relating to drugs—whether on, or off, school grounds is an essential part of the cure of the drug problem. Petitioners' incursion on *Frederick*'s speech, he argues, should be permitted because "student advocacy of illegal drug use at a school event is manifestly inconsistent with a public school's educational mission." . . . The virtually unlimited censorship powers advanced by the Solicitor General would not only result in grossly overbroad and unprecedented violation of the First Amendment by unwitting school officials, it would disserve students and the body politic.
>
> Likewise remarkable is the Solicitor General's appalling distortion of the *Tinker* progeny to advance these ends. . . . [The] circumstances [of *Fraser* and *Kuhlmeier*] are not even remotely close to this case. The Solicitor General's attempt to recast *Fraser* and *Kuhlmeier* into what is, in effect, "zero-tolerance" rhetoric with application throughout the community, in

order to squelch speech about drugs, is astounding and should be rejected as wholly inconsistent with those precedents and the Bill of Rights.[231]

During our interview, I asked John Whitehead about Rutherford's footnote eleven. I remarked: "Your footnote eleven seems to me almost the most important part of the brief. . . . How the [solicitor general] seeks to transform this from a school speech case into a zero-tolerance case." Whitehead replied: "Right—yeah, the drug thing, yeah. . . . I think that's partially true. But I think a lot that drives . . . it's the drug phobia. They're completely—what?—drug-o-phobes?"

Amicus briefs submitted by the Student Press Law Center (SPLC) et al. and the Christian Legal Society (CLS) exemplify two additional approaches to Schweitzer's "Answer the Other Side's Amici" brief. Both briefs can be said to counter what the SPLC brief characterizes as a "power grab."[232] For SPLC, the power grab takes the form of petitioners and their amici extending their control of student speech by a deceptive rhetorical shift. Actually, that shift is double-barreled. First, attention is transferred from Frederick's speech to the event during which he hoisted his banner. Deborah Morse legitimately demanded that Frederick take down his banner, so the petitioners' argument goes, less for what it said than for the circumstances surrounding his saying it. "They start by insisting that the Olympic torch relay—a commercially sponsored, international, public event—was in some way 'school-sponsored.'"[233] Second, the petitioners finesse the nature of the event by referring to it as "school-sanctioned." "Because the torch relay was clearly not 'school-sponsored,' petitioners and their amici resort to the more muted and legally meaningless phrase—'school-sanctioned.'"[234] These novel moves have "no support in the Constitution or the precedents"[235] of the Supreme Court. No matter. "According to Petitioners' argument, public schools apparently possess the power simply to declare or 'sanction' any commercial, private, public or community event they choose."[236]

The CLS brief specifically identifies the NSBA as a main culprit in seeking "undue power"[237] for school officials over students' speech. What particularly concerns CLS is that administrators will exercise their expanded discretion to punish speakers who "offend" others. Because religious speech often offends, such expression would be a ready target for sanctioning. "If this Court gives public school officials broad latitude to censor and punish expression that 'interferes with the rights of others,' one can be sure that many principals, superintendents, and school boards will invoke this power to forbid religious students from undertaking . . . benign and commonplace activity."[238]

I interviewed Gregory S. Baylor, director of the Christian Legal Society's Center for Law and Religious Freedom, and counsel of record on the CLS amicus brief. I observed: "Reading through the [CLS] brief, one of the things that comes out to me is it's almost like a brief particularly against the National [School Boards Association]." He replied:

Yeah, yeah . . . It's because of what they said in their brief. . . . I sat down with—I read— Juneau School Board's brief, and I read their amicus briefs, and I said, well, the stuff in the NSBA is what we really need to respond to. The other thing is, when you're writing an amicus brief, what you're trying to do is you're trying to offer something useful to the Court. . . . One of things that I think we tried to do in this brief was to not play the role of Joseph Frederick's lawyers by responding to everything that Deborah Morse's lawyers said. That's his job—["It's Doug Mertz's job?"—JCF]—right, he can do that, and he can do that well, and that's fine. But where do you think there might be place for us to say something that might cause a justice, one or more justices, to go "Humm . . . you've got a point there."[239]

The fifth, and final, of Schweitzer's categories that Joseph Frederick's amici demonstrate is "The 'Surprising Source' Brief." "Some amicus briefs are powerful," Schweitzer writes, "because they are written by entities that one would expect to be supporting the other side of the case. A brief can be particularly effective in rebutting the other side's contention regarding the practical implications of the case."[240] When applying Schweitzer's "Surprising Source" category to Frederick's amici, one needs to be discerning. There are five amici that, on first glance, appear to fall into this category: Alliance Defense Fund, American Center for Law and Justice, Christian Legal Society, Liberty Counsel, Liberty Legal Institute. These are the five organizations that I clustered together above under the heading "religious speech advocates." At a superficial level, one might conclude that associating such groups with Joe Frederick is curious, improbable—surprising. It is this conclusion, discussed and rejected above, that characterizes such an association as "odd bedfellows." As I say above: "Actually, Frederick's amici were not such odd bedfellows at all. They were united by their shared preventive task." Liberty Counsel's relationship to *Morse v. Frederick* illustrates this union.

The Liberty Counsel's brief unmistakably articulated how it understood its relationship to *Morse v. Frederick*. Liberty Counsel does an interesting "dance," balancing between dissociating and joining. It is a balance that recalls, while modifying, the cliché about hating the message but loving the messenger. Liberty Counsel loved neither Joe's "stunt" nor his message. Still, Liberty Counsel certainly fears the outcome of granting school administrators authority to sanction the Joes of the world and their "offensive" messages.[241] As Liberty Counsel's amicus brief puts it:

> Liberty Counsel does not endorse the message contained in Mr. Frederick's banner. However, Liberty Counsel supports individuals' rights to make such statements without the risk of censure, suspension or expulsion. Liberty Counsel is extremely concerned about the effects this case could have on the free speech rights of individuals and organizations who interact with public school officials, and seeks to ensure that this Court has the information necessary to review this case in the broader context.[242]

I interviewed Mary E. McAlister, senior litigation counsel for Liberty Counsel. McAlister spotlighted why Christian activist groups like Liberty Counsel aligned themselves with Frederick's cause:

> Part of the reason why we were interested in the case is that we were concerned that if the Court went further than it actually did—and went down the road that Morse wanted them to go—that it would affect religious speech. Like we say [in our brief], we obviously don't think that what [Frederick] said is acceptable to a Christian. But . . . part of our concern is the effect that this could have if it went the wrong way on [say] students . . . wearing a T-shirt

talking about Jesus, or any other religious figure. . . . We wanted to be able to participate to hopefully help convince the Court they don't want to open up this box to the extent that unpopular religious views—whether they're Christian or non-Christian—are scrutinized and restricted. . . . We didn't want students' religious speech restricted.[243]

I asked Ms. McAlister about Liberty Counsel's argument in its amicus brief that the petitioners' proposed "subjective approach is a move toward orthodoxy."[244] She replied:

The subjectivity argument is one that we make regularly when we have school speech cases. . . . Because . . . if there are no standards to govern the decision maker—no objective standards out there—and he or she is left to their discretion . . . that is the very problem. And we run into that with other school policies. If someone wants to come in and use a classroom, or if they want to distribute a flyer on campus, and the policy just says the Superintendent can approve or disapprove as he wants. Well, no—because he can just disapprove the Christian flyer, and approve the Muslim flyer, because he doesn't like Christians, and he likes Muslims. And that's not acceptable.

On Monday, March 19, 2007, the justices of the U.S. Supreme Court convened to hear arguments in *Morse v. Frederick*. Neither all of Deborah Morse's friends nor Joseph Frederick's were present in the courtroom on First Street NE that morning. By contrast, Deputy U.S. Solicitor General Edwin S. Kneedler had been granted ten minutes to argue as amicus on behalf of Principal Morse. Although mostly absent from oral argument, the other amici had raised their voices, articulating their respective legal cases in the briefs they submitted. We have seen that the not-so-brief battles in which amici on both sides engaged plausibly influenced the Court's decision to grant cert. It remains to be seen to what extent, and in what ways, these not-so-brief battles influenced the Court's eventual decision in *Morse v. Frederick*. Clearly apparent from the disputing I have analyzed in this chapter is that there are many more dimensions to the story of Joseph Frederick and Deborah Morse than their brief January 24, 2002, encounter on Glacier Avenue. Also apparent is how much their encounter put at stake.

"Up in Smoke at the High Court"

During oral argument, the most secretive branch of American national government goes public. The justices of the U.S. Supreme Court usually work out of sight, behind the red velvet curtains which hang in their Court Chamber, located at the east end of the Great Hall. The justices, their law clerks, and their support staff mostly labor in their respective chambers, cloistered in what sometimes are described as the nation's nine most elite law firms. Twice weekly members of the Court gather, strictly by themselves, in the main floor justices' conference room, to discuss matters before the Court. However, three days a week during the Court's term, in two-week intervals through April, the justices emerge from the curtains, in full regalia, to take their ordained seats as attorneys argue the cases the Court has elected to review.

Monday, March 19, 2007, the justices appeared at 10:03 a.m. to hear arguments in *Deborah Morse, et al., Petitioners v. Joseph Frederick*. Over the next hour, in a closely watched colloquy, the justices and the parties' lawyers energetically debated details of what actually took place that January 24, 2002, on Glacier Avenue. They weighed the law of student rights, gauged school administrators' authority—and talked drugs. Eight of the nine justices engaged counsel. (As usual, Justice Thomas said not a word.[1]) More or less far-fetched hypotheticals flew in barrages. Questions and answers largely supplanted formal argument. Ken Starr, Edwin Kneedler, and Doug Mertz each barely got a sentence or two in edgewise before a justice interrupted. Like a lot of first-year law school classes, the exchanges varied between high principle and "hide-the-ball."[2] Unlike many first-year law school classes, humor rather than angst punctuated the exchanges.

Washington Post columnist Dana Milbank saw the humor in the judicial repartee. The next day Milbank wrote a piece titled "Up in Smoke at the High Court."[3] His tongue planted firmly in his journalistic cheek, Milbank wrote that "[i]f the justices sounded as if they were doin' the doobies yesterday morning, the case invited a certain amount of reefer madness. . . . All that was missing in the chamber yesterday," Milbank jested, "was black light and Bob Marley." But Milbank also discerned the serious principles at stake. He noted that *Morse v. Frederick* is "a case in which a Dadaist slogan in Juneau will wind up setting a new precedent for students' speech":

> The case began when a high school kid unfurled a banner across the street from his Juneau, Alaska, high school in 2002 when the Olympic torch was passing through town. By the student's own admission, the sign had no meaning, but that didn't matter. The principal suspended him; he sued. Ken Starr and the Bush Administration sided with the principal. The ACLU and various Christian groups sided with the student. Thus does a high school prank become a federal case—an important First Amendment case before the high court, no less.

Milbank nicely captures the oral arguments in *Morse v. Frederick* as theater of the absurd— with no-nonsense consequences. The exchanges may, at times, have been less august than diverting.[4] In the end, one of the parties' cases was going to go up in smoke.

As with the amicus curiae briefs discussed in the previous chapter, a body of scholarly work exists which analyzes the relationship between "constitutional advocacy" and "constitutional outcomes."[5] I will look at salient aspects of this literature below. A useful point of departure, however, is the practitioners' point of view. What do experienced lawyers tell other lawyers who may be preparing to appear before the U.S. Supreme Court about "the importance of oral argument"?[6] These veterans advise that the Court takes oral argument seriously and, because of that, the justices place a premium on professional advocacy. In other words, the justices rely on their brief verbal interactions with members of the Supreme Court bar, and complain mightily about incompetence.

How do these veterans or, at least, the veterans who tender advice in places like the widely consulted *Supreme Court Practice*,[7] know this? They consult judges. "Only judges are in a position to give authoritative answers."[8] The authors of *Supreme Court Practice* prominently quote U.S. Supreme Court Chief Justice John G. Roberts Jr., himself a veteran of thirty-nine arguments before the body over which he now presides (Roberts prevailed in twenty-five of those cases).

> "Oral argument matters," then Judge Roberts wrote, "not just because of what the lawyers have to say," but because "[i]t is the organizing point for the entire judicial process." Oral argument is . . . a time "when ideas that have been percolating for some time begin to crystallize," and as the doors of receptivity to various ideas "begin to close at oral argument," because the "luxury of skepticism will have to yield to the necessity of decision," oral argument can often give a "push" to those doors.[9]

I want to highlight three related aspects of Roberts' acute observation, especially in light of the way in which oral argument in *Morse v. Frederick* unfolded. First, Roberts' use of the word *percolating* suggests that each justice brings a set of more or less fluid[10] predispositions to the courtroom on argument days. Although likely somewhat inclined toward an outcome in a case before the Court, each justice may still be mulling over options. Second, given this relative openness, a lawyer's performance during oral argument can be influential because that lawyer's arguments, and/or that lawyer's answers, may facilitate judicial closure. What a lawyer says might inch a justice closer toward discarding some options in lieu of embracing a particular result. Third, timing is of the essence. Because oral argument comes at that point in judicial process where the justices must shift from deliberating to deciding, a lawyer's arguments and/or answers can provide a pivotal "push"—moving a justice toward finality. Thus, Roberts' description of oral argument as, effectively, a crucial tipping point[11] is instructive. Although counsel likely will not change minds over the course of a half hour behind the lectern, an attorney can close the deal.

Conversely, a faltering performance can cause a deal to go up in smoke.[12] Gressman and his co-authors devote almost a quarter of their discussion of oral argument's importance to quoting Supreme Court justices voicing dissatisfaction over deficient presentations. Justice Lewis F. Powell Jr. voiced his "disappointment in the quality of briefs and oral arguments,"[13] in 1974, just over two years after he was appointed to the Court. "I had hoped for greater assistance from briefs and oral arguments[,]" Justice Powell wrote. "I certainly had expected that there would be relatively few mediocre performances before our Court. I regret to say that performance has not measured up to my expectations." The late Chief Justice Burger was an outspoken critic of lawyers appearing before the Court. He complained that "from one-third to one-half of the lawyers who appear in the serious cases are not really qualified to render fully adequate representation."[14] In 1984, then Justice Rehnquist expressed this complaint most succinctly, observing with his characteristic wry wit that "[many] advocates believe oral argument to be an opportunity to rehash their brief 'with gestures.'"[15]

Throughout the 1970s and 1980s, during the height of judicial displeasure with how counsel carried out oral argument, several state appellate courts, a few U.S. circuit courts, and some students of judicial process reconsidered the practice. One of these scholars, Robert J. Martineau, University of Cincinnati College of Law distinguished research professor emeritus, former appellate court executive, and respected expert on appellate practice, revisited oral argument in a much-discussed 1986 article.[16] Martineau subtitled his article a "Challenge to the Conventional Wisdom," conventional wisdom being that oral argument plays an indispensable role in judicial decision making. For Martineau, oral argument is expensive—hence, largely expendable. He wrote:

> Notwithstanding the generally accepted view that oral argument is a valuable and perhaps essential part of the appellate process, its real contribution to sound decisionmaking is questioned by an increasing number of commentators. The heart of the criticism is a realization that, in many if not most cases, oral argument adds little or nothing to the judge's understanding of a case that was not previously obtained through a study of the briefs and the record by the judges and their staffs. Simply stated, oral argument is not cost-effective.[17]

Martineau suggested reducing significantly the occurrence of oral argument. He offered two proposals. First, he says that the "threshold question"[18] triggering whether or not a judge, or a court, opts for oral argument should be whether a given case raises questions that cannot be addressed via written responses from the parties. Only if such replies do not suffice might an oral argument be scheduled.[19] Second, Martineau argues that the format of more infrequent oral arguments should be modified. He has in mind an arrangement resembling an informal conversation between judges and the parties. Give and take around a conference table would replace the more stylized and structured courtroom oral argument. Attorneys would be provided with judges' questions in advance in order to prepare adequate replies. The procedure would be more a problem-solving exercise than a ritual.[20]

Reform proposals targeting oral argument, like Martineau's, can be understood as artifacts. Saying that does not disparage the integrity of either his suggestions or the analysis supporting them. Rather, describing Martineau's take on oral argument as an artifact contextualizes his critique and his reform suggestions. An artifact is a creation of a particular time. Explaining Martineau's article as a product of the circumstances within which it was drafted connects his essay to the particular discontents prevailing in the mid-1980s when he wrote it. As I noted above, when Martineau wrote, a salient judicial complaint was incompetent lawyers performing badly during oral argument.[21] Judges and justices were dismayed by inferior oral advocacy precisely because they deemed oral argument essential. Judicial reliance on oral argument generated judicial frustration at its inadequacy. At the end of his essay, even Martineau, who dismisses unreformed oral argument as "a waste of time," writes that "[o]ral argument can and should continue to have a significant role in the appellate process."[22] It seems, then, that oral argument per se is less the problem than inept oral argument.

Four recent empirical studies of oral argument shed useful light on, while reinforcing, the nexus between competent advocacy and influential advocacy. In general, "lawyer capability"[23] is a key factor in explaining the effect of oral argument, specifically on decision making by the two North American Supreme Courts. In June 2007, three political scientists published an article in the influential *Law & Society Review* in which they examined "the impact of lawyer capability on the decisions of the Supreme Court of Canada (SCC)."[24] For their study, John Szmer, Susan Johnson, and Tammy Sarver operationalized "lawyer capability" via three independent variables which "reflected three alternative characteristics of litigation teams that could influence the justices: Litigation Experience, Queen's Counsel (QC), and Litigation Team Size."[25] Szmer, Johnson, and Sarver found that "overall the lawyer capability model was robust."[26] They concluded:

> Given the similar judicial processes in both systems, as well as the similar role of the lawyers in the processes, we expected that the lawyer capability theory would apply to the SCC in the same fashion that it applies in the United States. The results of our model seem to bear this out.[27]

In the same *Law & Society Review* issue as the Szmer, Johnson, and Sarver article, two other political scientists reported on their study of another aspect of the relation between competent advocacy and influential advocacy—as the relation plays out south of Ottawa, in Washington, D.C., Andrea McAtee and Kevin T. McGuire inquired into how "the impact of legal advocacy in the U.S. Supreme Court is conditioned by issue salience."[28]

McAtee and McGuire's findings add nuance to Chief Justice Roberts' observation, quoted above, that "[o]ral argument is . . . a time 'when ideas that have been percolating for some time begin to crystallize.'"[29] McAtee and McGuire argue that the more "salient," that is the more consequential, a case before the U.S. Supreme Court is, legal advocacy is less likely to influence the justices' votes. Using Chief Justice Roberts' imagery to summarize McAtee's and McGuire's hypothesis, in salient cases the justices come to oral argument with ideas more "crystallized" than "percolating." McAtee and McGuire's research tells a two-part tale. Initially, their findings confirm "the relevance of prior litigation experience, even after holding constant the quality of a lawyer's oral argument."[30] Halfway into their article, they summarize: "The story to this point emphasizes how experienced Supreme Court advocates affect the votes of the justices."[31] They then subject this preliminary finding to a fuller analysis, employing a "larger model [incorporating] a number of factors . . . that may well figure into the votes of the individual justices."[32] Among these factors are party status (including the solicitor general[33]) and justice's policy preferences. This supplementary analysis testifies "to the continued relevance of litigation experience, even after taking account of a number of competing considerations. . . . The model also confirms the significant effect of the justice's preferences."[34]

At this point, McAtee and McGuire come to the heart of their argument: less judicial certainty ("crystallization") heightens the influence of legal advocacy because uncertainty ("percolation") heightens openness to information that lawyers can provide. Judicial certainty results from cases in which justices are heavily invested. Such cases are most likely high-profile controversies. Conversely, judicial uncertainty results from cases about which justices are, if not necessarily indifferent, less ardent. As McAtee and McGuire put it:

> If a case involves a highly conspicuous legal or policy question, the members of the Court are likely to have given the issue a good deal of thought and to have formed reasonably strong preferences about the options for resolving it. If the justices come to a case with their mind already made up, it is doubtful that argument will have much of an effect. Where an experienced lawyer has a greater chance of affecting the justices' thinking are the cases involving issues that are less central to public discourse. Where the justices do not have firm preconceptions, there are greater opportunities for experienced lawyers to provide them with persuasive information.[35]

In short, "the justices' attitudes trump other considerations and seem to exclude a role for advocacy."[36] The key word in the previous sentence is *seem*. Based on their sophisticated statistical analysis, McAtee and McGuire can plausibly maintain that an inverse relationship exists between strong judicial preferences and effective lawyers' influence. Nevertheless, the probability that opinionated judges have less need for lawyers' information does not preclude skilled advocacy from dissolving crystalline certainty. The possibility for advocacy-induced "percolation" is documented by the work of other students of oral argument to which I now turn.

Timothy R. Johnson, James F. Spriggs II, and Paul J. Wahlbeck collaborated on two complementary articles, published in 2006[37] and 2007,[38] in which they inquire into the striking "divergence"[39] between lawyers' and judges' widely held view that oral argument matters, compared to the "almost dismissive viewpoint"[40] of political scientists that "there is no systematic empirical evidence that 'oral argument regularly, or even infrequently, determines who wins and who loses.'"[41] Johnson, Spriggs, and Wahlbeck investigated whether oral argument is "a dog and pony show"[42] or a way to "focus the minds of the justices and present the

possibility for fresh perspectives on a case."[43] They found that oral argument makes a difference. Specifically, by mining Harry A. Blackmun's archives for notes that the former justice
wrote during oral arguments,[44] they test their hypothesis that "oral arguments can influence
Supreme Court justices' decisions by providing information relevant to deciding a case."[45]
Because they posit that information conveyed during oral argument is key to the process
whereby counsel influence how justices decide, Johnson, Spriggs, and Wahlbeck hone in
on Justice Blackmun's differential ratings of lawyers who argued before the Court while he
served on the High Bench. The "quality" of legal advocacy is their crucial variable.

Basically, they make a two-step argument. First, they seek to show that "attorneys
with more litigating experience, better legal education and training, and greater resources
will receive higher evaluations because such attorneys will offer the Court more credible
and compelling arguments than less experienced or resourceful attorneys."[46] Why do
Johnson, Spriggs, and Wahlbeck believe that high scores from Justice Blackmun indicate
a quality oral argument? In other words, why equate high Blackmun marks with high
quality? They reply:

> First, ideology has a small substantive effect on his grades, which is a necessary (but not suf-
> ficient) condition for the grades' being a valid measure of argumentation quality. Second,
> these grades also evidence validity because they correlate with variables for attorney credibil-
> ity and experience. Third, we did not see Blackmun manifest a tendency to give higher grades
> to appellants. This latter result further suggests that he was not simply awarding higher grades
> to the lawyer he thought was on the winning side.[47]

In short, Johnson, Spriggs, and Wahlbeck offer the reasonable inference that "the substantial relationship between proxies for credibility and lawyers' grades" demonstrates that
Blackmun was evaluating quality.

Their quantitative argument is bulwarked by law professor Stephen A. Higginson's compelling qualitative analysis of oral arguments in his aptly titled article "Constitutional Advocacy
Explains Constitutional Outcomes."[48] Higginson himself advocates persuasively for a changed
focus in law teaching and legal scholarship. He urges shifting attention to the process of making
constitutional law—lawyers' performances before the Court. Higginson quotes Emily Dickinson: "To fill a Gap Insert the Thing that caused it." He responds, "[t]here is a gap in how
we understand the Constitution, and we should insert the thing that caused it."[49] The thing
causing the gap in our understanding is "the ways advocates frame their controversies."[50]
"Great and small cases," writes Higginson, "that stand in decisional edifice—as well as but-
tressed by scholarly scaffolding—are heard aloud and at inception by the Court as controversies compressed in courtroom clashes over constitutional syntax, origin, and purpose."[51]
Students of constitutional law need to ask the practitioner's question: "Which lawyer put
the Court where it came out, and how?"[52] Asking this question directs the interrogator to
the pith of constitutional lawmaking:

> [T]his shift in focus to advocacy illuminates three points no lawyer can overlook . . .
>   (1) whether positive facts are forcefully presented and negative ones effectively dealt with;

(2) whether pertinent points of law are forcefully presented;

(3) whether policy concerns are forcefully presented.

When robust scholarship considers the materials that the Supreme Court itself deems necessary to render its decision, inquiry will shift from the casebook holding to the adversarial making of that holding and to whether and how the Court's holding drew on specific argument submitted by lawyers.[53]

Whether quality Supreme Court lawyering is that which garners high grades from a sitting justice, per Johnson, Spriggs, and Wahlbeck, or that which convincingly assembles "propositions of fact, law, and policy,"[54] per Higginson—or, likely, both—these studies demonstrate that quality advocacy is the linchpin in explaining how oral argument shapes judicial outcomes. If either party's counsel is going to command the justices' attention, perhaps especially in high-profile, divisive cases, they must perform at a commensurately high level. Oral advocacy resembles a high-wire act. Executed proficiently, it is an awesome display in which talent, preparation, daring, and style converge. Poorly done . . . well, there is no safety net in the High Court.

Having established that quality oral argument counts, Johnson, Spriggs, and Wahlbeck turn to the second part of their two-part argument, asking, in effect, Does quality advocacy matter? That is: "Do Oral Arguments Affect the Justices' Votes"?[55] Their quantitative analysis supports an affirmative answer: "[W]e demonstrate that the justices are more likely to vote for the litigant whose attorney provided higher quality oral advocacy (as measured by Justice Blackmun), even after controlling for ideological considerations. This result . . . indicates that oral arguments do indeed enter into Supreme Court decision making."[56] Ultimately, the imagery that Johnson, Spriggs, and Wahlbeck use to describe why oral argument can matter returns us to Chief Justice Roberts' "crystallize" metaphor.[57] They write, in terms reminiscent of Stephen Higginson as well as John Roberts:

> The Justices . . . need an understanding of the legal status quo, the policy choices available to them, the likely effect that different legal rulings will have on the litigants and other similarly situated parties, and the like.
>
> It is in this context that lawyers appear before the Court and attempt to provide the Justices with information that will help their client's cause. Counsel appearing before the bench can do so by providing "a clear presentation of the issues, of the relationship of those issues to existing law, and of the implications of a decision for public policy." . . . These proceedings thus have the potential to crystallize Justices' views or to move them toward a particular outcome.[58]

On March 19, 2007, Kenneth W. Starr and Douglas K. Mertz sought to crystallize justices' views, moving them toward a particular outcome. Although we are not privy to the equivalent of Justice Blackmun's bench notes, we can draw on the imagery, analysis, and findings of the scholarship discussed above to parse the performances of Deborah Morse's and Joseph Frederick's attorneys. As we learn how effectively Starr and Mertz wove their respective factual narratives, reasoned from their reading of pertinent law, contrasted potential policy scenarios, and—mostly—responded to questions from the justices, we also can speculate who most effectively moved a majority toward a particular outcome. In the end, we will see how one lawyer was kept on track, while the other was thrown off balance.

Ken Starr addressed the Court first.[59] His primary task was to reinforce the "accountability narrative" underlying his clients' case. As I described it in Chapter 5, the accountability narrative tells a story "about a conscientious school principal who, during an official school event, observed a group of students raise a fourteen-foot-long banner displaying a message advocating drug use in violation of school district policy, and took decisive action."[60] In addition to telling a compelling tale, Starr needed to achieve two additional goals. First, he needed to connect his narrative to the law governing student speech rights, showing that, because it was disruptive speech, Frederick's banner was not protected speech. Second, he needed to demonstrate not only that failure to side with Principal Morse would put her at personal financial risk, failing to hold Frederick accountable would send a dispiriting message to America's school administrators, while crippling schools' efforts to combat epidemic illegal drug use by American adolescents.

Former Solicitor General Starr immediately got down to business.

> **MR. STARR**: Mr. Chief Justice, and may it please the Court:
>
> Illegal drugs and the glorification of the drug culture are profoundly serious problems for our nation. Congress has so recognized, as has this Court, time and again. The magnitude of the problem is captured . . . in the [D.A.R.E.] amicus brief of General McCaffrey, Secretary Bennett, and a number of organizations . . . the nature and the scope of the problem are well captured.[61]

In his first forty seconds at the lectern, Starr called attention to glorification of the drug culture, aligned his clients with Congress and the Court in identifying such celebration as a dire problem, and allied his clients with nationally known individuals and organizations dedicated to combating—not exalting—drugs. Starr did not mention Joseph Frederick's banner. He did not need to. For Deborah Morse and the Juneau School District, this case was not about a banner. It was about opposing drug use. Responding to Starr's opening gambit, Justice Kennedy interrupted, at :41, posing two highly cogent[62] questions.

> **JUSTICE KENNEDY**: Well, is this case limited to signs about drugs? What is the rule that you want us to adopt for deciding this case?[63]

Attorney Starr replied.

> **MR. STARR**: The rule of the Court—that it articulated in *Tinker*. The rule of the Court as articulated in *Tinker* is that there is, in fact, a right to political speech, subject to disruption, requirements that the speech not be disruptive.

Justice Kennedy probed further.

JUSTICE KENNEDY: Disruptive of what? Disruptive of the classroom order? There was no classroom here.

Notice that, at this very early point in the proceedings (just over one minute had elapsed), Justice Kennedy appears to doubt a crucial petitioner's claim, namely that Frederick's banner was disruptive. In his reply, Starr expanded his argument to encompass the nature of the Olympic torch run event.

MR. STARR: Including but not limited to. This was a school authorized event, this was education outside of the classroom. It was essentially a school simply out of doors. It was essentially—

At this point, a skeptical Justice Souter joined the interrogation.

JUSTICE SOUTER: Well, I can understand if they unfurled the banner in a classroom that it would be disruptive, but what did it disrupt on the sidewalk?

MR. STARR: The educational mission of the school.

JUSTICE SOUTER: No, but I mean, that's at a level of generality that doesn't get us very far. I mean, what specifically did it disrupt? Did it disrupt the parade, did it disrupt teaching, what was it?

MR. STARR: 5520,[64] a school policy of the board that says emphatically that political speech is protected, embracing *Tinker*.

JUSTICE SOUTER: Then if that's the rule, the school can make any rule that it wants on any subject restrictive of speech, and if anyone violates it, the result is, on your reasoning, it's disruptive under *Tinker*.

On the defensive, Starr tried to reply.

MR. STARR: Not at all. I think that in that form—

Souter interjected.

JUSTICE SOUTER: Then I'm missing the argument.

Starr persisted.

MR. STARR: The argument is that this Court in *Tinker* articulated a rule that allows the school boards considerable discretion both in identifying the educational mission and to prevent disruption of that mission, and this is disruptive of the mission—

At this point, Justice Kennedy asked the first of, by my count, a total of twenty hypothetical questions that various justices posed to either Starr or Mertz.

> **JUSTICE KENNEDY**: Well, suppose you have—suppose you have a mission to have a global school. Can they ban American flags on lapel pins?

Kennedy's conjecture created an opening for Starr, and he took it.

> **MR. STARR**: Absolutely not, because under *Tinker* that is political expression. Let me be very specific. This case is ultimately about drugs and other illegal substances.

Just over two and a half minutes into his allotted time, Ken Starr had accomplished two of his three tasks. He had told the Court that this case was about holding accountable student speech that disrupts the school's mission to combat illegal drug use. Furthermore, in so doing, Starr adroitly reasserted the pertinence of *Tinker*'s tentative endorsement of student speech: protecting "political speech" while legitimizing punishment of "disruptive speech."

Starr might as well have stopped while he was ahead, because a hypothetical put by Justice Ginsburg threatened to divert him. Immediately after Starr stated his view that *Morse v. Frederick* was "ultimately about drugs," Ginsburg inquired:

> **JUSTICE GINSBURG**: So if the sign had been "Bong Stinks for Jesus,"[65] that would be, and Morse had the same reaction, that this was demeaning to the Olympics and it was unruly conduct, that there would be a protected right under *Tinker* because the message was not promoting drugs?

Justice Ginsburg's somewhat confusing question appeared to throw Starr. His reply potentially exacerbated skepticism that any of the justices may have had about enlarging school administrators' discretion to interpret student speech. Starr appeared to contend that, if Morse had interpreted "Bong Stinks for Jesus" as disruptive, the principal's view was definitive.

> **MR. STARR**: . . . Under our theory, we think she could have interfered with that because it was disruptive to the event, it was disorderly to the event itself, but the—

Starr's seemingly broad-gauged conception again prompted Justice Souter to raise questions. Souter did so in a way that changed the subject to political speech and spotlighted arbitrary administrative discretion.

> **JUSTICE SOUTER**: What would be disorderly? I don't understand this disorder. If somebody holds up a sign and says change the marijuana laws, why is it disruptive of anything, simply because the school quite naturally has said we support the enforcement of the law, and the law right now does forbid the use of marijuana. . . . It's political speech, it seems to me. I don't see what it disrupts unless disruption simply means any statement of disagreement with a position officially adopted by the school. Is that what you mean by disruption?

Starr back-pedaled haltingly.

MR. STARR: No. Your Honor, first of all, this is, I think, an unusual characterization, namely for this to be called political speech. We would— . . . Your Honor, let's back up, if I may. Someone has to interpret the message and the front line message interpreter is the school official. . . .

JUSTICE SOUTER: . . . But as I understood the argument you were making, [political speech advocating change in marijuana laws] would still be regarded as an exception, as it were, to *Tinker*, because it was disruptive. And it was disruptive in the sense that it disagreed with official school policy, which was to enforce the law or support the law as it was. Is that your position on what disruption means under *Tinker*?

MR. STARR: But our—the answer is no. . . .

At this point, Justice Scalia came to Starr's rescue by refocusing the discussion on drugs.[66]

JUSTICE SCALIA: So you want to get away from a hypothetical then. I don't know why you try to defend a hypothetical that involves a banner that says amend marijuana laws. That's not the case as you see it, is it? . . . This banner was interpreted as meaning smoke pot, no?

A grateful Starr replied:

MR. STARR: It was interpreted—exactly, yes. It was interpreted as an encouragement of the drug culture . . .

Back on track, responding to questions from Justice Alito and Chief Justice Roberts,[67] Ken Starr returned to his argument that *Tinker* protects political speech, but not speech advocating use of illegal drugs. He seemed successfully to be charting a path between arbitrary and defensible interpretive discretion, until Justice Ginsburg posed another hypothetical.

Starr had just pointed out that one fact distinguishing *Tinker* from *Morse v. Frederick* was the absence of written school district policy governing student speech in Des Moines compared to Juneau. When Justice Ginsburg asked what difference this circumstance would make, her hypothetical question raised the specter of arbitrary administrative discretion in a way that piqued Justice Kennedy's skepticism.

JUSTICE GINSBURG: . . . If the school had a policy, defend our troops in Vietnam, would that have brought this into the category that you are now carving out? You said that *Tinker* had no policy, but suppose the school did have a policy, patriotism, we support our troops, no bad speech about the war in Vietnam. Should *Tinker* have come out the other way?

Starr responded, "No, it should not . . ." His reply caused Justice Kennedy to weigh back into the discussion.

JUSTICE KENNEDY: Yes, but the rule you proposed, I thought, in response to my question is that the school has wide discretion to define its educational mission and it can restrict speech that's inconsistent with that mission. . . . And it seems to me that's much broader than *Tinker*.

Now you said, well, there is an exception for political speech. Well, but then you're right with Justice Ginsburg's hypothetical, let's suppose that they have a particular view on a political issue, No Child Left Behind, or foreign intervention and so forth.

For a second time Starr floundered, offering something of a non sequitur reply.

> **MR. STARR**: Justice Kennedy, the words that you articulated are essentially quotes of *Fraser* or *Kuhlmeier*, so there is a broadening of the lens and a restoration, frankly, of greater school discretion in those two cases than one might see in *Tinker*. They of course drew, as you well know, from Justice Black's warning in dissent of *Tinker* that the federal courts, federal judiciary should not be extending itself unduly into the work of the school boards'—

Once again, Justice Scalia came to Starr's aid with a hypothetical of his own.

> **JUSTICE SCALIA**: Why do we have to get into the question of what the school board's policy is and what things they can make as policy? Surely it can be the—it must be the policy of any school to discourage breaking the law. I mean, suppose this banner had said kill somebody, and there was not explicit regulation of the school that said you should not, you should not foster murder. Wouldn't that be suppressible?

Vocalizing his relief, Starr sighed, "Of course . . . The answer is yes." Having been put back on track a second time, Starr stayed on message for another eighteen and a half minutes before reserving the remainder of his time. His core theme was "the [banner's] message here is in fact critical . . . that's why this case is here."[68] A corollary to Starr's core theme was that Deborah Morse was the "message interpreter" whose judgment should be vindicated.

Right at the end of his time, Starr turned yet another skeptical question from Justice Souter into an opportunity to address why Morse should not be held personally liable for her judgment that January day on Glacier Avenue. Justice Souter again had pressed Starr on the issue of disruption, opining that "'Bong Hits 4 Jesus' . . . sounds like just a kid's provocative statement to me." Starr replied:

> **MR. STARR**: Your Honor, with all due respect, the key is to allow the school official to interpret the message as long as that interpretation is reasonable. You might disagree with that just as Justice Brennan disagreed with whether Matt Fraser's speech[69] was all that terrible. But he said even though it wasn't all that terrible I nonetheless defer to the interpretation of school officials. That's what our educational system is all about.

Justice Ginsburg took issue with Starr's reference to *Fraser*.

> **JUSTICE GINSBURG**: But those were the words and characterizing them as offensive, but here [in *Morse*] one could look at these words and say it's just nonsense. Or one could say it's like "mares eat oats." It isn't clear that this is "smoke pot."

Starr stayed focused.

> MR. STARR: Your Honor, again, Deborah Morse, a conscientious principal, interpreted the
> message in light of the subculture of the school where drug use is a serious problem. And it
> was on-the-spot judgment. We believe that judgment was reasonable as opposed to a judg-
> ment reached in judicial chambers, but we know that that was also the judgment of the super-
> intendent and district judge—[70]

With this statement, Ken Starr articulated the third, and final, element in his accountability
narrative. He brought Deborah Morse front and center, lauding her professional exercise of
discretion, and urging as a matter of policy that the Court to defer to it. In spite of a couple
brief "detours," negotiated with Justice Scalia's obliging assistance, Starr remained focused
on his task. As we have seen, in theoretical terms, Starr's effectiveness can be evaluated in
terms of a threefold task: (1) whether positive facts are forcefully presented and negative
ones effectively dealt with; (2) whether pertinent points of law are forcefully presented; (3)
whether policy concerns are forcefully presented.[71] Assessed on these terms, Starr's performance can be judged impressive. The extent to which he successfully persuaded a majority
of Supreme Court's justices with his performance remains to be seen.

Before Doug Mertz took the lectern, Deputy Solicitor General Edwin S. Kneedler
argued on behalf of the United States as amicus curiae supporting Deborah Morse. By the
time Kneedler addressed the Court, he had been a career U.S. government lawyer since
1975. With the exception of a year, immediately after law school, as a clerk to Judge James
R. Browning on the Ninth Circuit, Kneedler worked in the U.S. Justice Department. After
three and a half years in the Office of Legal Counsel, Kneedler joined the solicitor general's
office in June 1979. He has been there ever since. Kneedler was appointed deputy solicitor
general in 1993.[72] No stranger to the Supreme Court, Kneedler argued his one-hundredth
case before the justices two days shy of a year after his appearance in *Morse v. Frederick*.[73]

Kneedler spoke and answered questions for about eleven minutes. His exchanges with
three of the justices shed light on the fault lines along which judicial opinion in *Morse v.
Frederick* were crystallizing. Kneedler began:

> MR. KNEEDLER: The First Amendment does not require public school officials to stand
> aside and permit students who are entrusted to their supervision and care to promote or
> encourage the use of illegal drugs. As this Court observed in *Earls*, the nationwide drug—
> drug epidemic makes the war against drugs a pressing concern in every school.[74]

Justice Kennedy stopped Kneedler to ask the same first question he had raised with Starr.

> JUSTICE KENNEDY: And is that the rationale on which you wish us to decide this case; noth-
> ing more broad?

Following suit with Starr, Kneedler agreed with Kennedy.

MR. KNEEDLER: The Court need not decide anything more broadly than that.

Hewing to requesting this narrow rule was prudent because, when Kneedler went on to speak more generally about schools not having "to tolerate a message that is inconsistent with its basic educational [mission]," he set off alarm bells for Justice Alito.

JUSTICE ALITO: Well, that's a very—I find that a very, very disturbing argument, because schools [can and they have] defined their educational missions so broadly that they can suppress all sorts of political speech and speech expressing fundamental values of the students, under the banner of . . . getting rid of speech that's inconsistent with educational mission.

Kneedler got Alito's message. He replied:

MR. KNEEDLER: That's why I think . . . it would make a lot of sense for the Court to articulate a rule that had to do with encouraging illegal conduct . . .

Justices Kennedy and Alito were expressing concern about administrators wielding unbridled discretion under the rubric of a school's "education mission." As Justice Kennedy said to Kneedler: "Well, then you're not arguing for the broad educational mission, which is what you said at the first." Kennedy's and Alito's comments and their questions sought guidance—and reassurance—from the plaintiffs' counsel and their amicus that the Court could embrace Deborah Morse's accountability narrative without creating a situation where she, and other school officials, would themselves lack accountability.

In sharp contrast, Justice Souter voiced skepticism about the entire accountability narrative itself. He doubted that Frederick had done anything for which he should answer.

JUSTICE SOUTER: Given the fact that this is a First Amendment case, isn't a court forced into the position if it's going to be consistent with what else we have said, even at the final appellate level, of giving pretty careful scrutiny to the statement itself in determining whether it may be suppressed or punished?

And if we do that, is it such a reasonable construction that this is an—an incitement to illegal drug use? I mean it's a statement which makes, makes the drug law look a little ridiculous, I think, but I'm not sure that that is very distinguishable from a statement saying "you ought to change the drug law."

Confronted with Justice Souter's qualms, Kneedler reasserted the need to defer to Principal Morse's discretion.

MR. KNEEDLER: Well, I . . . think in, in this Court's decisions dealing with public schools, this Court has, has a consistent theme as to give deference to the judgments by educators. . . .

Frustrated, Justice Souter replied:

JUSTICE SOUTER: [L]et me ask you this. And maybe this is the, as far as we can go with it here.

Is that the answer to the question here about what the statement means?

MR. KNEEDLER: Yes.

JUSTICE SOUTER: In other words, if we give deference, your argument wins. But if we don't give deference, then does anybody really know what the statement means?

MR. KNEEDLER: I don't think the question is what Mr. Frederick intended. The question is what a reasonable observer would think. And the words *bong hits* are slang that would be particularly, have a particular characteristic of getting across to other student[s], and they suggest a casual tolerance and encouragement of [drugs].

This Kneedler-Souter exchange is highly illuminating. It captures a central aspect of the controversy over which the justices were ruminating. Does a banner displaying the vague message "BONG HiTS 4 JESUS" rise to the level of "disruptive," hence, constitutionally unprotected speech—and who makes that call? In other words, should the Court defer to Deborah Morse's on-the-spot judgment that because Joe Frederick's banner advocated illegal drug use he should be held accountable? In a single sentence, Justice Souter went to the heart of this controversy, and provided the key to its outcome: "if we give deference," he told Kneedler, "your argument wins."

From the outset, it was clear that Doug Mertz was going to experience rougher sailing than either Ken Starr or Edwin Kneedler. Mertz began forthrightly enough:

MR. MERTZ: Mr. Chief Justice and may it please the Court: This is a case about free speech. It is not a case about drugs.[75]

At this point—a mere six seconds and twenty-three words into his argument—Chief Justice Roberts derailed Mertz.[76] Roberts parried Mertz's opening with nineteen telling words.

CHIEF JUSTICE ROBERTS: It's a case about money. Your client wants money from the principal personally for her actions in this case.

Straightaway put on the defensive, Mertz replied:

MR. MERTZ: [Frederick] does have a damages claim against the school district and the principal, but that's by no means his chief object here. The overwhelming object is to assert his free speech—

Again joining the interrogation at an early stage, Justice Kennedy pushed Mertz.

JUSTICE KENNEDY: Well, would you waive damages against this principal who has devoted her life to the school, and you're seeking damages from her for this sophomoric sign that was held up?

Apparently, by this time in the proceedings, with a total of almost half an hour elapsed, Justice Kennedy's previous uncertainty over whether or not Frederick's banner was disruptive had been supplanted by his distaste over Frederick's damages claim against Morse. Attorney Mertz's reply, by which he sought to assuage Kennedy from being vexed, gave Chief Justice Roberts an opening to express his general policy worry.

> **MR. MERTZ**: We are certainly willing to negotiate a minimum settlement of damages. That is not the object here.
>
> **CHIEF JUSTICE ROBERTS**: But there's a broader issue of whether principals and teachers around the country have to fear that they're going to have to pay out of their personal pocket whenever they take actions pursuant to established board policies that they think are necessary to promote the school's educational mission.

Mertz's acknowledgment of the chief justice's concern did not mollify Roberts.

> **MR. MERTZ**: That is indeed a legitimate fear, Your Honor, and we believe the existing law takes care of it by requiring before qualified immunity can be breached that there be a demonstration that under the existing law at the time available to her—
>
> **CHIEF JUSTICE ROBERTS**: And you think it was clearly established that she had to allow a student at a school-supervised function to hold a fifteen-foot banner saying "Bong Hits 4 Jesus"?
>
> **MR. MERTZ**: I think it was clearly established at the time, Your Honor, that a principal could not engage in viewpoint censorship of a nondisruptive expression, under both Ninth Circuit law and this Court's law . . .

This initial exchange set an uncongenial tone for Doug Mertz's half hour before the Court. More important, the exchange shaped the proceeding's trajectory. It seemed as though Mertz was thrown off balance, losing control of the exchange. Consequently, Mertz found it difficult to accomplish his primary task which, in a manner similar to Ken Starr, entailed conveying to the justices Frederick's injury narrative.

As I describe it in Chapter 5, Frederick's injury narrative is a "tale about a concerned student who, due to the rash actions of a school administrator, was deprived of his well-established First Amendment right to free expression. . . . Joseph Frederick attended the Olympic torch relay intending to exercise his First Amendment rights and was thwarted in doing so. But for Principal Morse's intemperate intervention, he and his friends would have hoisted their banner and had their innocuous nonsense message immortalized on television. Morse damaged Frederick by making what was just good fun into an incident followed by punishment."[77] Beyond telling a compelling story Mertz, again like Starr, also needed to link his narrative to prevailing legal precedent, showing that *Tinker* controlled, not *Fraser* or *Hazelwood*—nor *Vernonia* or *Earls*, for that matter. Third, Mertz needed to argue persuasively that, by siding with Principal Morse, the Court would stifle student expression while underwriting expansive, potentially arbitrary, administrative discretion. What transpired instead was, by and large, a confounding series of digressions, punctuated by occasional expressions of incredulity, bookended by Justice Roberts' "mantra" about monetary damages.

Roughly five minutes into Doug Mertz's time, Justice Scalia initiated an exchange that illustrates how the exchanges were both digressive and, from time to time, scornful. Frustrated by a meandering exchange about when and where a sign might be disruptive, Justice Scalia interjected:

> JUSTICE SCALIA: Well, but . . . the school has a program, an antidrug program that shows movies, it brings in policemen and social workers to preach against drug use and you're saying that—nevermind unfurling a banner[,] [y]ou're saying that it has to let students contradict this message it's trying to teach, to walk around, you know, with a button that says "Smoke Pot, It's Fun." . . .
>
>   Does the school have to do that?

Missing an opportunity to differentiate between Justice Scalia's loaded hypothetical and the circumstances on the ground on Glacier Avenue, and to reaffirm the pertinence of *Tinker* to Frederick's expression, Mertz instead tried to address Scalia's question.

> MR. MERTZ: I believe, Your Honor, that a nondisruptive pin, badge, whatever you want to call it, would have to be tolerated. However, they would not have to tolerate a student who interrupts a[n] antidrug presentation.

Mertz's response set him on a perilous path.

> JUSTICE SCALIA: But the school, even though it is trying to teach one point of view, can allow students to come in and undermine that point of view, assuming that it's legitimate to teach that point of view? It can allow students to come in and undermine what it's trying to teach? . . .
>
>   And that's not disruption in your view?
>
> MR. MERTZ: I think they cannot prevent presentations of a contrary viewpoint as long as it is done in such a way that it doesn't interfere with the school's own presentation of its viewpoint.
>
> JUSTICE KENNEDY: Can the student be allowed to wear a button that says "Rape Is Fun"?
>
> MR. MERTZ: No, I don't think so—
>
> JUSTICE KENNEDY: Why?
>
> MR. MERTZ: There is a distinction here.
>
> JUSTICE KENNEDY: Why?
>
> MR. MERTZ: Because when you're talking about hate speech, speech that advocates violence, then you're in another category of speech. There has been a general recognition—

Justice Scalia sprung his trap.

> JUSTICE SCALIA: Nonviolent crimes are okay, it's only violent crimes that you can't, you can not [*sic*] promote, right? Right? . . .
>
>   "Extortion is Profitable," that's okay?
>
> MR. MERTZ: Well—

JUSTICE SCALIA: This is a very, very, with all respect, ridiculous line. I mean, I can understand you're saying you cannot promote things that are unlawful, but to say, oh, it's only violent, where do you get that line from, only violent unlawful acts?[78]

Several of Mertz's liabilities are on display in this exchange. By taking Scalia's "Smoke Pot,
It's Fun" hypothetical at face value, Mertz necessarily embraced the justice's framing of the
situation. Scalia set up his hypothetical in a way that the "Smoke Pot, It's Fun" button is
unavoidably disruptive. Mertz's answer follows suit. Mertz is boxed in twice, initially by
not rejecting Justice Scalia's portrayal of an inherently disruptive expression, and then by
Mertz's response to Justice Kennedy's hypothetical about the "Rape Is Fun" button. Mertz's
rejecting the theoretical "Rape Is Fun" button while defending the supposed "Smoke Pot,
It's Fun" button is sort of "ridiculous." Although perhaps valid as a formal distinction
between violent speech versus political speech, as a defense of one form of "disruptive"
student expression over another, his reply is problematical. By responding to, instead of
retorting, these fraught questions, Mertz unwittingly played straight man, setting up Scalia's
quip. Damagingly, rather than employing the justices' comments and questions as grist for
his mill, aggressively engaging the justices in repartee to stay on message and pursue his
case, Mertz assumed the reactive posture of a resource instead of being resourceful.

Another example of how Mertz's time—and case—slipped away while he was bogged
down in minutiae is a five-minute exchange between Mertz and Justice Breyer. Without
reproducing the entire interaction, the excerpt below shows how "trees" (disputed facts)
swallowed Mertz's (narrative) "forest." The exchange began with Justice Breyer describing
the circumstances of the Olympic torch relay, with which Mertz took issue.

JUSTICE BREYER: . . . So it sounds to me like [teachers said] you're going to one place, stand
together, behave yourselves, watch the relay, and the teachers will be there and take you back
to class. Now is there something else in the record that suggests something different?

MR. MERTZ: There is a major dispute on that point, Your Honor. We presented several
affidavits that showed individual teachers—

JUSTICE BREYER: Just tell me where to look. Where are the conflicting affidavits? I'm
just reading from page 51 of the joint appendix. I didn't know there was a dispute.

MR. MERTZ: It would be on pages 32, 34, 36.

JUSTICE BREYER: Okay. I'll look at those. Another somewhat minor point. Can I ask you
another point about the record? . . .

Was there any—there was no requirement that they stay together, they didn't have to go
across the street or stay on campus, they could wander off distantly[?]

MR. MERTZ: They could, and many of them did. . . .

JUSTICE BREYER: Can I ask another record point, just to I know where to look?

MR. MERTZ: Yes.

By responding to Justice Breyer's series of narrowly specific questions, Mr. Mertz acceded
to the oral argument equivalent of being "nickel-and-dimed." No doubt, Justice Breyer did
not intend to drain attorney Mertz's time of substance and effect. Breyer sincerely sought

to clarify aspects of a record notoriously shot through with disagreements over basic facts. Nevertheless, by not utilizing Breyer's questions to change the subject and get back on track, Mertz spent scarce time on details at the expense of his narrative.

After wallowing in the factual swamp with Justice Breyer for almost five minutes, Mertz heard a familiar refrain from Chief Justice Roberts.[79] "Can we get back to what the case is about[?]," Roberts inquired.

> **CHIEF JUSTICE ROBERTS**: You think the law was so clearly established when this happened that the principal, that the instant that the banner was unfurled, snowballs are flying around, the torch is coming, should have said, oh I remember under *Tinker* I can only take the sign down if it's disruptive. But then under *Fraser* I can do something if it interferes with the basic mission, and under *Kuhlmeier* I got this other thing. So she should have known at that point that she could not take the banner down, and it was so clear that she should have to pay out of her own pocket because of it.
>
> **MR. MERTZ**: Mr. Chief Justice, there are two different time points we have to talk about. There's the heat of the moment out there on the street, but then later back in the office when she actually decided to levy the punishment after she had talked to him, after she heard why he did it and why he didn't do it, after she had had a chance to consult with the school district's counsel. At that point in the calmness of her office, then she should indeed have known it. And she did testify that she had taken a master's degree course in school law in which she studied *Kuhlmeier* and *Fraser* and *Tinker*. So—
>
> **CHIEF JUSTICE ROBERTS**: And so it should be perfectly clear to her exactly what she could and couldn't do.
>
> **MR. MERTZ**: Yes.

Here, Doug Mertz's nemesis chimed in:

> **JUSTICE SCALIA**: As it is to us, right? [*Laughter.*]

Mertz's qualified immunity argument prompted even Justice Souter, clearly dubious of the petitioners' case, immediately to voice his skepticism about Mertz's reasoning.

> **JUSTICE SOUTER**: I mean, we have had a debate here for going on fifty minutes about what *Tinker* means, about the proper characterization of the behavior, the nonspeech behavior. The school's terms in dealing with the kids that morning. The meaning of the, of the statement. We've been debating this in this courtroom for going on an hour, and it seems to me that however you come out, there is reasonable debate. Should the teacher have known, even in the, in the calm deliberative atmosphere of the school later, what the correct answer is?
>
> **MR. MERTZ**: We believe at the very least she should have known that one cannot punish a nondisruptive holding of a sign because it said something you disagree with.

Mertz's characterization of Joe Frederick's banner as "nondisruptive" provoked Justice Kennedy to proclaim:

JUSTICE KENNEDY: Of course, I disagree with the characterization on disruptive. It was completely disruptive of the message, of the theme that the school wanted to promote. Completely disruptive of the reason for letting the students out to begin with. Completely disruptive of the school's image that they wanted to portray in sponsoring the Olympics.

By this point, Justice Kennedy apparently had made up his mind on the "disruption" question. His pivotal declaration, fifty-one minutes into oral argument, encapsulates Doug Mertz's unavailing half hour. For Justice Kennedy, Joseph Frederick's banner was disruptive thrice over: of the Juneau School District's message and theme; of the Juneau School District's reason for excusing students to attend the Olympic torch relay; and of the Juneau School District's image in sponsoring the Olympics. Mertz replied gamely, once again correcting the record. "Well, they weren't sponsoring the Olympics," he amended, "they weren't even sponsoring the event actually. They simply let the students out to watch." Mertz replied resolutely, but inappositely. Instead of countering Justice Kennedy's conclusion on the key issue of disruptiveness, Mertz remained mired in marginalia. This Kennedy-Mertz exchange is akin to a batter whiffing—three strikes, you're out.

For the remainder of his time at the lectern, roughly six and a half minutes, several members of the Court (Ginsburg, Scalia, Kennedy, Roberts, and Breyer) quizzed Mertz about the circumstances and significance of Joe Frederick's truancy on January 24, 2002.[80] At the very end of this interrogation, in closing, Mertz managed briefly to return to his injury narrative.

MR. MERTZ: . . . We have two independent bases for defending [Frederick] here. One is the pure free speech in a public place argument. That's the one that hinges on the fact that he was not among the released students. The other argument, which we believe in equally, is that even if it were an on-campus or on an extension of campus like a field trip, then under *Tinker* because [Frederick's banner] was not disruptive they cannot punish it.

My time is up. I thank the Court.

Kenneth Starr had the final word. Earlier in the proceedings, eighteen and a half minutes into oral argument, Starr had reserved the balance of his time. When Doug Mertz sat down, Chief Justice Roberts turned to Starr: "Mr. Starr, you have a minute remaining." Petitioners' counsel made effective use of it.

MR. STARR: For the reasons that have been discussed, under no circumstances should Deborah Morse, a conscientious principal, be subjected to the possibility of punitive damages or compensatory damages.

A very brief factual point. In light of the richness of the discussion with respect to the facts, I would guide the Court to page 109[81] of the joint appendix. This is Deborah Morse's interrogatory answer and there she sets forth the facts, and that bleeds into the law.

To promote drugs—and this is our fundamental suggestion and submission. To promote drugs is utterly inconsistent with the basic educational mission of the school, and for this Court to suggest to the contrary would really be quite inconsistent with much of its drug jurisprudence, [*V*]*ernonia* and *Earls*. The opinion of the Court in *Earls* 2002 is especially powerful with respect to the scourge of drugs and their dangers.

More broadly, the Court does not need to go more broadly, but the Court has spoken with respect to the need to defer to school officials in identifying the educational mission. But we know that there are in fact constitutional limits. Those limits are captured in *Tinker*. A passive pure political speech that reflects on the part of the school board a standardless discretionary effort to squelch any kind of controversial discussion, that casts a pall of orthodoxy over the classroom. We are light-years away from that.

Starr sounded all the right notes. For openers, he addressed the emerging Achilles' heel of the defendant's case. Knowing with certainty that Chief Justice Roberts and Justice Kennedy—probably along with Justices Alito, Scalia, and Thomas, and likely including Justices Breyer and Souter—rejected Joseph Frederick's damages claim against Deborah Morse, Starr reiterated that "under no circumstances" should such damages be awarded. Next, Starr seemed to indulge in a bit of sarcasm, while turning again to precedent. Although one cannot be certain from the oral and written transcripts, one can visualize a knowing smile crossing Starr's face as he referenced "the richness of the discussion with respect to the facts." Given the exasperating fruitlessness of those discussions from the point of view of his opponent's case, it is easy to believe that Starr was sporting. In any event, reiterating his accountability narrative, Starr connected Principal Morse's interrogatory account of the ways Frederick's banner was disruptive, keying on promoting illegal drug use, to the Court's "drug jurisprudence, [*V*]*ernonia* and *Earls*." Finally, in a passage both dazzling and disingenuous, Starr invited the Court to rule broadly in favor of school officials' discretion, while reassuring the Court that *Tinker*'s "constitutional limits"—with which he aligned the petitioners—stood in the path of any "standardless discretionary effort to squelch any kind of controversial discussion." BONG HiTS 4 JESUS, Starr closed, is "light-years away from" such discussion.

Justice Kennedy and, to a lesser extent, Justice Souter, have played starring roles in my analysis of oral argument in *Morse v. Frederick*. They figure prominently because, in part, they participated actively in these proceedings. More important, Kennedy and Souter stand out because they are key players in contemporary Supreme Court decision making. The current U.S. Supreme Court is different from the group of justices that heard and decided *Vernonia* and *Earls*. As I wrote in Chapter 4, "A New Century, a Different Court": "We will never know how [Justice Sandra Day O'Connor] would have responded to the specific issues raised in *Morse v. Frederick*. . . . What we do know is that the Supreme Court to which Deborah Morse brought her appeal was not the same body that saw Justice O'Connor dissent in *Vernonia* and *Earls*."[82] The nature of the difference is decisive.

Following Justice O'Connor's departure on January 31, 2006, conventional wisdom assigned her pivotal "swing vote" status to Justice Anthony Kennedy. Here is how legal journalist Jeffrey Toobin described the transition in his influential book *The Nine: Inside the Secret World of the Supreme Court*:

At the Court, suddenly it was up to Anthony Kennedy. Even more than O'Connor had over the previous decade, Kennedy now controlled the outcome of case after case. During the

Rehnquist years, O'Connor and Kennedy had had idiosyncratic enough views that it wasn't always clear whose vote would turn out to be dispositive. But the Roberts Court had four outspoken conservatives—Roberts, Scalia, Thomas, and Alito—and four liberals, at least by contemporary standards—Stevens, Souter, Ginsburg, and Breyer. Kennedy, always, was in the middle. . . .[83]

Robert Barnes, *Washington Post* Supreme Court reporter, offered this complementary analysis.

It is easy to define Justice Anthony M. Kennedy's role on the Supreme Court . . . and difficult to exaggerate his importance.

To borrow President Bush's self-description, he's "The Decider."

He is the only justice to be in the majority in each of the [2006–2007] term's unusually high number of 5 to 4 decisions. At this midpoint of the court's rulings, he has been on the losing side in only two of the 40 opinions issued.

Because the court so far has shown itself to be strikingly—and evenly—divided on ideological issues, Kennedy holds enormous power in pivoting between the left and right, legal experts say. He stands alone in the middle—and that enhances his importance.

"There's nowhere else to go" when each side looks for a majority-clinching fifth vote, said Lee Epstein, a professor at the Northwestern University School of Law and an expert on the court's voting patterns. "There is this giant hurdle called Kennedy." . . .

"So Justice Kennedy is even more of an important swing vote than he was before," said Richard Dieter, executive director of the Death Penalty Information Center, which opposes capital punishment. . . .

"It's clearly going to be an important role he's playing," Dieter said. "People are speaking to him in their arguments."[84]

Lawyers who argue before the Supreme Court understand the late Justice Brennan's "rule of five," namely that five votes make a majority.[85] Such advocates also know that putting a majority together is a matter of coalition building, of which Brennan was a master.[86] Savvy lawyers realize that getting to five on a Court narrowly divided, four to four, requires persuading the justice in the middle. These days, the middle justice is Anthony Kennedy. That is why professor Lee Epstein said about Kennedy, "There's nowhere else to go."

Among Supreme Court scholars, when it comes to identifying the "go-to justice" on the Supreme Court in any given term, there is wide agreement. Students of the Court generally share the view that there is such a thing as the "Justice who is crucial to the outcome of a case and, thus, to the establishment of public policy."[87] Further, these legal academics and political scientists are convinced that, on a closely divided court, the reason one justice out of nine plays a pivotal role "is hardly a mystery."[88] As professors Andrew D. Martin, Kevin M. Quinn, and Lee Epstein explain:

[S]ince the publication of Duncan Black's seminal work we know that, under certain conditions, the outcome of a majority vote will "pull" towards the position favored by the median.

That is because, as Black demonstrated, the median voter is essential to secure a majority. In the context of judicial politics, this means that the legal policy desired by the median Justice will (again, under certain conditions and voting procedures) be the choice of the Court's majority and, as such, the median can serve as an appropriate way to characterize the preferences of "the Court" and the outcomes it reaches.[89]

Using Black's work as their point of departure, Martin, Quinn, and Epstein identify the median justice for the years 1937–2002. Between 1990, when Souter joined the Court, and 2002, four years before O'Connor left the Court, three justices played the median role: David Souter (1990–1991), Sandra Day O'Connor (1992, 1994, 1999–2002), and Anthony Kennedy (1993, 1995–1998).[90] In the process of reporting their findings Martin, Quinn, and Epstein also offer a couple of revealing observations. First, they note that "the median fluctuates considerably over time—even during periods of stability in Court membership (or what social scientists call 'natural courts')."[91] Second, they remark on the "high degree of uncertainty surrounding the identity of the median justice . . . certainty about the median's identity is far from the norm."[92] Both these comments suggest that many individual justices' policy preferences, hence the "center of gravity," as it were, of the Supreme Court, are relatively dynamic rather than static over time. In other words, the trajectory of judicial choices changes over time.

Martin, Quinn, and Epstein's observations are supported by analysis Andrew Martin and Kevin Quinn published three years before their article with Lee Epstein.[93] Employing a highly sophisticated "dynamic ideal point model,"[94] the authors plot individual justices' preferences between 1953 and 1999. They find that "it is clear that many justices trend."[95] By "trend" Martin and Quinn mean change direction in their voting preferences. Their data analysis shows that Justice Kennedy trended relatively little during his first eleven years on the High Bench (1988–1999), remaining squarely conservative vis-à-vis the median.[96] Subsequent analysis shows that, beginning in 2001 Justice Kennedy clearly began to move toward the median, a tendency even more noticeable following Justice O'Connor's departure from the Court in 2006.[97]

So the median justice is the "go-to" jurist on a closely divided Supreme Court. Currently, Justice Kennedy is that justice. But the picture is more multidimensional than median-justice theory suggests. There are other ways to identify the justice—or justices—to whom, as Richard Dieter, the death penalty opponent quoted above by journalist Robert Barnes, put it: "[p]eople are speaking . . . in their [oral] arguments." A mathematician and a law professor argue on behalf of an alternative methodology. Instead of analyzing decisions predictably closely split along a single dimension, on a Court narrowly divided by ideological difference, Paul H. Edelman and Jim Chen set their sights on unpredictable, multidimensional voting coalitions. "Supreme Court Justices' decisions," they point out, "may in some cases be structured along divergent or cross-cutting issues dimensions. These alternative issue dimensions can complicate the identification of the Court's pivotal justice."[98] Consequently, Edelman and Chen are less concerned to discover the median justice than to determine the "most powerful" justice.

With their scholarly tongues only somewhat planted in their respective cheeks, Edelman and Chen refer to the justice with more voting power relative to other colleagues as the "most dangerous Justice."[99] "[S]ophisticated observers have always understood," they write, "that the Supreme Court's internal dynamics are inherently political. 'Law, as it is generated by the Supreme Court, is the long-term product of short-term strategic decision making.' The politically savvy realize that possession of 'high political powers' heightens the value of 'strategy and tactics' to each of the Justices and to the court as an institution." Edelman and Chen conclude: "The Supreme Court, an institution designed to be a step removed from the maelstrom of partisan politics, yields its secrets only to those Justices who are willing and able to seize the weapons of politics."[100] Edelman and Chen fine-tuned their "power pageant" approach and responded to their critics in a series of four articles.[101]

In their fourth article, they rank "the Justices in terms of their individual ability to alter or shape Court outcomes" for the Rehnquist Natural Court, 1994–2004.[102] Edelman's and Chen's analysis yields a couple of surprises. First, "while others trumpet Justice O'Connor, we remain convinced that Kennedy held real power in the Rehnquist Court. . . . Justice Kennedy is now commonly assumed to occupy the power center on the Court, but it appears that he did so during the Rehnquist Court as well."[103] Why are Edelman and Chen convinced? The key is a justice's ability to form coalitions, defined as convergence of opinion—not merely agreement on the judgment. "While appearing to be a swing voter in any number of votes, Justice O'Connor in fact is less than willing to form coalitions outside the predictably conservative coalition of Rehnquist, Scalia, Kennedy, and Thomas, the usual suspects. . . . Justice O'Connor's exceedingly narrow approach thus may have won her majorities behind the judgment, but not allies with respect to her opinions."[104]

Second, Edelman and Chen's analysis crowns Justice David Souter first runner-up in their power pageant. They ask: "What to make of Justice Souter" when, "at least according to the median voter theory," since Souter "is among the most liberal Justices on the Court . . . it would appear unlikely . . . that he would wield any power on the Court."[105]

> That Justice Souter rates so high on [an index taking into account the credibility of a justice's threat to defect from a coalition] is indicative of his fluidity in structuring coalitions and his willingness to gather support wherever (and with whomever) he can. William Brennan is often lauded as a brilliant strategist within the Court; perhaps Souter has undertaken that role at least to the extent that he is able to form coalitions effectively and flexibly when it serves his policy objectives.[106]

As coalition builders, then, for a decade, Justices Kennedy and Souter were "dangerous" justices, that is, effective coalition builders relative to their colleagues on the Court. By Edelman and Chen's measures Kennedy and Souter held the balance of policy-making influence. This circumstance makes calling the 1994–2004 Court the "Rehnquist Court" a highly problematical misnomer. William Rehnquist may have presided over the tribunal, but Anthony Kennedy and, secondarily, David Souter shaped the voice with which the Court spoke. Further complicating the picture is the fact that, although William Rehnquist may have been chief justice, by Martin, Quinn, and Epstein's measures Sandra Day O'Connor and Anthony Kennedy (and, to a lesser extent, David Souter) alternatively were median justices. This means that these three justices variously were the pivot on which the

Court's judgment turned. From the standpoint of making law—handing down judgment supported by authoritative opinion—then, William H. Rehnquist may have reigned, but he did not rule.

The same situation existed in John Roberts' second year as chief justice. By whatever method one determines the go-to justice, the jurist to whom lawyers address their arguments and replies during their thirty minutes at the Supreme Court bar, on March 19, 2007, Justice Kennedy was that person. "Median" or "most dangerous" justice, when it came to deciding *Morse v. Frederick*, Kennedy was *el jefe*. Ken Starr's and Doug Mertz's primary task was to persuade Kennedy that their respective narratives rang true. As we have seen, their task entailed telling a compelling story, connecting their story to existing precedents, and making plain the policy consequences that would follow from adopting (or failing to adopt) their clients' argument. While Kennedy was the decisive justice, Souter captured the controversy. Recall that, during his colloquy with Deputy Solicitor General Edwin Kneedler, Justice Souter said: "if we give deference your argument wins." In the spirit of Dana Milbank's *Washington Post* column, Souter might have opined: if we give deference your opponent's argument goes up in smoke. The smoke clears in the following chapter in which I focus on how the justices voted and how they explained their votes.

8

Five Takes on a Single Event

ECISION DAY IN *Morse v. Frederick* was much anticipated. Handicapping the outcome began right after oral arguments ended. Journalists, bloggers, and academics
alike all speculated on possible outcomes. Although neither as inexact as reading tea leaves
nor as trivial as a parlor game, such conjecture is fallible. Reading list-serv postings, for
instance, one wonders if armchair guessing, for a few writers, has at least as much to do
with preening as with advancing understanding. Still, pre-announcement vote counting
and reading between the lines of oral argument are time-honored activities. The results of
these activities can be instructive.

New York Times reporter Linda Greenhouse was, until her summer 2008 retirement, one
of two "Deans" of journalists covering the Supreme Court. She anticipated that the justices
would rule for Deborah Morse and the Juneau School District. Her conclusion was based
on three observations. First, Ken Starr came to oral argument armed with the contention
that *Morse v. Frederick* was not about student free speech, but rather about student drug-
related speech. Just as revealing to Greenhouse, Starr managed to stay on message in the
face of numerous, repeated interruptions from the Bench. Second, Starr found an ally in
Chief Justice John Roberts, who expressed resistance to reading *Tinker v. Des Moines* broadly
as requiring high school teachers and administrators to tolerate even political speech running counter to their educational missions, be it teaching English literature or geometry—
or preventing adolescent drug abuse. Third, Greenhouse observed that over the course of
oral argument, Justice Anthony Kennedy, usually predisposed to support free speech rights,
clearly became convinced that Frederick's banner was disruptive, and Kennedy's vote was
key. Greenhouse's prediction? "A majority of the court seemed willing to create what would
amount to a drug exception to students' First Amendment rights, much as the court has in
recent years permitted widespread drug testing of students, even those not personally suspected of using drugs, under a relaxed view of the Fourth Amendment prohibition against

unreasonable searches."[1] Greenhouse thus foresaw a convergence of the Court's First and Fourth Amendment jurisprudence in the area of student rights.

The other Dean of Supreme Court reporters is Lyle Denniston. Having covered the Supreme Court for fifty years in a variety of media, he currently reports for *SCOTUSblog*. Denniston came to a similar conclusion as Greenhouse regarding how the Court would rule. He opened his analysis of oral argument in *Morse v. Frederick* saying: "The Supreme Court on Monday toyed with the notion that public school officials should have added discretion to censor student speech that they may interpret as advocating use of illegal drugs. But this was only a flirtation, not a warm embrace."[2] Denniston based his view that the Court would only halfheartedly endorse expanding school administrators' discretion on his observation that only Chief Justice Roberts and Justice Scalia appeared to support greatly broadening disciplinary authority. Denniston noted Justice Alito's dismay with the more widely sweeping argument of the plaintiffs and their amici on behalf of greater discretion. Denniston characterized Justice Kennedy, who, not surprisingly, Denniston also identified as the key vote in *Morse v. Frederick*, as "hostile" to the plaintiffs' proposition.[3] Toward the end of his analysis, Denniston made a sagacious connection. He linked his sense that the justices likely would accord Deborah Morse immunity from damages to his observation that "[m]uch of the one-hour hearing was taken up with . . . puzzled efforts by the justices to find out just what had happened in the student speech censorship incident outside a Juneau high school in early 2002."[4] Denniston noted Justice David Souter's wry observation that, since the justices themselves had devoted fifty minutes to debating *Tinker*, divining the meaning of "BONG HiTS 4 JESUS," and scrutinizing the January 24, 2002, event, the Court hardly could conclude that Principal Morse should have known what the correct answers were, thus holding her liable.

A third veteran Supreme Court reporter is Tony Mauro, correspondent for *Legal Times* and analyst for the First Amendment Center. A twenty-year Court-watcher, Mauro anticipated that the justices would split the difference in *Morse v. Frederick* between the Ninth Circuit's ringing endorsement of student speech rights, on the one hand, and blanket support for school officials' authority, on the other. Mauro said, "Somewhere in the middle is where the Court will likely rule, with a nod toward both student speech and the need for school discipline."[5] Mauro's speculation about just where "in the middle" the Court would come down was informed by two observations. First, he noted how Ken Starr suggested that the Court could create a narrow drug-speech exception to the basic *Tinker* rule. Doing so would recognize that drug abuse is a significant problem and the special responsibility school administrators have in combating this problem. "School officials, Starr argued, should be given special deference in the area of drugs to move against pro-drug speech—even messages like Frederick's banner, which are open to varying interpretations."[6] Second, Mauro detected scant support for Joseph Fredrick's damages claim again Deborah Morse. "Acknowledging the complexity of the precedents in [the student speech area], most justices . . . seemed eager to give Morse and other school officials in similar circumstances a break."[7] In light of what he heard on March 19, 2007, during oral argument, then, the "middle" position Mauro expected the Court to stake out would authorize narrow official discretion to proscribe student pro-drug speech, and shield school officials from damages when exercising that judgment.

Complicating attempts to predict accurately how the Court would decide *Morse v. Frederick* is the fact that, these days, the justices often do not rule unanimously. I say these days because, over time, voting behavior on the Court has followed two different patterns. These days, Americans are so used to a divided, often fragmented, Court that we assume that multiple and conflicting opinions are normal. It is not widely known that, for most of the Court's history, unanimity was the prevailing norm. Speaking with a single voice was an innovation adopted to fashion a "supreme" court out of what originally was a minor—and controversial—judicial body.

From 1790 until 1801, U.S. Supreme Court justices followed English practice, delivering their opinions seriatim—one after another, in a series. During these eleven years, three men served as chief justice.[8] One might characterize the body over which they reluctantly and briefly[9] presided as a contested backwater. The Court was a backwater because it was deemed less a co-equal branch of the national government than a subsidiary tribunal. Article III of the Constitution outlines the Court and its jurisdiction in only vague terms, and its membership not at all. It took an act of Congress, the Judiciary Act of 1789, to flesh out this sketch in ways enabling the Court to organize and to convene. For its first three terms, no cases were brought before the newly created court. The Supreme Court did not decide its first case until February 1792.[10] The Court was contested because the national judiciary was the object of intense political debate in the late eighteenth, early nineteenth centuries. Amidst highly partisan debates over, among other things, the role of the national judiciary in a federal system, the Court became a lightning rod. A pivotal issue was circuit riding. The 1789 Judiciary Act had required Supreme Court justices literally to ride circuit, that is, to personally preside over circuit courts that were established on a regional basis throughout the country. It was an onerous and widely resented duty. Circuit riding also dispersed the justices, limiting their capacity to sit as a Supreme Court. Just before John Adams' administration left office, after the Jeffersonians had defeated the Federalists in the watershed election of 1800, the lame-duck Federalist Congress adopted the Judiciary Act of 1801. That law's two most controversial passages rescinded circuit riding and, to replace the now-stationary Supreme Court justices, created sixteen judgeships for six judicial circuits. The outgoing Federalists industriously set about filling these positions with supporters, with less than three weeks remaining in office. These so-called "midnight judges" so incensed the Jeffersonians that they passed the Judiciary Act of 1802, repealing its predecessor and reestablishing the status quo ante.

John Marshall, fourth chief justice of the United States, served thirty-four and a half years, through the entire terms of four presidents and parts of two more (from John Adams to Andrew Jackson). Chief Justice Marshall turned a contested backwater tribunal into the Supreme Court of the United States. "It was Marshall who established the role of the Supreme Court as the authoritative expounder of the Constitution."[11] He accomplished this by cannily asserting and stalwartly husbanding the Court's "province and duty . . . to say what the law is."[12] A crucial tactic in Marshall's overall strategy was to create a single court out of several justices by forging them into one voice. Supreme Court historian Bernard Schwartz captures the mode and the consequence of Marshall's move:

The change from a number of individual opinions to the Court opinion was admirably suited to strengthen the prestige of the fledgling Court. Marshall saw that the needed authority and dignity of the Court could be obtained only if the principles it proclaimed were pronounced by a united tribunal. To win conclusiveness and fixity for its decisions, he strove for a Court with a single voice. How well he succeeded is shown by the reception accorded Justice William Johnson, who sought to express his own view in dissent. "During the rest of the session," he plaintively affirmed in a letter to Jefferson, "I heard nothing but lectures on the indecency of judges cutting at each other, and the loss of reputation which the Virginia appellate court had sustained by pursuing such a course."[13]

Thomas Jefferson perceived Marshall's new procedure quite differently. Replying to a letter from Justice William Johnson, whom he had appointed to the Supreme Court in 1804, Jefferson rejected the "conclusiveness and fixity" Marshall sought. Rather, Jefferson desired "the light which [the justices'] separate arguments threw on the subject, and the instruction communicated by their several modes of reasoning."[14] Although the current consensus is that Marshall's rejection of seriatim opinions was salutary because it elevated the Court to a co-equal branch of national government, there is a diversity of views assessing Supreme Court justices' contemporary centrifugal tendencies. Variations on the debate between Marshall and Jefferson on this score continue to be played out in present-day scholarly literature.

Just over twenty years ago, three political scientists published an article addressing the significant shift in Supreme Court opinion writing. The title of their work effectively captures the puzzle they explore: "On the Mysterious Demise of Consensual Norms in the United States Supreme Court."[15] By abandoning the practice of seriatim opinions in lieu of a single opinion for the Court, Chief Justice John Marshall instituted a "consensual norm." From 1801, on into the twentieth century, standard operating procedure was to minimize— or at least not publicize—internal disagreements among the justices in order to maximize institutional solidarity. "[O]n the early courts . . . public disagreement by dissent or concurrence, with or without opinion, was considered deviant behavior. Justices referred to the 'misfortune' of bringing their differences over law and policy to public attention."[16] This is not to say that there were no cracks in the institutional façade of unanimity.[17] There were. To cite one prominent example, in the landmark Commerce Clause decision, *Gibbons v. Ogden*, 9 *Wheaton* 1 (1824), Justice William Johnson, President Jefferson's appointment mentioned above, filed a concurring opinion. Johnson wrote that, although "[t]he judgment entered by the Court in this cause, has my entire approbation . . . having adopted my conclusions on views of the subject materially different from those of my brethren, I feel it incumbent on me to exhibit those views."[18] He continued: "I have also another inducement: in questions of great importance and great delicacy, I feel my duty to the public best discharged by an effort to maintain my opinions in my own way."[19] Marshall's consensual norm that disquieted Justice Johnson and aggravated Thomas Jefferson disappeared suddenly in 1941. The abrupt change represented "an apparently permanent alteration in the Court's decision-making regime."[20]

Scholars explore causes and weigh consequences of conflicts among Supreme Court justices over an array of issues.[21] Walker, Epstein, and Dixon's 1988 article pioneered discussion of the causes and consequences of non-unanimous opinions.[22] They approached explaining the "mysterious demise of consensual norms" in the manner of a detective. "As any good investigator knows," they wrote, "the first steps in solving a mystery are to establish a list of suspects and set criteria by which to eliminate them from culpability."[23] They identified five possible "culprits":

> Congressional enactment of the Judiciary Act of 1925.
> Changes in the Court's caseload.
> The promotion of a sitting associate to chief justice.
> Changes in the Court's composition.
> The leadership of the chief justice.[24]

While each of the five explanations is plausible at first sight, Walker, Epstein, and Dixon subjected them to various forms of analysis, eliminating all but the last from consideration.[25] They determined that Chief Justice Harlan Fiske Stone's approach to leading the Court largely contributed to institutionalizing an individualized style of opinion writing.[26] In light of the pivotal role John Marshall had played as chief justice in establishing the now-abandoned consensual norm in the first place, Walker, Epstein, and Dixon's conclusion is somewhat ironic. It also is unsurprising. "Many scholars have noted that the character of leadership provided by the chief justice has great influence on the operating norms of the Court."[27]

It also is true that, single-handedly, one person cannot effect a transformation—not even the chief justice who is primus inter pares[28] (first among equals) among his colleagues on the Court. Although the year 1941 marks a striking decline in the consensual norm, that year is more a culmination than a watershed. Building on Walker, Epstein, and Dixon's study, political scientist Stacia J. Haynie argues that the unraveling of the consensual norm among the justices began during Chief Justice Hughes' tenure (February 24, 1930–June 30, 1941). Haynie analyzed both patterns of dissenting and concurring over time. She found that the trend toward individualized opinion writing began prior to Stone becoming chief justice. The leadership style of Stone's predecessor, Charles Evans Hughes, contributed to undoing consensual behavior. "Under Hughes, cohorts became more willing to independently express themselves in concurring opinions, but they still remained unwilling to verbalize disagreements with the majority opinions via dissenting opinions. Under Chief Justice Stone, the willingness to disagree in both concurring and dissenting opinions became the norm rather than the exception."[29]

Having sophisticated her readers' understanding of the historical relationship between leadership style and opinion writing on the Court, Haynie opens the door to further complications. Pointing out that "[r]arely in social science are processes simply explained," Haynie continues: "It is unlikely that the leadership style of the chief justice was the only factor contributing to the rise of dissensus on the Court."[30] Two studies published within a year of one another in the late 1990s further add to our understanding of consensual norms and opinion writing. Gregory A. Caldeira and Christopher J. W. Zorn set out to demonstrate empirically, as opposed to merely assuming, that the level of dissent and concurrence writing by Supreme Court justices is related to institutional consensual norms. Their highly developed statistical analyses "show that the presence of [consensual norms] will manifest itself as a cointegrating relationship [correlation] between the levels of concurrences and dissents."[31] In other words, levels of concurrence and dissent writing on the Court are a function of consensual norms among the justices. Concluding their article, Caldeira and Zorn discuss what their results suggest:

> One critical implication of these findings is that one effect of external forces and events is to shape [consensual] norms; and, to the extent such "shocks" have permanent effects on overall levels of concurrences and dissents, they may fundamentally alter the equilibrium levels of those actions. Thus, in our reading of the results, consensual norms, far from being a fixed canon of judicial conduct, are a *dynamic* process; norms both influence, and are in turn influenced by, changes in the politics, procedures, and personnel of the Supreme Court.[32]

Caldeira and Zorn's work carries us a good way toward a nuanced understanding of how consensual norms relate to opinion writing behavior. First, and most basically, they conceive of such norms as internally created balancing mechanisms by means of which interactions among the justices are structured. To the extent that the justices comply with a social institution—say, consensus—they constitute a norm, which engenders equilibrium among them. But such norms are not permanent. Second, Caldeira and Zorn describe norms as fluid temporal phenomena, not fixed but rather dynamic over time. Although hardly ephemeral, neither are norms absolute. Third, Caldeira and Zorn conclude that changes in norms governing opinion writing behavior are driven by multiple factors, both internal and external to the Court. While a regime change plays an important part in normative variation, with one chief justice's leadership style replacing another, no single causal factor suffices to explain modification, weakening, failure, or outright disappearance of a consensual norm.

Caldeira and Zorn's insights point toward the second late-1990s study to which I alluded above. David O'Brien "reconsiders" explanations for the rise, and current prevalence, of individual opinion writing. O'Brien shifts analytical focus from differing leadership styles of chief justices to changing philosophies of justices. For O'Brien, Chief Justice Stone did less to erode institutional opinion writing than disputes among the eight associate justices, whom Franklin D. Roosevelt appointed, over their respective roles on the Court. "While Stone's conduct of the Court's deliberative process undoubtedly contributed to the rise in the number of individual opinions, too much weight has been given to his influence and too little to the impact of changes brought by FDR's other eight appointments."[33] O'Brien offers several subsidiary explanations for the erosion of consensual norms on the Court. He cites three internal changes that exacerbated institutional fragmentation while facilitating individual expression of opinion: (1) the practice of circulating draft opinions with the advent of typewriters; (2) relocation to their own home, in "the Marble Temple" Supreme Court building at One First Street, NE, congregated the justices in ways that intensified their interactions and heightened interpersonal tensions; (3) the number of law clerks doubled, from one to two.[34] Fundamentally, though, O'Brien attributes the erosion of consensual norms to a profoundly consequential shift in internal judicial philosophies, shaped externally by constitutional conflicts around the New Deal. "Simply put," he writes, "the arrival of the New Deal justices brought the full force of American Legal Realism and liberal legalism to bear on the Court." He continues:

> American Legal Realism was not a school of thought but rather an intellectual movement embracing a range of diverse, though generally progressive and pragmatic, positions on judging and legal reform . . . At the same time, precisely because Legal Realism debunked legal formalism, along with attacking the pre-1937 conservative Court's invalidation of progressive legislation, and taught that judges make law, the premium was raised on justifying the justices' decisions, individual and collective.
>
> Moreover, liberal legalism developed out of the progressive and Legal Realist movements and embraced diverse viewpoints but lacked coherence. . . . Although dominating the Court, FDR's New Deal Justices split into two camps: Frankfurter-Reed-and-Jackson stood for judicial self-restraint and became more conservative during their time on the bench, while Black-Douglas-Murphy-and-Rutledge pushed toward greater liberal judicial activism. . . . In short, as a result of their disagreements over the course of liberal legalism and constitutional interpretation, the New Deal Justices were inclined to articulate their distinctive views in individual opinions.[35]

O'Brien's explanation is that, primarily, individual opinion writing was spawned by basic jurisprudential disagreements among the New Deal justices themselves. Extending his account chronologically, O'Brien argues that, after Chief Justice Stone's death in 1946, the ongoing eclipse of institutional, consensual norms by individual opinion writing can be explained by several factors. During Fred Vinson's (June 24, 1946–September 8, 1953) and Earl Warren's (October 5, 1953–June 23, 1969) respective tenures as Chief Justice, the fact that the New Deal justices had become "socialized" to writing individual opinions played a decisive role, effectively transforming the prevailing norm. In this context, Warren Burger's ineffectiveness as chief, and William Rehnquist's lack of interest in building consensus, served to further normalize dissensus.[36] Thus, in the last half of the twentieth century, judicial fragmentation, originally fostered by philosophical disagreements, became standard operating procedure.

In a debate recapitulating aspects of the earlier dispute between John Marshall and Thomas Jefferson over the practice of seriatim opinion writing, contemporary students of the Court disagree over whether or not judicial fragmentation is a problem.[37] The argument can be summarized conveniently as two opposing understandings of judicial legitimacy. Some contend, like Marshall, that individual opinion writing undermines the force of Supreme Court judgments, diluting legitimacy with a welter of voices. From this vantage point, legitimacy results from cohesion; it is jeopardized by centrifugal tendencies.[38] Others disagree, holding with Jefferson that individual opinion writing undergirds the force of Supreme Court judgments, promoting legitimacy through freely voiced diverse views. From this point of view, legitimacy results from multiplicity; it is endangered by lockstep uniformity.[39] It bears noting that these two views are neither as absolute, nor as mutually exclusive, as this stark contrast, drawn to clarify differences, makes them appear. For instance,

I doubt that a contrived judicial unanimity, artificially created through stifling difference, would enhance the Court's legitimacy. Likewise, I am skeptical that concurring or dissenting merely as a mode of venting, point-scoring, or some other indulgence burnishes the Court's authority.

Regardless of where one locates oneself along the range of opinions—from judicial fragmentation as bane, to such fragmentation as boon—the fact remains that an individualist norm governs opinion writing on the contemporary Supreme Court. Chief Justice John G. Roberts realizes the existing equilibrium, and he bewails it even while reinforcing it. In 2006, at the end of Roberts' first term as chief justice, Jeffrey Rosen interviewed him for *The Atlantic*. The resulting article is titled "Roberts's Rules."[40] Unanimity appeared to be Roberts' Rule Number One, with John Marshall his proclaimed role model. I say "appeared" because, although Roberts placed great rhetorical stock in the Court speaking in one voice, his polarizing voting behavior elicits multiple opinions on a closely divided Tribunal. Roberts told Rosen that "[i]f the Court in Marshall's era had issued decisions in important cases the way this Court has over the past thirty years, we would not have a Supreme Court today of the sort we have."[41] In contrast to "reverting back to the English model," Roberts mused, "[i]nstead of nine justices moving in nine separate directions . . . 'it would be good to have a commitment on the part of the Court to acting as a Court, rather than being more concerned about the consistency and coherency of an individual judicial record.'"[42] The record shows that Roberts himself violates Roberts' Rules. As of this writing, in his four terms as chief justice, Roberts seems less interested in emulating Marshall as "a model of how to rein in a group of unruly prima donnas,"[43] than in pursuing a divisive policy agenda. Rosen describes the situation:

> [Roberts] had made it a priority of his first term to promote unanimity and collegiality on the Court. He was surprisingly successful in this goal: under his leadership, the Court issued more consecutive unanimous opinions than at any time in recent history. But the term ended in what Justice John Paul Stevens called a "cacophony" of discordant voices. Opposing justices addressed each other in unusually personal terms and generated a flurry of stories in the media about the divisions on the Court . . .[44]

Since the close of the 2005–2006 term, the abnormal nature of that series of unanimous decisions has become clear, with cacophony remaining the rule. Chief Justice Roberts' own decision making has fueled the dissonance.

For example, on June 28, 2007, the final day of the 2006–2007 term—three days after *Morse v. Frederick* was handed own—Chief Justice Roberts announced the decision in *Parents Involved in Community Schools v. Seattle School District No. 1*, 551 U.S. 701 (2007).[45] Roberts had written the lead opinion in a 4–1–4 ruling, in which a plurality of the justices, with Anthony Kennedy joining only the ruling, voided voluntary plans to integrate schools in Seattle, Washington, and Louisville, Kentucky, because the two districts took race into consideration as one factor in pupil assignment. Signaling a watershed shift in how a core of four Supreme Court justices reinterpreted Equal Protection jurisprudence in school integration cases, Roberts said: "The way to stop discrimination on the basis of race is to stop discriminating on the basis of race."[46] Justice Breyer strongly disagreed with Roberts' and Kennedy's opinions. Speaking for himself and his three colleagues in the minority, Justice Breyer dissented from the Bench, a relatively rare practice. Breyer began: "The majority is wrong."[47] Twenty-one minutes later, Breyer reached his climactic statement: "It is not often in the law that so few have so quickly changed so much."[48] Just one year after Rosen's interview, then, talk of Marshall Court–like unanimity was drowned out by stark policy differences on an "incoherent"[49] Court. Two years later, in July 2009, the Court under John Roberts remains deeply divided. Summing up the 2008–2009 term, *New York Times* Supreme Court reporter Adam Liptak described the justices as "remarkably polarized." "[I]n the 74 signed decisions [they] issued this term, [they divided] 5–4 or 6–3 in almost half of them, up from roughly a third in the three previous years."[50] Liptak explains the chief justice's role in present and future fragmentation on the Supreme Court:

> The court took mainly incremental steps in major cases concerning voting rights, employ-ment discrimination, criminal procedure and campaign finance. But the chief justice's fin-gerprints were on all of them, and he left clues that the court is only one decision away from fundamental change in many areas of the law.
>
> Chief Justice Roberts has certainly been planting seeds in this term's decisions. If his rea-soning takes root in future cases, the law will move in a conservative direction on questions as varied as what kinds of evidence may be used against criminal defendants and the role the government may play in combating race discrimination.[51]

The Court that decided *Morse v. Frederick* two years into John Roberts' tenure continued the well-established post–New Deal pattern of behavior; a pattern likely to continue. It is a doubly fragmented tribunal. First, the justices are deeply split. Standing on the cusp of potentially far-reaching doctrinal change in major areas of public policy, the Court is cleft into two opposing factions. Second, the justices also are fractious, inclined to write separate opinions staking out their own positions. As much as at any time in its history, the contemporary Supreme Court is less a unified body than a collection of discrete jurists loosely allied in rival camps. Under prevailing circumstances, perhaps "court" should be put in quotation marks.

Despite being doubly divided, as we have seen, the justices tipped their hands with regard to how *Morse v. Frederick* might come down. Professional tea-leaf readers and amateur arm chair prognosticators alike had access to an important clue. The dynamic at play during oral argument that Monday, March 19, 2007, provided a hint. More precisely, the dynamic is that "the party that gets the most questions is likely to lose."[52] Adam Liptak characterized this inter-action, in the title to his *New York Times* article on the nexus between questions asked and votes cast, as "When the Justices Ask Questions, Be Prepared to Lose the Case."[53] The logic of this nexus derives from how oral argument plays an influential role in shaping justices' opin-ions on the merits, a logic I explored in the previous chapter. The imagery I used there was that effective oral advocacy can serve to "crystallize" a justice's more or less incipient views about one side or the other's argument.[54] Oral argument resembles an elaborate mode of drama. Communication takes place as much via nonverbal cues—body language and posture, facial expressions and blank stares, dramatic pauses and silences—as through language. "'It's like a highly stylized Japanese theater,' says Ted Olson, a former U.S. solicitor general who has argued frequently before the court."[55] Predicting a resulting outcome from a given oral argument, thus, is not merely a matter of counting questions. It's about nuances.[56]

Oral argument in *Morse v. Frederick* underscores the importance of attending to subtleties. The question tallies are Ken Starr 38, Doug Mertz 64. On its face, this count looks like a rout. But these raw numbers tell only a superficial part of the tale. To begin with, these numbers are misleading. Starr was asked 38 questions to Mertz's 64, but Starr was only at the lectern for 18 minutes, 37 seconds.[57] Mertz was at the lectern for 30 minutes, 14 seconds. In both Starr's and Mertz's case, that computes to roughly two questions every sixty seconds. The result is a dead heat. If we add Deputy Solicitor General Edwin Kneedler to the mix, the picture grows even more interesting. Kneedler held the floor for 10 minutes, 32 seconds. He fielded twenty questions, for a rate of around two questions per minute. If Starr's thirty-eight questions are added to Kneedler's twenty questions (total = 58), then divided by their collective time at the lectern (29:09) the result is—once again—two questions per minute. Another draw. By this reckoning, during oral argument in *Morse v. Frederick*, the quizzical/skeptical nexus applied equally to both parties' counsel. Why?

Because *Morse v. Frederick* is a close case. *Morse v. Frederick* can be understood as a close case, in part, because of its persistently disputed facts. Going all the way back to the U.S. District Court's ruling on May 27, 2003,[58] Judge John W. Sedwick's reading of the disputed facts, on his way to granting summary judgment, did not resolve those disagreements. On the contrary, arguments over factual questions dogged the litigation as Joseph Frederick and Deborah Morse fought from Juneau to Anchorage (twice), eventually to Washington, D.C., to Pasadena, and ultimately back to Juneau. Second, the precedents in play, from *Tinker*[59] through *Kuhlmeier*,[60] and *T.L.O.*[61] through *Earls*,[62] are neither unequivocal nor univocal. They convey ambiguous messages. That ambiguity derives, to some extent,[63] from a third reason why *Morse* is a close case. Underlying all these much-debated precedents in *Morse v. Frederick* are two competing constitutional values, as contentious as they are time-honored: social order versus individual rights. Although the Court draws a line in each of the six precedential decisions, striking a balance between school authority and student liberty, its particular tilt toward one emphasis does not definitively preclude the other. The fundamental tension remains, to be contested another day.

If the quizzical/skeptical nexus does not take us very far toward predicting the outcome in *Morse v. Frederick*, perhaps a different approach might. This procedure compares salient words. Alderson Reporting Company, which publishes official transcripts of oral arguments before the U.S. Supreme Court, appends a tabular word tally to each written record. By looking at the frequency of key words that the lawyers and the justices used prominently in oral argument, one can obtain a feel for the ideas that shaped the exchanges. It is a rudimentary content analysis, of sorts. I have argued that one way to conceive of the dispute between Deborah Morse and Joseph Frederick is to see the conflict in terms of two competing narratives: Morse's "accountability narrative" versus Frederick's "injury narrative." In this context, the Alderson table contains two suggestive word pairings: variations on disrupt/drug, and variations on right/speech. It seems reasonable to associate disrupt/drug with Morse's "accountability narrative," while correlating right/speech with Frederick's "injury narrative." The former narrative urges holding Joe Frederick accountable for disrupting the Olympic torch run with his pro-drug advocacy. The latter narrative asserts that Deborah Morse behaved injuriously when she deprived a student of his First Amendment right to free speech. Variations on the words *disrupt/drug*[64] appear in the oral argument transcript 106 times. By contrast, variations on the words *right/speech*[65] appear in the transcript 77 times. By this elementary indicator, Principal Morse's narrative appears to have framed oral argument more effectively than student Frederick's. One might say that a frequency/credibility nexus was at work.

At 10:00 am, Monday, June 25, 2007, prognostication ended and scrutiny began. In just over five minutes, Chief Justice Roberts announced the Court's decision in *Morse v. Frederick*, No. 06-278, and noted that four other justices had filed opinions:

> Justice Thomas has filed a concurring opinion.
> Justice Alito has filed a concurring opinion in which Justice Kennedy has joined.
> Justice Breyer has filed an opinion concurring in the judgment in part and dissenting in part.
> Justice Stevens has filed a dissenting opinion joined by justices Souter and Ginsburg.[66]

Five separate opinions mentioned in the space of five minutes. Given this fragmented and fractious collection of justices, five separate opinions in a single case are less significant,[67] per se, than the dissonance those opinions convey. Usually, *Morse v. Frederick* is described as a 5–4 decision in favor of Deborah Morse. Although accurate, this conventional account is not very revealing. Parsing the justices' work products more thoroughly sophisticates the outcome. From another perspective, the 5–4 tally looks more like 2–1–2/1–3[68]—which amounts to five disparate takes on events on Glacier Avenue, and the resulting dispute. Another numerical way of illustrating the fractured *Morse* result is to point out that, at most, only three—a mere third—of the nine justices could agree on the legal rationale that ought to underpin *Morse*.[69] Now, such calculations may appear as sophistry, at best, or simply beside the point. After all, the numbers in the above series (2–1–2/3–1) represent votes. The backward-slash in that series stands for something, specifically that 2 + 1 + 2 = 5 votes. Five votes is a majority: Morse wins. Game over? I have more to say, below, about reducing Supreme Court decisions solely to a matter of winning and losing. For now, I want to continue plumbing the rich complexities of *Morse v. Frederick*, 551 U.S. 393 (2007).

Chief Justice Roberts' majority opinion runs just shy of fifteen pages.[70] At below 4,500 words, it is short by Supreme Court standards.[71] The opinion is comprised of brief introductory and concluding paragraphs as bookends to its four sections. Announcing his opinion for the Court, Chief Justice Roberts summarized its ruling in two sentences. "The question before us . . . ," he said from the Bench, "is whether a principal can restrict student's speech at a school event when that speech is reasonably viewed as promoting illegal drug use. We hold that she may."[72] The written opinion elaborates on these two sentences. Roberts' analysis is unsurprising in that he essentially recapitulates what I have termed the appellants' "accountability narrative." In other words, Roberts is working from materials scripted by counsel for Deborah Morse and the Juneau School Board, and articulated by Ken Starr during oral argument.

In his introduction, Chief Justice Roberts, like Starr, "make[s] clear]" that, under *Tinker*, "students do not 'shed their constitutional rights to freedom of speech or expression at the schoolhouse gate.'"[73] Roberts then immediately cites *Fraser* and *Kuhlmeier*, emphasizing what I have referred to as Tinker's tentative reach as a protection of student speech rights.[74] Roberts writes: "At the same time, we have held that 'the constitutional rights of students in public school are not automatically coextensive with the rights of adults in other settings,' *Bethel School Dist. No. 431 v. Fraser . . .* , and that the rights of students 'must be 'applied in light of the special characteristics of the school environment,'" *Hazelwood School Dist. v. Kuhlmeier* (quoting *Tinker*).[75] In Section I of his opinion, Chief Justice Roberts recounts a version of the facts centering on the drug-related message of Joseph Frederick's banner. Running through Roberts' account is the view that key persons involved in the dispute—Juneau-Douglas High School Principal Deborah Morse, Juneau School District Superintendent Bader, and U.S. District Court Judge Sedwick—all reasonably interpreted Frederick's banner as disruptive, hence as unprotected by the First Amendment. The Ninth Circuit, alone, disagreed. It is the Ninth's starkly divergent conclusion that the Supreme Court agreed to review.[76]

Sections II and III of the majority opinion are very short. In Section II, the chief justice dismisses the respondent's argument that *Morse v. Frederick* is not a school speech case, "as has every other authority to address the question." Roberts says "we agree with the superintendent that Frederick cannot 'stand in the midst of his fellow students, during school hours, at a school-sanctioned activity and claim he is not at school.'"[77] In Section III, Roberts aligns the majority squarely with Principal Morse's interpretation of the message displayed on Frederick's banner. He quotes Morse to the effect: "I told Frederick and the other members of his group to put the banner down because I felt that it violated the [school] policy against displaying . . . material that advertises or promotes use of illegal drugs."[78] Roberts then adds: "We agree with Morse."[79]

Section IV is the heart of the chief justice's opinion. Having adopted the petitioners' view of the facts that Frederick's pro-drug banner violated school policy, in this part Roberts lays out the legal basis for holding Frederick accountable. Notably, Section IV garnered only two votes: Roberts' and Scalia's. The other three justices in the majority all qualified their support with concurring opinions. Justice Thomas faulted the chief justice's legal analysis because it did not go far enough toward reversing *Tinker* outright. Robert's legal analysis troubled Justices Alito and Kennedy because of its potential to erode student speech rights grounded in *Tinker*. Thus, while five justices voted to hold Joe Frederick accountable, there is no unalloyed majority rationale underlying that conclusion.[80]

Roberts' analysis in Section IV is revealing for two reasons. First, he "distills"[81] *Fraser* down to a couple of "basic principles."[82] One principle, while debatable, is largely recognized. The second is problematic. The initial principle holds that students' constitutional rights "are not automatically co-extensive with the rights of adults in other settings."[83] As I said, this view that student rights occupy a second tier may be disputable; nevertheless it is well established. Not so, the second. Roberts next argues that *Fraser* can be understood to have shifted the "mode of analysis"[84] away from *Tinker*'s concern to protect nondisruptive speech to school administrators' "authority to determine what manner of speech in the classroom or in school assembly is inappropriate."[85] Under the chief justice's reading of

Fraser, the dispositive question no longer is whether or not any given content of student speech was "disruptive," but rather whether any given school official's judgment call about the content of student speech was "reasonable." Discretion replaces disruption as the decision rule, thereby putting students' rights inside the schoolhouse gate in the hands of the schoolhouse rulers.[86]

Having established that school administrators' discretion is decisive, Roberts next holds that the law requires judicial deference to those administrators' judgments when it comes to drugs. He arrives at this conclusion by wedding the Court's student speech rights jurisprudence under the First Amendment with its student privacy rights jurisprudence under the Fourth Amendment. Just as adolescent drug abuse justifies an attenuated expectation of privacy when searching students and drug testing students,[87] such illegal usage legitimizes school administrators proscribing student speech. "[T]hese [Fourth Amendment] cases . . . recognize that deterring drug use by schoolchildren is an 'important—indeed, perhaps compelling interest.' . . . Student speech celebrating illegal drug use at a school event, in the presence of school administrators and teachers, thus poses a particular challenge for school officials working to protect those entrusted to their care from the dangers of drug abuse."[88] In sum, for Roberts and Scalia, when it comes to drug-related cases and controversies, because the Court's precedents hold that students' rights are not coextensive with constitutional rights, and because those precedents also authorize school administrators' discretion, courts largely are relegated to the sidelines.[89]

Justice Clarence Thomas wants courts wholly confined to the sidelines with regard to student speech. When it comes to students' rights under the First Amendment, in Thomas' opinion there's no such thing as free speech.[90] With regard to judicial review of school administrators' judgments, and students' speech in school, Justice Thomas is a latter-day Hugo Black. As discussed in Chapter 2, Justice Black dissented forcefully from the Court's *Tinker* ruling. "By 1969, when the Court decided *Tinker*, Justice Black had long since publicly abandoned any hint of 'absolute' protection for nonverbal speech. He was testy about sit-ins and flag-burning, and the necessity for public order became a frequent theme."[91] Whatever factors led Black to reject the majority's view in *Tinker*,[92] his view of the case is remarkably similar to Thomas' assessment of *Tinker*. Black summarized *Tinker*'s key elements this way:

> [T]the crucial . . . questions are whether students and teachers may use the schools at their whim as a platform for the exercise of free speech—"symbolic" or "pure"—and whether the courts will allocate to themselves the function of deciding how the pupils' school day will be spent.[93]

Like Hugo Black, Clarence Thomas sees "no constitutional imperative requiring public schools to allow all student speech."[94] With Black, Thomas laments that "[i]n the place of [a] democratic regime, *Tinker* substituted judicial oversight of the day-to-day affairs of public schools."[95] Both jurists support expansive authority for teachers and administrators. Commensurately, Black and Thomas advocate strictly limited judicial oversight of how school officials govern student behavior. For them *Tinker* exemplifies federal judicial high-handedness, forcing a regime on local school districts which creates a situation where, in effect, the inmates run the asylum.[96]

Justice Thomas flatly rejects how the *Morse* majority continues what he characterizes as an "ad hoc" approach to "set[ting] the [*Tinker*] standard aside"[97]; an untenable approach he sees initiated in *Fraser* and perpetuated by *Kuhlmeier*. "I am afraid," Thomas writes, "that our jurisprudence now says that students have a right to speak in schools except when they don't—a standard continuously developed through litigation against local schools and their administrators. In my view, petitioners could prevail for a much simpler reason: As originally understood, the Constitution does not afford students a right to free speech in public schools."[98] One can almost hear Thomas drumming his fingers impatiently as he deplores:

> Today, the Court creates another exception. In doing so, we continue to distance ourselves from *Tinker*, but we neither overrule it nor offer any explanation of when it operates and when it does not. . . . I join the Court's opinion because it erodes *Tinker*'s hold in the realm of student speech, even though it does so by adding to the patchwork of exceptions to the *Tinker* standard. I think the better approach is to dispense with *Tinker* altogether, and given the opportunity, I would do so.[99]

Justice Thomas demands categorical action.[100] For him, if high school students are to be held accountable for running amok—in ways possibly more dangerous ways than sophomoric prankster Joe Frederick hoisting his BONG HiTS 4 JESUS banner during the Olympic torch relay—the Court must discard wholly its constitutionally indefensible *Tinker* ruling which curbs public school administrators from exercising their historically and legally sanctioned disciplinary authority. Why temporize any longer? insists Thomas. Rather than incrementally loosening the specious doctrinal fetters tying teachers' and principals' arms behind their backs, the Court should rearm them by liberating them from *Tinker*, so they can fight effectively in the war on drugs.

Justice Thomas insists that the Court break completely with *Tinker*. By contrast, at the opposite end of the doctrinal spectrum, Justice Alito, joined by Justice Kennedy's pivotal vote,[101] seeks to put the brakes on eroding *Tinker*. In a brief, four-page concurring opinion, Justice Alito characterizes as "correct"[102] the Court's reaffirming the "fundamental principle"[103] in *Tinker* "that students do not 'shed their constitutional rights to freedom of speech or expression at the schoolhouse gate.'"[104] He stipulates two provisos on the basis of which he joined the majority opinion. First: that the majority opinion "goes no further than to hold that a public school may restrict speech that a reasonable observer would interpret as advocating illegal drug use."[105] Second: that the majority opinion "provides no support for any restriction of speech that can plausibly be interpreted as commenting on any political or social issue, including speech on issues such as 'the wisdom of the war on drugs or of legalizing marijuana for medicinal use.'"[106] Both of Alito's conditions can be seen as seeking to fence *Tinker* off from any further exceptions. Regarding the specific *Morse* holding, Alito concurred with the majority solely because of his threshold acceptance of Morse's perception that Frederick's speech advocated illegal drug use. Consequently, Alito agreed that Frederick's banner was dangerous speech, threatening students' safety.[107] Frederick's dangerous drug-related speech thus was disruptive speech, hence it may be proscribed under the *Tinker-Fraser-Kuhlmeier* trilogy's understanding that "in-school student speech may be regulated by state actors in a way that would not be constitutional in other settings."[108] For Justices Alito and Kennedy, *Morse v. Frederick* stands for this narrowly limited proposition—nothing more. For them, "such regulation [stands] at the far reaches of what the First Amendment permits."[109]

It took Justice Alito just four pages to formulate the *Morse* constitutional outcome in circumscribed terms. Justice Breyer devotes nine pages to explaining why the Court should avoid reaching any constitutional outcome at all, confining its decision to the question of qualified immunity. Breyer's opinion reads like a gloss on the institutional wisdom contained in Justice Louis Brandeis' influential 1936 concurring opinion in *Ashwander v. Tennessee*, 297 U.S. 288. The so-called "Ashwander Rules" are seven precepts,[110] which Brandeis culled from Supreme Court precedents and practice, in order to implement the underlying prudential principle that in order to husband its authority the Court should refrain from deciding constitutional questions unless it cannot avoid doing so.[111] They are self-imposed "housekeeping" rules if you will, designed to guide the justices when choosing which cases and controversies to address, and the manner in which to address them. Justice Breyer clearly was troubled by the prospect that wading into the First Amendment aspects of the controversy between Deborah Morse and Joseph Frederick would put the Court squarely between the rock of impairing students' rights, on the one hand, and the hard place of restricting administrators' disciplinary authority. "All this is to say," Breyer wrote, "regardless of the outcome of the constitutional determination, a decision on the underlying First Amendment issue is both difficult and unusually portentous. And that is a reason for us not to decide the issues unless we must."[112]

Justice Breyer's exit strategy[113] centers on disposing of Frederick's damage claim by immunizing Morse. "In order to avoid resolving the fractious underlying constitutional question, we need only decide a different question that this case presents, the question of 'qualified immunity.' The principle of qualified immunity fits this case perfectly and, by saying so, we would diminish the risk of bringing about the adverse consequences I have identified."[114] For Breyer, his approach would have sidestepped the Court's lose-lose outcome by embracing a win-win result:

> In resolving the underlying constitutional question, we produce several differing opinions. It is utterly unnecessary to do so. Were we to decide this case on the ground of qualified immunity, our decision would be *unanimous*, for the dissent concedes that Morse should not be held liable in damages for confiscating Frederick's banner.... And the "cardinal principle of judicial restraint" is that "if it is not necessary to decide more, it is necessary not to decide more..."[115]

For Breyer, then, the Court overreaches when it could have problem solved. Worse, the Court's overreaching fractures it internally and muddles rather than resolve the First Amendment issues. The result is doubly self-defeating.

With Breyer's concurrence we have analyzed four of the five differing opinions that the nine justices wrote in *Morse v. Frederick*. The box score thus far: six justices, four opinions. The final—fifth—opinion, signed by Justices Stevens, Souter, and Ginsburg, is a full-blown dissent. I say "full-blown dissent" because, as I have argued, it is clear that the three opinions written, respectively, by Justices Thomas, Alito, and Breyer diverge significantly from the Opinion of the Court. The number and range of opinions in *Morse v. Frederick* exemplifies a fundamental institutional fact—perhaps the preeminent institutional fact—about the contemporary Supreme Court: fragmented decision making. Jeffrey Toobin writes: "In fact, Justices have a great deal of discretion—in which cases they take, in the results they reach, in the opinions they write." Toobin adds: "When it comes to interpreting the Constitution . . . there is frankly, no such thing as 'law.'"[116] When it comes to "law" in *Morse v. Frederick*, figuratively speaking, the justices are all over the map. The differences among the three concurring opinions and the Opinion of the Court, among the three concurring opinions themselves, and between the three concurring opinions and the dissent, are as deep as differences separating the dissent from the Opinion of the Court. Like the blind men and the elephant,[117] the justices part company over what sort of thing happened on January 24, 2002, on Glacier Avenue in Juneau, and what sort of rule—if any—should be formulated in response.

In the next to last paragraph of his opinion, Chief Justice Roberts seeks to minimize the distance between the majority and the dissenters:

> Stripped of rhetorical flourishes . . . the debate between the dissent and this opinion is less about constitutional first principles than about whether Frederick's banner constitutes promotion of illegal drug use. We have explained our view that it does. The dissent's contrary view on that relatively narrow question hardly justifies sounding the First Amendment bugle.[118]

The chief justice's assertion is both accurate and disingenuous. Roberts accurately notes that the majority and the dissenters differ significantly over key facts at issue in *Morse v. Frederick*. Less straightforwardly, the chief justice marginalizes the ways in which these factual disputes result in significantly different readings of *Tinker*. Justice Stevens may devote much of his fifteen-plus-page dissent to discrediting Deborah Morse's and the majority's interpretation of Joe Frederick's banner. Nevertheless, Stevens justifiably sounds "the First Amendment bugle" because he and his fellow dissenters believe the majority's application of *Tinker* to be "a gross non sequitur . . . that trivializes the two cardinal principles upon which *Tinker* rests."[119]

Conventional wisdom instructs that the Supreme Court weighs questions of law, not fact. Like most commonplaces, this description captures an important aspect of Supreme Court decision making while oversimplifying the process. Typically, the justices rely on the factual record received from lower courts, focusing their attention on interpreting legal materials relevant to the case at hand. When the record is incomplete, flawed, or, as in *Morse v. Frederick*, rife with starkly different accounts, facts come into play. Just how deeply in play were the competing narratives of Deborah Morse and Joe Frederick is apparent in this exchange between Justice Stevens and Kenneth Starr during oral argument:

> **JUSTICE STEVENS**: Let me just clear up one thing to be 100 percent sure I understand your position. It does—the message is the critical part of this case. If it was a totally neutral message on a fifteen-foot sign, that would be okay. You're not saying fifteen-foot signs are disruptive?
>
> **MR. STARR**: Not inherently disruptive, but in fact—the answer is yes. We're not saying that.
>
> **JUSTICE STEVENS**: And so we're focusing on the message and that's the whole crux of the case.
>
> **MR. STARR**: That's why this case is here because of the message.[120]

For five justices on the *Morse* Court, the message on Frederick's banner "advocated the use of illegal drugs."[121] The three dissenters saw Frederick's message completely differently. "[I]t is one thing to restrict speech that *advocates* drug use," writes Justice Stevens. "It is another thing entirely to prohibit an obscure message with a drug theme that a third party subjectively—and not very reasonably—thinks is tantamount to express advocacy."[122] A few pages later, Stevens elaborates on the dissenters' take on Frederick's banner:

> This is a nonsense message, not advocacy. The Court's feeble effort to divine its hidden meaning is strong evidence of that. . . . Frederick's credible and uncontradicted explanation for the message—he just wanted to get on television—is also relevant because a speaker who does not intend to persuade his audience can hardly be said to be advocating anything. But most importantly, it takes real imagination to read a "cryptic" message (the Court's characterization, not mine . . .) with a slanting drug reference as an incitement to use drugs. Admittedly, some high school students (including those who use drugs) are dumb. Most students, however, do not shed their brains at the schoolhouse gate and most students know dumb advocacy when they see it. The notion that the message on this banner would actually persuade either the average student or even the dumbest one to change his or her behavior is most implausible. That the Court believes such a silly message can be proscribed as advocacy underscores the novelty of its position, and suggests that the principle it articulates has no stopping point.[123]

Stevens' last sentence is crucial. It links the dissenters' understanding of the contested message on Frederick's banner—what in fact the banner said—with their criticism of how the majority misuses *Tinker*. The majority premises its ruling that Morse legitimately held Frederick accountable under *Tinker* on its agreement with Morse that Frederick's banner advocated illegal drug use. For the dissenters, the majority's agreement with Morse that "BONG HiTS 4 JESUS" was disruptive enables the Court to "trivialize"[124] *Tinker* by refusing to see the principal's actions as viewpoint discrimination, and by ignoring the distinction between advocacy and incitement—both "cardinal principles upon which *Tinker* rests."[125]

At the beginning of Kenneth Starr's time during oral argument, an insistently skeptical Justice Souter quizzed Starr: "Disruptive of what? Disruptive of the classroom? There was no classroom here. . . . [W]hat did [the banner] disrupt on the sidewalk?"[126] The dissenters' answer to Souter's question, in effect, is "nothing."[127] For them, since Frederick's banner is innocuously nonsensical, *Tinker* protects the expression. To rule otherwise is to strike "at 'the heart of the First Amendment' because it upholds a punishment meted out on the basis of a listener's disagreement with her understanding (or, more likely, misunderstanding) of the speaker's viewpoint."[128] Stated in terms I have used throughout my analysis, the dissenters argue that, by embracing the petitioners' "accountability narrative," the majority further injures Joseph Frederick. Moreover, the dissenters contend, in so ruling the majority also damages First Amendment protection of student speech. The sting of these criticisms is somewhat mitigated by the circumstance that the "majority" opinion is fraught with reservations and disagreements. In fine, *Morse v. Frederick*, 551 U.S. 393 (2007), is no less ambiguous than Frederick's banner at the bar of judgment.

Coda

Americans love a horse race. We tend to perceive complex political events, like presidential elections and Supreme Court decisions, more as matters of individual winners and losers than policy debates. In electoral politics, for instance, prevailing imagery depicts candidates breaking from the gate after Labor Day, rounding the back stretch in October, and heading for home the first Tuesday in November. Along the way, tracking polls—endlessly reported, repeated, and dissected by pundits and color commentators—offer a crescendo of snapshots, providing an exciting prelude to the climactic satisfaction of knowing who won. While aficionados, activists, and candidates and their staffers attend to the intricacies of national and state elections, most Americans, distanced from key activities, focus vicariously on the run for the finish line. It is as though a deeply embedded cultural predisposition toward dichotomies inclines us to conceive of electoral politics in terms of either winners or losers. Nuances are nugatory. Given such categorical thinking, zero-sum is the name of the game.

Reading judicial results, like the outcome in *Morse v. Frederick*, solely in zero-sum terms is highly misleading. To be sure, speaking only in such narrow terms, verdicts, judgments, and rulings are one-way outcomes, in which one party's victory assumes all other parties' defeat. From this attenuated perspective, in law as in poker, there can only be a single prevailing player: 5–4, game over, Morse wins. Guilty or not guilty; liable or not liable; petitioner or respondent, there are no shades of gray. Or are there?

Appellate court work products, especially U.S. Supreme Court decisions, are multi-dimensional. As I wrote above, referring to the precedents at play in *Morse*, they "are neither unequivocal nor univocal. They convey ambiguous messages." My analysis in this chapter of the five opinions in *Morse v. Frederick* further demonstrates this circumstance. U.S. Supreme Court outcomes, as distinct from the Court's specific holding, rarely have a single aspect. Supreme Court opinions are written speech acts. They are language products. Supreme Court opinions also result from the tugs and pulls of small group interaction. As such, they are shot through with ambiguity which renders them open textured. Even Supreme Court holdings (rulings) as distinct from Supreme Court opinions (reasoning) are not cut and dried. Linguistic substance and group process also render legal rules open to interpretation.[129] There is plentiful open space[130] in both rules and reasons. This is to say that both Supreme Court decisions, as well as the opinions written to elucidate and to justify them, are not conclusive in any ultimate sense of the word.[131]

Consider the iconic *Brown v. Board of Education*.[132] Portrayed conventionally as marking the definitive end of Jim Crow segregation, the *Brown* decision did nothing of the sort.[133] What the nine justices did accomplish was to declare legally segregated public school education unconstitutional.[134] Specifically, Chief Justice Warren wrote for a unanimous Court:

> We conclude that, in the field of public education, the doctrine of "separate but equal" has no place. Separate educational facilities are inherently unequal. Therefore, we hold that the plaintiffs and others similarly situated for whom the actions have been brought are, by reason of the segregation complained of, deprived of the equal protection of the laws guaranteed by the Fourteenth Amendment.[135]

Chief Justice Warren's rhetoric is inspired—one could say, per my discussion below, it is beautiful. Still, as a means of ending de jure racial segregation in the United States, the Court's ruling was, at most, a point of departure.[136] Chief Justice Warren's seemingly incontrovertible words[137] succeeded primarily in inflaming Southern opinion. The result was massive resistance.[138] While for the *Brown* Court the Constitution required that, "in the field of public education, the doctrine of 'separate but equal' has no place," for legions of Southerners, the Constitution guaranteed "separate but equal" as a way of life.

On March 12, 1956, nineteen U.S. Senators and seventy-seven members of the U.S. House of Representatives submitted a document titled "The Decision of the Supreme Court in the School Cases Declaration of Constitutional Principles."[139] This declaration has come to be called "The Southern Manifesto." In no uncertain terms, the Manifesto pronounces the U.S. Supreme Court's *Brown* decision unconstitutional:

> In the case of *Plessy* v. *Ferguson* in 1896 the Supreme Court expressly declared that under the 14th Amendment no person was denied any of his rights if the States provided separate but equal facilities. This decision has been followed in many other cases. . . .
>
> This interpretation, restated time and again, became a part of the life of the people of many of the States and confirmed their habits, traditions, and way of life. It is founded on elemental humanity and commonsense, for parents should not be deprived by Government of the right to direct the lives and education of their own children.
>
> Though there has been no constitutional amendment or act of Congress changing this established legal principle almost a century old, the Supreme Court of the United States, with no legal basis for such action, undertook to exercise their naked judicial power and substituted their personal political and social ideas for the established law of the land.[140]

It turns out that *Brown v. Board of Education*, indeed, is an iconic case. Ironically, however, *Brown* not only is emblematic as a clarion call for racial integration. It also is representative of how Supreme Court decisions and Supreme Court opinions, like those in *Morse v. Frederick*, are malleable.[141] Restating this characteristic in words I have used above, Supreme Court work products are inherently subject to interpretation.[142] From the High Court Bench in Washington, D.C., the nine justices believed they were saying one thing in *Brown*. To Americans living south of the Mason-Dixon Line, *Brown* said something entirely different.[143] The situation with regard to *Morse* is even more problematical. *Brown* was unanimous. *Morse* is a mess. It reaffirms *Tinker* while further qualifying it, and does so in the context of "facts"[144] deeply contested and thoroughly contestable.

Law's open texture, exemplified by *Brown*, its progeny, and *Morse*, raises the question of judicial authority. Putting the matter somewhat starkly, if collegial appellate courts speak ambiguously, how can they speak authoritatively? Since the very medium of judicial work products—language—and the essential process of producing judicial work products—group interaction—preclude being definitive, what is compelling about such outcomes? This most thorny of questions has shadowed U.S. Supreme Court jurisprudence from the beginning of the Republic.

On June 14, 1788, during debates over ratifying the U.S. Constitution, Alexander Hamilton famously addressed what I refer to as the paradox of judicial power. In a crucial paragraph of his essay on the Judiciary Department, *Federalist* no. 78, Hamilton addressed the objection raised by opponents of the recently drafted Constitution that the federal judiciary imperiled individual liberties. Hamilton's reply emphasized "the natural feebleness of the judiciary."[145]

> Whoever attentively considers the different departments of power must perceive, that, in a government in which they are separated from each other, the judiciary, from the nature of its functions, will always be the least dangerous to the political rights of the Constitution; because it will be least in a capacity to annoy or injure them. The Executive not only dispenses the honors, but holds the sword of the community. The legislature not only commands the purse, but prescribes the rules by which the duties and rights of every citizen are to be regulated. The judiciary, on the contrary, has no influence over either the sword or the purse; no direction either of the strength or of the wealth of the society; and can take no active resolution whatever. It may truly be said to have neither *force* nor *will*, but merely judgment; and must ultimately depend upon the aid of the executive arm even for the efficacy of its judgments.[146]

The paradox of judicial power is twofold.[147] Firstly, judicial power is vulnerable and invincible. Judicial power is vulnerable because, by themselves, mere words can neither coerce nor entice. Judicial power is invincible because words can change people's minds. Hamilton implicitly suggests this duality when he observes that the judiciary has "neither *force* nor *will*, but merely judgment." Of course, seeking to assuage anti-Federalists' fears of an independent federal judiciary, Hamilton attaches the modifier "merely" to judgment. Hamilton's move can be seen as adroit, disingenuous, or, more likely, both. Nevertheless, by identifying the source of judicial power as judgment, Hamilton points us toward the characteristic rendering Supreme Court determinations supreme, namely, the justices' ability to judge persuasively. Artfully crafted, words cut more deeply than any blade. Portraying the truth underlying the cliché "the pen is mightier than the sword,"[148] *New Yorker* cartoonist Charles Barsotti suggests the power of words in this drawing:

"You'd better cool it. Remember what he did to you last time."

The paradox that seemingly "mere" words, articulated winningly by justices in their work products, are powerfully moving can be explained in terms of what political scientist Lief Carter calls an "aesthetic" understanding of judging. Carter defines aesthetic "as fitting together the various parts of a subject coherently within a frame."[149] For Carter, judicial opinions are performances: "We use words and other forms of performance to demonstrate our virtue and trustworthiness to one another quite apart from the decisions and choices we make."[150] Aesthetically speaking, judicial work products are convincing to the extent that they are pleasing—that is, gratifying and delightful—to various communities interpreting them. Carter's approach to evaluating constitutional decisions "is grounded in a theory of morality based upon what can only be called communitarian dialogue . . . a plea for a new communitarian basis for legitimacy in a post-modern society."[151] In more colloquial terms, Carter says "in our day, people don't seem to agree about much of anything. . . . But we can converse and disagree in ways that connect us to each other."[152] Carter believes that "[t]he best we, or anyone, can do is to embrace what works for us and to try to persuade others that it can work for them, too."[153]

From this aesthetic point of view, *Morse v. Frederick* fails to please. In other words, *Morse* is not a pretty picture.[154] Now, Carter's aesthetic criterion may strike one as so lofty as to border on the ridiculous; that, or as simply inapt. After all, law is not art.[155] This is precisely my point: thinking of law and art as antithetical is problematical. To the extent that we think of law strictly in terms of defining winners and losers, as Hobbesian state-sanctioned rules in a zero-sum game, we reduce law to an elaborate playbook. By doing so, we impoverish our understanding of law and diminish law's place in our lives. When Oliver Wendell Holmes Jr. observed in 1880 that "[t]he life of the law has not been logic; it has been experience,"[156] he discerned that law shapes—and is shaped by—the stories of our lives. Like good art, law done well integrates human experience. Both activities help us to organize our world, to understand our place in our world, and to endow our world with meaning. Thus law, like art, is pragmatic.[157]

Let me approach Holmes' vantage point, and Carter's method of evaluating constitutional decisions, from a different angle. Shortly after *Morse v. Frederick* was announced Frederick Schauer published a critique of how the Court treated that case in the influential annual *Supreme Court Review*.[158] Schauer's purpose was not to evaluate whether *Morse* was rightly decided; his goal was "not to assess whether the Court in *Frederick* reached a correct or an incorrect constitutional decision."[159] Instead, Schauer argues that *Morse v. Frederick* typifies a troubling trend in Supreme Court jurisprudence. Specifically, Schauer thinks that, increasingly, the justices have abdicated their responsibility to provide guidance to other members of the political community of which the Court is a part. "Many of the Court's recent decisions exemplify this disturbing trend, but *Morse v. Frederick* . . . is among the most dramatic."[160] Schauer explains why:

> [W]hat *Frederick* did not decide, tellingly, is what standard school administrators should
> employ in deciding when to discipline students for verbal acts of in-school misbehavior, or
> what standard courts should use when such discipline is challenged on First Amendment
> grounds. In short, those who seek guidance from the Supreme Court—whether they be

judges, lawyers, teachers, or school administrators—about what the law is are certainly no better off after *Frederick* than before, and indeed they are arguably worse off.

Continuing, Schauer details his complaint:

> The uncertainty and confusion sown by *Frederick* are especially apparent with respect to *Tinker*'s substantial disruption standard. The *Tinker* structure itself was moderately plain. . . . *Fraser* muddied the waters . . . and *Kuhlmeier* added to the uncertainty[.] . . . After *Frederick*, the status of the *Tinker* standard is even less certain, for now the advocacy of illegal drug use also need not be likely to produce substantial disruption in order to be subject to restriction.[161]

"Tellingly," to use Schauer's word, *Morse v. Frederick* is incoherent. As a means of showing the way, the nominal Opinion of Court—not to mention the 2–1–2/3–1 result—fails.[162] More pertinent to my concern to connect Schauer's critique to Holmes and Carter, *Morse v. Frederick* abjectly fails to guide Americans how to proceed when grappling with reconciling student speech with school discipline in the context of adolescent drug use.

Holmes might say that *Morse v. Frederick* teaches nothing about navigating the treacherous passage between Scylla and Charybdis during stormy times. Carter likely would point out that, first, Schauer's complaint of lack of guidance resembles important aspects of his "cautious version of aesthetic jurisprudence,"[163] a version that confines "the aesthetic analysis to the world of law."[164] This version is concerned that "the difficulty in much modern jurisprudence [is] that the Court, even by the most cautious and limited definition of its audience, sends out noise, and the frequency of noisy opinions may be increasing." Carter continues, "[n]oise may communicate messages at rock concerts, but it is harder to communicate a jurisprudence of noise, particularly for an audience of lawyers and judges."[165] Second, Carter would apply Schauer's critical analysis to "a wider audience."[166] Aesthetically speaking, the "noisy" *Morse v. Frederick* result fails to guide Americans seeking to define how our community—we the People—can "fit," that is "harmonize,"[167] student speech with school discipline during dangerous times. Carter likely would rewrite Schauer's second sentence in the block quote on page 191 to read: "In short, those who seek guidance from the Supreme Court—whether they be judges, lawyers, teachers, or school administrators, *as well as students, parents, and other citizens*—about what the law is are certainly no better off after *Frederick* than before, and indeed they are arguably worse off*" (emphasis added).

What we have here, then, are three complementary understandings of the central task of constitutional law. I remind my constitutional law students that the root of the word *constitution* is to constitute—to bring into being.[168] Etymologically, *constitution* in the political sense of the word evolved from the Latin *constitutus*, past participle of *constituere*, "to fix, establish, and from constitution as in health, strength, and vitality." First and foremost, judging in constitutional law is about constituting vibrant community for, without community, there would be no use for the other trappings of a constitutional order. Carter's aesthetic approach to constitutional interpretation, Holmes' view that the life of the law has been experience, and Schauer's concern that Supreme Court decisions provide guidance—all three share the concern that the justices' work imparts political vision. I am using the word *vision* in the twofold sense that political philosopher Sheldon Wolin employed it in his classic *Politics and Vision*.[169] For Wolin, the political philosopher's vocation is to see clearly and imagine freely. That is my rendering. Wolin offers a play on the word *vision*, referring to the sense of sight and to the revelatory experience. However one articulates Wolin's frame of reference, his notion of doing political philosophy entails being creative. In this sense, constitutional law is necessarily, and beneficially, political. Here is how Lief Carter explains his understanding of Supreme Court justices' vocation, and how we might evaluate their work:

> My general point is that we find meaning in the world not by classifying our experience according to general rules but, as Martha Nussbaum . . . put it, "by burrowing down into the depths of the particular, finding images and connections that will permit us to see it more truly, describe it more richly." Good interpretation burrows into the depths of the particular and enriches us in the process. How well do [Supreme Court] opinions . . . empower us to see ourselves more truly and richly? How well do they build our trust in the virtue of [the] deciding justices? How well do they encourage us to converse and debate our character with each other? You be the judge.[170]

We can adapt Carter's questions, and his aesthetic concerns, to *Morse v. Frederick*.[171] What visions, we might ask, underpin the five *Morse* opinions? Do any of these judicial performances enlarge our understanding of drug use in public schools, stimulating imaginative approaches to adolescents and drugs while respecting student expression? More generally, do they help us to reconcile the tension between social control and individual expression— or do they exacerbate that opposition? Do any of these judicial performances enhance the dignity of the many teachers, school administrators, students, parents, and other citizens who genuinely care about student safety and student speech, helping us realize who we are as a people? Do the *Morse* judicial performances facilitate conversation, or are they conversation stoppers? Ultimately I suppose we might ask: Does *Morse v. Frederick* take us beyond sports metaphors? Abandoning the winner-take-all, zero-sum frame, does it help us burrow into details of our shared lives, conjuring images and forging connections, thereby enabling us to grapple with an intractable social problem in ways that honor us and burnish our cherished values? I turn to these matters toward the end of the following chapter.

9

Lost Opportunities and
Failure of Imagination

CHIEF JUSTICE John G. Roberts did not have the last word on the incident on Glacier Avenue. Roberts' nominally majority opinion, together with the four other opinions announced by the U.S. Supreme Court on June 25, 2007, comprise one episode in a dispute that refused to die. The nine justices' five different takes on BONG HiTS are an important episode, to be sure. They remain one installment nevertheless. Opposing counsel, representing Joe Frederick, and Deborah Morse and the Juneau School District, respectively, continued their "legal tit for tat"[1] for another seventeen months. It is as though the High Court outcomes provide an instructive sort of sidebar to the underlying story; certainly not incidental, and not entirely elemental. The visions informing that sidebar, realized as species of judicial performances, merit further analysis and assessment along the lines I discussed briefly in my coda to the previous chapter.

Before I address the questions I posed in concluding Chapter 8, I want to complete the story of how the incident on Glacier Avenue continued to reverberate, from the June 2007 U.S. Supreme Court constitutional outcome in *Morse v. Frederick*, 551 U.S. 393, until the November 2008 settlement between Joe Frederick and the Juneau School District. Comparing where the parties ended up, in relation to where their mutual distrust prevented them from going earlier, we will find that the trajectory of their fight smacks of déjà vu. Eventually, I want to return to the themes of pride, truth, and "surprising opportunities," treated in Chapter 1, with the goal of explaining my basic conviction that reconciling student speech rights with school authority entails imaginatively creating school forums where the enduring tension between liberty and order can be engaged. The story of Principal Morse's and student Frederick's interactions might have been a very different tale, if being disrespected in Juneau had been avoided by conversing in Juneau.

The *Juneau Empire* headline on June 26, 2007, read: "'Bong Hits' Ruling Sides with District: *Justices Say Juneau Principal Had a Right to Suspend Student*."[2] Greg Skinner, the reporter on the story, quotes Deborah Morse as saying that in light of the Supreme Court's decision

"[a]ny message 'perceived to promote drugs will be determined to be controlled speech[.]
It will be illegal.'" Skinner reports that "Morse thanked the Supreme Court for supporting
a principal's ability to control non-protected speech."[3] Clearly, Deborah Morse felt that her
exercise of control on Glacier Avenue had been vindicated. "You know, I never really had
any problems with students," she observed during our interview. "It was always—usually
when the student left my office, they were more upset they'd let me down, [as] opposed to
it being anything else. This is the first time. I mean this is just a—I don't know—real unique
situation. The first time I'd had an issue. And it's been goin' on forever."[4]

Needless to say, Joe Frederick and his attorney, Doug Mertz, reacted differently. "I was
actually pretty shocked," Joe recalls. "I knew that the Court was mostly conservative, but
I just didn't think there was any way a legal mind could possibly rule against me. And that
was judging from Mertz and other [lawyers] I've talked to. . . . [M]any legal minds thought
it was [as one lawyer put it] a 'hand's down case.'"[5] As far as Mertz was concerned, Morse's
actions amounted to viewpoint discrimination, pure and simple.

> Mertz said the Supreme Court applied a "viewpoint restriction" and "finessed the issue by limit-
> ing it to a pro-drug issue." . . . "This is an extremely dangerous precedent," Mertz told the *Juneau
> Empire*. 'This is the first time a subject matter is outside the protection of the First Amendment."
> Mertz said he and Frederick would confer about a final option, referring the case to the Alaska
> Supreme Court. "We are going to look at it very closely," Mertz said. "We believe the state con-
> stitution offers greater protection." . . . Mertz [continued, saying] the state constitution offers
> more protection from censorship than the federal constitution,[6] "unless there is a compelling
> reason." Such a compelling reason would be disruption to a classroom, he said. "The school
> district admits there was no disruption of the educational process[.]"[7]

The parties' response to the U.S. Supreme Court's decision in *Morse v. Frederick* added still
more takes on the Rorschach-like incident on Glacier Avenue.

Meanwhile, Joe Frederick's life continued to be eventful. Backtracking a bit to fill in
some blanks, he traces his whereabouts and his activities since June 2002.

> In June 2002, as soon as I graduated, me and my girlfriend took off to Hawaii for about four
> months, or so. . . . And from there I went straight to Texas. I had packed my car before I left,
> and had it barged to Seattle, and had a cousin pick it up there. So when I left Hawaii, I flew
> back to Seattle, picked up my car, and drove to Texas to university. I stayed down there awhile.
> ["What school were you at in Texas?"—JCF] Stephen F. Austin State University, in Nacogdo-
> ches, Texas. I went to school there for a year. . . .
>
> Then I, uh, . . . I ended up getting kicked out of school in Texas after getting charged
> with distribution of marijuana, after an incident with some other kids at the school. What
> happened was—I don't know—it's a long story. But I was charged with selling drugs after
> somebody told the police that I had sold him drugs. What happened was a bunch of us got
> together and ate some hallucinogenic mushrooms together—right? And I made some jokes
> about religion, or something, to this one kid, who I didn't know comes from this small town
> in Texas. And I didn't know that this kid still goes to Catholic church every Sunday and

Wednesday. Anyway, this kid walked off on his own and didn't have the mental capacity to know what a hallucination is, and ended up in the school library acting really weird. And security was called, and he was calling the security guards "demons," and telling them to go back to hell, and talking biblically, and really, really freaking out. So they arrested him. And after he calmed down he told the police like everybody he had eaten mushrooms with. And told them he had smoked marijuana. And where did it take place? It had taken place at my house. So, therefore, I was the person who took the blame for it. . . .

I didn't think they had any evidence. And they didn't have any evidence on me. They just had this kid's testimony—over a night where he was hallucinating the whole night, so his testimony shouldn't be admissible in court. I got an attorney down there, who recommended I take a plea bargain because [he said] there's something I had to understand: "This is Texas"—or, no—"This is Nacogdoches." "I'm not from Nacogdoches [Frederick's attorney told him] and, hell, I'm not even from Texas. That's more than enough to convict you." So I plea-bargained out for like a month and a half in jail with no probation, and a misdemeanor, or something like that.[8] Which, I think it was a good deal, because I got this attorney through an old friend of mine, and [he] would have taken care of me. But it caused me to have to drop out of that university, or be suspended for a year, which is long enough to consider just dropping out and starting at another school. . . .

After that I moved up to Marshall, Texas, not far from there, where I used to have grandparents, who have died since. I went and stayed with them, worked in some restaurants and stuff, for awhile, then got bored and moved back up to the Seattle area. [I] was there for a little bit, then . . . I moved back up to Juneau and worked construction, doing carpentry apprentice for probably a year, a year and a half. Then [I] went down to Idaho, University of Idaho at Moscow, and studied there for almost a year. Then, after that, I went to China. ["Where were you when the Supreme Court came down with your decision?"—JCF] I was in America, but I'd already been in China for a year. And I happened to be in America for the summer when the Supreme Court announced the decision.[9]

Joe resided in five states, and one foreign country, over the course of five years after he graduated, continuing the nomadic life he had been living prior to moving to Juneau in 2001. While the locales changed, Joe's self-professed modus operandus seemingly did not: "I want to do something, I do it," he observed. "I don't like to ask for permission. I like to do what I like to do."[10] It seems to me that Frederick's wanderlust was fueled not so much by a search for physical place as by Joe's search for a way he could feel at home with himself. His restlessness resulted not from where he was, but who he was.

In the wake of the Supreme Court's ruling in *Morse v. Frederick*, what Joe continued to want to do was to tell his story. "We started discussing on whether or not to take [the case] up in Alaska, in state court, on state constitutional rights."

We talked about whether we wanted to, whether it was plausible. I think what I ended up telling Doug [Mertz] on it was I'd like to, if he was willing to. Because I know this also was very exhausting for him. So, I told him that if he and the ACLU were still willing to fight, I was willing to stick with it. I have to consider them because this has been much more troublesome and strenuous for Doug and the ACLU, more than me, where all I have to do is really agree to continue or not. I mean all the hard work is [*chuckles*] definitely not mine. The hard work is all the legal things, preparing briefs, and all the technical stuff. So I told [Doug], if he still had the energy, and wanted to continue fighting it, I did too. I didn't want to be sort of an asshole and be like, "No, I still want to fight it!" if they're exhausted.[11]

Key to understanding Joe Frederick's decision to continue "fighting it" is Joe's desire to have his day in court. Primarily, he was fighting being silenced. His concern might seem odd. Even though three federal judicial tribunals—including the U.S. Supreme Court— had reviewed Frederick's case, he remained convinced that he had not been heard. Perhaps Frederick's belief is sour grapes. According to this view, Joe had been heard, and he had lost twice, the second time before the highest court in the country. Deborah Morse certainly felt validated. During our interview, with her attorney David Crosby present, Morse recalled, "[w]hen I left" following oral arguments before the justices, "I felt really good. I mean, I felt they had heard and really had dug in, and were really getting to the gist of it[.] . . . You know, it just really seemed that they got to the general points . . . surely, to support my part in the immunity, and my judgment at that time. . . . Now, if you talk to Mertz, even though we won, he would disagree [*laughter all around*]."[12] Morse's and Crosby's laughter was hard-edged.

Doug Mertz disagreed because no contest to weigh the contested facts at the heart of Joe Frederick's and Deborah Morse's dispute ever occurred. When I talked to Doug Mertz, it was clear that briefing and arguing one's case, on the one hand, and being heard are not identical experiences. He chafed at the preemptive way that the judicial process had unfolded, closing out Joe's voice.

[U.S. District Court Judge] Sedwick made his decision because he's the most conservative judge in the state—period. And he also did it in a vacuum of facts. . . . There's never been a hearing, never been a trial. And yet you had judges, from Sedwick on up through the Supreme Court, acting as if certain facts had been established—that weren't. And Joe never did have his day in court, never did get to explain what he was doing to any of the fact finders. So, as a pure matter of a case in the justice system, it was incomplete and, well frankly, troubling, because it was adjudicated on such an incomplete basis. You can understand why the Supreme Court did what it did, if you take what I think is accurate, that they really do not concern themselves with justice in individual cases. They concern themselves with setting broad policy. . . . So, the best way to look at the Supreme Court decision was, if circumstances like this occurred, this is what the legal result is—without really saying "this did occur."[13]

As a procedural matter, in order for Mertz and his client to continue to "fight it," they were initially required to return to Judge Sedwick's court. The final two sentences of Chief Justice Roberts' opinion for the U.S. Supreme Court in *Morse v. Frederick* read: "The judgment of the United States Court of Appeals for the Ninth Circuit is reversed, and the case is remanded for further proceedings consistent with this opinion. It is so ordered."[14] Accordingly, in July 2007, the Ninth Circuit reversed its ruling in *Frederick v. Morse*, 439 F. 3d 1114 (2006). On August 7, 2007, the Ninth Circuit returned the case to the U.S. District Court for the District of Alaska for further proceedings and, on September 10, 2007, entered an order referring the ongoing litigation to Judge Sedwick.

Basically, attorneys Crosby and Mertz sparred over whether Joe Frederick's lawsuit remained viable, or whether circumstances and previous court decisions rendered it moot. On August 2, 2007, David Crosby had filed with the district court a "suggestion of mootness and motion to dismiss, supported by the July 30, 2007, declaration of Juneau Superintendent of Schools, Peggy Cowan, who declared that all references to the discipline of the BONG HiTS 4 JESUS incident had been completely expunged from Frederick's records."[15] In his final judgment in *Frederick v. Morse*, No. J02-008 CV (JWS), issued October 10, 2007, Judge Sedwick agreed with the defendants. Judge Sedwick wrote:

> The only question left unresolved by the decision of the United States Supreme Court in *Morse v. Frederick*, 551 U.S. ____, 127 S.Ct 2618, 168 L.Ed.2d 290 (2007), is the fate of plaintiff Joseph Frederick's (Frederick's) claims for declaratory and injunctive relief under Article 1, Section 5, of the Alaska Constitution. . . . It appears from the record that Frederick has graduated from Juneau Douglas High School, and that the Superintendent of the Juneau School District has expunged all references to discipline of Frederick arising out of the Bong Hits 4 Jesus incident. Accordingly, Frederick's remaining claims for declaratory and injunctive relief under Alaska law are moot.[16]

Judge Sedwick's second, and final, ruling set the stage for a second trip to the Ninth Circuit Court of Appeals in September 2008. In the meantime, in a late 2007, early 2008 fusillade symptomatic of the deep roots of the "BONG HiTS" dispute, and exemplifying the ugly tone it had assumed, Crosby and Mertz fired broadsides at each other over another failed settlement effort and the school district's effort to recover court costs from Joe Frederick. In November, Doug Mertz approached the school district, offering to drop Frederick's lawsuit. In return for an $8,000 payment to Joe and $20,000 in legal fees, his client would settle.[17] The school district rejected the offer, and Doug Mertz filed an appeal of Judge Sedwick's ruling with the Ninth Circuit.[18] Not only did the Juneau School Board reject Frederick's latest offer, it filed a district court motion to compel Frederick to pay $5,000 in costs the school district said it incurred litigating at the U.S. Supreme Court, and the second U.S. District Court action.

According to *Juneau Empire* reporter Alan Suderman, Doug Mertz responded to the board's actions by saying: "'The only motive here is revenge, retaliation, and harassment.'" School board attorney David Crosby replied that "he was not harassing Frederick, but simply trying to get the money owed to his client." Mertz's rejoinder was that "lawyers typically wait until a case is settled before moving forward with financial requests such as Crosby's." "'If (Frederick) wants this thing to go away, it can go away,' Crosby [retorted]." "Mertz [answered] . . . Crosby is trying to punish [Joe Frederick] for having the 'effrontery' to take his case to the U.S. Supreme Court."[19] And so the tit-for-tat exchange went. The attorneys' mutual acrimony prompted the *Juneau Empire* to editorialize under the headline "Enough Already; Drop the Bong Hits Issue." The "BONG HiTS 4 JESUS" saga had "degenerated," the paper complained. To Frederick and Mertz, the *Empire* opined that "[w]hat started as a quest to ensure Alaska students' free speech rights—a worthy cause—has fizzled[,] . . . [i]t's time to move on." The *Empire* told the Juneau

School District and Crosby that "[t]he district appears to be acting out of spite[,] . . . [t]he amount Frederick owes is chump change to the district[.]" The editorial concluded: "This legal tit-for-tat must end. Let's drop the Bong Hits case once and for all."[20]

The BONG HiTS case was not about to go away. Year six, 2008, began with Doug Mertz and David Crosby filing briefs in Frederick's Ninth Circuit appeal of the "final" judgment[21] that Judge Sedwick had announced three months previously. Mertz made six arguments, based on the "overall question . . . [of] the proper process on remand of this case from the U.S. Supreme Court."[22] He grouped his arguments in three categories. First, referring back to Judge Sedwick's original May 27, 2003, ruling in the case, Mertz contended that the district court erred in dismissing his client's suit, because it mistakenly read Alaska state law as placing on Frederick "the burden of proving that the school district lacked a compelling state need for" suspending him, and did "not [recognize] that the student had carried this burden."[23] Second, Mertz turned to the mootness issue. He maintained that the district court was mistaken in assuming that, under Alaska state law, because it had ruled that school board officials were immune from money damages, Frederick was thereby precluded from suing for "declaratory relief, for injunctive relief, or for damages against the school board as a unit of government."[24] Further, the district court also erred by mooting Frederick's case based "on the belief that because the school district claims to have destroyed some of the records of the student's discipline, no further relief is possible."[25] Third, turning to federal claims, Mertz articulated what I think is his—and Frederick's—central objection, the lack of a trial:

> Since no court at any level has ever made findings on the material disputed facts in this case, the District Court erred in dismissing the federal counts without a trial, particularly since the student had made a prima facie showing that his speech was a serious nondisruptive protest of school district policies that had nothing to do with drugs. This is true not only for the dispute over display of the banner seized by the principal, but also the separate issue of whether the principal doubled the student's punishment because he quoted Thomas Jefferson on free speech to her.[26]

Mertz asked the Ninth Circuit either to order the district court hold a trial on the federal issues, or to certify the state issues to the Alaska Supreme Court. Clearly, Mertz sought a venue that would afford Joe Frederick the opportunity to explain his side of the story, contextualizing the incident on Glacier Avenue in a fact-finding forum, an opportunity thus far Frederick had been denied.

In his opposition brief, David Crosby essentially replied that Frederick had received ample chances to tell his story. Furthermore, Crosby argued, having heard Frederick's story, the U.S. District Court and the U.S. Supreme Court had responded with rulings that definitively precluded additional retellings. He organized his brief around two major headings: "The Supreme Court's Opinion Conclusively Disposed of All Frederick's Federal Claims"[27] and "Frederick's Alaska Law Claims Are Moot."[28] Crosby concluded his brief:

> The decision of the United States Supreme Court disposes of Frederick's First Amendment claims. His remaining state law claims have been rendered moot by: (1) his graduation; (2) his failure to contest the District Court's ruling granting Morse and JSB [Juneau School Board]

immunity from damages arising out of alleged violations of the Alaska Constitution; and (3) the removal of all references to the Bong Hits incident from Frederick's school records.[29]

Somewhat concurrently with the briefing process resulting in the documents just discussed, throughout the late winter and spring of 2008, mediation phone conferences occurred. Responding to Mertz filing an appeal of Judge Sedwick's decision, the Ninth Circuit had referred the parties to its Mediation and Settlement Program via an order to participate in a Settlement Assessment Conference. This conference is based on a Mediation Question-naire that the parties' counsel must complete.[30] Doug Mertz and David Crosby were offered the services of the Ninth Circuit's chief mediator, Claudia L. Bernard.

Mediation is confidential. Nevertheless, it is apparent that the telephone sessions did not go well, because they did not resolve the dispute. By now, the shoal on which mediation foundered is very familiar: lack of trust among the parties. Here is how the mediation pro-cess is described on the Ninth Circuit Web site:

> No matter what the content of the discussions, the mediator will facilitate negotiations among the parties to help them devise a mutually acceptable resolution of their dispute. The mediator will ask questions, reframe problems, facilitate communications, assist the parties to understand each other and help identify creative solutions. The mediator will not take sides, render decisions, offer legal advice or reveal confidences.
>
> Settlement occurs when the parties find a resolution that is preferable to continued liti-gation. Factors that frequently favor settlement over litigation include speed, cost, certainty, control, creativity and flexibility.[31]

Assessed according to these criteria, six years after the incident on Glacier Avenue, Joe Frederick's and Deborah Morse's dispute was nowhere near the point where finding "a resolution . . . is preferable to continued litigation." None of the main participants could see their way beyond the lack of understanding, and often animosity, characterizing their inter-actions from the outset. Two symptoms of their mutual failure of imagination stand out.

First, and perhaps most tellingly, both attorneys had taken the BONG HiTS dispute personally. By early 2008, opposing counsel had long since become adversaries. Ironically, as they went about castigating their opponent, both bewailed how the dispute had grown personal. During our interview, Deborah Morse speculated why Joe Frederick persisted in litigating. "I think Mertz was fanning this in a big way," she theorized. "I don't think Joe would have gone this far, or this long."[32] Then David Crosby joined in.

> This whole business about harassment, and this conspiracy against his client, that was thematic throughout this. I mean, Doug tried this case in the newspaper, which I've always tried not to do with my cases. But, given the nature of the case, and the nature of the community, I suppose it was a tactical decision. I don't like lawyers who do that, because it makes it very difficult to talk rationally about the case and to do things that lawyers can do, which is to try and solve problems, because, now, personalities are involved. . . . Doing anything with Doug Mertz is like punching the Tar Baby, you know, it just comes back at you in some other crazy form.[33]

Doug Mertz harbored his own critical view of opposing counsel. If Crosby saw Mertz as behaving unethically by, among other things, prolonging litigation and seeking publicity—making him a "sticky" person to deal with—Mertz pictured Crosby in commensurately pejorative terms. "A number of us have speculated," Mertz observed, "on the extent to which Crosby's actions were motivated by his own conflict of interest."

> He had clear very personal interest, which is why he volunteered for this role to begin with—former school board member, very conservative on drugs, although fairly liberal on other things. . . . I discovered very early on that my offers to settle were not being communicated to the school board. . . . And that, time after time, I made offers that should have been either accepted or at least opened up a dialogue. But Crosby came back and said: "The client won't do it." Now, in the end, I think he was identifying the client as the superintendent and the president of the school board, and maybe he was conveying my offers to them, and they weren't passing it on to the school board. But I think probably some things weren't even getting to them. . . . So, I don't know, but I came to distrust him very thoroughly. . . . I came to think of him as a real snake.[34]

Neither Crosby nor Mertz minced their words. Listening to them describe each other, first, I had a hard time recognizing the individual I had gotten to know as the person being depicted, and, second, I was struck by the sheer depth of their estrangement. Having been blown up from a tense encounter fraught with potential into a perfect constitutional storm, the incident on Glacier Avenue had become a grudge match. As I remarked to Doug Mertz upon hearing his views: "The level of hostility is amazing."[35]

Their hostility infected the Ninth Circuit's mediation efforts, likely dooming them from the outset. A second symptom of that enmity is how Doug Mertz interpreted changes his opponents made in the players involved in the mediation. In early February 2008, the named defendants in the ongoing litigation remained Deborah Morse and the Juneau School Board. David Crosby continued handling the case as their attorney. Three City of Juneau officials joined Crosby as participants in the Ninth Circuit mediations. Writing under the headline "City Joins 'Bong Hits' Mediation before Next Round of Litigation," *Juneau Empire* reporter Greg Skinner described the situation:

> The city recently became involved in the "Bong Hits 4 Jesus" litigation by appearing on behalf of the Juneau School District in settlement mediation required by the 9th U.S. Circuit Court of Appeals.
>
> The mediation was mandated before the appeals court will rehear the case on speech protections afforded under the Alaska Constitution. Juneau-Douglas High School Student Joe Frederick already lost his federal case, claiming his free-speech rights were violated, before the U.S. Supreme Court.
>
> Last Monday [February 11, 2008], City Manager Rod Swope, City Risk Manager Tim Allen and City Attorney John Hartle joined Juneau attorney Doug Mertz, representing Frederick, in a teleconferenced mediation session run by the San Francisco-based federal appeals court.

School district attorney David Crosby confirmed he was present for the mediation, but refused further comment. . . .

Hartle said the city's direct involvement in mediation came from its role as financier and risk manager for the school district.

"It's about money," he said. . . .

The city passed on any settlement offer that was discussed in mediation.

If the city agreed to any settlement, the first $25,000 of the agreed-upon amount would come from city coffers before insurance kicked in, Swope said.[36]

A plausible way of understanding the development that Skinner reported is that school board members were at least entertaining the possibility of ending six years of litigation by settling with Joe Frederick and, given that evolving posture, it was necessary that the city become involved. As Ann Gifford explained:

That's CBJ and APEI. ["And what do those acronyms stand for?"—JCF] City and Borough of Juneau, 'cause that's where the risk management pool that would pay like the stuff the insurance didn't cover. Because the district participates in this risk management pool and gets their insurance through CBJ. And so, CBJ kind of stands as their insurer. At this particular time, [the school district] had gone out and purchased a policy with APEI, and so like APEI was primarily doing it. But, like, there's a deductible on the policy, and CBJ would pay the deductible and APEI would pay the rest. ["What's APEI stand for, now?"—JCF] Alaska Public Entities Insurance. . . . And it's actually—it's a collective of public entities. . . . It's the insurance organization that a lot of school districts get their insurance through.[37]

One might perceive key Juneau personnel participating in the Ninth Circuit mediation as a potentially promising sign of movement on the negotiating front. Doug Mertz did not see the situation this way. Where suggestive tactical shuffling of the players may have been taking place, Mertz saw chicanery.

We were back in the Ninth Circuit, mediation going on . . . and at that time I perceived that we might have a school board much more willing to do something by way of settlement here. And so I said, "Okay, we're willing to do mediation. They're insisting that Joe be part of it— they'd hook him up by telephone [from China] at one point—and I said we want the other side to be there as well, the school board." And, at that point, Crosby said, "Well, my client is actually the borough." And so he showed up at the mediation with the city manager and the city risk manager, who had never had anything to do with the case, as if they were the clients. And the only reason it could have been was because the school board president, and probably a majority of the members of the school board, were not willing to go with Crosby's personal hard line. He cultivated the city manager so he basically could avoid having Mark [Choate, Juneau School Board President] there. . . . And I didn't make a big stink about it at the time, but it was very clear to me that Crosby was trying to manipulate it to get it his way. When you see your client drifting toward a result other than the one you want, you just change to a different client. And that's what he did.[38]

What we have here is a classic *Rashomon* situation: pride coloring perception. Like the dead samurai in Kurosawa's film, raw facts matter less than what, in the case of the failed Ninth Circuit mediation, two prideful opposing lawyers made of them. The fact is that by February 2008, it is likely that, as a group, the Juneau School Board was inclined to consider making the litigation lingering from the incident on Glacier Avenue go away.

Juneau lawyer Mark Choate had been elected to the Juneau School Board on October 3, 2006. During his campaign, Choate said he was running primarily because he was concerned about a "dropout crisis" which saw four in ten students in Juneau not graduating from high school. He also was concerned about uncertain funding for the operational costs of the then-proposed Thunder Mountain High School. Notably, Choate opposed the school district's decision to appeal the Ninth Circuit's decision in *Frederick v. Morse*, 439 F. 3d 1114 (2006). "'I think it's a waste of resources and I have serious concerns what we're trying to teach our children when we penalize what I think are speech issues,' Choate said. Kids are generally aware of drugs and alcohol and should be able to express their views, not have them suppressed, he said. Whether they are speaking in support of the war in Iraq or speaking out against racism, teenagers should be able to have their voices heard, Choate said. 'It's critical that kids get to express views—views that are unpopular,' he said."[39] Choate became Juneau School Board president on October 21, 2008. He was reelected on October 6, 2009.

The fact that the Juneau School Board, in February 2008, was not the same body that had voted, on May 2, 2006, to appeal *Frederick v. Morse* to the U.S. Supreme Court is, for my purposes, the equivalent of Kurosawa's samurai lying dead in a grove.[40] Both circumstances are true. In and of themselves, both circumstances also are without meaning. Legal scholar Cass R. Sunstein captured this situation when, in a different context, he wrote: "There is nothing that interpretation just is."[41] Sunstein argues that no single approach to interpreting the U.S. Constitution is either required, or self-evidently true. The dust jacket on Sunstein's book portrays the Constitution as a Rubik's Cube, suggesting the number of permutations available to a judge as she solves constitutional puzzles. Knowing that the district's posture toward Joe Frederick's continuing litigation was in flux, how did Doug Mertz and David Crosby interpret this situation? Therein hangs a revealing part of our tale.

We know how Doug Mertz read the board's evolving attitude. Seeing the change through the lenses of his suspicions about opposing counsel's motives, Mertz viewed the participation of three CBJ officials in the Ninth Circuit mediation as obstructing settlement. David Crosby did not discuss the Ninth Circuit mediation with me explicitly. Still, his views can be derived from other statements. First, as we have seen, Crosby was as distrustful of Doug Mertz as Mertz was of him. There was little love lost between them. Second, Crosby shared his clients' opinion that the U.S. Supreme Court's decision in *Morse v. Frederick* had definitively resolved the dispute in their favor. As far as they were concerned, the game was over, and their side had won. Consequently, they greeted Joe Frederick's continuing litigation with a mixture of impatience, frustration—and incredulity. We can get a flavor of their response in this exchange involving Crosby, Juneau Douglas High School Assistant Principal Dale Staley, and Peggy Cowan, then Juneau School district superintendent.

CROSBY: People got to the point where they couldn't believe *why* are they still doing this. They lost before the Supreme Court. Why is this still going on?! Sack your bats, and go home. . . . Let's drop it. We're ready to go.

COWAN: Right. People finally did tire of it—right.

STALEY: Some of us aren't schooled in law enough to know that you can go on beyond the Supreme Court [*laughs*]. They're really not the final word, I guess. . . .

COWAN: I know, because my family . . . when the Supreme Court ruling came down, I happened to be at a family reunion in Michigan. And we all turned on the national news, and Ken Starr was on the phone with me. And my cousins from England, and my nieces and nephews, anyways—and then [later] they would say, "What's going on?" "Oh, I still have a headache." "Whadda you mean, you still have a headache?!" [*Laughs.*] "How could you still have a headache? I thought it was over? You won." "No—not yet." . . .

["So you won. But, then, you got hauled back to court."—JCF]

COWAN: Yeah—that was a bit anticlimactic. [*Laughs all around.*]. . . .

CROSBY: There was a lot of outrage about the settlement demands that were being made, and that were being played in the press—and being misrepresented in the press. I mean, we had a settlement demand, the settlement demand was $108,000, and was represented by Mertz and the press as only being $28,000, or something like that. But it was an outrageously high demand. . . . And the feeling was, you know, millions for defense, and not a penny for tribute.[42]

David Crosby said two things during this conversation that shed telling light on what he thought of the Ninth Circuit mediation. Right at the beginning, he invokes a softball reference to criticize his opponent's continuing litigation: "Sack your bats, and go home." Three days earlier, Crosby had used the identical phrase, to the same effect, during my interview with Deborah Morse. "After the Supreme Court decision, it was clear that Frederick was not going to sack his bats and go home."[43] Crosby's being annoyed with Frederick's—and Mertz's—inability to accept what he considered their authoritative defeat likely hardened Crosby's resistance to settling. Being weary of Frederick's persistence is not the same thing as being willing to compromise. On the contrary, by invoking the alleged American retort to the French demand (made during the XYZ Affair, March 1797 to September 1800) to be paid a bribe and a loan—"millions for defense, and not a penny for tribute"[44]—Crosby suggests pretty conclusively that he and his clients were in no mood to arrive at any agreement that might remotely be understood as lending legitimacy to Frederick's indefensible position. Not yet, that is.

By July 2008, with its attempt to resolve the dispute between Frederick and Morse going the way of Avrum Gross' failed attempt to negotiate a settlement five years earlier, the Ninth Circuit Mediation Program ended its efforts, and oral argument was scheduled.[45] Oral argument was designated to be held at 3:00 p.m., Tuesday, September 9, 2008, before the same panel that, eighteen months previously, had ruled against Principal Morse and the school district in *Frederick v. Morse*, 439 F.3d 1114 (9th Cir. 2006). Judges Cynthia Holcomb Hall, Andrew J. Kleinfeld, and Kim McLane Wardlaw chose to retain control of the case on appeal to the Ninth Circuit—for the second time. Their decision is somewhat unusual, especially because the posture in which the case returned to the Ninth Circuit was as a procedural matter addressing the question of mootness. The reasons why the three panel members opted to hear a second appeal, only obliquely related to the merits of the case, are known only to them. Unsurprisingly, Frederick's and Morse's respective counsel speculate differently about what the Hall, Kleinfeld, and Wardlaw panel's decision to keep jurisdiction meant. In true *Rashomon* fashion, Crosby's and Mertz's interpretations are divergent views of a single fact. "Andy [Kleinfeld] is a civil libertarian" is how Doug Mertz articulated the fact of the matter. "He's a real Alaska judge in that sense, conservative and libertarian."[46] For David Crosby, the fact of the matter was that "[i]t was clear to me that . . . Judge Sedwick liked our case[.] . . . [And it] was equally clear that the Ninth Circuit hated our case."[47] While agreeing that Hall, Kleinfeld, and Wardlaw framed the dispute between Frederick and Morse in terms sympathetic to student rights, the two lawyers differed significantly over what to make of the judges' apparent attitude. The panel's attitude was lawless, in Crosby's opinion, because it was unconstrained by established precedents. He interpreted their vindicating Frederick's right to hoist his banner as "bias"[48] trumping fidelity to rules. For Mertz, the panel's attitude was laudable, in the sense of being in line with basic American constitutional values. "You've got all these well-educated people," Mertz remarked, "who will say, 'Oh, of course I support the First Amendment, free speech is tremendously important,' until it comes to a real world incidence where, somehow, they can't see it."[49] David Crosby viewed the Ninth Circuit panel as epitomizing the height of judicial arrogance in the face of an unambiguous legal answer. Doug Mertz understood the panel as adhering to First Amendment principles.

Oral argument before Judges Hall, Kleinfeld, and Wardlaw on September 9, 2008, did not go well for David Crosby.[50] From my vantage point, being present during the proceedings in the Ninth Circuit's beautiful courtroom in the historic Richard H. Chambers Courthouse in Pasadena, California,[51] Crosby was mauled. Judge Hall did not speak, but her colleagues Kleinfeld and Wardlaw interrogated Crosby sharply on the mootness issue. Clearly skeptical of the district's claim that no records existed that might cause harm to Frederick, these two judges gave him little quarter.[52] Their interactions smacked of yet another experience of déjà vu. Following the first round of Ninth Circuit oral argument, over four years earlier on July 8, 2004, Doug Mertz believed his exchanges with the court boded well. "I remember walking out," Mertz recalled, "and mentioning . . . to Crosby and [APEI Insurance Executive] Jeff Bush . . . and saying, 'Well, we all know you can't trust comments at oral argument,' . . . but it sure looks to me like we've got all three of them.' And they both said, "Well, looks to me like you've two out of three.'"[53] As we know from *Frederick v. Morse*, 439 F.3d 1114 (9th Cir. 2006), Mertz had all three judges. Based on the dynamics of the September 9, 2008, oral argument it appeared as though he again would have all three.

I say "would" because, in the event, Judges Hall, Kleinfeld, and Wardlaw did not have to render a decision. Following oral argument, the Ninth Circuit mediation was reopened, and the parties finally negotiated a settlement. Crosby recounts his perception of the aftermath of September 9, 2008:

> Before I went back to the Ninth Circuit and had that oral argument, the feeling was millions
> for defense and not a penny for tribute. And then it became clear that this panel was gonna

hold on to this case, and that this panel was just waiting to get to a merits decision on this [*taps table for emphasis*], and it was clear what they would do if they got to a merits on this. And, again, I want to stress, I don't agree with them. I think the panel was terribly wrong— and unfair—in this thing. I will say that about this panel. . . . And you [JCF] sat through that oral argument. . . . [A]t that point, then some of the arguments about economics, and the upset of the community, and everything, started to weigh much heavier. And that's when we started to get down to talking mediation, talking turkey about settlement.[54]

Watching Crosby being roughed up, pointedly yet decorously, by Judges Kleinfeld and Wardlaw, then listening to him reflect on what took place, it occurred to me that Crosby experienced a bittersweet epiphany that afternoon in Pasadena: it was time for him and his clients to sack *their* bats and go home. After all, hadn't his side already won the biggest prize before the highest court in the land? Hadn't five justices of the U.S. Supreme Court sided with Deborah Morse and the Juneau School District on the two key principles at issue? First, the Court ruled that the First Amendment shielded neither Joe Frederick's drug-related banner from being confiscated by the principal, nor from Morse suspending him. Second, the Court held that Morse was shielded from being liable for damages by qualified immunity. Given Crosby's clients' victory in *Morse v. Frederick*, 551 U.S. 393 (2007), continuing to answer Doug Mertz's niggling litigation before this particular Ninth Circuit panel needlessly placed Crosby's clients at risk. Yet, ending it entailed distasteful compromises. "I don't give Doug Mertz credit for many things," David Crosby remarked, "but I give him credit for persistence. You know, he and Frederick appeared to be ready to go for another seven years."[55] Under these circumstances, Crosby held his nose and recommended suing for peace.[56]

In yet another twist in this tangled tale, elements of the final settlement between Joseph Frederick, and Deborah Morse and the Juneau Board of Education, negotiated by the Ninth Circuit mediator, resemble the agreement Avrum Gross almost achieved in June 2002.[57] Gross' unsuccessful draft, and the eventual understanding are similar in two respects.[58] First both provide for some sort of activity pertaining to civil liberties. Gross' draft provides:

> The District will arrange for educational programs for administrators at which persons chosen by the Superintendent, who are recognized as knowledgeable in the field of civil liberties, will provide advice and expertise on the topic of student rights and responsibilities. Faculty and students will be permitted to attend these programs.[59]

The section of the Ninth Circuit settlement agreement about a civil liberties event is longer. It runs to over a full page and is full of particulars spelled out in five subsections. Instead of educational programs, the Ninth Circuit settlement specifies a single "forum on student free speech rights" to be held "[b]efore the end of the 2008/09 school year." The settlement specifies that the forum be organized in two consecutive presentations. During the first, "a knowledgeable neutral person," hired at District expense, will speak "on the subject of the current state of the law on student speech and its practical implications for students/faculty/staff." During the second, "one representative nominated by each party" will comment.[60]

Second, both documents address the underlying student speech controversy, albeit from different angles. Av Gross' draft is concerned with disciplinary charges and seeks to split off Frederick's expressive behavior from the other counts he faced:

> Frederick agrees that all of the disciplinary charges relating to truancy and to Frederick's failure to cooperate with Morse (2.07, 2.08, 2.05, and 2.17) shall stand. The defendants agree that in retrospect, both the wording of the sign and the circumstances under which it was displayed were sufficiently ambiguous as to justify a reversal of the decision upholding 2.14 "Display of Offensive Material." The defendants further agree that since the suspension was based on the existence of multiple offenses, and one has been removed, it is difficult to say now whether Frederick would have been suspended for any or all of the eight days actually served. Accordingly, the District agrees to remove all record of the suspension from Frederick's transcript.[61]

One might describe the compromise tactic that Av Gross adopted as a damage control approach. He parsed Morse's disciplinary charges against Frederick in order to expunge records held by the Juneau School District.[62] By contrast, the Ninth Circuit mediated settlement splits the difference by, first, invoking common ground then specifying where the parties agree to disagree:

> 3. The parties agree to the following statements of principle:
> A. Generally, students are not subject to discipline for speech that is controversial or in disagreement with policies or positions of the Juneau School Board or district;
> B. Issues related to application of state law to the banner incident and the subsequent discipline have not been resolved in this litigation;
> 4. FREDERICK maintains that his display of the banner was not intended in any way to be advocacy or encouragement of drug use.
> 5. THE JUNEAU SCHOOL BOARD maintains that Principal Morse's interpretation of the banner as constituting advocacy or encouragement of drug use was reasonable, regardless of FREDERICK'S subjective intent.[63]

These passages from the final settlement are symptomatic of just how deeply opposed the parties remained, despite exhaustion combining with prudence to curtail litigating. Point 3A of the agreement is inoffensive to the point of being meaningless (while being qualified by the word *generally*, to boot). Point 3B merely states the obvious (while containing an implicit threat of renewed litigation). Points 4 and 5 are, in effect, point-counterpoint (he says, she says). The whole document reads as much like a standoff as an agreement. It brings to mind an image of two neighborhood cats that have crossed paths on disputed territory. Backs arched, circling, yowling, spitting—they face each other off, locked eyeball to eyeball, neither able to stand down nor best their rival.[64]

One provision of the Ninth Circuit mediated settlement doubtless did little to ameliorate the underlying rift dividing Frederick, and Morse and the school district. Unlike Av Gross' 2002 draft, the Ninth Circuit 2008 settlement agreement mandated that the Juneau

School Board make a monetary payment to Joseph Frederick. The very first provision of the settlement agreement and mutual release ordered:

> 1. THE BOARD will pay FREDERICK $45,000 within five days of THE BOARD'S receipt of this Agreement executed by FREDERICK. Payment will be by check made payable to Douglas Mertz in trust for Joseph Frederick.[65]

Although "School Board President Mark Choate said . . . the school district's insurer will pay Frederick the settlement and . . . no funds will be diverted from educational programs,"[66] shelling out a "tribute" to Joe Frederick—amounting not just to a penny, but to four million, five hundred thousand pennies—was a bitter pill for some to swallow. Ann Gifford recalls that "the number came from Mertz. You know: 'This is what we want.' . . . I'm pretty sure that was just a number that he set . . ." she said, "in the course of negotiations. I think he demanded something more than that, because it was a mediated settlement. The Ninth Circuit mediator was involved."[67] It was galling enough that Doug Mertz drove the discussion of dollars and cents. Paying Joe Frederick, the board's nemesis, anything added insult to injury. "This kinda bugs me . . ." complained former school board president Mary Becker. "I was not opposed to us having that meeting [the student forum] with the kids. That was fine. But to give him any money really rubbed me the wrong way. I do not think we should have. I'm no longer on the board. I have no vote. . . . I know we needed to end it. And I'm glad we ended it. And I guess it's worth it that we ended it with $30,000, or whatever we did ["Forty-five."—JCF]. [*Laughs.*] Forty-five, it wasn't all that much. It was not much. It was the principle of the thing, not the money."[68]

When the parties signed the Ninth Circuit Settlement Agreement and Mutual Release on Monday, November 3, 2008, the incident on Glacier Avenue had come full circle. I mean full circle in a couple of senses of the term. First, it is one of the central ironies of this story that the parties ended up with an agreement not all that dissimilar to Av Gross' draft proposal that had come to naught. I asked Ann Gifford where the specific terms of the Ninth Circuit settlement agreement and mutual release originated. She replied, "Well, they were essentially just looking back at the [original offer]."[69] So, between the end of May 2002 and the beginning of November 2008, the parties expended significant amounts of scarce resources, while their ill feelings deepened, by litigating differences rather than seeking to mitigate conflict, only to settle on parallel terms. They had devoted six and a half years to getting back to where they started.

And yet, perhaps, under the circumstances, fighting was a necessary prerequisite to fixing. As Ann Gifford observed: "Well, it just seems a shame to have to invest those kind of resources. But I don't think the district really had a choice after the Ninth Circuit decision. You, know, they needed to do something. . . . Because I think that Ninth Circuit decision would have been terrible. It would have caused all kinds of trouble for a long time to come, if it had stood. . . . And the idea that it took all this [*laughs wryly*] to [reverse the Ninth] is kind of mind-boggling."[70] From the school district's perspective, there was no option but to challenge the Ninth Circuit Court of Appeals result, because its decision undermined the authority of school administrators like Deborah Morse and subjected them to being liable for damages. Joe Frederick did not see the situation this way. Still, he felt just as driven to litigate. Doug Mertz and his client found intolerable "the extent to which the school administration . . . was willing to go to be punitive and unthinking in its application of certain rules. . . . *Punitive* . . . isn't a very good word," Mertz continued, "I guess what I mean is draconian in general outlook. I mean, they've got their rules, and you follow 'em. . . . Now with Joe, there was an extra element, 'cause Joe was trouble. He was identified as a troublemaker, and they were out to get 'im. And it's—it's maybe to me . . . the single most troubling thing about the whole BONG HiTS business, is what they did to him without justification."[71] For Frederick and Mertz, Joe's arbitrary treatment could not go unchallenged.

Both adverse parties to this marathon commonly believed that they had been wronged. Consequently, both were convinced that they were litigating rightfully. The situation Joe Frederick and Deborah Morse locked themselves into for six and a half years gives new meaning to the legal phrase "exhausting all remedies."

Here is the second, more essential, way in which the incident on Glacier Avenue came full circle in November 2008. After suing, being sued, then suing some more, and eventually settling, Frederick and Morse remained as much at odds, likely more so, as they had been prior to their encounter that January 2002 morning. At the end of their costly jousting, each side credibly claimed victory. But what sort of victories were they? The roles that Frederick and Morse had already locked themselves into over half a decade earlier—roles precipitating their confrontation to begin with—merely had hardened over the course of successive court battles into burnished badges of honor. Each had vindicated their respective narratives, of accountability (Morse) and injury (Frederick). But these narratives were of a piece with the very Enforcer and Protester roles causing strife to begin with. Could their victories be anything but Pyrrhic?[72]

David Crosby undoubtedly would reject my rhetorical question. After all, he declared to me, in no uncertain terms: "You can read a Supreme Court opinion, or you can't."[73] Which, I suppose, is another way of asking "What part of a 5–4 opinion don't you understand?" Peggy Cowan would agree with Crosby. She drew a plausible analogy between *Morse v. Frederick*, 551 U.S. 393 (2007) and how *Miranda v. Arizona*, 384 U.S. 436 (1966) is understood. "*Miranda* was a 5–4 vote, as well," she noted. "You know what I mean? But does anybody today say that *Miranda* was a 5–4 vote? . . . In terms of when people talk about it, you watch the cop shows, and nobody says . . . we don't have to do this [warning], or whatever [because it was a 5–4 decision]."[74] As far as the Juneau School District is concerned, then, they triumphed by taking home the biggest prize. Nevertheless, a discordant note appears in even David Crosby's account. Toward the end of my interview with Deborah Morse, which Crosby sat in on and participated in, I was discussing with them the similarities between Av Gross' failed effort and the eventual final settlement. I proposed a metaphor: "In the end, sort of like Wagner's *Ring Cycle*, you start up in the Rhein and [after fifteen hours of opera over four nights] you end up in the Rhein, in the end they came back to the"—Crosby interrupted, and laughingly interjected—"except it's more like the city septic system."[75] At one level, I read Crosby's remark as acknowledging that the execrable, yet necessary, settlement with Joseph Frederick, especially its $45,000 payment, sullied an otherwise victorious outcome. More basically, one can construe his remark as evoking the sordid nature of the whole mean business.[76]

In the remainder of this chapter, I want to revisit the prize that Deborah Morse and the Juneau School District took home from Washington, D.C., on June 25, 2007. Ultimately, I also want to revisit the January 24, 2002, incident on Glacier Avenue, revising its aftermath. My intention is neither to play fox to the Supreme Court's *Morse v. Frederick* work product by grimacing at sour grapes, nor to rain on anyone's Olympic torch relay. On the contrary, I want to vindicate what I believe is the core value of the First Amendment speech clause, namely, conversing. My deeply held conviction is that we are most human when we converse, that is, when we exchange ideas, thoughts, opinions, and feelings through expressive acts—speech acts,[77] if you will. The activity of talking connects us. Talking, in an ongoing way, matters more than any particular outcome. Outcomes are more or less transitory, changeable way stations. It is conversing that counts.[78]

As keynotes to my ensuing discussion, I offer two quite different expressions of the same conviction: the indispensability of talking. Each addresses aspects of my embrace of conversing. The first keynote is sounded in a letter written by Juneau resident Kirk Ziegenfuss, published in the *Juneau Empire* on July 30, 2008. Mr. Ziegenfuss, who goes by "Ziggy," works in the mining industry, for AJ Mine/Gastineau Mill Enterprises.[79] He regularly writes letters to the editor of the *Juneau Empire*. Contextualizing Ziegenfuss' letter, by the time he wrote, Frederick and Morse had been at odds for over six years. The efforts of the Ninth Circuit Mediation Service to negotiate a settlement between the parties to *Frederick v. Morse*, No. 07-36013, were unraveling, thereby triggering the second round of oral arguments before Judges Hall, Kleinfeld, and Wardlaw the following September. Ziegenfuss wrote:

> Joseph Frederick, Deborah Morse and the city of Juneau have actually found themselves as co-defendants in a monumental case. Yes, I did say co-defendants.
>
> They are also joined by the Alaska judiciary system, the 9th U.S. Circuit Court of Appeals and the U.S. Supreme Court. What could link these opponents together as partners in crime? And who could try and judge such a case? Well, the judge and jury of this case will be history itself. And the charge is that the litigation and subsequent rulings to date in the "Bong Hits 4 Jesus" case have culminated into what may be the single most detrimental blow to the First Amendment to the Constitution of the United States of America.
>
> First we have a high school student, Frederick, who in what can clearly be considered a juvenile school-boy prank, displays a banner containing references to illicit drug use and religion on public property across the street from Juneau-Douglas High School, which has an open campus policy.
>
> Then we have a high school principal, Morse, who takes it upon herself to "confiscate" the banner displayed off school property. Morse then suspends Frederick from school, and he later parks his car in the Augustus Brown swimming pool parking lot, which is public property adjacent to the high school property. This prompted Morse to call the Juneau Police Department, which impounded, dismantled and searched Frederick's vehicle with only the implications of the confiscated banner as probable cause.

Now this obvious battle of wills is further escalated by a lawsuit, citing personal rights violations, against the city, which is obliged to defend its employees in the name of damage control.

Today this case has gone all the way to the Supreme Court where it was ruled on based upon the content of the banner rather than the rights of the individual guaranteed by our Constitution. In this precedent-setting judgment, the freedom of speech enjoyed by every citizen of our great nation has been compromised and undermined so that I believe even this letter of opinion could be scrutinized, its content deemed subversive and its author subject to persecution and even prosecution by the law. And this all because of a childish feud that went too far.

Hence these co-defendants judged by history will always be conjoined. Frederick is married to Morse as Roe is to Wade.

Kirk Ziegenfuss, Juneau[80]

Kirk Ziegenfuss' letter is a clever analysis of the perils of litigating instead of talking. The "crime" committed by "co-defendants" Frederick and Morse (not to mention their jurist "partners" in various state and federal judiciaries) was to allow their "childish feud" to go "too far." By lumping together Frederick and Morse and the several jurists involved in this saga, Ziegenfuss points us in the direction of understanding that, throughout, this story is about communication breakdowns in many ways, at several levels. To be sure, Ziegenfuss deplores that, by resorting to litigation, Frederick and Morse embarked on a path that resulted in a U.S. Supreme Court decision he believes threatens his own freedom of speech. That particular conclusion is dubious. Ziegenfuss' bit of hyperbole also is peripheral to the point of his letter, which eloquently, albeit implicitly, endorses discoursing. His core concern is the way in which Frederick's and Morse's "battle of wills" migrated into a prolonged series of court battles, by being "escalated by a lawsuit." His primary complaint is that Frederick and Morse did not figure out how to connect in ways other than being "conjoined" as litigants. In the end, Ziegenfuss pronounces Frederick and Morse "married." Whether intentional or not, the irony is delicious.

My second keynote is sounded by U.S. Supreme Court Justice Louis D. Brandeis. He wrote a concurring opinion in a 1927 case that came at the end of an eight-year series of four decisions involving "subversive speech," in which the Supreme Court endorsed silencing speakers deemed to have expressed various opinions threatening government.[81] In the annals of free speech doctrine, these four cases are seen as chapters in the halting evolution of First Amendment interpretation, from affording dissident speakers constricted constitutional protection, to providing them relatively less narrow safeguards. Justice Brandeis, and his colleague Justice Oliver Wendell Holmes Jr., are viewed as leading lights in this development.[82] Brandeis wrote in the 1927 case pitting Charlotte Anita Whitney against the State of California. A social activist and noted philanthropist in her early fifties, Ms. Whitney also was a member of the Oakland local of the Socialist Party. She ran afoul of a section of California's 1919 Criminal Syndicalism Act for having participated in a convention, held in Oakland, to organize the Communist Labor Party of California. She was arrested, convicted, and sentenced to prison (she never served hard time, and was pardoned by California Governor C. C. Young one month after *Whitney v. California* came down in May 1927).[83] On appeal to the U.S. Supreme Court, the justices unanimously upheld Whitney's state conviction. Curiously, Justice Brandeis concurred in that judgment, not because he agreed with his colleagues' First Amendment analysis on the merits, but due to his reading of the facts in *Whitney*, as they pertained to jurisdictional issues raised by the case.[84] Brandeis' puzzling vote has been almost totally eclipsed by his brilliant and accessible defense of free speech. I believe this paragraph from Justice Brandeis' defense pertains most directly to my concern with conversing instead of litigating:

> Those who won our independence by revolution were not cowards. They did not fear political change. They did not exalt order at the cost of liberty. To courageous, self reliant men, with confidence in the power of free and fearless reasoning applied through the processes of popular government, no danger flowing from speech can be deemed clear and present, unless the incidence of the evil apprehended is so imminent that it may befall before there is opportunity for full discussion. If there be time to expose through discussion the falsehood and fallacies, to avert the evil by the processes of education, the remedy to be applied is more speech, not enforced silence. Only an emergency can justify repression. Such must be the rule if authority is to be reconciled with freedom. Such, in my opinion, is the command of the Constitution. It is therefore always open to Americans to challenge a law abridging free speech and assembly by showing that there was no emergency justifying it.[85]

Brandeis' argument is compelling. To begin with, he assumes that speech is an asset, not a liability; a resource, not a problem. He shared the Founding Generation's "confidence in the power of free and fearless reasoning applied through the processes of popular government." Clearly, Brandeis understood speech as the means whereby Americans govern themselves. Given his point of departure, it followed that one need "not fear political change," nor "exalt order at the cost of liberty." The former position neuters speech out of anxiety. The latter stifles speech as unruly. Both stances presume that speech is inherently dangerous. For Brandeis, in stark contrast, speech only rises to the level of a "clear and present" danger in the absence of a timely occasion for speaking further—that is, lacking an "opportunity for full discussion." Only in a (fairly rare) emergency situation may speaking be silenced. Under what specific circumstances a situation amounts to an "emergency" entails a judgment based on the presence or absence of "time to expose through discussion the falsehood and fallacies." The default "remedy to be applied is more speech, not enforced silence." Brandeis' speech-centered "education" model of problem solving is enormously empowering.

Would that, in considering *Morse v. Frederick*, the U.S. Supreme Court had found ways to enact Kirk Ziegenfuss' preference for talking, embracing Louis Brandeis' understanding of speech. Five years previously, would that, on the morning of January 24, 2002, on Glacier Avenue, Joe Frederick and Deborah Morse had figured out how to talk their way through their confrontation. Had either of these scenarios unfolded, I would be telling a very different story (or no story at all). As it is, at the end of telling this story about a perfect constitutional storm in Alaska's capital city, I briefly want to shift gears from analyzing to diagnosing. My goal is political in the sense that I want to address the question: What is to be done?

Differently stated, I seek to offer preventive suggestions, along lines of: What might be done differently? However one poses the question, my baseline answer is the wisdom I have distilled from both keynotes: keep the conversation going.

.   There are no innocent bystanders in this story. There are no villains, either. Although some participants have, on occasion, fallen prey to reducing the incident on Glacier Avenue and its aftermath to a dichotomy pitting good persons against bad actors, we have seen that this saga is a lot more complex and nuanced than such zero-sum imagery allows. What we have here is variety of people, quite different, all decent, trying, as I put it in the previous chapter, "to define how our community—we the People—can 'fit,' that is 'harmonize,' student speech with school discipline during dangerous times." These words convey how I think about the central challenge lying at the heart of this story. What we have here is a daunting problem to solve. Addressing our predicament is made no easier by our tendency to read from established scripts, instead of thinking freely and acting imaginatively. By pridefully locking ourselves into our self-created roles, *Rashomon*-like, we miss an opportunity, likely to surprise each of us as much as it would others, of acting uncharacteristically. By reciting lines instead of co-authoring scenarios, we are merely mouthing words. What we have here is a failure to communicate.[86]

What is to be done? First, I suggest we revisit *Morse v. Frederick*, 551 U.S. 393 (2007), asking what the Court might have said.[87] Second, I propose that we return to that Thursday morning in January on Glacier Avenue and imagine how both immediate and subsequent interactions between Joe Frederick and Deborah Morse might have been played differently. Our two protagonists, and the justices of the U.S. Supreme Court, might have imagined ways to keep the conversation going about harmonizing student speech with school discipline.[88]

Informed by political scientist Lief Carter's aesthetic analysis, I posed these four questions in the coda to Chapter 8 with reference to the justices' performances in *Morse v. Frederick*:

> Do any of these judicial performances enlarge our understanding of drug use in public schools, stimulating imaginative approaches to adolescents and drugs while respecting student expression? More generally, do they help us to reconcile the tension between social control and individual expression—or do they exacerbate that opposition? Do any of these judicial performances enhance the dignity of the many teachers, school administrators, students, parents, and other citizens who genuinely care about student safety and student speech, helping us realize who we are as a people? Do the *Morse* judicial performances facilitate conversation, or are they conversation stoppers?

Then, following philosopher Martha Nussbaum, I asked:

> Ultimately . . . [d]oes *Morse v. Frederick* . . . help us burrow into details of our shared lives, conjuring images and forging connections, thereby enabling us to grapple with an intractable social problem in ways that honor us and burnish our cherished values?

The thematic thread linking these five questions is my concern that Supreme Court interpretations of the First Amendment Speech Clause further our ability to participate in common endeavors. The Latin word for common, *communis*, is the root of both communicate and community. One might say that these five questions assess *Morse v. Frederick* in terms of how effectively the justices speak to us as community members seeking to communicate who we are, and what we are thinking. In short, does *Morse v. Frederick* create common ground?

The glib answer is no—*Morse v. Frederick* does not create common ground. That bald statement is too uncomplicated and too absolute. "No" takes us nowhere. Ironically, just saying no to *Morse v. Frederick* is every bit as much of a conversation stopper as the majority decision itself. Rather than relegating the decision to being wrong, full stop, we need to recast it, responding to the justices' speech with more speech. The irony deepens. Dismissing *Morse v. Frederick* via the unambiguously negative linguistic construction—"no"—forecloses possibilities that are inherent in all Supreme Court work products precisely because they are linguistic creations. Since language is ambiguous, judges' words open doors as well as close them. Perhaps most ironically of all, categorically rejecting any common ground with *Morse v. Frederick* makes it difficult to create the very common ground sought. Keeping the conversation going about how we can harmonize student speech with school discipline during dangerous times entails conversing with the Court.

In this constructive spirit, I propose that the Court might have kept the conversation going by saying two things in *Morse v. Frederick*. First, the Court should have set off on a conciliatory foot by reversing the Ninth Circuit, and holding that Deborah Morse enjoyed qualified immunity, rendering her not liable for damages. Clearly, each of the nine justices rejected Frederick's claim for unspecified compensatory damages and punitive damages resulting from the incident on Glacier Avenue. Were I writing for the Court, for openers I would have coalesced their views into a single unanimous holding that removed the liability aspect of the case. Doing so would clear the air in a couple of ways. It would take the contentious question of money out of the picture. Deborah Morse would neither be at risk for compensating Joe Frederick (however unlikely her actually paying out of pocket was), nor would she suffer the stigma, indignity, and disability of having a judgment against her. Also, by taking money and reputation out of play, the Court could get on with crafting a more-speech remedy designed to privilege talking over litigating.

Second, the Court should have fashioned a remedy keyed on talking about drugs in high school instead of creating a First Amendment exception for purported drug speech. Were I writing for the Court, I would seek to thread the needle between acknowledging Principal Morse's authority, on the one hand, while respecting student Frederick's rights, on the other. How might I have accomplished this? I would begin by being skeptical of both Frederick's multiple explanations of his banner caper and of Morse's single-minded response. In line with my basic take on the whole incident on Glacier Avenue as being a matter of incommensurate stories told by prideful people, I would closely scrutinize both Frederick's injury narrative and Morse's accountability narrative. In other words, I would be "from Missouri," asking the narratives to show me that either was acting responsibly. My doubting would not be intended to cast aspersions, or to declare a pox on both houses. Rather, my doubting would be a solvent, employed to disperse certainty—a mode of ground clearing, if you will—in order to create space for conversing.[89]

The major flaw of Chief Justice Roberts' opinion for the Court, in my view, is that he accepts the appellants' story wholly without skepticism. Apparently, even inquiring minds do not want to know everything.[90] Having made up his mind, right at the start, that Principal Morse's version of the incident on Glacier Avenue was more plausible than student Frederick's, there was little left to talk about. Actually, Chief Justice Roberts came up with two fatal conversation stoppers in *Morse v. Frederick*. The first was his remark to Frederick's attorney, Doug Mertz, twenty-three words into Mertz's presentation during oral arguments on March 19, 2007:

> **MR. MERTZ**: Mr. Chief Justice, and may it please the Court: This is a case about free speech. It is not a case about drugs.
>
> **CHIEF JUSTICE ROBERTS**: It's a case about money. Your client wants money from the principal personally for her actions in this case.[91]

Having dismissively reduced Frederick's case to being about money in open court, when Chief Justice Roberts drafted his majority opinion, he began by framing the case as being about drugs. The first line of his opinion for the Court reads:

> At a school-sanctioned and school-supervised event, a high school principal saw some of her students unfurl a large banner conveying a message she reasonably regarded as promoting illegal drug use.[92]

I would say that the chief justice saw *Morse v. Frederick* as an open-and-shut case, except it is evident that Frederick never really had an opening. From the outset, Frederick could not get a word in edgewise. "Any astute reader knew as soon as he reached the end of [Roberts' first] sentence that school was out for Joseph Frederick and that the principal and the school board had won a complete victory from the Supreme Court."[93] It was game over for Joe Frederick, even before the game had begun.

Yet, Frederick's banner hardly "speaks for itself."[94] The chief justice observes that "[t]he message on Frederick's banner is cryptic." He notes that "[g]ibberish is surely a possible interpretation of the words on the banner."[95] One would think that the very ambiguity of Frederick's banner would invite, nay, demand further conversation about its meaning. Rather than "fixing on the principal's interpretation,"[96] thereby silencing Frederick, the Court should have validated Morse's authority to *speak to Joe* about his banner, as distinguished from affirming her authority to discipline Frederick. There is little question that, as principal, Morse had the authority to do *something* in response to Frederick unfurling his fourteen-foot banner emblazoned with BONG HiTS 4 JESUS. The crux of *Morse v. Frederick* is what she chose to do. Rather than finding a way to defuse the situation, clearly provoked by Frederick's sophomoric display, Morse exercised her undoubted authority in a manner that escalated the state of affairs.

Were I writing for the Court,[97] I would hold that precisely because Principal Morse reasonably concluded that student Frederick's banner was disruptive, under *Bethel School Dist. No. 403 v. Fraser*, 478 U.S. 675 (1986),[98] as drug speech, she was constitutionally obliged to engage Frederick in conversation in order to address the problem he created. A response from Morse to Frederick's provocation was completely legitimate. The punitive nature of her response was not. BONG HiTS 4 JESUS required being answered. Confiscating the banner while disciplining its maker was no answer. Suspending Frederick with a criminal trespass order was a riposte, of sorts. Sadly, Principal Morse's actions did not resolve the conflict, otherwise this case would not be before the Court. She ran afoul of the First Amendment when, at the time she perceived Frederick crossing the line on Glacier Avenue, she herself crossed the line separating problem solving from punishing. As Justice Brandeis reminds us: "If there be time to expose through discussion the falsehood and fallacies, to avert the evil by the processes of education, the remedy to be applied is more speech, not enforced silence," *Whitney v. California*, 274 U.S. 357, 377 (1927). I would conclude that while school officials in this case did not violate the First Amendment when they responded to the banner they plausibly deemed pro-drug, they did violate the First Amendment when they confiscated that banner and disciplined its creator. The character of the First Amendment breach consists not in curtailing Frederick's disruptive speech, but in penalizing it.

I can imagine the situation on Glacier Avenue unfolding something like this. The banner goes up, Principal Morse sees it, crosses the street, and says to the students holding it:

> **PRINCIPAL MORSE**: Hi folks, I want to talk to you. What's going on here? What's up with the banner? Whose idea was the message?
>
> **JOE FREDERICK**: There is no message.
>
> **PRINCIPAL MORSE**: No message?! What's BONG HiTS 4 JESUS mean?
>
> **JOE FREDERICK**: Nothing. It's nonsense.
>
> **PRINCIPAL MORSE**: Nonsense?! Then what's your point? Why go to all the trouble of making the banner and bringing it to the relay?
>
> **JOE FREDERICK**: To get on TV, and to test if free speech really exists at Juneau-Douglas.
>
> **PRINCIPAL MORSE**: Your speech rights aren't at issue here, Joe. The problem is wrong words at the wrong time. "BONG HiTS"? "JESUS"? What were you thinking? Not a good idea. Not acceptable. You need to take the banner down.
>
> **JOE FREDERICK**: What about my First Amendment rights?
>
> **PRINCIPAL MORSE**: Everybody has First Amendment rights, and nobody's rights are absolute. Please—let's fold up the banner then let's go talk about rights and responsibilities inside, in my office. C'mon everybody. It's cold and my feet are freezing.

In this hypothetical exchange, Principal Morse engages her errant students instead of commanding them. Frederick and Morse remain opposed, but their confrontation is muted. Now, it may seem presumptuous to rewrite history, second guessing a conscientious administrator doing her best under stressful and emergent circumstances. Unfortunately, Morse's best was not good enough. Why? Because her responses to Frederick's provocations set in motion a spiral of adversarial interactions whereby "a 2002 youthful street *farce* was being converted through [seven years] of tortured events into something of a First Amendment *tragedy*."[99] Courts cannot order common sense. Courts cannot mandate sound judgment. Courts can forestall abetting First Amendment tragedies by avoiding zero-sum dichotomous First Amendment outcomes. Such outcomes can be transcended by fashioning remedies that eschew either/or in lieu of both/and.[100] For example, in my imagined rewriting of *Morse v. Frederick* above, *both* Joseph Frederick's immature acting out *and* Deborah Morse's heavy-handed reaction are constitutionally problematical. Frederick's ambiguous, and plausibly harmful, banner undercuts his right to display it. Casting herself solely as an enforcer instead of being an educator undermines Principal Morse's authority. The judicious remedy? Hold *both* Frederick *and* Morse responsible for their actions and, as Kirk Ziegenfuss urges, give them a stake in talking instead of litigating.

In short, the Court can prompt people to rewrite their scripts, revising the roles in which we all so heavily invest. Such prompting is not always efficacious. Such prompting thoroughly challenges those cued, because responding often entails profound changes in identity and course. *Brown v. Board of Education*, 347 U.S. 483 (1954) comes to mind in this regard. As I suggested toward the end of Chapter 8, *Brown* is aesthetically valuable precisely because the Warren Court rewrote the script of race relations. That such reorientation incurred stiff resistance, unfolding glacially and incompletely, does not vitiate *Brown*'s beauty. In fact, the very disharmony *Brown* spawned in some circles results from *Brown*'s potent harmonizing. *Brown* lent profound constitutional dignity to everyone struggling to reconstruct race relations.[101] *Morse v. Frederick* might have achieved a similar result in the realm of school speech, with regard to relations between students and administrators.

Regrettably, the *Morse* majority missed its opportunity to do so. My sense is that the messy *Morse* outcome results, in large part, from a failure of judicial imagination.[102] Unable (because unwilling?) to conceive of a remedy in nondichotomous, relational terms, the *Morse* majority opinion contains no surprises. Chief Justice Roberts and Justices Alito, Kennedy, Scalia, and Thomas are not alone in their predictability. As law professor Stephen Kanter sagely recaps the incident on Glacier Avenue and its acrimonious aftermath, "There were many missteps along the way in Bong Hits." He continues:

> Joseph Frederick could have chosen a slightly different venue, or a more meaningful message. He could have acted more maturely as an eighteen-year-old young adult. Deborah Morse could have shown the wisdom of restraint, and calmed down a bit before acting. She could have let the essentially harmless situation play out, and marked Frederick tardy or absent depending on whether he deigned to make it to school later in the day. Subsequently, she could have admonished him for his immaturity, and suggested that he was only hurting himself and that it was time to grow up if he really wanted attention and respect. In the best of circumstances, she could have found a creative way to make this a productive learning experience. The superintendent or the school board could have expunged rather than just shortened the disciplinary suspension.
>
> Joseph Frederick and his lawyers could have restricted their legal claims to injunctive and declaratory relief or, if they were worried about potential mootness overtaking these claims, sought only nominal damages and voluntarily waived more substantial damages and especially punitive damages. These lawyers could have done a better job of persuading the district court that there was at least an issue of fact as to whether this controversy should be treated as

a full-on school speech case. The district court could have shielded the school officials from personal liability, but ruled that there was insufficient cause alleged by defendants to justify the suspension. The Ninth Circuit could have reversed on the merits of the First Amendment issue, but left the district court's qualified immunity ruling undisturbed. Counsel for petitioners in the Supreme Court, though they ultimately prevailed, might have been well advised to take a somewhat more restrained view of the school's powers over the students than they did. The Supreme Court could have denied certiorari. Once having taken the case, I suppose they could have followed Justice Breyer's lead and reversed the Ninth Circuit only on qualified immunity grounds, perhaps giving the principal the benefit of the doubt in the heat of a moment with an older subjective good faith standard of immunity, while remanding other aspects of the case. None of these things happened.[103]

Because none of the players in this saga deviated onto any of the available detours Professor Kanter identifies, Joseph Frederick and Deborah Morse did not move off the long and tortured road upon which they embarked together on January 24, 2002. But they did not have to set off on that path. Their dispute need not have come to litigating. They had other choices.[104] In the remainder of this chapter, and in culminating my treatment of the perfect constitutional storm in Juneau, Alaska, I want to discuss two other roads not taken—how the storm might have been averted.

The alternative routes I have in mind involve students, teachers, and administrators as participants in exchanging ideas, analysis, and opinions. Both activities share in common being more or less structured exchanges. One activity is a mock Supreme Court. The other is community dialogue. Two colleagues of mine, Lewis & Clark Law School professor Stephen Kanter, and Classroom Law Project (CLP) Executive Director Marilyn Cover, played important parts in a mock Supreme Court held at Tigard High School (THS) in fall 1987. Beginning in spring 2003, my Oregon State University–Cascades colleague Dr. Natalie Dollar has organized a series of community dialogues addressing pressing topical concerns. The fruits of my colleagues' creative efforts serve as promising "more-speech" models of dealing with conflict.

Not surprisingly perhaps, the Tigard story begins with an encounter between THS Principal C. A. "Al" Zimmerman and THS student J. R. Thomas.[105] Thomas had been sent to the principal's office for wearing to school a commercially manufactured T-shirt advertising Corona beer. Thomas had worn his T-shirt to THS the second day of the 1987–1988 school year, one day after Zimmerman, brand new to his THS administrative post, had promulgated a revised dress code. Provision B1 specified: "Clothing decorated or marked with illustrations, words or phrases which are in poor taste will not be acceptable. Clothing which displays alcohol or drug related advertising, symbols or logos is also unacceptable."[106] Thomas' attire choice on the very day after the new dress code was not unintentional. The similarities with Joe Frederick's acting out continue. "[A] number of students wore a variety of interesting T-shirts: a sampling includes a commercially produced Corona beer T-shirt, a Corona Extra shirt, a Corona Beach Club shirt in the same style as the beer shirt already noted, a Club Corona shirt, a shirt bearing the likeness of Budweiser's commercial hound Spuds McKenzie, a city pride shirt reading Munich, Deutschland with an image of a beer stein, and . . . a homemade shirt with small letters root on one line, and letters in approximately ten times larger font size beer on the next line.

root
beer"[107]

Only three members of the beer T-shirt–wearing crew were disciplined, and their sanctions varied from being driven home to change shirts to being suspended. An uproar ensued. Students' attempt to meet and talk with THS administrators about the dress code failed. *High Spots,* the THS newspaper, carried an article about "Corona-Gate." Students contacted the Oregon American Civil Liberties Union. Was a perfect storm brewing in Tigard, Oregon? I will leave it to readers interested in learning more about how the incident on S.W. Durham Road unfolded to access Steve Kanter's insightful and entertaining article and the sources he cites.[108] For my purposes, it suffices to answer, no, Principal Zimmerman acted to defuse the tempest.[109] He authorized students to organize a mock Supreme Court hearing—Case Number 1 *J.R. Thomas, Petitioner v. Tigard High School District 23J, Respondent*—to be held during an all-school assembly.

A couple of THS teachers, Cliff Sheldon and Joe Calpin, who are CLP alumni, played a key role in transforming the dispute over the student dress code into an occasion to debate student speech rights under the First Amendment. Marilyn Cover explains:

> These were wise teachers who wanted to make sure Mr. Zimmerman, as a brand-new principal, kinda got the message about how we did things here [at THS]. . . . They had been very active in my work with law-related education for years prior to even [the T-shirt dispute]. So, they'd been teaching Con. Law. They'd been using the "We The People" materials.[110] They had looked for student rights issues. . . . Really, the teachers said, "Why don't we make something out of this, because of it being the Bicentennial, with the Bill of Rights." And this would be a good thing. And they convinced the principal that he'd be open to these [student-authored] briefs being submitted and having this mock Supreme Court hearing.[111]

Cover emphasizes the teacher-driven genesis of the mock Supreme Court proposal:

> My impression was that these two teachers went in and kinda laid it out for [Principal Zimmerman]. "You know, you don't want to start here makin' a bunch of rules and not be sensitive to some of the places that that might take you. And could we help you kinda rethink this whole thing by doing this process." . . . I think it was more these savvy teachers, who'd been active in the Union and what-not, that wanted to make sure that they kinda got him on the right page. . . . Zimmerman was much more open after—or, my impression was—after he saw the Supreme Court hearing. He was so impressed with the arguments made by the students, with how serious the rest of the student body took this whole thing. The fact that half of the kids had to represent the school district, so this wasn't a one-sided kind of deal, and they did it zealously. And with the seriousness of the prominent people who were there as members

of the Court. All of that was just like, "Oh, this was a pretty good learning experience."["For him, as well?"—JCF] Yeah, yeah. So I don't know how much to say about who he was comin' in the door. I think it was more these teachers kinda pushing and then, after the fact, the feeling like, "Oh, this was pretty impressive."[112]

There were several reasons why Principal Zimmerman was justifiably impressed with the process to which he had agreed. He had taken THS students seriously enough, trusting their maturity and their ability, essentially to turn resolving the beer T-shirt controversy over to them as student advocates arguing their respective cases before neutral jurists.[113] The students did not disappoint, vindicating what might have been a risky choice. Second, the moot court activity took an intramural debate beyond school boundaries, thereby involving a broader range of people. In the process of allying with CLP, identifying and recruiting local lawyers willing to advise the student advocates or to serve as justices on the THS Supreme Court, and opening the event to the press, what might have remained a parochial dispute became a concern for a more inclusive and diverse community to address. Third, their moot Supreme Court provided THS students, faculty, and administrators a painless, cost-free means of debating weighty constitutional issues. The proceeding had all the gravity of actual litigation, without the downsides. On the contrary, by all accounts the experience was a classic win-win outcome. Fourth, by agreeing to the mock Supreme Court, Principal Zimmerman walked the talk of citizenship education, modeling the civic values public schools ostensibly seek to inculcate. As a concurring opinion written by mock Supreme Court jurists Chief Justice Kanter and Justice Stuart concluded: "The students and the community are fortunate to have a principal and staff committed to an exchange of ideas and the rule of law, rather than fiat, to resolve this issue."[114]

Although the November 12, 1987, Tigard High School Moot Supreme Court arose out of circumstances unique to that time and place, the conditions giving rise to this more-speech educational experience were not exclusive in the sense of constituting a class of one. The beneficial manner in which the THS community responded to its conflict over beer T-shirts is unusual, perhaps uncommon. It is not inimitable. Thinking about Tigard's tale as an example other schools might emulate, when they are experiencing discord resulting from student expression running afoul of school rules, it is useful to abstract several elements that facilitated the THS experience. Such components are not ingredients—a more-speech cookbook does not exist.

The presence of several circumstances are likely to make the Tigard experience more, rather than less, serviceable in any given student speech disagreement. To begin with, the openness of school administrators, especially the principal, to submitting to simulated judicial process in order to resolve First Amendment disputes, a path both novel and risky, is vital. Such openness, in turn, requires self-confident administrators possessing imagination, humility, and guts. The THS experience suggests that the other side of the responsiveness coin, and a second key factor, is the presence among faculty and students of people not merely eager to make a fuss over student speech rights, but willing and able to refine, research, and formally defend their assertions. In other words, if administrators are willing to transform in-house conflicts over discipline into quasi-legal First Amendment proceedings, students and their mentors need to be prepared to step up and assume responsibility for playing con-scientiously in the mock judicial arena. A third factor is the availability of legal practitioners and law professors as mentors, together with accessible resources, so students can prepare. THS students benefitted from having access to CLP's materials, and from getting referrals to lawyers with whom CLP networks. THS students and faculty also enjoyed the legitimacy conferred by working with such a reputable organization as CLP.[115] Ultimately, the absence of a shared conviction that everyone involved is acting in good faith can damage, maybe render stillborn, any salutary potential of the three factors above. As Professor Kanter notes, "Great boundary-testing moments, especially with teenagers, require great decisions and uncommon wisdom. There is rarely a chance to get a second bite at the apple to get things right unless a base of trust already has been established."[116]

In the absence of a base of trust, confidence-building measures are required. Under such circumstances, community dialogue potentially is helpful. Dialoguing can be helpful because engaging in this mode of communication can free us from being imprisoned within solipsistic pride and truth, the *Rashomon* effect I spoke of in Chapter 1, thereby creating space for "sur-prising opportunities." Whether or not dialogue's potential is realized, however, depends on how we go about it. Americans are great talkers. But mere talking is not the same as dialoguing. We use the term *dialogue* loosely, often synonymously with debating, discussing, negotiating, problem solving, etc. The manner in which we conventionally practice "dialogue" typically involves two or more individuals articulating their ideas, feelings, opinions. The emphasis is on speaking one's mind, often bent on changing others' minds. In dialogue, the emphasis is on thinking together in relationship. Thinking together is *dialogos*[117] founder William Isaacs' term. He offers this insightful comparison between talking and dialoguing:

> All too often our talk fails us. Instead of creating something new, we polarize and fight. Par-ticularly under conditions where the stakes are high and differences abound, we tend to harden into positions that we defend by advocacy. To advocate is to speak for your point of view. Usually, people do this unilaterally, without making room for others. . . . The headlines chronicle a multitude of times when people might have come together in a new way and yet somehow failed to do so. . . .
>
>   But dialogue is an altogether very different way of talking together. Generally, we think of dialogue as "better conversation." But there is much more to it. *Dialogue*, as I define it, is a *conversation with a center, not sides.* It is a way of taking the energy of our differences and chan-neling it toward something that has never been created before. It lifts us out of polarization and into a greater common sense, and is thereby a means for accessing the intelligence and coordinated power of groups of people.[118]

Isaacs' understanding of dialogue takes us far beyond eliminating differences. As he puts it: "Dialogue fills deeper, more widespread needs than simply 'getting to yes.'"[119] In her scholarship, and in her work with students and community members, speech communi-cation professor Natalie Dollar seeks to teach and to facilitate this synergistic sort of dia-loguing. She wants to create spaces, sometimes she calls them "scenes,"[120] where "relational talk"[121] can occur. During relational talk, speaking does not entail using words to convey suasive bits of information. Rather, relational talk involves connecting speakers—creating community—by means of words. Instead of clinging—*Rashomon*-like—to our self-defined roles as we recite well-rehearsed scripted lines, dialogue relaxes our "grip on certainty," and teaches us to "listen to the possibilities that result simply from being in a relationship with others . . ."[122]

As Dollar practices it, dialoguing can be understood as synonymous with building bridges, as distinguished from scoring points. Community dialogue is "an intentional type of communication and a way of being with others with whom we disagree."[123] This way of being seeks "the betwixt and between, the back and forth, the dialogic moment . . . [that] is not [an] agonistic playing off, but more playing with."[124]

Dollar's dialoguing clearly is just the sort of relationship-rich communication that many of the people involved, one way or another, with the incident on Glacier Avenue yearn for—and have no idea how to spark. Just as clearly, as this book documents, in the absence of "playing" with one another, Juneau residents chose sides, vis-à-vis Joseph Frederick and Deborah Morse, and played off each other.[125] Susan Christianson, who was communications manager for the Juneau School District from August 2007 until October 2008, and parent of a Juneau-Douglas High School student contemporary of Joe Frederick's, intuitively grasps what dialoguing entails. She speaks movingly of her citizen's longing, and her civic loss. Christianson eloquently summarizes perhaps the central issue in this book—healing a divided community:

> We are a community that splits 49/51 percent on almost every public issue. Whether it be the road—you know, to have a road or not have a road. Whether it's to have a mine or not have a mine. We're a 51/49 percent—sometimes we're scarily 50/50 on the politics. And what I've seen from my perspective is we have public officials that are . . . consistently putting their own personal political future, and polls, ahead of making decisions that could benefit the public good. And I don't know that the public good was benefitted by the outcome of this case. I think the public good in terms of Frederick versus Morse, and the issues that were raised, could have been so much better served by leadership taking a position that this is an opportunity for our community to have a discussion around some very difficult issues that we face as a community. Drugs in our community? Yes, they exist. Are young people taking drugs and selling drugs? Yes, it happens. Freedom of speech within the school? What's the student's rights? Ability for a school district to discipline our students outside the role of us being the parent of these students . . . What is that role? And where should that role be? And what does our community want that role to be? And an administrator's right to protect [her] individual personal assets . . . when they believe that they are influencing policy. We have a lot of public officials in this town. The majority of people in this town still work for a government. That's a huge issue for people in government. What's my role . . . if I'm following policy that I believe is set out by my superiors, where's the line? . . .
>
> My history goes back to being a newspaper reporter covering issues of the district, fifteen, twenty years—you know, beginning of my career here in Juneau, really. Watching the school district, having kids in it, being a member of this community. Being involved on both sides of very controversial issues that this community has faced. And the sad thing to me, and what

has led me, personally to leave it all behind, and give it up, and not allow myself to care—is that I feel that Juneau has never gotten to the point where it has . . . allowed itself to have true, open dialogue around the issues that truly face us as a state and as communities, that doesn't become polarized around the farthest away points of view that are not held by the majority of people who are too busy and too much involved in the difficulties of their own life to come to the public meeting[.] . . . And all the bogus public testimony, and public meetings that we have that never resolve any issues because they become so polarized around big money, and big issues and egos that prevent us, as a nation and as a state and as a community from resolving very, very important issues, like *Frederick*, that we face.[126]

Susan Christianson's powerful words shed light on how communities can split apart—and also how citizens of such communities can knit the break. She thus draws together key strands making up my account.

My account of the incident on Glacier Avenue and its aftermath has taken us many places. As that event recedes into the past, two matters remain. First, for the foreseeable future, we are stuck with the drug speech exception to protected student speech narrowly and divisively announced in *Morse v. Frederick*, 551 U.S. 393 (2007). *Morse* is a messy precedent providing little useful guidance to students, teachers, and administrators as we go about trying to harmonize the tension between First Amendment rights and school authority. A second, more fundamental challenge remains. How might people like Joseph Frederick and Deborah Morse, Doug Mertz and David Crosby—to name only our central players—how might they and others imagine breaking free from their self-defined rigid roles and seize the surprising opportunities that might result? Earlier in this chapter, I wrote: "By pridefully locking ourselves into our self-created roles, we miss an opportunity, likely to surprise each of us as much as it would others, of acting uncharacteristically. By reciting lines instead of co-authoring scenarios, we are merely mouthing words. What we have here is a failure to communicate." Those three sentences tell much, but not my whole story. Steve Kanter's and Marilyn Cover's Tale of Tigard, and Natalie Dollar's approach to dialogue, add another useful dimension: what we have here is a failure to connect.

Still, failure to connect is not the whole story either. This book is not primarily about loss and failure. While Susan Christianson sheds light on the causes and consequences of the breakdown I've referred to as a perfect constitutional storm in Juneau, she also points the way toward avoiding such rifts in the first place, as well as toward repairing breaches when they occur. Likewise, the title of this chapter—"lost opportunities and failure of imagination"—describes not just the formation but also the resolution of such perfect constitutional storms.[127] Implicit in lost opportunity is the possibility of rendering ominous circumstances favorable. Intrinsic in failing is the possibility of succeeding. In the dialectical spirit that has informed this entire project, my title refers to the immanent possibilities dwelling in even apparent inevitability. This is the basic lesson I glean from the perfect constitutional storm in Juneau.

Let me put what I have learned another way. Human beings live within the tension created by an existential paradox.[128] That paradox results from the twin circumstances that we engage in labeling as an essential survival skill, and that our very labeling can threaten our well-being. In order to reduce uncertainty, to render life meaningful, and to orient ourselves in the world, we necessarily engage in a mode of closure. We are born taxonomers. Without our ability to classify, negotiating social reality would be frightening and confusing. At the same time, our facility at ruling in aspects of our experience entails ruling much—most—experience out. We do this at our peril, because by boxing persons, places, and things out, we box ourselves in. Part of our challenge is to engage in self-completion self-consciously, realizing that our categories are both essential and illusory. Another part is to endeavor to embrace inclusive completion in lieu of zero-sum completion. To be concrete, what if Deborah Morse and Joe Frederick had managed to empathize with, instead of rubricizing, each other? What if they were able to suspend the labels to which they had consigned each other? What if they possessed the knack of thinking in discerning, sharp-minded ways? Had Deborah Morse and Joe Frederick managed to converse, my efforts in this book to kindle conversation would have been unnecessary.

Endnotes

● ● ●

Notes to the Introduction

1.   Linda Greenhouse, "Every Justice Creates a New Court," *New York Times*, May 26, 2009, http://www.nytimes.com/2009/05/27/opinion/27greenhouse.html.

2.   Ibid.

3.   Alan F. Westin, *The Anatomy of a Constitutional Law Case:* Youngstown Sheet and Tube v. Sawyer, *The Steel Seizure Case* (New York: Columbia University, 1990; originally published 1958, Macmillan).

4.   Frank B. Freidel, *Franklin D. Roosevelt: Launching the New Deal* (Boston: Little, Brown, 1973); and Frank B. Freidel, *Franklin D. Roosevelt: A Rendezvous with Destiny* (Boston: Little, Brown, 1990).

5.   John A. Garraty, ed., *Quarrels That Have Shaped the Constitution* (New York: Harper and Row, 1962). Westin and Freidel have essays in Garraty's book.

6.   Michael C. Dorf, ed., *Constitutional Law Stories* (New York: Foundation Press, 2004).

7.   Fred W. Friendly, *Minnesota Rag: The Dramatic Story of the Landmark Supreme Court Case that Gave New Meaning to Freedom of the Press* (New York: Random House, 1981).

8.   Anthony Lewis, *Gideon's Trumpet* (New York: Random House, 1964); and Anthony Lewis, *Make No Law: The Sullivan Case and the First Amendment* (New York: Random House, 1991).

9.   Peter H. Irons, *Justice at War* (New York: Oxford University Press, 1983); and Peter H. Irons, *The Courage of Their Convictions: Sixteen Americans Who Fought Their Way to the Supreme Court* (New York: Free Press, 1988).

10.   Richard Polenberg, *Fighting Faiths: The Abrams Case, The Supreme Court, and Free Speech* (New York: Viking Press, 1987).

11.   Clifford Geertz, *The Interpretation of Cultures* (New York: Basic Books, 1973).

12.   Jim Foster, Steve Robinson, and Steve Fisher, "Class, Political Consciousness, and Destructive Power in Appalachia," *Appalachian Journal* 5 (Spring 1978).

13.   Clifford Geertz, *Local Knowledge: Further Essays in Interpretive Anthropology* (New York: Basic Books, 1983), chap. 3.

14.   Ibid., 58.

15.   Ibid., 167.

16.   Moisés Kaufman and the Members of Tectonic Theater Project, *The Laramie Project* (New York: Dramatists Play Service, 2001), 88.

17.   My partner, Mindy Soules, suggested including this road map. I thank her for her good advice.

Notes to the Prologue

1. Source: http://www.royal.gov.uk/ImagesandBroadcasts/Historic%20speeches%20and%20broad casts/Annushorribilisspeech24November1992.aspx.

Notes to Chapter 1

1. Joe Friday is the L.A. Police Sergeant character created by actor Jack Webb for the radio and television drama *Dragnet*. Friday's catchphrase was "All we want are the facts, ma'am" (parodied as "Just the facts, ma'am"). See "Johnny Carson and Jack Webb," http://www.youtube.com/watch?v=F4RIBhQIkII.

2. Kurosawa based his film on two short stories by Ryunosuke Akutagawa, mostly "In a Bamboo Grove" and somewhat "Rashomon." In Kurosawa's version, four principals—the bandit, the woman, the dead husband (through a medium), and the woodcutter—offer contradictory accounts of how it happened that a woman was raped and her husband killed in the forest. See Ryunosuke Akutagawa, *Rashomon and Seventeen Other Stories*, Jay Rubin, trans., Haruki Murakami, intro. (New York: Penguin Classics, 2009), and Akira Kurosawa, *Rashomon* (Daiei Motion Picture Company, 1950).

3. Donald Richie, ed., *Rashomon* (New Brunswick, N.J.: Rutgers University Press, 1999), 11. Richie continued: "This is why Kurosawa could leave the [*Rashomon*] plot, insofar as there is one, dangling and unresolved. The fact that it *is* unresolved is itself one of the meanings of the film." Compare Austrian film writer-director Michael Haneke: "I try to construct stories so that several explanations are possible, to give the viewers the freedom to interpret. I do it by everything I don't show, and through all the questions I raise and don't answer. That way, the audience doesn't finish with the film as quickly as if I'd answered everything." Quoted in Stuart Klawans, "Fascism, Repression, and 'The White Ribbon,'" *New York Times*, October 30, 2009, http://www.nytimes.com/2009/11/01/movies/01klaw.html?ref=movies.

4. Richie, ed., *Rashomon*, 13. Compare Sir Walter Scott (1771–1832), "Oh what a tangled web we weave, when first we practice to deceive." Also see Karl G. Heider, "The Rashomon Effect: When Ethnographers Disagree," *American Anthropologist* 90 (March 1988): 73; and Richard A. Schweder, *Why Do Men Barbecue? Recipes for Cultural Psychology* (Cambridge, Mass.: Harvard University Press, 2003), "Introduction: Anti-Postculturalism or, The View from Manywheres," and "Conclusion: From Manywheres to The Civilizing Project, and Back." Compare Graham T. Allison, *Essence of Decision: Explaining the Cuban Missile Crisis* (Boston: Little, Brown, 1971); and Kathrin Day Lassila, "A Brief History of Groupthink," *Yale Alumni Magazine*, January/February 2008, http://www.yalealumnimagazine.com/issues/2008_01/groupthink.html.

5. Compare Kurt Vonnegut: "This is the only story of mine whose moral I know. I don't think it's a marvelous moral; I simply happen to know what it is: We are what we pretend to be, so we must be careful about what we pretend to be." *Mother Night* (New York: Avon Books, 1966), v.

6. Sally Smith interview, June 5, 2009, 14:18.

7. Ibid., 15:44.

8. Richie, ed., *Rashomon*, 11, 13.

9. W. I. Thomas and Dorothy Swaine Thomas, *The Child in America: Behavior Problems and Programs* (New York: Alfred A. Knopf, 1928), 572.

10. See Peter L. Berger and Thomas Luckmann: "Reification implies that man is capable of forgetting his own authorship of the human world, and further, that the dialectic between man, the producer, and his products is lost to consciousness. . . . In other words, reification can be described as an extreme step in the process of objectivation, whereby the objectivated world loses its comprehensibility as a human enterprise and becomes fixed as a non-human, non-humanizable, inert facticity. Roles may

be reified[.] . . . The paradigmatic formula for this kind of reification is the statement '*I have no choice in the matter, I have to act this way because of my position*'—as husband, father, general, archbishop, chairman of the board, gangster, or hangman, as the case may be [or, I would add, Principal or student]" (emphasis added). *The Social Construction of Reality: A Treatise in the Sociology of Knowledge* (New York: Anchor Books, 1967), 89, 91. Also see Hannah Fenichel Pitkin, "Rethinking reification," *Theory and Society* 16 (1987): 263. Pitkin quotes Franz Kafka's parable "A Little Fable" as her epigraph:

> "Alas," said the mouse, "the world is growing
> smaller every day. At the beginning it was so big
> that I was afraid. I kept running and running, and
> I was glad when at last I saw walls far away to
> the right and left, but these long walls have
> narrowed so quickly that I am in the last chamber
> already, and in the corner stands the trap
> that I must run into."
> "You only need to change your direction," said
> the cat, and ate it up."

Pitkin, "Rethinking Reification," 263. Pitkin maintains that, ironically, the concept of reification can itself "reify" because it "mystifies more than it reveals." Ibid., 285.

11. Richie, ed., *Rashomon*, 12. Compare Parker Tyler, "*Rashomon* as Modern Art," in Richie, ed., *Rashomon*.

12. Sally Smith interview, June 5, 2009, 29:11; 41:37.

13. "Most of us, I think, were pretty stunned at how it escalated. Then it became, in the thoughts of many, somebody trying to get someone." Sally Smith interview, June 5, 2009, 19:21.

14. See Hannah Arendt on the origin and character of "miracles," in *The Human Condition* (Garden City, N.Y.: Doubleday, 1959), 222–223; and "What Is Freedom?" in *Between Past and Future* (New York: Viking Press, 1961).

15. Richie, ed., *Rashomon*, 12.

16. Ibid., 13.

17. Remarking on what she saw as a key, and unfortunate, aspect of the "bad blood in Juneau," Anchorage School District Superintendent Carol Comeau criticized the "robot" behavior that seemed to her to characterize the conflict. Carol Comeau interview, June 2, 2009, 21:39; 24:10; 35:15.

18. Susan Spano, "A Five-Day Jaunt in Juneau," *New York Times*, September 7, 1997, http://www.nytimes.com/1997/09/07/travel/a-five-day-jaunt-in-juneau.html?scp=1&sq=five-day%20jaunt%20in%20juneau&st=cse. See Cornelia Dean, "36 Hours in Juneau, Alaska," *New York Times*, August 30, 2009, http://travel.nytimes.com/2009/08/30/travel/30hours.html?scp=3&sq=five-day%20jaunt%20in%20juneau&st=cse.

19. Jay Hammond, *Tales of Alaska's Bush Rat Governor* (Fairbanks: Epicenter Press, 1994), 237–238.

20. See Sean Cockerham, "Alaska Government Migrates to the North," *Anchorage Daily News*, December 21, 2008, http://www.adn.com/front/story/630232.html; and *Empire* Editorial: "Legislative Hall Bill Would Concentrate Power in Anchorage," *Juneau Empire*, March 23, 2008, http://www.juneauempire.com/stories/032308/opi_260769252.shtml.

21. On the *Weekly Standard* cruise aboard the MS *Oosterdam*, docking in Juneau on June 18, 2007, were William Kristol, Fred Barnes, and Michael Gerson. On the *National Review* cruise aboard the MS *Noordam*, docking in Juneau on August 1, 2007, were Rich Lowrey, Robert Bork, John Bolton, Victor Davis Hanson, and Dick Morris. See Jane Mayer, "The Insiders: How John McCain Came to Pick Sarah Palin," *New Yorker*, October 27, 2008, http://www.newyorker.com/reporting/2008/10/27/081027fa_fact_mayer?currentPage=1.

22. See artist Barry Blitt's satiric homage to Saul Steinberg in Blitt's cover drawing of Sarah Palin for *New Yorker*, October 6, 2008, http://www.newyorker.com/magazine/toc/2008/10/06/toc_20080929.

23. Richard Cohen, "Palin's Love Boats," *Washington Post*, October 28, 2008, http://www.washingtonpost.com/wp-dyn/content/article/2008/10/27/AR2008102702438.html.

24. On Monday, June 22, 2009 (roughly two years after the Court sided with Deborah Morse), the U.S. Supreme Court voted, 6–3, to reverse the Ninth Circuit in the Kensington Gold Mine case. *Coeur Alaska, Inc. v. Southeast Alaska Conservation Council*, 557 U.S. ____ (2009). See Kate Golden, "Coeur Alaska Wins Supreme Court Case," *Juneau Empire*, June 23, 2009, http://www.juneauempire.com/stories/062309/loc_453703862.shtml.

25. Mayer, "The Insiders: How John McCain Came to Pick Sarah Palin."

26. Compare, Roger Cohen, "Kiplin' vs. Palin," *New York Times*, October 6, 2008, http://www.nytimes.com/2008/10/06/opinion/06cohen.html; John Dickerson, "Palin's Campaign vs. McCain's," *Slate*, October 20, 2008, http://www.slate.com/toolbar.aspx?action=print&id=2202658; Maureen Dowd, "Bering Straight Talk," *New York Times*, September 14, 2008, http://www.nytimes.com/2008/09/14/opinion/14dowd.html; Timothy Egan, "Last-Frontier Follies," *New York Times*, November 12, 2008, http://egan.blogs.nytimes.com/2008/11/12/last-frontier-follies/; and Todd S. Purdum, "It Came from Wasilla," *Vanity Fair*, August 2009, http://www.vanityfair.com/politics/features/2009/08/sarah-palin200908. A cottage industry has sprung up around books about former governor Palin. See, for instance, Scott Conroy and Shushannah Walshe, *The Sudden Rise and Brutal Education of a New Conservative Superstar* (New York: Public Affairs, 2009); and Matthew Continetti, *The Persecution of Sarah Palin: How the Elite Media Tried to Bring Down a Rising Star* (New York: Sentinel, 2009). Compare Palin's own *Going Rogue: An American Life* (New York: HarperCollins, 2009).

27. Eric Morrison interview, June 4, 2009, 23:40. More pointedly, some refer to Juneau as a "suburb of Seattle." This characterization has less to do with Juneau being located only 300 miles further from Seattle (900 air miles) than from Anchorage (600 air miles) than the idea that, in terms of party alignment, Juneau more resembles the major city in Washington State than the state of which it is the capital.

28. A "sourdough" refers to a veteran Alaskan. By contrast, a "cheechako" is a newcomer. The late Kay Fanning, copublisher of the *Anchorage Daily News*, quotes a *Time* article reporting on her and her husband, Larry Fanning's, 1967 acquisition of the *Daily News*: "In the gold rush days, Alaska's Indians referred to intruders from the U.S. as *cheechakos*—a corruption of the word 'Chicago.'" The *Time* article referred to Larry Fanning as "a latter-day cheechako." Ironically, the Fannings relocated to Anchorage from Chicago. Kay Fanning with Katherine Field Stephen, *Kay Fanning's Alaska Story: Memoir of a Pulitzer Prize-Winning Newspaper Publisher on America's Northern Frontier* (Kenmore, Wash.: Epicenter Press, 2006), 27. Given the way Alaska state intramurals—some good natured, others not—play out, one wonders if, in the minds of non–southeastern Alaska residents, Juneau residents can ever be anything other than cheechakos. But then, all non-native Alaskans are "cheechakos." For a thoughtful and inspiring native account see Iñupiaq William L. Iġġiaġruk Hensley's *Fifty Miles from Tomorrow: A Memoir of Alaska and the Real People* (New York: Farrar, Straus and Giroux, 2009).

29. "There was one school of thought which held that it was less scary to fly into Juneau at night, when you could not see the closeness of the mountains. On the other hand, if the passengers could not see the mountains, neither could the pilot. And the Alaska Airlines crash a few years earlier—in which one hundred and eleven people had been killed—had come at night. In truth, there was no good way to fly to Juneau; just drink what they sell you and hope for the best." Joe McGinniss, *Going to Extremes* (New York: New American Library, 1980), 125. "Juneau, the only state capital that cannot be reached by road—'only by plane, boat or birth canal,' a resident told me, in what sounded like a well-worn witticism." Pico Iyer, "The Great Wide Open," *Smithsonian*, November 2009, 68.

30. The "road to nowhere" runs roughly forty miles, from Thane Road south of Juneau, north to Echo Cove on Berners Bay. See *The Milepost*, 61st ed. (Anchorage, Alaska: Morris Communications, 2009), 707–708. Also see Pat Forgey, "Court Halts Juneau Road Project," *Juneau Empire*, February 15, 2009, http://www.juneauempire.com/stories/021509/loc_388168240.shtml; and Pat Forgey, "Road Ruling Leaves Uncertainties," *Juneau Empire*, February 17, 2009, http://www.juneauempire.com/stories/021709/loc_389869758.shtml.

31. See "Juneau, Alaska," Alaska Travel, http://www.myalaskan.com/alaska-towns/juneau.html; "Juneau Alaska," Alaska Tour & Travel, http://www.alaskatravel.com/juneau/; and "Juneau," *The Milepost*, http://milepost.com/index.php?option=com_content&task=view&id=155&Itemid=199. Compare: "As one walked through Juneau—in the snow, in the sleet, in the rain—past all the pastel houses, up and down the wooden stairways, and through all the narrow, winding streets, this atmosphere, engendered by the presence of so many original structures, combined with the natural setting—the steepness, the mountains above, the water below—constantly asserted itself. Juneau staked out its own territory in your consciousness. To be there was to feel a sense of surroundings so powerful as to seem almost an extra dimension." McGinnnis, *Going to Extremes*, 126–127.

32. Sally Smith interview, June 5, 2009, 1:05.

33. Ibid., 22:36; 25:55; 15:02. Mary Becker, president of the Juneau-Douglas School Board at the time, underscored the importance of the Olympic torch relay to the school district: "This was the first time the torch has ever come to Alaska; not just Juneau, but to Alaska! . . . As the capital city, I think we go above and beyond sometimes. Because we went to Fairbanks, to Anchorage, to the rural areas, trying to find people who would be involved in this. ["As torch bearers?"—JCF] Yes. Just having representation. . . . We could have said, 'This ought to be our folks, after all, we're in Juneau.' But we did not do that. We were very inclusive of the state, because this was a state event. Even though it happened in the capital city, where it should have happened. . . . It was an Olympic torch, so naturally it was SPONSORED, in the big letters of the word, by someone else. We sponsored the events that involved the students. . . . It was a festive time. Let's put it that way. And we had really built this up. And it had been very much built up in the school district. . . . We bussed students all over the place—paid to bus students all over. If you were at a school that was not going to have the torch go by you, you weren't gonna be in the road, you got bussed to some place where you would see the torch. So, I mean, we had a lot of involvement. . . . I was very happy, at the end of this, that the city bought a torch and gave the school district a torch. And that was a part of the recognition. They gave it to us at a school board meeting. And at that [meeting] they recognized my part in it, and they recognized very strongly, this would not have been the event it was if the students hadn't been involved. Because it was a school day, and it was a work day, so you didn't have millions of people take—the state didn't say, "Everyone's excused, take half a day off." So we had people—a lot of people out—but it . . . was the students that really made the event as far as lining the streets. That was major." Mary Becker interview, June 6, 2009, 6:17; 9:24.

34. This narrative is derived mostly from two sources: (1) my interview with Joe Frederick, March 21, 2009; and (2) my interview with Frank Frederick, July 24, 2009. I quote Joe extensively, unfolding his story in his own words.

35. Clay Good took the widely distributed photograph (appearing on the front cover) recording Joe and his companions raising their banner as the Olympic torch relay passed by JDHS.

36. Clay Good interview, June 8, 2009, 0:14. Among Good's "suite of responses" to the BONG HiTS episode, "[o]ne is—I mean I love rascals. You know, I come from the School of Rascals, and remain a rascal in a lot of ways. And so, my first response may have been, "Oh, that's funny." Ibid., 16:25.

37. In line with my reading of the BONG HiTS story in terms of *Rashomon*, "[t]he name *Eulenspiegel* means 'Owl's Mirror' [in High German] and alludes to an old adage, 'One sees one's own faults no more clearly than an owl sees its own ugliness in a looking glass.'" Richard Freed, Program Note to National

Symphony Orchestra performance of "Till Eulenspiegel's Merry Pranks," January 13–15, 2005, http://www.kennedy-center.org/calendar/?fuseaction=composition&composition_id=2850. In Low German, the title is rendered in more earthy terms, *ul'n Spegel*, meaning to "wipe the arse." See Peter E. Carels, "Eulenspiegel and Company Visit the Eighteenth Century," *Modern Language Studies* 10 (Autumn 1980): 3.

38. John M. Gaustad and Walt Vogdes, "Till Eulenspiegel—The Merry Prankster," Stein Collectors International, Inc., http://www.steincollectors.org/library/articles/Eulenspiegel/Eulenspiegel.html. Compare Freed, Program Note to National Symphony Orchestra performance of "Till Eulenspiegel's Merry Pranks"; "Till Eulenspiegel," *Encyclopedia Britannica*, http://www.britannica.com/EBchecked/topic/195195/Till-Eulenspiegel; and Paul Oppenheimer, *A Pleasant Vintage of Till Eulenspiegel, Born in the Country of Brunswick; How He Spent His Life, 95 of His Tales* (Middleton, Conn.: Wesleyan University Press, 1972).

39. Frank Frederick interview, July 24, 2009, 4:21. Joe has two siblings, an older brother, Will, and a younger sister, Holly.

40. Joe wanted to move to Juneau for reasons other than his troubles at TJHS. He told his dad, "If we don't do it [move], we'll never experience Alaska." Frank replied, "Ah, that makes sense." Ibid., 3:10.

41. Ibid., 13:30; 12:08.

42. On vexatious high school social relations, see, for instance, the film *Heathers*, New World Pictures, 1989.

43. Tom Petty, "Into the Great Wide Open," MCA Records, 1991. Frank Frederick said, "I introduced [Joe] to Camus' writings. . . . In fact, Joe was the one that pointed out to me that, in *The Rebel*, . . . [Joe] says, 'Everybody gives Che Guevara credit for the quote . . . he stole it from Camus.' And I said: 'What quote are you talking about?' And he says, 'Right here in Camus' book: "I would rather die on my feet, than live on my knees."' [*Laughs.*] That's in Camus' book *The Rebel*. . . . Che Guevara stole it from Camus. Camus said it first." Frank Frederick interview, July 24, 2009, 13:23. This exchange reveals more about Joe and Frank than about the source of this particular quotation. I have seen versions of the quote attributed variously to Mikhail Bakunin, Albert Camus, Che Guevara, Dolores Ibárruri Gómez (*La Pasionaria*), and Emiliano Zapata.

44. Joe Frederick interview, March 21, 2009, 6:36.

45. The word *cast* conjures Kurosawa's insight that humans "cast," i.e., assign themselves roles, which then become "cast," i.e., shaped in stone. Possibility hardens into reified patterns of behavior.

46. Joe explains his frequent infractions in various terms, referring to Alaska's nineteen-year-old cigarette age limit, his inclination to push the envelope, having "lots of free time" because he had more than enough credits to graduate, the Juneau police being "like Nazis," and the city of Juneau citing and fining students as a lucrative source of revenue.

47. Joe Frederick interview, March 21, 2009, 12:50.

48. Ibid., 21:13.

49. "[JDHS administrators] have no idea about what students' rights are[,]" Joe complained. "They think that whatever their moral values are should be imposed upon the students. . . . They've got too many administrators down there, I think, because most of them appear to not have anything to do. Because they like to patrol the halls. They like to act like hall monitors. . . . I'm sure a high school vice principal makes much too high of a salary to be wasting time spent on writing parking tickets. But, I mean, I've always liked to push people's buttons." Ibid., 25:20; 25:34.

50. In literary terms, one might describe Joe as somewhat reminiscent of Meursault in Albert Camus' *The Stranger*, while bearing a strong resemblance to Jack Dawkins, the artful dodger in Charles Dickens' *Oliver Twist*.

51. Joe Frederick interview, March 21, 2009, 34:40.

52. This narrative is derived mostly from my interview with Deborah Morse, with her attorney David Crosby participating (Deb Morse would not meet with me without Crosby being present), June 5, 2009, and somewhat from Morse's deposition, given January 31, 2003. I quote Deb extensively, unfolding her story in her own words.

53. Deb's point of departure in our interview—the first thing she said—was: "There's a lot of misinformation in the media. You know, that's probably the most frustrating is that they didn't get the facts right, or didn't take the time to read the facts, and even how the facts seemed to have changed over some stories." Deborah Morse interview, June 5, 2009, 0:1.

54. Ibid., 1:13:59.

55. Ibid., 26:31, 23:32.

56. Ibid., 1:36:14.

57. While deposing Deborah Morse, Doug Mertz asked her: "When you saw the banner there, obviously you had choices you could do. What you did was one choice. I suppose you could've just turned back and walked away. Another choice might've been to go up to Joseph and the others and say, 'Look, that's incredibly stupid. Just put it down and go back to class,' or something of that sort where you're not actually ordering him to do it but telling him what you thought of it and telling him it was, say, an immature act and he needed to grow up. Why didn't you take that approach?"

Morse replied: "Because I did intend, when I asked him numerous times to come with me to my office, to discuss that with him at that time and talk about, you know, the—what happened, when it happened, that I felt it was inappropriate in that setting, and the reference to drugs."

Deposition of Deborah Lynn Morse, Friday, January 31, 2003, Juneau, Alaska, in author's possession, 61–62. Earlier in the deposition is this exchange between Mertz and Morse:

Q. You're obviously a polite person. When you say you asked [Joe to accompany you to your office], can you recall what words you used?

A. I did, I asked him. I said—I said, "Let's go talk. Come to my office we can talk about it there." . . .

Q. And when you said what you did to Joseph about coming to your office, was that a request or an instruction?

A. I asked him to come back to my office with me to discuss the matter, so I would perceive it was both; I asked him to come with me to my office.

Q. And you intended it as an instruction.

A. Right. And I restated it several times.

Ibid., 28.

Principal Morse also reflected on Joe's behavior, and her reactions, during their meeting in her office: "[L]ater as I'm filling out all the paperwork, I did decide to do—fill out a criminal trespass form because in my opinion Joseph clearly wasn't getting that this was inappropriate. In his interactions with me he was very agitative [sic]—agitated and just—just kept going on, 'Are you going to'—every time I talked about an offense, he would say, 'Are you going to suspend everybody who's skipping? Are you going to suspend everybody?' You know, he just kept saying that in a very agitated—'Show me. Show me.'" Ibid., 42.

In her testimony to the Juneau-Douglas School Board during Joe Frederick's disciplinary appeal hearing, Deb Morse said: "I asked Joseph—and there was another student directly behind him—and I asked both of them to please come with me to my office and we would talk about it. And that's what I asked them to do." Juneau School District, Transcript of Hearing in the Matter of Joseph Frederick, March 13, 2002, in author's possession, 104, 107.

Later, Morse had this exchange with Ann Gifford, the school district's attorney:

MS. GIFFORD: Did you talk to [Joe] about—did he—did he question you about why he was there in your office?

MS. MORSE: He did. He said—he did say something that were [sic] along that line and I said, "Because I asked you to come with me to my office and you didn't do that." And I did pull out the student handbook and pointed that that would be in violation of the discipline—on the discipline grid following a staff directive. I'd asked him to come with me, he had refused to come with me . . . Ibid., 107.

On Deb Morse's own accounts, it is not unambiguously clear whether she was inviting, requesting, instructing, or demanding that Joe accompany her to her office. It strikes me as puzzling that, given Morse's stated intention to talk through the banner incident with Joe, she would initiate that conversation by issuing an edict.

58. Eric Morrison interview, June 4, 2009, 18:00.

59. Recall Deb's initial reply, when I asked her to reflect on the whole experience: "I wish that we had never participated [smiles], and I never had to experience all this."

60. Eric Morrison interview, June 4, 2009, 22:08.

61. In the face of public criticism, Juneau School District Superintendent Gary Bader and Juneau School Board President Phyllis Carlson each felt constrained to write letters to the *Juneau Empire* editor defending Principal Morse's January 24, 2002, actions. Gary Bader, "My Turn: JDHS Principal Was Doing Her Job," *Juneau Empire*, May 9, 2002, http://www.juneauempire.com/stories/050902/opi_myturn2.shtml; Phyllis Carlson, "My Turn: 'Bong Hits' Deserves Supreme Court Test," *Juneau Empire*, May 24, 2006, http://www.juneauempire.com/stories/052406/opi_20060524001.shtml. Gary Bader: "There was a lot of really hateful stuff goin' on. I remember . . . at some point during this, the school board saying [to me], 'You've got to respond to this in the newspaper [*pounds on table for emphasis*]!' Because there was a lot of letters from Joseph's—from people identifying with Joseph . . . [saying] this is what's happening, and so on. And it wasn't the way we saw it. We didn't think that was happening. And the school board saying: 'You've gotta write a letter [*pounding on table*]!' And I say, 'They never work. It never works.' 'You gotta do it—we're telling ya to!' Okay, so I write a letter, and then fifty arrows come back at me. You just don't win in those things [*laughs*]. I think public officials like superintendents just need to be like a whale goin' through the water. You know, the little fish can come up and nibble at ya. You're not gonna catch 'em. You're not gonna win. You just gotta take your hits and go on doing what you think is right. . . . I think that those who are high school principals and superintendents have the most difficult job in public service. . . . There's no cookbook for a principal. Student holding up a banner [that] says this—there's no cookbook that says—you have to make those decisions. That's why I put the high school principal on the same footing as the superintendent. Superintendent generally has—has difficult political calls to make, but generally has some time to think them through. But the principals and high school administrators, where you have young people, with all of their energy, their hormones, and their enthusiasm and everything, and you can't just go back to your office saying 'Let me think about this' before I go address it." Gary Bader interview, June 6, 2009, 27:26; 47:16. Phyllis Carlson: "I did a 'My Turn' in the paper, so you can probably look that up . . . There was a couple of important things going on at the time, [there] was the exposure of our staff, our administrators. And the fact that one judge said our district was correct, and then the Ninth Circuit saying 'No, it wasn't,' reversing that. And then saying that Deb Morse, the principal at the time, would be held personally responsible. The impact of that on our administrators—to have to make those split-second judgments[.] . . . So, the exposure of our staff. When people of the court—judges—were not even clear on what's supposed to be so clear, was a real important piece for me." Phyllis Carlson interview, June 8, 2009, 3:05.

62. Julia O'Malley, "JDHS Renovation Making Progress," *Juneau Empire*, November 21, 2002, http://www.juneauempire.com/stories/112102/loc_jdhs.shtml; Joanna Markell, "Renovation Lags at JDHS," *Juneau Empire*, March 13, 2003, http://www.juneauempire.com/stories/031303/loc_

jdhsrenov.shtml; Eric Fry, "Schools Reopen as Renovation Stays on Course," *Juneau Empire*, August 28, 2003, http://www.juneauempire.com/stories/082803/loc_schoolopen.shtml.

63. Good's three references to gender relations pertain to a challenge by a group of women on the JDHS faculty to Deborah Morse remaining principal—a challenge apparently resulting from their dissatisfaction with her administration and management style. Corroborating Good's views, Margo Waring, a former Juneau School Board member, observed: "What I heard, before [Morse moved from being JDHS principal to being Juneau School District coordinator of facilities planning] was that . . . morale was extremely low. Some people said that they thought that she was 'agoraphobic' because she never left her office. I don't actually believe that, but I mean that's the kind of thing people were talking about; that she just didn't engage with students or faculty in any constructive kinds of ways. . . . There was a [faculty] petition—I don't remember whatever happened with the petition. But I mean it had reached that level." Margo Waring, interview, June 7, 2009, 0:01. In another interview, JDHS faculty member Gary Lehnhart commented: "I don't think it's any secret. The faculty—there was a group of women [on] the faculty who didn't like [Deborah Morse]. And they got together and they formed a committee. . . . And so, eventually . . . I think, the staff at [JDHS] had had enough; especially, there was some women who were upset with the way some of them were treated. I know they started documenting things and meeting. . . . The one thing [Deb] proved really good at . . . she was in charge of the High School during the remodel, and that was clearly her passion. . . . That was clearly what she cared about." Gary Lehnhart, interview, June 4, 2009, 42:20. See Eric Fry, "JDHS Principal to Depart Post," *Juneau Empire*, July 9, 2004, http://www.juneauempire.com/stories/070904/loc_principal.shtml.

64. Clay Good interview, June 8, 2009, 3:36.

65. "While the task leader concentrates on the Court's decision, the social leader concentrates on keeping the Court socially cohesive." David J. Danelski, "The Influence of the Chief Justice in the Decisional Process," in Walter F. Murphy, C. Herman Pritchett, Lee Epstein, and Jack Knight, eds., *Courts, Judges and Politics*, 6th ed. (Boston: McGraw-Hill, 2005), 676. Also see Stacia L. Haynie, "Leadership and Consensus on the U.S. Supreme Court," *Journal of Politics* 54 (November 1992): 1158; and Robert J. Steamer, *Chief Justice: Leadership and the Supreme Court* (Columbia: University of South Carolina Press, 1986).

66. In the high school context, the tidy distinction between being task proficient and being socially adept breaks down: *the* task is to help bring about a productive learning environment via collegial relations among students, faculty, and staff. In point of fact, as a practical matter, on the U.S. Supreme Court the analytically clear distinction between "task leadership" and "social leadership" can be messy.

67. Carol Comeau interview, June 3, 2009, 46:51.

68. At this point in my conversation with Eric, I interjected: "Isn't it interesting that that fifteen minutes on Glacier Avenue—I mean (I'm running a theory) Joe Frederick was just sort of out for a lark with a bunch of friends, probably smokin' dope that evening, and going, 'Hey, let's get on TV!' Unfurls the banner, Deborah Morse crosses and takes it down and, suddenly, they both become notorious; when neither of them probably intended to be notorious, at all [*laughter*]. Joe becomes this kind of civil liberty champion, and Deborah Morse becomes the symbolic heavy." Eric Morrison interview, June 4, 2009, 24:43.

69. Ibid., 22:08; 24:37; 34:20.

70. Carol Comeau interview, June 2, 2009, 7:00.

71. Sally Smith interview, June 5, 2009, 17:10. While indicating that people in her own circle shared what Sally Smith described as the "water-cooler-coffee-pot" assessment of Deb Morse's January 24 decisions, former Juneau-Douglas School Board President Mary Becker took issue with that judgment. "Even after [the U.S. Supreme Court's decision], even some friends of mine—even after we virtually won, at the Supreme Court, what else can you say?!—that we were right!—[friends] were still: 'That

was so stupid. You should have never taken that. That was such a waste of time.' I said: 'Wait a second. Did you hear the Supreme Court? They said students cannot advocate drug use in any kind of school setting, whether it's in or out of school. And they said that we have the authority over school—over students—under our policies and our rules when they are outside the doors of the school. Don't you think those are important?!' 'Oh, it's just a waste of time. [Deb] never should have done this to the kids.' . . . The truth of the matter was, she saw [the banner] immediately as drug language. She's very upright about that kind of stuff. She's the one that was working in a school that had drug problems. She didn't like that at all. And she didn't want her school embarrassed on national TV. I mean, it ended up being that we were on national TV [*laughs*]. But I would have done the very same thing. It was: 'Come on kids!' It's like doing any other kinds of obscene types of things that students could do to get attention from the press. You don't want them to do it. You try to stop it, if you can." Mary Becker interview, June 6, 2009, 48:13.

72. The two central characters in Ludwig Bemelmans' classic Caldecott Honor Book *Madeline* can be seen, in metaphorical terms, as Deb and Joe, respectively. Deb presided over JDHS in a manner reminiscent of Miss Clavel, conceiving of her role as principal in terms of maintaining order and expecting students, faculty, and staff to go about their business "in two straight lines." Joe resembles Madeline. No lines for him. He wanders off on his own, to "pooh-pooh" tigers at the zoo. Ludwig Bemelmans, *Mad about Madeline: The Complete Tales* (New York: Viking, 2001).

73. *Rubricize* is Abraham Maslow's term. In his chapter on the "Various Meanings of Transcendence," in *The Farther Reaches of Human Nature*, Maslow writes: "15. Transcending the opinions of others, i.e., of reflected appraisals. This means a self-determining Self. It means to be able to be unpopular when this is the right thing to do, to become an autonomous, self-deciding Self; *to write one's own lines*, to be one's own man, to be not manipulatable or seduceable. These are the resisters (rather than conformers) . . . Resistance to being rubricized, *to be able to be role-free, i.e., to transcend one's role and to be a person rather than being the role*. This includes resisting suggestion, propaganda, social pressures, being outvoted, etc." (emphasis added). Abraham Maslow, *The Farther Reaches of Human Nature* (New York: Viking, 1971), 273. See Abraham Maslow, "Resistance to Being Rubricized," in Bernard Kaplan and Seymour Wapner, *Perspectives in Psychological Theory: Essays in Honor of Heinz Werner* (New York: International Universities Press, 1960).

74. Joe's stories about the Glacier Avenue incident, his interactions with Principal Morse, and the aftermath are a composite derived primarily from two sources: (1) my interview with Joe Frederick, March 21, 2009; and (2) Deposition of Joseph Frederick, Wednesday, August 21, 2002, in author's possession. Compare, Juneau School District, Transcript of Hearing in the Matter of Joseph Frederick, March 13, 2002, in author's possession, 56–98.

75. Joe Frederick interview, March 21, 2009, 36:10.

76. Joe was deposed by attorney David Crosby.

77. Deposition of Joseph Frederick, 24–25.

78. Joe Frederick interview, March 21, 2009, 37:22.

79. Deposition of Joseph Frederick, 26, 28, 29, 30.

80. Joe Frederick interview, March 21, 2009, 36:51.

81. Deposition of Joseph Frederick, 44.

82. JDHS day custodian Chet Durand accompanied Deborah Morse when she crossed Glacier Avenue. See Deposition of Joseph Frederick, 40–43. Compare retired JDHS teacher, Clay Good: "I've got pictures of her [Morse] walking away with the banner in her hand. And then Joe's gesturing like 'What!'—you know, like—'What did I do?!' And the janitor's looking all snarly. And part of this has to be—the janitor has to be included in the story because, he's a janitor, but it was partly his delight to tell kids what to do. That was his persona. And here's a breach of etiquette and, by golly, the janitor's

gonna rush in and set things right. So, it's just a tag team. And it's also somewhat a courtesy, too. Deb's walking over to a gaggle of kids, it's good to have, you know, some authority with you—some physical authority. . . . They're working the job together." Clay Good interview, June 8, 2009, 15:01. Compare signed statement of Chet Durand, dated January 24, 2002, in author's possession.

83. Joe Frederick interview, March 21, 2009, 38:31.

84. Deposition of Joseph Frederick, 46.

85. Joe Frederick interview, March 21, 2009, 40:59.

86. Deposition of Joseph Frederick, 44–45.

87. Deb's stories about the Glacier Avenue incident, and her interactions with Joe in her office, are a composite derived primarily from two sources: (1) my interview with Deborah Morse, June 5, 2009; and (2) Deposition of Deborah Lynn Morse, Friday, January 31, 2003, Juneau, Alaska, in author's possession. Compare Juneau School District, Transcript of Hearing in the Matter of Joseph Frederick, March 13, 2002, in author's possession, 98–130.

88. Deborah Morse interview, June 5, 2009, 3:15.

89. Deb was deposed by attorney Doug Mertz.

90. Deposition of Deborah Lynn Morse, 63, 64, 65, 66.

91. Deborah Morse interview, June 5, 2009, 12:39.

92. Joe Frederick interview, March 21, 2009, 38:08.

93. Q. Did you at some point quote Voltaire as well as Jefferson?

A. Yes. The quote was "Freedom of speech may not be limited without being lost." I believe I was quoting Jefferson, but I believe Jefferson took the quote from Voltaire. I'm not exactly sure.

Q. So it's just one quote.

A. Yes. It's just one quote, but wasn't sure who it was.

Deposition of Joseph Frederick, 50. I believe the correct quote is from Thomas Jefferson, and reads: "our liberty depends on the freedom of the press, and that cannot be limited without being lost." Thomas Jefferson to Dr. James Currie, January 28, 1786, Thomas Jefferson Papers Series 1. General Correspondence. 1651–1827, The Library of Congress, http://memory.loc.gov/cgi-bin/ampage?collI d=mtj1&fileName=mtj1page005.db&recNum=0215.

94. Deposition of Joseph Frederick, 45, 49, 51–52.

95. Augustus Brown Pool and Juneau-Douglas High School are immediately adjacent, located at 1619 Glacier Avenue and 1639 Glacier Avenue, respectively.

96. Joe Frederick, interview, March 21, 2009, 53:38.

97. David Crosby is Deb Morse's attorney. (Morse would not meet with me without Crosby being present.)

98. Deborah Morse interview, June 5, 2009, 15:32, 17:45, 26:08; 23:32. Specifically, Frederick was suspended, January 24, 2002–February 6, 2002, for these five infractions: 2:05 Defiant/Disruptive Behavior, 2:07 Refusal to respond to staff directive regarding behavior, 2:08 Refusal to cooperate/assist in investigation, 2:12 Display of Offensive Material, and 2:17 Truancy/Skipping. Notification of Suspension, *Morse v. Frederick*, Joint Appendix, in author's possession, 106–107.

99. Deposition of Deborah Lynn Morse, 42–43; 44–46.

100. Gary Bader served as school superintendent from July 1999 until February 2003 when he resigned to become chief investment officer of the Alaska Department of Revenue's Treasury Division. See unofficial transcript of the superintendent's hearing, n.d., in author's possession.

101. Superintendent Bader played an unusual role in the criminal trespass episode. He explains: "My first contact that I recall with Joseph was that . . . he came to my office (principals aren't ordinarily directly accessible to students who have a grievance; you know, we have five thousand students). . . . [H]e was pretty insistent, and wanted to talk to the superintendent about this getting busted for being

on school property. . . . So I said, 'Okay. I'll talk to the young man.' And he came up, and we talked. And he said that the police had cited him; that he had to go to court—I think it was either that day, or tomorrow, or something like that. And [he] wanted somebody to tell 'em it wasn't on school property. And I said to Joseph, 'You know, Joseph, I'm not going to go to court and argue your case for you. But I will go to court and tell them that I think it is reasonable for somebody to think they're not on school property.' I didn't know exactly where he was. Him coming to me was my first knowledge of it. ["So, this was about the criminal trespass. It wasn't about the banner at all."—JCF] Right. It wasn't about the banner at all.

"So, I remember, I did go to court with Joseph. I don't think this made me very popular with the school administrators. But I thought it was the right thing to do. It turns out we went to court— Joseph, and his father and I. We sat there, probably for an hour and a half while they dealt with cases. I think it was Judge Froehlich—who said, [laughs] 'Well, Joseph, good for you if you have your superintendent here to talk on your behalf, but this isn't an arraignment.' So we had sat there for a couple of hours . . . it's a long part of my day, at any rate, and it was really for naught. . . . But what this did do . . . I can remember saying directly to Joseph—I can see it very clearly in the lobby of the courthouse—'Joseph, what do you want to have happen?' And Joseph said, 'I just want it to go away.' 'Just want it to go away.' I remember that very clearly. And the reason I bring that up is because— initially—I think that's all anybody wanted." Gary Bader interview, June 6, 2009, 2:34.

102. Ibid., 9:52.

103. Ibid., 17:26, 10:50. See Appendix H—Superintendent's Decision on Appeal Dated February 25, 2002, *Morse v. Frederick*, Appendix, in author's possession, 59a–67a.

104. See "Superintendent Upholds 'Banner' Suspension," *Juneau Empire*, February 28, 2002, http://www.juneauempire.com/stories/022802/Loc_suspension.shtml. Compare Ed Hein, "My Turn: How Will Students Learn Constitutional Values?" *Juneau Empire*, March 6, 2002, http://www. juneauempire.com/stories/030602/opE_myturn2.shtml.

105. Andrew Krueger, "School Board Hears Student Banner Case," *Juneau Empire*, March 14, 2002, http://www.juneauempire.com/stories/031402/loc_schoolboard.shtml.

106. Mary Becker, President, Chuck Cohen, Vice President, Daniel Peterson, Alan Schorr, Carolyn Spaulding, Deana Darnall, and Stan Ridgeway.

107. Appendix I—Minutes of the Juneau Board of Education Meeting of March 19, 2002, *Morse v. Frederick*, Appendix, in author's possession, 69a. See Andrew Krueger, "School Board Upholds Decision of Student Banner," *Juneau Empire*, March 20, 2002, http://www.juneauempire.com/ stories/032002/loc_stubanner.shtml. Gary Bader reflected: "I really felt like—and I know I have a bias in the case, I'm a school administrator, and now I had ownership in the decision and everything— but I really felt that Ann Gifford did an amazing job of making the case for the administration. And I also felt that Mr. Mertz hadn't prepared like he should of. 'Cause I didn't think it was close. I felt it was closer with me than with the school board. And this town is not known as being a right-wing town. And I think it was a unanimous decision at the board, if my memory serves me correct. . . . And it didn't take them long to decide. And they're not a—as I recall, I mean they were a good school board, and people doing the best job they can do, but not slavishly devoted [laughs] to administration. That doesn't happen in this town." Gary Bader interview, June 6, 2009, 20:35.

108. Mary Becker interview, June 6, 2009, 14:26.

109. Governor Hammond characterized Gross as "my brilliant attorney general." Gross argued Alaska's case before the U.S. Supreme Court in *Zobel v. Williams*, 457 U.S. 55 (1982). *Zobel* involved a challenge to the retroactive dividend provision of Alaska's Permanent Fund Program as violating the Equal Protection Clause of the Fourteenth Amendment. Alaska lost its case, 8–1. Hammond and his wife, Bella, had attended the oral arguments. Hammond's impressions of the experience

are interesting: "Av had argued in front of the U.S. Supreme Court before and he urged Bella and me to come and see for ourselves. 'You'll find it awe-inspiring; almost like an appearance before the Almighty.'

"Instead of awesome, we found it awful. The experience totally undermined my confidence in the court's ability to dispense justice or logic. From questions asked it was evident that few justices had personally reviewed the state's case. Not only did they interrupt with seemingly irrelevant questions, they never let Av present our basic arguments." Hammond, *Tales of Alaska's Bush Rat Governor*, 231, 234, 252.

110. It is not clear to me whether Av Gross was recruited, or volunteered. (I was unable to interview him.) Juneau attorney Ann Gifford, who represents the school district, remembers: "In this case the insurance company . . . actually had Av Gross come and try to negotiate a resolution of the thing. . . . Av is—he's a former attorney general here. He's retired now, but he had a, I guess, mostly an appellate practice. And I think he came and sort of volunteered, that he would try and do that." Ann Gifford interview, June 6, 2009, 11:22.

111. E-mail from William F. Cummings to James Foster, dated August 18, 2009, in author's possession.

112. Gary Bader interview, June 6, 2009, 26:08.

113. Mary Becker interview, June 6, 2009, 23:55.

114. Ann Gifford interview, June 6, 2009, 11:53.

115. Doug Mertz interview, June 7, 2009, 1:04:44.

116. Distrust—as well as control issues, and competing agendas. For Joe's part, we have already seen that willful behavior—insisting on having his own way—is not untypical. As for the school district, former Juneau school board member Margo Waring opined: "I say this about our school district . . . (and I've said it publicly at school board meetings), ours is a district in which the prime directive is to support the adults, even if it's at the expense of students. And I've seen it time, after time, after time. . . . And that's the whole tenor of that workplace environment." Margo Waring, interview, June 7, 2009, 36:45. (Margo Waring is married to Doug Mertz.) See handwritten memo from Av Gross to Ann Gifford, faxed May 29, 2002; "Acceptable Settlement Terms," hand dated 5/21; letter from Avrum M. Gross, dated June 4, 2002, hand delivered to Douglas Mertz; and unsigned, undated draft formal settlement agreement, all in author's possession.

117. U.S.C. § 1983 reads: "Every person who, under color of any statute, ordinance, regulation, custom, or usage, of any State or Territory or the District of Columbia, subjects, or causes to be subjected, any citizen of the United States or other person within the jurisdiction thereof to the deprivation of any rights, privileges, or immunities secured by the Constitution and laws, shall be liable to the party injured in an action at law, suit in equity, or other proper proceeding for redress, except that in any action brought against a judicial officer for an act or omission taken in such officer's judicial capacity, injunctive relief shall not be granted unless a declaratory decree was violated or declaratory relief was unavailable. For the purposes of this section, any Act of Congress applicable exclusively to the District of Columbia shall be considered to be a statute of the District of Columbia." U.S. Code Collection, Title 42 > Chapter 21 > Subchapter I > § 1983, Civil action for deprivation of rights, http://www.law.cornell.edu/uscode/42/usc_sec_42_00001983----000-.html.

118. Eric Fry, "Court Mulls over Protected Speech," *Juneau Empire*, April 14, 2003, http://www.juneauempire.com/stories/041403/loc_bonghits.shtml.

119. Judge Sedwick filled the seat vacated by Andrew J. Kleinfeld, whom George H. W. Bush had elevated to the Ninth Circuit Court of Appeals. Ironically, Kleinfeld wrote the opinion for the three-judge Ninth Circuit panel that unanimously overturned Sedwick in *Frederick v. Morse; Juneau School Board*, 439 F.3d 1114 (9th Cir. Alaska 2006).

120. Appendix B—Opinion and Order of the United States District Court for The District of Alaska, Dated and Filed May 27, 2003, 23a–40a; Appendix C—Order of the United States District Court for The District of Alaska, Dated and Filed on May 29, 2003 *Morse v. Frederick*, Appendix, in author's possession, 41–42a. See Eric Fry, "Judge: School District within Rights to Take Debated Banner," *Juneau Empire*, June 6, 2003, htp://www.juneauempire.com/stories/060603/loc_judge.shtml.

121. Opinion and Order of the United States District Court for The District of Alaska, Dated and Filed May 27, 2003, 34a.

122. "Summary Judgment," *The Free Legal Dictionary*, http://legal-dictionary.thefreedictionary.com/Summary+Judgment.

123. Federal Rules of Civil Procedure, VII Judgment, Rule 56. Summary Judgment, http://www.law.cornell.edu/rules/frcp/Rule56.htm.

124. Opinion and Order of the United States District Court for The District of Alaska, Dated and Filed May 27, 2003, 26a (emphasis added).

125. Ibid., 37a.

126. Moisés Kaufman and the Members of the Tectonic Theater Project, *The Laramie Project* (New York: Dramatists Play Service, 2001).

127. "New Details Emerge in Matthew Shepard Murder," *ABC News 20/20*, November 26, 2004, http://abcnews.go.com/2020/story?id=277685&page=1.

128. National Public Radio, "'Ten Years Later': The Matthew Shepard Story Retold," *All Things Considered*, October 12, 2009, http://www.npr.org/templates/transcript/transcript.php?storyId=113663235. See JoAnn Wypijewski, "A Boy's Life: For Mathew Shepard's Killers, What Does It Take to Pass As a Man?" *Harper's*, September, 1999, 61–74, http://www.harpers.org/archive/1999/09/0060647. Compare David Brooks: "We're all born late. We're born into history that is well under way. We're born into cultures, nations and languages that we didn't choose. On top of that, we're born with certain brain chemicals and genetic predispositions that we can't control. We're thrust into social conditions that we detest. Often, we react in ways we regret even while we're doing them.

"But unlike the other animals, people do have a drive to seek coherence and meaning. We have a need to tell ourselves stories that explain it all. We use these stories to supply the metaphysics, without which life seems pointless and empty.

"Among all the things we don't control, we do have some control over our stories. We do have a conscious say in selecting the narrative we will use to make sense of the world. Individual responsibility is contained in the act of selecting and constantly revising the master narrative we tell about ourselves.

"The stories we select help us, in turn, to interpret the world. They guide us to pay attention to certain things and ignore other things. They lead us to see certain things as sacred and other things as disgusting. They are the frameworks that shape our desires and goals. So while story selection may seem vague and intellectual, it's actually very powerful. The most important power we have is the power to help select the lens through which we see reality." "The Rush to Therapy," *New York Times*, November 10, 2009, http://www.nytimes.com/2009/11/10/opinion/10brooks.html?em.

129. *Rashomon*, video introduction by Robert Altman, Criterion, March 26, 2002.

130. See James C. Foster, "Rethinking Politics and Judicial Selection During Contentious Times," *Albany Law Review* 67 (2004): 821. Compare, C. Herman Pritchett, "The Development of Judicial Research," in *Frontiers of Judicial Research*, Joel B. Grossman, Joseph Tanenhaus, and Edward N. Muller, eds. (New York: Wiley, 1968); and Cass R. Sunstein, David Schkade, Lisa M. Ellman, and Andres Sawicki, *Are Judges Political? An Empirical Analysis of the Federal Judiciary* (Washington, D.C.: Brookings Institution Press, 2006).

Notes to Chapter 2

1. C. Wright Mills, *The Sociological Imagination* (New York: Oxford University Press, 1967), 3.

2. Ibid., 3–4.

3. William S. Geimer, "Juvenileness: A Single-edged Constitutional Sword," *Georgia Law Review* 22 (1988): 949.

4. For example, concurring in *Bethel School Dist. No. 403 v. Fraser,* 478 U.S. 675 (1986), Justice Brennan characterized *Tinker* as the "*unimpeachable proposition* that students do not 'shed their constitutional rights to freedom of speech or expression at the schoolhouse gate'" (emphasis added). Compare Erwin Chemerinsky, "Students Do Leave Their First Amendment Rights at the Schoolhouse Gate: What's Left of *Tinker,*" *Drake Law Review* 48 (2000): 527, 532.

5. Thomas C. Fischer, "Whatever Happened to Mary Beth Tinker and Other Sagas in the Academic 'Marketplace of Ideas,'" *Golden Gate University Law Review* 23 (1993): 352. Compare, Geimer, "Juvenileness: A Single-Edged Constitutional Sword."

6. *Schenck v. United States,* 249 U.S. 47 (1919).

7. *Meyer v. Nebraska,* 262 U.S. 390 (1923), and *Pierce v. Society of Sisters,* 268 U.S. 510 (1925).

8. *West Virginia State Board of Education v. Barnette,* 319 U.S. 624, 627 (1944).

9. *Barnette,* 642. In arriving at this result, the Court explicitly overruled its decision in *Minersville School District v. Gobitis,* 310 U.S. 586 (1940), decided only four years earlier, where the Court had upheld a mandatory flag salute policy challenged by Jehovah's Witnesses. By overruling *Gobitis* the *Barnette* Court rejected the assumption "that power exists in the State to impose the flag salute discipline upon school children in general. . . . We examine rather than assume existence of this power."

10. *Barnette* 634–635.

11. Compare *Schenck,* 52.

12. *Barnette,* 633–335.

13. *Barnette,* 631.

14. S. Elizabeth Wilborn, "Teaching the New Three Rs—Repression, Rights, and Respect: A Primer of Student Speech Activities," *Boston College Law Review* 31 (1995): 119, 130.

15. James E. Ryan, "The Supreme Court and Public Schools," *Virginia Law Review* 86 (2000): 1335, 1347.

16. Chemerinsky, "Students Do Leave Their First Amendment Rights at the Schoolhouse Gate," 535.

17. Akhil Reed Amar, "Hugo Black and the Hall of Fame," *Alabama Law Review* 53 (Summer 2002): 1221, 1238. Compare Alexander Meiklejohn, "The First Amendment Is an Absolute," *Superior Court Review* (1961): 245, and Alexander Meiklejohn, *Political Freedom: The Constitutional Powers of the People* (New York: Harper, 1960).

18. See Erwin Chemerinsky on the rhetoric and myth of discretion-free judging, "The Role of the Judge in the Twenty-first Century: Seeing the Emperor's Clothes: Recognizing the Reality of Constitutional Decision Making," *Boston University Law Review* 86 (December 2006): 1069. Compare Lief H. Carter, *Contemporary Constitutional Lawmaking: The Supreme Court and the Art of Politics* (New York: Pergamon, 1985); and Stanley Fish, "Does Constitutional Theory Matter?" *New York Times,* January 27, 2008, http://fish.blogs.nytimes.com. Wallace Mendelson's "Introduction" to his *The Supreme Court: Law and Discretion* (Indianapolis: Bobbs-Merrill, 1967) is an early, and thoughtful, reflection on the tension between judicial rule-following and judicial choice.

19. *Tinker v. Des Moines School Dist.,* 393 U.S. 503 (1969), 506.

20. Ibid.

21. Ibid., 507.

22. Ibid., 505.

23. *Blackwell v. Issaquena County Board of Education,* 363 F.2d 749, (5th Cir. 1966).

24. The absence of disorder at Booker T. Washington is especially notable because the school is located in Philadelphia, Mississippi, where civil rights workers Michael Schwerner, James Chaney, and Andrew Goodman had been murdered on June 21, 1964.

25. *Burnside v. Byars,* 363 F.2d 744, 749 (5ᵗʰ Cir. 1966) (emphasis added).

26. See, for instance, Fischer, "Whatever Happened to Mary Beth Tinker," 355; and James A. Whitson, *Constitution and Curriculum: Hermeneutical Semiotics of Cases and Controversies in Education, Law, and Social Science* (New York: Falmer Press, 1991), 41.

27. Fortas added an intriguing footnote to his first citation to *Burnside,* suggesting that he acknowledged the Fifth Circuit's concern with student responsibility: "In *Burnside,* the Fifth Circuit ordered that high school authorities be enjoined from enforcing a regulation forbidding students to wear 'freedom buttons.' It is instructive that in *Blackwell v. Issaquena County Board of Education,* 363 F2d. 749 (1966), the same panel on the same day reached the opposite result on different facts. It declined to enjoin enforcement of such a regulation in another high school where the students wearing freedom buttons harassed students who did not wear them and created much disturbance." *Tinker,* 505.

28. Fischer, "Whatever Happened to Mary Beth Tinker," 357.

29. See Chemerinsky, "Students Do Leave Their First Amendment Rights at the Schoolhouse Gate," 532. Compare Mark Yudof, "Tinker Tailored: Good Faith, Civility, and Student Expression," *St. John's Law Review* 69 (Summer/Fall 1995): 365.

30. Of course, as flights of soaring rhetoric go, Justice Fortas' *Tinker* dicta are not in the same league as Justice Jackson's defense of free opinion in *Barnette.* Jackson wrote: "If there is any fixed star in our constitutional constellation, it is that no official, high or petty, can prescribe what shall be orthodox in politics, nationalism, religion, or other matters of opinion or force citizens to confess by word or act their faith therein." Jackson's words have entered the First Amendment pantheon.

31. *Tinker,* 515.

32. Stewart quoted his concurring opinion from *Ginsberg v. New York,* 390 U.S. 629 (1968), decided just the previous term: "[A] State may permissibly determine that, at least in some precisely delineated areas, a child—like someone in a captive audience—is not possessed of that full capacity for individual choice which is the presupposition of First Amendment guarantees." Ibid., 515. See Mark Tushnet, "Free Expression and the Young Adult: A Constitutional Framework," *University of Illinois Law Review* 1976 (1976): 746.

33. *Tinker,* 515.

34. On the Warren Court's internal struggles with symbolic speech in another Vietnam War–era case—*United States v. O'Brien,* 391 U.S. 367 (1968)—see the discussion below, 50–52, and Michael R. Belknap, "The Warren Court and the Vietnam War: The Limits of Legal Liberalism," *Georgia Law Review* 33 (Fall 1998): 65.

35. *Tinker,* 516. Of these five, only Mary Beth and John Tinker and Christopher Eckhardt experienced any consequences for wearing black armbands to school, and these three are the plaintiffs in *Tinker v. Des Moines School Dist.* In all, only five Des Moines secondary school students were disciplined.

36. Ibid., 522.

37. Black observed: "It may be that the Nation has outworn the old-fashioned slogan that 'children are to be seen not heard' but one may, I hope, be permitted to harbor the thought that taxpayers send their children to school on the premise that at their age they need to learn, not teach." Ibid., 522. Compare Justice Mary Muehlen Maring, "'Children Should Be Seen and Not Heard': Do Children Shed Their Right to Free Speech at the Schoolhouse Gate?" *North Dakota Law Review* 74 (1998): 679.

38. Ibid., 326. Justice Harlan's dissent is more temperate and measured. He agreed that "state public school authorities in the discharge of their responsibilities are not wholly exempt from the requirements of the Fourteenth Amendment respecting the freedoms of expression and association."

Nevertheless, Harlan's primary concern lay with maintaining "discipline and good order," and he would put the burden of proof "upon those complaining . . . of showing that a particular school measure was motivated by other than legitimate concerns"; a burden the plaintiffs failed to carry. *Tinker,* 526.

39. Ibid., 520.

40. *Lochner v. New York,* 198 U.S. 45 (1905).

41. Stephen Kanter, "The *Griswold* Diagrams: Toward a Unified Theory of Constitutional Rights," *Cardozo Law Review* 28 (November 2006): 623, 671. Remainder of this quotation is from ibid.

42. *Tinker,* 519–520.

43. Ibid., 519.

44. Ibid., 518.

45. Ibid., 525.

46. "As *Tinker v. Des Moines Independent Community School District* demonstrated . . . the Justices were willing to shield with the First Amendment only the tamest and least menacing forms of dissent." Belknap, "The Warren Court and the Vietnam War," 65, 143.

47. Professor Joseph Russomanno nicely captures the *Tinker* paradox: "[B]eneath the surface, the ruling is broader in scope than simply examining the proper conduct of students. . . . The story of *Tinker* is a story that continues to resonate. Its lessons reinforce the value of speech that disagrees with prevailing viewpoints. But these lessons . . . are difficult ones. They are difficult to learn and apparently even more difficult to implement." "Dissent Yesterday and Today: The *Tinker* Case and Its Legacy," *Communication Law and Policy* 11, no. 367 (Summer 2006): 386, 371.

48. Maring, "'Children Should Be Seen and Not Heard,'" 679, 683.

49. Fischer, "Whatever Happened to Mary Beth Tinker?" 352, 366.

50. Yudof, "Tinker Tailored," 365, 367.

51. Fischer, "Whatever Happened to Mary Beth Tinker?" 368.

52. *Tinker,* 505, 508.

53. Russomanno, "Dissent Yesterday and Today," 375.

54. W. B. Gallie, "Essentially Contested Concepts," *Proceedings of the Aristotelian Society* 56 (1956): 167, 169. Compare William E. Connolly, *The Terms of Political Discourse,* 3rd ed. (Princeton, N.J.: Princeton University Press, 1993); and J. N. Gray, "On the Contestability of Social and Political Concepts," *Political Theory* 5 (August 1977): 331.

55. Samantha Beeson, *The Morality of Conflict: Reasonable Disagreement and the Law* (London: Hart, 2006), 72.

56. Ibid.

57. See Melville B. Nimmer, *Nimmer on Freedom of Speech: A Treatise of the Theory of the First Amendment* (New York: M. Bender, 1984), §3.06; compare Melville B. Nimmer, "The Meaning of Symbolic Speech under the First Amendment," *UCLA Law Review* 21 (1973): 29; and Nimmer, "Symbolic Speech," *Encyclopedia of the American Constitution,* 4 vols. (New York: Macmillan, 1986), 4: 1843.

58. Prior to *Stromberg,* the Court had a decidedly different take on political symbolism. See, for instance, Justice Harlan's opinion in *Halter v. Nebraska,* 205 U.S. 34 (1907) upholding a statute prohibiting display of the American flag for advertising purposes: "One who loves the Union will love the state in which he resides, and love both of the common country and of the state will diminish in proportion as respect for the flag is weakened. Therefore a state will be wanting in care for the well-being of its people if it ignores the fact that they regard the flag as a symbol of their country's power and prestige, and will be impatient if any open disrespect is shown towards it. By the statute in question the state has in substance declared that no one subject to its jurisdiction shall use the flag for purposes of trade and traffic, a purpose wholly foreign to that for which it was provided by the nation. Such a use tends to degrade and cheapen the flag in the estimation of the people, as well as to defeat

the object of maintaining it as an emblem of national power and national honor. And we cannot hold that any privilege of American citizenship or that any right of personal liberty is violated by a state enactment forbidding the flag to be used as an advertisement on a bottle of beer."

59. *Stromberg*, 362.

60. Ibid., 360.

61. Ibid., 369.

62. Ibid. As to displaying a flag in protest, Chief Justice Hughes opined: "The maintenance of the opportunity for free political discussion to the end that government may be responsive to the will of the people and that changes may be obtained by lawful means, an opportunity essential to the security of the Republic is a fundamental principle of our constitutional system." Ibid.

63. *Barnette*, 632–633.

64. Ibid., 636. On other categories of conduct that the Supreme Court has held to be "symbolic speech" see Joshua Waldman, "Symbolic Speech and Social Meaning," *Columbia Law Review* 97 (October 1997): 1844, 1863–1873.

65. *Barnette*, 652.

66. *Barnette*, 662.

67. The following account of the *O'Brien* story draws on Belknap, "The Warren Court and the Vietnam War"; and Geoffrey Stone, *Perilous Times: Free Speech in Wartime from the Sedition Act of 1798 to the War on Terrorism* (New York: W. W. Norton, 2004).

68. See Stanley Karnow, *Vietnam: A History* (New York: The Viking Press, 1983), chaps. 11, 12; and Steven Cohen, *Vietnam: Anthology and Guide to a Television History* (New York: Alfred Knopf, 1983), chaps. 4, 5.

69. Glen Silber and Barry Brown, First Run Features, 1979. Compare Errol Morris, *The Fog of War*, Sony Pictures, 2004.

70. Stone, *Perilous Times*, 472.

71. Ibid.

72. *United States v. O'Brien*, 391 U.S. 367 (1968), 369.

73. Ibid, 371.

74. Belknap, "The Warren Court and the Vietnam War," 130.

75. Ibid. "Larry Simon, who was one of his clerks during the term in which *O'Brien* was decided, explains Warren's position as follows: 'This was early in the Vietnam protest era. He, like a lot of people at the time, thought folks in O'Brien's shoes had plenty of [other] ways they could protest under American law.'" Ibid., n. 409.

76. Seventy thousand Viet Cong and North Vietnamese Communist soldiers launched the Tet Offensive on the Vietnamese lunar New Year, January 31, 1968, in the west. Militarily, the Tet Offensive was a Communist failure. Still, American officials' failure to anticipate the attacks, coupled with the casualties inflicted on American troops and horrific television coverage, dampened Americans' support for the policy. Tet also further isolated President Lyndon Johnson and led to his decision not to run for reelection, a decision he announced in a nationally televised speech on March 31, 1968. See Karnow, *Vietnam*, chap. 14. Compare James H. Willbanks, "Winning the Battle, Losing the War," *New York Times*, March 5, 2008, http://www.nytimes.com/2008/03/05/opinion/05willbanks.html.

77. Belknap, "The Warren Court and the Vietnam War," 132.

78. Ibid., 133–134.

79. *O'Brien*, 376-377.

80. Ibid., 388–389.

81. See, for instance, James M. McGoldrick Jr., "*United States v. O'Brien* Revisited: Of Burning Things, Waving Things, and G-Strings," *University of Memphis Law Review* 36 (Summer 2006): 903.

Professor McGoldrick identifies seven "mistakes" of the *O'Brien* test. Compare Peter Meijes Tiersma, "Nonverbal Communication and the Freedom of 'Speech,'" *Wisconsin Law Review* (November/ December 1993): 1525.

82. Justice Marshall recused himself, likely because he was solicitor general during the O'Brien prosecution. Opposed to the Vietnam War, Justice Douglas saw "[t]he underlying and basic problem in this case . . . [as] whether conscription is permissible in the absence of a declaration of war." Douglas advocated "the appropriateness of restoring the instant case to the calendar for reargument on the question of the constitutionality of a peacetime draft." *O'Brien*, 389, 391.

83. *Tinker*, 506 (emphasis added). We have already seen Justice Black's dissenting view that "public schools . . . are operated to give students an opportunity to learn, not to talk politics by actual speech or by 'symbolic' speech." Ibid., 523–524.

84. Ibid., 511.

85. Ibid.

86. Ibid., 512, quoting *Shelton v. Tucker,* 364 U.S. 479 (1960), 487.

87. Ibid. Compare Whitson, *Constitution and Curriculum*, 105–106.

88. William B. Senhauser, "Education and the Court: The Supreme Court's Educational Ideology," *Vanderbilt Law Review* 40 (May 1987): 939. Compare James E. Ryan, "The Supreme Court and Public Schools," *Virginia Law Review* 86 (October 2000): 1335. Ryan purports to offer a "quite different" explanation—"at least defensible"—of the Supreme Court's education cases: "Contrary to suggestions in the literature, the Court's cases do not reveal an elaborate and comprehensive theory of education; there is nothing close to a precise or complete vision of the permissible goals of public schools or the means by which those goals should be pursued. Rather, the cases seem to rest on a pragmatic and necessarily rough distinction between two functions: academic and social." Ryan, "The Supreme Court and Public Schools," 1340.

89. Senhauser, "Education and the Court: The Supreme Court's Educational Ideology," 942.

90. Citing "Development and the Aim of Education," *Harvard Education Review* 42 (1972): 449. Senhauser maintains that these ideologies, "although highly simplified, reflect the general philosophical scheme of education." Ibid., n. 18, 943.

91. Ibid., 948.

92. "The cultural transmission ideology defines education as the transmission of knowledge, skills, morals, and social rules to the student. . . . [T]he cultural transmissionists see the educational process as a guided acquisition of knowledge that reinforces desirable responses and eliminates undesirable ones. The cultural transmission ideology defines educational objectives . . . [as] the acquisition of knowledge and skills, measured in the short term by grades or report cards and in the long term by social status and power. . . . Thus, the purpose of education is not to encourage individual growth, but to assure the internalization of established norms, with the child's need to learn societal discipline receiving particular emphasis." Ibid., 943–944.

93. "[P]rogressive ideology . . . maintains that the touchstone of education is continued growth. . . . [T]he child is not viewed as a plant or a machine, but as a philosopher developing ideas through discourse. The objective of this process is not to stimulate behavior, but to reorganize and redefine the child's thought processes through confrontational discourse. . . . Child development must include exposure to more sophisticated thought requiring resolution of cognitive conflicts by active participation in the education process. . . . Progressivists encourage student expression and diversity because expressive behavior of students contributes to the learning environment." Ibid., 947–948.

94. Ibid., 956. Compare Richard L. Roe, "Valuing Student Speech: The Work of the Schools as Conceptual Development," *California Law Review* 79 (October 1991): 1271; and Rhonda Gay Hartman, "Adolescent Autonomy: Clarifying an Ageless Conundrum," *Hastings Law Journal* 51 (August 2000): 1265.

95. Kay S. Hymowitz, "*Tinker* and the Lessons from the Slippery Slope," *Drake Law Review* 48 (2000): 547, 548. Hymowitz is William E. Simon Fellow at the Manhattan Institute, a contributing editor of *City Journal*, and author of, among other books, *Ready or Not: What Happens When We Treat Children as Small Adults* (San Francisco: Encounter Books, 2000).

96. Hymowitz, "*Tinker* and the Lessons from the Slippery Slope," 556.

97. Ibid., 557.

98. Anne Proffitt Dupre, "Should Students Have Constitutional Rights? Keeping Order in the Public Schools," *George Washington Law Review* 65 (November 1996): 49, 53.

99. In fact, Dupre cites Senhauser when discussing both her models.

100. Ibid., 75, 74.

101. Ibid., 86.

102. Ibid., 101.

103. Ibid., 103.

104. Tushnet, "Free Expression and the Young Adult," 746.

105. Ibid., 760.

106. Ibid., 748. Tushnet continues: "Judges' images of school life derive from a time when schools were very different than they are today. Judges, therefore, are unlikely to appreciate fully the circumstances which exist in schools today."

107. Ibid., 753–758.

108. Ibid., 752–753. Tushnet cites Justice Brandeis' concurring opinion in *Whitney v. California*, 274 U.S. 357 (1927).

109. Dupre, "Should Students Have Constitutional Rights?" 105.

110. Tushnet, "Free Expression and the Young Adult," 758.

111. Ibid., 760.

112. Ibid. Compare Geimer, "Juvenileness: A Single-Edged Constitutional Sword," and Erwin Chemerinsky, "The Deconsitutionalization of Education," *Loyola University of Chicago Law Journal* 36 (Fall 2004): 111.

113. New York: W. W. Norton.

114. Blum refers to the "long-standing liberal belief in the beneficent possibilities of positive federal government." Ibid., 4. Compare Laura Kalman, *The Strange Career of Liberal Legalism* (New Haven, Conn.: Yale University Press, 1998).

115. Ibid., 216. See Alfred H. Kelly, et al., *The American Constitution: Its Origins and Development*, 2 vols., 7th ed. (New York: W. W. Norton, 1991), II: chap. 30.

116. Thomas I. Emerson, "Freedom of Expression in Wartime," *University of Pennsylvania Law Review* 116 (1968): 975.

117. Belknap, "The Warren Court and the Vietnam War," 153–154.

118. Chemerinsky, The Deconstitutionalization of Education," 124–125.

Notes to Chapter 3

1. John Morton Blum, *Years of Discord: American Politics and Society, 1961–1974* (New York: W. W. Norton, 1991), 475.

2. Ibid., 479.

3. Mark Tushnet dates what he terms the "real" Warren Court, as compared to the more "ambiguously liberal Warren Court," as existing from 1962 until 1969. Mark Tushnet, ed., *The Warren Court in Historical and Political Perspective* (Charlottesville: University of Virginia Press, 1993), 7.

4. Kalman, *The Strange Career of Liberal Legalism*; and Laura Kalman, "Law, Politics, and the New Deal(s)," *Yale Law Journal* 108 (1999): 101.

5. See, for example, James C. Foster, *The Ideology of Apolitical Politics: Elite Lawyers' Response to the Legitimation Crisis of American Capitalism, 1870–1920* (New York: Garland, 1990); William W. Fisher III, Morton J. Horwitz, and Thomas A. Reed, eds., *American Legal Realism* (New York: Oxford University Press, 1993); Morton J. Horwitz, *The Transformation of American Law, 1870–1960: The Crisis of Legal Orthodoxy* (New York: Oxford University Press, 1992); and G. Edward White, "From Sociological Jurisprudence to Realism: Jurisprudence and Social Change in Early Twentieth-Century America," in G. Edward White, *Patterns of American Legal Thought* (Indianapolis: Bobbs-Merrill, 1978).

6. *Lochner v. New York*, 198 U.S. 45 (1905). Compare Howard Gilman, *The Constitution Besieged: The Rise and Demise of Lochner Era Police Power Jurisprudence* (Durham, N.C.: Duke University Press, 1993); and G. Edward White, *The Constitution and the New Deal* (Cambridge, Mass.: Harvard University Press, 2000).

7. Tushnet, ed., *The Warren Court in Historical and Political Perspective*, 13–14. Compare Horwitz: "The legal consciousness of the Warren Court liberals had been shaped by the struggle between Progressivism and the *Lochner* Court, which culminated in the New Deal triumph after 1937." Morton J. Horwitz, *The Warren Court and the Pursuit of Justice* (New York: Hill and Wang, 1998), 114.

8. See Bernard Schwartz, *Super Chief: Earl Warren and His Supreme Court—A Judicial Biography* (New York: New York University Press, 1983), 280–282. In some conservative quarters, opposition remains unabated. See, for instance, Virginia C. Armstrong, "'Impeach Earl Warren': The Warren Court's Legacy Fifty Years Later, Part I," *Eagle Forum's Court Watch* 5 (February 21, 2003), http://www.eagleforum.org/court_watch/alerts/2003/feb03/02-21-03Brief.shtml. Professor Cass Sunstein locates the attack on the Warren Court as the first of three attacks that conservative politicians have launched against the federal judiciary in the last fifty years. "Constitution and the Law Now under Attack," University of Chicago, Law School *News*, April 24, 2005, http://www.law.uchicago.edu/news/law-under-attack.html. Also see Steven M. Teles, *The Rise of the Conservative Legal Movement: The Battle for Control of the Law* (Princeton, N.J.: Princeton University Press, 2008).

9. For a thought-provoking look back at one of those billboards, located in Columbus, Ohio, see Bob Greene, "On Main Street, Signs of the Times Tell Two Stories," *Jewish World Review*, July 20, 2000, http://www.jewishworldreview.com/bob/greene072000.asp.

10. Jack Harrison Pollock, *Earl Warren: The Judge Who Changed America* (Englewood Cliffs, N.J.: Prentice Hall, 1979), 283. Compare G. Edward White, *Earl Warren: A Public Life* (New York: Oxford University Press, 1982), chap. 12.

11. But see Lee Epstein and Jeffrey A. Segal, *Advice and Consent: The Politics of Judicial Appointments* (New York: Oxford University Press, 2005); Lee Epstein, et al., "Ideological Drift among Supreme Court Justices: Who, When, and How Important?" *Northwestern Law Review* 101 (Fall 2007): 1483; Lawrence Baum, *The Supreme Court*, 9th ed. (Washington, D.C.: Congressional Quarterly, 2006), chap. 5; and Christopher E. Smith and Thomas R. Hensley, "Unfulfilled Aspirations: The Court-Packing Efforts of Presidents Reagan and Bush," *Albany Law Review* 57 (Fall 1994): 1111.

12. The current conventional wisdom is that they were not, and that it was only with the appointments of Chief Justice John G. Roberts Jr. (September 2005) and Justice Samuel Alito (January 2006) that the Court's direction has been decisively altered. Even so, Justice Anthony Kennedy's continuing pivotal role as a fifth (swing) vote renders this judgment debatable. See Jeffrey Toobin, *The Nine: Inside the Secret World of the Supreme Court* (New York: Doubleday, 2006).

13. John T. Woolley and Gerhard Peters, *The American Presidency Project* [online]. Santa Barbara: University of California (hosted), Gerhard Peters (database). Available from http://www.presidency.ucsb.edu/ws/?pid=39572.

14. David M. O'Brien, "The Reagan Judges: His Most Enduring Legacy?" in Charles O. Jones, ed. *The Reagan Legacy* (Chatham, N.J.: Chatham House, 1988), 60-61. Even though Republican presidents since Nixon have tended to muddle the two, a concern with law-and-order and a "strict" interpretation of the Constitution do not necessarily follow from one another. (Thanks to my colleague Neil Browne for making this point.)

15. *New Jersey v. T.L.O.*, 469 U.S. 325 (1985), *Bethel School Dist. No 403 v. Fraser*, 478 U.S. 657 (1986), *Hazelwood School District v. Kuhlmeier*, 484 U.S. 260 (1988), *Vernonia School Dist. 47J v. Acton*, 515 U.S. 646 (1995), *Board of Education of Independent School District No. 92 of Pottawatomie County v. Earls*, 536 U.S. 822 (2002).

16. This is how my colleague, Susan Leeson, felicitously described a key aspect of *Morse v. Frederick*.

17. James E. Ryan, "The Supreme Court and Public Schools," *Virginia Law Review* 86 (October 2000): 1403.

18. Ibid., note 17, 1340.

19. Ibid., 1340–1341, 1342.

20. *New Jersey v. T.L.O.*, 469 U.S. 325 (1985), 336–337.

21. Ibid., 337.

22. Ibid., 329 (emphasis added).

23. Ibid., 330–331.

24. The New Jersey Supreme Court's conclusion resulted from its view that the mere presence of cigarettes in T.L.O.'s purse had no bearing on the charge that she had been smoking, much less providing Principal Choplick reason for "rummaging" through her purse. Justice White termed this application a "somewhat crabbed notion of reasonableness." Ibid., 331, 343. In his *T.L.O.* dissent Justice Brennan referred to "Principal Choplick's thorough excavation of T.L.O.'s purse." Ibid., 355.

25. Ibid., 340.

26. Ibid., 337.

27. Ibid., 340.

28. Ibid., 341.

29. Ibid., 342. To this passage, Justice White added a footnote in which he cited *Tinker* in support of this view: "The maintenance of discipline in the schools requires not only that students be restrained from assaulting one another, abusing drugs and alcohol, and committing crimes, but also that students conform themselves to the standards of conduct prescribed by school authorities. We have 'repeatedly emphasized the need for affirming the comprehensive authority of the States and of school officials, consistent with fundamental constitutional safeguards, to prescribe and control conduct in the schools.' *Tinker v. Des Moines Independent Community School District*, 393 U.S. 503, 507."

30. *Tinker v. Des Moines School Dist.*, 393 U.S. 503 (1969), 514–515.

31. *New Jersey v. T.L.O.*, 469 U.S. 325 (1985), 347.

32. Ibid., 348–349.

33. Ibid., 362.

34. Ibid., 354.

35. Ibid., 361.

36. Ibid., 362, quoting *Olmstead v. United States*, 277 U.S. 438 (1928), 478 (J. Brandeis, dissenting).

37. Ibid., 362. In the context of fears underlying the War on Drugs, it instructive to read Justice Brennan's observation: "Moved by whatever momentary evil has aroused their fears, officials—perhaps even supported by a majority of citizens—may be tempted to conduct searches that sacrifice the liberty of each citizen to assuage the perceived evil." Ibid., 361.

38. Ibid., 370.

39. Ibid.

40. Ibid., 369.

41. Ibid. Justice Brennan opines: "[T]he text of the Fourth Amendment does not grant a shifting majority of this Court the authority to answer all Fourth Amendment questions by consulting its momentary vision of the social good." Ibid., 370.

42. Ibid.

43. Fraser's speech runs 117 words. In its entirety it reads: "I know a man who is firm—he's firm in his pants, and he's firm in his shirt, his character is firm—but most . . . of all, his belief in you, the students of Bethel, is firm. Jeff Kuhlman is a man who takes his point and pounds it in. If necessary, he'll take an issue and nail it to the wall. He doesn't attack things in spurts—he drives hard, pushing and pushing until finally—he succeeds. Jeff is a man who will go to the very end—even the climax, for each and every one of you. So vote for Jeff for A.S.B. vice-president—he'll never come between you and the best our high school can be." *Bethel School Dist. No. 403 v. Fraser,* 478 U.S. 657 (1986), 687.

Fraser's sophomoric speech (delivered when he was a senior) brings to mind Justice Potter Stewart's description of the Connecticut statute at issue in *Griswold v. Connecticut* as "uncommonly silly." *Griswold v. Connecticut,* 381 U.S. 479 (1965), 528 (J. Stewart, dissenting).

44. *Bethel School Dist. No. 403,* 678. The wording of this rule appears to reproduce the "materially and substantially interferes" language of *Tinker.*

45. David Hudson, "Matthew Fraser Speaks Out on 15-year-old Supreme Court Free-Speech Decision," April 17, 2001, http://www.freedomforum.org/templates/document.asp?documentID=13701.

46. *Bethel School Dist. No. 403,* 683. Apparently, Fraser's speech was so offensive to Chief Justice Warren Burger that Burger couldn't bring himself to quote it.

47. As if adolescent males aren't preoccupied with sex. Compare:

RICK (HUMPHREY BOGART): How can you close me up? On what grounds?

CAPTAIN RENAULT (CLAUDE RAINES): I'm shocked, shocked to find that gambling is going on in here!

[*A croupier hands Renault a pile of money.*]

CROUPIER: Your winnings, sir.

CAPTAIN RENAULT: [*sotto voce*] Oh, thank you very much.

CAPTAIN RENAULT: [*aloud*] Everybody out at once!

Casablanca (1942), Michael Curtiz, director, Warner Bros.

48. *Bethel School Dist. No. 403,* 680.

49. Ibid., 679.

50. Ibid., 680.

51. Ibid., 681.

52. Burger cites *Tinker* to support his view that "The inculcation of these [fundamental] values is truly the 'work of the schools.' *Tinker,* 393 U.S., at 508." Ibid., 683. In fact, Justice Fortas' *Tinker* opinion does not specify the "work of the schools" in the particular passage Burger quoted.

53. Ibid., 682.

54. Ibid., 686. Revealingly, the language of in loco parentis makes an appearance in Burger's majority opinion. Citing *Ginsberg v. New York,* 390 U.S. 629 (1968) and the plurality opinion in *Board of Education v. Pico,* 457 U.S. 853 (1982), Burger says: "These cases recognize the obvious concern on the part of parents and school authorities acting *in loco parentis,* to protect children—especially a captive audience—from exposure to sexually explicit, indecent, or lewd speech." Ibid., 684.

55. As a kid, I collected bubblegum cards with funny sayings—funny to an eight-year-old. One of those sayings was "Keep your eye on the ball, your shoulder to the wheel, your nose to the grindstone, keep your feet on the ground—now try working in that position."

56. In his strategic decision to modify by joining, Justice Brennan's *Fraser* concurrence is reminiscent of Justice Brandeis' strategic concurrence in *Whitney v. People of State of California*, 274 U.S. 357 (1927). Of course, the long-term effectiveness of Justice Brennan's approach remains to be seen. Compare Lee Epstein and Jack Knight, *The Choices Justices Make* (Washington, D.C.: Congressional Quarterly Press, 1998); and Pablo T. Spiller, "Review of *The Choices Justices Make*," *American Political Science Review* 94 (December 2000): 943.

57. *Bethel School Dist. No. 403*, 689.

58. Justice Stevens also dissented, primarily on grounds that Fraser did not receive "fair notice" of the scope of the Bethel High School prohibition of offensive speech. See Ibid., 691–696.

59. Ibid., 690.

60. See, for instance, Sara Slaff, "Note: Silencing Student Speech: *Bethel School District No.403 v. Fraser*," *American University Law Review* 37 (Fall 1987): 219: "Although Justice Brennan claims that the Court has reaffirmed *Tinker's* deference to student's free expression rights, his concurrence bespeaks a dismembering of *Tinker*. This case [*Fraser*], he contends, involves neither school officials' attempt to ban inappropriate speech or speech they disagree with. Rather, he views the Court's holding as limited to the authority of school officials to restrict a high school student's use of 'disruptive' language. Justice Brennan, however, cites no examples of disruption. As Justice Marshall stated in his dissenting opinion, where speech is involved, a school official's assertion that certain speech interfered with education cannot be accepted without question. . . . This seventeen-year-old may just have wanted to tell his fellow classmates that he and the student he was nominating were willing to say something his fellow students would find witty and amusing but that school officials might find offensive."

61. The other case was *Bowsher v. Synar*, 478 U.S. 714 (1986), which addressed the question of whether specific functions, assigned by the Gramm-Rudman-Hollings Deficit Control Act of 1985 to the U.S. Comptroller General, violated constitutional separation of powers. *Fraser* and *Bowsher* were handed down on July 7, 1985.

62. U.S. 260 (1988). *Hazelwood* involved administrators censoring a high school newspaper that is produced by students under school sponsorship. The case raised the profile of high school journalism, and of controversies over censoring student journalists. But the problem was not new. See Jack Nelson, *Captive Voices: The Report of the Commission of Inquiry into High School Journalism* (New York: Schocken Books, 1974).

63. *Hazelwood School District v. Kuhlmeier*, 484 U.S. 260 (1988), 266.

64. Ryan, "The Supreme Court and Public Schools," 1423.

65. F. Supp. 1450 (1985).

66. *Hazelwood*, 264.

67. *Hazelwood*, 265.

68. See above, 61.

69. *Hazelwood*, 270, quoting *Perry Education Assn. v. Perry Local Educators' Assn.* 460 U.S. 37, 47 (1983).

70. Ibid., 270–271.

71. Ibid., 276.

72. Ibid., 271–272.

73. Ibid., 266–267.

74. See *Hazelwood*, 282–285 and, below, 39–43.

75. See Ibid., 277, 291. When I teach *Hazelwood*, I juxtapose White's and Brennan's opinions as alternative "civics lessons" informed by deeply opposing views on the roles, rights, and responsibilities of high school students.

76. Ibid., 278.

77. Ibid., 289.

78. Ibid., 287.

79. Ibid., (referencing White, J., Ibid., 272).

80. Ibid., 287–288, quoting *Shuttlesworth v. Birmingham*, 394 U.S. 147, 150 (1969).

81. Ibid., 288.

82. *Vernonia School Dist. 47J v. Acton*, 515 U.S. 646 (1995), 650.

83. Ibid., 649, quoting the District Court opinion, 796 F. Supp. 1354, 1357 (D. Ore. 1992).

84. The Actons also argued that the Vernonia policy violated Article I §9 of the Oregon Constitution. The U.S. Supreme Court rejected that argument: "The Ninth Circuit held that Vernonia's Policy not only violated the Fourth Amendment, but also, by reason of that violation, contravened Article I §9 of the Oregon Constitution. Our conclusion that the former holding was in error means that the latter holding rests on a flawed premise." Ibid., 666. On remand, concluding that "the Oregon Supreme Court would not offer greater protection under the provisions of Oregon Constitution in this case," a panel of the Ninth Circuit affirmed the District Court's original judgment (*Acton v. Vernonia School District 47J* 66 F.3d 217 [9th Cir. 1995]). Judge Reinhardt dissented. He characterized this outcome as "throw[ing] up our hands and simply proclaim[ing] that random, suspicionless drug tests are consistent with the Oregon Constitution as well [as the Fourth Amendment]." *Acton v. Vernonia School District*, 92-35520 D.C. No. CV-91-1154-MFM (September 15, 1995).

85. Justice Kennedy did not participate in *Hazelwood* because he had not yet joined the Court when it was argued. Given that he voted with the majority in *Vernonia*, it is not unreasonable to think that Kennedy would have joined the *Hazelwood* majority, which would have made *Hazelwood* a 6–3 decision.

86. See Justice Brennan's dissent in *Hazelwood*, 282–285.

87. Scalia was joined by Chief Justice Rehnquist, and Justices Breyer, Ginsburg, Kennedy, and Thomas.

88. *Hazelwood*, 266.

89. See Justice White above, 26, quoting *Fraser* (referencing *T.L.O.*), *Hazelwood*, 266.

90. *Vernonia*, 655 (emphasis added).

91. Ibid., 656.

92. Ibid., 655. Compare Ryan, "The Supreme Court and Public Schools," 1360–1364.

93. *Hazelwood*, 271.

94. Ibid., 271–272, quoting *Brown v. Board of Education*, 347 U.S. 483, 493 (1954).

95. *Vernonia*, 654.

96. O'Connor was joined by Justices Souter and Stevens.

97. Ibid., 679.

98. Ibid., 667.

99. Ibid., 680.

100. Ibid., 681.

101. Justice Ginsburg wrote a very short concurring opinion in *Vernonia* in which she appears to join the majority only because the Vernonia Student Athlete Drug Policy targets solely those voluntarily participating in sports, and because the most severe sanction is suspension from playing sports. Presciently, perhaps, she added: "I comprehend the Court's opinion as reserving the question whether the District, on no more than the showing made here, constitutionally could impose routine drug testing not only on those seeking to engage with others in team sports, but on all students required to attend school." Ibid., 666.

102. Bernard James and Joanne E. K. Larson, "The Doctrine of Deference: Shifting Constitutional Presumptions and the Supreme Court's Restatement of Student Rights after *Board of Education v. Earls*," *South Carolina Law Review* 56 (Autumn 2004): 1, 23.

103. James' ineligibility raised the question of standing to sue. The district court set aside that matter and allowed the suit to proceed due to Earls' clear standing. The U.S. Supreme Court agreed.

104. Kendra E. Fish and Stephanie Pfeffer, "*Board of Education of Independent School District No. 92 of Pottawatomie County, et al. v. Earls, Lindsay, et al.*" *On the Docket*, Medill Journalism, Northwestern University, posted June 23, 2004, http://docket.medill.northwestern.edu/archives/000605.php#relatedlinks.

105. *Board of Education v. Earls*, 828.

106. *Vernonia*, 665.

107. *Board of Education v. Earls*, 830, citing *Vernonia*. Compare Justice Breyer: "The law itself recognizes [the diverse] responsibilities [of public schools] with the phrase *in loco parentis*—a phrase that draws its legal force from the needs of younger students (who here are necessarily grouped together with older high school students) and which reflects, not that a child or adolescent lacks an interest in privacy, but that a child's or adolescent's school-related privacy interest, when compared to the privacy interests of an adult, has different dimensions." Ibid., 840.

108. Ibid., 838.

109. Ibid.

110. Compare James and Larson, "The Doctrine of Deference," passim.

111. *Board of Education v. Earls*, 843.

112. Ibid., 844.

113. Ibid., 845.

114. Ibid., 848.

115. Ibid., 846.

116. Ibid., 851. Compare: "[T]his case resembles *Vernonia* only in that the School Districts in both cases conditioned engagement in activities outside the obligatory curriculum on random subjection to urinalysis. The defining characteristics of the two programs, however, are entirely dissimilar." Ginsburg, J., Ibid., 853.

117. Ibid., 851–852.

118. A LexisNexis *Academic* search of Tinker [and] Pottawatomie [and] students [and] Fourth [and] First [and] Amendment yielded forty-one law review articles.

119. James and Larson, "The Doctrine of Deference," 4, 64. Compare, "[I]n the three decades since *Tinker*, the courts have made it clear that students leave most of their constitutional rights at the schoolhouse gate." Chemerinsky, "Students Do Leave Their First Amendment Rights at the Schoolhouse Gate," 527, 530.

120. Joseph Russomanno, "Dissent Yesterday and Today: The *Tinker* Case and Its Legacy," *Communications Law and Policy* 11 (Summer 2006): 387.

121. At a dramatic moment in his splendid *Peter and the Wolf*—just after the wolf has swallowed the duck—Sergei Prokofiev's narrator pauses to take stock: "This was now the situation: the cat was perched on one branch of the tree . . . /and the little bird on another . . . /a little way from the cat./And below them the wolf was pacing around the tree, looking up at them with greedy eyes." Sergei Prokofiev, *Peter and the Wolf*, 1936, http://library.thinkquest.org/C005400/musi/prokofievpnw.html.

122. Limbo: "**a:** a place or state of restraint or confinement **b:** a place or state of neglect or oblivion . . . **c:** an intermediate or transitional place or state **d:** a state of uncertainty." Merriam-Webster online search, http://www.merriam-webster.com/dictionary/limbo.

123. See above, 68.

124. *Hazelwood*, 283.

125. Ibid., 282. Here is Justice Brennan's take on the majority's "obscure tangle of three excuses": "[1] the public educator's prerogative to control curriculum; [2] the pedagogical interest in shielding the high school audience from objectionable viewpoints and sensitive topics; and [3] the school's

need to dissociate itself from student expression. None of the[se] excuses, once disentangled, support the distinction that the Court draws. *Tinker* fully addresses the first concern; the second is illegitimate; and the third is readily achievable through less oppressive means." Ibid., 282–283.

126. Ibid., 283. Brennan explained: "under *Tinker*, the school may constitutionally punish the budding political orator if he disrupts calculus class, but not if he holds his tongue for the cafeteria. . . . That is . . . because . . . student speech in the noncurricular context is less likely to disrupt materially any legitimate pedagogical purpose." Ibid.

127. Ibid., 283–284.

128. Ibid., 291, quoting *West Virginia State Board of Ed. v. Barnette*, 319 U.S. 624 (1943), 637.

129. Ibid., 290.

130. Ibid.

131. See note 122, above.

132. See note 122, above.

133. Compare James and Larson: "Due to the fragile majority in *Earls*, . . . Justice Breyer . . . is the controlling vote to hold the feet of educators to what little fire the Fourth Amendment produces in the area of student rights as long as the Court holds it current composition." "The Doctrine of Deference," 53–54.

Notes to Chapter 4

1. See Bruce Ackerman, *The Failure of the Founding Fathers: Jefferson, Marshall, and the Rise of Presidential Democracy* (Cambridge, Mass.: Harvard University Press, 2005).

2. David M. Silver, *Lincoln's Supreme Court* (Urbana: University of Illinois Press, 1998), 86–87.

3. See Gregory A. Caldeira, "Public Opinion and The U.S. Supreme Court: FDR's Court-Packing Plan," *American Political Science Review* 81 (December 1987): 1139. Compare Christopher Shea, "Supreme Switch: Did FDR's threat to 'pack' the court in 1937 really change the course of constitutional history?" Critical Faculties, *Boston Globe*, December 4, 2005, http://www.boston.com/news/globe/ideas/articles/2005/12/04/supreme_switch/.

4. See ch. 2, 55–56; ch. 3, 57–60.

5. John W. Dean, *The Rehnquist Choice: The Untold Story of the Nixon Appointment that Redefined the Supreme Court* (New York: John Wiley, 2001), 86.

6. Warren Burger had been an outspoken conservative voice on the D.C. Circuit Court of Appeals, especially critical of the defense of criminal defendants' rights under Chief Justice Earl Warren. See Earl M. Maltz, *The Chief Justiceship of Warren Burger, 1969–1986* (Columbia: University of South Carolina Press, 2000), chap. 1.

7. Jeffrey K. Tullis, "Constitutional Abdication: The Senate, the President, and Appointments to the Supreme Court," *Case Western Reserve Law Review* 47 (Summer 1997): 1331.

8. Quoted in Henry J. Abraham, *Justices and Presidents*, 3rd ed. (New York: Oxford University Press, 1992), 320.

9. See Tullis, "Constitutional Abdication"; and Jeff Yates and William Gillespie, "Supreme Court Power Play: Assessing the Appropriate Role of the Senate in the Confirmation Process," *Washington and Lee Law Review* 58 (Summer 2001): 1053. For details of the Fortas fight, see Laura Kalman, *Abe Fortas* (New Haven, Conn.: Yale University Press, 1990).

10. See, for instance, Gregory A. Caldeira and John R. Wright, "Lobbying for Justice: Organized Interests, Supreme Court Nominations, and the United States Senate," *American Journal of Political Science* 42 (April 1998): 499.

11. Adam Liptak, "The Memo That Rehnquist Wrote and Had to Disown," *New York Times*, September 11, 2005, http://www.nytimes.com/2005/09/11/weekinreview/11lipt.html.

12. Morris P. Fiorina, *Divided Government* (New York: Macmillan, 1992). Compare Mark Silverstein, *Judicious Choices: The Politics of Supreme Court Confirmations*, 2nd ed. (New York: W. W. Norton, 2007); and Kevin J. McMahon, "Presidents, Political Regimes, and Contentious Supreme Court Nominations: A Historical Institutional Model," *Law and Social Inquiry* 32 (Fall 2007): 919–922. Also compare Keith E. Whittington, "Presidents, Senates, and Failed Supreme Court Nominations," *Supreme Court Review* (2006): 401.

13. McMahon, "Presidents, Political Regimes, and Contentious Supreme Court Nominations," 943.

14. Stephen Skowronek quoted in McMahon, "Presidents, Political Regimes, and Contentious Supreme Court Nominations," 943. Compare Stephen Skowronek, *The Politics Presidents Make: Leadership from John Adams to George Bush* (Cambridge, Mass.: Harvard University Press, 1993). Following Skowronek, McMahon distinguishes President Nixon, who sought to preempt and disrupt New Deal Liberalism, from President Johnson, an architect of New Deal Liberalism, who was totally affiliated with that policy regime.

15. Russell Caplan, "The Paradoxes of Judicial Review in a Constitutional Democracy," *Buffalo Law Review* 30 (1981): 456.

16. Keith E. Whittington, "William H. Rehnquist: Nixon's Strict Constructionist, Reagan's Chief Justice," in Earl M. Maltz, ed., *Rehnquist Justice: Understanding the Court Dynamic* (Lawrence: University Press of Kansas, 2003), chap. 1.

17. Ibid., 10.

18. Alfred H. Kelly, Winfred A. Harbison, and Herman Belz, *The American Constitution: Its Origins and Development*, 7th ed., 2 vols. (New York: W. W. Norton, 1991), 2: 678.

19. Vincent Blasi, ed., *The Burger Court: The Counter-Revolution That Wasn't* (New Haven, Conn.: Yale University Press, 1983).

20. Ibid., ix.

21. Beverly B. Cook, "Justice Sandra Day O'Connor: Transition to a Republican Court Agenda," in Charles M. Lamb and Stephen C. Halpern, eds., *The Burger Court: Political and Judicial Profiles* (Urbana: University of Illinois Press, 1991), 239.

22. Ibid.

23. Skowronek, *The Politics Presidents Make*.

24. McMahon, "Presidents, Political Regimes, and Contentious Supreme Court Nominations," 933.

25. Ibid., 935.

26. Ibid.

27. Maltz, *The Chief Justiceship of Warren Burger, 1969-1986*, 10.

28. Charles M. Lamb, "Chief Justice Warren E. Burger: A Conservative Chief for Conservative Times," in *The Burger Court*, Lamb and Halpern, eds., 159.

29. See, for example, Melvin I. Urofsky, "Introduction," *Journal of Supreme Court History* 32 (November 2007): v–vii; Christopher P. Banks, "The Supreme Court and Precedent: An Analysis of Natural Courts and Reversal Trends," in Elliot E. Slotnick, *Judicial Politics: Readings from Judicature*, 2nd ed. (Lanham, Md.: Rowman and Littlefield, 1999), 378; and Linda Greenhouse, "Under the Microscope Longer Than Most," *New York Times*, July 10, 2005, http://www.nytimes.com/2005/07/10/weekinreview/10greenhouse.html.

30. Mark V. Tushnet, "Symposium on *Democracy and Distrust*: Ten Years Later: Foreword," *Virginia Law Review* 77 (May 1991): 634.

31. Two years after he proffered the "Brennan Court" description, Professor Tushnet qualified it: "That [name] . . . makes too much of Brennan's role within the Court. Labelling Courts is an exercise

in cultural analysis, and the real question is what the public understands about the Supreme Court and its history. Brennan was primarily a tactician devising ways to implement a vision clearly and properly associated with Warren. In that sense, there was a Warren Court, and not a Brennan Court." Mark V. Tushnet, ed., *The Warren Court in Historical and Political Perspective* (Charlottesville: University Press of Virginia, 1993), 33.

In another sense, Tushnet's original description is more accurate than his subsequent view. "Soon after his arrival ... Brennan formed a unique relationship with Earl Warren. A large man and a politician by trade, Warren led the Court by force of personality, but he was no one's idea of a brilliant lawyer. However, he soon had one working with him in Brennan. Together they set the agenda for the liberal Court of the 1960s." David G. Savage, *Turning Right: The Making of the Rehnquist Supreme Court* (New York: John Wiley & Son, 1992), 125–126. Compare Peter Irons' reference to the description of Justice Brennan, upon Brennan's 1990 retirement, as "the senior associate justice who some called the 'shadow chief justice' in the parlance of British politics." Peter Irons, *Brennan vs. Rehnquist: The Battle for the Constitution* (New York: Alfred A. Knopf, 1994), 322. Also compare Frank Michelman, "A Tribute to William J. Brennan, Jr." *Harvard Law Review* 104 (1990): 22; Mark V. Tushnet, "Themes in Warren Court Biographies," *N.Y.U. Law Review* 70 (1995): 748; and Laura Kalman, "Members of the Warren Court in Judicial Biography: Commentary: The Wonder of the Warren Court," *N.Y.U. Law Review* 70 (1995): 780, n. 23.

32. Savage, *Turning Right*, 126–127.

33. This was Attorney General Edwin Meese's assessment in recommending Rehnquist's nomination to Reagan. Savage, *Turning Right*, 15.

34. See Norman Vieira and Leonard Gross, *Supreme Court Appointments: Judge Bork and the Politicization of Senate Confirmations* (Carbondale: Southern Illinois University Press, 1998); and McMahon, "Presidents, Political Regimes, and Contentious Supreme Court Nominations," 935–937. Compare Robert H. Bork, *The Tempting of America: The Political Seduction of the Law* (New York: Simon and Schuster, 1991).

35. Savage, *Turning Right*, 23.

36. Ibid., 22.

37. Ibid., 37.

38. Ibid., 22.

39. Mark Silverstein, *Judicious Choices: The Politics of Supreme Court Confirmations*, 2nd ed. (New York: W. W. Norton, 2007), 151. Richard Nixon had adopted a similar tactic in 1971 when he simultaneously nominated William Rehnquist and Lewis Powell. In that instance, Rehnquist was a lightning rod shielding Powell. Amid an illustrious legal career, Powell had been Chair of the Richmond, Virginia, school board during the massive resistance to *Brown v. Board of Education*, he sat on several corporate boards including Philip Morris, and he had written a letter, known as the "Powell Memorandum," widely circulated among members of the U.S. Chamber of Commerce, in which Powell urged corporations to launch a defense of the free enterprise system in the face of what he saw as liberal attacks on business.

40. McMahon, "Presidents, Political Regimes, and Contentious Supreme Court Nominations," 937–938.

41. Justices Brennan and Marshall were replaced, respectively, by David Souter and Clarence Thomas.

42. These descriptions are Jeffrey Toobin's, from *The Nine: Inside the Secret World of the Supreme Court*, 7, 48, 129. Compare Diane Lowenthal and Barbara Palmer, "Justice Sandra Day O'Connor and Her Influence on Issues of Race, Religion, Gender and Class: Justice Sandra Day O'Connor: The World's Most Powerful Jurist?" *University of Maryland Law Journal of Race, Religion, Gender, and*

Class 4 (Fall 2004): 211. Compare Nancy Maveety, *Queen's Court: Judicial Power in the Rehnquist Era* (Lawrence: University Press of Kansas, 2008).

43. Jacob W. Landynski, "Justice Lewis F. Powell Jr.: Balance Wheel of the Court," in Lamb and Halpern, eds., *The Burger Court*, 276.

44. With regard to Justice O'Connor's pragmatism, I believe her colleague Justice Anthony M. Kennedy got it right: "As for the . . . issue of Justice O'Connor's overarching jurisprudential theory, please permit a brief observation. It would be too bold to ask Justice O'Connor, 'Are you a pragmatist?' Since the term is sometimes used to describe her approach, though, we can speculate on what her answer might be. She would say, it seems to me, that if the question asks whether she subscribes to the formal system described by James, Pierce, and Dewey, she would decline to embrace the entirety of their philosophy. For the formal pragmatist school, 'No abstract concept can be a valid substitute for a concrete reality.' I should think she could not accept this principle, because to do so would cast doubt upon belief in the innate spirituality of humankind. On the other hand, she would be pleased, I should think, to acknowledge that if by 'pragmatic' we mean paying serious attention to real-world consequences, this is a good attribute for a judge. Even in this limited sense, pragmatism does not suggest result-driven thinking. Awareness of real-world consequences is a far cry from having a preexisting purpose to achieve a particular outcome.

"Perhaps at this point in the hypothetical dialogue, Justice O'Connor would interject an additional observation: 'And just what do you think the case system is all about? One of its objects is to make judges aware of the consequences of their decisions. If pragmatism is used in this sense, without linking it to the formal philosophic school of that name, then the label is fine with me.' Her [autobiography] about the Lazy B, it is worth noting, describes a way of life in which utility, while not the sole value, cannot be shrugged off as irrelevant." Anthony M. Kennedy, "Tribute: William Rehnquist and Sandra Day O'Connor: An Expression of Appreciation," *Stanford Law Review* 58 (April 2006): 1669–1670. Compare Jeff Bleich, Anne Voigts, and Michelle Friedland, "A Practical Era: The Beginning (or the End) of Pragmatism," *Oregon State Bar Bulletin* 65 (August/September 2005): 19.

45. This term may have been coined by Circuit Judge J. Harvie Wilkinson III, in "The Rehnquist Court at Twilight: The Lures and Perils of Split-the-Difference Jurisprudence," *Stanford Law Review* 58 (April 2006): 1969. But compare Kathleen L. Sullivan, "The Supreme Court: 1991 Term—Foreword: The Justices of Rules and Standards," *Harvard Law Review* 106 (1992): 22; James F. Simon, *The Center Holds: The Power Struggle Inside the Rehnquist Court* (New York: Simon and Schuster, 1995); and Jeffrey Rosen, "Dialogue: Who Cares?" *N.Y.U. Law Review* 40 (1996): 899.

Also compare Lyle Denniston, "Rehnquist to Roberts: The 'Reagan Revolution' Fulfilled?" *University of Pennsylvania Law Review* 154 (June 2006): 63, esp. n. 13; John F. Basiak Jr., "The Roberts Court and the Future of Substantive Due Process: The Demise of 'Split-the-Difference' Jurisprudence?" *Whittier Law Review* 28 (Spring 2007): 861; and Richard A. Epstein, "The Federalism Decisions of Justices Rehnquist and O'Connor: Is Half a Loaf Enough?" *Stanford Law Review* 58 (April 2006): 1793.

46. Cass R. Sunstein, *One Case at a Time: Judicial Minimalism on the Supreme Court* (Cambridge, Mass.: Harvard University Press, 1999). Compare Jay D. Wexler, "Defending the Middle Way: Intermediate Scrutiny as Judicial Minimalism," *George Washington Law Review* 66 (January 1998): 298.

47. Wilkinson, "The Rehnquist Court at Twilight," 1972; and Thomas M. Keck, *The Most Activist Supreme Court in History: The Road to Modern Judicial Conservatism* (Chicago: University of Chicago Press, 2004), 292–293.

48. Ibid.

49. Ibid., 1971, 1972. Jeffrey Toobin writes that O'Connor's "judicial approach was indefensible in theory and impeccable in practice." Toobin, *The Nine*, 226.

50. *Planned Parenthood of Southeastern Pennsylvania v. Casey,* 505 U.S. 833 (1992), 877. Justice O'Connor first embraced the undue burden standard, dissenting in *City of Akron v. Akron Center for Reproductive Health,* 462 U.S. 416 (1983), 461. The standard itself makes its first appearance in the abortion context in *Maher v. Roe,* 432 U.S. 464 (1977), 473–474. Compare *Carey v. Population Services International,* 311 U.S. 678 (1977), 688.

51. *Grutter v. Bollinger,* 539 U.S. 306 (2003), 324.

52. Bleich, Voigts, and Friedland, "A Practical Era," 19.

53. *New Jersey v. T.L.O.,* 469 U.S. 325 (1985), 337.

54. Ibid., 340.

55. Ibid., 350.

56. The two quotes in this sentence are from ibid.

57. Ibid., 349–350.

58. Ibid., 349.

59. The two quotes in this sentence are from *Vernonia School District 47J v. Acton,* 515 U.S. 646 (1995), 667.

60. See *T.L.O.,* 348.

61. *Vernonia,* 678–679.

62. Ibid., 686.

63. *Board of Education of Independent School District No. 92 of Pottawatomie County v. Earls,* 536 U.S. 822 (2002), 842.

64. See, for instance, Savage, *Turning Right;* Stanley H. Friedelbaum, *The Rehnquist Court: In Pursuit of Judicial Conservatism* (Westport, Conn.: Greenwood Press, 1994); Edward Lazarus, *Closed Chambers: The Rise, Fall, and Future of the Modern Supreme Court* (New York: Penguin Books, 1999); Stephen E. Gottlieb, *Morality Imposed: The Rehnquist Court and Liberty in America* (New York: New York University Press, 2000); Tinsley E. Yarbrough, *The Rehnquist Court and the Constitution* (New York: Oxford University Press, 2000); Martin H. Belsky, ed., *The Rehnquist Court: A Retrospective* (New York: Oxford University Press, 2002); Martin Garbus, *Courting Disaster: The Supreme Court and the Unmaking of American Law* (New York: Times Books, 2002); Herman Schwartz, ed., *The Rehnquist Court: Judicial Activism on the Right* (New York: Hill and Wang, 2002); Earl M. Maltz, ed., *Rehnquist Justice: Understanding the Court Dynamic* (Lawrence: University Press of Kansas, 2003); and Mark Tushnet, *A Court Divided: The Rehnquist Court and the Future of Constitutional Law* (New York: W. W. Norton, 2005).

65. Linda Greenhouse, "Foreword: The Third Rehnquist Court," in Craig M. Bradley, *The Rehnquist Legacy* (New York: Cambridge University Press, 2006).

66. Thomas W. Merrill, "The Making of the Second Rehnquist Court: A Preliminary Analysis," *St. Louis Law Journal* 47 (Spring 2003): 569. Compare John O. McGinnis, "Continuity and Coherence in the Rehnquist Court," *St. Louis Law Journal* 47 (Spring 2003): 875; and Tushnet, *A Court Divided,* 67–70.

For a different explanation of the Court's work under Chief Justice Rehnquist, see Keck, *The Most Activist Supreme Court in History.*

67. "[D]ifferences in personnel and rates of change in personnel; differences in the number of cases heard by the Court; a shift in emphasis from cases presenting social issues to cases presenting issues of constitutional federalism; differences in the number of 5–4 decisions and the willingness of the Justices to adopt important legal innovations in 5–4 decisions; and differences in the number of plurality decisions. Merrill, "The Making of the Second Rehnquist Court," 573–574.

68. The so-called "attitudinal model," "internal strategic actor hypothesis," "external strategic actor hypothesis," and "Court in flux/Court in stasis hypothesis."

69. All quotations in this paragraph, subsequent to the previous footnote, are from Merrill, "The Making of the Second Rehnquist Court," 652. Merrill also offers this final lesson: "for both lawyers and political scientists . . . that far too little attention has been given in the past to the rate of turnover on collegial courts. One can distinguish three states of affairs: normal turnover, which historically has been about one new Justice every two years; above normal turnover; and subnormal turnover. The first Rehnquist Court was a Court of above normal turnover; the second Rehnquist Court a Court of subnormal turnover. I have argued in a preliminary fashion that a Court with above normal turnover is more likely to experience important changes in institutional inputs—the norms that govern institutional behavior. A Court with subnormal turnover is more likely to develop stable and powerful coalitions that produce important changes in institutional outputs—the legal doctrine produced by such Courts." Ibid., 652–653.

70. Linda Greenhouse, "The Year Rehnquist May Have Lost His Court," *New York Times*, July 4, 2004, A1.

71. Greenhouse, "Foreword," xiv.

72. *Rasul v. Bush*, 542 U.S. 466 (2004) (jurisdiction over Guantanamo detainees); *Tennessee v. Lane*, 541 U.S. 509 (2004) (Eleventh Amendment immunity); *Lawrence v. Texas*, 539 U.S. 558 (2003) (sodomy laws); *Grutter v. Bollinger*, 539 U.S. 982 (2003) (affirmative action); *Blakely v. Washington*, 542 U.S. 296 (2004) (criminal-sentencing guidelines); *McConnell v. Federal Election Commission*, 540 U.S. 93 (2003) (campaign finance law); *Elk Grove Unified School District v. Newdow*, 542 U.S. 1 (2004) ("under God" in Pledge of Allegiance); *Brown v. Legal Foundation of Washington*, 538 U.S. 216 (2003) (takings); *Sosa v. Alvarez-Machain*, 542 U.S. 692 (2004) (human rights claims by foreigners); *Vieth v. Jubelirer*, 541 U.S. 267 (2004) (gerrymandering as a justiciable claim); *Roper v. Simmons*, 543 U.S. 551 (2005) (juvenile death penalty); *Jackson v. Birmingham Board of Education*, 544 U.S. 167 (2005) (Title IX retaliation case); *Gonzales v. Raich*, 545 U.S. 1 (2005) (medical marijuana); *Kelo v. City of New London*, 545 U.S. 469 (2005) (takings).

73. Greenhouse, "Foreword," xv.

74. *Seminole Tribe of Florida v. Florida*, 517 U.S. 44 (1996), *City of Boerne v. Flores*, 521 U.S. 507 (1997), *Kimel v. Florida Board of Regents*, 528 U.S. 62 (2000), *Board of Trustees of the University of Alabama v. Garrett*, 531 U.S. 356 (2001). Compare Rehnquist's opinion twenty-eight years earlier in *Fry v. United States*, 421 U.S. 542 (1975); and *Hans v. Louisiana*, 134 U.S. 1 (1890).

75. "The Congress shall have power to enforce, by appropriate legislation, the provisions of this article."

76. Greenhouse, "Foreword," xviii.

77. *Nevada Dept. of Human Resources v. Hibbs*, 538 U.S. 721 (2003), 735.

78. *Zelman v. Simmons-Harris*, 536 U.S. 639 (2002). Compare Rehnquist's opinion nineteen years previously in *Mueller v. Allen*, 463 U.S. 388 (1983).

79. *Locke v. Davey*, 540 U.S. 712 (2004), 718, quoting *Walz* v. *TaxComm'n of City of New York*, 397 U. S. 664 (1970), 669.

80. *Locke*, 725.

81. Greenhouse, "Foreword," xvii.

82. Sunstein, *One Case at a Time*.

83. Greenhouse, "Foreword," xx.

84. Ibid., xviii, xx.

85. O'Connor's balance also is evident in Justice Steven's majority opinion in *Tennessee v. Lane*, 541 U.S. 509 (2004). (States liable to suits under the Americans with Disabilities Act to enforce a due process right of access to courts.) Justice O'Connor joined the *Lane* majority, parting company with Rehnquist for the first time in a state immunity case. Chief Justice Rehnquist dissented: "the fact that

the majority had decided the case narrowly and saved the harder issues for another day bought it no credit with the Chief Justice; to the contrary, he stops just short of accusing the majority of having pulled off an intellectually dishonest trick." Ibid., xx.

86. For "comfort level" and "felt need" see ibid., xviii.

87. For "surrounding constitutional culture" see ibid. Greenhouse derives the term from Robert C. Post, "Foreword: Fashioning the Legal Constitution: Culture, Courts, and the Law," *Harvard Law Review* 117 (2003): 4.

88. Greenhouse, "Foreword," xix, quoting John C. Jeffries Jr., "*Bakke* Revisited," *Supreme Court Review* (2003): 1, at 24, 21.

89. Referring to Justice O'Connor's pivotal role on the Court during Rehnquist's tenure, Greenhouse says: "the Court's center of gravity lies where it so often has." Ibid., xv.

90. Shakespeare, *Henry IV*, part 1, V, iv. (As my English professor colleague, Neil Browne, observes, Falstaff was, among other things, variously a coward, liar, cheat, and drunkard. Falstaff also was a masterful wit, raconteur par excellence, and true friend.)

Mark Tushnet points out that "judicial minimalism paradoxically maximizes judicial power." Thomas M. Keck quoting Mark Tushnet in Keck, *The Most Activist Supreme Court in History*, 292. Compare Alexander M. Bickel, "The Passive Virtues," *Harvard Law Review* 75 (November 1961): 40; Gerald Gunther, "The Subtle Vices of the 'Passive Virtues'—A Comment on Principle and Expediency in Judicial Review," *Columbia Law Review* 64 (1964): 1; and Henry J. Abraham, *The Judicial Process: An Introductory Analysis of the Courts of the United States, England, and France*, 4th ed. (New York: Oxford University Press, 1980), 295ff.

91. See, for instance, Lee Epstein, Andrew D. Martin, Kevin M. Quinn, and Jeffery A. Segal, "Ideological Drift among Supreme Court Justices: Who, When, and How Important?" *Northwestern University Law Review* 101 (Fall 2007): 1483; Linda Greenhouse, "Justices Who Change: A Response to Epstein et al.," *Northwestern University Law Review* 101 (Fall 2007): 1885; and Toobin, *The Nine*, chap. 25 and Epilogue.

92. See, for example, *Baze v. Rees*, 553 U.S. 35 (2008), a death penalty decision from Kentucky in which six of the seven justices making up the fragmented majority wrote separate opinions.

93. See Erwin Chemerinsky, "The Kennedy Court: October Term 2005," *Green Bag* 2, no. 9 (Summer 2006): 335; compare Paul H. Edelman and Jim Chen, "The Rehnquist Court in Empirical and Statistical Retrospective: The Most Dangerous Justice Rides into the Sunset," *Constitutional Commentary* 24 (Spring 2007): 199.

94. Ann Carey McFeatters, *Sandra Day O'Connor: Justice in the Balance* (Albuquerque: University of New Mexico Press, 2005), chap. 12.

95. Joan Biskupic, *Sandra Day O'Connor: How the First Woman on the Supreme Court Became Its Most Influential Member* (New York: Harper, 2005).

96. Nancy Maveety, *Justice Sandra Day O'Connor: Strategist on the Supreme Court* (Lanham, Md.: Rowman and Littlefield, 1996), chap. 8. Actually, Maveety began formulating her view of Justice O'Connor in 1993. See Nancy Maveety and Robert C. Bradley, "Justice O'Connor: A Different Kind of Court Leader?" *Southeastern Political Review* 21 (1993): 39.

97. Maveety, *Justice Sandra Day O'Connor*, ix.

98. Ibid., chap. 1.

99. Contextual conservatism: "her conservatism is not categorical and rule bound, but sensitive to the particular elements and history of specific fact situations"; coalitional propensities: "she seems to consider the influence potential of being part of, if not necessary to, minimal winning coalitions on a collegial decision-making body"; pragmatic centrism: "she pursues the alternative leadership tactic of writing concurring opinions to shape the development of legal doctrine." Ibid., 4.

100. Ibid., 5.

101. The three quotes immediately above are from ibid., 5, 6. Compare Maveety, *Queen's Court: Judicial Power in the Rehnquist Era.*

102. Ibid., 3–4.

103. Wilson Ray Huhn, "The Constitutional Jurisprudence of Sandra Day O'Connor: A Refusal to 'Foreclose the Unanticipated,'" *Akron Law Review* 39 (2006): 373, 374.

104. Significantly, immediately after rejecting foreclosure of the unanticipated, Justice O'Connor cites two passages from the dissenting opinion in *Poe v. Ullman*, 367 U.S. 497 (1961) written by another highly respected judicial conservative, John M. Harlan, to wit: "Due process has not been reduced to any formula; its content cannot be determined by reference to any code"; and "there is no 'mechanical yard-stick,' no 'mechanical answer.'"

105. *Capitol Square Review and Advisory Board v. Pinnett*, 515 U.S. 753 (1995), 782–783. Given Justice O'Connor's proclivity toward contextualizing, it is useful to read the passage from which these eight words are excerpted: "To be sure, the endorsement test depends on a sensitivity to the unique circumstances and context of a particular challenged practice and, like any test that is sensitive to context, it may not always yield results with unanimous agreement at the margins." *Allegheny*, 492 U.S., at 629 (O'CONNOR, J., concurring in part and concurring in judgment). "In my view, however, this flexibility is a virtue and not a vice."

106. Huhn, "The Constitutional Jurisprudence of Sandra Day O'Connor," 374.

107. Most famously, and acerbically, Justice Scalia ridiculed Justice O'Connor's statement, concurring in *Webster v. Reproductive Health Service*, 492 U.S. 490 (1989), that "a 'fundamental rule of judicial restraint' requires us to avoid reconsidering *Roe* [*v. Wade*]," saying "her assertion . . . cannot be taken seriously." Twelve years later, dissenting in another abortion case, *Stenberg v. Carhart*, 530 U.S. 914 (2000), Justice Scalia took Justice O'Connor to task twice. First, he restated his view that the undue burden test (perhaps O'Connor's most notable contribution to constitutional jurisprudence) "created a standard that was 'as doubtful in application as it is unprincipled in origin'; . . . '[is] hopelessly unworkable in practice'; . . . '[and] ultimately standardless.'" Second, Scalia targeted O'Connor's *Stenberg* concurrence, saying: "I cannot understand why those who *acknowledge* that, in the opening words of Justice O'Connor's concurrence, '[t]he issue of abortion is one of the most contentious and controversial in contemporary American society,' . . . persist in the belief that this Court, armed with neither constitutional text nor accepted tradition, can resolve that contention and controversy rather than be consumed by it."

Notes to Chapter 5

1. Foreword to David C. Frederick, *Rugged Justice: The Ninth Circuit Court of Appeals in the American West, 1891–1941* (Berkeley: University of California Press, 1994), x.

2. Alaska, Arizona, California, Hawaii, Idaho, Montana, Nevada, Oregon, Washington, and the U.S. Territory of Guam and the Commonwealth of the Northern Mariana Islands.

3. Districts of Alaska, Arizona, Northern California, Central California, Eastern California, Southern California, Hawaii, Idaho, Montana, Nevada, Oregon, Eastern Washington, Western Washington, the U.S. Territory of Guam and the Commonwealth of the Northern Mariana Islands.

4. *U.S. Term Limits, Inc. v. Thornton*, 514 U.S. 779, 838-839 (1995).

5. See http://www.uscourts.gov/courtlinks.

6. Erwin Surrency reports that, from early in the nineteenth century, although required by statute to preside over courts within their assigned circuit, U.S. Supreme Court justices did so only irregularly. See his *History of the Federal Courts* (New York: Oceana, 1987). For one particularly harrowing story of

the rigors of circuit riding, see the accounts of a fateful encounter between David S. Terry and Stephen J. Field, the U.S. Supreme Court justice assigned to the Ninth Circuit, by Robert H. Kroninger, *Sarah and the Senator* (Berkeley, Calif.: Howell-North, 1964); and Carl Brent Swisher, *Stephen J. Field: Craftsman of the Law* (Chicago: University of Chicago Press, 1969 c1930).

7. Frederick, *Rugged Justice*, 15.

8. Ibid.

9. Congress had established the basic regional outline of the nine circuits in 1866. The circuit courts, originally established in 1789 (not to be confused with the circuit courts of appeal created in 1891) continued to exist and to share original jurisdiction with federal district courts until Congress abolished circuit courts in 1911.

10. In 1900, Congress assigned the judicial district of the Territory of Alaska to the Ninth Circuit and provided for appeals from the district court to the U.S. Circuit Court of Appeals for the Ninth Circuit. See also *The Coquitlam et al v. United States*, 163 U.S. 346 (1896).

11. The composition of the Ninth Circuit bench also is uniquely diverse in terms of its gender composition. See Rorie Spill Solberg, "Court Size and Diversity: The Ninth Circuit and Its Sisters," *Arizona Law Review* 48 (Summer 2006): 247.

12. F. 3d 1114 (2006).

13. Of course, judicial decisions also are shaped by the jurists who craft them and, on collegial courts, by the interactions among these jurists. Analyzing these factors is beyond the scope of this chapter. See, for instance, Lawrence Baum, *The Puzzle of Judicial Behavior* (Ann Arbor: University of Michigan Press, 1977); Lawrence Baum, *Judges and Their Audiences: A Perspective on Judicial Behavior* (Princeton, N.J.: Princeton University Press, 2006); Lee Epstein and Jack Knight, *The Choices Justices Make* (Washington, D.C.: Congressional Quarterly Press, 1998); and Cass Sunstein, et al., *Are Judges Political?: An Empirical Analysis of the Federal Judiciary* (Washington, D.C.: Brookings Institution Press, 2006).

14. The "cases and controversies" terminology is from Article III, Section 2 of the U.S. Constitution: "The judicial power shall extend to all cases, in law and equity, arising under this Constitution, the laws of the United States, and treaties made, or which shall be made, under their authority; —to all cases affecting ambassadors, other public ministers and consuls; —to all cases of admiralty and maritime jurisdiction; —to controversies to which the United States shall be a party; —to controversies between two or more states; —between a state and citizens of another state; —between citizens of different states; —between citizens of the same state claiming lands under grants of different states, and between a state, or the citizens thereof, and foreign states, citizens or subjects."

The Ninth Circuit Court of Appeals, like the other eleven Circuit Courts of Appeal, are "Article III courts" in that they were created by Congress under its Article III authority to create "such inferior courts as the Congress may from time to time ordain and establish."

15. Frederick, *Rugged Justice*, 240.

16. "100 Years of Ninth Circuit History in San Francisco Courthouse," http://www.ce9.uscourts. gov/history/100_years.pdf.

17. 138 F. 775 (9th Cir. 1905).

18. Order No. 34 was adopted pursuant to Executive Order 9066. The Roosevelt administration promulgated Executive Order 9066 on February 19, 1942. Its operative language reads: "I hereby authorize and direct the Secretary of War, and the Military Commanders whom he may from time to time designate, whenever he or any designated Commander deem such action necessary or desirable to prescribe military areas in such places and of such extent as he or the appropriate Military Commander may determine, from which any or all persons may be excluded, and with respect to which, the right of any person to enter, remain in, or leave shall be subject to whatever restriction the Secretary of War or the appropriate Military Commander may impose in his discretion." See Peter Irons, *Justice at*

War (Berkeley: University of California Press, 1993; and Peter Irons, *Justice Delayed: The Record of the Japanese-American Internment Cases* (Middletown, Conn.: Wesleyan University Press, 1989).

19. *Korematsu v. United* States, 140 F. 2d 289 (9th Cir. 1943b).

20. Compare Justice Hugo Black's majority opinion in *Korematsu v. United States*, 323 U.S. 214 (1944).

21. F. 2d 774 (9th Cir. 1947) (en banc).

22. U.S. 483 (1954). See David S. Ettinger, "The History of School Desegregation in the Ninth Circuit," *Loyola of Los Angeles Law Review* 12, no. 481 (1979); Vicki L. Riuz, "We Always Tell Our Children They Are Americans: *Mendez v. Westminster," Brown Quarterly* 6 (2004), http://brownvboard. org/brwnqurt/06-3/; Frederick P. Aguirre, "*Mendez v. Westminster School District*: How It Affected *Brown v. Board of Education," Journal of Hispanic Higher Education* 4, no. 321 (2005); and "*Mendez vs. Westminster*: For All the Children/Para Todos los Ninos," KOCE television (2002).

23. The two colleagues were Robert L. Carter, who worked with Marshall as assistant special counsel to the National Association for the Advancement of Colored People, Legal Defense and Education Fund, and Loren Miller who was a California attorney and civil rights activist, specializing in challenging racially restrictive housing covenants.

24. *Mendez v. Westminster*, 64 F. Supp. 544 (C.D. Cal. 1946).

25. See 161 F. 2d 774, 779–780, 781 (9th Cir. 1947) (en banc), fn. 5

26. F. 2d 774, 780–781 (9th Cir. 1947) (en banc).

27. Ibid., 780.

28. *Brown v. Board of Education,* 347 U.S. 483 (1954).

29. Jonathan Matthew Cohen, *Inside Appellate Courts: The Impact of Court Organization on Judicial Decision Making in the United States Courts of Appeals* (Ann Arbor: University of Michigan Press, 2002), ix.

"Cathy Catterson is Circuit and Court of Appeals Executive for the Ninth Circuit. She documents the stunning growth in workload: In 1971 . . . [t]he Ninth Circuit had 1936 appeals and thirteen judgeships. Nationally, there were 12,788 appeals filed and ninety-six permanent judgeships. Today, according to the 2005 statistics from the Administrative Office of the United States Courts, there were 15,236 appeals filed in the Ninth Circuit, and 65,418 appeals filed nationally with 179 judges. That's almost a 500% increase in filings and a 77% increase in judgeships." Cathy Catterson, "Caseload and Mechanisms for Dealing with It: Changes in Appellate Caseload and its Processing," *Arizona Law Review* 48 (Summer 2006): 288. Catterson's one-word summary of how courts manage caseload is "technology": "It has not only changed the world, it has changed how courts operate, and it will continue to do so in the coming years, in an even more dramatic fashion." Catterson, "Caseload and Mechanisms for Dealing with It," 294.

30. See Cohen, *Inside Appellate Courts*; and Arthur D. Hellman, ed., *Restructuring Justice: The Innovations of the Ninth Circuit and the Future of the Federal Courts* (Ithaca, N.Y.: Cornell University Press, 1990).

31. F. 3d 1114 (2006).

32. For analysis of these multiple reasons, see Stephen L. Wasby, "The Supreme Court and Courts of Appeal *En Bancs," McGeorge Law Review* 33 (2001): 17, 29.

33. See Arthur D. Hellman, "Getting It Right: Panel Error and the *En Banc* Process in the Ninth Circuit Court of Appeals," *Davis Law Review* 34 (2000): 425.

34. The congressional Omnibus Judgeship Act of 1978 authorized any appellate court with more than fifteen active judges to "perform its *en banc* function by such numbers of its members as may be prescribed by rule of the court of appeals."

35. Arthur D. Hellman tells the story of circumstances and debates culminating in the Ninth's adoption of these Rule 35-3 procedures in "Maintaining Consistency in the Law of the Large Circuit,"

in Hellman, *Restructuring Justice*, 62–70. Compare Amendments to the Local Rules for the Ninth Circuit Court of Appeals, effective July 1, 2007: http://www.ca9.uscourts.gov/ca9/documents.nsf/ 174376a6245fda7888256ce5007d5470/d1888830399260d78825730d007532de?OpenDocument.

36. See Judith A. McKenna, ed., *Structural and Other Alternatives for the Federal Courts of Appeal* (Washington, D.C.: Federal Judicial Center, 2003), 96.

37. See Judge Pamela Ann Rymer, "The 'Limited' En Banc: Half Full, or Half Empty?" *Arizona Law Review* 48 (Summer 2006): 317; compare McKenna, *Structural and Other Alternatives for the Federal Courts of Appeal*, fn. 183, 96.

38. Although Rule 35-3 provides that "In appropriate cases, the Court may order a rehearing by the full court following a hearing or rehearing en banc" this procedure has not been used. See: http:// www.ca9.uscourts.gov/ca9/documents.nsf/174376a6245fda7888256ce5007d5470/d1888830399260d7 8825730d007532de?OpenDocument.

39. McKenna, *Structural and Other Alternatives for the Federal Courts of Appeal*, 97. Compare Hellman, "Maintaining Consistency in the Law of the Large Circuit," in *Restructuring Justice*," 70–90; and Pamela A. MacLean, "9th Circuit Steps Up En Banc Reviews," Law.com, February 6, 2007, http:// www.law.com/jsp/article.jsp?id=1170682661753.

40. Rymer, "The 'Limited' En Banc," 323.

41. "The selection of a Supreme Court justice is front-page news. At times, it may dominate the headlines for days or weeks[.] . . . But throughout American history we find little such national attention given to the selection of lower federal court judges." Sheldon Goldman, *Picking Federal Judges: Lower Court Selection from Roosevelt to Reagan* (New Haven, Conn.: Yale University Press, 1997), 1.

In a blog she wrote in conjunction with her July 18, 2008, retirement as U.S. Supreme Court reporter for the *New York Times*, Linda Greenhouse responds to a reader's question as to whether Supreme Court nominations "really make a difference": "The first, and most direct, answer is, yes, [nominations do] matter—especially today, when the court is so closely balanced and when so many cases have been decided by votes of 5 to 4. It has made a substantial difference these past 20 years that Anthony Kennedy is sitting in the seat intended for Robert Bork, for example." *New York Times*, July 14, 2008, http://www.nytimes.com/2008/07/14/business/media/14askthetimes.html?pagewanted=all.

Sheldon Goldman gets more specific about why Supreme Court nominations matter: "Were Bork on the Court instead of Anthony Kennedy, who filled the slot originally slated for Bork, *Roe v. Wade*—a woman's constitutional right of privacy to terminate a non-viable fetus from an unwanted pregnancy—would be history." Sheldon Goldman, "Judicial Confirmation Wars: Ideology and the Battle for the Federal Courts," *University of Richmond Law Review* 39 (March 2005): 871, 877.

42. Harold W. Chase, *Federal Judges: The Appointing Process* (Minneapolis: University of Minnesota Press, 1972). Compare Elliot E. Slotnick, "Appellate Judicial Selection During the Bush Administration: Business as Usual or a Nuclear Winter?" *Arizona Law Review* 48 (Summer 2006): 225–228.

43. Chase, *Federal Judges*, 27.

44. See David R. Mayhew, *Congress: The Electoral Connection* (New Haven, Conn.: Yale University Press, 1974, 2004).

45. Chase, *Federal Judges*, 35.

46. As the reader, who asked Linda Greenhouse whether Supreme Court nominations really make a difference, complained: "Conservative presidents will appoint conservative justices, liberal presidents will appoint liberal justices, yada yada yada." *New York Times*, July 14, 2008, http://www. nytimes.com/2008/07/14/business/media/14askthetimes.html?pagewanted=all.

47. Fifth Circuit Judge Edith H. Jones puts it this way: "As the social policy stakes have gotten higher, confirmation battles have extended from the Supreme Court to a large portion of appellate court

appointments." Edith H. Jones, "Observations on the Status and Impact of the Judicial Confirmation Process," *University of Richmond Law Review* 39 (March 2005): 833, 835.

48. Carl Tobias, "The Federal Appellate Court Appointments Conundrum," *Utah Law Review* (2005): 743, 749.

49. Chase, *Federal Judges*, 195. Compare William P. Marshall, "The Judicial Nominations Wars," *University of Richmond Law Review* 39 (March 2005): 819, 820–827.

50. Joel B. Grossman, *Lawyers and Judges: The ABA and the Politics of Judicial Selection* (New York: Wiley, 1965), 219, quoted in Chase, *Federal Judges*, 196.

51. Tobias, "The Federal Appellate Court Appointments Conundrum," 750. Tobias argues: "Many political factors that accompanied judicial selection contributed significantly to the present situation. The Chief Executives and the senators—including the Majority Leaders, members and leaders of the Judiciary Committees, and individual senators—were mainly responsible for numerous phenomena that constitute the existing difficulty. These public officials—alone or synergistically—could have resolved or ameliorated a number of complications, if they exercised the requisite political will." Ibid., 752.

Unfortunately, "political will" is not synonymous with statesmanship, or with "good politics," as Harold W. Chase referred to nonpartisan pressure. Chase observed in 1972: "On the whole, in any administration of modern times, [judicial] selections made as a consequence of the pressure of 'good politics' have been few in number, the exceptions and not the rule." Chase, *Federal Judges*, 34.

52. The three Huston quotations are from Goldman, *Picking Federal Judges*, 206. Tom Huston also was the author of the infamous June 1970 "Huston Plan" which marshaled the resources of the FBI, the CIA, and various military intelligence agencies to spy on domestic opponents of the Vietnam War. See Assassination Archives and Research Center, vol. 2: Huston Plan, at http://www.aarclibrary.org/publib/contents/church/contents_church_reports_vol2.htm; and Athan G. Theoharis, *Spying on Americans: Political Surveillance from Hoover to the Huston Plan* (Philadelphia: Temple University Press, 1978). Also see Rick Perlstein, *Nixonland: The Rise of a President and the Fracturing of America* (New York: Scribner, 2008).

53. Slotnick, "Appellate Judicial Selection during the Bush Administration," 228.

54. The particulars of these developments are analyzed in Goldman, *Picking Federal Judges*; Goldman, "Judicial Confirmation Wars"; and Slotnick, "Appellate Judicial Selection during the Bush Administration." Also see Jeff Alworth, "Poisoning the Well," *Blue Oregon*, May 15, 2005, at http://www.blueoregon.com/2005/05/poisoning_the_w.html.

55. Slotnick, "Appellate Judicial Selection during the Bush Administration," 237–238.

56. David M. O'Brien, *Judicial Roulette* (New York: Priority Press, 1988), 19. Ironically, while both Democrats and Republicans are fully aware that appellate judges make policy decisions and that those decisions make a social difference, and while as a consequence of their shared awareness both Democrats and Republicans strive to put judges on federal appellate benches who likely will advance their preferred policy agendas, both Democrats and Republicans decry judicial policy making as "legislating from the bench" and both Democrats and Republicans accuse each other of attempting to "politicize" judicial appointments. "[E]ach side argues that the other is interested in appointing people who will merely vote to uphold their side's policies as constitutional, but not the policies of the other side. . . . Neither side in the debate concedes that the other's criteria for judicial selection are legitimate." Michael J. Gerhardt, "Judicial Selection as . . . Talk Radio," *University of Richmond Law Review* 39 (March 2005): 909, 917. Compare Sheldon Goldman, "Judicial Appointments and the Presidential Agenda," in Paul Brace, Christine B. Harrington, and Gary Kings, eds., *The Presidency in American Politics* (New York: New York University Press, 1989).

57. I realize this is a much debated claim. Indeed, underlying current fights over judicial selection, at both the state and federal levels, are deep differences over the nature of law and of judging. Nevertheless,

in terms of political practice, that is, what politicians do when they make judicial appointments, it is incontrovertible that the prevailing assumption is that "judges are merely policymakers who wear robes." Gerhardt, "Judicial Selection as . . . Talk Radio," 917. On judicial discretion see James C. Foster, "Rethinking Politics and Judicial Selection During Contentious Times," *Albany Law Review* 67 (2003–2004): 821. On law as a linguistic phenomenon, as opposed to reducing judicial interpretation to merely a matter of linguistic science, see Alani Golanski, "Linguistics in Law," *Albany Law Review* 66 (2002): 61. Also see "Sorites Paradox" (The Heap Paradox), *Stanford Encyclopedia of Philosophy*, http://plato.stanford.edu/entries/sorites-paradox; and "Law and Language," *Stanford Encyclopedia of Philosophy*, http://plato.stanford.edu/entries/law-language.

58. I am talking here especially, but not exclusively, about appellate judges. See C. K. Rowland and Robert A. Carp, *Politics and Judgment in Federal District Courts* (Lawrence: University Press of Kansas, 1996).

59. As Alani Golanski puts it: "Whether plain is defined as 'ordinary' or 'unambiguous,' judicial scrutiny of plain meaning is always embedded in a context of competing policy interests. Accordingly, at times there may be little to distinguish two pieces of statutory language that the court construes quite differently on policy grounds." Alani Golanski, "Linguistics in Law," 64.

60. Goldman, "Judicial Confirmation Wars," 873. "[I]ndividuals come to the bench with personal preferences and particular experiences that often affect their perspective on the law. Simply put, women and minorities may provide perspectives that differ from their male and white counterparts. While debate continues regarding the factors that influence judicial decisionmaking, it is generally agreed that the person who occupies a seat on the bench will have an impact on the outcome of a case." Solberg, "Court Size and Diversity," 247.

61. See, for instance, David S. Law and Sanford Levinson, "Why Nuclear Disarmament May Be Easier to Achieve Than an End to Partisan Conflict over Judicial Appointments," *University of Richmond Law Review* 39 (March 2005): 923.

62. See 91, 94–98, above.

63. Stephen J. Wermiel, "Exploring the Myths About the Ninth Circuit," *Arizona Law Review* 48 (Summer 2006): 355, 364.

64. Jonathan D. Glater, "Lawmakers Trying Again to Divide Ninth Circuit," *New York Times*, June 19, 2005, http://www.nytimes.com/2005/06/19/politics/19court.html.

65. For example, Article III of the 1855 treaty negotiated by Oregon Territory Governor Isaac Stevens and Superintendent of Indian Affairs Joe Stevens with the Yakima Nation guaranteed the Yakima their right to fish "at their usual and accustomed places in common with the citizens of the territory." Cited in Martin H. Belsky, "Indian Fishing Rights: A Lost Opportunity for Ecosystem Management," *Journal of Land Use & Environmental Law* 12 (Fall 1996): 45, 47.

See Joane Nagel, *American Indian Ethnic Renewal: Red Power and the Resurgence of Identity and Culture* (New York: Oxford University Press, 1996); Alexandra Harmon, *Indians in the Making: Ethnic Relationships and Indian Identities around Puget Sound* (Berkeley: University of California Press, 1998); and Donna Hightower Langston, "American Indian Women's Activism in the 1960s and 1970s," *Hypatia: Journal of Feminist Philosophy* 18 (Spring 2003): 114.

66. *United States v. Washington*, 384 F. Supp. 312 (W.D. Wash. 1974). Compare *Sohappy v. Smith*, 302 F. Supp. 899 (D. Or. 1969).

67. Ibid., 343.

68. "[W]hile it must be recognized that these large harvests by non-treaty fishermen cannot be regulated with any certainty or precision by the state defendants, it is incumbent upon such defendants to take all appropriate steps within their actual abilities to assure as nearly as possible an equal sharing of the opportunity for treaty and non-treaty fishermen to harvest every species of fish to which the

treaty tribes had access at their usual and accustomed fishing places at treaty times. Some additional adjustments in the harvesting scheme under state jurisdiction may be necessary to approach more nearly an equal allocation of the opportunity to harvest fish at usual and accustomed grounds and station." Ibid., 344.

69. See Charles Wilkinson, *Messages from Frank's Landing* (Seattle: University of Washington Press, 2000).

70. F.2d 676 (9th Cir. 1975).

71. Martin H. Belsky, "Indian Fishing Rights," 52. The citations for the two Washington Supreme Court decisions are *Puget Sound Gillnetters Ass'n. v. Moos*, 565 P.2d 1151 (Wash. 1977); and *Washington Commercial Passenger Fishing Vessel Ass'n. v. Tollefson*, 571 P.2d 1373 (Wash. 1977).

72. Tim Burke, *The Legal Relationship between Washington State and Its Reservation-Based Indian Tribes* (Olympia, Wash.: Office of Program Research, House of Representatives, 1977), 104.

73. Previously, the U.S. Supreme Court had, in effect, upheld Judge Boldt's decision sub silentio when it refused to hear an appeal of the Ninth Circuit's affirmation of *United States v. Washington, cert. denied*, 423 U.S. 1086 (1976).

74. *Newdow v. U.S. Congress*, 292 F. 3d 597, 602 (CA9 2002) *(Newdow I)*.

75. The Ninth Circuit's holding in *Newdow I* brings to mind Charles Evan Hughes' remark about "self-inflicted wounds." Charles Evans Hughes, *The Supreme Court of the United States* (New York: Columbia University Press, 1928), 50.

76. The literature treating the Supreme Court's Establishment Clause jurisprudence is vast. A few recent, thought-provoking places to slice into it are: Lisa Shaw Roy, "History, Transparency, and the Establishment Clause: A Proposal for Reform," *Penn State Law Review* 112 (Winter 2008): 683; Richard M. Esenberg, "You Cannot Lose If You Choose Not to Play: Toward a More Modest Establishment Clause," *Roger Williams University Law Review* 12 (Fall 2006): 1; Alex Geisinger and Ivan E. Bodensteiner, "An Expressive Jurisprudence of the Establishment Clause," *Penn State Law Review* 112 (Summer 2007): 77; Steven G. Gey, "Vestiges of the Establishment Clause," *First Amendment Law Review* 5 (Fall 2006): 1; Amit Patel, "The Orthodoxy Opening Predicament: The Crumbling Wall of Separation between Church and State," *University of Detroit Mercy Law Review* (Spring 2006): 195; and Christopher B. Harwood, "Evaluating the Supreme Court's Establishment Clause Jurisprudence in the Wake of *Van Orden v. Perry* and *McCreary County v. ACLU*," *Missouri Law Review* 71 (Spring 2006): 317.

77. The remaining three participating Court members, Chief Justice Rehnquist and Justices O'Connor and Thomas, wanted to take on the Ninth Circuit's Establishment Clause ruling and overturn it. One reasonable reading of the *Newdow* voting alignment is that the five justices in the majority, persuaded that Dr. Newdow had the winning argument based on precedent and knowing that to side with him would supercharge an already overheated political environment, fashioned a way to avoid a decision on the merits.

78. *Elk Grove Unified School Dist. v. Newdow*, 542 U.S. 1, 16 (2004).

79. Ibid., 17.

80. Alexander M. Bickel, "The Supreme Court, 1960 Term—Foreword: The Passive Virtues," *Harvard Law Review* 75 (1961): 40.

81. "I've been talking to law professors this afternoon and I think this decision is dead on arrival either in the full 9th Circuit or in the United States Supreme Court. It really seems to be outside the mainstream of American legal opinion." Jeffrey Toobin, CNN.com/lawcenter, June 27, 2002, http://archives.cnn.com/2002/LAW/06/26/toobin.pledge.cnna/index.html.

82. The Ninth Circuit handed down three decisions in the Newdow matter. In *Newdow I*, 292 F. 3d 597 (CA9 2002), the three-judge panel, Alfred T. Goodwin, Ferdinand F. Fernandez, and Stephen

Reinhardt, unanimously upheld Dr. Newdow's standing to challenge both the Elk Grove School District policy and the 1954 Act of Congress adding "under God" to the Pledge of Allegiance. That panel split 2–1, Fernandez dissenting, on the merits of Newdow's challenges. In *Newdow II*, 313 F. 3d 500 (CA9 2002), the panel reconsidered Dr. Newdow's standing to sue in light of Sandra Banning filing a petition that resulted in the California Superior Court issuing an order enjoining Newdow from suing on behalf of his daughter. The Ninth Circuit held that Newdow retained standing to challenge alleged unconstitutional governmental action under Article III of the U.S. Constitution. In *Newdow III*, 328 F. 3d 466 (CA9 2003), after a majority of the twenty-three then-active Ninth Circuit judges had voted against a request to rehear the case en banc, the Court entered an order denying petitions for such a rehearing. Nine of the active judges dissented in writing from this denial.

83. Evelyn Nieves, "Judges Ban Pledge of Allegiance from Schools, Citing 'Under God,'" *New York Times*, June 27, 2002, http://query.nytimes.com/gst/fullpage.html?res=9E0DE2DE123EF934A15755 C0A9649C8B63&sec=&spon=&&scp=2&sq=reaction%20to%20newdow%20I&st=cse

84. Justice Scalia was speaking at a Religious Freedom Day rally in Fredricksburg, Virginia. See "Scalia Attacks Church-State Court Rulings," *New York Times*, January 13, 2003, http://query.nytimes. com/gst/fullpage.html?res=9B05E5D81431F930A25752C0A9659C8B63. Compare Dahlia Lithwick, "Scaliapalooza: The Supreme Court's Pocket Jeremiah," *Slate*, October 30, 2003, http://slate.msn. com/id/2090532; and Tony Mauro, "Scalia Recusal Revives Debate over Judicial Speech, Ethics," Law. com, October 20, 2003, http://www.law.com/jsp/article.jsp?id=1066080440869.

85. I have found these writings helpful in sorting out "wars" over the Ninth Circuit: Cohen, *Inside Appellate Courts*; Hellman, ed., *Restructuring Justice*; Erwin Chemerinsky, "The Myth of the Liberal Ninth Circuit," *Loyola L. Annual Law Review* 37 (Fall 2003): 1; Jeffrey O. Cooper and Douglas A. Berman, "Passive Virtues and Casual Vices in the Federal Courts of Appeal," *Brooklyn Law Review* 66 (Winter 2000/Spring 2001): 685; Jerome Farris, "The Ninth Circuit—Most Maligned Circuit in the Country—Fact or Fiction?" *Ohio State Law Journal* 58 (1997): 1465; Susan B. Haire, "Judicial Selection and Decisionmaking in the Ninth Circuit," *Arizona Law Review* 48 (Summer 2006): 267; Marybeth Herald, "Reversed, Vacated, and Split: The Supreme Court, the Ninth Circuit, and the Congress," *Oregon Law Review* 77 (Summer 1998): 405; Kevin M. Scott, "Supreme Court Reversals of the Ninth Circuit," *Arizona Law Review* 48 (Summer 2006): 341; Slotnick, "Appellate Judicial Selection During the Bush Administration"; Frank Tamulonis III, "Splitting the Ninth Circuit: Necessity or Environmental Gerrymandering?" *Pennsylvania State Law Review* 112 (Winter 2008): 859; Carl Tobias, "The Impoverished Idea of Circuit-Splitting," *Emory Law Journal* 44 (Fall 1995): 1357; Wasby, "The Supreme Court and Courts of Appeal *En Bancs*"; Stephen L. Wasby, "How the Ninth Circuit fares in the Supreme Court: The Intercircuit Conflict Cases," *Seton Hall Circuit Review* 1 (Spring 2005): 119; and Wermiel, "Exploring the Myths About the Ninth Circuit."

86. Did Roosevelt lose the court-packing battle, but win the war over the constitutionality of New Deal programs? Or had Roosevelt already won the war before the decisive battles over his court-packing plan? See Howard Gillman, *The Constitution Besieged: The Rise and Demise of Lochner Era Jurisprudence* (Durham, N.C.: Duke University Press, 1993); Joseph Rauh, "An Unabashed Liberal Looks at a Half-Century of the Supreme Court," *North Carolina Law Review* 69 (1990): 213; and G. Edward White, *The Constitution and the New Deal* (Cambridge, Mass.: Harvard University Press, 2000).

87. 439 F. 3d 1114 (2006).

88. Any sitting Article III judge may take "senior status" upon meeting the requirements of the "Rule of Eighty": the jurist's age and years of service must add up to eighty, (s)he must be at least sixty-five years old, and must have been on the bench for at least ten years. Senior status is neither retirement nor resignation, and senior judges continue to provide useful service to their respective courts. See Fredric Block, "Senior Status: An 'Active' Senior Judge Corrects Some Common Misunderstandings,"

Cornell Law Review 92 (2007): 533. Also see Sara C. Benesh, "Caseload and Mechanisms for Dealing with It: The Contribution of 'Extra' Judges," *Arizona Law Review* 48 (Summer 2006): 301; and Stephen L. Wasby, "'Extra' Judges in a Federal Appellate Court: The Ninth Circuit," *Law & Society Review* 15 (1980): 369.

89. Joseph Frederick, appellant, vs. Deborah Morse and the Juneau School Board, appellees, Appellant's Opening Brief, Ninth Circuit Court of Appeals No. 03-35701, in author's possession, 4, 6.

90. Joseph Frederick, appellant, vs. Deborah Morse and the Juneau School Board, appellees, Appellee's Brief, Ninth Circuit Court of Appeals No. 03-35701, in author's possession, 4, 8.

91. Appellant's Opening Brief, Ninth Circuit Court of Appeals No. 03-35701, 9.

92. Appellee's Brief, Ninth Circuit Court of Appeals No. 03-35701, 8.

93. See above, chapter 3, 73–74.

94. F.2d 524 (9th Cir. 1992).

95. Ibid., 529. Compare Circuit Judge Goodwin concurring.

96. Ibid.

97. Ibid.

98. Appellant's Opening Brief, Ninth Circuit Court of Appeals No. 03-35701, 10–11.

99. Ibid., 10.

100. Ibid., 12–22.

101. Ibid., 20.

102. Ibid., 22.

103. Ibid., 22–28.

104. Ibid., 28.

105. Ibid., 30.

106. Ibid., 31.

107. Ibid., 32–39.

108. Ibid., 35.

109. Appellee's Brief, Ninth Circuit Court of Appeals No. 03-35701, 39. Citing *United States v. Wise*, 550 F.2d 1180, 1186 (9th Cir. 1977); *United States v. Tidwell*, 191 F.3d 976, 980 (9th Cir. 1999); and *United States v. Bohonus*, 628 F.2d 1167, 1774 (9th Cir. 1980).

110. Appellee's Brief, Ninth Circuit Court of Appeals No. 03-35701, 10–21.

111. Ibid., 10–12.

112. Ibid., 10, 11.

113. Ibid., 12.

114. Ibid., 13–14.

115. Ibid., 13.

116. Ibid., 14–21.

117. Ibid., 16.

118. Ibid., 16, 19.

119. Ibid., 19.

120. Ibid., 22–25.

121. Ibid., 22 fn. 73.

122. As Henry J. Abraham wrote in the opening line of the preface to the first edition (1967) of his influential *Freedom & the Court: Civil Rights & Liberties in the United States*, "This is essentially a study of the lines that must be drawn by a democratic society as it attempts to reconcile individual freedom with the rights of the community." Henry J. Abraham and Barbara A. Perry, *Freedom & the Court: Civil Rights & Liberties in the United States*, 6th ed. (New York: Oxford University Press, 1994), ix.

123. *Frederick v. Morse*, 439 F.3d 2461, 2464 (9th Cir 2006).

124. Ibid., 2465–2466.

125. Ibid., 2465.

126. Ibid., 2467.

127. Ibid., 2469.

128. See Ibid., 2470–2471.

129. See Ibid., 2471–2472.

130. Ibid., 2473.

131. Ibid., 2469.

132. Ibid., 2471.

133. See 2477, fn. 44: "The word 'offensive' is not a catch-all to embrace any speech that might offend some hearers. Nor was *Fraser* an invitation to censor and punish any speech that offends school authorities. . . . By Appellees' standard, distributing photocopies of the Alaska Supreme Court decision in *Ravin v. State*, in which it declared that there is 'no adequate justification for the state's intrusion into the citizen's right to privacy by its prohibition of possession of marijuana,' . . . would also undermine the school's anti-drug mission. However, it could not seriously be contended that handing out copies of *Ravin* on the sidewalk across the street from the school while students were released from classes could be punished. *Fraser* only enables schools to prevent the sort of vulgar, obscene, lewd, or sexual speech that, especially with adolescents, readily promotes disruption from the *educational curriculum*."

134. John Stuart Mill, "On Liberty," in *Three Essays*, Richard Wollheim, intro. (New York: Oxford University Press, 1975), 9–10.

Notes to Chapter 6

1. The Drug Free America Foundation, Inc.; National Families in Action; Save Our Society from Drugs; former Secretary of Education and first Director of the Office of National Drug Control Policy, William J. Bennett; and fourth Director of the Office of National Drug Control Policy, Gen. Barry R. McCaffrey joined the D.A.R.E. America amicus brief.

2. The American Association of School Administrators and the National Association of Secondary School Principals joined the National School Boards Association amicus brief.

3. On the brief with the solicitor general were Assistant Attorney General Peter D. Keisler, U.S. Department of Education General Counsel Kent D. Talbert, and Edward H. Jurith, General Counsel of the Office of National Drug Control Policy, plus eight other attorneys from these three government organizations. The Supreme Court granted Solicitor General Clement permission to participate in oral argument as an amicus for Morse. Deputy Solicitor General Edwin S. Kneedler actually represented the United States during the March 19, 2007, argument.

4. Stuart Banner, "The Myth of the Neutral *Amicus*: American Courts and Their Friends, 1790–1890," *Constitutional Commentary* 20 (Spring 2003): 111. See the reference to the line from Shakespeare's *As You Like It*, (II. vii.): "friendship is feigning," in Michael J. Harris, "*Amicus Curiae*: Friend or Foe? The Limits of Friendship in American Jurisprudence," *Suffolk Journal of Trial & Appellate* 5 (2000): 1, 6. But compare Ethan J. Leib, "Friendship & the Law," *UCLA Law Review* 54 (February 2007): 631; and Ruben J. Garcia, "A Democratic Theory of *Amicus* Advocacy," *Florida State University Law Review* 35 (Winter 2008): 315.

5. See David Gossett, "Friendship: *Amicus* Briefs in the Supreme Court," *Green Bag 2d* 8 (Summer 2005): 363.

6. Michael K. Lowman, "The Litigating *Amicus Curiae*: When Does the Party Begin after the Friends Leave?" *American University Law Review* 41 (Summer 1992): 1243, 1245.

7. Ibid., 1247.

8. See Linda Sandstrom Simard, "An Empirical Study of *Amici Curiae* in Federal Court: A Fine Balance of Access, Efficiency, and Adversarialism," *Review of Litigation* 27 (Summer 2008): 669. Compare Kelly J. Lynch, "Best Friends? Supreme Court Law Clerks on Effective *Amicus Curiae* Briefs," *Journal of Law and Politics* 20 (Winter 2004): 33.

9. Lowman, "The Litigating *Amicus Curiae*," 1248, quoting Samuel Krislov, "The *Amicus Curiae* Brief: From Friendship to Advocacy," *Yale Law Journal* 72 (1963): 694, 695. Compare Stephen L. Wasby, *The Supreme Court in the Federal Judicial System*, 4th ed. (Chicago, Ill.: Nelson-Hall, 1994).

10. Lowman, "The Litigating *Amicus Curiae*," passim.

11. For instance, Frank M. Covey Jr., "*Amicus Curiae*: Friend of the Court," *DePaul Law Review* 9 (1959–1960): 30, argues that English practice more closely resembled the American. Compare Ernest Angell, "The *Amicus Curiae*: American Development of English Institutions," *International and Comparative Law Quarterly* 16 (1967): 1017.

12. Simard, "An Empirical Study of *Amici Curiae* in Federal Court," 675. Simard quotes from English lexicographer, Henry James Holthouse's 1850 *A New Law Dictionary*: "When a judge is doubtful or mistaken in a matter of law, a bystander may inform the court thereof as *amicus curiae*. Counsel in court frequently act in this capacity when they happen to be in possession of a case which the judge has not seen or does not at the moment remember." Simard, "An Empirical Study of *Amici Curiae* in Federal Court," 676, fn. 29.

13. F.2d 1196 (1st Cir. 1979).

14. Ibid., 1200, 1201.

15. Ibid., fn. 3, 1198. Compare similar conceptions articulated in *United States v. Michigan*, 940 F.2d 143 (6th Cir. 1991), 164–165, and the cases cited in Banner, "The Myth of the Neutral *Amicus*," fns. 1, 2, 111–112.

16. Garcia, "A Democratic Theory of *Amicus* Advocacy," 320.

17. Harris, "*Amicus Curiae*: Friend or Foe?" 2. In a similar—more pointed—vein, see Judge Richard A. Posner's three related opinions inhospitable to amicus briefs in *Ryan v. CFTC*, 125 F.3d 1062 (7th Cir. 1997), *Nat'l Org. for Women v. Scheidler*, 223 F.3d 615 (7th Cir. 2000), and *Voices for Choices v. Illinois Bell Tel. Co.*, 339 F.3d 542 (7th Cir. 2003). Also see Justice Robert Jackson's view articulated in *Craig v. Harney*, 331 U.S. 367 (1947). Compare Luther T. Munford, "When Does the *Curiae* Need an *Amicus*?" *Journal of Appellate Practice* 1 (Summer 1999): 279. But see John Harrington, "*Amici Curiae* in the Federal Courts of Appeals: How Friendly Are They?" *Case Western Research* 5 (Spring 2005): 667.

18. Banner, "The Myth of the Neutral *Amicus*."

19. Ibid., 112.

20. Ibid., 114.

21. Ibid., 111. Compare Krislov, "The *Amicus Curiae* Brief." More broadly, see Lucius Barker, "Third Parties in Litigation: A Systemic View of the Judicial Function," *Journal of Politics* 29 (1967): 41.

22. Ibid., 119.

23. Ibid., 119–120. Banner defined "neutrality" as when counsel "was not representing anyone and he was not unambiguously for one side or the other." Banner defined "partisan" if counsel "participated in the case in order to advance the interests of someone he represented, or, in cases where it was unclear whether he was representing someone, if he unambiguously appeared on the side of one party or the other." Ibid., 116. Applying these definitions, Banner identified 45 neutral cases and 207 partisan cases. In 56 cases he was unable to determine the amicus's motive for appearing. Ibid., 114, 116.

24. Ibid., 121–122.

25. Steven K. Gragert, ed., *Will Rogers' Weekly Articles*, Vol. 4, *The Hoover Years: 1929–1931* (Stillwater: Oklahoma State University, 1981), 77.

26. Karen O'Connor and Lee Epstein, "*Amicus Curiae* Participation in U.S. Supreme Court Litigation: An Appraisal of Hakman's Folklore," *Law and Society Review* 16 (1981–1982): 317. Compare Lee Epstein and C. K. Rowland, "Interest Groups in Courts: Do Groups Fare Better," in Allan J. Cigler and Burdett A. Loomis, eds., *Interest Group Politics*, 2nd ed. (Washington, D.C.: CQ Press, 1986), and Lee Epstein, "Courts and Interest Groups," in John B. Gates and Charles A. Johnson, eds., *The American Courts: A Critical Assessment* (Washington, D.C.: CQ Press, 1991).

Epstein and O'Connor also published two other important analyses of *amicus* advocacy in the early 1980s: Karen O'Connor and Lee Epstein, "Court Rules and Workload: A Case Study of Rules Governing *Amicus Curiae* Participation," *Justice System Journal* 8 (1983): 35; and Karen O'Connor and Lee Epstein, "The Rise of Conservative Interest Group Litigation," *Journal of Politics* 45 (1983): 479. Also see Steven Puro's pioneering "The Role of *Amicus Curiae* in the United States Supreme Court: 1920–1966," unpublished Ph.D. dissertation, State University of New York at Buffalo, 1971.

27. O'Connor and Epstein, "*Amicus Curiae* Participation in U.S. Supreme Court Litigation," 318.

28. Nathan Hakman, "Lobbying the Supreme Court—An Appraisal of the Political Science 'Folklore,'" *Fordham Law Review* 35 (1966): 50. Also see Nathan Hakman, "The Supreme Court's Political Environment: The Processing of Noncommercial Litigation," in Joel Grossman and Joseph Tanenhaus, eds., *Frontiers of Judicial Research* (New York: John Wiley, 1969).

29. Krislov, "The *Amicus Curiae* Brief: From Friendship to Advocacy." Since Hakman died in September 2001, he obviously did not see Stuart Banner's 2003 corrective analysis of Krislov.

30. "Whatever the validity of Hakman's conclusions for the time period he studied, current research on interest group participation cast doubt on their current utility." O'Connor and Epstein, "*Amicus Curiae* Participation in U.S. Supreme Court Litigation," 312.

31. Ibid., 312, 314, 318.

32. "Academics followed Hakman's advice; for more than a decade [1966–1981], work on interest group litigation was virtually nonexistent. The scholarly community seemed to agree that it was fruitless to study a phenomenon that was almost certainly episodic." Epstein and Rowland, "Interest Groups in Courts," 279.

33. Judithanne Scourfield McLauchlan, *Congressional Participation as* Amicus Curiae *before the U.S. Supreme Court* (New York: LFB Scholarly Press, 2005), 9.

34. Gregory A. Caldeira and John R. Wright, "Organized Interests and Agenda Setting in the U.S. Supreme Court," *American Political Science Review* 82 (December 1988): 1109.

35. Ibid., 1115–1116.

36. Ibid., 1114–1115.

37. Ibid., 1111. Caldeira and Wright add: "the primary informational value of *amicus* briefs lies in their presence or absence alone, not in the direction of the legal arguments advanced within. . . . The direction of [our] statistical result suggests that what matters most is the presence or absence of an *amicus* brief per se, not the direction of the substantive arguments presented. . . . Briefs *amicus curiae* in opposition, plainly and simply, pique the Court's interest in a case." Ibid., 1113, 1119.

38. Ibid., 1119.

39. Gregory A. Caldeira and John R. Wright, "*Amici Curiae* before the Supreme Court: Who Participates, When, and How Much?" *Journal of Politics* 52 (August 1990): 782.

40. Ibid., 794.

41. Adam Chandler, "Cert.-stage *Amicus* Briefs: Who Files Them and to What Effect?" *SCOTUSBlog*, September 27, 2007, http://www.scotusblog.com/wp/cert-stage-amicus-briefs-who-files-them-and-to-what-effect-2/.

42. What Chandler terms the "sweet sixteen" of top amicus-stage participants includes (in the order of the number of briefs filed): Chamber of Commerce of the United States of America, National

Association of Criminal Defense Lawyers, Washington Legal Foundation, Pacific Legal Foundation, National Association of Manufacturers, National Association of Home Builders, New England Legal Foundation, International Municipal Lawyers Association, National League of Cities, Mountain States Legal Foundation, Council on State Taxation, Pharmaceutical Research and Manufacturers of America, Product Liability Advisory Council, Inc., Reporters Committee for Freedom of the Press, Society of Professional Journalists, Association of American Railroads.

43. Marc Galanter, "Why the 'Haves' Come Out Ahead: Speculations of the Limits of Legal Change," *Law and Society Review* 9 (1974): 95.

44. See table at http://www.scotusblog.com/movabletype/archives/Top%2016%20Amici.pdf.

45. Chandler, "Cert.-stage *Amicus* Briefs."

46. Lee Epstein and C. K. Rowland, "Debunking the Myth of Interest Group Invincibility in the Courts," *American Political Science Review* 85 (1991): 205. Compare Donald R. Songer and Reginald S. Sheehan, "Interest Group Success in the Courts: *Amicus* Participation in the Supreme Court," *Political Research Quarterly* 46 (1993): 339. Songer and Sheehan contend that "[o]verall, the evidence on the extent of the impact of *amici* is fragmentary." Ibid., 341. Their research leads them to conclude that "[w]hile there may be particular cases in which the argument presented by groups appearing as *amici* decisively influenced the Court's thinking, there is no general pattern which suggests that a litigant's chances for success depend on whether or not an *amicus curiae* is filed in the litigant's behalf." Ibid., 351.

One should not confuse apples with oranges: Epstein and Rowland's and Songer and Sheehan's respective studies focus on the merits stage, not the cert. stage, of Supreme Court review process. Thus, these two studies do not bear directly on research about amicus advocacy and granting cert.

47. Richard J. Lazarus, "Advocacy Matters Before and Within the Supreme Court: Transforming the Court by Transforming the Bar," *Georgetown Law Journal* 96 (June 2008): 1487.

Compare Kevin T. McGuire, *The Supreme Court Bar: Legal Elites in the Washington Community* (Charlottesville: University Press of Virginia, 1993); and Kevin T. McGuire, "The Supreme Court Bar and Institutional Relationships," in Howard Gillman and Cornell Clayton, eds., *The Supreme Court in American Politics: New Institutionalist Interpretations* (Lawrence: University Press of Kansas, 1999). Also see Jack Greenberg, *Crusaders in the Courts: How a Dedicated Band of Lawyers Fought for the Civil Rights Revolution* (New York: Basic Books, 1994); and Stephen L. Wasby, *Race Relations in an Age of Complexity* (Charlottesville: University Press of Virginia, 1995).

48. Lazarus, "Advocacy Matters Before and Within the Supreme Court," 1497.

49. Lazarus quoting Jill Abramson, "Mayer, Brown's 'Shadow' Solicitors," *Legal Times*, November 24, 1986, 1. See ibid., 1491–1503.

50. Ibid., 1507.

51. Ibid., 1522–1540.

52. "Interviews with former clerks confirm the obvious: the clerks pay special attention to the petitions filed by prominent Supreme Court advocates and to the *amicus* briefs those advocates succeed in having filed in support of review. When they see the name of an attorney whose work before the Court they know, at least by reputation, that attorney's involvement in the case, by itself, conveys an important message about the significance of the legal issues being presented and the credibility of the assertions being made." Ibid., 1526.

Compare the analysis of criminal court communities in James Eisenstein and Herbert Jacob, *Felony Justice: An Organizational Analysis of Criminal Courts* (Boston: Little, Brown, 1977); James Eisenstein, Roy B. Flemming, and Peter F. Nardulli, *The Contours of Justices: Communities and Their Courts* (Boston: Little, Brown, 1988); Peter F. Nardulli, James Eisenstein, and Roy B. Flemming, *The Tenor of Justice: Criminal Courts and the Guilty Plea Process* (Urbana: University of Illinois Press, 1988); and

Roy B. Flemming, Peter F. Nardulli, and James Eisenstein, *The Craft of Justice: Politics and Work in Criminal Court Communities* (Philadelphia: University of Pennsylvania Press, 1992).

53. Lazarus, "Advocacy Matters Before and within the Supreme Court," 1530.

54. Ibid., 1555–1557.

55. Ibid., 1557.

56. B.A., Brigham Young University (1983), J.D., The George Washington University (1986), President, The George Washington University Chapter of the Federalist Society, 1984–1986, joined Kirkland & Ellis in 1989, becoming a partner in 1993. Richmond is now managing partner at Jenner & Block in Los Angeles.

57. Notes from interview with Rick Richmond, September 9, 2008. My partner, Melinda Soules, also participated in the Richmond interview. Follow-up telephone conversation, February, 25, 2009. The materials in the following two paragraphs are taken from these conversations.

58. Richmond opined that he believed there usually is not enough pro bono done in big firms. Ibid.

59. Rick Richmond interview, September 9, 2008.

60. Justice John Paul Stevens and, more recently, Justice Samuel Alito do not participate in the cert. pool. See Adam Liptak, "A Second Justice Opts Out of a Longtime Custom: The 'Cert. Pool,'" *New York Times*, September 25, 2008, http://www.nytimes.com/2008/09/26/washington/26memo. html?_r=1&scp=1&sq=alito%20and%20cert.%20pool&st=cse.

61. Eugene Gressman, et al., *Supreme Court Practice: For Practice in the Supreme Court of the United States*, 9th ed. (Arlington, Va.: Bureau of National Affairs, 2007). See 58–65 for an analysis of these long odds.

62. Rick Richmond interview, September 9, 2008. Richmond joked about the ambiguous phrase in Joseph Frederick's banner. Did it mean that Frederick loved Jesus so much that he wanted to share bong hits with Jesus, or was Frederick mocking Jesus? In any event, Richmond speculated that the "odd and interesting" banner might catch the attention of the young people who clerk at the Supreme Court.

63. Ibid.

64. Ibid.

65. See Margaret Meriwether Cordray and Richard Cordray, "The Supreme Court's Plenary Docket," *Washington & Lee Law Review* 58 (Summer 2001): 737; and Margaret Meriwether Cordray and Richard Cordray, "The Philosophy of *Certiorari*: Jurisprudential Considerations in Supreme Court Case Selection," *Washington University Law Quarterly* 82 (Summer 2004): 389. Also see Kevin M. Scott, "Shaping the Supreme Court's Federal *Certiorari* Docket," *Justice System Journal* 27 (2006): 191. Compare H. W. Perry, *Deciding to Decide* (Cambridge, Mass.: Harvard University Press, 1991); and Doris Marie Provine, *Case Selection in the United States Supreme Court* (Chicago: University of Chicago Press, 1980).

66. See David M. O'Brien, "Join-3 Votes, the Rule of Four, the Cert. Pool, and the Supreme Court's Shrinking Plenary Docket," *Journal Law & Politics* 13 (Fall 1997): 779.

67. On the D.A.R.E. brief were three other organizations, the Drug Free America Foundation, Inc., National Families in Action, and Save Our Society from Drugs, together with William J. Bennett and Gen. Barry R. McCaffrey (see *Amicus curiae* brief for D.A.R.E. America in support of petitioners on writ of *certiorari*, Appendix A, 1a-3a). Rick Richmond was instrumental in enlisting General McCaffrey to join the D.A.R.E. brief. Richmond said that one key task facing the petitioners was to persuade the Court that the issues raised by *Morse* were "much broader than a kid holding up a banner and the Principal responding." Getting General McCaffrey, former U.S. Drug Czar (2/29/96–1/4/01), whom Richmond knows well, to sign on the D.A.R.E. brief as an amici would help to "educate" the Court about the dangers of allowing students to advocate drug use. Notes from interview with Rick Richmond, September 9, 2008. Follow-up telephone conversation, February, 25, 2009.

The American Association of School Administrators joined the National School Boards Association brief (see *Amicus curiae* brief for National School Boards Association In Support of Petition for Writ of *Certiorari*, Motion for leave to file brief as *amici curiae* in support of the petition for writ of *certiorari*, unpaginated).

68. See 118 above.

69. Gregory A. Caldeira, John R. Wright, and Christopher J. W. Zorn, "Sophisticated Voting and Gate-Keeping in the Supreme Court," *Journal of Law, Economics, and Organization* 15 (1999): 549.

70. Ibid., 550.

71. Ibid., 566.

72. James S. Thomson, "Review Essay: Inside the Supreme Court: A Sanctum Sanctorum?" *Mississippi Law Journal* 66 (Fall 1996): 177. Compare, Laura Krugman Ray, "America Meets the Justices: Explaining the Supreme Court to the General Reader," *Tennessee Law Review* 72 (Winter 2005): 573; and Frank B. Cross and Stephanie Lindquist, "The Chief Justice and the Institutional Judiciary: Doctrinal and Strategic Influences of the Chief Justice: The Decisional Significance of the Chief Justice," *University of Pennsylvania Law Review* 154 (June 2006): 1665; and David Ray Papke, "From Flat to Round: Changing Portrayals of the Judge in American Popular Culture," *Journal of Legal Professionals* 31 (2007): 127.

73. *Amicus curiae* brief for National School Boards Association In Support of Petition for Writ of *Certiorari*, i.

74. Ibid.

75. Ibid., 2.

76. Ibid., 8 (emphasis added; citation omitted).

77. Ibid., 9 (emphasis added).

78. *Bethel School District No 403 v. Fraser*, 478 U.S. 675 (1987).

79. *Amicus curiae* brief for National School Boards Association in Support of Petition for Writ of *Certiorari*, 16.

80. Ibid., 17. The other five NSBA derivative clarifications are: B. This Court Should Clarify That Schools May Enforce Their Educational Mission in All Settings Where Students Are Entrusted to Their Care and Tutelage; C. This Court Should Clarify the Meaning of "Plainly Offensive" Speech; D. This Court Should Resolve the Differences Among Federal Courts Regarding Whether *Fraser* Applies to Manner or to Content of Student Speech, or Both; E. This Court Should Clarify Whether *Tinker* Establishes a Two Prong Analysis of Student Speech or Requires Only Substantial Disruption. Ibid., 9–15.

81. Ibid., 18–20.

82. Ibid., 5.

83. Ibid (emphasis added).

84. *Amicus curiae* brief for D.A.R.E. in Support of Petition for Writ of *Certiorari*, ii.

85. Ibid., 8.

86. Ibid., 4–8.

87. Ibid., 13–18.

88. Ibid., 6 (citations omitted).

89. Ibid., 13 (emphasis added).

90. *Vernonia School District 47J v. Acton*, 515 U.S. 646 (1995).

91. *Board of Education v. Earls*, 536 U.S. 822 (2002).

92. Ibid., 834.

93. *Amicus curiae* brief for D.A.R.E. in Support of Petition for Writ of *Certiorari*, 9.

94. Ibid., 11.

95. Joining Starr on the petition were Rick Richmond and Eric W. Hagen, formerly of Kirkland & Ellis. When he learned that his colleagues were taking on Deborah Morse and the Juneau School Board's case pro bono, Hagen asked to join the cause. Notes from interview with Rick Richmond, September 9, 2008. Follow-up telephone conversation, February, 25, 2009.

96. Ibid. The material in the remainder of this paragraph is taken from these conversations.

97. Petition for writ of *certiorari, Juneau School Board; Deborah Morse v. Joseph Frederick*, 1.

98. Ibid., 12–23.

99. 439 F.3d 1114 (9th Cir. 2006).

100. Petition for writ of *certiorari, Juneau School Board; Deborah Morse v. Joseph Frederick*, 12–14. *Tinker v. Des Moines Independent Community School District*, 393 U.S. 503 (1969); *Bethel School District No. 403 v. Fraser*, 478 U.S. 675 (1986); *Hazelwood School District v. Kuhlmeier*, 484 U.S. 260 (1988).

101. Petition for writ of *certiorari, Juneau School Board; Deborah Morse v. Joseph Frederick*, 14.

102. "Disruptive" student speech (*Tinker*), "vulgar, lewd, indecent, obscene and plainly offensive" student speech (*Fraser*), speech that "might reasonably bear the imprimatur of the school" (*Kuhlmeier*).

103. Petition for writ of *certiorari, Juneau School Board; Deborah Morse v. Joseph Frederick*, 20. See ibid., 15–21.

104. Ibid., 20.

105. Ibid., 21.

106. Ibid.

107. Ibid. For instance the petitioners cite the "custodial and tutelary" language of *Vernonia School District 47J v. Acton*, 515 U.S. 646, 655 (1995) (quoted in *Davis Next Friend LaShonda D. v. Monroe County Board of Education*, 526 U.S. 629, 646 (1999)).

108. Petition for writ of *certiorari, Juneau School Board; Deborah Morse v. Joseph Frederick*, 21.

109. Ibid., 22.

110. Ibid., 22–23.

111. Ibid., 23. The Kirkland & Ellis lawyers argued, secondly, that by holding Deborah Morse personally liable: "The Decision Below Radically Departs From Well-Established Principles Of Qualified Immunity." Their argument consists of four parts. First, the Ninth Circuit departed from the principle that "[i]f judges . . . disagree on a constitutional question, it is unfair to subject [governmental actors] to money damages for picking the losing side of the controversy." Ibid., 24. Second, the Ninth Circuit's error results from its misapplication of the correct two-part qualified immunity test, a test the Supreme Court announced (in the course of overturning another Ninth Circuit decision) in *Saucier v. Katz*, 533 U.S. 194 (2001). Ibid., 25–27. Third, the Ninth Circuit decision is a "disruptive judicial development in the multi-State mega-Circuit of the Ninth [that] threatens to compromise public school administration in the West—and beyond—in a fundamental way." Ibid., 28. Fourth, '[i]n view of the manifest error infecting the Ninth Circuit's qualified immunity analysis, [the Supreme Court] may wish to consider summary reversal." Ibid., 28.

112. On the opposition brief with Mertz is Jason Brandeis of the American Civil Liberties Union of Alaska Foundation.

113. Brief in Opposition to Petition for Writ of *Certiorari, Juneau School Board and Deborah Morse v. Joseph Frederick*, 1.

114. Ibid.

115. J. D. Tuccille, "Joe Frederick's Free-Speech Battle," *Disloyal Opposition*, March 20, 2007, http://www.tuccille.com/blog/2007/03/joe-fredericks-free-speech-battle.html.

116. See generally, chapter 5, 103–104.

117. Brief in Opposition to Petition for Writ of *Certiorari, Juneau School Board and Deborah Morse v. Joseph Frederick*, 5–6.

118. The previous two quotations are from ibid., 10.

119. Ibid., 11.

120. Ibid., 12.

121. Ibid., 13.

122. These four quotations are from Petitioner's Reply Memorandum, *Juneau School Board and Deborah Morse v. Joseph Frederick*, 1.

123. Ibid., 2–5.

124. Ibid., 3.

125. Ibid.

126. Ibid.

127. Ibid., 5–9.

128. Ibid., 6, 7, and 8, respectively.

129. Ibid., 9–10.

130. Ibid., 10. Rick Richmond observed, when asked to reflect on striking a correct balance between students' rights and school authority, "We don't want to inhibit young people's views. We want to allow healthy debate; don't restrict robust healthy debate. We want education debate, religious debate, free and open—but drug use? Sex speech? We can't allow speech to become disruptive. The balance needs to be toward healthy debate that's civil." Notes from interview with Rick Richmond, September 9, 2008. Follow-up telephone conversation, February, 25, 2009.

131. Listed alphabetically, Frederick's amici were Alliance Defense Fund (http://www.alliance defensefund.org/main/default.aspx), American Center for Law and Justice (http://www.aclj.org), Center for Individual Rights (http://www.cir-usa.org), Christian Legal Society (http://www.clsnet. org), Drug Policy Alliance (http://www.drugpolicy.org/homepage.cfm), Lambda Legal Defense and Education Fund (http://www.lambdalegal.org), Liberty Counsel (http://www.lc.org), Liberty Legal Institute (http://www.libertylegal.org), National Coalition Against Censorship (http://www. ncac.org), Rutherford Institute (http://www.rutherford.org), Student Press Law Center (http:// www.splc.org), Students for Sensible Drug Policy (http://ssdp.org/index.php).

132. Paul M. Collins Jr. and Lisa A. Solowiej, "Interest Group Participation, Competition, and Conflict in the U.S. Supreme Court," *Law & Social Inquiry* 32 (Fall 2007): 959–960.

133. Andrea McAtee and Kevin T. McGuire, "Convincing the Court: Two Studies of Advocacy: Lawyers, Justices, and Issue Salience: When and How Do Legal Arguments Affect the U.S. Supreme Court," *Law & Society Review* 41 (June 2007): 274.

134. See above, 116–119.

135. Bruce J. Ennis, "Effective Amicus Briefs," *Catholic University Law Review* 33 (Spring 1984) 603.

136. Compare Chief Justice Roberts' opinion for the Court and Justice Alito's concurrence, *Morse v. Frederick*, 551 U.S. 393 (2007).

137. See above, 117.

138. Caldeira and Wright, "*Amici Curiae* before the Supreme Court: Who Participates, When, and How Much."

139. Collins and Solowiej, "Interest Group Participation, Competition, and Conflict in the U.S. Supreme Court." See esp. 956–961.

140. Ibid., 958.

141. Joseph D. Kearney and Thomas W. Merrill, "The Influence of *Amicus Curiae* Briefs on the Supreme Court," *Pennsylvania Law Review* 148 (January 2000): 743. Compare Lee Epstein and Jack Knight, "Mapping Out the Strategic Terrain: The Informational Role of *Amicus Curiae*," in Cornell W.

Clayton and Howard Gillman, eds., *Supreme Court Decision-Making: New Institutionalist Approaches* (Chicago: University of Chicago Press, 1999).

142. Kearney and Thomas W. Merrill, "The Influence of *Amicus Curiae* Briefs on the Supreme Court," 775–788.

143. Ibid., 815–817. See 816–820 for Kearney and Merrill's discussion of the four reasons they conclude their results show that law matters.

144. Ibid., 819. Compare McAtee and McGuire, "Convincing the Court"; and Simard, "An Empirical Study of *Amici Curiae* in Federal Court."

145. "The quality of mercy is not strain'd," observes Portia during her defense of Antonio, William Shakespeare, *Merchant of Venice*, VI, I. For Kearney and Merrill, the quality of Supreme Court advocacy is not dispensable. They write: "The Court grants *certiorari* in only about 4% of all cases in which it is sought. Thus, there is a strong presumption against review, and a petitioner's counsel must carry a heavy burden in persuading the Court to hear her case in preference to thousands of others. The lawyer who can carry this burden must typically be highly skilled." (To the last sentence Kearney and Merrill add this footnote: "This proposition, of course, is not always true. There will be instances where cases present such square circuit conflicts or issues of such clear national importance that any lawyer could secure review. We are speaking of the general case.") Kearney and Merrill continue: "In contrast, respondents obviously do not have to be represented by able counsel in order to have the Court grant review; indeed, the Court is more likely to grant review if the respondent is not represented by able counsel who can distinguish circuit conflicts and offer prudential reasons why review should be denied." (To this sentence, Kearney and Merrill add this footnote: "Of course, respondent's counsel was skilled enough to prevail in the court below. But Supreme Court advocacy is a specialized discipline. Often petitioners who succeed in obtaining a grant of review will have switched to specialized Supreme Court lawyers; the respondent below may be less inclined to shop for new counsel once the case moves to the Supreme Court.") Ibid., 817; fns. 192, 193. Kearney and Merrill's observations appear to resonate with my story, given that, after losing in the Ninth Circuit, Deborah Morse and the Juneau School Board sought out Kirkland & Ellis to represent them, while Joseph Frederick stayed with Douglas Mertz throughout.

Nevertheless, that said, Kearney and Merrill's observations about Supreme Court advocacy must be understood within the context they made them. They offer four reasons supporting their interpretation of their data that law matters. The first of these is "we find a fairly consistent pattern in which *amicus* briefs supporting respondents show more success . . . than do *amicus* briefs supporting petitioners." Ibid., 816. They then ask: "Why might *amicus* filers supporting respondents achieve more success than filers supporting petitioners?" Ibid., 817. It is in this context that they speculate that ability matters: "The explanation *may* be that petitioners *typically* must be represented by able counsel in order to convince the Court to grant review." Ibid., (emphasis added).

Whether or not Kearney and Merrill's conjecture is valid, their use of the word "able" is infelicitous. Following their own analysis, the more apt description would be "specialized"; or, perhaps, "repeat player." See Kevin T. McGuire, "Repeat Players in the Supreme Court: The Role of Experienced Lawyers in Litigation Success," *Journal of Politics* 57 (February 1995): 187.

146. Paul M. Collins Jr., "Friends of the Court: Examining the Influence of *Amicus Curiae* Participation in U.S. Supreme Court Litigation," *Law & Society Review* 38 (December 2004): 808, 828 (citations omitted).

147. Ibid., 808.

148. Ibid., 822. Like Kearney and Merrill, Collins is circumspect about his findings. He cautions: "[W]hile I am confident in the result that a relative advantage of *amicus* participants does not increase the likelihood of litigation success, I am hesitant to call the affected group hypothesis lifeless. . . . In particular, it is possible that the Court reacts to affected groups in the form of briefs and not participants.

If the Court believes that the number of participants on a brief is a less credible information source than the number of briefs filed, it may simply be responding to the number of briefs filed as indicative of affected groups. In other words, if the Court considers the amount of resources interest groups spend as indicative of truly potentially affected groups, and if the costs of filing an *amicus* brief are within a relatively homogeneous range, then we would expect the Court to consider the number of briefs filed as a proxy for the amount of resources expended and not the number of participants joining briefs." Ibid., 828.

Collins has published subsequent research that complements the results discussed here. In "Lobbyists before the U.S. Supreme Court: Investigating the Influence of *Amicus Curiae* Briefs," Collins closed the findings section of his article: "Given the above [data] analyses, I can reasonably conclude that the robust support for the influence of *amicus* briefs on the Court's decision making ... reflects the important role organized interests play in Supreme Court decision making." Paul M. Collins Jr., "Lobbyists before the U.S. Supreme Court: Investigating the Influence of *Amicus Curiae* Briefs," *Political Research Quarterly* 60 (March 2007): 65. Collins' most recent work is *Friends of the Supreme Court: Interest Groups and Judicial Decision Making* (New York: Oxford University Press, 2008), a book that, if not definitive, significantly "moves forward," as Collins says, our understanding the role *amici* play in the Supreme Court policy process. See *Friends of the Supreme Court*, 10–12.

149. Paul M. Chen, "The Informational Role of *Amici Curiae* in *Gonzales v. Raich*," *Illinois University Law Journal* 31 (Winter 2007): 217. Compare Ruth Colker, "Justice Sandra Day O'Connor's Friends," *Ohio State Law Journal* 68 (2007): 517.

150. "[B]ecause these studies measure the AC [amicus curiae] brief's impact by correlating the number or type of briefs with specific case outcomes (for example, granting or denying *cert.*, winning or losing on the merits), they cannot tell us precisely how the justices actually use the arguments or information from the briefs to help them rule one way or another in a case. Even those studies that code specific arguments in the brief, while they show that AC arguments do appear in Supreme Court opinions, they cannot tell us whether the arguments appearing in the opinion were rejected of approved by the opinion-writer, which is important in determining what kind of impact the AC brief had." Chen, "The Informational Role of *Amici Curiae*," 220.

151. Ibid., 239.

152. Ibid., 240. Compare Collins, "Friends of the Court"; Susan Behuniak-Long, "Friendly Fire: *Amici Curiae* and *Webster v. Reproductive Health Services*," *Judicature* 74 (1991): 261; and James F. Spriggs and Paul J. Wahlbeck, "*Amici Curiae* and the Role of Information at the Supreme Court," *Policy Research Quarterly* 50 (1997): 365. Also see Susanne U. Samuels, *First Among Friends: Interest Groups, the U.S. Supreme Court, and the Right to Privacy* (Westport, Conn.: Praeger, 2004).

153. Brief for Petitioner, *Deborah Morse; Juneau School Board v. Joseph Frederick*, 14.

154. Ibid., 17.

155. "In reversing the district court's grant of summary judgment in favor of the Juneau School Board and Deborah Morse, the Ninth Circuit embraced an unduly narrow reading of this Court's teachings with respect to the free speech rights of public school students. To make very bad matters profoundly worse, the court below fashioned an approach to qualified immunity doctrine that conflicts with this Court's precedents and is dangerously unsettling to thousands of public school educators and administrators across the country." Ibid., 14.

156. Ibid., 18.

157. Ibid., 25–26.

158. Ibid., 27.

159. Ibid., 32.

160. Ibid., 38.

161. William J. Bennett and Gen. Barry R. McCaffrey.

162. Compare the critique of the "bad tendency" theory in Brief for the Drug Policy Alliance and the Campaign for New Drug Policies as *Amici Curiae* supporting Respondent, 6–10.

163. Brief for D.A.R.E. America, et al. as *Amici Curiae* in support of Petitioners, 1.

164. These passages are from ibid., 1, 2, 14, 21.

165. Ibid., 21.

166. Joining the NSBA were the American Association of School Administrators and the National Association of Secondary School Principals.

167. Brief of *Amici Curiae* National School Boards Association, American Association of School Administrators, and the National Association of Secondary School Principals, In Support of Petitioners, 15.

168. Ibid., 18. The NSBA brief continues: "In no way does this mean that school officials have unbridled discretion to define and promote their educational mission in a manner that capriciously tramples on students' First Amendment rights. Indeed, local school officials experienced at establishing their schools' educational mission through adoption and implementation of district policies are trained to take many factors into consideration in developing school policies. A school's educational mission as defined through its policies is constrained and sometimes mandated by voluminous and expanding legal rules and regulations; informed by scientific research, educational expertise, and community input; and ultimately subject to the censure of the ballot box." Ibid., 18–19.

169. Ibid., 27.

170. Interview with Naomi Gittins, November 5, 2008. "[W]e have an internal process that we go through, which includes vetting by the legal staff and then also approval by what we call our executive committee, which is a subset of our board of directors. And they have to—we write them a memo about why we think the case is important, how it will affect schools across the nation, does it align with positions we have taken before in similar cases, does it align with what we call our beliefs and policies . . . and then it's up to them to vote on whether we will actually participate in the case. They usually take the recommendations of the legal staff; but not always. They have final say-so on our participation." Ibid.

171. Ibid.

172. Ibid.

173. Ibid.

174. Lincoln Kaplan, *The Tenth Justice: The Solicitor General and the Rule of Law* (New York: Knopf, 1987).

175. See Kearney and Merrill, "The Influence of *Amicus Curiae* Briefs on the Supreme Court," 772–775 and notes accompanying.

176. Rebecca Mae Salokar, *The Solicitor General: The Politics of Law* (Philadelphia: Temple University Press, 1992), 135.

177. Collins, *Friends of the Supreme Court*, 182 (also see 182, fn. 146). Collins continued: "A growing body of scholarship . . . indicates that the quality of argumentation and the status of litigants (and perhaps *amici*) can shape judicial choice[.] . . . As applied to *amicus* briefs, this implies that courts might be particularly attentive to the arguments advanced by highly experienced advocates, giving those briefs favorable attention." Ibid., 183. Compare McGuire, "Repeat Players in the Supreme Court."

Recalling that on the brief with the solicitor general were Assistant Attorney General Peter D. Keisler, U.S. Department of Education General Counsel Kent D. Talbert, and Edward H. Jurith, General Counsel of the Office of National Drug Control Policy, plus eight other attorneys from these three federal government organizations, it is not unreasonable to speculate that experience and status enhanced the weight of the SG's brief on behalf of the Petitioners.

178. Brief for the United States as *Amicus Curiae* Supporting Petitioners, 1.

179. Ibid., 3, quoting Deborah Morse in Pet App. 2a.

180. Ibid., 10.

181. See ibid., 10–12.

182. Ibid., 14. Compare ibid., 19.

183. Respondent's Brief, 7. Joining Mertz on the Respondent's Brief were Jason Brandeis of the American Civil Liberties Union of Alaska, and Steven R. Shapiro, Catherine N. Crump, and Jonathan B. Miller of the American Civil Liberties Union Foundation.

184. Ibid., 8.

185. Ibid., 29–30. Referencing the SG's brief (U.S. Br. 27), Mertz noted that the United States "argues that even speech advocating reform of drug laws can properly be subject to school discipline." Ibid., 31.

186. Ibid., 13–16; 21–29.

187. Ibid., 30–31.

188. For good measure, Mertz added that Frederick's speech might be understood to have occurred outside the Juneau-Douglas High School gate: "The Record Supports a Finding That This Is Not a Student Speech Case Because Frederick Was Not Subject to the School's Authority When He Was Told to Take Down His Banner." Ibid., 33–36.

Compare Reply Brief for Petitioners, filed by Kirkland & Ellis attorneys one week before oral argument, on March 12, 2007. This brief reasserted that *Morse v. Frederick* is a student speech case, maintained again that illegal drug speech is unprotected speech, and reaffirmed school officials' need to exercise discretion in order to hold students accountable.

189. Listed in the order they appear on the Supreme Court Docket Sheet, the full list of *amici* are: (1) Rutherford Institute; (2) Liberty Counsel; (3) Alliance Defense Fund; (4) Student Press Law Center (with Feminists for Free Expression, the First Amendment Project, The Freedom to Read Foundation, and the Thomas Jefferson Center for the Protection of Free Expression); (5) Liberty Legal Institute; (6) Students for Sensible Drug Policy; (7) Christian Legal Society; (8) National Coalition Against Censorship (with the American Booksellers Foundation for Free Expression); (9) American Center for Law and Justice; (10) Drug Policy Alliance (with the Campaign for New Drug Policies); (11) Lambda Legal Defense and Education Fund; (12) Center for Individual Rights.

190. Stephen M. Shapiro, "*Amicus* Briefs in the Supreme Court," *Litigation* 10 (Spring 1984): 21–22. Shapiro also is one of the five coauthors of the influential *Supreme Court Practice: For Practice in the Supreme Court of the United States*, 9th ed. (Arlington, Va.: Bureau of National Affairs, 2007). On the perils of "me too" briefs, compare Dan Schweitzer, "Development and Practice Note: Fundamentals of Preparing a United States Supreme Court *Amicus* Brief," *Journal of Appellate Practice & Process* 5 (Fall 2003): 538.

191. See above, 129–131.

192. **Free expression advocates**: Center for Individual Rights, Lambda Legal Defense and Education Fund, National Coalition Against Censorship, Rutherford Institute, Student Press Law Center; **religious speech advocates**: Alliance Defense Fund, American Center for Law and Justice, Christian Legal Society, Liberty Counsel, Liberty Legal Institute; **drug policy reform advocates**: Drug Policy Alliance, Students for Sensible Drug Policy.

193. "While it is hardly surprising to find the American Civil Liberties Union and the National Coalition Against Censorship on Mr. Frederick's side, it is the array of briefs from organizations that litigate and speak on behalf of the religious right that has lifted *Morse v. Frederick* out of the realm of the ordinary." Linda Greenhouse, "Free Speech Case Divides Bush and Religious Right," *New York Times*, March 18, 2007, http://www.nytimes.com/2007/03/18/washington/18scotus.html?pagewanted=1&_r=1.

Compare Jon Katz: "At first blush, Mr. Frederick and his counsel, the American Civil Liberties Union, may seem like strange bedfellows with such organizations, but they all have recognized that robust First Amendment protections for students and everyone else is critical to the ACLU's broad First Amendment protection interests and the interests of the other organizations listed here against government officials not favorably disposed to their agendas." "'Bong Hits 4 Jesus:' Strange bedfellows justifiably rally behind . . ." *Underdog*, April 2, 2007, http://katzjustice.com/underdog/archives/448-Bong-Hits-4-Jesus-Strange-bedfellows-justifiably-rally-behind-the-First-Amendment.html. Also see David Masci, "Strange Bedfellows: Why Are Some Religious Groups Defending 'Bong Hits 4 Jesus'?" *The Pew Forum on Religion and Public Life*, March 27, 2007, http://pewforum.org/docs/?DocID=184; Ed Brayton, "Strange Bedfellows on Bong hits Case," *Dispatches from the Culture Wars: Thoughts from the Interface of Science, Religion, Law and Culture*, March 19, 2007, http://scienceblogs.com/dispatches/2007/03/strange_bedfellows_on_bong_hit.php; and Daniel Burke, "Supreme Court Hears 'Bong Hits 4 Jesus' Case: Christian legal groups file briefs supporting banner," *Christianity Today*, March 20, 2007, http://www.christianitytoday.com/ct/2007/marchweb-only/112-22.0.html.

194. The ACLU informed amici of other groups participating. Alex D. Kreit, who helped author the Students for a Sensible Drug Policy (SSDP) amicus brief, observed: "We got information from ACLU . . . the folks who were sort of coordinating the *amici* about who else is going to be filing *amicus* briefs on [Frederick's] side. . . . That . . . helped guide what SSDP is going to bring to the table that's unique from these other groups. Because, when you've got a case like this that has a lot of *amici*, you want to make sure that what your brief is bringing to the table is going to be sort of distinct enough. It's going to have its own voice. It's going to have its own purpose, and it's not just overlapping what a different *amicus* group is saying." Interview with Alex D. Kreit, November 23, 1008.

195. Schweitzer, "Fundamentals of Preparing a United States Supreme Court *Amicus* Brief," 531.

196. Ibid., 531–538. Schweitzer's other ideas, the first two of which seem more suited to Petitioner amici, are: "The 'Go Further Than the Party' Brief," "The 'More Restrained Than the Party' Brief," "The 'Practical Implications' or 'Brandeis' Brief," and "the 'Historical Background' Brief." The analysis that follows focuses on an aspect, or aspects, of each brief discussed that primarily situates them in one or more of Schweitzer's categories. The briefs so identified contain more arguments than the one(s) I single out.

197. Ibid., 534.

198. *Amicus* Brief of the American Center for Law and Justice in Support of Respondent, 3, 4. ACLJ asserted that "[d]ismissal of the present writ . . . would not preclude . . . review. Already pending on this Court's docket are two other cases on the same topic. *See Harper v. Poway Unified Sch. Dist..*, U.S. No. 06-595; *Marineau v. Guiles*, U.S. No. 06-757." Ibid., 4. (The Supreme Court vacated the Ninth Circuit's *Harper* decision without a hearing, *Harper v. Poway Unified School Dist.*, 127 S. Ct. 1484 (2007) (No. 06-595). In *Marineau* the Court denied *cert.*, *Marineau v. Guiles*, 75 USLW 3313 (U.S. June 29, 2007) (No. 06-757)).

Compare: "In the quite likely event that the Court can make no confident judgment about the meaning of [Frederick's] sign, the legal issues are presented only in a hypothetical and alternative way. In that event, the proper course is to dismiss the writ as improvidently granted." Brief of the Liberty Legal Institute as *Amicus Curiae* in Support of Respondent, 5.

Also see: "Although the School wants this Court to rely upon 'the facts as determined by two lower courts,' it does not explain what business those courts had *determining* facts on summary judgment motions. 'By its very nature, a summary judgment does not involve the determination of disputed questions of fact, but is confined to purely legal issues.' With that standard in mind, the judgment of the Ninth Circuit denying defendants summary judgment can be affirmed for a variety of reasons not relied upon by the Ninth Circuit." Brief of *Amicus Curiae* Center for Individual Rights in Support of Respondent, 18 (citation omitted).

199. Brief for *Amicus Curiae* Lambda Legal Defense and Education Fund, Inc. in Support of Respondent, 26 (citations omitted).

200. Ibid., 27.

201. Brief of the National Coalition Against Censorship and the American Booksellers Foundation for Free Expression as *Amici Curiae* in Support of Respondent, 21, 22.

202. Ibid., 27.

203. Ibid., 28.

204. Ibid., 29.

205. Ibid.

206. Brief on Behalf of Students for Sensible Drug Policy as *Amicus Curiae* in Support of Respondent, 20-23.

207. Ibid., i, 4–11.

208. Interview with Alex D. Kreit, November 23, 1008. The remaining quotations from Kreit on pages 137–138 are from this interview.

At the time Alex was involved in drafting the SSDP amicus brief, he was an associate at Morrison & Foerster, LLP in San Francisco. Currently, Kreit is assistant professor and director, Center for Law & Social Justice, at the Thomas Jefferson School of Law.

209. Schweitzer, "Fundamentals of Preparing a United States Supreme Court *Amicus* Brief," 535.

210. Interview with Alex D. Kreit, November 23, 2008.

211. Brief of *Amicus Curiae* Center for Individual Rights in Support of Respondent, 1.

212. Ibid., 4, 10, 15.

213. Of the process that led to his writing an amicus brief for CIR supporting Frederick, Rosman observed: "Basically [Terry Pell, my boss] . . . asked me for an evaluation of whether we could say something intelligent, 'cause just writing an *amicus* brief that's 'yeah, what the Plaintiff says, and me too'—that's not something that really interests us. There's something that my friends at the Institute for Justice call the 'Mr. Ed Rule': you shouldn't speak unless you have something to say." Interview with Michael E. Rosman, November 6, 2008.

214. Ibid. The remaining quotations from Rosman in this paragraph are from this interview.

215. Brief of The Liberty Legal Institute as *Amicus Curiae* in Support of Respondent, 1. Kelly J. Shackelford (counsel of record), Hiram S. Sasser, III, Douglas Laycock, and Robert A. Destro were listed on the brief.

216. http://www.libertylegal.org.

217. Brief of The Liberty Legal Institute as *Amicus Curiae* in Support of Respondent, 2.

218. Ibid., 2, 14 (emphasis added). "*Amicus* is unwilling to trade the protections *Tinker* affords religious speech for some marginal 'victory' over the ambiguous message at issue in this case." Ibid., 1.

219. Schweitzer, "Fundamentals of Preparing a United States Supreme Court *Amicus* Brief," 535.

220. Respondent's Brief, 33–36.

221. F.3d 1114 (9th Cir. 2006).

222. Brief of The Rutherford Institute, *Amicus Curiae*, In Support of Respondent, 3–8.

223. James J. Knicely (counsel of record), John W. Whitehead, and David Cadell.

224. Brief of The Rutherford Institute, *Amicus Curiae*, In Support of Respondent, 8.

225. Ibid., fn. 3, 3.

226. Ibid., 6. The other crucial disputed fact is "[t]he meaning of Frederick's message 'Bong Hits 4 Jesus.'" Ibid., 7.

227. Ibid., 11. Compare Brief for *Amicus Curiae* Liberty Counsel in Support of Respondent, 11–14.

228. Ibid., 23.

229. Whitehead observed that he and James Knicely "write briefs and we flip-flop our names [as] Counsel of Record. It doesn't matter.... He and I have been working together for—gee—twenty-eight years, something like that." Interview with John W. Whitehead, December 3, 2008. See John W. Whitehead, *The Change Manifesto: Join the Block by Block Movement to Remake America* (Naperville, Ill.: Sourcebooks, Inc. 2008); and R. Jonathan Moore, *Suing for America's Soul: John Whitehead, The Rutherford Institute, and Conservative Christians in Court* (Grand Rapids, Mich.: William B. Eerdmans, 2007).

The remaining quotations from Whitehead on pages 141, 142 are from my December 3, 2008, interview.

230. Schweitzer, "Fundamentals of Preparing a United States Supreme Court *Amicus* Brief," 536.

231. Brief of The Rutherford Institute, *Amicus Curiae*, In Support of Respondent, fn. 11, 23–24.

232. Brief for the Student Press Law Center, Feminists for Free Expression, The First Amendment Project, The Freedom to Read Foundation, and the Thomas Jefferson Center for The Protection of Free Expression as *Amici Curiae* Supporting Respondent, 13.

233. Ibid., 11.

234. Ibid., 12

235. Ibid., 13.

236. Ibid.

237. Brief *Amicus Curiae* of The Christian Legal Society in Support of Respondent, 4.

238. Ibid., 7.

239. Interview with Gregory S. Baylor, Christian Legal Society Center for Law and Religious Freedom, November 13, 2008.

240. Schweitzer, "Fundamentals of Preparing a United States Supreme Court *Amicus* Brief, 534.

241. Compare the sentiment conventionally (inaccurately) ascribed to Voltaire: "I disapprove of what you say, but I will defend to the death your right to say it."

242. Brief for *Amicus Curiae* Liberty Counsel in Support of Respondent, 1–2. Compare: "The Alliance Defense Fund ('ADF') is a not-for-profit public interest legal organization providing strategic planning, training, funding, and direct litigation services to protect our first constitutional liberty— religious freedom." Brief of *Amicus Curiae* Alliance Defense Fund Supporting Respondent, 1.

243. Interview with Mary E. McAlister, December 3, 2008. The subsequent quote, below, from Ms. McAlister also is from this interview.

244. Brief for *Amicus Curiae* Liberty Counsel in Support of Respondent, 24.

Notes to Chapter 7

1. See Adam Liptak, "Reticent Justice Opens Up to a Group of Students," *New York Times*, April 13, 2009, http://www.nytimes.com/2009/04/14/us/14bar.html.

2. "Students in these [first-year law school] classes know that they will have to present more than memorized formulas: they will face detailed questioning in a situation of intense and public competition with fellow students. Along with pressure to keep up or excel, there is often excitement, as students put aside their instinctive reactions and their laypersons' reasoning about cases to try in earnest to 'think like a lawyer.' Although generations of disgruntled students (and some observers) have noted that the case-dialogue method easily degenerates into a game of 'hide the ball'—a sort of Twenty Questions without clear pedagogical point—there is no denying that these practices carry a profound mystique. They also produce lasting results." William M. Sullivan, et al., *Educating Lawyers: Preparation for the Profession of Law* (San Francisco: Jossey-Bass/Wiley, 2007), 2.

Compare John Brigham: "The debates between the attorneys and the justices are not all that technical, perhaps not unlike the conduct of case discussion in a law school class." "May It Please the Court: Symposium on Oral Argument," *Law and Courts* 5 (Spring 1995): 3.

3. Dana Milbank, "Up in Smoke at the High Court," *Washington Post*, March 20, 2007, http://www.washingtonpost.com/wp-dyn/content/article/2007/03/19/AR2007031901696.html. The Milbank quotes in the remainder of this paragraph are from this source.

4. "While Justice Jackson has likened oral argument to the stately process of 'building a cathedral,' counsel is apt to conclude, after completing a first argument, that the experience is more akin to an intense athletic contest, hedged by rigid time restrictions and potentially fatal fumbles and missteps." Stephen M. Shapiro, "Oral Argument in the Supreme Court of the United States," *Cath. U. Law Review* 33 (Spring 1984): 529.

On another occasion, Justice Jackson observed: "I used to say that, as Solicitor General, I made three arguments in every case. First came the one that I planned—as I thought, logical, coherent, complete. Second was the one actually presented—interrupted, incoherent, disjointed, disappointing. The third was the utterly devastating argument that I thought of after going to bed that night." Robert H. Jackson, "Advocacy Before the United States Supreme Court," *Cornell L. Q.* 37 (1951): 6.

5. See Stephen A. Higginson, "Constitutional Advocacy Explains Constitutional Outcomes," *Fla. Law Review* 60 (September 2008): 857.

6. Eugene Gressman et al., *Supreme Court Practice*, 9th ed. (Arlington, Va.: Bureau of National Affairs Books, 2007), 748–752. Compare, Stephen L. Wasby, Anthony A. D'Amato, and Rosemary Metrailer, "The Function of Oral Argument in the U.S. Supreme Court," *Q. J. Speech* 62 (December 1976): 410; and Peter H. Irons and Stephanie Guitton, eds., *May It Please the Court: The Most Significant Oral Arguments Made before the Supreme Court Since 1955* (New York: The New Press, 1993).

7. Gressman, et al, *Supreme Court Practice*. See ibid., notes 1–9, 748–750 citing several sitting and former appellate judges, and scholars, on the importance of oral advocacy.

8. Ibid., 748.

9. Ibid., 749, quoting John G. Roberts Jr. "Oral Advocacy and the Re-emergence of a Supreme Court Bar," *J. Sup Ct. History* 30 (2005): 68, 69, 70.

Reviewing Cass R. Sunstein's 2009 book on constitutional interpretation, Ronald Dworkin employs imagery similar to Chief Justice Robert's. Assessing what he terms Sunstein's "more nuanced kind of minimalism" approach to constitutional interpretation (which Dworkin ultimately criticizes), Dworkin writes: "[Such m]inimalism would permit the Court to develop doctrine slowly, responding to experience and public discussion in expanding or contracting its rulings later. It would allow public opinion to mature through continuing debate and experimentation in state and local politics, perhaps crystallizing emerging political trends that would allow the Court to rule more generously later with fewer social costs." Ronald Dworkin, "Looking for Cass Sunstein," *New York Review of Books*, April 30, 2009, 30. Compare John Brigham: "Stern and Gressman publish extensive commentary from justices like Charles Evans Hughes who said that his ideas about a case crystallize at oral argument." "May It Please the Court: Symposium on Oral Argument," *Law and Courts* 5 (Spring 1995): 3.

10. See J. Woodford Howard Jr., "On the Fluidity of Judicial Choice," *Am. Pol. Sci. Rev.* 62 (1968): 43–56. Compare, Nancy Maveety and John Anthony Maltese, "J. Woodford Howard, Jr.: Fluidity, Strategy and Analytical Synthesis in Judicial Studies," in Nancy Maveety, ed., *Pioneers of Judicial Behavior* (Ann Arbor: University of Michigan Press, 2003).

11. Compare Malcolm Gladwell, *The Tipping Point: How Little Things Can Make a Big Difference* (Boston: Little, Brown, 2000).

12. "Not many cases . . . are won on the oral argument alone, but a case can be lost if a lawyer is unable or unwilling to answer a justice's question honestly and persuasively." Justice Ruth Bader Ginsburg, "Remarks on Appellate Advocacy," *S.C. Law Review* 50 (1999): 569.

13. Gressman, et al., *Supreme Court Practice*, 751. The remaining quotations in this paragraph are from this source. See ibid., notes 10–11, 751 citing Justices Douglas, Powell, (then Justice) Rehnquist, and Chief Justice Burger.

14. Justice Douglas fixed the proportion of "incompetent" lawyers at 40 percent. Ibid.

15. Note that these criticisms date from the 1970s and 1980s. Apropos of the rise of an elite Supreme Court Bar at the end of the twentieth century—a development discussed above in Chapter 6, 118–119—Gressman, et al., note that "[i]n more recent years, a resurgent and increasingly specialized private Supreme Court bar, multiple law school clinics, Supreme Court advocacy institutes, and a concerted effort by state and local officials to improve argument have enhanced the quality of oral argument before the Court." Gressman, et al, *Supreme Court Practice*.

16. See Robert J. Martineau, "The Value of Appellate Oral Argument: A Challenge to the Conventional Wisdom," *Iowa Law Review* 72 (October 1986): 1. Compare Myron H. Bright, "The Power of the Spoken Word: In Defense of Oral Argument," *Iowa Law Review* 72 (October 1986): 35; and Mark R. Kravitz, "Book Review: Words to the Wise," *Journal of Appellate Practice & Process* 5 (Fall 2003): 543.

17. Martineau, "The Value of Appellate Oral Argument," 22.

18. Ibid., 29.

19. For a complementary argument to Martineau's preference for written communication in law, see Suzanne Ehrenberg, "Embracing the Writing-Centered Legal Process," *Iowa Law Review* 89 (April 2004): 1159.

20. Martineau cites the late U.S. Fifth Circuit Judge Albert Tate Jr.'s conception of oral argument as a "court conference" as "the basis for developing a more suitable [oral argument] format than the traditional one." Martineau, "The Value of Appellate Oral Argument, 31. See Albert Tate Jr., "Federal Appellate Advocacy in the 1980s," *American Journal of Trial Advocacy* (1981): 78–79.

21. Judges also complained about crushing workloads. Given the deleterious consequences of ballooning filings, oral argument seems a lesser problem, and identifying oral argument as a major cause of a severe judicial time crunch seems something of a red herring. Indeed, it is plausible that *competent* oral argument might mitigate judges' burden by facilitating their work.

22. Both quotes are from Martineau, "The Value of Appellate Oral Argument," 33.

23. John Szmer, Susan W. Johnson, and Tammy A. Sarver, "Does the Lawyer Matter? Influencing Outcomes on the Supreme Court of Canada," *Law & Society Review* 41 (June 2007): 280–282.

24. Szmer, Johnson, and Sarver, "Does the Lawyer Matter?" 279. Szmer and his colleagues argue that "[w]hile Canada (and its judicial system) is similar to the United States (and its judicial system) in many respects, there are still significant differences between the two states. For example, until recently Canada did not have the functional equivalent of a Bill of Rights (the Charter of Rights and Freedoms is barely 20 years old). . . . Given the differences between Canada and the United States, if the attorney capability theory extends to the merits decisions by the [Supreme Court of Canada], it only bolsters the importance, and in particular, the generalizability of the theory." Ibid., 279–280.

25. Ibid., 284. "QC . . . [is an] honorific designation from the provincial government. . . . [T]he criteria in Canada are . . . a function of experience and reputation. . . . Given that the Litigation Experience variable controlled for the experience aspect of the QC designation, we could assume that the coefficient for the QC variable reflects the 'professional or public repute' element." Ibid., 287.

26. Ibid., 293.

27. Ibid., 298.

28. Andrea McAtee and Kevin T. McGuire, "Lawyers, Justices, and Issue Salience: When and How Do Legal Arguments Affect the U.S. Supreme Court?" *Law & Society Review* 41 (June 2007): 260.

29. See 146.

30. McAtee and McGuire, "Lawyers, Justices, and Issue Salience," 266.

31. Ibid., 267.

32. Ibid.

33. But see Helen J. Knowles, "May It Please the Court? The Solicitor General's Not-So-'Special' Relationship: Archibald Cox and the 1963–1964 Reapportionment Cases," *Journal of Supreme Court History* 31 (2006): 279.

34. McAtee and McGuire, 269, 271.

35. Ibid., 272. Jeffrey Toobin observes: "When Antonin Scalia joined the Court, in 1986, he brought a new gladiatorial spirit to oral arguments, and in subsequent years the Justices have often used their questions as much for campaign speeches as for requests for information. Roberts . . . has taken this practice to an extreme, and now, even more than the effervescent Scalia, it is the Chief Justice, with his slight Midwestern twang, who dominates the court's public sessions." Jeffrey Toobin, "No More Mr. Nice Guy," *New Yorker*, May 25, 2009, 44.

36. Ibid., 275. Compare Lawrence Baum, "May It Please the Court: Symposium on Oral Argument," *Law and Courts* 5 (Spring 1995): 4.

37. Timothy R. Johnson, Paul J. Wahlbeck, and James F. Spriggs II, "The Influence of Oral Arguments on the U.S. Supreme Court," *American Political Science Review* 100 (February 2006): 99. Compare Timothy R. Johnson, *Oral Arguments and Decision Making on the United States Supreme Court* (Albany: State University of New York Press, 2004).

38. Timothy R. Johnson, James F. Spriggs II, and Paul J. Wahlbeck, "Oral Advocacy before the United States Supreme Court: Does It Affect the Justices' Decisions?" *Washington University Law Review* 85 (2007): 457.

39. Johnson, Spriggs, and Wahlbeck, "Oral Advocacy before the United States Supreme Court," 460.

40. Ibid.

41. Ibid., quoting Jeffrey A. Segal and Harold J. Spaeth, *The Supreme Court and the Attitudinal Model Revisited* (Cambridge: Cambridge University Press, 2002), 280.

42. Ibid., 458, quoting Justice Antonin Scalia's initially disdainful opinion of oral argument, before spending almost two decades listening to lawyers' advocacy caused him to revise his view.

43. Johnson, Wahlbeck, and Spriggs, "The Influence of Oral Arguments on the U.S. Supreme Court," 99, quoting David O'Brien, *Storm Center: The Supreme Court in American Politics*, 4th ed. (New York: W. W. Norton, 1996), 275.

44. "In each case, [Blackmun] took notes that include information perfectly tailored for investigating the role of oral arguments. Among other things, his oral argument notes record a grade for each attorney's oral presentation before the Court and contain comments raised by his colleagues. His oral argument notes even go so far as to predict the other Justices' final votes on the merits in many cases." Johnson, Spriggs, and Wahlbeck, "Oral Advocacy before the United States Supreme Court," 460–461.

45. Johnson, Wahlbeck, and Spriggs, "The Influence of Oral Arguments on the U.S. Supreme Court," 99.

46. Ibid., 107. Johnson, Wahlbeck, and Spriggs employed nine independent variables to explain Justice Blackmun's assessment of the quality of oral argumentation before the Court. Of these, eight proved more or less valid predictors of high grades: "litigating experience," "Solicitor General," "federal government attorney," "attorney attended elite law school," "Washington elite," "law professor," "attorney argues for interest group," and "former law clerk." Ibid., 105–106; 107–108. The authors' negative findings regarding their ninth independent variable, "ideological compatibility with

attorney," "indicates that our measure of oral argument quality is not appreciably tainted by Justice Blackmun's ideology." Ibid., 108. Compare Johnson, Spriggs, and Wahlbeck, "Oral Advocacy before the United States Supreme Court," 469–481.

47. Johnson, Spriggs, and Wahlbeck, "Oral Advocacy before the United States Supreme Court," 485. In their 2006 article, Johnson, Spriggs, and Wahlbeck elaborate: "Combined, [our] findings suggest that the credibility of the attorney plays a role in Justice Blackmun's grading scheme. Taking each variable in isolation, as we have done, artificially diminishes the effect of credibility, because attorney profiles usually comprise combinations of these attributes.... For us, this confirms the validity of Blackmun's evaluations as reflecting the quality of argumentation, especially in light of ideology's small substantive effect." Johnson, Wahlbeck, and Spriggs, "The Influence of Oral Arguments on the U.S. Supreme Court," 108. Compare Johnson, Spriggs, and Wahlbeck, "Oral Advocacy before the United States Supreme Court," 484–485.

48. Stephen A. Higginson, "Constitutional Advocacy Explains Constitutional Outcomes," 857.

49. Both quotes are from ibid., 893–894.

50. Ibid., 858.

51. Ibid., 861.

52. Ibid., 866.

53. Ibid., 867. Compare Frederick Liu, "Citing the Transcript of Oral Argument: Which Justices Do It and Why," *Yale Law Journal Pocket Part* 118 (2008): 32.

54. Higginson, 888.

55. Johnson, Wahlbeck, and Spriggs, "The Influence of Oral Arguments on the U.S. Supreme Court," 108.

56. Ibid., 111–112. Compare Johnson, Spriggs, and Wahlbeck, "Oral Advocacy before the United States Supreme Court," 489–502.

57. See pp. 146–147, 151.

58. Johnson, Spriggs, and Wahlbeck, "Oral Advocacy before the United States Supreme Court," 462 (internal citation omitted).

59. By the time Starr approached the lectern, he had twice hired the person sitting in the center of the nine justices before whom he stood. First, as chief of staff for William French Smith, President Reagan's attorney general, Starr hired John Roberts in 1981 as Smith's special assistant. Second, in 1988 Solicitor General Starr hired John Roberts as his principal deputy.

60. Chapter 5, 103–104.

61. The Oyez Project, http://www.oyez.org/, Oral Argument Transcript, *Morse v. Frederick*, March 19, 2007, 2. Compare Official Transcript, oral argument, *Morse v. Frederick*, No. 06-278, http://www.supremecourtus.gov/oral_arguments/argument_transcripts/06-278.pdf.

62. Given the Court's eventual ruling and Kennedy's posture in concurring, these first two questions from the Bench proved both revealing and decisive.

63. The Oyez Project, Oral Argument Transcript, *Morse v. Frederick*, 2. Subsequent quotations on the following pages, drawn from Kenneth Starr's allotted time, are from ibid., 2–7.

64. Board Policy No. 5520R, Disruption and Demonstration, Joint Appendix, *Deborah Morse; Juneau School Board*, Petitioners, v. *Joseph Frederick*, Respondent, On Writ of Certiorari to the United States Court of Appeals for the Ninth Circuit, 81–83, in author's possession.

65. Other hypotheticals of student messages the justices rendered were: "bong hits should be legal," "vote Republican, vote Democrat," "Smoke Pot, It's Fun," "Rape Is Fun," and "Extortion Is Profitable."

66. "Scalia's interactions with lawyers are notoriously aggressive.... Scalia also has a habit of telling lawyers whose position he agrees with how to make their arguments; this term, his guidance

prompted one lawyer to say, 'Thank you for throwing me a life preserver.'" Margaret Talbot, "Supreme Confidence," *New Yorker*, March 28, 2005, 46–47.

67. **JUSTICE ALITO**: Are you arguing that there should be a *sui generis* rule for speech that advocates illegal drug use, or this broader argument that the school can suppress any speech that is inconsistent with its educational mission as the school . . . defines it?

MR. STARR: . . . The Court can certainly decide this on very narrow grounds, that there are certain substances, illegal drugs, we would include alcohol and tobacco, that's part of the school's policy, because those are illegal substances which are very injurious to health. And this Court has noted that in *Vernonia* and in *Earls*, time and again, it is that these are very dangerous substances and we have a clear policy sanctioned by Congress, and also noted by courts across the country, that illegal drugs are so dangerous that schools are entitled to have a message going—

CHIEF JUSTICE ROBERTS: But the problem—the problem, Mr. Starr, is that school boards these days take it upon themselves to broaden their mission well beyond education or protection from illegal substances, and several of the briefs have pointed out school boards have adopted policies taking on the whole range of political issues. Now, do they get to dictate the content of speech on all of those issues simply because they have adopted that as part of their educational mission?

MR. STARR: No, because that may very well be inconsistent with *Tinker*. *Tinker* articulates a baseline of political speech is, in fact, protected . . .

68. I reversed the original order of Starr's two phrases for syntactical purposes.

69. Chief Justice Burger referred to Matt Fraser's speech as "an elaborate, graphic, and explicit sexual metaphor." *Bethel Sch. Dist. v. Fraser*, 478 U.S. 675, 678 (1986).

The speech, in its entirety, reads: "I know a man who is firm—he's firm in his pants, he's firm in his shirt, his character is firm—but most . . . of all, his belief in you, the students of Bethel, is firm. Jeff Kuhlman is a man who takes his point and pounds it in. If necessary, he'll take an issue and nail it to the wall. He doesn't attack things in spurts—he drives hard, pushing and pushing until finally—he succeeds. Jeff is a man who will go to the very end—even the climax, for each and every one of you. So vote for Jeff for A.S.B. vice-president—he'll never come between you and the best our high school can be." Ibid., 687.

70. Shortly after these remarks, eighteen minutes and thirty-five seconds into oral argument, Starr said he would "like to reserve the remainder of my time."

71. See discussion of Stephen A. Higginson's work, and citations, above, 150–151.

72. Right at the end of his term in office, President George W. Bush appointed Kneedler acting solicitor general. Kneedler served in that post for about two months until the Senate confirmed Elena Kagan, President Barack Obama's nominee as solicitor general, on March 19, 2009.

73. *Republic of the Philippines v. Mariano J. Pimentel*, 553 U.S. ___ (2008), argued March 17, 2008.

74. The Oyez Project, Oral Argument Transcript, *Morse v. Frederick*, 7. Subsequent quotations on the following pages, drawn from Edwin Kneedler's allotted time are from ibid., 7–10.

75. The Oyez Project, Oral Argument Transcript, *Morse v. Frederick*, 10. Subsequent quotations on the following pages, drawn from Douglas Mertz's allotted time, are from ibid., 10–19.

76. Jeffrey Toobin characterizes Roberts' approach to oral argument as "hard-edged" and "pugnacious." Toobin, "No More Mr. Nice Guy," 44, 47.

77. Chapter 5, 103.

78. Justice Ginsburg initiated another line of questioning that further illustrates how digressions and sarcasm from the Bench undermined Mertz's ability to make his case.

JUSTICE GINSBURG: . . . I couldn't understand that somehow you got mileage out of [Frederick] being truant that morning. . . . Does the case turn on the fact that he was late to school that day?

MR. MERTZ: We believe it would be a closer question, but the fact that he was not there in school today [*sic*], and intentionally was not there today [sic], turns this into a pure free speech case where you have a citizen in a public place in a public event who was not acting like a student.

JUSTICE GINSBURG: So he's not a school child, he would be playing hooky?

MR. MERTZ: Because he was playing hooky because he chose not to be there, because he was not part of the class. . . .

JUSTICE SCALIA: He wasn't playing hooky. He showed up late, that's all, right? I mean, he actually came and joined his classmates at an event that he knew was an event that the school told the classes to go to. . . .

MR. MERTZ: He joined a public crowd on a private . . . sidewalk in front of private homes. The crowd happened to have some other students in that school there. . . .

JUSTICE KENNEDY: So under your view, if the principal sees something wrong in the crowd across the street, had to come up and say now, how many here are truants and how many here are—I can't discipline you because you're a truant, you can go ahead and throw the bottle. [*Laughter.*]

MR. MERTZ: No, I don't think she needs to do that in the heat of the moment. But later on once she's discovered the true facts, then at that point she loses a basis for punishing him as a student if he was not there as a student.

JUSTICE SCALIA: Because you're both truant and a disrupter, you get off. [*Laughter.*] Had you been just a disrupter, tough luck.

79. Chief Justice Roberts' return to his "leitmotif" of monetary damages is reminiscent of the late Anna Russell's satirical take on Richard Wagner's "Der Ring des Niebelungen"—except that Supreme Court oral argument and musical comedy have decidedly different stakes. The conclusion of Russell's thirty-minute parody is: "Well then the River Rhine overflows its banks. D'y'remember the Rhine? And the waters come in over the ashes. And who d'you think turns up next? The *Rhinemaidens*. So they take their lump of gold, I mean the Ring, which is of course their lump of gold, and they put it back where it came from. And after sitting through this whole operation, what do you hear? You hear: [*Plays and sings Rheinmaidens' leitmotif*]. YOU'RE EXACTLY WHERE YOU STARTED TWENTY HOURS AGO!" Anna Russell, "The Ring of the Nibelungs (An Analysis)," http://www.markelliswalker.net/music/albums/anna-russell-ring.html.

80. See footnote 78, above, for an excerpt from this series of exchanges.

One measure of the futility of these exchanges, especially for the appellee's case, is that they begin and end with Justice Ginsburg posing essentially the identical question. At 52:22 Ginsburg asked: "[W]ould you be making any different argument if [Frederick] got to school on time and was released with the rest of [the students]?" Six minutes and twelve seconds later, at 58:34, Justice Ginsburg asked: "You would still be making the argument about the free speech right if he had diligently showed up for his math class first period in the morning, gone out with the others, and had his banner to unfurl when the torch came by?"

81. Interrogatory No. 5 and Response [on disruption], Joint Appendix, *Deborah Morse; Juneau School Board*, Petitioners, v. *Joseph Frederick*, Respondent, On Writ of Certiorari to the United States Court of Appeals for the Ninth Circuit, 109, in author's possession.

82. Chapter 4, 90.

83. Toobin, *The Nine*, 327.

84. Robert Barnes, "Justice Kennedy: The Highly Influential Man in the Middle," *Washington Post*, May 13, 2007, http://www.washingtonpost.com/wp-dyn/content/article/2007/05/12/AR2007051201586.html. Blogger Terence Kane, of Generations United, offers an insightful analysis of Justice Kennedy's median role, in the context of Justice Souter's resignation from the Court. "Consider the current court

make-up on an ideological spectrum," writes Kane. "Stevens-Ginsburg-Breyer-Souter-**Kennedy**-Roberts-Alito-Scalia-Thomas.

"In order to make a dramatic change on the court's direction, President Obama would have to replace Justice Kennedy, or a judge to his right on the ideological spectrum, with a more liberal judge. This, of course, is a simplification; different aspects of law can produce different coalitions and ideological alignments, like Justice Scalia's vote to strike down a flag-burning law.

"We tend to think that the court is divided by a liberal and a conservative bloc and that decisions depend on whichever bloc has a majority of members, but it's much more accurate to describe the current as being driven by the jurist that sits fifth along a nine-member spectrum.

"It's true that the current court has liberal and conservative blocs, but that thinking is an outgrowth of how a median voter operates. To move the court substantively to one ideological side or the other requires changing the median vote, and President Obama, presumably, has no interest in appointing someone more conservative than Justice Kennedy." Terence Kane, "SCOTUS and Median Voter Theory," *The Hill's Pundits Blog*, May 1, 2009, http://pundits.thehill.com/2009/05/01/scotus-and-median-voter-theory.

Also see Helen J. Knowles, *The Tie Goes to Freedom: Justice Anthony M. Kennedy on Liberty* (Lanham, Md.: Rowman and Littlefield, 2009).

85. "Each year Brennan asked his law clerks to name the most important rule in constitutional law. Brennan gave them the answer after they stumbled around, naming one great case after another. 'This,' he said, holding up one hand with his fingers spread, 'is the most important rule in constitutional law.' Brennan knew that it took five votes to do anything, and, he may have thought, with five votes you can do anything." Mark Tushnet, *A Court Divided: The Rehnquist Court and the Future of Constitutional Law* (New York: W.W. Norton, 2005), 35.

86. "It really isn't very mysterious or complex, what we do . . . in these chambers," [said Brennan]. "We debate the issues, the merits, and when it comes time to write, we discuss the various possible approaches. We ask about some of the approaches. Will this be rejected by Lewis Powell or Harry Blackmun? Will Thurgood agree with this? Has John Stevens written any cases which may suggest how he is thinking and about which we should be aware? What does Sandra think? You try to get, in advance of circulation, a sense of what will sell, what the others can accept. And you write it that way, and when it works out—and maybe you have suggestions that come in and perhaps you make substantial revisions—but when it works out and you have a Court, you are delighted." Nina Totenberg, "A Tribute to Justice William A. Brennan, Jr.," *Harvard Law Review* 104 (November 1990): 37–38, quoting Jeffrey T. Leeds, "A Life on the Court," *New York Times Magazine*, October 5, 1986, 74–75. Compare Bernard Schwartz, *Decision: How the Supreme Court Decides Cases* (New York: Oxford University Press, 1996), 170.

87. Andrew D. Martin, Kevin M. Quinn, and Lee Epstein, "The Median Justice on the United States Supreme Court," *North Carolina Law Review* 83 (2005): 1277. See the scholarship cited in Martin et al., notes 1–14, and Bernard Grofman and Timothy Brazill, "Identifying the Median Justice on the Supreme Court through Multidimensional Scaling: Analysis of 'Natural Court' 1953–1991," *Public Choice* 112 (2002): 55.

88. Martin, Quinn, and Epstein, 1278.

89. Ibid. The work to which Martin, Quinn, and Epstein refer is Duncan Black, "On the Rationale of Group Decision-Making," *Journal of Political Economics* 56 (1948): 23; and Duncan Black, *The Theory of Committees and Elections* (Cambridge: Cambridge University Press, 1958).

But compare Jeffrey R. Lax and Charles M. Cameron, "Beyond the Median Voter: Bargaining and Law in the Supreme Court," paper prepared for the 2005 Annual Meeting of the Midwest Political Science Association, April 6, 2005, on file with the author; Jeffrey R. Lax and Charles M. Cameron,

"Bargaining and Opinion Assignment on the U.S. Supreme Court," *Journal of Law, Economics, and Organization* 23 (2007): 276; Cliff Carrubba, et al., "Does the Median Justice Control the Content of Supreme Court Opinions?" Working paper presented at Second Annual Conference on Empirical Legal Studies, November 2007, in author's possession; and Chris W. Bonneau, Thomas H. Hammond, Forrest Maltzman, and Paul J. Wahlbeck, "Agenda Control, the Median Justice, and the Majority Opinion on the U.S. Supreme Court," *American Journal of Political Science* 51 (October 2007): 891.

90. Martin, Quinn, and Epstein, "The Median Justice on the United States Supreme Court," Table 4, 1303–1304.

Not coincidentally, Justices Souter, O'Connor, and Kennedy collaborated on the key plurality opinion in *Planned Parenthood v. Casey*, 505 U.S. 833 (1992) which upheld the "essential holding" in *Roe v. Wade*, 410 U.S. 113 (1973).

91. Ibid., 1301.

92. Ibid., 1304.

93. Andrew D. Martin and Kevin M. Quinn, "Dynamic Ideal Point Estimation via Markov Chain Monte Carlo for the U.S. Supreme Court, 1953–1999," *Political Analysis* 10 (2002): 134. Also see Lee Epstein, et al., "Ideological Drift among Supreme Court Justices: Who, When, and How Important?" *Northwestern University Law Review* 101 (2007): 1483; and Lee Epstein, et al., "Ideological Drift among Supreme Court Justices: Who, When, and How Important?" *Northwestern University Law Review Colloquy* (2007), and responses by Stephen Burbank, Linda Greenhouse, and David Strauss, http://www.law.northwestern.edu/lawreview/colloquy/2007/8.

94. Martin and Quinn, "Dynamic Ideal Point Estimation," 137–145.

95. Ibid., 147.

96. Ibid., Figure 1, 148.

97. See Martin and Quinn's chart, "Placing Justices on an Ideological Line," accompanying Adam Nagourney and Jeff Zeleny, "Washington Prepares for Fight Over Any Nominee," *New York Times*, May 1, 2009, http://www.nytimes.com/2009/05/02/us/02court.html?emc=eta1.

98. Paul H. Edelman and Jim Chen, "The Most Dangerous Justice Rides into the Sunset," *Constitutional Communications* 24 (2007): 300. As an example, Edelman and Chen cite *Philip Morris v. Williams*, 549 U.S. 346 (2007). "Voting in the majority were Justices Roberts, Alito, Breyer, Kennedy, and Souter. In dissent were Justices Ginsburg, Stevens, Thomas, and Scalia. These odd coalitions clearly fail to conform to expectations concerning the Justices' shared policy preferences. In short, such an outcome is inconsistent with the notion that the Justices' votes are best described in all cases as the product of a single ideological dimension." Ibid.

For another example, see blogger Terence Kane's reference, in footnote 84 above, to Justice Scalia's "different" ideological alignment in the flag-burning cases, *Texas v. Johnson*, 491 U.S. 397 (1989); *United States v. Eichman*, 496 U.S. 310 (1990). Also see Amy Davidson's question-and-answer with *New Yorker* writer Margaret Talbot, who had profiled Justice Scalia. Davidson asked: "Just how conservative is Scalia?" Talbot replied: "I think we can surmise that socially he's pretty conservative[.] . . . And it's true that he sometimes comes to conclusions that don't seem to comport with his own political or social beliefs. He likes to cite his vote in a flag-burning case, for instance, when he voted with liberals on the Court to protect flag desecration as symbolic political speech. 'Scalia did not like to vote that way,' he said in a speech at the University of Michigan. 'He does not like sandal-wearing, bearded weirdoes who go around burning flags.'" Amy Davidson, "The Scalia Court," *New Yorker*, March 28, 2005, http://www.newyorker.com/archive/2005/03/28/050328on_onlineonly01. Talbot, "Supreme Confidence."

99. In 2005, Dr. James C. Dobson, founder of Focus on the Family, described Justice Kennedy as "the most dangerous man in America." Quoted in Dana Milbank, "And the Verdict on Justice Kennedy

Is: Guilty," *Washington Post*, April 9, 2006, 3; and Jason DeParle, "In Battle to Pick Next Justice, Right Says, Avoid a Kennedy," *New York Times*, June 27, 2006, 1.

100. Paul H. Edelman and Jim Chen, "The Most Dangerous Justice Rides Again: Revisiting the Power Pageant of the Justices," *Minnesota Law Review* 86 (2001): 133–134; 221–222, internal citations omitted.

Edelman and Chen write: "There remain diehards who believe that the Court can be purged of its partisan stench. 'When the Court no longer ultimately determines the great controversies of the day,' so the faithful believe, 'the other actors in the political system will not place so much importance on controlling the selection of the Justices.' For the foreseeable future, though, the Court will continue to exert 'pervasive influence on a wide range of issues that can only in a partial and peripheral way be considered legal rather than political.' Until further notice, the Power Pageant of the Justices will matter." Ibid., 221, internal citations omitted.

101. Paul H. Edelman and Jim Chen, "The Most Dangerous Justice: The Supreme Court at the Bar of Mathematics," *Southern California Law Review* 70 (1996): 63; Paul H. Edelman and Jim Chen, "'Duel' Diligence: Second Thoughts about the Supremes as the Sultans of Swat," *Southern California Law Review* 70 (1996): 219; Edelman and Chen, "The Most Dangerous Justice Rides Again," 131; and Edelman and Chen, "The Most Dangerous Justice Rides into the Sunset," 299.

Compare Lynn A. Baker, "Interdisciplinary Due Diligence: The Case for Common Sense in the Search for the Swing Justice," *Southern California Law Review* 70 (1996): 187.

Edelman and Chen write: "We do not mean to be dismissive of the search for the median Justice. As Martin et al., make clear, there are many situations in which knowledge of the median Justice is useful as an input to other positive political models of the Court. However, for the purposes of understanding the coalitional nature of the Court, and the power that structure imparts to the various Justices, we think that the data indicate that the one dimensional spatial voting model does not adequately capture the data." Edelman and Chen, "The Most Dangerous Justice Rides into the Sunset," 309–310. As they put it—twice—the "median is not the message." Edelman and Chen, "'Duel' Diligence," 230–233; and Edelman and Chen, "The Most Dangerous Justice Rides into the Sunset," 303–310.

102. Edelman and Chen, "The Most Dangerous Justice Rides into the Sunset," 300.

103. Ibid., 316, 319.

104. Ibid., 317.

105. Ibid., 316.

106. Ibid., 317. Edelman and Chen speculate that, with Justice O'Connor's departure and the arrival of Justice Alito, Souter's ability to forge coalitions, hence his power, may decrease.

Compare Tonja Jacobi and Matthew Sag, "Taking the Measure of Ideology: Empirically Measuring Supreme Court Cases," draft working paper, January 13, 2009, University of Chicago Workshop on Judicial Behavior, copy in author's possession; and student blogger, "Can Obama Influence the Court?" University of Chicago Faculty Blog, February 9, 2009, http://uchicagolaw.typepad.com/faculty/2009/02/can-obama-shape-supreme-court-jurisprudence.html.

Notes to Chapter 8

1. Linda Greenhouse, "Court Hears Whether a Drug Statement Is Protected Free Speech for Students," *New York Times*, March 20, 2007, http://query.nytimes.com/gst/fullpage.html?res=9A0CE3DE1730F933A15750C0A9619C8B63&sec=&spon=&pagewanted=1.

2. Lyle Denniston, "Analysis: A New Exception to 'Tinker'?" SCOTUSblog, March 19, 2007, http://www.scotusblog.com/wp/analysis-a-new-exception-to-tinker.

3. Ibid.

4. Ibid.

5. Tony Mauro, "Justices May Take Centrist View of 'Bong Hits' Case," First Amendment Center, March 20, 2007, http://www.firstamendmentcenter.org/analysis.aspx?id=18309.

6. Ibid.

7. Ibid.

8. The information in this overview paragraph is derived from Henry J. Abraham, *Justices, Presidents, and Senators: A History of the U.S. Supreme Court Appointments from Washington to Bush II*, 5th new and rev. ed. (Lanham, Md.: Rowman and Littlefield, 2008); and Bernard Schwartz, *A History of the Supreme Court* (New York: Oxford University Press, 1993).

9. While still chief justice, John Jay left the country to serve as special ambassador to England in 1794, where he negotiated the treaty bearing his name, after which he resigned from the Court to accept a "promotion" to the governorship of New York. (Alexander Hamilton refused President Washington's offer of the post.) Jay's successor, John Rutledge, served but six months in a recess appointment, only to have his nomination rejected by the Senate on December 15, 1795. Oliver Ellsworth found time, simultaneously, to be special envoy to France as well as being third chief justice.

10. The Supreme Court had no permanent home until 1935, being left out of original planning for a federal city (Washington, D.C.) and shunted around the Capitol Building as an orphan.

11. Schwartz, *A History of the Supreme Court*, 34.

12. *Marbury v . Madison*, 1 Cranch 137 (1803): 137, 177

13. Schwartz, *A History of the Supreme Court*, 39. Schwartz seems to have obtained the "conclusiveness and fixity" phrase from an article by Donald G. Morgan, "Mr. Justice William Johnson and the Constitution," *Harvard Law Review* 57 (1944): 328.

14. Thomas Jefferson to Justice William Johnson, October 27, 1822, "From Revolution to Reconstruction," University of Groningen, http://www.let.rug.nl/usa/P/tj3/writings/brf/jefl269.htm. Jefferson's vantage point on opinion writing provides such an instructive counterpoint to Marshall's prevailing approach that it deserves reading in full: "You know that from the earliest ages of the English law, from the date of the year-books, at least, to the end of the IId George, the judges of England, in all but self-evident cases, delivered their opinions *seriatim*, with the reasons and authorities which governed their decisions. If they sometimes consulted together, and gave a general opinion, it was so rarely as not to excite either alarm or notice. Besides the light which their separate arguments threw on the subject, and the instruction communicated by their several modes of reasoning, it shewed whether the judges were unanimous or divided, and gave accordingly more or less weight to the judgment as a precedent. It sometimes happened too that when there were three opinions against one, the reasoning of the one was so much the most cogent as to become afterwards the law of the land. When [Lord] Mansfield came to the bench he introduced the habit of caucusing opinions. The judges met at their chambers, or elsewhere, secluded from the presence of the public, and made up what was to be delivered as the opinion of the court. On the retirement of Mansfield, [Lord] Kenyon put an end to the practice, and the judges returned to that of *seriatim* opinions, and practice it habitually to this day, I believe. I am not acquainted with the late reporters, do not possess them, and state the fact from the information of others. To come now to ourselves I know nothing of what is done in other states, but in this our great and good Mr. Pendleton was, after the revolution, placed at the head of the court of Appeals. He adored [Lord] Mansfield, & considered him as the greatest luminary of law that any age had ever produced, and he introduced into the court over which he presided, Mansfield's practice of making up opinions in secret & delivering them as the Oracles of the court, in mass. Judge Roane, when he came to that bench, broke up the practice, refused to hatch judgments, in Conclave, or to let others deliver opinions for him. At what time the *seriatim* opinions ceased in the Supreme Court of the US., I am not informed. They continued I know to the end of the 3d Dallas in 1800. Later than which I have no Reporter of that court. About

that time the present C. J. [Marshall] came to the bench. Whether he carried the practice of Mr. Pendleton to it, or who, or when I do not know; but I understand from others it is now the habit of the court, & I suppose it true from the cases sometimes reported in the newspapers, and others which I casually see, wherein I observe that the opinions were uniformly prepared in private. Some of these cases too have been of such importance, of such difficulty, and the decisions so grating to a portion of the public as to have merited the fullest explanation from every judge *seriatim*, of the reasons which had produced such convictions on his mind. It was interesting to the public to know whether these decisions were really unanimous, or might not perhaps be of 4. against 3. and consequently prevailing by the preponderance of one voice only. The Judges holding their offices for life are under two responsibilities only. 1. Impeachment. 2. Individual reputation. But this practice compleatly withdraws them from both. For nobody knows what opinion any individual member gave in any case, nor even that he who delivers the opinion, concurred in it himself. Be the opinion therefore ever so impeachable, having been done in the dark it can be proved on no one. As to the 2d guarantee, personal reputation, it is shielded compleately. The practice is certainly convenient for the lazy, the modest & the incompetent. It saves them the trouble of developing their opinion methodically and even of making up an opinion at all. That of *seriatim* argument shews whether every judge has taken the trouble of understanding the case, of investigating it minutely, and of forming an opinion for himself, instead of pinning it on another's sleeve. It would certainly be right to abandon this practice in order to give to our citizens one and all, that confidence in their judges which must be so desirable to the judges themselves, and so important to the cement of the union. During the administration of Genl. Washington, and while E. Randolph was Attorney General, he was required by Congress to digest the judiciary laws into a single one, with such amendments as might be thought proper. He prepared a section requiring the Judges to give their opinions *seriatim*, in writing, to be recorded in a distinct volume. Other business prevented this bill from being taken up, and it passed off, but such a volume would have been the best possible book of reports, and the better, as unincumbered with the hired sophisms and perversions of Counsel."

15. Thomas G. Walker, Lee Epstein, and William J. Dixon, "On the Mysterious Demise of Consensual Norms in the United States Supreme Court," *Journal of Politics* 50 (1988): 361. Compare Steven A. Peterson, "Dissent in American Courts," *Journal of Politics* 43 (1981): 412; and Nancy Maveety, "Concurrence and the Study of Judicial Behavior in American Political Science," *Juridica International* I (2003), http://www.juridica.ee/print_article_et.php?document=en/international/2003/1/65317.ART.0.pub.php.

16. Beverly Blair Cook, "Justice Brennan and the Institutionalization of Dissent Assignment," in Elliot E. Slotnick, ed., *Judicial Politics: Readings from Judicature* (Chicago: American Judicature Society, 1992), 363.

17. Political scientist Stacia J. Haynie refers to "a myth of unanimity" in "Leadership and Consensus on the U.S. Supreme Court," *Journal of Politics* 54 (November 1992): 1160. Karl M. ZoBell discusses "judicial disintegration" in "Division of Opinion in the Supreme Court: A History of Judicial Disintegration," *Cornell Law Quarterly* 44 (1959): 186.

18. *Gibbons v. Ogden*, 9 Wheaton 1 (1824): 223. Justice Johnson served on the Court from May 7, 1804, until his death, August 4, 1834. One-third of Johnson's opinions were either concurrences or dissents. See Morgan, "Mr. Justice William Johnson and the Constitution"; and Meredith Kolsky, "Justice William Johnson and the History of Supreme Court Dissent," *Georgetown Law Journal* 83 (1995): 2069.

19. *Gibbons v. Ogden*, Wheaton 9, 1 (1824): 223. See G. Edward White and Gerald Gunther, *The Marshall Court and Cultural Change, 1815–1835* (New York: Macmillan, 1988); and Carl Brent Swisher, *The Taney Period, 1836–64* (New York: Macmillan, 1974).

20. Walker, Epstein, and Dixon, "On the Mysterious Demise of Consensual Norms in the United States Supreme Court," 362. Compare Figure 1, "Dissent and Concurrence per 100 Majority Opinions in the United States Supreme Court, 1800–1981." Ibid., 363, with Figure 4.1. "Opinion-writing, 1800–1994," David M. O'Brien, "Institutional Norms and Supreme Court Opinions: On Reconsidering the Rise of Individual Opinions," in Cornell W. Clayton and Howard Gillman, eds., *Supreme Court Decision-making: New Institutional Approaches* (Chicago: University of Chicago Press, 1999), 92. Also see C. Herman Pritchett, "Divisions of Opinion among Justices of the U.S. Supreme Court," *American Political Science Review* 35 (1941): 890; C. Herman Pritchett, "The Coming of the New Dissent: The Supreme Court, 1942–1943," *University of Chicago Law Review* 11 (1943): 49; and C. Herman Pritchett, "Dissent on the Supreme Court, 1943–1944," *American Political Science Review* 39 (1945): 42.

21. For example, see the unique study of justices' disagreements over the "Rule of Four" and the "hold rule" by Richard L. Revesz and Pamela S. Karlan, "Nonmajority Rules and the Supreme Court," *University of Pennsylvania Law Review* 136 (April 1988): 1067.

22. But see David J. Danelski, "The Influence of the Chief Justice in the Decisional Process," in Walter F. Murphy and C. Herman Pritchett, eds., *Courts, Judges and Politics*, 6th ed. (New York: Random House, 2006); and David J. Danelski, "Causes and Consequences of Conflict and Its Resolution in the Supreme Court," in Sheldon Goldman and Charles M. Lamb, eds., *Judicial Conflict and Consensus* (Lexington: University of Kentucky Press, 1986). Compare Walter F. Murphy, *Elements of Judicial Strategy* (Chicago: University of Chicago Press, 1964), esp. chap. 3; Lee Epstein and Jack Knight, *The Choices Justices Make* (Washington, D.C.: Congressional Quarterly Press, 1998); and Forrest Maltzman, James F. Spriggs II, and Paul J. Wahlbeck, *Crafting Law on the Supreme Court: The Collegial Game* (New York: Cambridge University Press, 2000).

23. Walker, Epstein, and Dixon, "On the Mysterious Demise of Consensual Norms in the United States Supreme Court," 363.

24. Ibid., 364.

25. See ibid., 364–378. Compare Stephen C. Halpern and Kenneth N. Vines, "Institutional Disunity, the Judge's Bill and the Role of the Supreme Court," *Western Politics Quarterly* 30 (December 1977): 471.

26. "[Stone's] conception of the chief justiceship radically differed from his predecessors. He rejected the 'no dissent unless absolutely necessary' rule and believed that good law was the product of the clash of individually expressed positions. Importantly, Stone refused to enforce consensus expectations, always remaining a participant rather than a leader. He led by example in maintaining high rates of concurring and dissenting opinions." Walker, Epstein, and Dixon, "On the Mysterious Demise of Consensual Norms in the United States Supreme Court," 384.

27. Ibid., 378.

28. "The Chief Justice may be only *primus inter pares*; but [s]he is *primus*." Bernard Schwartz, *Decision: How the Supreme Court Decides Cases* (New York: Oxford University Press, 1996), 74.

29. Haynie, "Leadership and Consensus on the U.S. Supreme Court," 1167. "The comparison of the two dependent series suggests that the deterioration of the consensus norm on the Court began with Hughes . . . [t]his was reinforced by the *collapse* of consensus under Chief Justice Stone." Ibid. Compare the findings on "regime shift" reported by Gregory A. Caldeira and Christopher J. W. Zorn, "Of Time and Consensual Norms in the Supreme Court," *American Journal of Political Science* 42 (July 1998): 892–893.

30. Haynie, "Leadership and Consensus on the U.S. Supreme Court," 1164. For analysis of other aspects and explanations of Supreme Court "dissensus," see S. Sidney Ulmer, "Exploring the Dissent Patterns of the Chief Justices: John Marshall to Warren Burger," in Goldman and Lamb, *Judicial Conflict and Consensus*; Robert W. Bennett, "Styles of Judging," *Northwest University Law Review* 84 (Spring/Summer 1990): 853; Terry Bowen, "Consensual Norms and the Freshman Effect on

the United States Supreme Court," *Social Science Quarterly* 76 (March 1995): 222; Scott D. Gerber and Keeok Park, "The Quixotic Search of Consensus on the U.S. Supreme Court: A Cross-Judicial Empirical Analysis of Rehnquist Court Justices," *American Political Science Review* 91 (June 1997): 390; David K. Scott and Robert H. Gobetz, "The U.S. Supreme Court, 1969–1992: A Shift Toward an Individualistic Style of Judging," *Communication Studies* 54 (Summer 2003): 211; and Jeffrey Davis, "Adversarial Jurisprudence: Legal Education and the Demise of the Consensual Norm," *Politics & Policy* 30 (December 2002): 763.

31. Caldeira and Zorn, "Of Time and Consensual Norms in the Supreme Court," 875.

32. Ibid., 900.

33. O'Brien, "Institutional Norms and Supreme Court Opinions," 103.

34. Ibid., 102–103. On how increasing numbers of law clerks and expanding support personnel affected consensual norms, see Bradley Best, *Law Clerks, Support Personnel, and the Decline of Consensual Norms on the United States Supreme Court, 1935–1995* (New York: LFB Publishing, 2002).

35. Ibid., 101–102.

36. Ibid., 107–111. Compare William A. Galston, "Political Polarization and the U.S. Judiciary," *UMKC Law Review* 77 (Winter 2008): 307; and Bradley W. Joondeph, "The Many Meanings of 'Politics' in Judicial Decision Making," *UMKC Law Review* 77 (Winter 2008): 347. For cross-national comparative analysis of consensual norms, see Russell Smyth, "Historical Consensual Norms in the High Court," *Australian Journal of Political Science* 37 (2002): 255; Russell Smyth, "What Explains Variations in Dissent Rates? Time Series Evidence from the High Court," *Sydney Law Review* 10 (2004), http://www.austlii.com/au/journals/SydLRev/2004/10.html; Paresh Kumar Narayan and Russell Smyth, "The Consensual Norm on the High Court of Australia, 1904–2001," *International Political Science Review* 26 (2005): 147; and Rebecca Wood, "Institutional Considerations in Locating Norms of Consensus: A Cross-National Investigation," paper presented at the 2008 Annual Meeting of the Midwest Political Science Association, Chicago, Ill., April 3–6, in author's possession.

37. See, for instance, discussion and sources cited in Peterson, "Dissent in American Courts," 425–433; Walker, Epstein, and Dixon, "On the Mysterious Demise of Consensual Norms in the United States Supreme Court," 386–387; Gerber and Park, "The Quixotic Search of Consensus on the U.S. Supreme Court," 404–405; Scott and Gobetz, "The U.S. Supreme Court 1969–1992," 220–223; O'Brien, "Institutional Norms and Supreme Court Opinions: On Reconsidering the Rise of Individual Opinions," 111–112; and Best, *Law Clerks, Support Personnel, and the Decline of Consensual Norms on the United States Supreme Court, 1935–1995*, 232–236.

38. For analysis in a similar vein, see R. Dean Moorhead, "Concurring and Dissenting Opinions," *American Bar Association Journal* 38 (1952): 821–824, 884; Nancy Staudt, Barry Friedman, and Lee Epstein, "On the Role of Ideological Homogeneity in Generating Consequential Constitutional Decisions," *University of Pennsylvania Journal of Constitutional Law* 10 (January 2008): 361; and Lee Epstein, Barry Friedman, and Nancy Staudt, "On the Capacity of the Roberts Court to Generate Consequential Precedent," *North Carolina Law Review* 86 (June 2008): 1299. Compare Frank Cross and Emerson H. Tiller, "Understanding Collegiality on the Court," *University of Pennsylvania Journal of Constitutional Law* 10 (January 2008): 257.

39. See, for instance, J. Louis Campbell III, "The Spirit of Dissent," *Judicature* 66 (February 1983): 304; Kevin M. Stack, "The Practice of Dissent in the Supreme Court," *Yale Law Journal* 105 (June 1996): 2235; and Lani Guinier, "Foreword: Demosprudence through Dissent," *Harvard Law Review* 122 (November 2008): 4.

40. Jeffrey Rosen, "Robert's Rules," *The Atlantic*, January/February 2007, http://www.theatlantic.com/doc/200701/john-roberts.

41. Ibid.

42. Ibid.

43. Ibid.

44. Ibid. Compare Linda Greenhouse, "The Law: At the Bar; Name-Calling in the Supreme Court: When the Justices Vent Their Spleen, Is There a Social Cost?" *New York Times*, July 28, 1989, http://www.nytimes.com/1989/07/28/us/law-bar-name-calling-supreme-court-when-justices-vent-their-spleen-there-social.html. Also see Judge Richard Posner: "Holmes is said to have described the Justices of the Supreme Court as 'nine scorpions in a bottle.' An alternative metaphor is an arranged marriage by indifferent parents in a system with no divorce. Judges do not pick their colleagues; most of those colleagues serve until retirement; and the appointing authorities give little weight to the interest in judicial collegiality in deciding whom to appoint." *The Problems of Jurisprudence* (Cambridge, Mass.: Harvard University Press, 1993), fn. 46, 190.

45. Decided together with *Meredith, Custodial Parent and Next Friend of McDonald v. Jefferson County Bd. of Ed. et al.*

46. Linda Greenhouse, "Justices Limit the Use of Race in School Plans for Integration," *New York Times*, June 29, 2007, http://www.nytimes.com/2007/06/29/washington/29scotus.html?_r=1&oref=slogin.

47. Ibid.

48. Ibid. In his written solo dissent, Justice Stevens wrote: "There is cruel irony in the Chief Justice's reliance on our decision in *Brown v. Board of* Education, 349 U.S. 294 (1955). . . . [T]he Chief Justice rewrites the history of one of this Court's most important decisions. . . . It is my firm conviction that no Member of the Court that I joined in 1975 would have agreed with today's decision." *Parents Involved in Community Schools v. Seattle School District No. 1*, 551 U.S. 701 (2007). For an analysis of the entire 2006–2007 term, see Charles Whitebread, "The Conservative Kennedy Court—What a Difference a Single Justice Can Make: The 2006–2007 Term of the United States Supreme Court," *Whittier Law Review* 29 (Fall 2007): 1.

49. See Neal Devins, "The Big Picture: External and Internal Influences on the Roberts Court's Handling of Precedents: Ideological Cohesion and Precedent (or Why the Court Only Cares about Precedent when Most Justices Agree with Each Other)," *North Carolina Law Review* 86 (June 2008): 1399. Compare, Epstein, Friedman, and Staudt, "On the Capacity of the Roberts Court to Generate Consequential Precedent"; and Lee Epstein, Andrew D. Martin, Kevin M. Quinn, and Jeffrey A. Segal, "Why Conservatives Should Continue to Yearn and Liberals Should Not Fear," *Tulsa Law Review* 43 (Spring 2008): 651.

50. Adam Liptak, "Roberts Court Shifts Right, Tipped by Kennedy," *New York Times*, July 1, 2009, http://www.nytimes.com/2009/07/01/us/01scotus.html.

51. Ibid. Compare Nancy Maveety, *Queen's Court: Judicial Power in the Rehnquist Era* (Lawrence, KS: University Press of Kansas, 2008).

52. Sarah Levien Shullman quoted in Adam Liptak, "When the Justices Ask Questions, Be Prepared to Lose the Case," *New York Times*, May 26, 2009, http://www.nytimes.com/2009/05/26/us/26bar.html. See Sarah Levien Shullman, "The Illusion of Devil's Advocacy: How the Justices of the Supreme Court Foreshadow Their Decisions during Oral Argument," *Journal of Appellate Practice & Process* 6 (Fall 2004): 271. Compare John G. Roberts Jr., "Oral Advocacy and the Re-emergence of a Supreme Court Bar," *Journal of Supreme Court History* 30 (2005): 68; and Timothy R. Johnson, Ryan C. Black, Jerry Goldman, and Sarah A. Treul, "Inquiring Minds Want to Know: Do Justices Tip Their Hands with Questions at Oral Argument in the U.S. Supreme Court?" *Washington University Journal of Law & Policy* 29 (2009): 241, http://papers.ssrn.com/sol3/papers.cfm?abstract_id=1373965.

53. Ibid. Compare Tony Mauro, "Counting Questions: Adding Up High Court Outcomes," *Legal Times Law.com*, May 12, 2005, http://www.law.com/jsp/article.jsp?id=1115802310553; Tony Mauro,

"When in Doubt, Look to Roberts for Outcome of Supreme Court Cases," *Legal Times Law.com*, June 11, 2007, http://www.law.com/jsp/article.jsp?id=1184058397113; and Lawrence S. Wrightsman, *Oral Arguments before the Supreme Court: An Empirical Approach* (New York: Oxford University Press, 2008), esp. chap. 7. Also see Washington University Law, "Supreme Court Forecasting Project 2002," http://wusct.wustl.edu/index.php, and two manuscripts cited there.

54. See Chapter 7, 146–147, 151.

55. Joan Biskupic, "Justices Make Points by Questioning Lawyers," *USA Today*, October 5, 2006, http://www.usatoday.com/news/washington/judicial/2006-10-05-oral-arguments_x.htm. "David Frederick, a Washington lawyer who argued four cases before the court last term, says he considers oral arguments a kind of 'three-way' conversation, among a justice, the lawyer at the lectern and a potentially persuadable justice." Ibid.

56. But see Johnson, Black, Goldman, and Treul, "Inquiring Minds Want to Know." They quantified their hypothesis that the side that "garners the most attention from the bench is most likely to lose its case" by employing two variables: "question difference" (counting the difference between the number of questions asked the petitioner and the number of questions asked the respondent), and "words difference" (counting the difference between the number of words used to discuss the case with the petitioner and the number of words used to discuss the case with the respondent), http://papers.ssrn.com/sol3/papers.cfm?abstract_id=1373965. Compare the methodology Sarah Shullman employed in "The Illusion of Devil's Advocacy," 273–276.

57. Adding to Starr's total the 1:01 speaking time he had reserved, and took at the very end of oral argument, during which Starr was asked no questions, does not significantly change my computations.

58. The many factual disputes pervading this story actually originate prior to the January 24, 2002, events on Glacier Avenue. Indeed, factual disputes could be said to *define* this story.

59. *Tinker v. Des Moines Independent Community School District*, 393 U.S. 503 (1969).

60. *Hazelwood School District v. Kuhlmeier*, 484 U.S. 260 (1988).

61. *New Jersey v. T.L.O.*, 469 U.S. 325 (1985).

62. *Board of Ed. of Independent School Dist. No. 92 of Pottawatomie City v. Earls*, 536 U.S. 822 (2002).

63. Ambiguity also is intrinsic to precedent. See my discussion, Coda, 188–193, below.

64. Disrupt, disrupter, disrupting, disruption, disruptive/drug, drugs.

65. Right, rights.

66. The Oyez Project, *Morse v. Frederick*, 551 U.S. 393 (2007), http://oyez.org/cases/2000-2009/2006/2006_06_278.

67. For example, four other decisions were announced the same day as *Morse v. Frederick*. All had multiple opinions: *Federal Election Commission v. Wisconsin Right to Life, Inc*, 551 U.S. 449 (2007) (majority + 2 concurrences, 1 dissent); *Wilkie v. Robbins*, 551 U.S. 537 (2007) (majority + 1 concurrence, 1 concurrence/dissent); *Hein v. Freedom from Religion Foundation, Inc.*, 551 U.S. 587 (2007) (plurality + 2 concurrences, 1 dissent); *National Assn. of Homebuilders v. Defenders of Wildlife*, 551 U.S. 644 (2007) (majority + 1 dissent). Three days after announcing *Morse*, on the final day of its 2006–2007 term, a deeply divided Court handed down *Parents Involved in Community Schools v. Seattle School Dist. No. 1*, 551 U.S. 701 (2007). *Parents Involved* has six opinions: opinion of the Court, plurality + 2 concurrences + 2 dissents.

68. Roberts, Scalia (2); Thomas (1); Alito, Kennedy (2); Breyer (1); Stevens, Ginsburg, Souter (3). See Joshua Azriel, "The Supreme Court's Decision in *Morse v. Frederick*: The Majority Opinion Revealed Sharp Ideological Differences on Student Speech Rights among the Court's Five Justice Majority," *UC Davis Journal of Juvenile Law & Policy* 12 (Summer 2008): 427.

69. Ironically, those three justices are the dissenters: Stevens, Ginsburg, and Souter.

70. *Morse v. Frederick*, 551 U.S. 393 (2007), http://www.supremecourtus.gov/opinions/06pdf/06-278.pdf, Opinion of the Court, 1–15.

71. The opinion also is minimalist in the sense that it carves out a narrow drug-related-speech-at-school-event exception to *Tinker*, which is probably the furthest the Court could modify *Tinker* without losing Justices Alito's and Kennedy's votes. See my discussion of Alito's concurrence, below.

72. The Oyez Project, *Morse v. Frederick*, 551 U.S. 393 (2007), http://oyez.org/cases/2000-2009/2006/2006_06_278.

73. *Morse v. Frederick*, 551 U.S. 393 (2007), http://www.supremecourtus.gov/opinions/06pdf/06-278.pdf, Opinion of the Court, 1.

74. See Chapter 2. *Tinker v. Des Moines Independent School Dist.* 393 U.S. 503 (1969), itself not an unqualified endorsement of student speech, has been further limited by the Court's subsequent rulings in *Bethel School Dist. v. Fraser*, 478 U.S. 675 (1986) and *Hazelwood School Dist. v. Kuhlmeier*, 484 U.S. 260 (1988).

75. *Morse v. Frederick*, 551 U.S. 393 (2007), http://www.supremecourtus.gov/opinions/06pdf/06-278.pdf, Opinion of the Court, 1–2.

76. "We granted certiorari on two questions: whether Frederick had a First Amendment right to wield his banner, and, if so, whether that right was so clearly established that the principal may be held liable for damages. . . . We resolve the first question against Frederick, and therefore have no occasion to reach the second." Ibid., 5.

77. Ibid., 6.

78. Ibid., 7.

79. Ibid.

80. Not even a plurality of the Court unequivocally endorsed any one of the three legal rationales propounded for holding Joe Fredericks accountable. As noted above, ironically, the only plurality that exists in *Morse v. Frederick* is the three dissenting justices.

81. *Morse v. Frederick*, 551 U.S. 393 (2007), http://www.supremecourtus.gov/opinions/06pdf/06-278.pdf, Opinion of the Court, 10.

82. Ibid.

83. Ibid.

84. Ibid.

85. Ibid., 9–10 (quoting *Fraser*).

86. Compare Chief Justice Roberts' observation during oral argument: "I guess my question goes to how broadly we should read *Tinker*. I mean, why is it that the classroom ought to be a forum for political debate simply because the students want to put that on their agenda? Presumably the teacher's agenda is a little bit different and includes things like teaching Shakespeare or the Pythagorean Theorem, and just because political speech is on the student's agenda, I'm not sure that it makes sense to read *Tinker* so broadly as to include protection of those, that speech. "The Oyez Project, *Morse v. Frederick* , 551 U.S. 393 (2007), http://oyez.org/cases/2000-2009/2006/2006_06_278.

87. See *New Jersey v. T.L.O.*, 469 U.S. 325 (1985); *Vernonia School Dist. 47J v. Acton*, 515 U.S. 646 (1995); *Board of Ed. of Independent School Dist. No. 92 of Pottawatomie City v. Earls*, 536 U.S. 822 (2002). Compare *Safford Unified School Dist. No. 1 v. Redding*, 557 U.S. ___ (2009), http://www.supremecourtus.gov/opinions/08pdf/08-479.pdf.

88. *Morse v. Frederick*, 551 U.S. 393 (2007), http://www.supremecourtus.gov/opinions/06pdf/06-278.pdf, Opinion of the Court, 12, 13.

89. Compare, *Safford Unified School Dist. No. 1 v. Redding*, 557 U.S. ___ (2009), http://www.supremecourtus.gov/opinions/08pdf/08-479.pdf. Also see Joan Biskupic, "Ginsburg: Court Needs Another Woman," *USA Today*, May 5, 2009, http://www.usatoday.com/news/washington/

judicial/2009-05-05-ruthginsburg_N.htm; and Neil A. Lewis, "Debate on Whether Female Judges Decide Differently Arises Anew," *New York Times*, June 3, 2009, http://www.nytimes.com/2009/06/04/us/politics/04women.html?_r=3&scp=1&sq=female%20justices&st=cse.

90. I appropriated the title of Stanley Fish's thought-provoking book in this context. Stanley Fish, *There's No Such Thing as Free Speech: And It's a Good Thing, Too* (New York: Oxford University Press, 1994).

91. Dennis J. Hutchinson, "Hugo Black among Friends, Review of Roger K. Newman, *Hugo Black: A Biography* (New York: Pantheon, 1994)," *Michigan Law Review* 93 (May 1995): 1886–1887. Black wrote in *Tinker*, "One does not need to be a prophet or the son of a prophet to know that, after the Court's holding today, some students in Iowa schools—and, indeed, in all schools—will be ready, able, and willing to defy their teachers on practically all orders. This is the more unfortunate for the schools since groups of students all over the land are already running loose, conducting break-ins, sit-ins, lie-ins, and smash-ins. Many of these student groups, as is all too familiar to all who read the newspapers and watch the television news programs, have already engaged in rioting, property seizures, and destruction. They have picketed schools to force students not to cross their picket lines, and have too often violently attacked earnest but frightened students who wanted an education that the pickets did not want them to get." *Tinker v. Des Moines Independent School Dist.*, 393 U.S. 503, 525 (1969).

92. Compare Hutchinson, "Hugo Black among Friends"; Laura Kalman, *Abe Fortas: A Biography* (New Haven, Conn.: Yale University Press, 1990); and Michael Klarman, Book Review, *Law & History Review* 12 (1994): 399.

93. *Tinker*, 517.

94. *Morse v. Frederick*, 551 U.S. 393 (2007), http://www.supremecourtus.gov/opinions/06pdf/06-278.pdf, Thomas, J., concurring, 11. Justice Thomas' rejection of the *Tinker* Court's view of student First Amendment speech rights derives from his reading of public school history, underpinned by his interpretation of the doctrine of in loco parentis. His foray led him to conclude—*contra Tinker*—that: "In short, in the earliest public schools, teachers taught, and students listened. Teachers commanded, and students obeyed. Teachers did not rely solely on the power of ideas to persuade; they relied on discipline to maintain order. . . . Through the legal doctrine of in loco parentis, courts upheld the right of schools to discipline students, to enforce rules, and to maintain order. . . . *Tinker* effected a sea change in students' speech rights, extending them well beyond traditional bounds." Ibid., 3–4, 8.

95. Ibid., 11.

96. Black: "[*Tinker*] . . . wholly without constitutional reasons, in my judgment, subjects all the public schools in the country to the whims and caprices of their loudest-mouthed, but maybe not their brightest, students. I, for one, am not fully persuaded that school pupils are wise enough, even with this Court's expert help from Washington, to run the 23,390 public school systems in our 50 States." *Tinker*, 525–526. Thomas: "'Once a society that generally respected the authority of teachers, deferred to their judgment, and trusted them to act in the best interest of school children, we now accept defiance, disrespect, and disorder as daily occurrences in many of our public schools.' Dupre, "Should Students Have Constitutional Rights? Keeping Order in the Public Schools," *George Washington Law Review* 65 (1996): 49, 50. We need look no further than *Morse v. Frederick* for an example: Frederick asserts a constitutional right to utter at a school event what is either '[g]ibberish,' *ante*, at 7, or an open call to use illegal drugs. 'To elevate such impertinence to the status of constitutional protection would be farcical and would indeed be to 'surrender control of the American public school system to public school students.' *Tinker* (Black, J., dissenting).'" *Morse v. Frederick*, 551 U.S. 393 (2007), http://www.supremecourtus.gov/opinions/06pdf/06-278.pdf, Thomas, J., concurring, 12–13.

97. *Morse v. Frederick*, 551 U.S. 393 (2007), http://www.supremecourtus.gov/opinions/06pdf/06-278.pdf, Thomas, J., concurring, 9.

98. Ibid., 9–10. Compare fn. 162, below.

99. Ibid., 9, 13.

100. See William D. Araiza, "*Morse v. Frederick*: History, Policy and Temptation," Legal Studies Paper No. 2007-43, Loyola Law School, Los Angeles (November 2007), http://papers.ssrn.com/sol3/papers.cfm?abstract_id=1024322.

101. See Daniel Gordon, "America's Constitutional Dad: Justice Kennedy and His Intricate Children," *Idaho Law Review* (2007): 161.

102. *Morse v. Frederick*, 551 U.S. 393 (2007), http://www.supremecourtus.gov/opinions/06pdf/06-278.pdf, Alito and Kennedy, J.J., concurring, 1.

103. Ibid.

104. Ibid.

105. Ibid. Compare Justice Alito's reply to Deputy U.S. Solicitor General Edwin S. Kneedler, during oral argument:

MR. KNEEDLER: I think [this case] is a manifestation of the principle articulated in *Earls* and repeated in *Hazelwood* that a school does not have to tolerate a message that is inconsistent with its basic educational [mission].

JUSTICE ALITO: Well, that's a very—I find that a very, a very disturbing argument because schools have and they can defined their educational mission so broadly that they can suppress all sorts of political speech and speech expressing fundamental values of the students, under the banner of, of—of getting rid of speech that's inconsistent with educational missions.

The Oyez Project, *Morse v. Frederick*, 551 U.S. 393 (2007) available at http://oyez.org/cases/2000-2009/2006/2006_06_278.

Also compare Justice Kennedy to Kenneth Starr:

MR. STARR: The argument is that this Court in *Tinker* articulated a rule that allows the school boards considerable discretion both in identifying the educational mission and to prevent disruption of that mission, and [Frederick's banner] is disruptive of the mission[.]

JUSTICE KENNEDY: Well, suppose you have—suppose you have a mission to have a global school. Can they ban American flags on lapel pins?

The Oyez Project, *Morse v. Frederick* , 551 U.S. 393 (2007), http://oyez.org/cases/2000-2009/2006/2006_06_278.

106. *Morse v. Frederick*, 551 U.S. 393 (2007), http://www.supremecourtus.gov/opinions/06pdf/06-278.pdf, Alito and Kennedy, J.J., concurring (quoting Stevens, J. dissenting in *Morse v. Frederick*).

107. Ibid., 3–4.

108. Ibid., 1–2.

109. Ibid., 4. Alito wrote: "I do not read the [Court's] opinion to mean that there are necessarily any grounds for such regulation that are not already recognized in the holding of this Court. . . . I join the opinion of the Court on the understanding that the opinion does not hold that the special characteristics of the public schools necessarily justify any other speech restrictions." Ibid., 2. Justice Alito's cautious concurring opinion in *Morse* is foreshadowed by an opinion he wrote over six years earlier while he still was serving on the U.S. Third Circuit Court of Appeals. *Saxe v. State College Area School Dist.*, 240 F.3d 200 (3d Cir. 2001) arose when David Saxe, a parent of two children enrolled in the Pennsylvania State College Area School District (SCASD), filed suit arguing that the 1999 SCASD Anti-Harassment Policy was facially unconstitutional under the First Amendment. A three-judge Third Circuit panel unanimously overturned the SCASD policy as overly broad, reversing the District Court for the Middle District of Pennsylvania's ruling that the First Amendment does not protect harassing speech. Turning to the specific question of whether SCASD's policy was a permissible regulation of speech in public schools, Judge Alito argued

that, even considering the *Fraser* and *Kuhlmeier* modifications, the policy was unconstitutionally overbroad under *Tinker*: "In short, the Policy, even narrowly read, prohibits a substantial amount of non-vulgar, non-sponsored student speech. SCASD must therefore satisfy the *Tinker* test by showing that the Policy's restrictions are necessary to prevent substantial disruption or interference with the work of the school of the rights of other students. Applying this test, we conclude that the Policy is substantially overbroad."

Judge Alito's *Saxe* opinion is notable because, as in his *Morse* concurrence, first, he reverts to the *Tinker* substantial disruption rule and, second, because he reads the *Tinker* rule as requiring "that a school must reasonably believe that speech will cause actual, material disruption before prohibiting it." (Of course—in *Morse*, unlike in *Saxe*—Alito was persuaded that Principal Deborah Morse "reasonably believed" that Joe Frederick's banner would "cause actual, material disruption.")

110. "1. The Court will not pass upon the constitutionality of legislation in a friendly, nonadversary, proceeding, declining because to decide such questions 'is legitimate only in the last resort, and as a necessity in the determination of real, earnest and vital controversy between individuals. It never was the thought that, by means of a friendly suit, a party beaten in the legislature could transfer to the courts an inquiry as to the constitutionality of the legislative act.' 2. The Court will not 'anticipate a question of constitutional law in advance of the necessity of deciding it.' 3. The Court will not 'formulate a rule of constitutional law broader than is required by the precise facts to which it is to be applied.' 4. The Court will not pass upon a constitutional question, although properly presented by the record, if there is also present some other ground upon which the case may be disposed of. This rule has found most varied application. Thus, if a case can be decided on either of two grounds, one involving a constitutional question, the other a question of statutory construction or general law, the Court will decide only the latter. 5. The Court will not pass upon the validity of a statute upon complaint of one who fails to show that he is injured by its operation. 6. The Court will not pass upon the constitutionality of a statute at the instance of one who has availed himself of its benefits. 7. 'When the validity of an act of the Congress is drawn in question, and even if a serious doubt of constitutionality is raised, it is a cardinal principle that this Court will first ascertain whether a construction of the statute is fairly possible by which the question may be avoided.'" *Ashwander v. Tennessee*, 297 U.S. 288, 346–348 (internal citations omitted).

111. Compare Felix Frankfurter's advice that "[c]ourts ought not to enter [the] political thicket." Justice Frankfurter was referring to controversies over the constitutionality of state legislative apportionment schemes. *Colegrove v. Green*, 328 U.S. 549, 556 (1946).

112. *Morse v. Frederick*, 551 U.S. 393 (2007), http://www.supremecourtus.gov/opinions/06pdf/06-278.pdf, Breyer, J., concurring, 3. "This Court need not and should not decide this difficult First Amendment issue on the merits. Rather, I believe that it should simply hold that qualified immunity bars the student's claim for monetary damages and say no more." Ibid., 1. Given Justice Breyer's posture on the constitutional issue, it is interesting to speculate how he voted on granting *cert.* in *Morse v. Frederick*. Would he have voted yes solely to review the Ninth Circuit's damage award?

113. As Breyer himself says, avoidance strategy probably is a more accurate description. See next sentence.

114. *Morse v. Frederick*, 551 U.S. 393 (2007), http://www.supremecourtus.gov/opinions/06pdf/06-278.pdf, Breyer, J., concurring, 4.

115. Ibid., 7.

116. Jeffrey Toobin, "Answers to Questions," *New Yorker*, July 27, 2009, 19. Toobin continues: "In such instances, Justices make choices, based largely, though not exclusively, on their political views of the issues involved. In reaching decisions this way, the Justices are not doing anything wrong; there is no other way to interpret the majestic vagueness of the Constitution." Ibid.

117. Compare: "A camel is a horse designed by a committee."

118. *Morse v. Frederick*, 551 U.S. 393 (2007), http://www.supremecourtus.gov/opinions/06pdf/06-278.pdf, Opinion of the Court, 15.

119. Ibid., Stevens, Souter, and Ginsburg, JJ., dissenting, 2, 5.

120. The Oyez Project, *Morse v. Frederick*, 551 U.S. 393 (2007), http://oyez.org/cases/2000-2009/2006/2006_06_278.

121. *Morse v. Frederick*, 551 U.S. 393 (2007), http://www.supremecourtus.gov/opinions/06pdf/06-278.pdf, Opinion of the Court, 7.

122. Ibid., Stevens, Souter, and Ginsburg, JJ., dissenting, 7. Compare Justice Breyer: "[T]o hold, as the Court does, that 'schools may take steps to safeguard those entrusted to their care from speech that can reasonably be regarded as encouraging illegal drug use' (and that 'schools' may 'restrict student expression that they reasonably regards as promoting illegal drug use') . . . based as it is on viewpoint restrictions, raises a host of serious concerns." Ibid., Breyer, J. concurring, 1–2.

123. Ibid., Stevens, Souter, and Ginsburg, JJ., dissenting, 11–12.

124. Ibid., 5.

125. Ibid.

126. The Oyez Project, *Morse v. Frederick*, 551 U.S. 393 (2007), http://oyez.org/cases/2000-2009/2006/2006_06_278.

127. Starr's reply to Justice Souter was: "The educational mission of the school." Ibid.

128. *Morse v. Frederick*, 551 U.S. 393 (2007), http://www.supremecourtus.gov/opinions/06pdf/06-278.pdf, Stevens, Souter, and Ginsburg, dissenting, 5.

129. Take the Court's ruling in *Morse*, for example: "The 'special characteristics of the school environment,' *Tinker* . . . , and the governmental interest in stopping student drug abuse—reflected in the policies of Congress and myriad school boards, including JDHS—allow schools to restrict student expression that they reasonably regard as promoting illegal drug use." *Morse v. Frederick*, 551 U.S. 393 (2007), http://www.supremecourtus.gov/opinions/06pdf/06-278.pdf, Opinion of the Court, 14. All four of the key phrases in this holding are open to debate and interpretation: (1) "special characteristics of the school environment"; (2) governmental interest in stopping student drug abuse; (3) student expression; and (4) promoting illegal drug use.

130. Adam Liptak, "Sotomayor Confirmed by Senate, 68–31: Back Story with the *Times'* Adam Liptak," *New York Times*, August 6, 2009, http://www.nytimes.com.

131. See Stanley Fish, "What Kind of Judges Do We Want?" blog post, *New York Times*, June 22, 2009, http://fish.blogs.nytimes.com/2009/06/22/what-kind-of-judges-do-we-want.

132. 347 U.S. 483 (1954).

133. Paraphrasing Winston Churchill: "Now [*Brown*] is not the end. [*Brown*] is not even the beginning of the end. But [*Brown*] is, *perhaps*, the end of the beginning" (emphasis added). The Lord Mayor's Luncheon, Mansion House, London, November 10, 1942. Compare Gerald N. Rosenberg, *The Hollow Hope: Can Courts Bring about Social Change?* 2nd ed. (Chicago: University of Chicago Press, 2008), and the review of Rosenberg, and sources cited, by Wayne D. Moore, *Law and Politics Book Review* 18 (November 2008), http://www.bsos.umd.edu/gvpt/lpbr/subpages/reviews/rosenberg1108.htm. Also see Gerald N. Rosenberg, "*Brown* Is Dead! Long Live *Brown*! The Endless Attempt to Canonize a Case," *Virginia Law Review* 80 (February 1994): 161; David J. Garrow, "Hopelessly Hollow History: Revisionist Devaluing of *Brown v. Board of Education*," *Virginia Law Review* 80 (February 1994): 151; Mark V. Tushnet, "The Significance of *Brown v. Board of Education*," *Virginia Law Review* 80 (February 1994): 173; and Michael J. Klarman, "*Brown v. Board of Education*: Facts and Political Correctness," *Virginia Law Review* 80 (February 1994): 185.

134. Compare Lincoln's January 1, 1863, Emancipation Proclamation, which, as a practical matter, freed no one. See Burrus M. Carnahan, *Act of Justice: Lincoln's Emancipation Proclamation and the Law of War* (Lexington: University Press of Kentucky, 2007); and the review of Carnahan's book by James C. Foster, *Law and Politics Book Review* 19 (January 2009), http://www.bsos.umd.edu/gvpt/lpbr/reviews/2009/01/act-of-justice-lincolns-emancipation.html.

135. 347 U.S. 483, 495 (1954).

136. As for ending de facto racial segregation in schools, *Brown*'s impact was negligible. See *Freeman v. Pitts*, 503 U.S. 467 (1992), and *Parents Involved in Community Schools v. Seattle School Dist. No. 1* and *Meredith v. Jefferson County Board of Education*, 551 U.S. 701 (2007).

137. Only in retrospect are Warren's words are incontrovertible. They were anything but incontrovertible on May 17, 1954, the day *Brown* was announced. The justices themselves had been divided over whether or not to overturn *Plessy v. Ferguson*, 163 U.S. 537 (1896), where the Court had upheld the constitutionality of racial segregation. In fact, as we have seen, William H. Rehnquist, eventually to become Chief Justice in 1986, wrote a memo to Justice Robert H. Jackson, for whom he was clerking at the time, arguing that *Plessy* should not be overturned. See Mark Tushnet with Katya Lezin, "What Really Happened in *Brown v. Board of Education*," *Columbia Law Review* 91 (December 1991): 1867. Compare Jack Balkin, ed., *What Brown v. Board of Education Should Have Said: The Nation's Top Legal Experts Rewrite America's Landmark Civil Right Decision* (New York: New York University Press, 2002).

138. See *Green v. School Board of New Kent County, Va.*, 391 U.S. 430 (1968). Compare Kristin Luker, *Abortion and the Politics of Motherhood* (Berkeley: University of California Press, 1984), on *Roe v. Wade*, 410 U.S. 113 (1973), fanning resistance to legal abortions.

139. *Congressional Record*, 84th Congress Second Session. Vol. 102, part 4 (March 12, 1956) (Washington, D.C.: Government Printing Office, 1956), 4459–4460.

140. Ibid.

141. Having said all this, assessed according to the aesthetic criteria explained below, 191–193, *Brown v. Board of Education* is a beautifully executed decision.

142. But see Stefanie A. Lindquist and Frank B. Cross, "Empirically Testing Dworkin's Chain Novel Theory: Studying the Path of Precedent," *N.Y.U. Law Review* 80 (October 2005): 1156.

143. Comparing the Court's ruling in *Brown v. Board of Education*, 394 U.S. 294 (1955) (*Brown II*) with its opinion in *Green v. School Board of New Kent County, Va.*, 391 U.S. 430 (1968), provides another dramatic example of how pliable Supreme Court holdings and opinions are. In *Brown II* the Court declared a remedy by means of which its ruling on the constitutional principle in *Brown I* was to be implemented. Chief Justice Warren wrote: ". . . the cases are remanded to the District Courts to take such proceedings and enter such orders and decrees consistent with this opinion as are necessary and proper to admit to public schools on a racially nondiscriminatory basis with *all deliberate speed* the parties to these cases" (emphasis added), *Brown v. Board of Education*, 394 U.S. 294, 301 (1955). Fourteen years and ten days later, frustrated by stubbornly ingenious sabotage of efforts to create desegregated (unitary) school districts, Justice Brennan wrote for a unanimous Court: "This deliberate perpetuation of the unconstitutional dual system can only have compounded the harm of such a system. Such delays are no longer tolerable[.] . . . Moreover, a plan that, at this late date, fails to provide meaningful assurance of prompt and effective disestablishment of a dual system is also intolerable. 'The time for mere *deliberate speed*' has run out'" . . . (citation omitted). *Green v. School Board of New Kent County, Va.*, 391 U.S. 430, 438 (1968). What, for the *Brown* II Court, meant (deliberate) speed was read by Southern politicians and school administrators as deliberate (speed)—if not deliberate obstruction. See J. W. Peltason, *Fifty-eight Lonely Men: Southern Federal Judges and School Desegregation* (Urbana: University of Illinois Press, 1971). Compare *Cooper v. Aaron*, 358 U.S. 1 (1958).

144. I am reluctant to use the word *facts* with reference to the contested circumstances underlying *Morse v. Frederick*. Beyond the actuality that Deborah Morse and Joseph Frederick stood across Glacier Avenue from each other the morning of January 24, 2002, the day the Olympic torch run came through Juneau, Alaska, and that as the torch bearer approached, Frederick and others hoisted a fourteen-foot banner reading "BONG HiTS 4 JESUS"—aside from these "facts," objective reality vanishes.

145. *The Federalist Papers*, Clinton Rossiter, ed. (New York: Mentor, 1961), 465.

146. Ibid.

147. I focus on the first aspect of the paradox here. The second aspect of the paradox is that judicial power is fragile and essential. See James C. Foster and Susan M. Leeson, *Constitutional Law: Cases in Context*, 2 vols. (Upper Saddle River, N.J.: Prentice-Hall, 1998), I: 2.

148. Edward Bulwer-Lytton, "Beneath the rule of men entirely great/The pen is mightier than the sword," *Richelieu; Or the Conspiracy*. Compare Cicero: "*cēdant arma togae*" (let military power yield to civil authority), *De Officiis*, I.lxxvii; Shakespeare, "many wearing rapiers are afraid of goose-quills," *Hamlet,* Act 2, Scene II; "a goose quill is more dangerous than a lion's claw," English proverb; and Thomas Jefferson to Thomas Paine: "Go on then in doing with your pen what in other times was done with the sword: shew that reformation is more practicable by operating on the mind than on the body of man, and be assured that it has not a more sincere votary nor you a more ardent well-wisher than Y[ou]rs. &c. Thomas Jefferson," June 19, 1792. Also see Egyptian King Akhtov III's advice to his son, Marikare: "Be a craftsman in speech, for the tongue is a sword to man, and speech is more valorous than fighting." Quoted in Lief H. Carter, *Contemporary Constitutional Lawmaking: The Supreme Court and the Art of Politics* (New York: Pergamon Press, 1985), 170. Carter obtained the Akhtov III quote from Henry Fairlie, "The Decline of Oratory," *New Republic*, May 28, 1984, 15. Fairlie's original is well worth reading, especially in the context of this chapter's discussion.

149. Lief Carter, review of Richard Posner, *The Problems of Jurisprudence, Law and Politics Book Review* 1 (April 1991), http://www.bsos.umd.edu/gvpt/lpbr/subpages/reviews/posner2.htm.

150. Ibid. Also see Carter, *Contemporary Constitutional Lawmaking*.

151. Albert R. Matheny, Review of Lief Carter, *An Introduction to Constitutional Interpretation; Cases in Law and Religion, Law and Politics Book Review* 1 (August 1991), http://www.bsos.umd.edu/gvpt/lpbr/subpages/reviews/vangeel.htm.

152. Lief Carter, *An Introduction to Constitutional Interpretation: Cases in Law and Religion* (New York: Longman, 1991), xi.

153. Lief Carter paraphrasing Richard Rorty, "No Ivory Tower: CC's 124th Anniversary Symposium," Colorado College Symposium, Cultures in the 21st Century: Conflicts and Convergences, February 4–6, 1999, http://www.coloradocollege.edu/Publications/TheBulletin/Summer99/125.html. In another place, Carter writes: "I . . . had the fortunate chance . . . to ask Richard Rorty . . . 'Suppose, while flying over some remote and primitive land, you are forced to parachute out of a crippled plane. You land among a people with no experience of western values. Given your 'supernaturally' sudden arrival, you are treated with great respect and deference. While waiting for a rescue, you discover that the tribe practices female genital mutilation (FGM). What do you say to persuade them to stop the practice?' Rorty's answer was . . . 'I would explain that we don't practice FGM and that we find our women are happier. That makes our men happier. Try it, you might like it.'" Rorty's reply to Carter's question captures Rorty's persuasive strategy, as well as Carter's understanding of how judicial words can move us. Lief Carter, review of Steven L. Winter, *A Clearing in the Forest: Law, Life and the Mind, Law and Politics Book Review* 12 (June 2002), http://www.bsos.umd.edu/gvpt/lpbr/subpages/reviews/winterclear.html. Compare Richard A. Schweder on FGM, *Why Do Men Barbecue: Recipes for Cultural Psychology* (Cambridge, Mass.: Harvard University Press, 2003), chap. 4 ; and Rolando Díaz-Loving

and Rogelio Díaz-Guerrero, "Some Thoughts on Schweder's 'Why Do Men Barbecue,'" *Cross Cultural Psychiatry Bulletin* 38 (2004): 4.

154. *Pretty* being understood as compelling, beautiful, and true.

155. Carter titles one section of his *Contemporary Constitutional Lawmaking*, "'For God's Sake, Don't Think of It As Art!'" 197. Earlier in his book Carter traces this quotation "reportedly" to James Agee, 9. The accurate quote is "Above all else: in God's name don't think of it as Art." The source is James Agee and Walker Evans, *Let Us Now Praise Famous Men* (New York: Houghton Mifflin, 1941), 15. Carter's point is that confining *art* to merely modes of entertainment trivializes the activity of making meaning.

156. Holmes continued: "The felt necessities of the time, the prevalent moral and political theories, intuitions of public policy, avowed or unconscious, even the prejudices which judges share with their fellow men, have had a good deal more to do than the syllogism in determining the rules by which men should be governed. The law embodies the story of a nation's development through many centuries, and it cannot be dealt with as if it contained only the axioms and corollaries of a book of mathematics." Oliver Wendell Holmes Jr., Lowell Lecture, November 23, 1880, http://www.law.harvard.edu/library/collections/special/online-collections/common_law/index.php. Compare Lief Carter on Stephen L. Winter: "'[T]he life of the law is not logic but persuasion' (p. 317). Since each individual brain creates its own ongoing stream of image-driven schema, it is persuasion ('selling,' to put it more crassly) that converts an individual cognition into a collective one. However, persuasive conversions can only happen within the framework of what the listener already believes. 'I am not arguing that people can never be persuaded to change their beliefs, only that one must be able to refer to some other aspects of their believes [*sic*], values, and understandings in order to effect that change' (p. 320). 'What a given judge will do in a case depends on what she thinks will fly with the much larger constituency to which she must appeal both for her legitimacy and efficacy' (p. 312)." Lief Carter, review of Winter, *A Clearing in the Forest.*

157. "Art is, as Dewey suggested, that method of simplifying our raw experience so that we can find some meaning in it." Carter, *Contemporary Constitutional Lawmaking*, 187. See John Dewey, *Art as Experience* (New York: Minton, Balch and Company, 1934); and Louis Menand, *The Metaphysical Club: A Story of Ideas in America* (New York: Farrar, Straus and Giroux, 2002).

158. Frederick Schauer, "Abandoning the Guidance Function: *Morse v. Frederick*," *Supreme Court Review* (2007), 205.

159. Ibid., 219.

160. Ibid., 208.

161. Ibid., 219–220. "[T]he gap between the issue that the Supreme Court took on in *Frederick* and the issues that have dominated the lower court litigation about student speech is vast. As the cases below the Supreme Court show, therefore, there are multiple recurring issues in the domain of student speech, but these issues are not the ones that the Court decided, either directly or indirectly, to address. Instead, the Court elected to hear a highly unrepresentative case, and having done so then proceeded to issues a series of opinions, including the opinion of the Court, that gave virtually no additional guidance to lower state and federal courts on how the cases that actually do arise with some frequency in the lower courts ought to be decided." Ibid., 225.

162. Schauer's criticism recalls Justice Thomas' complaint in his *Morse* concurring opinion: "Today, the Court creates another exception. In doing so, we continue to distance ourselves from *Tinker*, but we neither overrule it nor offer an explanation of when it operates and when it does not. . . . I am afraid that our jurisprudence now says that students have a right to speak in schools except when they don't—a standard continuously developed through litigation against local schools

and their administrators." *Morse v. Frederick*, 551 U.S. 393 (2007), http://www.supremecourtus.gov/opinions/06pdf/06-278.pdf, Thomas, J., concurring, 9–10.

163. Carter, *Contemporary Constitutional Lawmaking*, 172–178.

164. Ibid., 173.

165. This and the immediately previous quote are ibid., 178.

166. Ibid., 179–182.

167. "Fit" is the key concept in Carter's aesthetic approach to constitutional interpretation. He first uses "fittedness," ibid., xv of his Preface. "Fits" (3 times) and "fitting" appear on the last page of his final chapter, ibid., 195. "Harmonize"—a variation on fit—appears occasionally throughout *Contemporary Constitutional Interpretation*. "[W]ithin the frame of experience of audiences, the 'fittedness' of the elements of the performance and the coherence of the thinking the performance conveys explain the reactions to painting, concerts, poems, television shows, and judicial opinions. Aesthetics examines not objects of art but the relationships between performers and audiences. Aesthetics is, in other words, a version of communications theory wherein the audience matters as much as the performer." Ibid., xv.

168. "[Humans], though they must die, are not born in order to die but in order to begin." Hannah Arendt, *The Human Condition* (New York: Doubleday Anchor, 1959), 222.

169. Sheldon S. Wolin, *Politics and Vision: Continuity and Innovation in Western Political Thought* (Boston: Little, Brown, 1960), 17–21.

170. Carter, *An Introduction to Constitutional Interpretation*, 124. Carter is quoting Martha Nussbaum, "Our Pasts, Ourselves," Review of Charles Taylor's *Sources of the Self: The Making of Modern Identity*, *New Republic*, April 9, 1990, 27. Compare Lief H. Carter, "Law and Politics as Play," *Chicago-Kent Law Review* 83 (2008): 1333.

171. In so doing, we also address Schauer's concerns and exemplify Holmes' conception of law.

Notes to Chapter 9

1. Editorial, "Enough Already; Drop the Bong Hits Issue," *Juneau Empire*, January 25, 2008, http://www.juneauempire.com/stories/012508/opi_240253928.shtml.

2. Greg Skinner, "'Bong Hits' Ruling Sides with District," *Juneau Empire*, June 26, 2007, http://www.juneauempire.com/stories/062607/loc_20070626018.shtml.

3. Ibid. "Morse also thanked the justices for language that absolved her from personal liability."

4. Deborah Morse interview, June 5, 2009, 1:26:26.

5. Joe Frederick interview, March 21, 2009, 1:12:41.

6. See G. Alan Tarr, "The New Judicial Federalism in Perspective," *Notre Dame Law Review* 72 (1996–1997): 1097; William J. Brennan Jr., "State Constitutions and the Protection of Individual Rights," *Harvard Law Review* 90 (1977): 489; Robert K. Fitzpatrick, "Neither Icarus nor Ostrich: State Constitutions as an Independent Source of Rights," *N.Y.U. Law Review* 79 (November 2004): 1833; Hans E. Linde, "Without 'Due Process': Unconstitutional Law in Oregon," *Oregon Law Review* 49 (1970): 125; Susan P. Fino, *The Role of State Supreme Courts in the New Judicial Federalism* (Westport, Conn.: Greenwood Press, 1987); and Michael E. Solimine and James L. Walker, *Respecting State Courts: The Inevitability of Judicial Federalism* (Westport, Conn.: Greenwood Press 1999). Also see Stephen L. Wasby, "The Road Not Taken: Judicial Federalism, Student Athletes, and Drugs," *Albany Law Review* 59 (1996): 1699.

7. Skinner, "'Bong Hits' Ruling Sides with District." I changed the order in which one of Mertz's quotes appears in the article.

The three journalist/prognosticators to whose predictions I refer in Chapter 8 likely were pleasantly unsurprised by the Court's *Morse v. Frederick* ruling. I quoted Linda Greenhouse: "A majority of the court seemed willing to create what would amount to a drug exception to students' First Amendment rights, much as the court has in recent years permitted widespread drug testing of students, even those not personally suspected of using drugs, under a relaxed view of the Fourth Amendment prohibition against unreasonable searches." Greenhouse was spot on. Lyle Denniston wrote: "The Supreme Court on Monday toyed with the notion that public school officials should have added discretion to censor student speech that they may interpret as advocating use of illegal drugs. But this was only a flirtation, not a warm embrace." In the event, the flirtation Denniston had noted turned into a fragmented embrace. I summarized Tony Mauro's view as: In light of what he heard on March 19, 2007, during oral argument, then, the "middle" position Mauro expected the Court to stake out would authorize narrow official discretion to proscribe student pro-drug speech, and shield school officials from damages when exercising that judgment. Mauro also was on the mark. Unlike his two colleagues, who confined themselves to reporting the outcome, Lyle Denniston ventured this speculation about *Morse*'s potential significance: "[I suggest] caution about taking *Morse* as a this-case-this-day-only ruling by the Court. Between the Roberts opinion, the concurrences, and the dissent, the Justices are deeply divided about standards for regulating student speech, and *Morse* makes only a modest beginning on settling on some new standards. The dominant thrust of the principal opinion appears, in potential, at least, to be toward a considerable expansion of school officials' authority over student expression. No longer is it necessary to regulation, for example, to find that the expression disrupts school life, or that it is crudely and profanely offensive, or that it is an utterance done during assigned or immediately supervised school work. If it is close enough to the schoolhouse gate, it appears to be subject to regulation—at least when it is perceived, by school officials, as promoting a drug-use message. . . . There is, perhaps, not as much judicial modesty here as originally meets the eye of the reader." Lyle Denniston, "Commentary: Beyond the schoolhouse gate," *SCOTUSBlog*, June 25, 2007, http://www.scotusblog.com/wp/commentary-beyond-the-schoolhouse-gate/#more-5645.

8. Frank Frederick had this to say about his son's arrest and conviction: "I told Joe that you make choices in life. There're basically no excuses in life. You're responsible for who you are, and what you become, and nothin' besides. You are your own destiny, and nothing besides. What happened was, they got somebody on drugs. . . . They put the guy back on campus, and this guy set up other people. . . . And so, anyway, they come in and they got about twenty-five college students on various drug charges, and all this stuff. And apparently Joe went and got this guy some marijuana from someone else and sold it to him. And, you know: 'Yeah, I can get you some marijuana.' And, you know, I said, 'Joe, nice guys finish last.' But, you know, I said, 'You know what, there are no excuses in life. You know that the drug was illegal. And you're responsible for who you are, and what you become.'" Frank Frederick, interview, July 24, 2009, 1:16:09. Once again, when it comes to key biographical events, even father and son apparently cannot get their stories straight.

9. Joe Frederick interview, March 21, 2009, 1:04:07.

10. Ibid., 1:37:01.

11. Ibid., 1:14:57. Margo Waring, Doug Mertz's wife, said: "I can tell you, just in our private lives, the numbers of times Doug has gone: "Oh, my God, do I have to keep on supporting [*laughs*] this case!" [Doug interjects, "Yeah."] "Will this never end!" Doug Mertz and Margo Waring, interview, June 7, 2009, 1:42:34.

12. Deborah Morse interview, June 5, 2009, 1:17:10. At this remark, David Crosby interjected: "There was a flat five Justices who agreed with the majority opinion. You know, I can't understand

Doug Mertz runnin' around sayin' that there was not a majority for the decision. You can read a Supreme Court opinion, or you can't." Ibid., 1:18:34.

13. Doug Mertz and Margo Waring interview, June 7, 2009, 1:15:18.

14. *Morse v. Frederick*, 551 U.S. 393 (2007).

15. *Joseph Frederick v. Deborah Morse and the Juneau School Board*, Opposition Brief of Appellees, No. 07-36013, in author's possession, 5. See Greg Skinner, "'Bong Hits' Case Goes Back to Court," *Juneau Empire*, September 6, 2007, http://www.juneauempire.com/stories/090607/loc_20070906004.shtml.

16. *Frederick v. Morse*, Order partially vacating judgment of May 29, 2003, and directing entry of final judgment in favor of defendants, Case No. J02-008 CV (JWS), in author's possession, 1–2. The Alaska Constitution, Article I, Declaration of Rights, § 5. Freedom of Speech, reads: "Every person may freely speak, write, and publish on all subjects, being responsible for the abuse of that right." See Greg Skinner, "Judge: District Won't Pay Damages in Bong Hits Case: Officials Describe Ruling As End of Suit," *Juneau Empire*, October 14, 2007, http://www.juneauempire.com/stories/101407/loc_20071014025.shtml.

17. David Crosby disputes the $28,000 figure. He says that Mertz demanded more like $108,000.

18. Greg Skinner, "School Board Mulls Offer for Settlement in Bong Hits Case," *Juneau Empire*, November 21, 2007, http://www.juneauempire.com/stories/112107/loc_20071121023.shtml.

19. Alan Suderman, "School Board Tries to Recover 'Bong Hits' Court Fees," *Juneau Empire*, January 24, 2008, http://www.juneauempire.com/stories/012408/loc_239777207.shtml.

20. Editorial, "Enough Already; Drop the Bong Hits Issue."

21. As circumstances eventually turned out, because Judge Sedwick's court was the last adjudicatory stop in the litigation, John Sedwick had the last word regarding the disposition of important issues in the BONG HiTS dispute, in *Frederick v. Morse*, Case No. J02-008 CV (JWS).

22. *Frederick v. Morse*, Appellant's Opening Brief, in the United States Court of Appeals for the Ninth Circuit, No. 07-36013, in author's possession, 8.

23. Ibid., 8–9.

24. Ibid., 9.

25. Ibid.

26. Ibid., 9–10.

27. *Frederick v. Morse*, Opposition Brief of Appellees Deborah Morse and Juneau School Board, in the United States Court of Appeals for the Ninth Circuit, No. 07-36013, in author's possession, 8–14. Under this heading, Crosby advanced two arguments: "The Supreme Court ruled that the words used by Frederick constituted advocacy of illegal drug use and were not protected by the First Amendment"; and "Frederick failed to appeal Judge Sedwick's ruling that his suspension was not increased for supposedly quoting Thomas Jefferson."

28. Ibid., 14–31. Under this heading, Crosby advanced six major arguments (with subsidiary points under B and C): A. As a General Rule, Graduation Moots a Challenge to Discipline Imposed While the Plaintiff Was a Student; B. Frederick Has No Viable Claim for Damages Arising from Alleged Violations of His Rights Under the Alaska Constitution; C. Frederick Has No Viable Claim for Expungement of Disciplinary Records, Either; D. The Exception to Mootness for Actions "Capable of Repetition Yet Avoiding Review" Does Not Apply to Frederick's "As Applied" Challenge; E. Morse and JSB [Juneau School Board] Have Not "Voluntarily Ceased" Any Conduct Challenged in the Complaint; and F. Frederick Can Not Assert the Rights of Other Students.

29. Ibid., 31.

30. See Mediation Questionnaire, http://www.ca9.uscourts.gov/datastore/uploads/Mediation_Questionnaire.pdf.

31. "Mediation in the Ninth Circuit, C. The Mediation Process," http://www.ca9.uscourts.gov/mediation/mediation_c.php.

32. Deborah Morse interview, June 5, 2009, 1:37:11.

33. Ibid., 1:38:10.

34. Doug Mertz interview, June 7, 2009, 1:35:00. Compare Joe's view: "We didn't trust that the school's attorney was actually presenting the school board with our offers, and that's why we couldn't come to a settlement. . . . When we decided to [appeal] it on state grounds, immediately both sides decided we wanted to try and mediate this. But we made many reasonable offers, and the offers Crosby was coming back with were not—he was just saying like flat-out 'no' to everything; saying, 'No, we'll give you this,' and this ridiculous offer. And Doug had suspicions that the school board was not being given any of the offers. [We] went back and forth on mediation for quite a while." Joe Frederick interview, March 21, 2009, 1:16:39.

35. Doug Mertz interview, June 7, 2009, 1:37:37.

36. Greg Skinner, "City Joins 'Bong Hits' Mediation before Next Round of Litigation," *Juneau Empire*, February 17, 2008, http://www.juneauempire.com/stories/021708/loc_247904339.shtml.

37. Ann Gifford interview, June 6, 2009, 51:31.

38. Doug Mertz interview, June 7, 2009, 1:37:33. Joe Frederick shared Doug Mertz's distrust. He also expressed misgivings with the manner in which the Ninth Circuit mediator conducted the negotiations. "We had to go through some mediations on the telephone. . . . There were quite a few times we had to call into the Ninth Circuit to Mediations. And there were some weird things about it me and Doug didn't like. We didn't like what the mediator was doing. Like, for instance, we didn't trust that the school's attorney was actually presenting the school board with our offers, and that's why we couldn't come to a settlement. But the mediator also refused to require—here's something that was weird—what was weird about it [was] the mediator wouldn't have a mediation unless I was present, at least via phone. Right? But she didn't care about anything on their side. Their attorney was enough. And I was like, 'Can't Doug talk for me, because I'm in China and I have to be up at 2 a.m. on the phone, when I have to work in the morning.' Like, 'No, you have to be there.' And . . . I told the mediator, 'If I have to be there, why doesn't the superintendent or at least one representative of the school board have to be here, so we are at least sure that this mediation offer is even given to the school?' Which me and Doug are pretty sure 90 percent of our offers were not even offered to the school board; that their attorney was misleading them because he wanted the case to continue." Joe Frederick interview, March 21, 2009, 1:16:39.

39. Eric Morrison, "Candidates Vie for Seat on School Board: Mark Choate Sees Crisis in High School Dropout Rate," *Juneau Empire*, August 25, 2006, http://www.juneauempire.com/stories/092506/loc_20060925005.shtml. The day after Election Day 2006, the *Juneau Empire* reported: "Choate . . . said the now infamous 'Bong Hits 4 Jesus' case was a deciding factor in the election. The controversial case—which derives from a student being suspended for displaying a sign, 'Bong Hits 4 Jesus,' at the 2002 Winter Olympic Torch relay—has led some to believe the Juneau School District is trying to suppress free speech. The district, which lost the case, is appealing the decision to the U.S. Supreme Court. . . . Choate sad [sic] pursuing the case is the wrong priority for the School Board, and that the electorate agrees with him. 'I would say 80 percent of the people I talked to were unhappy about the 'Bong Hits 4 Jesus' writ,' Choate said. 'When I get on the board, I hope to show why we should concentrate on other matters.'" Will Morris, "Incumbents Keep School Board Seats," *Juneau Empire*, October 4, 2006, http://www.juneauempire.com/stories/100406/loc_20061004033.shtml.

40. Editorial, "A Silly Banner and a Stupid Court Appeal," *Juneau Empire*, May 7, 2006, http://www.juneauempire.com/stories/050706/opi_20060507013.shtml.

41. Cass R. Sunstein, *A Constitution of Many Minds: Why the Founding Document Doesn't Mean What It Meant Before* (Princeton, N.J.: Princeton University Press, 2009), chap. 1.

42. Peggy Cowan and Dale Staley (with David Crosby) interview, June 8, 2009, 33:26; 34:12; 43:30.

43. Deborah Morse (with David Crosby) interview, June 5, 2009, 1:33:24.

44. The retort Crosby quotes is usually ascribed to Charles Cotesworth Pinckney, one of three commissioners that President John Adams sent to France in an attempt to negotiate a treaty ending an undeclared naval war and normalizing commercial relations. What Pinckney more likely said, if anything at all, was "No! No! Not a sixpence."

45. Associated Press, "'Bong Hits' Case Back in Court," *Anchorage Daily News*, July 24, 2008, http://www.adn.com/news/alaska/story/474150.html. Compare Alan Suderman, "'Bong Hits' Case Going Back to Court," *Juneau Empire*, July 24, 2008, http://www.juneauempire.com/stories/072408/loc_309068471.shtml; and Greg Skinner, "'Bong Hits' Case Goes Back to Court."

46. Doug Mertz interview, June 7, 2009, 1:53:21.

47. Deborah Morse (with David Crosby) interview, June 5, 2009, 1:26:46.

48. Ibid., 1:28:11.

49. Doug Mertz interview, June 7, 2009, 2:31:30.

50. An audio record of oral argument can be found at *Frederick v. Morse*, Ninth Circuit Court of Appeals, No. 07-36013, http://www.ca9.uscourts.gov/media/view_subpage.php?pk_id=0000000031.

51. See Richard H. Chambers, U.S. Court of Appeals, Pasadena, CA, U.S. General Services Administration, http://www.gsa.gov/Portal/gsa/ep/buildingView.do?pageTypeId=17109&channelPage=/ep/channel/gsaOverview.jsp&channelId=-25241&bid=825.

52. Right at the beginning of David Crosby's time at the lectern, there was this exchange that set the tone:

> **JUDGE KLEINFELD**: Counsel, I need some help from you . . . on mootness. . . . I was thinking, of course, now they [school district] want the case to be moot, but they've never given any promise about the future. And they won in the Supreme Court—the school district won the case. I would think that when it's all over, it might be very satisfying for the Juneau School Board, and the superintendent of schools, and retired Principal Morse, to put a big blackboard notice in Fredrick's file saying this kid was disciplined for advocating drug use.
>
> **CROSBY**: Well, let's talk for a minute about the records.
>
> **JUDGE KLEINFELD**: Is there anything to stop them from doing that?
>
> **CROSBY**: Well, yes there is.
>
> **JUDGE KLEINFELD**: What?
>
> **CROSBY**: Because they cannot release any records, any student records, without the consent of the student. So that's the very first question that comes in.
>
> **JUDGE WARDLAW**: But if they're in the file—we've seen this over and over—even though there're laws that say that the records cannot be turned over without the consent of the subject of the records, they're leaked all the time, if they exist[.] . . . So the point is, one, [Superintendent Peggy] Cowan's declaration doesn't speak to whether there are any records at the high school so, for all we know there might be some, and two, could they be used to harm Frederick sometime in the future. . . .
>
> **CROSBY**: Mootness is a jurisdictional question, it's a very serious question for the federal courts to proceed—
>
> **JUDGE WARDLAW**: —yes, you don't need to tell us that. We know that.

Frederick v. Morse, Ninth Circuit Court of Appeals, No. 07-36013, http://www.ca9.uscourts.gov/media/view_subpage.php?pk_id=0000000031.

53. Doug Mertz interview, June 7, 2009, 1:49:38.

54. Peggy Cowan and Dale Staley (with David Crosby) interview, June 8, 2009, 46:22. Crosby added: "I mean, frankly, I thought this was a crazy panel, and you'd have to be crazy to put your fate in their hands. (And, since I'm retired, you can say that.) [*Laughter all around.*]" Ibid., 48:34. Three days previously, during my interview with Deborah Morse, Crosby and I had the following exchange: ["I just want to be clear here, David. So your sense is that the Nines (Ninth Circuit panel) would have decided this (case on the merits) rather than certifying it (to the Alaska Supreme Court)."—JCF]. That's right, they were not gonna let this one go. They wanted to decide this case. ["So, was that the decisive factor in the School District deciding to settle?"—JCF] You know, I . . . can't tell you what I said to them [the School Board members] when I was in that room with them, and I can't answer for them. . . . But . . . you [JCF] heard the argument. It was clear to me that they [Ninth Circuit panel] were going to rule against me on the mootness issue, which shocks me! I don't think there's another panel of that Court that would have treated the District's case that way on mootness. [Frederick's] records were gone. That's the only remedy that a federal court can issue. And they [Ninth Circuit panel] were stretching to find some reason why the case was not moot. Because you could always find somebody—if it was the school janitor—who would blab about . . . What every litigant wants in every mootness case is to have a federal court declare what his rights are. And the whole mootness doctrine says that you're not entitled to that. You're not entitled to have a federal court issue an opinion, with no consequences, about what your rights are. But it was clear that this panel was prepared to do that. . . . I thought we might get a different panel, since the only issue was a procedural issue of mootness. But they wanted this case. And I think they wanted to poke a finger in the eye of the United States Supreme Court, which they could have done, by ruling on the state . . . if they ever got the state constitutional issue. [If] they ruled on that, it would not be appealable to the United States Supreme Court. . . . At that point, I said [to the school board] 'You got your decision before the United States Supreme Court. The next time around, if it gets challenged, it's gonna have to get challenged in [Alaska] state court, and you'll win on that [*Morse v. Frederick*, 551 U.S. 393 (2007)]. So why tempt fate by hangin' around that panel. ["So your sense is that it was on your advice—the advice you just tendered—that the school board decided to pull the plug? The reason I ask is because other parts of the story float around that, the insurance company—the meter was running too long and too high—and the insurance company wanted to pull the plug. Another piece of it was community resistance was building—why is the school district spending all this time on this kid (Frederick) and this issue? Were those other pieces of it?"—JCF] Yeah, those were other pieces of it. . . . And, you know, everybody was just tired of it. It had been—what?—by this time, seven years, seven years that we'd been doin' this." Deborah Morse (with David Crosby) interview, June 5, 2009, 1:29:17.

55. Deborah Morse (with David Crosby) interview, June 5, 2009, 1:34:26.

56. Here is how Ann Gifford described the aftermath of the September 9 oral argument during our interview: "Well then, it's talking to the insurance company about, 'Okay, what makes sense here.' Because, obviously, if there's not something simple and clean, then you're looking at a lot of litigation to get it resolved, because of all this procedural stuff. And then it's like, it's not worth it. You know, it's not worth it to keep going on this. The costs exceed the benefits. ["Who was in on the decision to pull the plug?"—JFC] Well, primarily the ones who were paying the money; that's CBJ and APEI. ["So, it's primarily a cost-benefit analysis that leads to the decision to try and settle?"—JCF] It's pretty much all a cost-benefit analysis." Ann Gifford interview, June 6, 2009, 51:31.

57. Eric Morrison, "School Board, Frederick Reach Settlement in 'Bong Hits' Case," *Juneau Empire*, November 5, 2008, http://www.juneauempire.com/stories/110508/loc_352352563.shtml. During our interview, Eric Morrison observed: "I was surprised when they announced that they were actually . . . that the school board was gonna give a settlement. . . . It did seem odd, after all that time,

how many twists and turns the story had. . . . As I recall, [School Board President] Mark Choate . . . he's a lawyer himself . . . [thought] the district has other priorities that it should be focusing on rather than this pissing match, if you will." Eric Morrison interview, June 4, 2009, 30:50.

58. In the United States District Court for the District of Alaska, *Joseph Frederick, plaintiff vs. Deborah Morse and the Juneau School Board, defendants*, No. J02 008 CV (JWS), Settlement Agreement; and Settlement Agreement and Mutual Release, both in the author's possession.

59. *Frederick vs. Morse* Settlement Agreement, 4–5.

60. The five quotations just above are from Settlement Agreement and Mutual Release, 2. The remainder of the five subsections detail format, scheduling and access, and decorum.

61. *Frederick vs. Morse* Settlement Agreement, 4.

62. Ann Gifford connects the record removal issue to the mootness issue, as the district saw it: "[Expunging his records] was originally what [Frederick] asked for. They did that anyway. . . . When all the legal issues were resolved at the Supreme Court level, there was no reason not to expunge the records anymore and, so, they did that. Yes, that was part of what he wanted, but he already got that. I mean, that was a huge part of why, clearly, the thing was moot at that point." Ann Gifford interview, June 6, 2009, 54:18.

63. Settlement Agreement and Mutual Release, 2–3.

64. An alternative image is of two punch-drunk fighters, so battered and exhausted that they must cling to one another so as to remain standing.

65. Settlement Agreement and Mutual Release, 1.

66. Morrison, "School Board, Frederick Reach Settlement in 'Bong Hits' Case."

67. Ann Gifford interview, June 6, 2009, 55:19.

68. Mary Becker interview, June 6, 2009, 53:40. Gary Bader observed: "I'm glad this case is over. I regret that it ended up costing money. I think it was, probably at the end of the day, a good business decision for the School District to just pay up and get it done with." Gary Bader interview, June 6, 2009, 55:41. Phyllis Carlson said of the final settlement: "It was a tough pill for me to swallow. . . . The final settlement, for me, it was $50,000, or whatever we were—["Forty-five."—JCF]—45. It was not an easy thing for me because, I felt like I just didn't want to give that any more energy at all—or any, but, on the other hand, what's the point. I mean, you could just drag this thing out. I just wanted it done. I think most people just wanted it done. We just want to move on with the district. And . . . looking through the lens as a board member, put that behind us [*claps her hands*], move on. We've got kids to educate." Phyllis Carlson interview, June 8, 2009, 29:19. Sally Smith put the settlement in this context: "There was a lot of anger in many sectors of the community that the school board was spending money on this litigation. They thought they should'a just dropped it; settled with the kid [*claps her hands*], and been done with it. There were others who were sayin', 'No, you can't let a kid jerk your chain like this.' . . . But I think, by and large, the people thought that this was silliness at this point; that the school district was too ground down. But I also think they maybe didn't understand how serious Doug and Joe really were in getting big bucks out of this, and that the school district needed to try to save its bacon." Sally Smith interview, June 5, 2009, 33:57.

69. Ann Gifford interview, June 6, 2009, 55:05.

70. Ibid., 56:08.

71. Doug Mertz interview, June 7, 2009, 18:25.

72. Toward the end of my interview with Doug Mertz and Margo Waring, the two of them reflected candidly on this episode in their lives.

WARING: I guess that's another thing. . . . In a small community, the enormous power of people with a passion, who find themselves in—or create—the right time, the right moment to mount a crusade.

MERTZ: Yeah. And I will say, Crosby's one of them. And I probably was another one of them. More than Joe ever was. At a certain point I got the feeling that Joe just wanted to move on. And, well (laughingly) Crosby and I fought about this. And Crosby's and my commitments to our respective points of view were—had become so much the motivating factors in everything that went on that he and I were just carrying the whole controversy. And the rest of the community had long since moved past it.

As I observed in Chapter 1, "Pride goeth before a fall." Doug Mertz (with Margo Waring) interview, June 7, 2009, 5:40.

73. Deborah Morse (with David Crosby) interview, June 5, 2009, 1:18:48.

74. Peggy Cowan and Dale Staley interview, June 8, 2009, 42:31.

75. Deborah Morse (with David Crosby) interview, June 5, 2009, 1:34:56. See Anna Russell, "The Ring of the Nibelungs (An Analysis)," *Anna Russell Sings! Again?* Columbia Masterworks, ML4594/ML4733, 1953. I replied, "Okay, whatever metaphor one uses, didn't they basically end up with the settlement that was offered four or five years earlier, in substance?" To which Crosby said: "Basically, basically—except, in the meantime, the School District has gotten a very powerful, helpful interpretation from the Supreme Court." Deborah Morse (with David Crosby) interview, June 5, 2009, 1:35:10.

76. Toward the end of my interview with Joe Frederick, I asked him: "Looking back at it from this vantage point, of March of 2009, what's the whole saga look like to you?" Joe's reply was candid, and ambivalent: "I don't know, the whole thing's ridiculous. What does it all look like? . . . [W]ell, in hindsight, I see the importance of the case more now. . . . Like, originally I was sort of regretting the case after the Supreme Court, of course, because it did set bad precedent and that was something I'd never really expected or thought about the consequences until afterward. And like realizing, actually, if I had just dropped this before, then this Supreme Court decision would never have been made, and students would still have more rights than they do after my case. And my case actually limited those. Yeah, when the case started, I didn't have any idea of the magnitude—the potential magnitude—of it. Which Doug and them clearly warned me. The ACLU—well there's no way you can really explain how big this could be, but I thought they all were getting ahead of themselves. Saying, like, 'Hang on now.' After we'd lost at the school with this thing, 'now we can take this further, but this is gonna take a big commitment on your part. This could take up five, six, maybe even ten years to fight this. This could be big . . . there could be media, and you'll be watched and everything you do will be scrutinized.' And I sort of didn't believe it. Also, Doug and them explaining the importance of it in society right now, especially after the Patriot Act had demolished free speech. The more that time went by, the more I could see the significance of the case. I sort of understood it at the time. But I didn't understand it nearly as well as I do now, the importance of a sign like that that is absurd. Early on in the case, like when the ACLU told me why they would like to do the case, is because it is absurd, and doesn't really mean anything. And it really begs the question, do we have free speech, or not. So, yeah, looking back, I realize more and more how important it turned out to be." Joe Frederick interview, March 21, 2009, 1:21:23.

77. John R. Searle, *Speech Acts: An Essay in the Philosophy of Language* (Cambridge: Cambridge University Press, 1969).

78. I do not discount the value of other forms of expression, such as written speech. My view is that, of the rich range of human means of communicating, the immediacy and engagement inherent in conversing makes talking an essential vehicle for fashioning civil society. Neither do I romanticize conversing. Talk can go terribly wrong. When communicating goes awry, only more talking will suffice.

79. See Melanie Plenda, "Princess Announces Winners of Awards for Onshore Tours," *Juneau Empire*, September 18, 2001, http://www.juneauempire.com/stories/091801/Biz_princess.shtml.

80. Kirk Ziegenfuss, Letter to the Editor, "In Bong Hits History, Players Are Partners," *Juneau Empire*, July 30, 2008, http://www.juneauempire.com/stories/073008/let_311382174.shtml.

81. *Schenck v. United States*, 249 U.S. 47 (1919); *Abrams v. United States*, 250 U.S. 616 (1919); *Gitlow v. New York*, 268 U.S. 652 (1925); and *Whitney v. California*, 274 U.S. 357 (1927).

82. See James C. Foster and Susan M. Leeson, *Constitutional Law: Cases in Context*, 2 vols. (Upper Saddle River, N.J.: Prentice-Hall, 1998), II: 167–198.

83. See Vincent Blasi, "The First Amendment and the Ideal of Civic Courage: The Brandeis Opinion in *Whitney v. California*," *William and Mary Law Review* 29 (Summer 1988): 653.

84. See Ronald K. L. Collins and David M. Skover, "Curious Concurrence: Justice Brandeis' Vote in *Whitney v. California*," *Superior Court Review* (2005): 333.

85. *Whitney v. California*, 274 U.S. 357, 377 (1927).

86. Stuart Rosenberg, director, and Donn Pearce and Frank Pierson, screen writers, of *Cool Hand Luke*, Warner Brothers, 1967.

87. Compare Jack M. Balkan, ed., *What Brown v. Board of Education Should Have Said: The Nation's Top Legal Experts Rewrite America's Landmark Civil Rights Decision* (New York: New York University Press, 2001).

88. Obviously, had Frederick and Morse found ways to talk through their differences, the Supreme Court would not have come into the picture. Given the Court's failure to envision a "more speech" remedy in *Morse v. Frederick*, not involving the Court would have been the preferable outcome. Still, one can imagine an ideal outcome whereby, under different circumstances (i.e., a differently constituted Court) a majority would fashion a rule facilitating, instead of frustrating, schoolhouse conversation.

89. See John Dewey, *The Quest for Certainty: A Study of the Relation of Knowledge and Action* (New York: Minton, Balch, 1929).

90. "The reason for the Chief's likely 'error' was that the Superintendent (administratively), the board, and both the district court and the Ninth Circuit, all previously had accepted the same factual conclusions, either as a finding of fact or as an assumed or already decided fact. The Supreme Court is not a trial court, does not take evidence, and normally accepts historical record facts found in proceedings below. Still, at a minimum, Chief Justice Roberts should have discussed the facts more critically. . . . It is said that 'hard cases make bad law;' it may even be more true that 'bad or inaccurate records make bad law.'" Stephen Kanter, "*Bong Hits 4 Jesus* As a Cautionary Tale of Two Cities," *Lewis & Clark Law Review* 12 (Spring 2008): 85.

91. Official transcript of Oral Argument in *Deborah Morse, et al. v. Joseph Frederick*, No. 06-278, March 19,2007, http://www.supremecourtus.gov/oral_arguments/argument_transcripts/06-278.pdf.

92. *Morse et al. v. Frederick*, No. 06-278, slip opinion, June 25, 2007, Opinion of the Court, 1, http://www.supremecourtus.gov/opinions/06slipopinion.html.

93. Kanter, "*Bong Hits 4 Jesus* As a Cautionary Tale of Two Cities," 85. Kanter continues: "If the opening sentence did not fully decide the case, it at least framed the issue in a way that colored the analysis and led almost ineluctably to the Court's result in favor of the [petitioners]." Ibid.

94. Ibid., fn. 123, 86. Roberts continues, "but it is not the only [interpretation], and dismissing the banner as meaningless ignores its undeniable reference to illegal drugs." Ibid.

95. *Morse et al. v. Frederick*, No. 06-278, slip opinion, Opinion of the Court, 7.

96. Kanter, "*Bong Hits 4 Jesus* As a Cautionary Tale of Two Cities," 88.

97. It is not inconceivable that my more-speech remedy would attract five, perhaps six votes on its merits. In addition to the *Morse v. Frederick* dissenters—Justices Ginsburg, Souter, and Stevens—

Justice Breyer might find my alternative resolution of the First Amendment issue less "portentous" than the outcome in *Morse v. Frederick*. *Morse et al. v. Frederick*, No. 06-278, slip opinion, Opinion of Breyer, J., 3. As for Justices Alito and Kennedy, I read the former's concurring opinion, on to which the latter signed, as a reluctant, limited, and contingent join with the majority in *Morse v. Frederick*. Justice Alito concurred that "public schools may ban speech advocating illegal drug use" because such speech "poses a threat." Any further silencing transcends "what the First Amendment permits." *Morse et al. v. Frederick*, No. 06-278, slip opinion, Alito, J. concurring, 4. If punishing Joe Frederick for displaying his banner stands at the outer limits of an acceptable response under the First Amendment, then it is plausible that a less punitive response, like engaging in conversation about why BONG HiTS 4 JESUS is problematical, might earn his vote. See Kanter, "*Bong Hits 4 Jesus* As a Cautionary Tale of Two Cities," 93–97, arguing that "Justice Alito's independent views and analytical work in *Morse*, and the craft and fine writing he displays in his opinion, portend a much more interesting Court. Particularly given his *partnering-up* with Justice Kennedy in *Morse*, there is cause to hope that he and Justice Kennedy might form the core of a new, flexible center, at least in some doctrinal areas of the Court's work, that could begin to thaw the assumed icebound coalitions on the Court's left and right flanks." Ibid., 97.

98. See *Morse et al. v. Frederick*, No. 06-278, slip opinion, Opinion of the Court, 10.

99. Kanter, "*Bong Hits 4 Jesus* As a Cautionary Tale of Two Cities," 105.

100. Also see my discussion, below, 222ff, of the uniquely nondichotomous character of dialoguing.

101. See Michael J. Klarman, *From Jim Crow to Civil Rights: The Supreme Court and the Struggle for Racial Equality* (New York: Oxford University Press, 2004). Also see Carl M. Brauer, *John F. Kennedy and the Second Reconstruction* (New York: Columbia University Press, 1977); Myriam E. Gilles and Risa Lauren Goluboff, eds., *Civil Rights Stories* (New York: Foundation Press, 2008); Manning Marable, *Race, Reform and Rebellion: The Second Reconstruction and Beyond in Black America, 1945–2006* (Jackson: University Press of Mississippi, 2007); Clive Webb, ed., *Massive Resistance: Southern Opposition to the Second Reconstruction* (New York: Oxford University Press, 2005).

102. Frederick Schauer likely would attribute the *Morse* Court's mess, *inter alia*, to "the incentive of reputation." He writes: "Those who have the ability to make or break judicial reputations—lawyers, other judges, law professors, historians, and journalists, most prominently—rarely focus on the Court as an institution. . . . [I]t is the individual performance that matters. Rare is the praise for the Justice who subjugated her or his own point of view in order to help make a clear majority (or unanimity), and even rarer is the praise for the Justice whose opinion is nonliterary, crystal clear, and oversimplified, even though these are among the most important hallmarks of an opinion likely to guide successfully." Frederick Schauer, "Abandoning the Guidance Function: *Morse v. Frederick*," *Superior Court Review* (2007): 234.

103. Kanter, "*Bong Hits 4 Jesus* As a Cautionary Tale of Two Cities," 109–110.

104. I say "they" because Joseph Frederick's behavior sparked the incident on Glacier Avenue. He could have chosen to act differently. Nevertheless, as a practical matter, once Frederick's BONG HiTS 4 JESUS banner went up, the ball passed squarely into Deborah Morse's court. At that point, it was up to her, together with her Juneau-Douglas High School administrative and faculty colleagues, to choose what to make of Frederick's provocation. Her choices became decisive. Susan Christianson was communications manager for the Juneau School District from August 2007 until October 2008. Additionally, her daughter was a Juneau-Douglas High School student contemporary of Joe Frederick's. Her dual vantage points led Christianson to conclude (a conclusion corresponding to my *Rashomon* take on this whole story) that Frederick's issues and Morse's leadership style locked them into roles preventing their dispute from being "settled very

differently, earlier on." "If you wanted to have a poster child for free speech," Christianson remarked, "it wouldn't be Joseph Frederick, because he had so many other issues that he was known for in the community—of anyone who had kids going through the school at that time—that he was kind of a creep. [He was] a kid that had issues with authority, issues with the school." As for Deborah Morse's regime, Christianson opined: "I believe a different type of school leadership may have been able to take a more active role in finding a solution and crafting a message around the solution much, much earlier on in the process, that would have been agreeable to all concerned and would have benefited the district and the community. And I still believe that. I believe that this community would have been better served had this issue been solved in the front—in the very beginning— through dialogue. Through open dialogue the issue—through clear communication on the part of the city public entity, which is the school district in this case, about its concerns, its issues, and also a clear discussion about free speech within our school district, our society. When and where is [speech] appropriate? A discussion with the students about where is the line crossed, from our perspective. I mean, I think that could have easily happened in an assembly early on that would have made everybody—would have allowed both sides to have integrity." Susan Christianson interview, June 8, 2009, 26:04; 37:38; 10:30; 41:30. It ironic that by clinging tightly to the integrity of their respective Protester and Enforcer roles, Frederick and Morse lost the opportunity to validate one another in more imaginatively expansive roles.

105. My account of the Tigard story relies on Kanter, "*Bong Hits 4 Jesus* As a Cautionary Tale of Two Cities," and my interview with Stephen Kanter and Marilyn Cover, December 14, 2009.

106. Kanter, "*Bong Hits 4 Jesus* As a Cautionary Tale of Two Cities," 64.

107. Ibid.

108. Ibid.

109. "This was the moment of truth for Principal Zimmerman. Did he act as a bureaucrat? Hunker down with a touch of paranoia? Ratchet up the pressure with more severe sanctions and threats? No, no, and no. Instead, he metaphorically must have counted to ten, at least, and decided to use the controversy as a true teaching moment." Ibid., 66.

110. See the Classroom Law Project Web site: http://www.classroomlaw.org.

111. Stephen Kanter and Marilyn Cover interview, December 14, 2009, 2:10.

112. Stephen Kanter and Marilyn Cover interview, December 14, 2009, 8:41.

113. For discussion of the students' briefs, their oral argument, and the moot Court's opinion, see Kanter, "*Bong Hits 4 Jesus* As a Cautionary Tale of Two Cities," 67–82.

114. Ibid., 82. For another Tigard High School student speech controversy that took a very different path, see *Barcik v. Kubiaczyk*, 912 P.2d 408 (Or. Ct. App. 1996).

115. The Resources page on the CLP Web site informs: "Over the last 25 years, Classroom Law Project has accumulated an extensive collection of civics education materials—mock trials, lesson plans, case studies, supplementary resources, and knowledge—to help put the importance of civics education in closer reach for teachers, young citizens, and community members alike," http://www.classroomlaw.org/resources. Local and state bar associations can be of assistance in connecting high school students and faculty with lawyer-mentors.

116. Kanter, "*Bong Hits 4 Jesus* As a Cautionary Tale of Two Cities," 65.

117. http://www.dialogos.com/index.html.

118. William Isaacs, "A Conversation with a Center, Not Sides," in John Robert Stewart, ed., *Bridges Not Walls*, 9th ed. (Boston: McGraw-Hill, 2006), 606–607. Issacs informs us: "The roots of the word *dialogue* come from the Greek words *dia* and *logos*. *Dia* means 'through'; *logos* translates to 'word' or 'meaning.' In essence, a dialogue is a *flow of meaning*. But it is more than this too. In the most ancient meaning of the word, *logos* meant 'to gather together,' and suggested an intimate awareness of the

relationships among thing in the natural world. In that sense, *logos* may best be rendered in English as 'relationship.' The Book of John in the New Testament begins: 'In the beginning was the Word (*logos*).' We could now hear this as 'In the beginning was the Relationship.'" Ibid., 607.

119. Ibid.

120. Natalie Dollar, "Community Dialogue Workshop as Civil Society: A Preliminary Analysis of 'Getting Below the Sound Bite' to the Betwixt and Between," paper presented at the annual meeting of the Western States Communication Association, Seattle, Wash., February 2007, unpublished paper in author's possession, 3.

121. Ibid., 5.

122. Isaacs, "A Conversation with a Center, Not Sides," 607.

123. Natalie Dollar, "Community Dialogue Workshop, Winter 2008," document in author's possession.

124. Dollar, "Community Dialogue Workshop as Civil Society," 21, 24. The rules and strategies that Professor Dollar provides community dialogue workshop participants shed more specific light on what dialoguing entails:

Rules for Participating in Our Community Dialogue Workshops

The instructor facilitates the dialogue. When we break into small groups, students are co-facilitators.

No interrupting.

Speak calmly. Speak slowly.

No personal attacks. Don't demonize those with whom you disagree.

No yelling or raising your voice.

Respond to ideas not individuals.

Be aware of your nonverbals as others tend to rely on facials, gestures, body position, and other nonverbal cues to interpret our interaction.

All communication must be respectful of other participants. Disagree with ideas without attacking, insulting, or name calling.

Keep an open mind with the goal of understanding other's views.

When someone says something you vehemently oppose, stop and consider the above rules in formulating your response.

Dollar, "Community Dialogue Workshop, Winter 2008."

Community Dialogue Strategies
Community Dialogue Workshop, Winter 2008

Ask clarifying questions

How are you defining "Intelligent Design"?

Would you provide an example of what you believe to be a "hole" in the theory of evolution?

Ask for details: engage the complexity rather than leveling or oversimplifying

What has influenced your ideas on the origin of the world?

Who? What? Where? When? How? Etc.

Paraphrase: restate what you think is being said

Are you saying that all beliefs are equal?

Paraphrase plus: paraphrase and engage

I think I hear you saying that the origin of our world can be explained through a scientific process. Are there other ways it can be explained?

Context building refers the need to explain your frame of reference for your statements and encourage others to explain their context.

I have been skeptical of what my children have been taught in school about evolution because of our religious background but I understand the importance of alternative views.

Identify and explore points of commonality

Everyone seems to agree that beliefs and theories about the origin of our world are important. What impact do these beliefs and theories have on our daily lives?

Identify connections and explore connections between contributions.

I've heard several person address biblical explanations and the big bang theory. What I'd like to explore is if and how the two support one another.

Identify what we have created.

We've identified and clarified arguments for Intelligent Design and for the Theory of Evolution. We seem to agree that there exists some validity in all theories. We seem to disagree about the type of evidence we find convincing. We seem hopeful that we can maintain our open-minded approach as we continue our dialogue.

Dollar, "Community Dialogue Strategies, Community Dialogue Workshop, Winter 2008," document in author's possession.

125. Compare Lief H. Carter, "Law and Politics as Play," *Chicago Kent Law Review* 83 (2008), 1333; and Henry S. Kariel, *Beyond Liberalism, Where Relations Grow* (San Francisco: Chandler and Sharp, 1977).

126. Susan Christianson interview, June 8, 2009, 0:01.

127. I thank my colleague Michele DeSilva for the formulation in this sentence.

128. I thank Bjorn Peterson and the other students in my class PS 363, "Gender and Race in American Political Thought," for the conversation that generated the ideas in this paragraph.

Works Cited

● ● ●

Books

Abraham, Henry J. *The Judicial Process: An Introductory Analysis of the Courts of the United States, England, and France.* 4th ed. New York: Oxford University Press, 1980.

———. *Justices and Presidents.* 3rd ed. New York: Oxford University Press, 1992.

———. *Justices, Presidents, and Senators: A History of the U.S. Supreme Court Appointments from Washington to Bush II.* 5th new and rev. ed. Lanham, Md.: Rowman and Littlefield, 2008.

Abraham, Henry J., and Barbara A. Perry. *Freedom and the Court: Civil Rights and Liberties in the United States.* 6th ed. New York: Oxford University Press, 1967, 1994.

Ackerman, Bruce. *The Failure of the Founding Fathers: Jefferson, Marshall, and the Rise of Presidential Democracy.* Cambridge, Mass.: Harvard University Press, 2005.

Agee, James, and Walker Evans. *Let Us Now Praise Famous Men.* New York: Houghton Mifflin, 1941.

Akutagawa, Ryunosuke. *Rashomon and Seventeen Other Stories.* Jay Rubin, trans. New York: Penguin Classics, 2009.

Allison, Graham T. *Essence of Decision: Explaining the Cuban Missile Crisis.* Boston: Little, Brown, 1971.

Arendt, Hannah. *The Human Condition.* Garden City, N.Y.: Doubleday, 1959.

Balkin, Jack, ed. *What* Brown v. Board of Education *Should Have Said: The Nation's Top Legal Experts Rewrite America's Landmark Civil Rights Decision.* New York: New York University Press, 2002.

Baum, Lawrence. *The Puzzle of Judicial Behavior.* Ann Arbor: University of Michigan Press, 1977.

———. *Judges and Their Audiences: A Perspective on Judicial Behavior.* Princeton, N.J.: Princeton University Press, 2006.

———. *The Supreme Court.* 9th ed. Washington, D.C.: Congressional Quarterly, 2006.

Belsky, Martin H. ed. *The Rehnquist Court: A Retrospective.* New York: Oxford University Press, 2002.

Bemelmans, Ludwig. *Mad about Madeline: The Complete Tales.* New York: Viking, 2001.

Berger, Peter L., and Thomas Luckmann. *The Social Construction of Reality: A Treatise in the Sociology of Knowledge.* New York: Anchor Books, 1967.

Besson, Samantha. *The Morality of Conflict: Reasonable Disagreement and the Law.* Oxford, U.K.: Hart, 2006.

Best, Bradley. *Law Clerks, Support Personnel, and the Decline of Consensual Norms on the United States Supreme Court, 1935–1995.* New York: LFB Publishing, 2002.

Biskupic, Joan. *Sandra Day O'Connor: How the First Woman on the Supreme Court Became Its Most Influential Member.* New York: Harper, 2005.

Black, Duncan. *The Theory of Committees and Elections.* Cambridge: Cambridge University Press, 1958.

Blasi, Vincent, ed. *The Burger Court: The Counter-Revolution That Wasn't.* New Haven, Conn.: Yale University Press, 1983.

Blum, John Morton. *Years of Discord: American Politics and Society, 1961–1974.* New York: W. W. Norton, 1991.

Bork, Robert H. *The Tempting of America: The Political Seduction of the Law.* New York: Simon and Schuster, 1991.

Brauer, Carl M. *John F. Kennedy and the Second Reconstruction.* New York: Columbia University Press, 1977.

Bulwer-Lytton, Edward. *Richelieu.* New York: D. Appleton and Co., 1930.

Burke, Tim. *The Legal Relationship between Washington State and Its Reservation-Based Indian Tribes.* Olympia, Wash.: Office of Program Research, House of Representatives, 1977.

Camus, Albert. *The Stranger.* New York: Vintage International, 1989.

Carnahan, Burrus M. *Act of Justice: Lincoln's Emancipation Proclamation and the Law of War.* Lexington: University Press of Kentucky, 2007.

Carter, Lief H. *Contemporary Constitutional Lawmaking: The Supreme Court and the Art of Politics.* New York: Pergamon, 1985.

———. *An Introduction to Constitutional Interpretation: Cases in Law and Religion.* New York: Longman, 1991.

Chase, Harold W. *Federal Judges: The Appointing Process.* Minneapolis: University of Minnesota Press, 1972.

Cohen, Jonathan Matthew. *Inside Appellate Courts: The Impact of Court Organization on Judicial Decision Making in the United States Courts of Appeals.* Ann Arbor: University of Michigan Press, 2002.

Cohen, Steven. *Vietnam: Anthology and Guide to a Television History.* New York: Alfred A. Knopf, 1983.

Collins, Paul, Jr. *Friends of the Supreme Court: Interest Groups and Judicial Decision Making.* New York: Oxford University Press, 2008.

Connolly, William E. *The Terms of Political Discourse.* 3rd ed. Princeton, N.J.: Princeton University Press, 1993.

Conroy, Scott, and Shushannah Walshe. *Sarah from Alaska: The Sudden Rise and Brutal Education of a New Conservative Superstar.* New York: Public Affairs, 2009.

Continetti, Matthew. *The Persecution of Sarah Palin: How the Elite Media Tried to Bring Down a Rising Star.* New York: Sentinel, 2009.

Dean, John W. *The Rehnquist Choice: The Untold Story of the Nixon Appointment That Redefined the Supreme Court.* New York: John Wiley, 2001.

Dewey, John, *The Quest for Certainty: A Study of the Relation of Knowledge and Action* New York: Minton, Balch, 1929.

———. *Art as Experience.* New York: Minton, Balch, 1934.

Dickens, Charles. *Oliver Twist.* New York: Dodd, Mead, 1941.

Dorf, Michael C., ed. *Constitutional Law Stories.* New York: Foundation Press, 2004.

Dyck, Andrew R. *A Commentary on Cicero (Marcus Tullius), De Officiis.* Ann Arbor: University of Michigan Press, 1996.

Eisenstein, James, and Herbert Jacob. *Felony Justice: An Organizational Analysis of Criminal Courts.* Boston: Little, Brown, 1977.

Eisenstein, James, Roy B. Flemming, and Peter F. Nardulli. *The Contours of Justices: Communities and Their Courts.* Boston: Little, Brown, 1988.

Epstein, Lee, and Jack Knight. *The Choices Justices Make.* Washington, D.C.: Congressional Quarterly Press, 1998.

Epstein, Lee, and Jeffrey A. Segal. *Advice and Consent: The Politics of Judicial Appointments.* New York: Oxford University Press, 2005.

Fanning, Kay, with Katherine Field Stephen. *Kay Fanning's Alaska Story: Memoir of a Pulitzer Prize-Winning Newspaper Publisher on America's Northern Frontier.* Kenmore, Wash.: Epicenter Press, 2006.

Federalist Papers, The. Clinton Rossiter, ed. New York: Mentor, 1961.

Fino, Susan P. *The Role of State Supreme Courts in the New Judicial Federalism.* Westport, Conn.: Greenwood Press, 1987.

Fiorina, Morris P. *Divided Government.* New York: Macmillan, 1992.

Fish, Stanley. *There's No Such Thing as Free Speech: And It's a Good Thing, Too.* New York: Oxford University Press, 1994.

Fisher, William W., III, Morton J. Horwitz, and Thomas A. Reed, eds., *American Legal Realism.* New York: Oxford University Press, 1993.

Flemming, Roy B., Peter F. Nardulli, and James Eisenstein. *The Craft of Justice: Politics and Work in Criminal Court Communities.* Philadelphia: University of Pennsylvania Press, 1992.

Foster, James C. *The Ideology of Apolitical Politics: Elite Lawyers' Response to the Legitimation Crisis of American Capitalism, 1870–1920.* New York: Garland, 1990.

Foster, James C., and Susan M. Leeson. *Constitutional Law: Cases in Context.* 2 vols. Upper Saddle River, N.J.: Prentice Hall, 1998.

Freidel, Frank B. *Franklin D. Roosevelt: Launching the New Deal.* Boston: Little, Brown, 1973.

———. *Franklin D. Roosevelt: A Rendezvous with Destiny.* Boston: Little, Brown, 1990.

Friedelbaum, Stanley H. *The Rehnquist Court: In Pursuit of Judicial Conservatism.* Westport, Conn.: Greenwood Press, 1994.

Friendly, Fred W. *Minnesota Rag: The Dramatic Story of the Landmark Supreme Court Case that Gave New Meaning to Freedom of the Press.* New York: Random House, 1981.

Garbus, Martin. *Courting Disaster: The Supreme Court and the Unmaking of American Law.* New York: Times Books, 2002.

Garraty, John A., ed. *Quarrels That Have Shaped the Constitution.* New York: Harper and Row, 1962.

Geertz, Clifford. *The Interpretation of Cultures.* New York: Basic Books, 1973.

———. *Local Knowledge: Further Essays in Interpretive Anthropology.* New York: Basic Books, 1983.

Gilles, Myriam E., and Risa Lauren Goluboff, eds. *Civil Rights Stories.* New York: Foundation Press, 2008.

Gilman, Howard. *The Constitution Besieged: The Rise and Demise of Lochner Era Police Power Jurisprudence.* Durham, N.C.: Duke University Press, 1993.

Gladwell, Malcolm. *The Tipping Point: How Little Things Can Make a Big Difference.* Boston: Little, Brown, 2000.

Goldman, Sheldon. *Picking Federal Judges: Lower Court Selection from Roosevelt to Reagan.* New Haven, Conn.: Yale University Press, 1997.

Gottlieb, Stephen E. *Morality Imposed: The Rehnquist Court and Liberty in America.* New York: New York University Press, 2000.

Gragert, Steven K., ed. *Will Rogers' Weekly Articles.* Vol. 4, *The Hoover Years: 1929–1931.* Stillwater: Oklahoma State University, 1981.

Greenberg, Jack. *Crusaders in the Courts: How a Dedicated Band of Lawyers Fought for the Civil Rights Revolution.* New York: Basic Books, 1994.

Gressman, Eugene, et al. *Supreme Court Practice: For Practice in the Supreme Court of the United States.* 9th ed. Arlington, Va.: Bureau of National Affairs, 2007.

Grossman, Joel B., *Lawyers and Judges: The ABA and the Politics of Judicial Selection.* New York: Wiley, 1965.

Hammond, Jay. *Tales of Alaska's Bush Rat Governor.* Fairbanks, Alaska: Epicenter Press, 1994.

Harmon, Alexandra. *Indians in the Making: Ethnic Relationships and Indian Identities around Puget Sound.* Berkeley: University of California Press, 1998.

Hellman, Arthur D., ed. *Restructuring Justice: The Innovations of the Ninth Circuit and the Future of the Federal Courts.* Ithaca, N.Y.: Cornell University Press, 1990.

Hensley, William L. Iġġiaġruk. *Fifty Miles from Tomorrow: A Memoir of Alaska and the Real People.* New York: Farrar, Straus and Giroux, 2009.

Horwitz, Morton J. *The Transformation of American Law, 1870–1960: The Crisis of Legal Orthodoxy*. New York: Oxford University Press, 1992.

———. *The Warren Court and the Pursuit of Justice*. New York: Hill and Wang, 1998.

Hughes, Charles Evans. *The Supreme Court of the United States*. New York: Columbia University Press, 1928.

Hymowitz, Kay S. *Ready or Not: What Happens When We Treat Children as Small Adults*. San Francisco: Encounter Books, 2000.

Irons, Peter H. *Justice at War*. New York: Oxford University Press, 1983.

———. *The Courage of Their Convictions: Sixteen Americans Who Fought Their Way to the Supreme Court*. New York: Free Press, 1988.

———. *Brennan vs. Rehnquist: The Battle for the Constitution*. New York: Alfred A. Knopf, 1994.

Irons, Peter H., and Stephanie Guitton, eds. *May It Please the Court: The Most Significant Oral Arguments Made before the Supreme Court Since 1955*. New York: New Press, 1993.

Johnson, Timothy R. *Oral Arguments and Decision Making on the United States Supreme Court*. Albany: State University of New York Press, 2004.

Kalman, Laura. *Abe Fortas*. New Haven, Conn.: Yale University Press, 1990.

———. *The Strange Career of Liberal Legalism*. New Haven, Conn.: Yale University Press, 1998.

Kaplan, Lincoln. *The Tenth Justice: The Solicitor General and the Rule of Law*. New York: Alfred A. Knopf, 1987.

Kariel, Henry S. *Beyond Liberalism: Where Relations Grow*. San Francisco: Chandler and Sharp, 1977.

Karnow, Stanley. *Vietnam: A History*. New York: Viking, 1983.

Keck, Thomas M. *The Most Activist Supreme Court in History: The Road to Modern Judicial Conservatism*. Chicago: University of Chicago Press, 2004.

Kelly, Alfred H., Winfred A. Harbison, and Herman Belz. *The American Constitution: Its Origins and Development*. 7th ed. 2 vols. New York: W. W. Norton, 1991.

Klarman, Michael J. *From Jim Crow to Civil Rights: The Supreme Court and the Struggle for Racial Equality*. New York: Oxford University Press, 2004.

Knowles, Helen J. *The Tie Goes to Freedom: Justice Anthony M. Kennedy on Liberty*. Lanham, Md.: Rowman and Littlefield, 2009.

Kroninger, Robert H. *Sarah and the Senator*. Berkeley, Calif.: Howell-North, 1964.

Lazarus, Edward. *Closed Chambers: The Rise, Fall, and Future of the Modern Supreme Court*. New York: Penguin, 1999.

Lewis, Anthony. *Gideon's Trumpet*. New York: Random House, 1964.

———. *Make No Law: The* Sullivan *Case and the First Amendment*. New York: Random House, 1991.

Maltz, Earl M. *The Chief Justiceship of Warren Burger, 1969–1986*. Columbia: University of South Carolina Press, 2000.

Maltz, Earl M., ed. *Rehnquist Justice: Understanding the Court Dynamic* Lawrence: University Press of Kansas, 2003.

Maltzman, Forrest, James F. Spriggs II, and Paul J. Wahlbeck. *Crafting Law on the Supreme Court: The Collegial Game*. New York: Cambridge University Press, 2000.

Marable, Manning. *Race, Reform and Rebellion: The Second Reconstruction and Beyond in Black America, 1945–2006*. Jackson: University Press of Mississippi, 2007.

Maslow, Abraham. *The Farther Reaches of Human Nature*. New York: Viking, 1971.

Maveety, Nancy. *Justice Sandra Day O'Connor: Strategist on the Supreme Court*. Lanham, Md.: Rowman and Littlefield, 1996.

———. *Queen's Court: Judicial Power in the Rehnquist Era*. Lawrence: University Press of Kansas, 2008.

Mayhew, David R. *Congress: The Electoral Connection.* New Haven, Conn.: Yale University Press, 1974, 2004.

McFeatters, Ann Carey. *Sandra Day O'Connor: Justice in the Balance.* Albuquerque: University of New Mexico Press, 2005.

McGinniss, Joe. *Going to Extremes.* New York: New American Library, 1980.

McGuire, Kevin T. *The Supreme Court Bar: Legal Elites in the Washington Community.* Charlottesville: University Press of Virginia, 1993.

McKenna, Judith A., ed. *Structural and Other Alternatives for the Federal Courts of Appeal.* Washington, D.C.: Federal Judicial Center, 2003.

McLauchlan, Judithanne Scourfield. *Congressional Participation as* Amicus Curiae *before the U.S. Supreme Court.* New York: LFB Scholarly Press, 2005.

Meiklejohn, Alexander. *Political Freedom: The Constitutional Powers of the People.* New York: Harper, 1960.

Menand, Louis. *The Metaphysical Club: A Story of Ideas in America.* New York: Farrar, Straus and Giroux, 2002.

Mendelson, Wallace. *The Supreme Court: Law and Discretion.* Indianapolis: Bobbs-Merrill, 1967.

Mills, C. Wright. *The Sociological Imagination.* New York: Oxford University Press, 1967.

Moore, R. Jonathan. *Suing for America's Soul: John Whitehead, The Rutherford Institute, and Conservative Christians in Court.* Grand Rapids, Mich.: William B. Eerdmans, 2007.

Murphy, Walter F. *Elements of Judicial Strategy.* Chicago: University of Chicago Press, 1964.

Nagel, Joane. *American Indian Ethnic Renewal: Red Power and the Resurgence of Identity and Culture.* New York: Oxford University Press, 1996.

Nardulli, Peter F., James Eisenstein, and Roy B. Flemming. *The Tenor of Justice: Criminal Courts and the Guilty Plea Process.* Urbana: University of Illinois Press, 1988.

Nelson, Jack. *Captive Voices: The Report of the Commission of Inquiry into High School Journalism.* New York: Schocken Books, 1974.

Nimmer, Melville B. *Nimmer on Freedom of Speech: A Treatise of the Theory of the First Amendment.* New York: M. Bender, 1984.

O'Brien, David M. *Judicial Roulette.* New York: Priority Press, 1988.

———. *Storm Center: The Supreme Court in American Politics.* 4th ed. New York: W. W. Norton, 1996.

Oppenheimer, Paul. *A Pleasant Vintage of Till Eulenspiegel, Born in the Country of Brunswick; How He Spent His Life, 95 of His Tales.* Middleton, Conn.: Wesleyan University Press, 1972.

Palin, Sarah. *Going Rogue: An American Life.* New York: HarperCollins, 2009.

Peltason, J. W. *Fifty-eight Lonely Men: Southern Federal Judges and School Desegregation.* Urbana: University of Illinois Press, 1971.

Perlstein, Rick. *Nixonland: The Rise of a President and the Fracturing of America.* New York: Scribner, 2008.

Perry, H. W. *Deciding to Decide.* Cambridge, Mass.: Harvard University Press, 1991.

Polenberg, Richard. *Fighting Faiths: The Abrams Case, the Supreme Court, and Free Speech.* New York: Viking Press, 1987.

Pollock, Jack Harrison. *Earl Warren: The Judge Who Changed America.* Englewood Cliffs, N.J.: Prentice Hall, 1979.

Posner, Richard. *The Problems of Jurisprudence.* Cambridge, Mass.: Harvard University Press, 1993.

Provine, Doris Marie. *Case Selection in the United States Supreme Court.* Chicago: University of Chicago Press, 1980.

Richie, Donald, ed. *Rashomon.* New Brunswick: N.J.: Rutgers University Press, 1999.

Rosenberg, Gerald N. *The Hollow Hope: Can Courts Bring about Social Change?* 2nd ed. Chicago: University of Chicago Press, 2008.

Rowland, C. K., and Robert A. Carp. *Politics and Judgment in Federal District Courts.* Lawrence: University Press of Kansas, 1996.

Salokar, Rebecca Mae. *The Solicitor General: The Politics of Law.* Philadelphia: Temple University Press, 1992.

Samuels, Susanne U. *First Among Friends: Interest Groups, the U.S. Supreme Court, and the Right to Privacy.* Westport, Conn.: Praeger, 2004.

Savage, David G. *Turning Right: The Making of the Rehnquist Supreme Court.* New York: John Wiley and Son, 1992.

Schwartz, Bernard. *Super Chief: Earl Warren and His Supreme Court—A Judicial Biography.* New York: New York University Press, 1983.

———. *A History of the Supreme Court.* New York: Oxford University Press, 1993.

———. *Decision: How The Supreme Court Decides Cases.* New York: Oxford University Press, 1996.

Schwartz, Herman, ed. *The Rehnquist Court: Judicial Activism on the Right.* New York: Hill and Wang, 2002.

Searle, John R. *Speech Acts: An Essay in the Philosophy of Language.* Cambridge: Cambridge University Press, 1969.

Segal, Jeffrey A., and Harold J. Spaeth. *The Supreme Court and the Attitudinal Model Revisited.* Cambridge: Cambridge University Press, 2002.

Shweder, Richard A. *Why Do Men Barbecue? Recipes for Cultural Psychology.* Cambridge, Mass.: Harvard University Press, 2003.

Silver, David M. *Lincoln's Supreme Court.* Urbana: University of Illinois Press, 1998.

Silverstein, Mark. *Judicious Choices: The Politics of Supreme Court Confirmations.* 2nd ed. New York: W. W. Norton, 2007.

Simon, James F. *The Center Holds: The Power Struggle Inside the Rehnquist Court.* New York: Simon and Schuster, 1995.

Skowronek, Stephen. *The Politics Presidents Make: Leadership from John Adams to George Bush.* Cambridge, Mass.: Harvard University Press, 1993.

Solimine, Michael E., and James L. Walker. *Respecting State Courts: The Inevitability of Judicial Federalism.* Westport, Conn.: Greenwood Press 1999.

Steamer, Robert J. *Chief Justice: Leadership and the Supreme Court.* Columbia: University of South Carolina Press, 1986.

Stone, Geoffrey. *Perilous Times: Free Speech in Wartime from the Sedition Act of 1798 to the War on Terrorism.* New York: W. W. Norton, 2004.

Sullivan, William M., et al. *Educating Lawyers: Preparation for the Profession of Law.* San Francisco: Jossey-Bass/Wiley, 2007.

Sunstein, Cass R. *One Case at a Time: Judicial Minimalism on the Supreme Court.* Cambridge, Mass.: Harvard University Press, 1999.

———. *A Constitution of Many Minds: Why the Founding Document Doesn't Mean What It Meant Before.* Princeton, N.J.: Princeton University Press, 2009.

Sunstein, Cass R., et al. *Are Judges Political? An Empirical Analysis of the Federal Judiciary.* Washington, D.C.: Brookings Institution Press, 2006.

Surrency, Erwin. *History of the Federal Courts.* New York: Oceana, 1987.

Swisher, Carl Brent. *Stephen J. Field: Craftsman of the Law.* Chicago: University of Chicago Press, 1930, 1969.

———. *The Taney Period, 1836–1864.* New York: Macmillan, 1974.

Teles, Steven M. *The Rise of the Conservative Legal Movement: The Battle for Control of the Law.* Princeton, N.J.: Princeton University Press, 2008.

Theoharis, Athan G. *Spying on Americans: Political Surveillance from Hoover to the Huston Plan.* Philadelphia: Temple University Press, 1978.

Thomas, W. I., and Dorothy Swaine Thomas. *The Child in America: Behavior Problems and Programs.* New York: Alfred A. Knopf, 1928.

Toobin, Jeffrey. *The Nine: Inside the Secret World of the Supreme Court.* New York: Doubleday, 2006.

Tushnet, Mark V. *A Court Divided: The Rehnquist Court and the Future of Constitutional Law.* New York: W. W. Norton, 2005.

Tushnet, Mark V., ed. *The Warren Court in Historical and Political Perspective.* Charlottesville: University of Virginia Press, 1993.

Vieira, Norman, and Leonard Gross. *Supreme Court Appointments: Judge Bork and the Politicization of Senate Confirmations.* Carbondale: Southern Illinois University Press, 1998.

Vonnegut, Kurt, Jr. *Mother Night.* New York: Avon Books, 1966.

Wasby, Stephen L. *The Supreme Court in the Federal Judicial System.* 2nd ed. New York: Holt, Reinhart, and Winston, 1984.

———. *Race Relations in an Age of Complexity.* Charlottesville: University Press of Virginia, 1995.

Webb, Clive, ed., *Massive Resistance: Southern Opposition to the Second Reconstruction.* New York: Oxford University Press, 2005.

Westin, Alan F. *The Anatomy of a Constitutional Law Case:* Youngstown Sheet and Tube v. Sawyer, *The Steel Seizure Case.* New York: Columbia University, 1990; originally published 1958, Macmillan.

White, G. Edward. *Earl Warren: A Public Life.* New York: Oxford University Press, 1982.

———. *The Constitution and the New Deal.* Cambridge, Mass.: Harvard University Press, 2000.

White, G. Edward, and Gerald Gunther. *The Marshall Court and Cultural Change, 1815–1835.* New York: Macmillan, 1988.

Whitehead, John W. *The Change Manifesto: Join the Block by Block Movement to Remake America.* Naperville, Ill.: Sourcebooks, 2008.

Whitson, James A. *Constitution and Curriculum: Hermeneutical Semiotics of Cases and Controversies in Education, Law, and Social Science.* New York: Falmer Press, 1991.

Wilkinson, Charles. *Messages from Frank's Landing.* Seattle: University of Washington Press, 2000.

Wolin, Sheldon S. *Politics and Vision: Continuity and Innovation in Western Political Thought.* Boston: Little, Brown, 1960.

Wrightsman, Lawrence S. *Oral Arguments before the Supreme Court: An Empirical Approach.* New York: Oxford University Press, 2008.

Yarbrough, Tinsley E. *The Rehnquist Court and the Constitution.* New York: Oxford University Press, 2000.

Chapters in Books

Arendt, Hannah. "What Is Freedom?" In *Between Past and Future,* Hannah Arendt. New York: Viking Press, 1961.

Banks, Christopher P. "The Supreme Court and Precedent: An Analysis of Natural Courts and Reversal Trends." In *Judicial Politics: Readings from Judicature,* 2nd ed, Elliot E. Slotnick. Lanham, Md.: Rowman and Littlefield, 1999.

Cook, Beverly B. "Justice Sandra Day O'Connor: Transition to a Republican Court Agenda." In *The Burger Court: Political and Judicial Profiles,* Charles M. Lamb and Stephen C. Halpern, eds. Urbana: University of Illinois Press, 1991.

———. "Justice Brennan and the Institutionalization of Dissent Assignment." In *Judicial Politics: Readings from Judicature,* Elliot E. Slotnick, ed. Chicago: American Judicature Society, 1992.

Danelski, David J. "Causes and Consequences of Conflict and Its Resolution in the Supreme Court." In *Judicial Conflict and Consensus,* Sheldon Goldman and Charles M. Lamb, eds. Lexington: University of Kentucky Press, 1986.

————. "The Influence of the Chief Justice in the Decisional Process." In *Courts, Judges and Politics*, 6th ed., Walter M. Murphy, C. Herman Pritchett, Lee Epstein, and Jack Knight, eds. Boston: McGraw-Hill, 2006.

Epstein, Lee. "Courts and Interest Groups." In *The American Courts: A Critical Assessment*, John B. Gates and Charles A. Johnson, eds. Washington, D.C.: CQ Press, 1991.

Epstein, Lee, and Jack Knight. "Mapping Out the Strategic Terrain: The Informational Role of Amicus Curiae." In *Supreme Court Decision-Making: New Institutionalist Approaches,* Cornell W. Clayton and Howard Gillman, eds. Chicago: University of Chicago Press, 1999.

Epstein, Lee, and C. K. Rowland. "Interest Groups in Courts: Do Groups Fare Better." In *Interest Group Politics*, 2nd ed., Allan J. Cigler and Burdett A. Loomis, eds. Washington, D.C.: CQ Press, 1986.

Goldman, Sheldon. "Judicial Appointments and the Presidential Agenda." In *The Presidency in American Politics,* Paul Brace, Christine B. Harrington, and Gary Kings, eds. New York: New York University Press, 1989.

Greenhouse, Linda. "Foreword: The Third Rehnquist Court." In *The Rehnquist Legacy,* Craig M. Bradley, ed. New York: Cambridge University Press, 2006.

Hakman, Nathan. "The Supreme Court's Political Environment: The Processing of Noncommercial Litigation." In *Frontiers of Judicial Research,* Joel Grossman and Joseph Tanenhaus, eds. New York: John Wiley, 1969.

Isaacs, William. "A Conversation with a Center, Not Sides." In *Bridges Not Walls*, 9th ed., John Robert Stewart, ed. Boston: McGraw-Hill, 2006.

Lamb, Charles M. "Chief Justice Warren E. Burger: A Conservative Chief for Conservative Times." In *The Burger Court: Political and Judicial Profiles,* Charles M. Lamb and Stephen C. Halpern, eds. Urbana: University of Illinois Press, 1991.

Landynski, Jacob W. "Justice Lewis F. Powell, Jr.: Balance Wheel of the Court." In *The Burger Court: Political and Judicial Profiles,* Charles M. Lamb and Stephen C. Halpern, eds. Urbana: University of Illinois Press, 1991.

Maslow, Abraham. "Resistance to Being Rubricized." In *Perspectives in Psychological Theory: Essays in Honor of Heinz Werner,* Bernard Kaplan and Seymour Wapner, eds. New York: International Universities Press, 1960.

McGuire, Kevin T. "The Supreme Court Bar and Institutional Relationships." In *The Supreme Court in American Politics: New Institutionalist Interpretations,* Howard Gillman and Cornell Clayton, eds. Lawrence: University Press of Kansas, 1999.

Maveety, Nancy, and John Anthony Maltese. "J. Woodford Howard, Jr.: Fluidity, Strategy and Analytical Synthesis in Judicial Studies." In *Pioneers of Judicial Behavior,* Nancy Maveety, ed. Ann Arbor: University of Michigan Press, 2003.

Mill, John Stuart. "On Liberty." In *Three Essays*, Richard Wollheim, intro. New York: Oxford University Press, 1975.

O'Brien, David M. "The Reagan Judges: His Most Enduring Legacy?" In *The Reagan Legacy,* Charles O. Jones, ed. Chatham, N.J.: Chatham House, 1988.

————. "Institutional Norms and Supreme Court Opinions: On Reconsidering the Rise of Individual Opinions." In *Supreme Court Decision-making: New Institutional Approaches*, Cornell W. Clayton and Howard Gillman, eds. Chicago: University of Chicago Press, 1999.

O'Connor, Sandra Day. Foreword to David C. Frederick, *Rugged Justice: The Ninth Circuit Court of Appeals in the American West, 1891–1941*. Berkeley: University of California Press, 1994.

Pritchett, C. Herman. "The Development of Judicial Research." In *Frontiers of Judicial Research,* Joel B. Grossman, Joseph Tanenhaus, and Edward N. Muller, eds. New York: Wiley, 1968.

Tyler, Parker. "Rashomon as Modern Art." In *Rashomon*, Donald Richie, ed. New Brunswick, N.J.: Rutgers University Press, 1999.

Ulmer, S. Sidney. "Exploring the Dissent Patterns of the Chief Justices: John Marshall to Warren Burger." In *Judicial Conflict and Consensus*, Sheldon Goldman and Charles M. Lamb, eds. Lexington: University of Kentucky Press, 1986.

White, G. Edward. "From Sociological Jurisprudence to Realism: Jurisprudence and Social Change in Early Twentieth-Century America." In *Patterns of American Legal Thought*, G. Edward White, ed. Indianapolis: Bobbs-Merrill, 1978.

Whittington, Keith E. "William H. Rehnquist: Nixon's Strict Constructionist, Reagan's Chief Justice." In *Rehnquist Justice: Understanding the Court Dynamic*, Earl M. Maltz, ed. Lawrence: University Press of Kansas, 2003.

Journal and Law Review Articles

Aguirre, Frederick P., "*Mendez v. Westminster School District*: How It Affected *Brown v. Board of Education*." *Journal of Hispanic Higher Education* 4 (2005): 321.

Amar, Akhil Reed. "Hugo Black and the Hall of Fame." *Alabama Law Review* 53 (Summer 2002): 1221.

Angell, Ernest. "The Amicus *Curiae*: American Development of English Institutions." *International & Comparative Law Quarterly* 16 (1967): 1017.

Azriel, Joshua. "The Supreme Court's Decision in *Morse v. Frederick*: The Majority Opinion Revealed Sharp Ideological Differences on Student Speech Rights among the Court's Five Justice Majority." *UC Davis Journal of Juvenile Law & Policy* 12 (Summer 2008): 427.

Baker, Lynn A. "Interdisciplinary Due Diligence: The Case for Common Sense in the Search for the Swing Justice." *Southern California Law Review* 70 (1996): 187.

Banner, Stuart. "The Myth of the Neutral Amicus: American Courts and Their Friends, 1790–1890." *Constitutional Commentary* 20 (Spring 2003): 111.

Barker, Lucius. "Third Parties in Litigation: A Systemic View of the Judicial Function." *Journal of Politics* 29 (1967): 41.

Basiak, John F., Jr. "The Roberts Court and the Future of Substantive Due Process: The Demise of 'Split-the-Difference' Jurisprudence?" *Whittier Law Review* 28 (Spring 2007): 861.

Behuniak-Long, Susan. "Friendly Fire: *Amici Curiae* and *Webster v. Reproductive Health Services*." *Judicature* 74 (1991): 261.

Belknap, Michael R. "The Warren Court and the Vietnam War: The Limits of Legal Liberalism." *Georgia Law Review* 33 (Fall 1998): 65.

Belsky, Martin H. "Indian Fishing Rights: A Lost Opportunity for Ecosystem Management." *Journal of Land Use & Environmental Law* 12 (Fall 1996): 45.

Benesh, Sara C. "Caseload and Mechanisms for Dealing with It: The Contribution of 'Extra' Judges." *Arizona Law Review* 48 (Summer 2006): 301.

Bennett, Robert W. "Styles of Judging." *Northwestern University Law Review* 84 (Spring/Summer 1990): 853.

Bickel, Alexander M. "The Passive Virtues." *Harvard Law Review* 75 (November 1961): 40.

Blasi, Vincent. "The First Amendment and the Ideal of Civic Courage: The Brandeis Opinion in *Whitney v. California*." *William and Mary Law Review* 29 (Summer 1988): 653.

Black, Duncan. "On the Rationale of Group Decision-Making." *Journal of Political Economy* 56 (1948): 23.

Bleich, Jeff, Anne Voigts, and Michelle Friedland. "A Practical Era: The Beginning (or the End) of Pragmatism." *Oregon State Bar Bulletin* 65 (August/September 2005): 19.

Block, Frederic. "Senior Status: An 'Active' Senior Judge Corrects Some Common Misunderstandings." *Cornell Law Review* 92 (2007): 533.

Bonneau, Chris W., et al. "Agenda Control, the Median Justice, and the Majority Opinion on the U.S. Supreme Court." *American Journal of Political Science* 51 (October 2007): 890.

Bowen, Terry. "Consensual Norms and the Freshman Effect on the United States Supreme Court." *Social Science Quarterly* 76 (March 1995): 222.

Brennan, William J., Jr. "State Constitutions and the Protection of Individual Rights." *Harvard Law Review* 90 (1977): 489.

Bright, Myron H. "The Power of the Spoken Word: In Defense of Oral Argument." *Iowa Law Review* 72 (October 1986): 35.

Caldeira, Gregory A. "Public Opinion and the U.S. Supreme Court: FDR's Court-Packing Plan." *American Political Science Review* 81 (December 1987): 1139.

Caldeira, Gregory A., and John R. Wright. "Organized Interests and Agenda Setting in the U.S. Supreme Court." *American Political Science Review* 82 (December 1988): 1109.

———. "*Amici Curiae* before the Supreme Court: Who Participates, When, and How Much?" *Journal of Politics* 52 (August 1990): 782.

———. "Lobbying for Justice: Organized Interests, Supreme Court Nominations, and the United States Senate." *American Journal of Political Science* 42 (April 1998): 499.

Caldeira, Gregory A., and Christopher J. W. Zorn. "Of Time and Consensual Norms in the Supreme Court." *American Journal of Political Science* 42 (July 1998): 874.

Caldeira, Gregory A., John R. Wright, and Christopher J. W. Zorn. "Sophisticated Voting and Gate-Keeping in the Supreme Court." *Journal of Law, Economy, and Organization* 15 (1999): 549.

Campbell, J. Louis, III. "The Spirit of Dissent." *Judicature* 66 (February 1983): 304.

Caplan, Russell. "The Paradoxes of Judicial Review in a Constitutional Democracy." *Buffalo Law Review* 30 (1981): 451.

Carels, Peter E. "Eulenspiegel and Company Visit the Eighteenth Century." *Modern Language Studies* 10 (Autumn 1980): 3.

Carter, Lief H. "Law and Politics as Play." *Chicago-Kent Law Review* 83 (2008): 1333.

Catterson, Cathy. "Caseload and Mechanisms for Dealing with It: Changes in Appellate Caseload and its Processing." *Arizona Law Review* 48 (Summer 2006): 287.

Chemerinsky, Erwin. "Students Do Leave Their First Amendment Rights at the Schoolhouse Gate: What's Left of *Tinker*." *Drake Law Review* 48 (2000): 527.

———. "The Myth of the Liberal Ninth Circuit." *Loyola of Los Angeles Law Review* 37 (Fall 2003): 1.

———. "The Deconsitutionalization of Education." *Loyola University Chicago Law Journal* 36 (Fall 2004): 111.

———. "The Kennedy Court: October Term 2005." *Green Bag* 9, no. 2 (Summer 2006): 335.

———. "The Role of the Judge in the Twenty-First Century: Seeing the Emperor's Clothes: Recognizing the Reality of Constitutional Decision Making." *Boston University Law Review* 86 (December 2006): 1069

Chen, Paul M. "The Informational Role of *Amici Curiae* in *Gonzales v. Raich*." *Illinois University Law Journal* 31 (Winter 2007): 217.

Colker, Ruth. "Justice Sandra Day O'Connor's Friends." *Ohio State Law Journal* 68 (2007): 517.

Collins, Paul M., Jr. "Friends of the Court: Examining the Influence of Amicus *Curiae* Participation in U.S. Supreme Court Litigation." *Law & Society Review* 38 (December 2004): 807.

———. "Lobbyists before the U.S. Supreme Court: Investigating the Influence of Amicus *Curiae* Briefs." *Political Research Quarterly* 60 (March 2007): 55.

Collins, Paul M., Jr., and Lisa A. Solowiej. "Interest Group Participation, Competition, and Conflict in the U.S. Supreme Court." *Law & Social Inquiry* 32 (Fall 2007): 955.

Collins, Ronald K. L., and David M. Skover. "Curious Concurrence: Justice Brandeis' Vote in *Whitney v. California.*" *Supreme Court Review* (2005): 333.

Cooper, Jeffrey O., and Douglas A. Berman. "Passive Virtues and Casual Vices in the Federal Courts of Appeal." *Brooklyn Law Review* 66 (Winter 2000/Spring 2001): 685.

Cordray, Margaret Meriwether, and Richard Cordray. "The Supreme Court's Plenary Docket." *Washington & Lee Law Review* 58 (Summer 2001): 737.

———. "The Philosophy of *Certiorari*: Jurisprudential Considerations in Supreme Court Case Selection." *Washington University Law Quarterly* 82 (Summer 2004): 389.

Covey, Frank M., Jr. "Amicus *Curiae*: Friend of the Court." *DePaul Law Review* 9 (1959–1960): 30.

Cross, Frank B., and Stephanie Lindquist. "The Chief Justice and the Institutional Judiciary: Doctrinal and Strategic Influences of the Chief Justice: The Decisional Significance of the Chief Justice." *University of Pennsylvania Law Review* 154 (June 2006): 1665.

Cross, Frank, and Emerson H. Tiller. "Understanding Collegiality on the Court." *University of Pennsylvania Journal of Constitutional Law* 10 (January 2008): 257.

Davis, Jeffrey. "Adversarial Jurisprudence: Legal Education and the Demise of the Consensual Norm." *Politics & Policy* 30 (December 2002): 763.

Devins, Neal. "The Big Picture: External and Internal Influences on the Roberts Court's Handling of Precedents: Ideological Cohesion and Precedent (or Why the Court Only Cares about Precedent when Most Justices Agree with Each Other)." *North Carolina Law Review* 86 (June 2008): 1399.

Denniston, Lyle. "Rehnquist to Roberts: The 'Reagan Revolution' Fulfilled?" *University of Pennsylvania Law Review* 154 (June 2006): 155.

Díaz-Loving, Rolando, and Rogelio Díaz-Guerrero. "Some Thoughts on Schweder's 'Why Do Men Barbecue.'" *Cross-Cultural Psychology Bulletin* 38 (2004): 4.

Dupre, Anne Proffitt. "Should Students Have Constitutional Rights? Keeping Order in the Public Schools." *George Washington Law Review* 65 (November 1996): 49.

Edelman, Paul H., and Jim Chen. "'Duel' Diligence: Second Thoughts about the Supremes as the Sultans of Swat." *Southern California Law Review* 70 (1996): 219.

———. "The Most Dangerous Justice: The Supreme Court at the Bar of Mathematics." *Southern California Law Review* 70 (1996): 63.

———. "The Most Dangerous Justice Rides Again: Revisiting the Power Pageant of the Justices." *Minnesota Law Review* 86 (2001): 131.

———. "The Rehnquist Court in Empirical and Statistical Retrospective: The Most Dangerous Justice Rides into the Sunset." *Constitutional Commentary* 24 (Spring 2007): 199.

Ehrenberg, Suzanne. "Embracing the Writing-Centered Legal Process." *Iowa Law Review* 89 (April 2004): 1159.

Emerson, Thomas I. "Freedom of Expression in Wartime." *University of Pennsylvania Law Review* 116 (1968): 975.

Epstein, Lee, and C. K. Rowland. "Debunking the Myth of Interest Group Invincibility in the Courts." *American Political Science Review* 85 (1991): 205.

Epstein, Lee, et al. "Ideological Drift Among Supreme Court Justices: Who, When, and How Important?" *Northwest Law Review* 101 (Fall 2007): 1483.

Epstein, Lee, et al. "Why Conservatives Should Continue to Yearn and Liberals Should Not Fear." *University of Tulsa Law Review* 43 (Spring 2008): 651.

Epstein, Lee, Barry Friedman, and Nancy Staudt. "On the Capacity of the Roberts Court to Generate Consequential Precedent." *North Carolina Law Review* 86 (June 2008): 1299.

Epstein, Richard A. "The Federalism Decisions of Justices Rehnquist and O'Connor: Is Half a Loaf Enough?" *Stanford Law Review* 58 (April 2006): 1793.

Esenberg, Richard M. "You Cannot Lose If You Choose Not to Play: Toward a More Modest Establishment Clause." *Roger Williams University Law Review* 12 (Fall 2006): 1.

Ettinger, David S. "The History of School Desegregation in the Ninth Circuit." *Loyola of Los Angeles Law Review* 12 (1979): 481.

Farris, Jerome. "The Ninth Circuit—Most Maligned Circuit in the Country—Fact or Fiction?" *Ohio State Law Journal* 58 (1997): 58.

Fischer, Thomas C. "Whatever Happened to Mary Beth Tinker and Other Sagas in the Academic 'Marketplace of Ideas.'" *Golden Gate University Law Review* 23 (1993): 352.

Fitzpatrick, Robert K. "Neither Icarus nor Ostrich: State Constitutions as an Independent Source of Rights." *New York University Law Review* 79 (November 2004): 79.

Foster, James C. "Rethinking Politics and Judicial Selection During Contentious Times." *Albany Law Review* 67 (2004): 821.

Foster, Jim [James C.], Steve Robinson, and Steve Fisher. "Class, Political Consciousness, and Destructive Power in Appalachia." *Appalachian Journal* 5 (Spring 1978).

Galanter, Marc. "Why the 'Haves' Come Out Ahead: Speculations of the Limits of Legal Change." *Law & Society Review* 9 (1974): 95.

Gallie, W. B. "Essentially Contested Concepts." *Proceedings of the Aristotelian Society* 56 (1956): 167.

Galston, William A. "Political Polarization and the U.S. Judiciary." *University of Missouri-Kansas City Law Review* 77 (Winter 2008): 307.

Garcia, Ruben J. "A Democratic Theory of Amicus Advocacy." *Florida State University Law Review* 35 (Winter 2008): 315.

Garrow, David J. "Hopelessly Hollow History: Revisionist Devaluing of *Brown v. Board of Education.*" *Virginia Law Review* 80 (February 1994): 151.

Geimer, William S. "Juvenileness: A Single-edged Constitutional Sword." *Georgia Law Review* 22 (1988): 949.

Geisinger, Alex, and Ivan E. Bodensteiner. "An Expressive Jurisprudence of the Establishment Clause." *Dickinson School of Law Penn State Law Review* 112 (Summer 2007): 77.

Gerber, Scott D., and Keeok Park. "The Quixotic Search for Consensus on the U.S. Supreme Court: A Cross-Judicial Empirical Analysis of Rehnquist Court Justices." *American Political Science Review* 91 (June 1997): 390.

Gerhardt, Michael J. "Judicial Selection as . . . Talk Radio." *University of Richmond Law Review* 39 (March 2005): 39.

Gey, Steven G. "Vestiges of the Establishment Clause." *First Amendment Law Review* 5 (Fall 2006): 1.

Ginsburg, Ruth Bader. "Remarks on Appellate Advocacy." *South Carolina Law Review* 50 (1999): 567.

Golanski, Alani. "Linguistics in Law." *Albany Law Review* 66 (2002): 61.

Goldman, Sheldon. "Judicial Confirmation Wars: Ideology and the Battle for the Federal Courts." *University of Richmond Law Review* 39 (March 2005): 871.

Gordon, Daniel. "America's Constitutional Dad: Justice Kennedy and His Intricate Children." *Idaho Law Review* 44 (2007): 161.

Gossett, David. "Friendship: Amicus Briefs in the Supreme Court." *Green Bag* 8, no. 2 (Summer 2005): 363.

Gray, J. N. "On the Contestability of Social and Political Concepts." *Political Theory* 5 (August 1977): 331.

Greenhouse, Linda. "Justices Who Change: A Response to Epstein et al." *Northwestern University Law Review* 101 (Fall 2007): 1885.

Grofman, Bernard, and Timothy Brazill. "Identifying the Median Justice on the Supreme Court through Multidimensional Scaling: Analysis of 'Natural Court' 1953–1991." *Public Choice* 112 (2002): 55.

Guinier, Lani. "Foreword: Demosprudence Through Dissent." *Harvard Law Review* 122 (November 2008): 4.

Gunther, Gerald. "The Subtle Vices of the 'Passive Virtues'—A Comment on Principle and Expediency in Judicial Review." *Columbia Law Review* 64 (1964): 1.

Haire, Susan B. "Judicial Selection and Decisionmaking in the Ninth Circuit." *Arizona Law Review* 48 (Summer 2006): 267.

Hakman, Nathan. "Lobbying the Supreme Court—An Appraisal of the Political Science 'Folklore.'" *Fordham Law Review* 35 (1966): 15.

Halpern, Stephen C., and Kenneth N. Vines. "Institutional Disunity, the Judge's Bill and the Role of the Supreme Court." *Western Political Quarterly* 30 (December 1977): 471.

Harrington, John. "Amici Curiae in the Federal Courts of Appeals: How Friendly Are They?" *Case Western Reserve Law Review* 55 (Spring 2005): 667.

Harris, Michael J. "Amicus Curiae: Friend or Foe? The Limits of Friendship in American Jurisprudence." *Suffolk Journal of Trial & Appellate Advocacy* 5 (2000): 1.

Hartman, Rhonda Gay. "Adolescent Autonomy: Clarifying an Ageless Conundrum." *Hastings Law Journal* 51 (August 2000): 1265.

Harwood, Christopher B. "Evaluating the Supreme Court's Establishment Clause Jurisprudence in the Wake of *Van Orden v. Perry* and *McCreary County v. ACLU*." *Missouri Law Review* 71 (Spring 2006): 317.

Haynie, Stacia L. "Leadership and Consensus on the U.S. Supreme Court." *Journal of Politics* 54 (November 1992): 1158.

Heider, Karl G. "The *Rashomon* Effect: When Ethnographers Disagree." *American Anthropologist* 90 (March 1988): 90.

Hellman, Arthur D. "Getting It Right: Panel Error and the En Banc Process in the Ninth Circuit Court of Appeals." *Davis Law Review* 34 (2000): 425.

Herald, Marybeth. "Reversed, Vacated, and Split: The Supreme Court, the Ninth Circuit, and the Congress." *Oregon Law Review* 77 (Summer 1998): 405.

Higginson, Stephen A. "Constitutional Advocacy Explains Constitutional Outcomes." *Florida Law Review* 60 (September 2008): 857.

Howard, J. Woodford, Jr. "On the Fluidity of Judicial Choice." *American Political Science Review* 62 (1968): 43.

Huhn, Wilson Ray. "The Constitutional Jurisprudence of Sandra Day O'Connor: A Refusal to 'Foreclose the Unanticipated.'" *Akron Law Review* 39 (2006): 373.

Hutchinson, Dennis J. "Hugo Black among Friends." Review of Roger K. Newman, Hugo Black: A Biography. *Michigan Law Review* 93 (May 1995): 1885.

Hymowitz, Kay S. "Tinker and the Lessons from the Slippery Slope." *Drake Law Review* 48 (2000): 547.

Jackson, Robert H. "Advocacy before the United States Supreme Court." *Cornell Law Quarterly* 37 (1951): 1.

James, Bernard, and Joanne E. K. Larson. "The Doctrine of Deference: Shifting Constitutional Presumptions and the Supreme Court's Restatement of Student Rights after *Board of Education v. Earls*." *South Carolina Law Review* 56 (Autumn 2004): 1.

Jeffries, John C., Jr. "*Bakke* Revisited." *Supreme Court Review* (2003): 1.

Johnson, Timothy R., Paul J. Wahlbeck, and James F. Spriggs II. "The Influence of Oral Arguments on the U.S. Supreme Court." *American Political Science Review* 100 (February 2006): 99.

Johnson, Timothy R., James F. Spriggs, II, and Paul J. Wahlbeck. "Oral Advocacy before the United States Supreme Court: Does It Affect the Justices' Decisions?" *Washington University Law Review* 85 (2007): 457.

Johnson, Timothy R., Ryan C. Black, Jerry Goldman, and Sarah A. Treul. "Inquiring Minds Want to Know: Do Justices Tip Their Hands with Questions at Oral Argument in the U.S. Supreme Court?" *Washington University Journal of Law & Policy* 29 (2009): 241.

Jones, Edith H. "Observations on the Status and Impact of the Judicial Confirmation Process." *University of Richmond Law Review* 39 (March 2005): 833.

Joondeph, Bradley W. "The Many Meanings of 'Politics' in Judicial Decision Making." *University of Missouri–Kansas City Law Review* 77 (Winter 2008): 347.

Kalman, Laura. "Members of the Warren Court in Judicial Biography: Commentary: The Wonder of the Warren Court." *New York University Law Review* 70 (1995): 780.

Kanter, Stephen. "The *Griswold* Diagrams: Toward a Unified Theory of Constitutional Rights." *Cardozo Law Review* 28 (November 2006): 623.

———. "Bong Hits 4 Jesus as a Cautionary Tale of Two Cities." *Lewis & Clark Law Review* 12 (Spring 2008): 61.

Kearney, Joseph D., and Thomas W. Merrill. "The Influence of Amicus Curiae Briefs on the Supreme Court." *Pennsylvania Law Review* 148 (January 2000): 743.

Kennedy, Anthony M. "Tribute: William Rehnquist and Sandra Day O'Connor: An Expression of Appreciation." *Stanford Law Review* 58 (April 2006): 1663.

Klarman, Michael. Book Review. *Law and History Review* 12 (1994).

———. "*Brown v. Board of Education*: Facts and Political Correctness." *Virginia Law Review* 80 (February 1994): 185.

Kolsky, Meredith. "Justice William Johnson and the History of Supreme Court Dissent." *Georgetown Law Journal* 83 (1995): 2069.

Knowles, Helen J. "May It Please the Court? The Solicitor General's Not-So-'Special' Relationship: Archibald Cox and the 1963–1964 Reapportionment Cases." *Journal of Supreme Court History* 31 (2006): 279.

Kohlberg, Lawrence, and Rochelle Mayer. "Development and the Aim of Education." *Harvard Education Review* 42 (1972): 44.

Kravitz, Mark R. "Book Review: Words to the Wise." *Journal of Appellate Practice & Process* 5 (Fall 2003): 543.

Krislov, Samuel. "The *Amicus Curiae* Brief: From Friendship to Advocacy." *Yale Law Journal* 72 (1963): 694.

Langston, Donna Hightower. "American Indian Women's Activism in the 1960s and 1970s." *Hypatia: Journal of Feminist Philosophy* 18 (Spring 2003): 114.

Law, David S., and Sanford Levinson. "Why Nuclear Disarmament May Be Easier to Achieve Than an End to Partisan Conflict over Judicial Appointments." *University of Richmond Law Review* 39 (March 2005): 923.

Lax, Jeffrey R., and Charles M. Cameron. "Bargaining and Opinion Assignment on the U.S. Supreme Court." *Journal of Law, Economy, and Organization* 23 (2007): 276.

Lazarus, Richard J. "Advocacy Matters Before and Within the Supreme Court: Transforming the Court by Transforming the Bar." *Georgetown Law Journal* 96 (June 2008): 1487.

Leib, Ethan J. "Friendship and the Law." *UCLA Law Review* 54 (February 2007): 631.

Linde, Hans E. "Without 'Due Process': Unconstitutional Law in Oregon." *Oregon Law Review* 49 (1970): 125.

Lindquist, Stefanie A., and Frank B. Cross. "Empirically Testing Dworkin's Chain Novel Theory: Studying the Path of Precedent." *New York University Law Review* 80 (October 2005): 1156.

Liu, Frederick. "Citing the Transcript of Oral Argument: Which Justices Do It and Why." *Yale Law Journal Pocket Part* 118 (2008): 32.

Lowenthal, Diane and Barbara Palmer. "Justice Sandra Day O'Connor and Her Influence on Issues of Race, Religion, Gender and Class: Justice Sandra Day O'Connor: The World's Most Powerful Jurist?" *University of Maryland Law Journal of Race, Religion, Gender, and Class* 4 (Fall 2004): 211.

Lowman, Michael K. "The Litigating Amicus Curiae: When Does the Party Begin after the Friends Leave?" *American University Law Review* 41 (Summer 1992): 1243.

Lynch, Kelly J. "Best Friends? Supreme Court Law Clerks on Effective *Amicus Curiae* Briefs." *Journal of Law & Politics* 20 (Winter 2004): 33.

Maring, Justice Mary Muehlen. "'Children Should Be Seen and Not Heard': Do Children Shed Their Right to Free Speech at the Schoolhouse Gate?" *North Dakota Law Review* 74 (1998): 679.

Marshall, William P. "The Judicial Nominations Wars." *University of Richmond Law Review* 39 (March 2005): 819.

Martin, Andrew D., and Kevin M. Quinn. "Dynamic Ideal Point Estimation via Markov Chain Monte Carlo for the U.S. Supreme Court, 1953–1999." *Political Analysis* 10 (2002): 134.

Martin, Andrew D., Kevin M. Quinn, and Lee Epstein. "The Median Justice on the United States Supreme Court." *North Carolina Law Review* 83 (2005): 1275.

Maveety, Nancy, and Robert C. Bradley. "Justice O'Connor: A Different Kind of Court Leader?" *Southeastern Political Review* 21 (1993): 39.

McAtee, Andrea, and Kevin T. McGuire. "Lawyers, Justices, and Issue Salience: When and How Do Legal Arguments Affect the U.S. Supreme Court." *Law & Society Review* 41 (June 2007): 259.

McGinnis, John O. "Continuity and Coherence in the Rehnquist Court." *St. Louis Law Journal* 47 (Spring 2003): 875.

McGoldrick, James M., Jr. "*United States v. O'Brien* Revisited: Of Burning Things, Waving Things, and G-Strings." *University of Memphis Law Review* 36 (Summer 2006): 903.

McGuire, Kevin T. "Repeat Players in the Supreme Court: The Role of Experienced Lawyers in Litigation Success." *Journal of Politics* 57 (February 1995): 187.

McMahon, Kevin J. "Presidents, Political Regimes, and Contentious Supreme Court Nominations: A Historical Institutional Model." *Law & Social Inquiry* 32 (Fall 2007): 919.

Martineau, Robert J. "The Value of Appellate Oral Argument: A Challenge to the Conventional Wisdom." *Iowa Law Review* 72 (October 1986): 1.

Meiklejohn, Alexander. "The First Amendment Is an Absolute." *Supreme Court Review* (1961): 245.

Merrill, Thomas W. "The Making of the Second Rehnquist Court: A Preliminary Analysis." *St. Louis Law Journal* 47 (Spring 2003): 569.

Michelman, Frank. "A Tribute to William J. Brennan, Jr." *Harvard Law Review* 104 (1990): 22.

Moorhead, R. Dean. "Concurring and Dissenting Opinions." *American Bar Association Journal* 38 (1952): 821.

Morgan, D. "Mr. Justice William Johnson and the Constitution." *Harvard Law Review* 57 (1944): 328.

Munford, Luther T. "When Does the Curiae Need an Amicus?" *Journal of Appellate Practice* 1 (Summer 1999): 279.

Narayan, Paresh Kumar, and Russell Smyth. "The Consensual Norm on the High Court of Australia, 1904-2001." *International Political Science Review* 26 (2005): 147.

Nimmer, Melville B. "The Meaning of Symbolic Speech under the First Amendment." *UCLA Law Review* 21 (1973): 29.

O'Brien, David M. "Join-3 Votes, the Rule of Four, the Cert. Pool, and the Supreme Court's Shrinking Plenary Docket." *Journal of Law & Politics* 13 (Fall 1997): 779.

O'Connor, Karen, and Lee Epstein. "*Amicus Curiae* Participation in U.S. Supreme Court Litigation: An Appraisal of Hakman's Folklore." *Law and Society Review* 16 (1981–1982): 311.

———. "Court Rules and Workload: A Case Study of Rules Governing Amicus Curiae Participation." *Justice System Journal* 8 (1983): 35.

———. "The Rise of Conservative Interest Group Litigation." *Journal of Politics* 45 (1983): 479.

Papke, David Ray. "From Flat to Round: Changing Portrayals of the Judge in American Popular Culture." *Journal of the Legal Profession* 31 (2007): 127.

Patel, Amit. "The Orthodoxy Opening Predicament: The Crumbling Wall of Separation between Church and State." *University of Detroit Mercy Law Review* 83(Spring 2006): 195.

Peterson, Steven A. "Dissent in American Courts." *Journal of Politics* 43 (1981): 412.

Pitkin, Hannah Fenichel. "Rethinking Reification." *Theory and Society* 16 (1987): 263.

Post, Robert C. "Foreword: Fashioning the Legal Constitution: Culture, Courts, and the Law." *Harvard Law Review* 117 (2003): 4.

Pritchett, C. Herman. "Divisions of Opinion among Justices of the U.S. Supreme Court." *American Political Science Review* 35 (1941): 890.

———. "The Coming of the New Dissent: The Supreme Court, 1942–1943." *University of Chicago Law Review* 11 (1943): 49.

———. "Dissent on the Supreme Court, 1943–1944." *American Political Science Review* 39 (1945): 42.

Rauh, Joseph. "An Unabashed Liberal Looks at A Half-Century of the Supreme Court." *North Carolina Law Review* 69 (1990): 213.

Ray, Laura Krugman. "America Meets the Justices: Explaining the Supreme Court to the General Reader." *Tennessee Law Review* 72 (Winter 2005): 573.

Revesz, Richard L., and Pamela S. Karlan. "Nonmajority Rules and the Supreme Court." *University of Pennsylvania Law Review* 136 (April 1988): 1067.

Roberts, John G., Jr. "Oral Advocacy and the Re-emergence of a Supreme Court Bar." *Journal of Supreme Court History* 30 (2005): 68.

Roe, Richard L. "Valuing Student Speech: The Work of the Schools as Conceptual Development." *California Law Review* 79 (October 1991): 1271.

Rosen, Jeffrey. "Dialogue: Who Cares?" *New York University Law Review* 40 (1996): 899.

Rosenberg, Gerald N. "Brown Is Dead! Long Live Brown! The Endless Attempt to Canonize a Case." *Virginia Law Review* 80 (February 1994): 161.

Roy, Lisa Shaw, "History, Transparency, and the Establishment Clause: A Proposal for Reform." *Penn State Law Review* 112 (Winter 2008): 683.

Russomanno, Joseph. "Dissent Yesterday and Today: The Tinker Case and Its Legacy." *Communication Law & Policy* 11 (Summer 2006): 367

Ryan, James E. "The Supreme Court and Public Schools." *Virginia Law Review* 86 (2000): 1335.

Rymer, Judge Pamela Ann. "The 'Limited' En Banc: Half Full, or Half Empty?" *Arizona Law Review* 48 (Summer 2006): 317.

Schauer, Frederick. "Abandoning the Guidance Function: *Morse v. Frederick*." *Supreme Court Review* (2007): 205.

Schweitzer, Dan. "Development and Practice Note: Fundamentals of Preparing a United States Supreme Court Amicus Brief." *Journal of Appellate Practice & Process* 5 (Fall 2003): 523.

Scott, David K., and Robert H. Gobetz. "The U.S. Supreme Court 1969–1992: A Shift Toward an Individualistic Style of Judging." *Communication Studies* 54 (Summer 2003): 211.

Scott, Kevin M. "Shaping the Supreme Court's Federal Certiorari Docket." *Justice System Journal* 27 (2006): 191.

———. "Supreme Court Reversals of the Ninth Circuit." *Arizona Law Review* 48 (Summer 2006): 341.

Senhauser, William B. "Education and the Court: The Supreme Court's Educational Ideology." *Vanderbilt Law Review* 40 (May 1987): 939.

Shapiro, Stephen M. "Amicus Briefs in the Supreme Court." *Litigation* 10 (Spring 1984): 21.

———. "Oral Argument in the Supreme Court of the United States." *Catholic University Law Review* 33 (Spring 1984): 529.

Shullman, Sarah Levien. "The Illusion of Devil's Advocacy: How the Justices of the Supreme Court Foreshadow Their Decisions during Oral Argument." *Journal of Appellate Practice & Process* 6 (Fall 2004): 271.

Simard, Linda Sandstrom. "An Empirical Study of *Amici Curiae* in Federal Court: A Fine Balance of Access, Efficiency, and Adversarialism." *Review of Litigation* 27 (Summer 2008): 669.

Slaff, Sara. "Note: Silencing Student Speech: *Bethel School District No. 403 v. Fraser.*" *American University Law Review* 37 (Fall 1987): 203.

Slotnick, Elliot E. "Appellate Judicial Selection during the Bush Administration: Business As Usual or a Nuclear Winter?" *Arizona Law Review* 48 (Summer 2006): 225.

Smith, Christopher E., and Thomas R. Hensley. "Unfulfilled Aspirations: The Court-Packing Efforts of Presidents Reagan and Bush." *Albany Law Review* 57 (Fall 1994): 1111.

Smyth, Russell. "Historical Consensual Norms in the High Court." *Australian Journal of Political Science* 37 (2002): 255.

Solberg, Rorie Spill. "Court Size and Diversity: The Ninth Circuit and Its Sisters." *Arizona Law Review* 48 (Summer 2006): 247.

Songer, Donald R., and Reginald S. Sheehan. "Interest Group Success in the Courts: Amicus Participation in the Supreme Court." *Political Research Quarterly* 46 (1993): 339.

Spiller, Pablo T. "Review of *The Choices Justices Make.*" *American Political Science Review* 94 (December 2000): 943.

Spriggs, James F., and Paul J. Wahlbeck. "*Amici Curiae* and the Role of Information at the Supreme Court." *Political Research Quarterly* 50 (1997): 365.

Stack, Kevin M. "The Practice of Dissent in the Supreme Court." *Yale Law Journal* 105 (June 1996): 2235.

Staudt, Nancy, Barry Friedman, and Lee Epstein. "On the Role of Ideological Homogeneity in Generating Consequential Constitutional Decisions." *University of Pennsylvania Journal of Constitutional Law* 10 (January 2008): 361.

Sullivan, Kathleen L. "The Supreme Court: 1991 Term—Foreword: The Justices of Rules and Standards." *Harvard Law Review* 106 (1992): 22.

Szmer, John, Susan W. Johnson, and Tammy A. Sarver. "Does the Lawyer Matter? Influencing Outcomes on the Supreme Court of Canada." *Law & Society Review* 41 (June 2007): 279.

Tamulonis, Frank, III. "Splitting the Ninth Circuit: Necessity or Environmental Gerrymandering?" *Penn State Law Review* 112 (Winter 2008): 859.

Tarr, G. Alan. "The New Judicial Federalism in Perspective." *Notre Dame Law Review* 72 (1996–1997): 1097.

Tate, Albert, Jr. "Federal Appellate Advocacy in the 1980's." *American Journal of Trial Advocacy* 5 (1981): 63.

Thomson, James S. "Review Essay: Inside the Supreme Court: A Sanctum Sanctorum?" *Mississippi Law Journal* 66 (Fall 1996): 177.

Tiersma, Peter Meijes. "Nonverbal Communication and the Freedom of 'Speech.'" *Wisconsin Law Review* (November–December 1993): 1525.

Tobias, Carl. "The Impoverished Idea of Circuit-Splitting." *Emory Law Journal* 44 (Fall 1995): 1357.

———. "The Federal Appellate Court Appointments Conundrum." *Utah Law Review* (2005): 743.

Totenberg, Nina. "A Tribute to Justice William A. Brennan, Jr." *Harvard Law Review* 104 (November 1990): 33.

Tullis, Jeffrey K. "Constitutional Abdication: The Senate, the president, and Appointments to the Supreme Court." *Case Western Reserve Law Review* 47 (Summer 1997): 1331.

Tushnet, Mark V. "Free Expression and the Young Adult: A Constitutional Framework." *University of Illinois Law Review* 746 (1976): 746.

———. "Symposium on Democracy and Distrust: Ten Years Later: Foreword." *Virginia Law Review* 77 (May 1991): 631.

———. "The Significance of *Brown v. Board of Education*." *Virginia Law Review* 80 (February 1994): 173.

———. "Themes in Warren Court Biographies." *New York University Law Review* 70 (1995): 748.

Tushnet, Mark, with Katya Lezin. "What Really Happened in *Brown v. Board of Education*." *Columbia Law Review* 91 (December 1991): 1867.

Urofsky, Melvin I. "Introduction." *Journal of Supreme Court History* 32 (November 2007): v.

Waldman, Joshua. "Symbolic Speech and Social Meaning." *Columbia Law Review* 97 (October 1997): 1844.

Walker, Thomas G., Lee Epstein, and William J. Dixon. "On the Mysterious Demise of Consensual Norms in the United States Supreme Court." *Journal of Politics* 50 (May 1988): 361.

Wasby, Stephen L. "'Extra' Judges in a Federal Appellate Court: The Ninth Circuit." *Law & Society Review* 15 (1980–1981): 369.

———. "The Road Not Taken: Judicial Federalism, Student Athletes, and Drugs." *Albany Law Review* 59 (1996): 1699.

———. "The Supreme Court and Courts of Appeal En Bancs." *McGeorge Law Review* 33 (2001): 17.

———. "How the Ninth Circuit Fares in the Supreme Court: The Intercircuit Conflict Cases." *Seton Hall Circuit Review* 1 (Spring 2005): 119.

Wasby, Stephen L., Anthony A. D'Amato, and Rosemary Metrailer. "The Function of Oral Argument in the U.S. Supreme Court." *Quarterly Journal of Speech* 62 (December 1976): 410.

Wermiel, Stephen J. "Exploring the Myths About the Ninth Circuit." *Arizona Law Review* 48 (Summer 2006): 355.

Wexler, Jay D. "Defending the Middle Way: Intermediate Scrutiny as Judicial Minimalism." *George Washington Law Review* 66 (January 1998): 298.

Whitebread, Charles. "The Conservative Kennedy Court—What a Difference a Single Justice Can Make: The 2006–2007 Term of the United States Supreme Court." *Whittier Law Review* 29 (Fall 2007): 1.

Whittington, Keith E. "Presidents, Senates, and Failed Supreme Court Nominations." *Supreme Court Review* (2006): 401.

Wilborn, S. Elizabeth. "Teaching the New Three Rs—Repression, Rights, and Respect: A Primer of Student Speech Activities." *Boston College Law Review* 31 (1995): 119.

Wilkinson, J. Harvie, III. "The Rehnquist Court at Twilight: The Lures and Perils of Split-the-Difference Jurisprudence." *Stanford Law Review* 58 (April 2006): 1969.

Yates, Jeff, and William Gillespie. "Supreme Court Power Play: Assessing the Appropriate Role of the Senate in the Confirmation Process." *Washington & Lee Law Review* 58 (Summer 2001): 1053.

Yudof, Mark. "*Tinker* Tailored: Good Faith, Civility, and Student Expression." *St. John's Law Review* 69 (Summer–Fall 1995): 365.

ZoBell, Karl M. "Division of Opinion in the Supreme Court: A History of Judicial Disintegration." *Cornell Law Quarterly* 44 (1959): 186.

Miscellaneous

"100 Years of Ninth Circuit History in San Francisco Courthouse," http://www.ce9.uscourts.gov/history/100_years.pdf.

Alaska Constitution, Article I, Declaration of Rights, § 5.

Altman, Robert, video introduction to *Rashomon*, Criterion, March 26, 2002.

Amicus curiae Brief for D.A.R.E. America in support of petitioners on writ of certiorari, *Morse v. Frederick*, 06-278.

Amicus curiae Brief for National School Boards Association in support of Petition for writ of certiorari, motion for leave to file Brief as amici curiae in support of the Petition for writ of certiorari, *Morse v. Frederick*, 06-278.

Amicus Brief of the American Center for Law and Justice in support of respondent, *Morse v. Frederick*, 06-278.

Appellant's Opening Brief, Joseph Fredrick, appellant, vs. Deborah Morse and the Juneau School Board, appellees, Ninth Circuit Court of Appeals No. 03-35701.

Appellee's Brief, Joseph Fredrick, appellant, vs. Deborah Morse and the Juneau School Board, appellees, Ninth Circuit Court of Appeals No. 03-35701.

Appellant's Opening Brief, in the United States Court of Appeals for the Ninth Circuit, *Frederick v. Morse*, No. 07-36013.

Appendix, *Morse v. Frederick*, 06-278, Appendix B—Opinion and Order of the United States District Court for The District of Alaska, dated and filed May 27, 2003.

Appendix, *Morse v. Frederick*, 06-278, Appendix C—Order of the United States District Court for the District of Alaska, dated and filed on May 29, 2003.

Appendix, *Morse v. Frederick*, 06-278, Appendix H—Superintendent's decision on Appeal dated February 25, 2002.

Appendix, *Morse v. Frederick*, 06-278, Appendix I—Minutes of the Juneau Board of Education meeting of March 19, 2002.

Assassination Archives and Research Center, vol. 2: Huston Plan, at http://www.aarclibrary.org/publib/contents/church/contents_church_reports_vol2.htm.

Board Policy No. 5520R, Disruption and Demonstration, Joint Appendix, *Deborah Morse; Juneau School Board, Petitioners, v. Joseph Frederick, Respondent*, On Writ of Certiorari to the United States Court of Appeals for the Ninth Circuit.

Brief of Amicus Curiae Alliance Defense Fund supporting respondent, *Morse v. Frederick*, 06-278.

Brief for Amicus *Curiae* Lambda Legal Defense and Education Fund, Inc. in support of respondent, *Morse v. Frederick*, 06-278.

Brief for Amicus *Curiae* Liberty Counsel in Support of Respondent, *Morse v. Frederick*, 06-278.

Brief Amicus *Curiae* of the Christian Legal Society in support of respondent, *Morse v. Frederick*, 06-278.

Brief for Petitioner, Deborah Morse; Juneau School Board v. Joseph Frederick, *Morse v. Frederick*, 06-278.

Brief for the Student Press Law Center, Feminists for Free Expression, The First Amendment Project, The Freedom to Read Foundation, and the Thomas Jefferson Center for the Protection of Free Expression as *Amici Curiae* supporting respondent, *Morse v. Frederick*, 06-278.

Brief for the United States as Amicus *Curiae* supporting petitioners, *Morse v. Frederick*, 06-278.

Brief in Opposition to Petition for Writ of Certiorari, Juneau School Board and Deborah Morse v. Joseph Frederick, *Morse v. Frederick*, 06-278.

Brief of Amicus *Curiae* Center for Individual Rights in support of respondent, *Morse v. Frederick*, 06-278.

Brief of the National Coalition against Censorship and the American Booksellers Foundation for Free Expression as *Amici Curiae* in support of respondent, *Morse v. Frederick*, 06-278.

Brief of the Liberty Legal Institute as Amicus *Curiae* in Support of Respondent, *Morse v. Frederick*, 06-278.

Brief of the Rutherford Institute, Amicus *Curiae* in Support of Respondent, *Morse v. Frederick*, 06-278.

Brief on Behalf of Students for Sensible Drug Policy as Amicus *Curiae* in Support of Respondent, *Morse v. Frederick*, 06-278.

"Can Obama Influence the Court?" The University of Chicago Faculty Blog, February 9, 2009. http://uchicagolaw.typepad.com/faculty/2009/02/can-obama-shape-supreme-court-jurisprudence.html.

Carrubba, Cliff, et al. "Does the Median Justice Control the Content of Supreme Court Opinions?" Working paper presented at Second Annual Conference on Empirical Legal Studies, November 2007.

Chandler, Adam. "Cert.-stage Amicus Briefs: Who Files Them and to What Effect?" SCOTUS Blog, September 27, 2007. http://www.scotusblog.com/wp/cert-stage-amicus-briefs-who-files-them-and-to-what-effect-2.

Churchill, Winston. The Lord Mayor's Luncheon, Mansion House, London, November 10, 1942.

Classroom Law Project Web site, http://www.classroomlaw.org/resources/.

Cummings, William F. E-mail to James Foster, dated August 18, 2009.

Curtiz, Michael. *Casablanca*. Warner Bros., 1942.

Deposition of Deborah Lynn Morse, Friday, January 31, 2003.

Deposition of Joseph Frederick, Wednesday, August 21, 2002.

Dialogos Web site, http://www.dialogos.com/index.html.

Dollar, Natalie. "Community Dialogue Workshop as Civil Society: A Preliminary Analysis of 'Getting Below the Sound Bite' to the Betwixt and Between," paper presented at the annual meeting of the Western States Communication Association, Seattle, WA, February 2007.

———. "Community Dialogue Workshop." Winter 2008.

———. "Community Dialogue Strategies, Community Dialogue Workshop." Winter 2008.

Durand, Chet. Signed statement, dated January 24, 2002.

Executive Order 9066, February 19, 1942.

Federal Rules of Civil Procedure, VII Judgment, Rule 56. Summary Judgment. http://www.law.cornell.edu/rules/frcp/Rule56.htm.

Freed, Richard. Program note to National Symphony Orchestra performance of "Till Eulenspiegel's Merry Pranks," January 13–15, 2005. http://www.kennedy-center.org/calendar/?fuseaction=composition&composition_id=2850.

Gaustad, John M., and Walt Vogdes. "Till Eulenspiegel—The Merry Prankster," Stein Collectors International, Inc. http://www.steincollectors.org/library/articles/Eulenspiegel/Eulenspiegel.html.

Holmes, Oliver Wendell Jr. Lowell Lecture, November 23, 1880. http://www.law.harvard.edu/library/collections/special/online-collections/common_law/index.php.

Hudson, David. "Matthew Fraser Speaks Out on 15-Year-Old Supreme Court Free-Speech Decision," April 17, 2001. http://www.freedomforum.org/templates/document.asp?documentID=13701.

Interrogatory No. 5 and Response [on disruption], Joint Appendix, *Deborah Morse; Juneau School Board, Petitioners, v. Joseph Frederick, Respondent*, On Writ of Certiorari to the United States Court of Appeals for the Ninth Circuit.

Jacobi, Tonja, and Matthew Sag. "Taking the Measure of Ideology: Empirically Measuring Supreme Court Cases." Draft working paper, January 13, 2009, University of Chicago Workshop on Judicial Behavior.

Jefferson, Thomas, to Dr. James Currie, January 28, 1786. The Thomas Jefferson Papers Series 1. General Correspondence. 1651–1827, The Library of Congress. http://memory.loc.gov/cgi-bin/ampage?collId=mtj1&fileName=mtj1page005.db&recNum=0215.

Jefferson Thomas, to Justice William Johnson, Monticello, October 27, 1822. "From Revolution to Reconstruction," University of Groningen. http://www.let.rug.nl/usa/P/tj3/writings/brf/jefl269.htm.

"Johnny Carson and Jack Webb." http://www.youtube.com/watch?v=F4RIBhQIkII.

Joint Appendix. *Morse v. Frederick*, 06-278.

"Juneau, Alaska." Alaska Tour and Travel. http://www.alaskatravel.com/juneau.

"Juneau, Alaska." Alaska Travel. http://www.myalaskan.com/alaska-towns/juneau.html.

Juneau School District. Transcript of Hearing in the Matter of Joseph Frederick, March 13, 2002.

Kaufman, Moisés, and the Members of the Tectonic Theater Project. *The Laramie Project*. New York: Dramatists Play Service, 2001.

Kurosawa, Akira. *Rashomon*. Daiei Motion Picture Company, 1950.

Lax, Jeffrey R., and Charles M. Cameron. "Beyond the Median Voter: Bargaining and Law in the Supreme Court." Paper prepared for the 2005 Annual Meeting of the Midwest Political Science Association, April 6, 2005.

"Mediation in the Ninth Circuit, C. The Mediation Process." http://www.ca9.uscourts.gov/mediation/mediation_c.php.

Mediation Questionnaire. http://www.ca9.uscourts.gov/datastore/uploads/Mediation_Questionnaire.pdf.

Mendez vs. Westminster: For All the Children/Para Todos los Ninos. KOCE television (2002).

Morris, Errol. *The Fog of War*. Sony Pictures, 2004.

Morse et al. v. Frederick, No. 06-278, slip opinion, June 25, 2007, http://www.supremecourtus.gov/opinions/06slipopinion.html.

National Public Radio. "'Ten Years Later': The Matthew Shepard Story Retold." *All Things Considered*, October 12, 2009. http://www.npr.org/templates/transcript/transcript.php?storyId=113663235.

"New Details Emerge in Matthew Shepard Murder." *ABC News 20/20*, November 26, 2004. http://abcnews.go.com/2020/story?id=277685&page=1.

Opinion and Order of the United States District Court for The District of Alaska, dated and filed May 27, 2003.

Opposition Brief of Appellees Deborah Morse and Juneau School Board, in the United States Court of Appeals for the Ninth Circuit, *Frederick v. Morse*, No. 07-36013.

Oral argument, *Frederick v. Morse*, Ninth Circuit Court of Appeals, No. 07-36013, http://www.ca9.uscourts.gov/media/view_subpage.php?pk_id=0000000031.

Oral argument, *Morse v. Frederick*, No. 06-278, March 19, 2007. http://www.supremecourtus.gov/oral_arguments/argument_transcripts/06-278.pdf.

Order partially vacating judgment of May 29, 2003, and directing entry of final judgment in favor of defendants, *Frederick v. Morse*, Case No. J02-008 CV (JWS).

Oyez Project. The oral argument in *Morse v. Frederick*, 551 U.S. 393 (2007). http://oyez.org/cases/2000-2009/2006/2006_06_278.

Pearce, Donn, and Frank Pierson. *Cool Hand Luke*. Directed by Stuart Rosenberg. Warner Brothers, 1967.

Petition for Writ of Certiorari, Juneau School Board; Deborah Morse v. Joseph Frederick, *Morse v. Frederick*, 06-278.

Petitioner's Reply Memorandum, Juneau School Board; Deborah Morse, v. Joseph Frederick, *Morse v. Frederick*, 06-278.

Petty, Tom. "Into the Great Wide Open." MCA Records, 1991.

Prokofiev, Sergei. *Peter and the Wolf*. 1936. http://library.thinkquest.org/C005400/musi/prokofievpnw.html.

Puro, Steven. "The Role of Amicus Curiae in The United States Supreme Court: 1920–1966." Ph.D. diss., State University of New York at Buffalo, unpublished, 1971.

Reply Brief for Petitioners, Deborah Morse; Juneau School Board v. Joseph Frederick, *Morse v. Frederick*, 06-278.

Respondent's Brief, Deborah Morse; Juneau School Board v. Joseph Frederick, *Morse v. Frederick*, 06-278.

Richard H. Chambers U.S. Court of Appeals, Pasadena, Calif., U.S. General Services Administration. http://www.gsa.gov/Portal/gsa/ep/buildingView.do?pageTypeId=17109&channelPage=/ep/channel/gsaOverview.jsp&channelId=-25241&bid=825.

Shakespeare. *Hamlet*, Act 2, Scene II.

Silber, Glen, and Barry Brown. *The War at Home*. First Run Features, 1979.

Russell, Anna. The Ring of the Nibelungs (An Analysis), Anna Russell Sings! Again? Columbia Masterworks, ML4594/ML4733, 1953.

———. "*The Ring of the Nibelungs* (An Analysis)." http://www.markelliswalker.net/music/albums/anna-russell-ring.html.

Settlement Agreement, in the United States District Court for the District of Alaska, Joseph Frederick, Plaintiff vs. Deborah Morse and the Juneau School Board, Defendants, No. J02 008 CV (JWS).

Settlement Agreement and Mutual Release.

Unofficial transcript of Juneau School District Superintendent's hearing, n.d.

U.S. Code Collection, Title 42, Chapter 21, Subchapter I, § 83, Civil Action for Deprivation of Rights. http://www.law.cornell.edu/uscode/42/usc_sec_42_00001983----000-.html.

U.S. Congress. *Congressional Record*. 84th Cong., 2d sess., 1956. Vol. 102, pt. 4. Washington, D.C., 1956.

Washington University Law. "Supreme Court Forecasting Project 2002." http://wusct.wustl.edu/index.php.

Wood, Rebecca. "Institutional Considerations in Locating Norms of Consensus: A Cross-National Investigation." Paper presented at the 2008 Annual Meeting of the Midwest Political Science Association, Chicago, Ill., April 3–6.

Woolley, John T., and Gerhard Peters. *The American Presidency Project*. Santa Barbara: University of California. http://www.presidency.ucsb.edu/ws/?pid=39572.

Newspapers, Magazines, and Web Articles

"A Silly Banner and a Stupid Court Appeal." *Juneau Empire*, n.d. http://www.juneauempire.com/stories/050706/opi_20060507013.shtml.

Abramson, Jill. "Mayer, Brown's 'Shadow' Solicitors." *Legal Times*, November 24, 1986.

Alworth, Jeff, "Poisoning the Well," *Blue Oregon*, May 15, 2005, at http://www.blueoregon.com/2005/05/poisoning_the_w.html.

Araiza, William D. "*Morse v. Frederick*: History, Policy and Temptation," Legal Studies Paper No. 2007-43, Loyola Law School, Los Angeles (November 2007). http://papers.ssrn.com/sol3/papers.cfm?abstract_id=1024322.

Armstrong, Virginia C. "'Impeach Earl Warren:' The Warren Court's Legacy Fifty Years Later, Part I." *Eagle Forum's Court Watch* 5, February 21, 2003. http://www.eagleforum.org/court_watch/alerts/2003/feb03/02-21-03Brief.shtml.

Associated Press. "'Bong Hits' Case Back in Court." *Anchorage Daily News*, July 24, 2008. http://www.adn.com/news/alaska/story/474150.html.

Bader, Gary. "My Turn: JDHS Principal Was Doing Her Job." *Juneau Empire*, n.d. http://www.juneauempire.com/stories/050902/opi_myturn2.shtml.

Barnes, Robert. "Justice Kennedy: The Highly Influential Man in the Middle." *Washington Post*, May 13, 2007. http://www.washingtonpost.com/wp-dyn/content/article/2007/05/12/AR2007051201586.html.

Baum, Lawrence. "May It Please the Court: Symposium on Oral Argument." *Law and Courts* 5 (Spring 1995). http://www1.law.nyu.edu/lawcourts/pubs/newsletter/index.html.

Brayton, Ed. "Strange Bedfellows on Bong Hits Case." In *Dispatches from the Culture Wars: Thoughts from the Interface of Science, Religion, Law and Culture*, http://scienceblogs.com/dispatches/2007/03/strange_bedfellows_on_bong_hit.php.

Biskupic, Joan. "Justices make points by questioning lawyers." *USA Today*, October 5, 2006. http://www.usatoday.com/news/washington/judicial/2006-10-05-oral-arguments_x.htm.

———. "Ginsburg: Court Needs Another Woman." *USA Today*, May 5, 2009. http://www.usatoday.com/news/washington/judicial/2009-05-05-ruthginsburg_N.htm.

Brigham, John. "May It Please the Court: Symposium on Oral Argument." *Law and Courts* 5 (Spring 1995). http://www1.law.nyu.edu/lawcourts/pubs/newsletter/index.html.

Brooks, David. "The Rush to Therapy." *New York Times*, November 10, 2009. http://www.nytimes.com/2009/11/10/opinion/10brooks.html?em.

Burke, Daniel. "Supreme Court Hears 'Bong Hits 4 Jesus' Case: Christian Legal Groups File Briefs Supporting Banner." *Christianity Today*, March 20, 2007. http://www.christianitytoday.com/ct/2007/marchweb-only/112-22.0.html.

Carlson, Phyllis. "My Turn: 'Bong Hits' Deserves Supreme Court Test." *Juneau Empire*, n.d. http://www.juneauempire.com/stories/052406/opi_20060524001.shtml.

Carter, Lief.Review of Richard Posner, *The Problems of Jurisprudence*." *Law and Politics Book Review* 1 (April 1991). http://www.bsos.umd.edu/gvpt/lpbr/subpages/reviews/posner2.htm.

———. "No Ivory Tower: CC's 124th Anniversary Symposium," Colorado College Symposium, "Cultures in the 21st Century: Conflicts and Convergences, February 4–6, 1999. http://www.coloradocollege.edu/Publications/TheBulletin/Summer99/125.html.

———. Review of Steven L. Winter, *A Clearing in the Forest: Law, Life and the Mind. Law and Politics Book Review* 12 (June 2002). http://www.bsos.umd.edu/gvpt/lpbr/subpages/reviews/winterclear.html.

Cockerham, Sean. "Alaska Government Migrates to the North." *Anchorage Daily News*, December 21, 2008. http://www.adn.com/front/story/630232.html.

Cohen, Richard. "Palin's Love Boats." *Washington Post*, October 28, 2008. http://www.washingtonpost.com/wp-dyn/content/article/2008/10/27/AR2008102702438.html.

Cohen, Roger. "Kiplin' vs. Palin." *New York Times*, October 6, 2008. http://www.nytimes.com/2008/10/06/opinion/06cohen.html

Davidson, Amy. "The Scalia Court." *New Yorker*, March 28, 2005. http://www.newyorker.com/archive/2005/03/28/050328on_onlineonly01.

Dean, Cornelia. "36 Hours in Juneau, Alaska." *New York Times*, August 30, 2009. http://travel.nytimes.com/2009/08/30/travel/30hours.html?scp=3&sq=five-day%20jaunt%20in%20juneau&st=cse.

Denniston, Lyle. "Analysis: A New Exception to 'Tinker'?" *SCOTUSBlog*, March 19, 2007. http://www.scotusblog.com/wp/analysis-a-new-exception-to-tinker/.

———. "Commentary: Beyond the schoolhouse gate," *SCOTUSBlog*, June 25, 2007. http://www.scotusblog.com/wp/commentary-beyond-the-schoolhouse-gate/#more-5645.

DeParle, Jason. "In Battle to Pick Next Justice, Right Says, Avoid a Kennedy." *New York Times*, June 27, 2006.

Dickerson, John. "Palin's Campaign vs. McCain's." *Slate*, October 20, 2008. http://www.slate.com/id/2202658/?GT1=38001.

Dowd, Maureen. "Bering Straight Talk." *New York Times*, September 14, 2008. http://www.nytimes.com/2008/09/14/opinion/14dowd.html.

Dworkin, Ronald. "Looking for Cass Sunstein." *New York Review of Books*, April 30, 2009.

Egan, Timothy. "Last-Frontier Follies." *New York Times*, November 12, 2008. http://egan.blogs.nytimes.com/2008/11/12/last-frontier-follies/.

Encyclopedia Britannica. "Till Eulenspiegel." http://www.britannica.com/EBchecked/topic/195195/ Till-Eulenspiegel.

"Enough Already; Drop the Bong Hits Issue." *Juneau Empire*, January 25, 2008. http://www.juneauempire. com/stories/012508/opi_240253928.shtml.

Epstein, Lee, et al. "Ideological Drift among Supreme Court Justices: Who, When, and How Important?" *Northwestern University Law Review Colloquy* (2007), and responses by Stephen Burbank, Linda Greenhouse, and David Strauss. http://www.law.northwestern.edu/lawreview/colloquy/2007/8/.

Fairlie, Henry. "The Decline of Oratory." *New Republic*, May 28, 1984.

Fish, Kendra E., and Stephanie Pfeffer. "Board of Education of Independent School District No. 92 of Pottawatomie County, et al. v. Earls, Lindsay, et al." *On the Docket*, Medill Journalism, Northwestern University, posted June 23, 2004. http://docket.medill.northwestern.edu/ archives/000605.php#relatedlinks.

Fish, Stanley. "Does Constitutional Theory Matter?" *New York Times*, January 27, 2008, http://fish.blogs. nytimes.com/.

———. "What Kind of Judges Do We Want?" *New York Times*, June 22, 2009. http://fish.blogs.nytimes. com/2009/06/22/what-kind-of-judges-do-we-want.

Forgey, Pat. "Court Halts Juneau Road Project." *Juneau Empire*, February 15, 2009. http://www. juneauempire.com/stories/021509/loc_388168240.shtml.

———. "Road Ruling Leaves Uncertainties." *Juneau Empire*, February 17, 2009. http://www. juneauempire.com/stories/021709/loc_389869758.shtml.

Foster, James C. Review of Burrus M. Carnahan's *Act of Justice: Lincoln's Emancipation Proclamation and the Law of War*. *Law and Politics Book Review* 19 (January 2009). http://www.bsos.umd.edu/gvpt/ lpbr/reviews/2009/01/act-of-justice-lincolns-emancipation.html.

"Free Speech Case Divides Bush and Religious Right," *New York Times*, March 18, 2007. http://www. nytimes.com/2007/03/18/washington/18scotus.html?pagewanted=1&_r=1.

Fry, Eric. "Court Mulls over Protected Speech." *Juneau Empire*, n.d. http://www.juneauempire.com/ stories/041403/loc_bonghits.shtml.

———. "Judge: School district within rights to take debated banner." *Juneau Empire*, n.d. htp://www. juneauempire.com/stories/060603/loc_judge.shtml.

———. "Schools reopen as renovation stays on course." *Juneau Empire*, n.d. http://www.juneauempire. com/stories/082803/loc_schoolopen.shtml.

———. "JDHS principal to depart post." *Juneau Empire*, n.d. http://www.juneauempire.com/stories/ 070904/loc_principal.shtml.

Glater, Jonathan D. "Lawmakers Trying Again to Divide Ninth Circuit." *New York Times*, June 19, 2005. http://www.nytimes.com/2005/06/19/politics/19court.html.

Golden, Kate. "Coeur Alaska Wins Supreme Court Case." *Juneau Empire*, June 23, 2009. http://www. juneauempire.com/stories/062309/loc_453703862.shtml.

Greene, Bob. "On Main Street, Signs of the Times Tell Two Stories." *Jewish World Review*, July 20, 2000. http://www.jewishworldreview.com/bob/greene072000.asp.

Greenhouse, Linda. "The Law: At the Bar; Name-Calling in the Supreme Court: When the Justices Vent Their Spleen, Is There a Social Cost?" *New York Times*, July 28, 1989. http://www.nytimes. com/1989/07/28/us/law-bar-name-calling-supreme-court-when-justices-vent-their-spleen- there-social.html.

———. "The Year Rehnquist May Have Lost His Court." *New York Times*, July 4, 2004, A1.

———. "Under the Microscope Longer Than Most." *New York Times*, July 10, 2005. http://www.nytimes. com/2005/07/10/weekinreview/10greenhouse.html.

———. "Court Hears Whether a Drug Statement Is Protected Free Speech for Students." *New York Times*, March 20, 2007. http://query.nytimes.com/gst/fullpage.html?res=9A0CE3DE1730F933A 15750C0A9619C8B63&sec=&spon=&pagewanted=1.

———. "Justices Limit the Use of Race in School Plans for Integration." *New York Times*, June 29, 2007. http://www.nytimes.com/2007/06/29/washington/29scotus.html?_r=1&oref=slogin.

———. "Talk to the Newsroom: Supreme Court Reporter." *New York Times*, July 14, 2008. http://www. nytimes.com/2008/07/14/business/media/14askthetimes.html?pagewanted=all

———. "Every Justice Creates a New Court." *New York Times*, May 26, 2009. http://www.nytimes. com/2009/05/27/opinion/27greenhouse.html?scp=1&sq=every%20justice%20creates%20a%20 new%20court&st=cse.

Hein, Ed. "My Turn: How Will Students Learn Constitutional Values?" *Juneau Empire*, n.d. http://www. juneauempire.com/stories/030602/opE_myturn2.shtml.

Iyer, Pico. "The Great Wide Open." *Smithsonian*, November 2009.

"Juneau." The Milepost. http://milepost.com/index.php?option=com_content&task=view&id=155&I temid=199.

Kane, Terence. "SCOTUS and Median Voter Theory." The Hill's Pundits Blog, May 1, 2009. http:// pundits.thehill.com/2009/05/01/scotus-and-median-voter-theory/.

Katz, Jon. "'Bong Hits 4 Jesus:' Strange bedfellows justifiably rally behind . . ." Underdog, April 2, 2007. http://katzjustice.com/underdog/archives/448-Bong-Hits-4-Jesus-Strange-bedfellows-justifiably-rally-behind-the-First-Amendment.html.

Klawans, Stuart. "Fascism, Repression, and 'The White Ribbon.'" *New York Times*, October 30, 2009. http://www.nytimes.com/2009/11/01/movies/01klaw.html?ref=movies.

Krueger, Andrew. "School Board Hears Student Banner Case." *Juneau Empire*, n.d. http://www. juneauempire.com/stories/031402/loc_schoolboard.shtml.

———. "School Board Upholds Decision of Student Banner," *Juneau Empire*, n.d. http://www. juneauempire.com/stories/032002/loc_stubanner.shtml.

Lassila, Kathrin Day. "A Brief History of Groupthink." *Yale Alumni Magazine*, January–February 2008. http://www.yalealumnimagazine.com/issues/2008_01/groupthink.html.

"Law and Language." Stanford Encyclopedia of Philosophy. http://plato.stanford.edu/entries/law-language.

Leeds, Jeffrey T. "A Life on the Court." *New York Times Magazine*, October 5, 1986.

"Legislative Hall Bill Would Concentrate Power in Anchorage." *Juneau Empire*, March 23, 2008. http:// www.juneauempire.com/stories/032308/opi_260769252.shtml.

Lewis, Neil A. "Debate on Whether Female Judges Decide Differently Arises Anew." *New York Times*, June 3, 2009. http://www.nytimes.com/2009/06/04/us/politics/04women.html?_r=3&scp=1&sq= female%20justices&st=cse.

Lithwick, Dahlia. "Scaliapalooza: The Supreme Court's Pocket Jeremiah." *Slate*, October 30, 2003, http:// slate.msn.com/id/2090532.

Liptak, Adam. "A Second Justice Opts Out of a Longtime Custom: The 'Cert. Pool.'" *New York Times*, September 25, 2008. http://www.nytimes.com/2008/09/26/washington/26memo.html?_r= 1&scp=1&sq=alito%20and%20cert.%20pool&st=cse.

———. "Reticent Justice Opens Up to a Group of Students." *New York Times*, April 13, 2009. http:// www.nytimes.com/2009/04/14/us/14bar.html.

———. "Roberts Court Shifts Right, Tipped by Kennedy." *New York Times*, July 1, 2009. http://www. nytimes.com/2009/07/01/us/01scotus.html.

———. "Sotomayor Confirmed by Senate, 68–31: Back Story with the *Times'* Adam Liptak." *New York Times*, August 6, 2009. http://www.nytimes.com.

———. "The Memo That Rehnquist Wrote and Had to Disown." *New York Times*, September 11, 2005. http://www.nytimes.com/2005/09/11/weekinreview/11lipt.html.

———. "When the Justices ask Questions, Be Prepared to Lose the Case." *New York Times*, May 26, 2009. http://www.nytimes.com/2009/05/26/us/26bar.html.

MacLean, Pamela A. "9th Circuit Steps Up En Banc Reviews." Law.com, February 6, 2007. http://www.law.com/jsp/article.jsp?id=1170682661753.

Markell, Joanna. "Renovation Lags at JDHS." *Juneau Empire*, March 13, 2003. http://www.juneauempire.com/stories/031303/loc_jdhsrenov.shtml.

Masci, David. "Strange Bedfellows: Why Are Some Religious Groups Defending 'Bong Hits 4 Jesus'?" *The Pew Forum on Religion and Public Life*, March 27, 2007. http://pewforum.org/docs/?DocID=184.

Matheny, Albert R. Review of Lief Carter, *An Introduction to Constitutional Interpretation; Cases in Law and Religion*. Law and Politics Book Review 1 (August 1991). http://www.bsos.umd.edu/gvpt/lpbr/subpages/reviews/vangeel.htm.

Mauro, Tony. "Scalia Recusal Revives Debate over Judicial Speech, Ethics." Law.com, October 20, 2003. http://www.law.com/jsp/article.jsp?id=1066080440869.

———. "Counting Questions: Adding Up High Court Outcomes." *Legal Times* Law.com, May 12, 2005. http://www.law.com/jsp/article.jsp?id=1115802310553.

———. "Justices May Take Centrist View of 'Bong Hits' Case." First Amendment Center, March 20, 2007. http://www.firstamendmentcenter.org/analysis.aspx?id=18309.

———. "When in Doubt, Look to Roberts for Outcome of Supreme Court Cases." *Legal Times* Law.com, June 11, 2007. http://www.law.com/jsp/article.jsp?id=1184058397113.

Maveety, Nancy. "Concurrence and the Study of Judicial Behavior in American Political Science." *Juridica International* I (2003). http://www.juridica.ee/print_article_et.php?document=en/international/2003/1/65317.ART.0.pub.php.

Mayer, Jane. "The Insiders: How John McCain Came to Pick Sarah Palin." *New Yorker*, October 27, 2008. http://www.newyorker.com/reporting/2008/10/27/081027fa_fact_mayer?currentPage=1.

Milbank, Dana. "Up in Smoke at the High Court." *Washington Post*, March 20, 2007. http://www.washingtonpost.com/wp-dyn/content/article/2007/03/19/AR2007031901696.html.

———. "And the Verdict on Justice Kennedy Is: Guilty." *Washington Post*, April 9, 2006.

Moore, Wayne D. Review of Gerald Rosenberg, *The Hollow Hope: Can Courts Bring About Social Change? Law and Politics Book Review* 18 (November 2008). http://www.bsos.umd.edu/gvpt/lpbr/subpages/reviews/rosenberg1108.htm.

Morris, Will. "Incumbents Keep School Board Seats." *Juneau Empire*, October 4, 2006. http://www.juneauempire.com/stories/100406/loc_20061004033.shtml.

Morrison, Eric. "Candidates Vie for Seat on School Board: Mark Choate Sees Crisis in High School Dropout Rate." *Juneau Empire*, September 25, 2006. http://www.juneauempire.com/stories/092506/loc_20060925005.shtml.

———. "School Board, Frederick Reach Settlement in 'Bong Hits' Case." *Juneau Empire*, November 5, 2008. http://www.juneauempire.com/stories/110508/loc_352352563.shtml.

Nagourney, Adam, and Jeff Zeleny. "Washington Prepares for Fight over Any Nominee." *New York Times*, May 1, 2009. http://www.nytimes.com/2009/05/02/us/02court.html?emc=eta1.

Nieves, Evelyn. "Judges Ban Pledge of Allegiance from Schools, Citing 'Under God.'" *New York Times*, June 27, 2002. http://query.nytimes.com/gst/fullpage.html?res=9E0DE2DE123EF934A15755C0A9649C8B63&sec=&spon=&&scp=2&sq=reaction%20to%20onewdow%20I&st=cse.

Nimmer, Melville B. "Symbolic Speech." *Encyclopedia of the American Constitution.* 4 vols. New York: Macmillan, 1986, 4.

Nussbaum, Martha. "Our Pasts, Ourselves." Review of Charles Taylor's *Sources of the Self: The Making of Modern Identity. The New Republic,* April 9, 1990.

O'Malley, Julia. "JDHS Renovation Making Progress." *Juneau Empire,* November 21, 2002. http://www.juneauempire.com/stories/112102/loc_jdhs.shtml.

Plenda, Melanie. "Princess Announces Winners of Awards for Onshore Tours." *Juneau Empire,* September 18, 2001. http://www.juneauempire.com/stories/091801/Biz_princess.shtml.

Purdum, Todd S. "It Came from Wasilla." *Vanity Fair,* August 2009. http://www.vanityfair.com/politics/features/2009/08/sarah-palin200908.

Rosen, Jeffrey. "Robert's Rules." *The Atlantic,* January–February 2007. http://www.theatlantic.com/doc/200701/john-roberts.

Riuz, Vicki L. "We Always Tell Our Children They Are Americans: *Mendez v. Westminster." Brown Quarterly* 6 (2004). http://brownvboard.org/brwnqurt/06-3.

"Scalia Attacks Church-State Court Rulings." *New York Times,* January 13, 2003. http://query.nytimes.com/gst/fullpage.html?res=9B05E5D81431F930A25752C0A9659C8B63.

Shea, Christopher. "Supreme Switch: Did FDR's Threat to 'Pack' the Court in 1937 Really Change the Course of Constitutional History?" *Boston Globe,* December 4, 2005. http://www.boston.com/news/globe/ideas/articles/2005/12/04/supreme_switch/.

Skinner, Greg. "Bong Hits' Ruling Sides with District." *Juneau Empire,* June 26, 2007. http://www.juneauempire.com/stories/062607/loc_20070626018.shtml.

———. "'Bong Hits' Case Goes Back to Court." *Juneau Empire,* September 6, 2007. http://www.juneauempire.com/stories/090607/loc_20070906004.shtml.

———. "Judge: District Won't Pay Damages in Bong Hits Case: Officials Describe Ruling As End of Suit." *Juneau Empire,* October 14, 2007. http://www.juneauempire.com/stories/101407/loc_20071014025.shtml.

———. "School Board Mulls Offer for Settlement in Bong Hits Case." *Juneau Empire,* November 21, 2007. http://www.juneauempire.com/stories/112107/loc_20071121023.shtml.

———. "City Joins 'Bong Hits' Mediation before Next Round of Litigation." *Juneau Empire,* February 17, 2008. http://www.juneauempire.com/stories/021708/loc_247904339.shtml.

Smyth, Russell. "What Explains Variations in Dissent Rates? Time Series Evidence from the High Court." *Sydney Law Review* 10 (2004). http://www.austlii.com/au/journals/SydLRev/2004/10.html.

"Sorites Paradox" (The Heap Paradox). *Stanford Encyclopedia of Philosophy.* http://plato.stanford.edu/entries/sorites-paradox/.

Spano, Susan. "A Five-Day Jaunt in Juneau." *New York Times,* September 7, 1997. http://www.nytimes.com/1997/09/07/travel/a-five-day-jaunt-in-juneau.html?scp=1&sq=five-day%20jaunt%20in%20juneau&st=cse.

"Summary judgment." The Free Legal Dictionary, http://legal-dictionary.thefreedictionary.com/Summary+Judgment.

Sunstein, Cass. "Constitution and the Law Now under Attack." University of Chicago Law School *News,* April 24, 2005. http://www.law.uchicago.edu/news/law-under-attack.html.

Suderman, Alan. "School Board Tries to Recover 'Bong Hits' Court Fees." *Juneau Empire,* January 24, 2008. http://www.juneauempire.com/stories/012408/loc_239777207.shtml.

———. "'Bong Hits' Case Going Back to Court." *Juneau Empire,* July 24, 2008. http://www.juneauempire.com/stories/072408/loc_309068471.shtml.

"Superintendent Upholds 'Banner' Suspension." *Juneau Empire*, February 28, 2002. http://www.juneauempire.com/stories/022802/Loc_suspension.shtml.

Talbot, Margaret. "Supreme Confidence." *New Yorker*, March 28, 2005.

The Milepost. 61st ed. Anchorage, Alaska: Morris Communications, 2009.

Toobin, Jeffrey. "Pledge Ruling Likely 'Dead on Arrival.'" CNN.Com/LAWCENTER, June 27, 2002. http://archives.cnn.com/2002/LAW/06/26/toobin.pledge.cnna/index.html.

———."No More Mr. Nice Guy." *New Yorker*, May 25, 2009.

———. "Answers to Questions." *New Yorker*, July 27, 2009.

Willbanks, James H. "Winning the Battle, Losing the War." *New York Times*, March 5, 2008. http://www.nytimes.com/2008/03/05/opinion/05willbanks.html.

Wypijewski, JoAnn. "A Boy's Life: For Mathew Shepard's Killers, What Does It Take to Pass as a Man?" *Harper's*, September 1999. http://www.harpers.org/archive/1999/09/0060647.

Ziegenfuss, Kirk. Letter to the Editor, "In Bong Hits History, Players Are Partners." *Juneau Empire*, July 30, 2008. http://www.juneauempire.com/stories/0.

List of Interviews

● ● ●

Rick Richmond, 9/9/08
Naomi Gittens, 11/5/08
Michael Rosman, 11/6/08
Greg Baylor, 11/13/08
Alex Kreit, 11/23/08
John Whitehead, 12/3/08
Mary McAlister, 12/3/08
Joseph Frederick, 3/21/09
Carol Comeau, 6/2/09
Jason Brandeis, 6/4/09
Eric Morrison, 6/4/09
Gary Lehnhart, 6/4/09
Deborah Morse (with David Crosby), 6/5/09
Sally Smith, 6/5/09
Ann Gifford, 6/6/09
Gary Bader, 6/6/09
Doug Mertz and Margo Waring, 6/7/09
Clay Good, 6/8/09
Susan Christianson, 6/8/09
Peggy Cowan and Dale Staley (with David Crosby), 6/8/09
Phyllis Carlson, 6/8/09
Frank Frederick, 7/24/09
Steve Kanter and Marilyn Cover, 12/14/09

Table of Cases

• • •

Index

• • •

Page numbers in *italics* refer to figures.